ELISA HOVEN AND THOMAS WEIGEND (Eds.)

Justice in Criminal Law

Beiträge zum Internationalen und
Europäischen Strafrecht

Studies in International and
European Criminal Law and Procedure

Herausgegeben von / Edited by
Prof. Dr. Dr. h.c. Kai Ambos, Richter am Kosovo Sondertribunal
Berater (amicus curiae) Sondergerichtsbarkeit für den Frieden, Bogotá, Kolumbien

Band / Volume 62

Justice in Criminal Law

Global Perspectives

Edited by

Elisa Hoven and Thomas Weigend

Duncker & Humblot · Berlin

Unter Beteiligung des Göttinger Vereins zur Förderung der Strafrechtswissenschaft
und Kriminologie sowie ihrer praktischen Anwendung e. V.

Bibliographic information of the German national library

The German national library registers this publication in
the German national bibliography; specified bibliographic data
are retrievable on the Internet about http://dnb.d-nb.de.

Typesetting: 3w+p GmbH, Rimpar
Printing: Prime Rate Zrt., Budapest, Hungary

ISSN 1867-5271
ISBN 978-3-428-19449-0 (Print)
ISBN 978-3-428-59449-8 (E-Book)

Printed on no aging resistant (non-acid) paper
according to ISO 9706 ♾

Duncker & Humblot GmbH, Carl-Heinrich-Becker-Weg 9,
12165 Berlin, Germany | E-Mail: info@duncker-humblot.de
https://www.duncker-humblot.de

Table of Contents

Duncker & Humblot · Berlin | https://doi.org/10.3790/978-3-428-59449-8.2025.415906

I. Introduction

By *Elisa Hoven* and *Thomas Weigend*

Justice is an elusive ideal in many spheres of life, but to achieve justice in criminal law is perhaps the greatest challenge of all. It is difficult even to define what "justice" means in this context, given the various purposes of criminal punishment that have been proposed. Regardless of whether criminal punishment is to achieve retribution or crime prevention or both, we can say that punishment is "just" if it fulfills a number of conditions. First, punishment must be understood as a reaction to conduct defined as criminal because it is causing harm or an imminent risk for an important individual or social interest. Second, a person can be held responsible for such conduct if the harm or endangerment can be attributed to him, except when his conduct is justified because he is pursuing a more important legal interest. Third, punishment can be imposed on the actor only if he can be blamed for the conduct because he was able to recognize the legal prohibition and could be expected, in the given situation, to comply with the demands of the law. Finally, the sanction imposed should not be disproportionate to the seriousness of the violation. Beyond these general requirements, there are many areas in which criminal law must accommodate conflicting interests, for example between an aggressor and a defender, and between an offender's interest in being left alone after many years have passed since he committed the offense and the victim's – or society's – interest in pursuing retributory justice even decades later.

Our starting point in devising this volume was the hypothesis that similar concepts of justice in criminal law exist in most jurisdictions worldwide and that the conflicts of interest mentioned above are resolved in similar ways. We sought to test this proposition by positing a list of "hard cases" and presenting them to jurists from several jurisdictions, asking for their assessment. We did not ask our respondents for abstract statements; instead, we devised ten case vignettes which were meant to address key issues in criminal law. The Vignettes cover these themes:

(1) Trolley Problem – Killing one Person to Save Many

(2) Attribution of Death

(3) Torture to Save a Life

(4) Lethal Self-Defense

(5) Criminal Responsibility of Subordinates for Systemic Offenses

(6) Limits of Consent

(7) Withdrawal from an Attempt

(8) Criminal Responsibility of Minors

Duncker & Humblot · Berlin | https://doi.org/10.3790/978-3-428-59449-8.2025.415907

(9) Statute of Limitations

(10) Life Imprisonment without Parole

26 experts from 16 countries, spread out all over the globe, have written national reports, explaining how the domestic laws of their jurisdictions, as interpreted by courts and scholars, would resolve each of the ten cases represented in the vignettes. Some of these scholars kindly agreed to write a synopsis on one of the ten case Vignettes, reviewing the relevant parts of the various national reports, describing similarities and differences between national perspectives, and drawing conclusions from comparing them.

In the summer of 2024, all participants in the project came together in a day-long online conference, discussing the draft synopses and trying to draw some general conclusions from the rich information and thought-provoking ideas that can be found in the various contributions. The broad range of ideas that were put forward during the conference went into the Concluding Observations which can be found in the final part of this publication. Our findings suggest that general ideas of justice in criminal law are indeed shared across legal systems, but that they do not necessarily lead to the same outcomes when applied to specific cases. Similarities appear more in the way judges, lawyers and scholars argue than in the results at which they arrive. This holds true even where systems are considered to belong to the same "legal family". Globalization may well have promoted some assimilation of people's sense of justice; but criminal law – more than other areas of the legal system – reflects basic value judgments of each society, hence national criminal laws and their interpretation can be expected to differ significantly from each other.

Apart from these general observations, the very process of collecting and comparing solutions to "hard cases" from 16 different jurisdictions has turned out to be a great intellectual pleasure and has greatly enriched our understanding of criminal law, given the large scope of possible approaches to justice as a response to crime. We hope that you, as readers of this volume, share our feeling of opening a treasure trove of new ideas.

We owe all this to the fantastic cooperation of the rapporteurs from the various jurisdictions and, to an even greater extent, to the analytical skills of the authors of the ten Synopses. We are most grateful to these wonderful colleagues. We also owe great thanks to Ms. Vanessa Kempe of the University of Leipzig, who has most ably assisted in the process of editing the contributions to this volume and has brought her intelligence, her attention to detail, and her patience to bear to make the product perfect.

Leipzig and Cologne, June 2025

Elisa Hoven
Thomas Weigend

II. National Reports

1. Australia

By *Andrew Dyer**, *Michael Peng***, *Thomas Crofts**** and *Arlie Loughnan*****

Vignette 1: Trolley Problem – Killing one Person to Save Many

Five young children are playing on railway tracks. An express train is approaching, and it is too late to stop the train before it hits the children, probably killing them. Operator D recognizes the emergency situation. He electronically flips a switch and thus deflects the train from its regular track to a little-used sidetrack. However, the lone repairman V is busy on the sidetrack, and the deflected train kills V, as D had anticipated. Is D criminally responsible for murder of V?

In the largest Australian jurisdiction, New South Wales ("NSW"), it is unclear whether D would be held criminally responsible for the murder of V. All would depend on whether he could successfully raise the "shadowy, uncertain"[1] common law "defence"[2] of necessity, which is "often treated as though it were only a justification but sometimes [is] also recognised as an excuse"[3] – and which, relatedly, has some-

* Associate Professor, University of Melbourne Law School.

** Solicitor, Commonwealth Director of Public Prosecutions, Sydney. Sessional Lecturer in Criminal Law at the University of New South Wales. The views expressed here are Michael's, and not those of his employer.

*** Associate Dean and Professor, Department of Law and Behavioural Sciences, City University of Hong Kong.

**** Professor of Criminal Law and Criminal Law Theory, University of Sydney Law School.

1 *The King v Anna Rowan – A Pseudonym* (2024) 98 ALJR 508, 525 [86] (Edelman J) ("*Anna Rowan*").

2 We place this term within inverted commas because Australian courts have repeatedly made it clear that, where, as with necessity (*Rogers v The Queen* (1996) 86 A Crim R 542, 550), the ultimate onus lies on the Crown to disprove a ground of exculpation, it is inaccurate to describe that matter as a defence. See, e.g., *R v Youssef* (1990) 50 A Crim R 1, 2–4 (Hunt J, with whom Wood J agreed at 12 and Finlay agreed at 12); *CTM v The Queen* (2008) 236 CLR 440, 446 [6] (Gleeson CJ, Gummow, Crennan and Kiefel JJ); *R v Dziduch* (1990) 47 A Crim R 378, 380–1 (Hunt J, with whom Enderby J agreed at 384 and Sharpe J agreed at 384). In the last of these authorities, Hunt J noted that "it is very unwise ever to refer to the issue of self-defence as a 'defence', unless it is only to point out that it is not really a defence at all": at 380.

3 *Anna Rowan* (2024) 98 ALJR 508, 525 [86] (Edelman J).

Duncker & Humblot · Berlin | https://doi.org/10.3790/978-3-428-59449-8.2025.415908

times been said to be unavailable to a person accused of murder.[4] But in certain other Australian jurisdictions the matter is more clear-cut. In Victoria, for instance, D would very probably avoid murder liability on the basis of the "defence" of sudden or extraordinary emergency[5] – which is expressly stated to be available to a person accused of murder where, as here, he or she might have believed that the emergency involved a "risk of death or really serious injury".[6] Likewise, in Queensland and Western Australia ("WA") D would be likely successfully to raise the (extraordinary) emergency excuse, provided for by s 25 of the *Criminal Codes* of those States. Moreover, it is submitted that D *should* not be held criminally liable. Reasonable minds might differ about whether D was *justified* in acting as he did.[7] But certainly he was *excused* – "he [...] behaved as any reasonable person in his situation might be expected to behave"[8] – and we contend that that is "the right [...] [question] for a criminal court".[9]

In *The Queen v Dudley and Stephens*,[10] the Divisional Court, in a judgment authored by Lord Coleridge CJ, famously held that the "defence" of necessity was unavailable to the prisoners, who had killed and eaten "an innocent and unoffending"[11] cabin boy who had been shipwrecked with them on the high seas for 20 days without very much food or water. The Court clearly conceived of necessity as a justification: that is, as applying only where the conduct of the accused was "rightful"[12] or, at least, "socially acceptable or tolerable"[13] – something of which society would approve[14] or that it would consider to be permissible. In other words, while acknowledging "how awful the [prisoners'] suffering"[15] had been, and while suggesting that the rule the Court had laid down was one that "we could not ourselves satisfy",[16] Lord Coleridge

4 The case that has been said to lay down this rule is of course *The Queen v Dudley and Stephens* (1884) 14 QBD 273 ("*Dudley*"). See, e.g., *The Queen v Howe* [1987] 1 AC 417, 429 (Lord Hailsham), 453 (Lord Mackay) ("*Howe*"). Cf. Glanville Williams, "A Commentary on *R v Dudley and Stephens*" (1977) 8 *Cambrian Law Review* 94, 99; *In re A (Children) (Conjoined Twins: Surgical Separation)* [2001] Fam 147, 239–240 (Brooke LJ) ("*In Re A*").

5 *Crimes Act 1958* (Vic) s 322R.

6 *Crimes Act 1958* (Vic) s 322R(3).

7 Compare, e.g., JC Smith, *Justification and Excuse in the Criminal Law* (Stevens & Sons, 1989) 74, 76–7 with *Perka v The Queen* [1984] 2 SCR 232, 278 (Wilson J) ("*Perka*"). See too Joshua Dressler, "Reflections on *Dudley and Stephens* and Killing the Innocent: Taking a Wrong Conceptual Path", in: Dennis J Baker and Jeremy Horder, *The Sanctity of Life and the Criminal Law* (Cambridge University Press, 2013) 126, 141–3.

8 Smith (n 7) 126.

9 Ibid. 13.

10 (1884) 14 QBD 273.

11 Ibid. 280.

12 *Anna Rowan* (2024) 98 ALJR 508, 523 [76] (Edelman J). See too, e.g., George P Fletcher, "Should Intolerable Prison Conditions Generate a Justification or Excuse for Escape?" (1979) 26(6) *UCLA Law Review* 1355, 1358.

13 Joshua Dressler, "Foreword – Justifications and Excuses: A Brief Review of the Concepts and Literature" (1987) 33(4) *Wayne Law Review* 1155, 1161.

14 Smith (n 7) 11.

15 *Dudley* (1884) 14 QBD 273, 288.

16 Ibid.

CJ also indicated that Dudley's and Stephens' conduct had not been "pure".[17] "In this case", his Lordship said, "the weakest, the most unresisting, was chosen. Was it more necessary to kill him than one of the grown men?"[18] Lord Coleridge CJ returned a negative response to this question. And he added that, if Dudley and Stephens were to be acquitted of murder, the principle that facilitated such an outcome "might be made the legal cloak for unbridled passion and atrocious crime".[19]

Dudley and Stephens, then, gives little encouragement to D – and the same is true of two later cases, *The Queen v McConnell*,[20] decided by the NSW Court of Criminal Appeal ("NSWCCA") in 1976, and *The Queen v Howe*,[21] decided by the House of Lords just over 10 years later. In the first of these authorities, the Court held that the "defence" of duress is unavailable to a person charged with murder as a principal in the first degree. In the second, their Lordships held that that "defence" is also unavailable to those who are alleged to be accessories to murder. Importantly, in so holding, Lord Hailsham of Marylebone expressly associated himself[22] with the justificatory reasoning of Lord Coleridge CJ in *Dudley*, and he expressly dissociated himself[23] from the view that the criminal law must always "set up standards"[24] with which the average person can comply. His Lordship accepted that many persons would "succumb to temptation"[25] and kill an innocent, in the face of a threat from a criminal that, if they did not do this, they and/or their family would be killed. "But", he said, "I have known of too many acts of heroism by ordinary human beings to regard as either 'just or humane' a law"[26] that excused those who *did* succumb.

However, the later English case of *In re A (Children) (Conjoined Twins: Surgical Separation)*[27] might be more helpful to D. In that case, Brooke LJ held[28] that necessity would render doctors not guilty of murder if they were to perform an operation on conjoined twins that would certainly result in the death of one (Mary), but would save the other (Jodie) – who currently was sustaining her sister's life, but who would die within three to six months unless doctors were to intervene. His Lordship thought the case distinguishable from *Dudley* – and such reasoning has attracted academic support. It will be recalled that, in *Dudley*, the defendants had "selected to be killed"[29] the most vulnerable person aboard. There was no such problem of selection in *In Re A.*

---

17 Ibid.

18 Ibid. 287–8.

19 Ibid. 288.

20 [1977] 1 NSWLR 714.

21 [1987] 1 AC 417.

22 Ibid. 430–1.

23 Ibid. 431.

24 *Dudley* (1884) 14 QBD 273, 288.

25 *Howe* [1987] 1 AC 417, 432.

26 Ibid.

27 [2001] Fam 147.

28 Ibid. 239–240.

29 David Ormerod and Karl Laird, *Smith, Hogan and Ormerod's Criminal Law* (Oxford University Press, 2021, 16th ed.) 394.

Rather, Mary had been "selected by the circumstances":[30] she would certainly die within the year, whether the doctors performed the operation or not.[31] Admittedly, the scenario with which we are currently dealing is slightly different. There was no imminent prospect of V's dying before D flipped the switch.[32] But the choice that D has made – to kill V and to avoid the deaths of the children – seems far less morally questionable than that made by Dudley and Stephens. Unlike those defendants, but as with the doctors in *In Re A*, V is disinterested. He has nothing personally to gain by proceeding in the way that he has.

That said, it is far from certain that a NSW court would acquit V on the basis of necessity.[33] Perhaps a court would regard necessity as a justification and consider V's conduct, however reasonable and lacking in culpability, to be wrongful. And perhaps, in so reasoning, it would attach determinative moral and legal weight to the circumstances that, unlike Mary in *In Re A*, V: (i) was imperilling no one's life; and (ii) would have lived indefinitely had it not been for the choice D made. On the other hand, the judge might be inclined to see necessity as an excuse. He or she might reason that, whether or not D's conduct was "right", or permissible, it was a reasonable response to the emergency with which he was faced – and that that should be enough for him to avoid criminal liability.

This brings us to the final matter that we wish to address. As suggested above, in certain Australian jurisdictions D would seemingly be acquitted of murder. In Victoria, for instance, a person will not be guilty of that offence where (leaving the onus of proof to one side):

(a) s/he reasonably believes that there is a "sudden or extraordinary emergency"[34];

(b) s/he believes that that emergency involves a risk of death or really serious injury;[35]

(c) s/he reasonably believes that his or her conduct is the only reasonable way to deal with the emergency;[36] and

(d) his or her conduct is a reasonable response to the emergency.[37]

It will be observed that requirements (a)–(c) are clearly satisfied in D's case and that, while (d) would be a matter for the jury to decide, a jury would seem very likely

---

30 Ibid.

31 JJ Child et al., *Simester and Sullivan's Criminal Law: Theory and Doctrine* (Hart Publishing, 8th ed. 2022) 920.

32 That is, unlike Mary, he was not "marked for death": Paul A Fairall and Malcolm Barrett, *Criminal Defences in Australia* (Lexis Nexis Butterworths, 2017) 182 [6.37].

33 Brent Fisse, *Howard's Criminal Law* (The Law Book Co Ltd, 5th ed., 1990) 558 states that the question of whether necessity is available as a "defence" to murder in NSW "can hardly be regarded as concluded".

34 *Crimes Act 1958* (Vic) s 322R(2)(a)(i).

35 *Crimes Act 1958* (Vic) s 322R(3). Oddly, this belief need not be reasonable.

36 *Crimes Act 1958* (Vic) s 322R(2)(a)(ii).

37 *Crimes Act 1958* (Vic) s 322R(2)(b).

to consider it possibly[38] reasonable for D, in the agony of the moment, to have made the choice that he did. It will also be observed that the Victorian "defence" just noted "operates by way of excuse".[39] In our view, this is the normatively correct approach.

There are at least two reasons why we consider that the "defence" available to D – whether necessity or sudden or extraordinary emergency – should be conceived of and defined as an excuse. The first is that, if it were otherwise – if, that is, D could avoid criminal liability only if his act were justified – the law would potentially involve jurors in a complex moral reasoning process for which they are ill-equipped. It takes only a brief perusal of the relevant literature to realise that there is no certain boundary between justification and excuse.[40] A jury that attempted to determine whether D had acted rightly, or acceptably – which is it? – would be attempting to resolve an issue that divides philosophers. But, secondly, and most importantly, "a liberal and humane criminal law"[41] should impose criminal liability only on those who had a "fair opportunity"[42] to act differently. To treat as a criminal the person who has acted reasonably but not heroically is to impose a harsh and unforgiving standard. And to do so on the basis that, otherwise, the floodgates might be opened to "unbridled passion and atrocious crime",[43] is to speculate impermissibly about the capacity of "exceptionally rare"[44] cases to operate as examples.

Vignette 2: Attribution of Death

D intends to kill his neighbour V. Hidden near V's house, D waits for V and stabs him several times with a knife. V is taken to the hospital, where his wounds are treated. His injuries are not life-threatening and V is kept overnight for observation. During the night, a technical defect in the hospital kitchen leads to the outbreak of a fire, which kills V and other persons. Can D be held criminally responsible for V's death?

It would seem that, as a matter of Australian law – the law relating to causation does not differ greatly across the various States and Territories[45] – D would certainly

38 In other words, where there is evidence of sudden or extraordinary emergency, the Crown must disprove that "defence" beyond reasonable doubt: *Crimes Act 1958* (Vic) s 322I.

39 To use the language of Kyrou and Niall JA in *Rowan (a Pseudonym) v The Queen* [2022] VSCA 236, [59] – although their Honours were there referring to the common law "defence" of duress.

40 One question that divides commentators is whether the reasonably mistaken self-defender is justified or excused. Compare, e. g., Heidi M Hurd, "Justification and Excuse: Wrongdoing and Culpability" (1999) 74(5) *Notre Dame Law Review* 1551, especially 1563–5, with Kent Greenawalt, "Distinguishing Justifications from Excuses" (1986) 49(3) *Law and Contemporary Problems* 89, 101–2.

41 *Perka* [1984] 2 SCR 232, 248 (Dickson J, with whom Ritchie, Chouinard and Lamer JJ agreed).

42 HLA Hart, "Negligence, *Mens Rea* and Criminal Responsibility", in: *Punishment and Responsibility: Essays in the Philosophy of Law* (Oxford University Press, 2008, 2nd ed) 136, 152.

43 *Dudley* (1884) 14 QBD 273, 288.

44 *In Re A* [2001] Fam 147, 240 (Brooke LJ).

45 See Eric Colvin, "Causation in Criminal Law" (1989) 1 *Bond Law Review* 253, 254.

not be criminally responsible for V's death. At the very least, a jury at any murder trial in which D was the defendant would be capable of finding that he performed no act "causing the death" of V within the meaning of a provision such as s 18(1)(a) *Crimes Act 1900* (NSW);[46] and that, therefore, no murder liability could attach to him. Certainly, but for D's stabbing of V, V would not have died when he did. And certainly, as McHugh J put it in *Royall v The Queen*,[47] "the 'but for' test is a useful tool in criminal law for determining whether a causal link existed between an accused's act or omission and the relevant injury or damage". But the satisfaction of that test is insufficient for criminal causation to be established.[48] As the Australian Courts have repeatedly indicated,[49] and as is stated in a highly-respected textbook,[50] a person can be liable for homicide only if his or her conduct "substantially [or significantly[51]] contributed to the subsequent death of V, taking into account the actual time at which and the manner in which the death occurred."[52] In the above case, V's death occurred, not immediately, and not because of the wounds that resulted from the stabbing,[53] and not because of any event that D could reasonably have foreseen[54] – but because of "the extraordinary [...] operation of [...] [non-human] forces".[55] While Australian law is perhaps not entirely clear on this point, it does appear that, in such circumstances, it would attribute the death to "the 'Act of God'"[56] and not to "the act of the party inflicting the wound".[57]

46 This provision creates the offence of murder in NSW, stating that the actus reus of that offence is an act or omission of the accused "causing the death charged". Section 18(1)(b) then goes on to state that "[e]very other punishable homicide shall be manslaughter". As noted by the NSWCCA in *Lane v The Queen* (2013) 241 A Crim R 321, 334 [46], there is no "detailed definition [...] in s 18 [...] of what constitutes manslaughter". Nevertheless, it is clear that the actus reus of that offence is the same as for murder: at 335 [50], 337 [57], 338 [62].

47 (1991) 172 CLR 378, 440 ("*Royall*").

48 *Swan v The Queen* (2020) 269 CLR 663, 674 [24] (The Court) ("*Swan*").

49 See, e.g., ibid; *Royall* (1991) 172 CLR 378, 398 (Brennan J), 411 (Deane and Dawson JJ), 423 (Toohey and Gaudron JJ).

50 Fisse (n 33) 33.

51 Cf. Child et al. (n 31) 94.

52 Whether such a person *would* be liable for murder or manslaughter would depend on his or her mental state at the time of the relevant conduct. If he or she had the requisite mental state, it would also depend on whether he or she could successfully raise any defence, "defence" or partial defence.

53 Though if these *had* been the medical cause of his death, this would not have been determinative of the causal question: Colvin (n 45) 260. Cf. *R v Blaue* [1975] 1 WLR 1411, 1415 (Lawton LJ for the England and Wales Court of Appeal).

54 In the circumstances of this case, if it *had*, that would seemingly have led the causal question to be determined adversely to him: see *R v Hallett* [1969] SASR 141, 149–150 (The Court).

55 Ibid. 150 (The Court).

56 Rollin M Perkins, "The Law of Homicide" (1946) 36(6) *Journal of Criminal Law and Criminology* 391, 393.

57 HLA Hart and Tony Honore, *Causation in the Law* (Clarendon Press, 1985, 2nd ed) 342, discussing *Bush v Commonwealth* (1880) 78 Ky 268.

To say that conduct will be the legal cause of a result only if it is "a substantial or significant cause of [that result] […]"[58] – or, alternatively, a "sufficiently substantial"[59] cause of that result – is to provide no very specific guidance about when criminal causation will, and will not, be established. Moreover, to use Smith & Hogan's language, in Australia, as in England, "[t]he courts have struggled to produce a clear approach in this complex area", instead developing principles that, in some cases, "openly […] conflict" with one another.[60] That said, one such principle is clear: where "the voluntary and informed act of an adult"[61] intervenes between the accused's conduct and the relevant consequence, the accused will be "relieve[d] […] of criminal responsibility"[62] in respect of that consequence. This is so because of "the philosophy of autonomy"[63] that underlies our criminal law. Certainly, if A supplies B with a prohibited drug, or if A attacks B near a busy road, this makes it foreseeable (or "predictable"[64]) that B will, respectively, self-administer the drug or run onto the road in an attempt to escape the threatened violence. Nevertheless, if B does act in such a way and dies in consequence, A will not necessarily be guilty of homicide. Provided that B is a "sane adult", whose decision to take the drug/run onto the road was not vitiated by a factor such as "intimidation" or "mistake",[65] the law will regard his or her "volitional" (or autonomous) act as "setting a new 'chain of causation' going".[66]

Kadish has noted that rules such as the one just described are "the product […] of the pervasive conviction, widely manifested in the law, that […] human action differ[s] […] from all other natural events in the world".[67] He is referring to an "individualistic"[68] and "self-determinist"[69] ethic, under which human beings, as autonomous choosers, are seen as responsible for the choices that they make. That said, where, as

58 *Swan* (2020) 269 CLR 663, 674 [24] (The Court), quoting *Royall* (1991) 172 CLR 378, 411 (Deane and Dawson JJ).

59 Ibid, quoting *Royall* (1991) 172 CLR 378, 412 (Deane and Dawson JJ).

60 Ormerod and Laird (n 29) 70.

61 *Burns v The Queen* (2012) 246 CLR 334, 364 [86] (Gummow, Hayne, Crennan, Kiefel and Bell JJ) ("*Burns HCA*").

62 Hart and Honore (n 57) 326.

63 Glanville Williams, "*Finis* for *Novus Actus*" (1989) 48(3) *Cambridge Law Journal* 391, 397–8.

64 *Burns v The Queen* (2011) 205 A Crim R 240, 270 [151].

65 *Burns HCA* (2012) 246 CLR 334, 364 [86] (Gummow, Hayne, Crennan, Kiefel and Bell JJ).

66 Williams (n 63) 392. Note that, normally, in a "fright or self-preservation" case such as the busy road scenario, A's attack will render B's response other than autonomous. That said, if a jury considers it reasonably possible that B's response was an unreasonable one, it must find that A's conduct did not cause B's death: *Royall* (1991) 172 CLR 378, 412–3 (Deane and Dawson JJ), 425 (Toohey and Gaudron JJ). See too *McAuliffe v The Queen* (1995) 183 CLR 108, 118–19 (The Court) and *RIK v R* [2004] NSWCCA 282, [14]–[16] and [21] (Hodgson JA, with whom Hulme J agreed at [25] and Smart AJ agreed at [26]).

67 Sanford H Kadish, "Reckless Complicity" (1997) 87(2) *Journal of Criminal Law and Criminology* 369, 393.

68 Ibid. 391.

69 Ibid. 392.

in the hypothetical to which we are responding, a *non*-human natural event intervenes between a human attack on another and that other's death, Australian law will not always regard the human attack as the cause of the death. Rather, certain such natural events will be viewed in the same light as – or, at the very least, will be held to be capable of being viewed by a jury in the same light as – the "free, deliberate, and informed intervention of a second person".[70]

The leading case on this point is the Full Court of the Supreme Court of South Australia's decision in *The Queen v Hallett.*[71] In that case, the appellant had assaulted the deceased and then left him unconscious on a beach, whereupon the deceased was eventually drowned by the incoming tide. The Court held, without very much hesitation, that "the action of the sea on the deceased" could not be regarded as "breaking the chain of causation".[72] However, their Honours then quickly added that they were:[73]

> not concerned to deny that there may be causes where the extraordinary as opposed to the ordinary operation of natural forces might be regarded as breaking the chain of causation [...] So here if the deceased had been placed in a situation safe from the ordinary operations of the sea and had been engulfed by an extraordinary tidal wave as the result of an earthquake in the sea it may be that the earthquake and not the act of the appellant would be regarded as the cause of the death.

If we apply this dictum to the scenario with which we are currently dealing, surely the technical defect in the hospital kitchen would be an "extraordinary" non-human event, analogous to a natural event such as an earthquake – which might prevent D from being convicted of V's murder?

Indeed, it seems that we can go further than this. The words "may" and "might" in the above passage from *Hallett* could be taken as indicating that, in our scenario, the question of causation would be left with the jury to resolve. It would be open to that jury to resolve the causal question adversely to the accused. But it "might" not. All would depend on whether, in the jury's view, D's act should properly be seen "as having a sufficiently substantial causal effect which subsisted up to [V's death]",[74] despite the occurrence of the fire. But we doubt whether, if such a question were to arise, the matter would be left with the jury.[75] And we do not think that it *should* be. Rather, where an extraordinary event such as the one with which we are concerned intervenes between the conduct of the accused and the death of the deceased, it seems that that event must be regarded as replacing the accused's conduct as the legal cause of the

70 Hart and Honore (n 57) 326.

71 [1969] SASR 141.

72 Ibid. 149.

73 Ibid. 150.

74 Ibid. 149.

75 Academic commentators seem to agree that, in such a case, causation would clearly not be established: i. e., there would be nothing to be decided by the jury (although the jury would have to satisfy itself that it is reasonably possible that the fire occurred and that, but for it, V would have survived). See, e. g., Perkins (n 56) 393–4; Hart and Honore (n 57) 340–2; Ormerod and Laird (n 29) 70–1; Colvin (n 45) 257–8.

death. At the very least, that should be the case where, as here, the wounds caused by the accused would certainly not have killed the deceased.

Consider a case where A's mother dies, not because she has drunk the (non-fatal) dose of poison that A had placed in her drink, but because of an unrelated heart attack.[76] Or a case, similar to the present one, where A seriously injures B, who would have survived, but is then killed in a car accident on her way to hospital.[77] Or a case where B would have lived had it just been for the serious injuries that A had intentionally inflicted on him, but dies after contracting scarlet fever from the surgeon who had operated on those injuries.[78] Even assuming that, in each of these cases (as in our one), A intended to bring about the result (B's death) that in fact then occurred,[79] he should not be convicted of murder. In each of these scenarios, the injuries inflicted by A were not the physical cause of B's death. Indeed, without the intervening event, B would have survived. But, most importantly, while B's death was the foreseeable result of A's conduct, it occurred in an entirely unforeseeable way. Such cases thus seem broadly analogous to those in which a person's "voluntary and informed" act has intervened between the accused's conduct and the deceased's death. A death made foreseeable by the accused's conduct has actually resulted from an event that is so unpredictable, and thus "so independent"[80] of that conduct, as to render the accused's acts "merely part of the history".[81]

Vignette 3: Torture to Save a Life

> Kidnapper K has abducted an 8-year-old girl G and hidden her in a small cave in the woods. K is trying to extort money from G's parents for her release. The police manage to arrest K. Although being questioned for 24 hours, K steadfastly refuses to disclose where he hid G. Police officer D correctly assumes that G may soon die of thirst if she cannot be found. He therefore severely beats K to make him tell the truth. Fearing even more violence, K eventually leads the police to the cave, where they find G still barely alive. Should D be punished for torturing K?

If such events were to occur in Australia, D would probably be convicted of the federal offence of torture, created by s 274.2(1) of the *Criminal Code* (Cth) ("the *Criminal Code*").[82] That is because D has seemingly engaged in conduct: (i) that inflicted

---

76 These facts are based on those in *The King v White* [1910] 2 KB 124 ("*White*").

77 This case is imagined by Colvin (n 45) 257.

78 (1880) 78 Ky 268.

79 In the poisoning example, this would be because the accused, as in *White*, mistakenly thought that the dose was fatal: *White* [1910] 2 KB 124, 129.

80 *R v Cheshire* [1991] 1 WLR 844, 852 (Beldam LJ for the England and Wales Court of Appeal). Note, however, that where there is an intervening "informed and voluntary act", the second cause is of course usually seen as being entirely independent of the accused's conduct, not because the act is unpredictable, but because it was the autonomous act of an adult.

81 *R v Smith* [1959] 2 QB 35, 43 (Lord Parker CJ for the England and Wales Court of Appeal).

82 Assuming that the Crown prosecuted him. In a similar NSW case, which seems possibly to have occurred before the enactment of the *Criminal Code*, the police officers faced no criminal charges: cf. *Gäfgen v Germany* (2011) 52 EHRR 1. According to an account given by the former NSW police officer, John Blacker, in that case a woman had filled up her car's tank

severe physical suffering on K;[83] (ii) for the purpose of obtaining "information or a confession" from K;[84] and (iii) "in the capacity of a public official".[85] The *Criminal Code* does create the "defence" of "self-defence", which applies in circumstances where, relevantly, it is reasonably possible that: (i) the accused believed that his or her conduct was necessary to defend another person; and (ii) the conduct was a reasonable response in the circumstances as the accused perceived them.[86] And, certainly, there seems a strong chance that, if such a "defence" were left with the jury in D's case, the jury would acquit him on this basis. In other words, where the police believe that a child is in imminent danger of dying of thirst, and where the person whom they correctly believe to be responsible for the threat to the child's life "steadfastly refuses" to tell them where the child is, most people would accept that: (i) they might genuinely think that severe violence is necessary to preserve the life of the child; and (ii) such violence might be a reasonable response to the emergency that they perceive to exist. But the clear effect of s 274.4(a) of the *Criminal Code* would seem to be to prevent a trial judge, in a case such as D's, from charging the jury about self-defence. Section 274.4 provides that "[i]t is not a defence" to "an offence under this Division" – including torture – that the conduct constituting the offence was "done out of necessity arising from the existence of a state of war, a threat of war, internal political instability, a public emergency *or any other exceptional circumstance*" (emphasis added). While self-defence is not explicitly mentioned, the italicized words seem to leave little doubt that that "defence" may not be pleaded in response to a torture charge.

Whether this *should* be the case seems doubtful. Of course, it might be said that, by torturing K, D has infringed K's human dignity, and that he should for that reason be convicted of a serious offence. But such reasoning appears to be misconceived. If a police officer shoots a person in the leg just because the police officer is "feeling brutal and does not like the look of the particular prisoner",[87] the police officer undoubtedly breaches that person's human dignity. Yet that would not be so if the police officer "took the shot as the minimum measure necessary to incapacitate a person who is in the process of attacking the police officer or a nearby third party with a knife".[88]

---

with petrol at the height of the Australian summer, leaving the keys in the ignition and her 3-year-old son in the backseat while she went inside to pay. A man then entered the car and drove off in it, but he soon abandoned it. Upon arresting the offender at a nearby railway station, police demanded that he tell them where the car was; but, despite numerous inducements and threats, he refused to provide them with the relevant information. They then bashed him severely until he told them where the car was. The child was saved and, as noted above, the police were not prosecuted. See Seumas Miller, "Torture", in: Edward N Zalta and Uri Nodelman (eds.), The Stanford Encyclopedia of Philosophy (Winter 2012 Edition), https://plato.stanford.edu/entries/torture/.

83 *Criminal Code* (Cth) s 274.2(1)(a).

84 *Criminal Code* (Cth) s 274.2(1)(b).

85 *Criminal Code* (Cth) s 274.2(1)(c)(i).

86 *Criminal Code* (Cth) s 10.4(2).

87 Natasa Mavronicola, "Güler and Öngel v Turkey: Article 3 of the European Convention on Human Rights and Strasbourg's Discourse on the Justified Use of Force" (2013) 76(2) *Modern Law Review* 370, 379.

88 Ibid.

Why not? It is essentially because, whereas the first person is treated as an object – the police officer deals with him or her not as a person who is "autonomous, responsible, and deserving of the special kind of treatment due that status",[89] but rather as a thing to be intimidated into submission – the second person's "agency is respected".[90] The shot is a proportionate response to, and has been made "strictly necessary by",[91] his or her conduct.

If we return to the above scenario, D's conduct towards K seems analogous to that of the police officer in the second case just noted, not the first. As in that second case, it is defensive action that goes no further than is necessary to ward off the unjust threat posed by the person against whom the action is taken (and does in fact ward off that threat).[92]

That said, even if that is accepted, some might feel some unease about a law that facilitated the acquittal of a person such as D. It might be said, in other words, that if a judge were to leave self-defence with the jury in such a case, and if that jury were then to acquit, the floodgates might be opened. State torture might come to be practised in far less sympathetic circumstances. But while such a concern is understandable, perhaps it is overstated.[93] Even if a jury were to acquit D, such a decision would have no precedential value. It would amount merely to a decision by a particular jury that in particular, very exceptional circumstances, an act of state torture must attract no criminal liability. Such a decision might not give very much encouragement to police officers to torture detainees. Moreover, the very act of putting D on trial, combined perhaps with non-criminal consequences such as the loss of his job, might sufficiently convey the message that state torture can never be practised with impunity.

Vignette 4: Lethal Self-Defence

> R, a well-trained young man armed with a knife, accosts 50-year-old D, who is on her way home from a party in the early morning hours. R threatens her with the

---

89 Jeffrie G Murphy, "Cruel and Unusual Punishments", in: Jeffrie G Murphy, Retribution, Justice, and Therapy: Essays in the Philosophy of Law (D Reidel Publishing Company, Dordrecht 1979) 223, 233.

90 Natasa Mavronicola, "Is the Prohibition Against Torture and Cruel, Inhuman and Degrading Treatment Absolute in International Human Rights Law? A Reply to Steven Greer" (2017) 17(3) *Human Rights Law Review* 479, 487.

91 *Bouyid v Belgium* [2015] V Eur Court HR 457, [100].

92 It is sometimes suggested in the literature that, in circumstances such as those that arise in our scenario, the proper "defence" for the accused is necessity or sudden or extraordinary emergency. But whereas the conduct that is rendered non-criminal by such "defences" is normally directed at an innocent person or his or her property, K is by no means innocent. As indicated in the text, he is responsible for an unjust threat to G. And because, as also indicated in the text, D's otherwise criminal conduct is directed at K and is aimed at removing the threat he poses, this seems to be a case of defence of others. See Jeremy Horder, "Self-defence, Necessity and Duress: Understanding the Relationship" (2011) 11(1) *Canadian Journal of Law and Jurisprudence* 143, especially 143–8, 150–5.

93 See Steven Greer, "Is the Prohibition against Torture, Cruel, Inhuman and Degrading Treatment Really 'Absolute' in International Human Rights Law? A Reply to Graffin and Mavronicola" (2018) 18 *Human Rights Law Review* 297, 300–1.

knife and takes away her purse filled with 500 € and her wristwatch worth 1,000 €. As R turns to run away, D draws a pistol she is secretly carrying in her jacket, and shoots and kills R in order to retrieve her property. Is D guilty of murder?

If these events were to occur in Australia, D would be guilty of murder.[94] In NSW[95] and Victoria,[96] a person will not be guilty of an offence if it is reasonably possible that he or she: (i) believed that his or her conduct was necessary to protect property; and (ii) that conduct was a reasonable response in the circumstances that the person subjectively perceived to exist. But, in the former jurisdiction, the relevant statute provides that the "defence" just noted – self-defence – is unavailable to a person who "uses force that involves the intentional or reckless infliction of death only […] to protect property";[97] and, in the latter, self-defence is available in murder proceedings only if it is reasonably possible that the accused believed that the conduct was nec-

94 The only possible exception is this. In South Australia, a person who kills *without an intention to cause death* will be guilty of manslaughter, not murder, if (i) it is reasonably possible that he or she believed that his or her conduct was "necessary and reasonable […] to protect property from unlawful appropriation"; but (ii) that conduct "was not, in the circumstances as the defendant genuinely believed them to be, reasonably proportionate to the threat that the defendant genuinely believed to exist": *Criminal Law Consolidation Act 1935* (SA) s 15A(2). Did D lack an intent to cause death? If so, then perhaps she would be convicted of manslaughter, rather than murder – although, with that said, s 15A is seemingly capable of operating in a less than rational way. If D *did* lack an intent to cause death and, also, (ignoring the onus of proof): (i) she genuinely believed that her conduct was "necessary and reasonable to protect property from unlawful appropriation"; and (ii) her conduct *was* "reasonably proportionate to the threat" that she "genuinely believed to exist" (the latter admittedly seems unlikely: see n 97), s 15A(2) seems to make it clear that she would not be guilty of manslaughter. But, strangely, she might be guilty of murder. That is because of s 15A(1)(b), which provides that a person who kills to protect property will have no "defence" if he or she acted with an intent to cause death *or* "recklessly realising that the conduct could result in death". Might not D have realised that her firing of the gun could result in R's death?

95 *Crimes Act 1900* (NSW) s 418(2).

96 *Crimes Act 1958* (Vic) s 322K(2) and see also the "Notes" after s 322K(3).

97 *Crimes Act 1900* (NSW) s 420. Perhaps s 420 only prevents self-defence from operating in a case of murder where the accused had an intent to kill or displayed "reckless indifference to human life" (*Crimes Act 1900* (NSW) s 18(1)(a)), that is, foresaw the probability that his or her conduct would result in death, but proceeded with it anyway: *Royall* (1991) 172 CLR 378, 395 (Mason CJ), 405 (Brennan J), 415 (Deane and Dawson JJ), 430–1 (Toohey and Gaudron JJ), 455 (McHugh J); *R v Solomon* [1980] 1 NSWLR 321, 337 (Begg J, with whom Street CJ agreed at 327). But even if that is so – in other words, even if s 420 does not apply in a case where a person is prima facie guilty of murder because he or she has killed with an "intent to […] inflict grievous harm on some person" (*Crimes Act 1900* (NSW) s 18(1)(a)) – D would still seem to be guilty of murder (assuming that D acted only with such an intent). That is because a jury would be most likely to conclude her conduct was not a reasonable – that is, proportionate (*R v Katarzynski* [2002] NSWSC 613, [23]) – response in the circumstances that she perceived to exist (a thief turning to run away from her, with some of her property). It is true that, under *Crimes Act 1900* (NSW) s 421, a person will be guilty of manslaughter if his or her conduct is not a reasonable response in the circumstances as he or she perceives them, but he or she might have believed that the conduct was necessary to achieve certain purposes. But, as noted below in the text, one of those purposes is not the protection of property. In other words, even if R might have believed that her conduct was necessary to "protect property from unlawful taking" (*Crimes Act 1900* (NSW) s 418(2)(c)), this could not lead her liability to be downgraded from murder to manslaughter.

essary to defend himself or herself or another person "from the infliction of death or really serious injury."[98] Like rules exist in the other Australian States and Territories. In WA, for example, while it is lawful for the possessor of "movable property" to "use such force as is reasonably necessary [...] in order to retake [the property] from a trespasser", the relevant provision states that this is only so if the "force used is not intended, and is not such as is likely to cause death or grievous bodily harm to the trespasser".[99] And in the Northern Territory ("NT"), a person cannot rely on self-defence if he or she uses "force that involves the intentional infliction of death or serious harm [...] to protect property."[100]

At common law in Australia, the position was different. Certainly, there was not very much common law authority regarding the criminal liability of the defender of property.[101] But, under such authority as existed, D would seemingly be guilty of manslaughter rather than murder. The leading case was *R v McKay*,[102] which was decided by the Full Court of the Supreme Court of Victoria well before the enactment of the Victorian provisions just noted. The social context in which that case was decided perhaps helps us to see why their Honours took the approach they did.

In *McKay*, the appellant lived with his wife and children on a poultry farm owned by his father. In the three-and-a-half year period leading up to the events at issue, there had been "an unbroken series of thefts of fowls, the total number of birds lost being at least 1000".[103] The McKays took a number of measures to prevent the thefts, but none of them had any effect, and McKay began sleeping with a rifle close by.[104] At "first light"[105] on the day in question, McKay became aware that an intruder was on the farm. He went outside with the rifle and, upon seeing a man stealing chickens, he fired a shot at him.[106] The man started running away, and McKay fired a second shot, whereupon the man dropped the chickens.[107] McKay then fired three more shots, and the man died.[108] It was unclear which shot, or shots, had killed him.[109]

98 *Crimes Act 1958* (Vic) s 322K(3). It seems clear that R had no such belief. We are told that D has turned "to run away" and that R has killed him "in order to retrieve her property", and not because she thought that D was just about to kill or inflict really serious injury on her.

99 *Criminal Code Act 1913* (WA) s 251. See too *Criminal Code Act 1924* (Tas) s 43. In Queensland, the possessor may use "such force as is reasonably necessary in order to [...] retake [the property] from a possessor, provided that the person does not do grievous bodily harm to the trespasser."

100 *Criminal Code Act 1983* (NT) s 43BD(3)(a)(i); and see also s 29(3)(a). See too *Criminal Code Act 2002* (ACT) s 42(3)(a)(i).

101 Fairall and Barrett (n 32) 268 [10.16].

102 [1957] VR 560 ("*McKay*").

103 Ibid. 569 (Smith J).

104 Ibid.

105 Ibid.

106 Ibid. 569–570.

107 Ibid. 570.

108 Ibid.

109 Ibid. 561 (Lowe J).

At McKay's trial for murder, the trial judge, Barry J, instructed the jury that there were three "possible lines of justification"[110] open to the defendant: that he was acting in reasonable defence of property; that he had used reasonable force to prevent the commission of a felony; or that he had used reasonable force to apprehend a felon. His Honour clearly did not think that any of these justifications should succeed. The prisoner's conduct, he suggested to the jury, was *un*reasonable.[111] Nevertheless, Barry J also told the jury that it should find McKay guilty of manslaughter, not murder, if he had acted "honestly [...] to protect his property [...] [or] to prevent the commission of a felony, or [...] to apprehend a felon", but had used "more force than [was] reasonably necessary".[112] The jury so instructed convicted McKay of manslaughter; and, on appeal, the Full Court seems to have taken essentially the same view of the law as Barry J had.[113] According to Lowe J, "[i]f the occasion warrants action in self-defence or for the prevention of felony or the apprehension of the felon, but the person taking action acts beyond the necessity of the occasion and kills the offender, the crime is manslaughter – not murder."[114]

The "balance"[115] the judiciary achieved in *McKay* – the person who used lethal force to defend property would not be acquitted, but would be convicted of manslaughter rather than murder – seems to have represented a compromise between two competing ideas. The first of these is that, as McKay himself had essentially put it,[116] and as many of his contemporaries seemed to think,[117] the deceased had got his just deserts. In other words, by acting unlawfully, the deceased had declared war on the legal order, and McKay was entitled "to use whatever force [was] necessary to restore"[118] the equilibrium. The second is the more liberal notion that, however badly the deceased had behaved, he did *not* deserve to die. According to such a view, the law must ensure that, in cases of defensive self-help, there is a proper relationship of proportionality between "the defended interest and the means of defence."[119] If it does not – if it instead allows us, say, to kill those who pose a threat merely to our

---

110 Norval Morris, "The Slain Chicken Thief: Some Aspects of Justifiable and Excusable Homicide" (1958) 2(3) *Sydney Law Review* 414, 418.

111 *McKay* [1957] VR 560, 564. See too ibid. 417.

112 *McKay* [1957] VR 560, 564.

113 As Morris notes: Morris (n 110) 425.

114 *McKay* [1957] VR 560, 563. For a discussion of the Australian common law's acknowledgement of the existence of the partial defence of excessive self-defence, see Arlie Loughnan, Self, Others and the State: Relations of Criminal Responsibility (CUP, 2020) 126–8.

115 Morris (n 110) 435.

116 *McKay* [1957] VR 560, 570. "Serve him right", McKay said, shortly after the events in question.

117 Morris notes the "sympathetic publicity" that McKay had received (Morris (n 110) 432), and that "[t]he whole tone of the press reports of the case was to stress the provocation to which [he] had been subjected": at 433.

118 George P. Fletcher, "Proportionality and the Psychotic Aggressor: A Vignette in Comparative Criminal Theory" (1973) 8(3) *Israel Law Review* 367, 381.

119 Fiona Leverick, *Killing in Self-Defence* (OUP, 2006) 135.

property – it is said to make "a value judgment that property [...] is worth more than human life."[120]

From time to time in Australia, there has been pressure on judges and legislators to place greater weight on the first of these ideas than the second. So it was when the *McKay* litigation was on foot, and so it was in the 1990s in NSW. At that latter time, in the wake of a media-fuelled moral panic about "home invasions",[121] the NSW Parliament enacted the *Home Invasion (Occupant Protection) Act* 1998 (NSW) ("the *Home Invasion Act*"). Under that Act, "an occupant of a dwelling-house" was immunised from criminal liability if he or she killed "an intruder", reasonably believing that such action was necessary to defend "any property of, or within, the dwelling-house".[122]

In calmer times, however, Australian parliamentarians and judges have given priority to the second of these ideas. In the words of a former justice of the High Court of Australia ("HCA"), once "public concern" about "home invasions" evaporated in NSW, the NSW Parliament "gracefully repealed"[123] the *Home Invasion Act.* It replaced it with a statutory self-defence scheme that contained some of the provisions noted above. As we have seen, one of those provisions renders self-defence unavailable to the person who has intentionally or recklessly killed to protect property.[124] And, indeed, that same provision goes further than this. We have seen that, according to the common law as stated by *McKay*,[125] a person would be convicted of manslaughter, not murder, if (essentially) an unlawful attack caused him or her reasonably to fear for his or her life "or the safety of his [or her] person from injury",[126] but his or her response went beyond what he or she could reasonably believe to have been "necessary for his [or her] protection."[127] Section 421 of the *Crimes Act 1900* (NSW) takes the same approach. That section creates the "partial defence" of excessive self-defence. The "partial defence" reduces a killing from murder to manslaughter if, although the accused might have believed that his or her conduct was necessary for certain defensive purposes, that conduct was not a "reasonable response in the circumstances as he or she perceive[d] them".[128] Crucially, however, excessive self-defence is unavailable to the accused, like D, who kills with the requisite mental state for

---

120 Ibid.

121 There was in fact no evidence that "home invasions" had become more prevalent in NSW: Gareth Griffith, *Home Invasion and Self-Defence: An Update*, NSW Parliament Briefing Paper 17/98 (October 1998).

122 *Home Invasion (Occupants Protection) Act* 1998 (NSW) s 8 (repealed).

123 Virginia Bell, "Keeping the Criminal Law in 'Serviceable Condition': A Task for the Courts or the Parliament?" (2016) 27(3) *Current Issues in Criminal Justice* 335, 340.

124 *Crimes Act 1900* (NSW) s 420.

125 See text accompanying n 114. See, too, *The Queen v Howe* (1958) 100 CLR 448 ("*Howe*"); *Viro v The Queen* (1978) 141 CLR 88. Cf. *Zecevic v Director of Public Prosecutions* (1987) 162 CLR 645, 652–4 (Mason CJ), 664 (Wilson, Dawson and Toohey JJ); *Palmer v The Queen* [1971] AC 814, 831–2; *R v Clegg* [1995] 1 AC 482, 498–501.

126 *Howe* (1958) 100 CLR 448, 460 (Dixon CJ).

127 Ibid. 461.

128 *Crimes Act 1900* (NSW) s 421(1)(b).

murder because she believes that such conduct is necessary to protect property.[129] By legislating to this effect, the NSW Parliament – in common with other Australian legislatures – has committed itself to the view that such a person has erroneously valued property more than human life. Such an error, it says, is grave and obvious. Indeed, according to the view now taken by Australian law, it is so grave and obvious as to mean that s/he who makes it is owed no mitigation at all. His or her crime is not manslaughter; it is murder. Such an accused, the law says, has displayed sufficient culpability to be justifiably convicted of the latter offence.

Vignette 5: Criminal Responsibility of Subordinates for Systemic Offences

D is a soldier in the army of a country ruled by a junta of generals who have come to power through a violent coup. When an opposition group demands the return to a democratic system, the government orders the soldiers to shoot and kill any person who resists arrest. Following this order, D kills three young men who take part in a protest demonstration and hit a police officer who tries to arrest them. When D is tried after a change of regime, he says that he did not like to shoot the protesters but that he thought that he had to obey his commanders' orders. D knew that if he had refused to shoot, he might have been demoted, but no physical harm would have occurred to him. Should D be convicted of murder? If so, should his sentence be mitigated because of his situation?

If these events were to occur in Australia, D would be convicted of murder, and it is likely that D's situation would have limited (if any) mitigatory effect on his sentence.

a) Liability

Regarding liability, the only question that arises is whether D could successfully raise the "defence" of duress.[130] Depending on which Australian jurisdiction is being considered, there are a number of reasons why he could not.

The first of these reasons is that, in certain Australian jurisdictions, duress is not available to a person, like D, who is a principal in the first degree to murder. As noted above,[131] that is the effect of the NSWCCA's decision in *McConnell*[132] – and, in NSW, where the common law "defence" of duress still applies, that decision remains authoritative. It is true that there are persuasive arguments, grounded in principle and

---

129 Cf. *McKay* [1957] VR 560, 563.

130 The "defence" of superior orders appears to be unknown to the common law of Australia: *A v Hayden* (1984) 156 CLR 532, 540 (Gibbs CJ), 550 (Mason J), 562 (Murphy J), 580 (Brennan J), 593 (Deane J). Such a "defence" is provided for by the *Criminal Codes* of WA and Queensland (*Criminal Code Act 1913* (WA) s 31(1) and *Criminal Code Act 1899* (Qld) s 31(1)(b)) – but the Queensland "defence" is not available to a person charged with murder (*Criminal Code Act 1899* (Qld) s 31(2)) and the WA "defence" does not apply where, as in the case of D, the order was "manifestly unlawful" (*Criminal Code Act 1913* (WA) s 31(1)(b)), i.e. was one that the accused knew or ought to have known was unlawful: Fairall and Barrett (n 32) 251–2 [9.23]–[9.24]; Fisse (n 33) 554–5.

131 See text accompanying nn 20–22.

132 [1977] 1 NSWLR 714, 718 (Street CJ, with whom Taylor CJ at CL agreed at 723 and Begg J agreed at 723).

morality, against this position.[133] It is also true that this common law rule might one day be overturned. But that is by no means certain – and it can also be noted that, in particular Australian jurisdictions, a rule similar to the *McConnell* one has been placed on a statutory foundation. Section 40(2) of the *Criminal Code Act 1983* (NT) provides that the "excuse" created by s 40(1) – duress – "does not extend to an act, omission or event that would constitute an offence of which serious harm or an intention to cause such harm is an element". Section 20(1) of the *Criminal Code Act 1924* (Tas) provides that the Tasmanian "defence" of compulsion – which operates relatively similarly to duress at common law – "shall be an excuse for the commission [...] of any offence other than", relevantly, "murder". And, in South Australia ("SA"), duress is expressly stated not to be a defence to "a prescribed offence".[134] One such prescribed offence is murder.[135]

Secondly, in certain Australian jurisdictions, a person is prevented from relying on duress unless the threat to which he or she responded (by committing what would otherwise be a crime) was one of death or really serious injury.[136] It is debatable whether it is sound, as a matter of policy, to limit duress in such a fashion.[137] Indeed, other Australian jurisdictions have taken a different approach. For example, in Victoria,[138] SA,[139] the Australian Capital Territory ("ACT"),[140] the NT[141] and WA,[142] a person might be able to raise duress successfully if he or she performed the relevant conduct due to a *threat of any kind* that would otherwise have been carried out. But it can be noted that, even in those jurisdictions, this requirement might render duress unavailable to D. It is true that, if duress is to be raised successfully, the threat

133 See, for example, *Abbott v The Queen* [1977] AC 755, 772–4 (Lords Wilberforce and Edmund-Davies); Criminal Law Officers Committee of the Standing Committee of Attorneys-General, *Model Criminal Code, Chapters 1 and 2, General Principles of Criminal Responsibility* (December 1992) 65, where the Committee pithily observed: "Where free will is overborne by duress, the nature of the offence is not relevant".

134 *Criminal Law Consolidation Act 1935* (SA) s 15D(1).

135 *Criminal Law Consolidation Act 1935* (SA) s 15D(4).

136 This is the position at common law in Australia. *Carr v R* [2023] NSWCCA 269, [48] (Davies J, with whom Fagan J agreed at [80]), quoting *R v Hurley and Murray* [1967] VR 526, 543 (Smith J) ("*Hurley*"). See too, e.g., *R v Abusafiah* (1991) 24 NSWLR 531, 545 (Hunt J, with whom Gleeson CJ agreed at 532 and Mahoney relevantly agreed at 532–3) ("*Abusafiah*"). It is also the position in Tasmania: *Criminal Code Act 1924* (Tas) s 20(1).

137 See, for example, Criminal Law Officers Committee of the Standing Committee of Attorneys-General (n 133) 65, where the Committee agreed with a submission by Stanley Yeo that the "crime demanded might be trivial or serious but it has no necessary connection with the type of threat confronting the accused": Stanley Yeo, "Private Defences, Duress and Necessity" (1991) 15 *Criminal Law Journal* 139, 143.

138 *Crimes Act 1958* (Vic) s 322O(2)(a)(i).

139 *Criminal Law Consolidation Act 1935* (SA) s 15D(1)(a)(i).

140 *Criminal Code Act 2002* (ACT s 40(2)(a).

141 See *Criminal Code Act 1983* (NT) s 40(1)(a)–(b), (d).

142 *Criminal Code Act 1913* (WA) s 32(2) (a)(i).

need not have been an explicit one; it may have been implicit or unstated.[143] But, in D's case, was there even an implied *threat* of demotion?

Thirdly, and most fundamentally, even if there *was* an implied threat, D's situation is one that plainly would not meet the basal requirements of the "defence". For example, at common law in Australia, duress will be available:

> Where a person does acts otherwise criminal by reason only of his mind being then overborne by threats of death or serious bodily violence [...], provided that an average person of ordinary firmness of mind, of a like age and sex, in like circumstances, would have done the acts.[144]

It is worth emphasising here that the question is not one of whether such a hypothetical individual *could* or *might* have committed the acts – but, rather, whether he or she *would* have done so.[145] Additionally, in determining whether an accused would have so yielded, it is plain that the factfinder "should have regard [...] to the nature of the threat and its proportion to the crime committed".[146] The combination of those matters means that the factual threshold that must be satisfied for duress is a high one – particularly in circumstances where, as here, the accused has committed three intentional killings.

If we return to the scenario involving D, the significant disparity between any threat to him (demotion) and D's response to such a threat, is self-evident. Accordingly, it is inconceivable that D's will was in fact *overborne* by this threat, or that an average person of ordinary firmness of mind would have responded as D did.[147]

---

143 *Anna Rowan* (2024) 98 ALJR 508, 516 [39], 519–20 [56]–[62] (Gageler CJ, Gordon, Jagot and Beech-Jones JJ).

144 *R v Lawrence* [1980] 1 NSWLR 122, 143 (Moffitt P, with whom Nagle CJ at CL and Yeldham J agreed at 166).

145 *Abusafiah* (1991) 24 NSWLR 531, 540–2, 545 (Hunt J, with whom Gleeson CJ agreed at 532 and Mahoney JA generally agreed at 532). Cf. *R v Palazoff* (1986) 23 A Crim R 86; *R v Brown* (1986) 21 A Crim R 288, 293 (King CJ). It is true that, in *Hurley* [1967] VR 526, 543, Smith J stated that the question was whether "the circumstances were such that a person of ordinary firmness *would have been likely* to yield to the threat in the way that the accused did" (emphasis added). It is also true that the HCA has observed that his Honour's "statement of the elements of the common law defence has frequently been treated as authoritative": *Taiapa v The Queen* (2009) 240 CLR 95, 105 [28] fn. 46. See also *Anna Rowan* (2024) 98 ALJR 508, 515 [34]–[35] (Gageler CJ, Gordon, Jagot and Beech-Jones JJ). But, when supporting this statement, their Honours in *Taiapa* cited the three cases noted at the start of this footnote – *Abusafiah, Palazoff* and *Brown* (as well as *R v Dawson* [1978] VR 536 and *Lawrence* [1980] 1 NSWLR 122). Because *Abusafiah* is the most recent of these decisions, we assume that it correctly states the objective test for duress (although, if that is wrong, D would also not satisfy the slightly less demanding *Hurley* threshold).

146 *Abusafiah* (1991) 24 NSWLR 531, 544 (Hunt J, Gleeson CJ and Mahoney JA agreeing at 532).

147 A similar analysis applies in those Australian jurisdictions where duress is on a statutory footing and is available to a person, like D, who is charged with murder. In Victoria, for example, the accused will successfully raise duress only if he or she can establish that it is reasonably possible that, relevantly: (i) he or she reasonably believed "carrying out the conduct [was] the only reasonable way that the threatened harm [could] be avoided"; and (ii) "the conduct [was] a reasonable response to the threat": *Crimes Act 1958* (Vic) s 322O(2)(a)(ii)–(b). Killing three people is not a reasonable response to a threat of demotion. It is also not a

b) Sentencing

D's situation would also seemingly afford him little, if any, mitigation at sentence.

When sentencing an offender, Australian courts will take into account as a mitigating factor that the offender was acting under duress.[148] This is described as non-exculpatory duress. It refers to a situation where duress does not remove liability, but where the duress suffered by the offender renders him or her less culpable than an offender not operating under such circumstances.[149] In such a case, a court might also find a "reduced likelihood of future offending and a favourable expectation of rehabilitation once the duress has ceased to be operative".[150]

Non-exculpatory duress has, in appropriate cases, mitigated an offender's sentence for murder. For example, in *R v Robertson*,[151] the offender was 18 years old when he murdered the deceased with a cricket bat. The Court accepted that the offender's fear of violence at the hands of a third party, as well as his youth and immaturity, operated as non-exculpatory duress, and was thereby relevant at sentence.[152] But D's factual scenario makes it unlikely that the duress will have significant mitigatory effect. Indeed, it would seem likely that, rather than D's situation affording him mitigation in sentence, it might in fact *increase* the length of any sentence.

It must first be observed that the non-exculpatory duress might not even be established in the immediate case. If non-exculpatory duress is to be taken into account, the offender must establish, on the balance of probabilities, that he or she was acting under duress.[153] Consistently with what was noted above, it could be argued with some force that D was not, in fact, acting under the *threat* of demotion – but, rather, was motivated by a speculative or unsubstantiated fear that, if he behaved differently, he might lose his rank. If that argument were to be accepted, non-exculpatory duress would have no relevance.

Even if D were to be found to be acting under duress, however, it seems unlikely that the duress would have any mitigatory effect. The Courts determine on a case-by-case basis whether duress requires a reduction in penalty.[154] Because any duress here

---

"reasonable way" to avoid such threatened harm (let alone the "only" reasonable way). See also *Criminal Code Act 2002* (ACT) s 40(2) and *Criminal Code Act 1913* (WA) s 32(2). In both the ACT and WA, duress will succeed only if it is reasonably possible that the accused's conduct was "a reasonable response to the threat": *Criminal Code Act 2002* (ACT) s 40(2)(c); *Criminal Code Act 1913* (WA) s 32(2)(b).

148 See, e.g., *Crimes (Sentencing Procedure) Act 1999* (NSW) s 21A(3)(d).

149 *R v Day* [2009] SASC 84, [35] (Sulan J, with whom Doyle CJ agreed at [1] and White J agreed at [51]) ("*Day*"); *Tiknius v R* (2011) 221 A Crim R 365, 375–6 [41] (Johnson J, with whom Tobias AJA agreed at 367 [1] and Hall J agreed at 383 [104]) ("*Tiknius*").

150 *DG v R (No 1)* [2023] NSWCCA 30, [31] (The Court).

151 [2021] NSWSC 861.

152 Ibid. [173] (Ierace J). See also, for example, *R v ZT* [2022] NSWSC 511, [166]–[170] (Walton J).

153 See, e.g., *Filippou v The Queen* (2015) 256 CLR 47, 69–70 [64], 71 [66] (French CJ, Bell, Keane, and Nettle JJ, with whom Gageler J relevantly agreed at 73 [74]).

154 *Day* [2009] SASC 84, [35] (Sulan J, with whom Doyle CJ agreed at [1] and White J agreed at [51]).

is very minor, and because D's response to it so disproportionate, it seems likely that the sentencing court would find that D's moral culpability was not reduced on this account. And it would be difficult for a court to conclude that, due to the presence of such duress, D's prospects of rehabilitation were improved or his chances of reoffending reduced.

Additionally, in non-exculpatory duress cases, courts have emphasised the importance of general deterrence. In *R v Liu*,[155] the NSWCCA observed that, even where non-exculpatory duress had been established so as to mean that an offender may be unlikely to re-offend, "the sentence which [the offender] receives must be sufficient to remind others considering similar criminal activity that, if caught, a lengthy prison term will almost certainly follow".[156] And, in *R v Roach*,[157] the Victorian Court of Appeal similarly observed that "[g]eneral deterrence is not excluded by threats. On the contrary, general deterrence may provide a counter-threat". Given the seriousness of the offending in question here, a court would probably give significant weight to the sentencing aim of general deterrence,[158] when crafting the sentence for D. In other words, it would probably conclude that a very lengthy sentence was necessary to – among other things – disincentivise such activity.

Vignette 6: Limits of Consent

> V is a 21-year-old ambitious athlete and short-distance runner. He has learned that certain artificial limbs can enhance a runner's speed. He decides that he would rather have an artificial limb instead of his right lower leg. He approaches D, a surgeon in private practice, and asks him to amputate his leg below the knee and replace it with an artificial limb. D complies with V's request. Should D be punished for mayhem?

While Australian law delivers no clear answer to this question, it is likely that D would be convicted of a serious offence due to his amputation of V's right lower leg.

In NSW, the offence that D is prima facie liable for is inflicting grievous bodily harm with intent to do so;[159] in Victoria, the least serious offence with which D would be charged is causing serious injury intentionally;[160] and in SA, likewise, D would, on

---

155 [2005] NSWCCA 378, [34] (McClellan CJ at CL, with whom Hoeben J agreed at [68]).

156 See also *R v Riddell* (2009) 194 A Crim R 524, 536–9 [54]–[63] (Beazley JA, with whom Blanch J agreed at 544 [88] and Howie J agreed at 544 [89]); *Tiknius* (2011) 221 A Crim R 365, [51] (Johnson J, with whom Tobias AJA agreed at 367 [1] and Hall J agreed at 383 [104]).

157 [2005] VSCA 162, [15] (Callaway JA, with whom Ormiston JA agreed at [20] and Charles JA agreed at [21]).

158 See, e.g., *Crimes (Sentencing Procedure) Act 1999* (NSW) s 3A(b); *Sentencing Act 1991* (Vic) s 5(1)(b).

159 *Crimes Act 1900* (NSW) s 33(1).

160 *Crimes Act 1958* (Vic) s 16. We say "the least serious offence" because, in fact, D seems to have performed the elements of the more serious offence of causing serious injury intentionally in circumstances of gross violence: *Crimes Act 1958* (Vic) s 15A(1). See *Crimes Act 1958* (Vic) s 15A(2)(a) and (f).

the face of it, be guilty of causing serious harm to another with intent to do so.[161] Similar offences exist in the other Australian jurisdictions.[162] But would V's consent to the amputation give D an answer to the relevant charge?

At common law in Australia,[163] outside of well-established exceptions, consent is not available as an answer to a charge of inflicting "significant physical injury"/[164] grievous bodily harm.[165] It is true that surgery is a "well-established exception" to the rule just stated. In other words, in an appropriate case, an individual may successfully defend a serious injury charge on the basis that the relevant act was one of surgery, and the recipient consented to it.[166] But this exception almost certainly does not cover all consensual surgical procedures, and it would seem that it would not cover D's activities here.[167]

a) What is the precise ambit of the surgical exception?

In 1877, Sir James Fitzjames Stephen wrote, "Every one has a right to consent to the infliction of any bodily injury in the nature of a surgical operation upon him-

161 *Criminal Law Consolidation Act 1935* (SA) s 23(1).

162 See, e.g., *Crimes Act 1900* (ACT) s 19(1); *Criminal Code Act 1899* (Qld) s 317(1).

163 *Russell v R* (2023) 112 NSWLR 533, 562 [91] (The Court) ("*Russell*"); *R v Stein* (2007) 18 VR 376, 381 [21] (Kellam JA, with whom Vincent JA agreed at 377 [1] and Neave JA agreed at 377 [2]). This is consistent with the position in the United Kingdom. See, e.g., *R v M(B)* [2019] QB 1 ("*M(B)*"); *R v Brown* [1994] 1 AC 212 ("*Brown*"); and *Attorney-General's Reference (No 6 of 1980)* [1981] 1 QB 715. The NSWCCA in *Russell* expressly approved each of these decisions (at 562 [91]) – although only insofar as they concerned, or shed light on, the question of when 'consent lies as a defence to a count of infliction of *grievous bodily harm*': at 549 [54] (emphasis added).

164 To use the words of Vincent J in *R v McIntosh* [1999] VSC 358, [13].

165 *Russell* (2023) 112 NSWLR 533, 549 [54] (The Court).

166 See, e.g., *Attorney-General's Reference (No 6 of 1980)* [1981] QB 715, 719 (Lord Lane CJ for the England and Wales Court of Appeal); *Brown* [1994] 1 AC 212, 231 (Lord Templeman), 242, 245 (Lord Jauncey), 258–9, 266 (Lord Mustill), 277 (Lord Slynn).

167 In certain Australian jurisdictions, statute, rather than the common law, deals with the circumstances in which consent to surgery shields the surgeon from a serious injury charge. But it would seem that these provisions would not lead the present case to be decided any differently from how it would be at common law. For example, s 22(3) of the *Criminal Law Consolidation Act 1935* (SA) provides that: "A person may consent to harm (including serious harm) if the nature of the harm and the purpose for which it is inflicted fall within limits that are generally accepted in the community". It seems at least doubtful that a South Australian court would conclude that the amputation of a limb for non-medical reasons is generally acceptable to the community. Likewise, s 51 of the *Criminal Code Act 1924* (Tas) provides that it is lawful for "a person to perform in good faith and with reasonable care and skill a surgical operation upon another person, with his consent and for his benefit", *only if* "the performance of such an operation is reasonable, having regard to all the circumstances." It is hard to imagine a Tasmanian court holding that the amputation contemplated here is "reasonable." Section 26(3) of the *Criminal Code Act 1983* (NT) might seem more promising from D's point of view. It states, relevantly, that a person cannot "authorize or permit" another "to cause him serious harm" "*except in the case of medical treatment*" (emphasis added). But the sub-section stops short of stating that *all* serious harm that a surgeon consensually inflicts on a patient, is lawful – and it is doubtful that V's consent would cause D to avoid liability if these events were to occur in the Northern Territory.

self'.[168] Nearly 150 years after this pronouncement, the precise ambit of the exception has not been made clear. All that can be said is that, from time to time, courts have dealt with activities clearly falling *outside* the bounds of the exception, without making any clear statement as to which conduct will fall *inside* it.

Judicial statements about the exception and its scope have been sparse and vague. In *Attorney-General's Reference (No 6 of 1980)*,[169] after holding that "it is not in the public interest that people should try to cause, or should cause, each other actual bodily harm for no good reason", the England and Wales Court of Appeal ("EWCA") immediately made it clear that activities such as "reasonable surgical interference" stood on a different footing. This exception, their Lordships said, *was* "needed in the public interest"[170] – and a like approach was taken by various members of the House of Lords in *R v Brown.*[171] In this latter case, it was said that bodily harm could lawfully be inflicted in the course of "surgery",[172] or "necessary surgery", [173] or "reasonable surgery",[174] or "surgical treatment [...] if performed in accordance with good medical practice",[175] or surgery in the course of "proper medical treatment", [176] or "surgical operations".[177] In *Russell v R*,[178] the NSWCCA referred with evident approval to certain of the statements just noted. According to their Honours, "surgery" is an "established exception" to the rule that the complainant's consent is no answer to a grievous bodily harm charge.[179] But the Court provided no detail about exactly which surgical procedures this exception covers. It was not required to do so, because, as in the English cases,[180] the facts in *Russell* did not raise this matter squarely for decision.

---

168 Sir James Fitzjames Stephen, *A Digest of the Criminal Law (Crimes and Punishments)* (Macmillan (London) 1877, 1st ed) Article 204, 128. In a footnote, Sir James remarked: "I know of no authority for these propositions, but I apprehend they require none. The existence of surgery as a profession assumes their truth". Sir James did not expand on the ambit of this apparent exception, except to say that, plainly, a medical professional would nevertheless be subject to duties in the performing of such surgeries. No breach of duty question is presently relevant. There is no suggestion that D either provided negligent advice about the need for surgery (cf. *R v Patel* [2011] QCA 81, [4]–[5]) or failed to exercise reasonable care and skill when performing the amputation.

169 [1981] QB 715, 719 (Lord Lane CJ for the Court).

170 Ibid.

171 [1994] 1 AC 212.

172 Ibid. 231 (Lord Templeman).

173 Ibid. 242 (Lord Jauncey).

174 Ibid. 245 (Lord Jauncey).

175 Ibid. 258–259 (Lord Mustill).

176 Ibid. 266 (Lord Mustill).

177 Ibid. 277 (Lord Slynn).

178 (2023) 112 NSWLR 533, 551 [61], 554 [72], 555 [73] (The Court).

179 Ibid. 558 [82].

180 The question in *Brown* was whether the appellants had rightly been convicted of wounding and actual bodily harm offences, in circumstances where they had inflicted such injuries on the complainants in the course of consensual sado-masochistic activities. See, e. g., *Brown* [1994] 1 AC 212, 230, 236 (Lord Templeman). The question in *Attorney-General's Reference (No 6 of 1980)* was whether a person could be convicted of assault in circumstances

b) Cases falling outside the scope of the surgical exception

Courts have occasionally provided guidance about cases that clearly fall *outside* the scope of the surgical exception (or any other exception to the general rule that consent is no answer to a charge of causing grievous bodily harm). But those cases are best viewed as cases where there was, in truth, no consent, or where, as in *Russell*, the exception did not apply, because the surgery was performed by someone other than a doctor.

In *Ian Paterson v The Queen*,[181] the applicant was a surgeon who had been convicted of multiple counts of wounding and grievous bodily harm. The applicant's offending comprised his performance of unnecessary surgical procedures, including mastectomies, in circumstances where he had "deliberately misrepresented the contents of medical reports [...] [and] exaggerated the complainants' risk of cancer".[182] The case was accordingly dealt with on the basis that any consent by the victims was vitiated,[183] and is therefore irrelevant to the case with which we are dealing. V's consent to the amputation was clearly a fully informed one.

In *Russell*[184] the NSWCCA was concerned with body modification procedures performed by a person who, as indicated above, was not a medical practitioner. The same was so in the English case of *R v M(B)*,[185] where the applicant had consensually: (i) removed a customer's ear; (ii) removed a further customer's nipple; and (iii) split a third customer's tongue. In both cases, the Court held that the complainants' consent provided the defendant with no answer to the charges against him.[186] This was primarily due to his not being a doctor: according to the respective courts, surgical procedures performed by laypersons could hardly fall within the ambit of the surgical exception.[187] Those cases are, accordingly, of no immediate assistance. They offer no real guidance concerning when the surgical exception will, and will not, shield *surgeons* from criminal liability.[188]

---

where he or she had struck another in a consensual fight "otherwise than in the course of sport": *Attorney-General's Reference (No 6 of 1980)* [1981] QB 715, 717.

181 [2022] EWCA 456.

182 Ibid. [6].

183 The EWCA remarked at [33] that "in substance, the patients were deceived about the true position by the applicant, who dishonestly and for an improper collateral purpose misrepresented the position to them, thus vitiating their purported consent to the procedures he then carried out".

184 (2023) 112 NSWLR 533.

185 [2019] QB 1.

186 Ibid. 12–13 [41]–[45] (Lord Burnett CJ for the England and Wales Court of Appeal); *Russell* (2023) 112 NSWLR 533, 560–1 [87]–[88], 562 [91] (The Court).

187 *M(B)* [2019] QB 1, 12 [42] (Lord Burnett CJ for the England and Wales Court of Appeal), endorsed by the NSWCCA in *Russell* (2023) 112 NSWLR 533, 561 [88]–[89], 562 [91]. Lord Burnett CJ observed that the "implication" arising from Lord Lane's remarks in the *AG No 6* as to "reasonable surgical inference" was that "elective surgery would only be reasonable if carried out by someone qualified to perform it".

188 In *M(B)* [2019] QB 1, 13 [45], Lord Burnett CJ did refer disapprovingly to the applicant's argument that "consent to surgical treatment provid[es] [...] a defence to the person performing the surgery whether or not that person is a suitably qualified as a doctor, *and whether or not*

c) The immediate case[189]

If we return to the facts of the present case, it can first be noted that a scenario such as this seems unlikely to arise. As observed in *M(B)*, "[t]here are good reasons why reputable medical practitioners will not remove parts of the body simply when asked by a patient".[190] Yet it is far from unimaginable. In Scotland, a surgeon named Robert Smith amputated a leg from each of two patients – one in 1997 and one in 1999 – in circumstances where they had a "body dysmorphic disorder known as apotemnophilia, in which patients are convinced from childhood that they will be normal only once a limb has been removed".[191] No prosecution appears to have been contemplated there; but that could hardly be taken as demonstrating that the activities were lawful (or, still less, that they would be lawful if performed in Australia).

It appears that an Australian court applying the common law would decide that V's consent provided D with no answer to the charge against him. In so holding, it would seemingly attach much weight to the seriousness of the procedure in question (an amputation) and the absence of any compelling justification or need for it. It would also seemingly be influenced by what Lord Burnett CJ in *M(B)* described as "the values of society recognised from time to time by the judges"[192] – that is, by the absence of anything approaching a consensus in the community that D's activities are acceptable.

In *Russell*, the NSWCCA held that:[193]

---

there is a medical (including psychological) justification for the surgery" (emphasis added). But it is submitted that *M(B)* is not authority for the proposition that a surgeon will be able to rely on the surgical exception only if there is a "medical [...] justification" for the surgery. Rather, the ratio decidendi of the case concerns the legality of body modification procedures performed by people, like M(B), who are *not* medical practitioners.

189 Michael Peng extends his sincere thanks to Dr Emily O'Keefe, for assisting him in understanding the outcomes for patients who undergo amputation, the ethical quandaries that exist for medical practitioners on the question of amputation, and also for drawing his attention to the extensive relevant literature on this topic. This assisted him greatly to prepare this section of this response.

190 *M(B)* [2019] QB 1, 13 [43] (Lord Burnett CJ for the England and Wales Court of Appeal). Similarly, in *Russell*, Senior Counsel for the appellant observed that "registered medical practitioners [...] of course would not be prepared to do such procedures in the first place": *Russell v R* (2023) 112 NSWLR 533, 548 [50].

191 Claire Dyer, "Surgeon Amputated Healthy Legs" (2000) 320 (7231) *BMJ* 332.

192 *M(B)* [2019] QB 1, 8 [24].

193 *Russell v R* [2023] NSWCCA 272, [92] (note that this passage was not reported). In making this statement, the Court adopted the approach taken by Lord Burnett CJ in *M(B)* [2019] QB 1, [41]. It is worth observing that the conservative approach taken here by the NSWCCA (and by the EWCA) to this public policy question is different from the approach taken in New Zealand ("NZ"), which is also a common law jurisdiction. The NZ Court of Appeal in *R v Lee* [2006] NZLR 42 indicated a willingness to engage with public policy questions and create new exceptions to the general rule that a person cannot consent to GBH outside of well-established exceptions (see [261], [312]–[318]). As noted in *Russell* (2023) 112 NSWLR 533, 558 [82], however, "the decision in *Lee* represents a radical departure from the prevailing state of the law in Australia, Canada and England [...] It contemplates that consent may be a defence to the infliction of grievous bodily harm in certain circumstances (beyond the established exceptions such as boxing and surgery). Not even Lord Mustill's dissent in *Brown* went so far".

> Certainty is an important quality in the law and the weight of judicial authority in common law jurisdictions is that lines must be drawn subject to exceptions which are well established. The corollary of this is that, outside well-established exceptions, a case-by-case judicial inquiry into the social utility or disutility of particular conduct is best left for the legislature.

Of course, it could be argued that D's amputation of V's leg falls within the "well-established" surgical exception. But, as noted above, the ambit of this exception is unclear; and it seems that the common law judges who have acknowledged its existence, had in mind, when doing so, rather more conventional surgical procedures than the one at issue here. Admittedly, this takes us only so far. When Stephen made the statement quoted above, he presumably did not have cosmetic surgery in contemplation. Yet it seems clear that such surgery is lawful in Australia. Given that that is so, why would D's activities be treated any differently?

It could be argued that the removal of a vital body part is so significant – and so inherently dangerous – as to prevent any analogy being drawn between the operation performed by D and cosmetic surgery. Medical literature is replete with studies on the outcomes for individuals who undergo amputation of lower limbs, and the following perhaps suffices to illustrate the difficulties they face:[194]

> Loss of a limb has a profound impact on health indicators, including physical, mental, and emotional health. Associations between lower limb loss (LLL) and impaired functional mobility, an aspect of physical health, have been well documented. Limited mobility often persists in the months and years following limb amputation. LLL is also associated with other physical and mental health problems, such as pain (e. g., phantom limb, residuum, and back pain) and depression.

But also, perhaps more tellingly, there would appear to be an array of different views in the community about the acceptability of a procedure like D's.[195] Accordingly, this is just the kind of case to which Lord Atkin was referring when he said that: "the mere consent of the patient to an operation which may be considered contrary to public policy, or likely to be an injury to the public generally, is not such an operation

---

194 Dagmar Amtmann et al., "Health-related Profiles of People with Lower Limb Loss" (2016) 96(8) *Archives of Physical Medicine and Rehabilitation* 1474 (citations omitted). See also, e. g., Robert Gailey et al., "Review of Secondary Physical Conditions Associated with Lower-limb Amputation and Long-term Prosthesis Use" (2008) 45(1) *Journal of Rehabilitation Research & Development* 15; Matthijs Oosterhoff et al., "More than Half of Persons with Lower Limb Amputation Suffer from Chronic Back Pain or Residual Limb Pain: A Systematic Review with Meta-analysis" (2022) 44(6) *Disability and Rehabilitation* 834; Shruti Turner et al., "Issues Faced by People with Amputation(s) During Lower Limb Prosthetic Rehabilitation: A Thematic Analysis" (2022) 46(1) *Prosthetics and Orthotics International* 61.

195 The degree of controversy concerning this issue is fairly self-evident, but can be seen in, e. g., the following texts, which demonstrate extensive debate on whether individuals should be allowed to amputate healthy limbs: Peter Barry, "The Ethics of Voluntary Amputation" (2012) 26(1) *Public Affairs Quarterly* 1; Richard Gibson, "No Harm, No Foul? Body Integrity Identity Disorder and the Metaphysics of Grievous Bodily Harm" (2020) 20(1) *Medical Law International* 73; Tim Bayne and Neil Levy, "Amputees by Choice: Body Integrity Identity Disorder and the Ethics of Amputation" (2005) 22(1) *Journal of Applied Philosophy* 75; Sabine Müller, "Body Integrity Identity Disorder (BIID) – Is the Amputation of Healthy Limbs Ethically Justified?" (2009) 9(1) *The American Journal of Bioethics* 36.

as would relieve the surgeon from [criminal] responsibility".[196] In other words, in the face of controversy about whether the amputation of limbs for non-medical purposes should be lawful, an Australian court would be likely to leave it to Parliament to legalise such conduct if, after hearing from interested parties and taking account of the community's views, it considered such a course to be appropriate.

Vignette 7: Withdrawal from an Attempt

> 25-year-old D is deeply upset with her former boyfriend V, who had ended their relationship to be with another woman. To punish V, D plans to stab him with a large knife. D knows that the stab wounds can be fatal and accepts V's death as a possible outcome. When V goes jogging, D attacks him from behind and stabs him in the back three times. V breaks down. D realises that she has injured him but that the injuries will not cause his death. She realises that she could kill him by stabbing him again but decides to leave him alone. Should D be punished for attempted murder?

If these events were to occur in Australia, D would seemingly avoid being convicted of attempted murder. That is not because Australian law provides a person with an answer to an attempt charge if it is possible[197] (or if he or she can prove[198]) that he or she voluntarily abandoned the attempt. It does not.[199] Rather, it is because, at the time of stabbing V, D seems to have lacked the requisite mental state for attempted murder – an intent to kill.[200] That said, if this is wrong – that is, if D did have an intent to kill V when she stabbed him – D *would* be convicted of attempted murder. Her later voluntary desistance from the attempt would, however, seemingly be a mitigating factor at sentencing.[201]

The first point to note here is that, throughout Australia, a person commits an attempt if, to use the language of s 321N(1) of the *Crimes Act 1958* (Vic), he or she performs an act that is "more than merely preparatory to the commission of [...] [an] offence" and is "immediately and not remotely connected with the commission of the offence" (the physical element), with the intention of committing that offence (the mental element).[202] There can be no doubt that, in the above hypothetical, D has

---

196 Penney Lewis, "The Medical Exception" (2012) 65(1) *Current Legal Problems* 355, 357, quoting Lord Justice Atkin, who was responding to Lord Riddell, "The Legal Responsibility of the Surgeon" 19 *Transactions of the Medico-Legal Society* 83, *Discussion*, 93–97, 95.

197 See RA Duff, *Criminal Attempts* (OUP, 1996) 72.

198 See Child et al. (n 31) 387.

199 See, e.g., *R v Page* [1933] VLR 351, 353–5 (Mann ACJ, delivering the judgment of the Court); *Criminal Code Act 1899* (Qld) s 4(2); *Criminal Code Act 1924* (Tas) s 2(2); *Criminal Code Act 1913* (WA) s 4; *Criminal Code Act 1983* (NT) s 4(2).

200 See, e.g., *Cutter v R* (1997) 143 ALR 498, 499 (Brennan CJ and Dawson J), 503 (McHugh J), 503 (Gummow J), 507, 509 (Kirby J); *McGhee v The Queen* (1995) 183 CLR 82, 85–6 (Brennan J), 97 (Dawson J); *Knight v The Queen* (1992) 175 CLR 495, 501 (Mason CJ, Dawson and Toohey JJ); *Alister v The Queen* (1984) 154 CLR 404, 421 (Gibbs CJ).

201 See, most starkly, *Criminal Code Act 1899* (Qld) s 538. But see also, e.g., *Criminal Code Act 1924* (Tas) s 2(2); *Criminal Code Act 1913* (WA) s 4; *Criminal Code Act 1983* (NT) s 4(2).

202 *Crimes Act 1958* (Vic) s 321N(2)(a). See also, e.g., *Criminal Code Act 1913* (WA) s 4.

performed the physical element of attempted murder. By thrice stabbing D in the back, she has clearly performed more than merely preparatory conduct. Indeed, D has gone *well* beyond mere preparation. She has done "what is (for all [s]he knows) the last act necessary to complete the offence".[203] However, as Brennan J explained in *McGhee v The Queen*,[204] a person can only have an intention to commit murder if he or she intends to cause the result that must be caused before that crime is complete – death – and, as just indicated, D seems to have lacked such an intent. According to the facts with which we have been provided, D "accepts V's death as a possible outcome" – which is a very different mental state from an intention to kill V.[205] It is true that D must have had an intention to inflict grievous bodily harm upon V.[206] It is also true that an intention to cause grievous bodily harm is a sufficient mental state for murder throughout Australia.[207] But, as we have already twice indicated, the mental threshold for attempted murder is higher than for the completed offence.

The second point to note is that if we are wrong and, when D stabbed V, she had an intent to kill him, she would be guilty of attempted murder as a matter of Australian law. D has undoubtedly *voluntarily* desisted from any attempt of hers to murder V. In other words, it seems that she has abandoned such an attempt, not because she suddenly realised that she was under "police observation",[208] or because "completion [was] [...] harder than [...] expected",[209] or for any other "objectionable"[210] reason – but, rather, because she realised "that what she [...] [was] trying to do [...] [was] wrong."[211] But Australian law is clear. According to s 4 of the *Criminal Code Act 1899* (Qld), "[i]t is immaterial, except so far as regards punishment [...] whether the offender desists of his or her own motion from the further prosecution of" an attempt. Section 4 of the *Criminal Code Act 1913* (WA) and s 4(2) of the *Criminal*

---

203 Duff (n 197) 69.

204 (1995) 183 CLR 82, 86. See too, e.g., *R v Whybrow* (1951) 35 Cr App R 141, 146–7 (Lord Goddard CJ for the England and Wales Court of Appeal).

205 *Zaburoni v The Queen* (2016) 256 CLR 482, 489 [10] (Kiefel, Bell and Keane JJ).

206 Grievous bodily harm is so "obvious and inevitable" a consequence of thrice stabbing another person in the back, as to mandate the inference that the stabber's intent was to cause that consequence: *Parker v The Queen* (1963) 111 CLR 610, 649 (Windeyer J).

207 See, e.g., *Crimes Act 1900* (NSW) s 18(1)(a); *The Queen v Crabbe* (1985) 156 CLR 464, 467–9 (The Court).

208 See Child et al. (n 31) 387.

209 Gideon Yaffe, *Attempts: In the Philosophy of Action and the Criminal Law* (OUP, 2011) 298.

210 Ibid.

211 Duff (n 197) 68. Duff notes that a person may desist, "not for any moral reason, nor because he suddenly realizes that he might well be caught, but because he has a prudential change of mind about whether it is worth risking punishment to commit this crime": at 69. He concludes that this person's desistance should be viewed as voluntary: at 397. But whether or not that is so – and Duff's reasoning does seem sound – D would not seem to be such a person. If she had killed V, she would presumably have had a better chance of escaping detection that she now does. By allowing him to live, she has made it practically inevitable that she will be convicted of a very serious offence.

Code Act 1983 (NT) say exactly the same thing.[212] Section 2(2) of the *Criminal Code Act 1924* (Tas) states that "[t]he offence of attempting to commit a crime may be committed, although the offender voluntarily desists from the actual commission of the crime itself". And in the leading common law case, *R v Page*,[213] the Full Court of the Supreme Court of Victoria held that, to use the language of the headnote:

> Where the prisoner has so far prosecuted his criminal purpose as otherwise to be guilty of an attempt, he is not exculpated by the fact that owing to a mere change of mind he desists, of his own free will, from completion of his purpose.

The third point to note is that, in all Australian jurisdictions, D would seemingly have her sentence for attempted murder reduced on account of her voluntary abandonment of this attempt. The position is clearest in Queensland. Section 538(1) of the *Criminal Code Act 1899* (Qld) provides that a person who is convicted of an attempt will be "liable to one-half only of the punishment to which the person would otherwise be liable" if he or she proves that he or she "desisted of [...] [his or her] own motion from the further prosecution of [...] [his or her] intention". And s 538(2) goes on to provide that where, as is the case with attempted murder,[214] the maximum penalty is normally life imprisonment, "the greatest punishment" that can be imposed on the offender who has voluntary desisted, is 14 years' imprisonment. But in other Australian jurisdictions, too, it would seem that D's desistance would cause her sentence to be mitigated. We have seen that the *Criminal Codes* of WA and the NT state that voluntary desistance from an attempt is immaterial "*except so far as regards punishment*" (emphasis added). Similarly, when sentencing D, courts in the other Australian States and Territories would be likely to reason that her abandonment: (i) was evidence of remorse,[215] and/or (ii) showed her "to be someone who recognizes sufficient reason to refrain" from criminal wrongdoing, "even in the face of a lower sanction"[216] – and who is therefore less in need of specific deterrence.[217]

Our fourth and last point concerns *why* Australian law takes the approach that it does. As Yaffe has indicated, while there is a prevalent and powerful intuition that the attempter who voluntarily desists "is importantly different, and ought to be treated differently under the law",[218] commentators disagree about what the appropriate legal

---

212 Though they use sexist language: "It is immaterial,' they provide", "except so far as regards punishment, whether the offender [...] desists of his own motion from the further prosecution of his intention."

213 [1933] VLR 351, 351. *Page* remains authoritative in Victoria, as well as in NSW, SA and the ACT.

214 *Criminal Code Act 1899* (Qld) s 306(1).

215 See in this regard *R v BBF* [2007] QCA 262, [21] (Keane JA, with whom de Jersey CJ agreed at [1] and Jerrard JA agreed at [2]). It is well-established that remorse is a mitigating factor at sentencing. See, e. g., *Crimes (Sentencing Procedure) Act 1999* (NSW) s 21 A(3)(i); *Sentencing Act 1991* (Vic) s 5(2C).

216 Yaffe (n 209) 309.

217 In all Australian jurisdictions, specific deterrence is one of the purposes of punishment. See, e. g., *Crimes (Sentencing Procedure) Act 1999* (NSW) s 3 A(b); *Sentencing Act 1991* (Vic) s 5(1)(b).

218 Yaffe (n 209) 288.

response is.[219] Should such an attempter merely be granted mitigation? Or should he or she be acquitted? According to Yaffe, mitigation is the correct legal response. "An attempter who abandons", he says, "has committed a crime – the crime of attempt – and this fact is not erased by his abandonment, nor are most of the reasons for punishing attempts negated by it."[220] In other words, Yaffe's reasoning seems to be that this person has performed the actus reus of attempt, with the requisite mens rea, and has acted culpably enough to warrant being convicted. According to Simester & Sullivan, however, "there is something inapt about such an unyielding analysis."[221] "A genuine change of heart by D prior to bringing about harm", the authors continue, "indicates that intervention and restraint were not required for that occasion. Further, some voluntary withdrawals can considerably reduce D's culpability."[222] And for Duff, likewise, if we convict and punish certain voluntary desisters, we show scant regard for their autonomy. They have chosen to "alter the character of [...] [their] whole course of conduct by abandoning the attempt", he reasons;[223] they have voluntarily desisted before doing all they can to bring about the relevant harm; and they should not be treated as though they *have* "crossed the Rubicon and burnt [...] [their] boats."[224]

There is much to be said for such reasoning. But, consistently with what an Australian textbook has observed,[225] it has no application to the case of D. When she stabbed V, she *did* "cross the Rubicon": from her point of view, she performed the last act that was necessary to bring about his death. And Duff is explicit about such cases. After observing that, under the *Model Penal Code*, a person would be acquitted of attempted murder if, "after shooting his victim, completely and voluntarily renounced his criminal purpose and secured life-saving treatment for her",[226] Duff makes clear his disagreement with such an approach. His basic argument is that, if a person does "what would, for all he knew, put it beyond his power to prevent the crime's completion",[227] it is not at all disrespectful of his autonomy to convict him of an attempt. We agree. Assuming still that D had an intent to kill when she stabbed V, she completed what she thought was a murderous attack on him. Should not such a person – a person, that is, who has culpably[228] done all that she can to bring about a

219 Ibid. 288–9. See also Duff (n 197) 66.

220 Yaffe (n 209) 291–2. See too Ormerod and Laird (n 29) 455.

221 Child et al. (n 31) 386.

222 Ibid.

223 Duff (n 197) 396.

224 *Director of Public Prosecutions v Stonehouse* [1978] AC 55, 68 (Lord Diplock).

225 Simon Bronitt and Bernadette McSherry, *Principles of Criminal Law* (Lawbook Co, 2017, 4th ed) 470 [8.60]. "The policy for allowing desistance to exculpate an accused", the authors say, "obviously makes more sense the further back the conduct is from the substantive offence."

226 Duff (n 197) 70.

227 Ibid. 396.

228 Like Duff, Simester & Sullivan draw a distinction between such an actor and the person who voluntarily abandons an attempt at an earlier stage. "[S]hould D take aim at V and shoot with intent to kill", they say, "D's innate culpability remains the same whether or not she

death – be convicted of attempted murder if, for reasons beyond her control, the victim survives?

Vignette 8: Criminal Responsibility of Minors

D is a 13-year-old boy. He abducts and rapes V, a girl of the same age. Should D be punished for a criminal offence?

Whether D could and should be punished for a criminal offence are different questions. Addressing first whether D could be punished: since 2000, the age of 10 had been the minimum age of criminal responsibility ("MACR") in all Australian jurisdictions.[229] Recently, some jurisdictions have raised this minimum age level to 12 or 14 years of age, with some planning an increase to the age of 14 in the near future.[230] This means that currently D *could* be liable to prosecution, a finding of guilt and the imposition of punishment in all Australian jurisdictions. However, beyond the minimum age of criminal responsibility, until the age of 14, there is a rebuttable presumption that a child lacks the capacity to be criminally responsible for his or her acts (at common law called the presumption of *doli incapax*). This presumption is anchored in legislation in some jurisdictions[231] but remains a matter of common law in NSW and SA.

---

succeeds in killing V. Yet, if D should take aim and then voluntarily desist, the survival of V is to D's credit": Child et al. (n 31) 387.

229 See, e.g., *Children (Criminal Proceedings) Act 1987* (NSW) s 5. Historically, in common law systems, this was fixed at the age of 7. Many common law jurisdictions raised this age level to 10 from the 1960s onwards. The last Australian jurisdictions to do so, in 2000, were the ACT and Tasmania. This was in response to the Australian Law Reform Commission and the Equal Opportunity Commission calling on all Australian jurisdictions in 1997 to agree on a uniform MACR because it was seen to be wrong that, depending on the child's age, he or she could be liable to be charged in one jurisdiction but not another for the same behaviour (Australian Law Reform Commission and the Equal Opportunity Commission, "Seen and Heard: Priority for Children in the Legal Process", Report No 84 (1997) [18.20]). For a discussion of the history of the age of criminal responsibility in an Australian context, see Thomas Crofts, "The Common Law Influence over the Age of Criminal Responsibility – Australia" (2016) 67(3) *Northern Ireland Legal Quarterly* 283.

230 See, e.g., *Justice (Age of Criminal Responsibility) Legislation Amendment Act 2023* (ACT), amending *Criminal Code 2002* (ACT) s 25. See also *Youth Justice Act* (Vic) s 10. While the MACR is now 14 in the ACT, there is a 'carve-out' such that a child aged 12 but not yet 14 can be held liable for certain serious offences provided that he or she knew that his or her conduct was wrong. Tasmania has committed to raising the MACR to 14 with no exceptions by 2029: see Tasmanian Government, Department for Education, Children and Young People Youth Justice Blueprint 2024–2034, "Keeping Children and Young People Out of the Youth Justice System" (2023): https://publicdocumentcentre.education.tas.gov.au/library/Shared%20Documents/Youth-Justice-Blueprint.pdf, viewed 1 September 2025. While the NT was the first jurisdiction to raise the MACR to 12 years of age in 2022 it was returned to the age of 10 in 2024 following a change of government: *Criminal Code Amendment Act 2024* (NT) s 4.

231 The presumption is legislatively embedded in all the Code criminal jurisdictions of Australia: *Criminal Code 2002* (ACT) s 26; *Criminal Code* (Cth) s 7.2; *Criminal Code 1983* (NT) s 38(2); *Criminal Code 1899* (Qld) s 29(2); *Criminal Code 1924* (Tas) s 18(2); *Criminal Code 1913* (WA) s 29 second para. It has also been given a statutory form in Victoria: *Youth Justice Act 2024* (Vic) s 11. It should also be noted that there are variations throughout Australia in how this presumption is formulated. It is debatable whether these differences in wording are intended to make a difference in application: see Dominique Moritz and

To rebut the presumption of *doli incapax*, the prosecution must bring proof of all elements of the offence, as well as proof that the child knew that what they were doing was seriously wrong, as distinct from an act of mere naughtiness or mischief.[232] In *R v M*, [233] Bray CJ explained that this requires proof that the child knew that the act was wrong according to the ordinary standards of reasonable people. Recently, in *RP v The Queen*, the HCA confirmed this formulation – noting that, aside from establishing that the child knew that the offence was seriously wrong in a moral sense, there was "the further dimension of proof of knowledge of serious wrongness as distinct from mere naughtiness".[234] The HCA also confirmed that the child's understanding "must be proved by express evidence, and cannot in any case be presumed from the mere commission of the act".[235] In all Australian jurisdictions, the common law irrebuttable presumption that a male child under 14 was incapable of having, or intending to have, sexual intercourse, has been abolished.[236]

When seeking to rebut the presumption, the prosecution may rely on evidence from a range of sources.[237] While evidence of the age of the child or type of act committed cannot in itself be used to rebut the presumption, it may be used to indicate how much other evidence is required to rebut the presumption. The closer the child is to 14[238] and the more serious the offence, the easier it will be to rebut the presumption.[239] Other evidence may come from what the child says to the police or to others,[240] and how the child behaved before, during or after performing the relevant conduct. This may include behaviour showing planning (for example, using sophisticated subterfuge to lure the victim away to a secluded space to commit a sexual/indecent assault),[241] taking steps to cover up the offence (for example, only attacking when adults

---

Mac Tuomi, "Four Thresholds of Doli Incapax in Australia: Inconsistency or Uniformity for Children's Criminal Responsibility?" (2022) 48(1) *Alternative Law Review* 25; Thomas Crofts, "Prosecuting Child Offenders: Factors Relevant to Rebutting the Presumption of Doli Incapax" (2018) 40(3) *Sydney Law Review* 339, 345–6.

232 Older writers spoke of the ability to "discern between good and evil at the time of the offence committed": Matthew Hale, *The History of the Pleas of the Crown* (London, 1736) vol. 1, 26. In *R v Gorrie* (1919) 83 JP 136, Salter J explained that proof that the child had "mischievous discretion" necessitated that the prosecution "must satisfy the jury that when the boy did this he knew that he was doing what was wrong – not merely what was wrong, but what was gravely wrong, seriously wrong".

233 (1977) 16 SASR 589, 591 ("*M*").

234 (2016) 259 CLR 641, 650 [11] ("*RP*").

235 Ibid. See also *C v DPP* [1996] AC 1, 38.

236 *Crimes Act 1900* (NSW) s 61S; *Crimes Act 1958* (Vic) s 62(1); *Criminal Code (Qld) 1899* s 29; *Criminal Code 1913* (WA) s 29; *Criminal Law Consolidation Act 1935* (SA) s 73(2); *Crimes Act 1900* (ACT) s 68; *Criminal Code 1983* (NT) s 38.

237 For detailed discussion of the types of factors that can be drawn on to rebut the presumption of doli incapax, see Crofts (n 231).

238 *B v The Queen* [1958] 44 Cr App R 1, 3; *RH v DPP (NSW)* [2013] NSWSC 520. In *RP* (2016) 259 CLR 641, 651 [12], Kiefel, Bell, Keane and Gordon JJ were critical of this approach because it is "apt to suggest that children mature at a uniform rate".

239 *C v DPP* [1996] AC 1, 39; *RH v DPP (NSW)* [2013] NSWSC 520, [12].

240 *IPH v Chief Constable of South Wales* [1987] Crim LR 42; *R v EI* [2009] QCA 177.

241 *R v Sheldon* [1996] 2 Cr App R 50 ("*Sheldon*").

are away,[242] covering the victim's mouth,[243] attempting to cast blame on others,[244] or making threats to prevent reporting of the assault[245]). Evidence may also be drawn from the child's educational or family background,[246] or a previous criminal record;[247] and it is also possible for an expert to be called to assess the child's understanding.[248]

This means that whether D could be found guilty for an offence would depend on what evidence the prosecution could bring about the elements of these offences and of his understanding of the wrongfulness of his behaviour. Any evidence which may show that he had the requisite understanding would have to be carefully balanced against evidence which might point in the other direction. This is well-illustrated by *RP*, a case involving a boy aged 11-and-a-half who had committed sexual acts against his younger brother. Here, there was evidence showing that RP was in the borderline range of intellectual disability. Furthermore, evidence such as RP's use of a condom when sexually assaulting his brother was thought to indicate that he himself may have been subject to sexual abuse, or exposed to inappropriate sexual material, which would have affected his ability to understand the wrongfulness of his behaviour.[249]

Applying these factors to the scenario involving D, that D was in the older age range at which the presumption applies, and that he committed serious and obviously wrong conduct, might mean that it will not take a great deal of further evidence for the prosecution to rebut the presumption of *doli incapax*. Evidence of D's understanding of the wrongfulness of his conduct might come from the fact that he abducted the victim before committing a sexual assault, suggesting careful planning. Furthermore, it is likely that the victim's distress would have been evident to D: continuing a sexual assault in disregard of that distress might strengthen a conclusion that he understood that this behaviour was seriously wrong. Such evidence would need to be balanced against any evidence contextualising this conclusion and indicating that D might lack such understanding – for example, evidence of his level of mental development or evidence of the circumstances of his upbringing.

The second, and distinct question, which ought to be briefly addressed, is whether D *should* be punished for his behaviour. While D has committed seriously wrong conduct, the question is whether the criminal justice system is the best place to respond to such behaviour. When viewed in an international context, Australia – in common

242 *RP* (2016) 259 CLR 641.

243 *RP* (2016) 259 CLR 641; *BP v The Queen* [2006] NSWCCA 172.

244 *Sheldon* [1996] 2 Cr App R 50; *RP* (2016) 259 CLR 641; *AL v The Queen* [2017] NSWCCA 34 ("*AL*").

245 *AL* [2017] NSWCCA 34.

246 *RP* (2016) 259 CLR 641, 652–3 [18]–[19]; *AL* [2017] NSWCCA 34; *M v J* [1989] Tas R 212.

247 *M* (1977) 16 SASR 589, 594–5; *R v F; Ex parte A-G (Qld)* [1998] QCA 97; *GW v The Queen* (2015) 20 DCLR (NSW) 236, 240–1 [17]–[22].

248 *R v EI* [2009] QCA 177. See *RP* (2016) 259 CLR 641, 652–3 [16]–[19] for discussion of the use of reports not specifically prepared about the child's understanding in the relevant case.

249 *RP* (2016) 259 CLR 641, 652–3 [18]–[19].

with other common law jurisdictions – has a low MACR. This is something that has been criticised by the UN Committee on the Rights of the Child, which has repeatedly called on Australia – and other common law jurisdictions – to raise the MACR to an internationally acceptable minimum level.[250] While in 2007 this was thought to be the age of 12,[251] in 2019 the UN Committee revised this upwards to at least the age of 14,[252] but preferably higher. The UN Committee emphasised that this should be a minimum, and it cautioned against countries with a higher MACR reducing it.[253]

In Australia, there have been growing calls for an increase in the MACR. These calls have come from a diverse range of sources, including academics, campaigners, NGOs, politicians and professional bodies.[254] The airing in August 2016, on ABC television, of a *Four Corners* episode that exposed the cruel treatment of children in detention in the NT, shocked the Australian public and gave a rare public insight into the treatment of children who get into trouble with the law. This added fuel to calls for change. Only a few days later, a Royal Commission into the Protection and Detention of Children in the Northern Territory ("Royal Commission") was established, which recommended increasing the MACR to 12 and removing children under 14 from detention.[255] One year after the Commission published its report, the Commonwealth Attorney-General agreed in November 2018 to establish a Council of Attorneys-General Age of Criminal Responsibility Working Group to examine whether to raise the MACR. While some Australian jurisdictions are waiting for unified action on whether to raise the MACR (as well as on the related question of, if it is to be raised, what age it should be raised to), other jurisdictions are independently pressing ahead with change. For example, Victoria has raised the MACR to 12, the ACT has raised it to 14 (although a child aged 12 or 13 may be held criminally responsible for certain serious offences if it is proved that he or she knew that his or her conduct was wrong) and Tasmania is planning to increase the MACR to 14 with no exceptions by 2029. Bucking this trend, the Northern Territory, which was the first jurisdiction to raise the MACR to the age of 12 in 2022, has recently taken the MACR back to 10 following a change in government.

As the UN Committee and the Royal Commission note, one major reason for increasing the MACR is that this would bring the law closer into line with recent research – particularly from developmental psychology and neuroscience – that children, even beyond teenage years, are in the process of developing the capacities

250 United Nations, Committee on the Rights of the Child: Concluding Observations: Australia (2005) (UN Doc CRC/C/15/Add.268) para 74a; United Nations, Committee on the Rights of the Child: Concluding Observations: Australia (2012) (UN Doc CRC/C/AUS/CO/4) para 84(a).

251 United Nations Committee on the Rights of the Child (2007) General Comment No 10 (UN Doc CRC/C/GC/10) [30].

252 United Nations Committee on the Rights of the Child (2019) General Comment No 24 (UN Doc CRC/C/GC/24) [22] ("UNCRC 2019").

253 Ibid.

254 For recent discussion see, Thomas Crofts, "Act Now: Raise the Minimum Age of Criminal Responsibility" (2023) 35(1) *Current Issues in Criminal Justice* 118.

255 Royal Commission into the Protection and Detention of Children in the Northern Territory, *Final Report* (2017, Volume 2B) 418.

thought to underlie an ascription of criminal responsibility.[256] Such research is showing that children are in a period of neuro-developmental immaturity, where they are prone to impulsive, sensation-seeking behaviour, and have an underdeveloped capacity to gauge the consequences of actions. They tend to be less future-oriented with their decisions, weigh gains more heavily than losses compared to adults and to have a heightened vulnerability to peer influence.[257] This can be impacted by brain trauma caused by factors such as "poor prenatal care, a lack of early life access to appropriate physical and mental health support from families […] exposure to violence and other traumatic experiences […] as well as exposure to things that may damage brain development such as head injuries, drugs and alcohol, and the effect of poor socio-economic conditions".[258] Furthermore, the typical characteristics of children inside the child justice system indicates that these are the very children who need help and support. Children who engage in wrongdoing, or who are at risk of engaging in such behaviour, experience complex needs. This term refers to "individuals who have a combination of: mental health problems; cognitive disability, including intellectual and developmental disability; physical disability; behavioural difficulties; precarious housing; social isolation; family dysfunction; and problematic drug or alcohol use".[259] In an Australian context, there is also the issue of the chronic overrepresentation of Indigenous children in the child justice system.[260]

There is therefore little to be gained, and much to be lost, by drawing children into the criminal justice system. Involvement with the criminal justice system can inflict harms that permanently prevent children from developing into fully autonomous adults.[261] This means that D should not be liable to prosecution in any Australian jurisdiction for his behaviour, and in the future it is likely that he could not be. This does not of course mean that nothing can or should be done with a child who has engaged in behaviour that could constitute a criminal offence – especially where the conduct is as serious as that engaged in by D. Such conduct might indicate the need for interventions though the social welfare system to address the root causes of the child's behaviour and support those responsible for his or her welfare.

---

256 UNCRC 2019, [22]; Royal Commission into the Protection and Detention of Children in the Northern Territory *Final Report* (2017, Volume 1) 134.

257 Research summarised in Sentencing Advisory Council Victoria, *Sentencing Children and Young People in Victoria* (2021): http://www.sentencingcouncil.vic.gov.au/sites/default/files/publication-documents/Sentencing%20Children%20and%20Young%20People%20in%20Victoria.pdf; for further summary and references, see Thomas Crofts "Age of Criminal Responsibility: Getting Older and Wiser" (2024) 47(4) *Criminal Law Journal* 470.

258 Thomas Crofts, Enys Delmage and Laura Janes "Deterring Children from Crime Through Sentencing: Can It Be Justified?" (2022) *Youth Justice* 11.

259 Morag McArthur, Aoni Suomi and Belinda Kendall, *Review of the service system and implementation requirements for raising the minimum age of criminal responsibility in the Australian Capital Territory: Final Report* (2021) 18.

260 Chris Cunneen, *Arguments for Raising the Minimum Age of Criminal Responsibility*, Research Report, Comparative Youth Penality Project, University of New South Wales (2017).

261 Kathryn Hollingsworth, "Theorising Children's Rights in Youth Justice: The Significance of Autonomy and Foundational Rights", (2013) 76(6) *Modern Law Review* 1046; Ray Arthur, "Exploring childhood, criminal responsibility and the evolving capacities of the child" (2016) 67(3) *Northern Ireland Legal Quarterly* 269.

Vignette 9: Statute of Limitations

In 1995, D violently raped V, a 35-year-old woman, using a knife. D managed to escape and was not apprehended until 2023. Traces of his DNA taken from the victim's body leave no doubt that D is the perpetrator. Should D be convicted despite the long delay?

If these events were to occur in Australia, the answer would almost certainly be "yes" – and we will substantiate this conclusion primarily through reference to the law of the largest Australian jurisdiction, NSW.

In that jurisdiction, while there is a six-month limitation period for the commencement of summary proceedings,[262] there are no general limitation periods associated with indictable offences.[263] Certainly, no limitation periods attach to the offences that appear to be relevant to D's case – namely, sexual assault and aggravated sexual assault.[264] However, a permanent stay may be ordered in an exceptional case; and permanent stay applications made wholly or partially on the basis of delay are reasonably common (even if, as will be seen, they are very rarely granted). In substance, a permanent stay would have the same effect as a limitation period, because permanent stays prevent criminal proceedings continuing against an accused. That said, the situation here would be unlikely to give rise to a permanent stay.

a) The existence of the power to grant a permanent stay in an appropriate case

In *Dupas v The Queen*,[265] the HCA unanimously confirmed that, at common law in Australia, the power to order a permanent stay is an exceptional remedy; and their Honours held that the following is an authoritative statement of principle:

> A permanent stay will only be ordered in an extreme case and there must be a fundamental defect "of such a nature that nothing that a trial judge can do in the conduct of the trial can relieve against its unfair consequence.[266]

262 *Criminal Procedure Act 1986* (NSW) s 179. The limitation period in relation to the commencement of summary offences does not apply to indictable offences that are being dealt with summarily: *Criminal Procedure Act 1986* (NSW) s 179(2)(b).

263 While this is the general position in relation to indictable offences, from time-to-time Parliament will prescribe limitation periods for more serious offences. An example of a current limitation period can be found in s 12GB(6) of the *Australian Securities and Investments Commission Act 2001* (Cth), which imposes a three-year limitation period on the commencement of proceedings for offences such as that of misleading and deceptive conduct in s 12DA of that Act. Regarding historic limitation periods, a notable example is provided by the former s 78 of the *Crimes Act 1900* (NSW). Up until its repeal, on 3 May 1992, by the *Criminal Legislation (Amendment) Act 1992* (NSW), s 78 imposed a 12-month limitation period on the offences of carnal knowledge, attempted carnal knowledge, and indecent assault, in circumstances where the complainant was between 14 and 16 years of age.

264 *Crimes Act 1900* (NSW) ss 61I-61J.

265 (2010) 241 CLR 237 ("*Dupas*").

266 Ibid. 245 [18], approving and quoting from *The Queen v Glennon* (1992) 173 CLR 592, 605–6 (Mason CJ and Toohey J) ("*Glennon*"). See also *Jago v District Court (NSW)* (1989) 168 CLR 23, 31 (Mason CJ) ("*Jago*").

In the same case, the HCA observed that "[t]here is no definitive category of extreme cases in which a permanent stay of criminal proceedings will be ordered".[267] That being said, and as set out in decisions before and after *Dupas*, the question is one of "whether, in all the circumstances, the continuation of the proceedings would involve unacceptable injustice or unfairness", or whether the "continuation of the proceedings would be 'so unfairly and unjustifiably oppressive' as to constitute an abuse of process".[268] That is, and as explained by Bathurst CJ in *R v RD*,[269] the precondition for the granting of a permanent stay is that "the proceedings must inevitably, rather than possibly, have that effect".[270]

b) Delay: An enlivening factor for a permanent stay?

In D's case, it would seem that the basis for any application for a permanent stay would principally be that of *delay*. The applicable test was set out by Mason CJ in *Jago v District Court (NSW)*.[271] "Where delay is the sole ground of complaint," his Honour said, "an accused seeking a permanent stay must be 'able to show that the lapse of time is such that any trial is necessarily unfair so that any conviction would bring the administration of justice into disrepute'".[272]

A couple of observations can be made about any application for a permanent stay made on the basis of delay. First, the question of delay in such a case is not one about the effluxion of time by itself. Rather, it is concerned with prejudice to an accused by reason of that delay.[273] In such cases, an accused might argue that, due to the passage of time, evidence has been lost. An accused might also point to the obvious difficulties that delay could have on their ability to recall matters. However, concerning the latter point, Deane J's observation in *Jago* is apt:

> It is relevant to note that, in the context of an accused being entitled to the benefit of any reasonable doubt, the vagueness and uncertainty of memory and evidence which is likely to result from delay is more likely to be damaging to the prosecution than to the defence case.[274]

Secondly, even assuming that prejudice can be established, a fair trial is not the same as a *perfect* trial.[275] In *The Queen v Edwards*,[276] the HCA explained:

---

267 *Dupas* (2010) 241 CLR 237, 250 [35].

268 *Walton v Gardiner* (1993) 177 CLR 378, 392 (Mason CJ, Deane and Dawson JJ). See also, e.g., *The Queen v Edwards* (2009) 83 ALJR 717, 721 [24] (The Court) ("*Edwards*"); *R v RD* [2016] NSWCCA 84, [54] (Bathurst CJ, with whom Johnson J agreed at [75] and RS Hulme AJ agreed at [76]) ("*RD*").

269 *RD* [2016] NSWCCA 84.

270 Ibid. [54] (Bathurst CJ, with whom Johnson J agreed at [75] and RS Hulme AJ agreed at [76]).

271 (1989) 168 CLR 23.

272 Ibid. 34 (Mason CJ), quoting *R v Clarkson* [1987] VR 962, 973.

273 See, e.g., *Macri v R* (2022) 110 NSWLR 1, 36 [166] (N Adams J) ("*Macri*").

274 *Jago* (1989) 168 CLR 23, 60 (Deane J).

275 Affirmed, most recently, in *Koschier v R* (2024) 113 NSWLR 491, 507 [73] (Bell CJ, with whom Harrison CJ at CL agreed at 507 [76] and Chen J agreed at 508 [77]).

276 (2009) 83 ALJR 717, 722 [31].

Trials involve the reconstruction of events and it happens on occasions that relevant material is not available; documents, recordings and other things may be lost or destroyed. Witnesses may die. The fact that the tribunal of fact is called upon to determine issues of fact upon less than all of the material which could relevantly bear upon the matter does not make the trial unfair.

c) Managing delay with jury directions

In the context of delay and its consequential effects – and to return to the question of what a trial judge "can do in the conduct of the trial [that] can relieve against its unfair consequences"[277] – in NSW, the primary action that may be taken is the giving of directions to a jury. Pursuant to s 165B of the *Evidence Act 1995* (NSW), where the matter is being tried by a jury, and where the delay has caused the accused to suffer a significant forensic disadvantage, the trial judge must "inform the jury of the nature of that disadvantage and the need to take that disadvantage into account when considering this evidence".[278] While the exact form of such a direction will depend on the precise circumstances of the immediate case and the nature of any forensic disadvantage, it may include, for example, commenting on matters such as the unavailability of documentary evidence, difficulties with memory, the unavailability of witnesses, or an inability to obtain fresh forensic evidence that would have been available at the time of the alleged offending.[279]

Concerning the interaction between the question of a permanent stay and the directions referred to above, it must also be observed that applications for a permanent stay made wholly (or even partially) on the basis of delay are very frequently rejected in NSW.[280] As a recent example, and one which involved a delay of a similar length to the immediate case, in the 2022 case of *Macri*,[281] the Court was concerned with an accused who had been charged with numerous historical child sexual assault offences

---

277 *Dupas* (2010) 241 CLR 237, 245 approving and quoting from *Glennon* (1992) 173 CLR 592, 605–6 (Mason CJ and Toohey J).

278 *Evidence Act 1995* (NSW) s 165B(2). Cf. the rule that previously existed at common law: *Longman v The Queen* (1989) 168 CLR 79; *Crampton v The Queen* (2000) 206 CLR 161, 181–2 [45] (Gaudron, Gummow and Callinan JJ). It can be observed, however, that s 165B is a discretionary power, with s 165B(3) providing that a judge may refuse to make such a direction if he or she considers there are "good reasons for not doing so". See also *TO v R* (2017) 265 A Crim R 191, 217–18 [167] (Price J).

279 See, e. g., *Groundstroem v R* [2013] NSWCCA 237, [63] (Adams J, with whom Macfarlan JA agreed at [1] and Button J agreed at [67]); *PM v R* [2017] NSWCCA 108. See also Judicial Commission of NSW, *Criminal Trial Courts Bench Book*, "Delay in complaint and forensic disadvantage to the accused", [5–070]: https://www.judcom.nsw.gov.au/publications/benchbks/criminal/complaint_evidence_in_sexual_assault_trials.html#p5-055 (viewed 27 November 2024).

280 See, for example, *R v H* (2002) 132 A Crim R 551, which involved a delay of between 27 and 32 years; *RD* [2016] NSWCCA 84, which involved a delay of about 17 years; *R v Richards* [2020] NSWDC 763, which involved a delay of about 50 years; *Dawson v R* (2021) 108 NSWLR 96, which concerned a charge of murder and a delay of about 38 years; *Camelo-Gomez v R* [2022] NSWCCA 108, which similarly concerned a charge of murder and a delay of about 20 years; and *Kitchingman v R* [2023] NSWCCA 4, which involved a delay of about 40 years.

281 *Macri* (2022) 110 NSWLR 1.

that were alleged to have taken place between 1986 and 1991.[282] The trial against the accused did not commence until more than three decades later, in 2021. Despite this delay, N Adams J concluded that the high bar for the granting of a permanent stay had not been reached, and that the forensic disadvantages caused by the delay were curable by directions made pursuant to s 165B.[283] Her Honour observed that it was "to be accepted that the applicant defended the allegations by 'blunt and basic denials of the alleged events', but that does not mean that he could not and did not receive a fair trial".[284]

As compared with the significant number of cases in which permanent stays have been refused, it appears that *R v Littler*[285] is the only NSW case in which a permanent stay has been ordered predominantly on the basis of delay.[286] In that case, however, the permanent stay was not solely ordered on the basis of the Crown's delay in bringing charges of sexual assault (the relevant events were alleged to have taken place between 38 and 46 years prior).[287] Rather, the NSWCCA did not see how directions could adequately address "the difficulties in this case resulting from delay, the absence of relevant evidence, the possibility of the loss of potential witnesses and the health and psychological condition of the applicant".[288] The final consideration there was particularly important, in circumstances where the accused's health problems included significant long term and short term memory deficits.[289]

d) The likely outcome in D's case

Applying all of this to the immediate case: without D's advancing specific instances of serious (and perhaps unusual) prejudice that he will suffer by reason of the delay, it seems exceedingly unlikely that he would be granted a permanent

282 Ibid. 7 [16].

283 Ibid. 3 [175] (N Adams J, with whom Beech-Jones CJ at CL agreed at [6] and Lonergan J agreed at [206]).

284 Ibid. Earlier in her Honour's judgment, at 36 [166], N Adams J observed that "[l]apse of time and the impact of memory is a feature of most historical child sexual assault trials and trials have been conducted with far greater delays than this one. That is not to say that such a trial would never be stayed; only that more than mere effluxion of time is required".

285 (2001) 120 A Crim R 512 ("*Littler*").

286 We note for completeness that a permanent stay was also granted in *R v Westley* [2004] NSWCCA 192, in circumstances where one of the grounds on which a permanent stay was sought was the extensive delay of about 25 or 26 years: at [3]. That ground was not determinative, however, and the permanent stay was instead ordered due to the operation of a limitation period, the effect of which was that the prosecution was "ultimately doomed to failure": at [50] (Dunford J, with whom Hidden J agreed at [52] and Adams J agreed at [53]).

287 *Littler* (2001) 120 A Crim R 512, 515 [22] (Adams J).

288 Ibid. 529 [57] (Adams J, with whom Hodgson JA agreed at 513 [10] and Greg James J agreed at 514 [14]. See also Greg James J's remarks at 514 [20].

289 Ibid. 522–3 [40] (Adams J). See also *R v RWO* [2002] NSWCCA 133, [81]–[89] (Bell J, with whom Ipp AJA agreed at [1] and Smart AJ agreed at [110]). Cf. *Austin v The Queen* (1995) 84 A Crim R 374, which was a case where the accused was in poor health and had impaired capacity, but where a permanent stay was not ordered. Courts tend to take a different approach with respect to prosecution witnesses' memory deficiencies: see, e.g., *Brown v R* [2022] NSWCCA 116, [46] (Bell CJ, with whom Kirk JA agreed at [58] and Price J agreed at [59]).

stay. This is particularly so in circumstances where the delay does not appear to be the fault of the prosecuting authorities,[290] and there is no suggestion of a loss of an opportunity to obtain evidence. Rather, the opposite appears true – that is, in this case, so strong is the DNA evidence that there is "no doubt that D is the perpetrator". It would accordingly seem that this is far from the "extreme case" that would enliven a permanent stay, and that any significant forensic disadvantages could be cured through appropriate directions made under s 165B.

Vignette 10: Life Imprisonment without Parole

> The Penal Code of State S provides for imprisonment for life as the maximum penalty for murder, but also authorises the court to order an offender's early release after a minimum of 15 years if the offender is no longer dangerous. Reacting to cases of particularly heinous murders, the legislature of S wishes to introduce a penalty of life imprisonment without any possibility of early release, regardless of the offender's continued dangerousness. Would this amendment be acceptable?

The short answer to the question posed is that this amendment would be acceptable in all Australian jurisdictions.

In the largest Australian jurisdiction, NSW, the legislature may authorise – and indeed has authorised[291] – sentencing judges to impose irreducible life sentences on offenders for purely retributive reasons. NSW judges are slow to impose such sentences, which, they have said, must be reserved for "the worst type of case".[292] But they have imposed them on certain offenders;[293] and, in many cases where the charge is murder and the victim was a police officer, they are obliged to do so.[294] Without a human rights charter in NSW, or even a separation of powers,[295] mandatory sentencing provisions of the kind just noted are constitutionally valid.[296] And, even more worryingly, the HCA has unanimously upheld[297] the validity of s 154A of the *Crimes (Administration of Sentences) Act 1999* (NSW), which provides that certain life sentence prisoners, whose sentences were reducible when passed, may now be granted parole only when they are in imminent danger of dying, or are incapacitated, and further conditions are satisfied.

In three Australian jurisdictions, a statutory human rights charter does exist.[298] And it appears that, as in many jurisdictions elsewhere in the world,[299] if a judge, or the

---

290 *Jago* (1989) 168 CLR 23, 61 (Deane J).

291 See, e.g., *Crimes Act 1900* (NSW) s 19 A(1)–(2). The same is true in most other Australian jurisdictions. See, e.g., *Sentencing Act 1991* (Vic) s 11(1); *Sentencing Act 1995* (WA) s 90(1)(b), (3) and (4); *Sentencing Act 1997* (Tas) s 18(1)(a), (2) and (4).

292 *R v Garforth* (Unreported, NSW Court of Criminal Appeal, 23 May 1994).

293 See, e.g., ibid.

294 *Crimes Act 1900* (NSW) s 19B.

295 *Kable v Director of Public Prosecutions (NSW)* (1996) 189 CLR 51, 65 (Brennan CJ), 77–80 (Dawson J), 92–4 (Toohey J), 109 (McHugh J) ("*Kable*").

296 See, e.g., *Wynbyne v Marshall* (1997) 7 NTLR 97 ("*Wynbyne*").

297 *Crump v State of New South Wales* (2012) 247 CLR 1 ("*Crump*").

298 *Human Rights Act 2004* (ACT) ("ACT Charter"); *Charter of Rights and Responsibilities Act 2006* (Vic) ("Victorian Charter"); *Human Rights Act 2019* (Qld).

legislature,[300] imposes an irreducible life sentence on a criminal offender in these jurisdictions, this will amount to a breach of at least one charter guarantee.[301] But does that mean that, in these Australian jurisdictions at least, such sentences are not being imposed and served? It does not. That is because Australian human rights charters are "weak-form"[302] instruments. If Parliament wishes to disapply these charters for the purposes of particular legislation, or if it wishes to ignore a judicial declaration that legislation is contrary to one or more charter guarantees, then it may do so.[303] Of course, Parliament will have to accept any political cost of acting in such a way. But given the punitiveness of the Australian media and public, and taking account too of the widespread Australian indifference to the rights of prisoners, governments in this country will often in fact sustain no political damage if they do take such action.[304] On the contrary, at least in some circumstances, a government that *does not* except prisoners from the protection of any charter guarantee, is taking a major political risk.

We can now expand slightly on what has just been said. Since the coming into force of the *Crimes (Life Sentences) Amendment Act 1989* (NSW), s 19A(2) of the *Crimes Act 1900* (NSW) has provided that a person who is sentenced to life imprisonment for murder must serve that sentence for the term of his or her natural life. This does not oblige a judge to pass such a sentence on a person convicted of murder in NSW. Indeed, normally, he or she will not do so. What it does mean is that, where a judge considers a life sentence to be appropriate in a murder case, that sentence will be irreducible.[305] In *R v Garforth*,[306] the NSWCCA acknowledged the "terrible significance of a sentence of life imprisonment [without parole]". Such a sentence, their Honours continued, may only be imposed where "the level of culpability is so extreme that the community interest in retribution and punishment can only be met through the imposition of the maximum penalty".[307] Nevertheless, such sentences can be, and have been, imposed – including in *Garforth* itself – and, in 1996, the NSW Parliament

---

299 See, e.g., *R v Bissonette* [2022] SCC 23; *Makoni v Commissioner of Prisons* [2016] ZWCC 8.

300 *Corrections Act 1986* (Vic) ss 74AA and 74AB.

301 *Minogue v State of Victoria* (2019) 268 1, 20 [30] (Gageler J) ("*Minogue 2019*"); *Minogue v State of Victoria* (2018) 264 CLR 252, 276 [72] (Gageler J). See also 272–3 [52]–[56] (Kiefel CJ, Bell, Keane, Nettle and Edelman JJ).

302 This terminology seems to have first been used by Mark Tushnet, "New Forms of Judicial Review and the Persistence of Rights- and Democracy-Based Worries" (2003) 38(2) *Wake Forest Law Review* 813, 814.

303 See, e.g., Victorian Charter, ss 31, 36 and 37. Note that, in the ACT, Parliament may not make an "override declaration", but it may ignore a judicial declaration that a legislative provision is incompatible with human rights: ACT Charter, ss 32(3) and 33.

304 Cf. George Williams, "The Victorian *Charter of Human Rights and Responsibilities:* Origin and Scope" (2006) 30 *Melbourne University Law Review* 880, 900.

305 *R v Harris* (2000) 50 NSWLR 409.

306 (Unreported, NSW Court of Criminal Appeal, 23 May 1994).

307 Ibid.

saw fit to codify the principle just stated.[308] Parliament has also provided that a judge may pass such a sentence for certain crimes other than murder;[309] and, as indicated above, it is also now the case that a NSW judge *must* impose an irreducible life sentence on many of those convicted of murdering a police officer.[310]

The casual observer might be forgiven for thinking that mandatory sentencing provisions of this nature amount to a legislative usurpation of judicial power. It might be thought, that is, that while the judge pronounces sentence, that sentence has been dictated to him or her by the elected branches of government. But Australian judges have not seen the force of such logic. In *Liyanage v The Queen*,[311] the Privy Council did seem to regard as a legislative exercise of judicial power a provision that required at least a sentence of 10 years' imprisonment to be imposed on *particular, identifiable* participants in a failed *coup d'etat*, if they were convicted of an offence that the Ceylon legislature had "added ex post facto to meet the circumstances of the abortive coup".[312] But where the mandatory sentencing provision speaks *generally*, the orthodox position is that stated by Barwick CJ in *Palling v Corfield*.[313] "If the statute nominates the penalty and imposes on the court a duty to impose it", his Honour said, "no judicial function or power is invaded".[314] That said, even if that were not so, because of the absence of a separation of powers in NSW the NSW Parliament can seemingly exercise at least many judicial functions.[315]

If we return to the *Crimes (Life Sentences) Amendment Act 1989* (NSW), another change effected by that Act concerned those prisoners who were serving life sentences at the time of its enactment. Before 1989 in NSW, while there was a mandatory life sentence for murder, sentencing judges had no power to impose an irreducible life sentence on a person convicted of that offence.[316] And once a judge passed the mandatory sentence, the judiciary had no further role to play. Whether and when

308 *Crimes Act 1900* (NSW) s 61(1). For commentary, see Nicholas Cowdery QC, "Mandatory Life Sentences in New South Wales" (1999) *UNSW Law Journal* 290.

309 See, e.g., *Crimes Act 1900* (NSW) s 61JA(2).

310 *Crimes Act 1900* (NSW) s 19B.

311 [1967] 1 AC 259, 290–1.

312 Ibid. 280.

313 (1970) 123 CLR 52.

314 Ibid. 58.

315 *Kable* (1996) 189 CLR 51, 109 (McHugh J). Cf. *Crump* (2012) 247 CLR 1, 18 [33] (French CJ). *Kable* establishes that a NSW Court may not exercise any non-judicial function that would be incompatible with its exercise of "the judicial power of the Commonwealth" (see *Commonwealth Constitution* ss 71 and 77(iii)) – and, on the face of it, there is a powerful argument that a Court that imposes a sentence mandated by Parliament has exercised such a function because it has not acted independently. See *North Australian Aboriginal Legal Aid Service Inc v Bradley* (2004) 218 CLR 146, 163 [29] (The Court). But the Full Court of the Supreme Court of the NT has dismissed such an argument, with Mildren J (with whom Bailey J agreed at 112) asserting that the mandatory minimum sentencing provision at issue in that case in fact did "not interfere with the independence of the judiciary": *Wynbyne* (1997) 7 NTLR 97, 112.

316 As noted, e.g., in: *Baker v The Queen* (2004) 223 CLR 513, 527 [27] (McHugh, Gummow, Hayne and Heydon JJ), 549 [105] (Kirby J) ("*Baker*").

to release the prisoner was a matter for the executive to decide.[317] In certain cases, sentencing judges did recommend that the offender(s) never be released. But such recommendations had no binding effect.[318] Accordingly, when the 1989 Act gave the judiciary the power to re-determine the sentences of existing life sentence prisoners, it was open to the judges to provide a determinate sentence to those NSW prisoners in respect of whom a non-release recommendation had been made. And, on 24 April 1997, this is precisely what McInerney J did.[319] In 1974, when sentencing Kevin Crump, Taylor J had recommended that Crump and his co-offender, Allan Baker, never be released.[320] But 23 years later, McInerney J re-determined Crump's sentence, imposing on him a non-parole period of 30 years' imprisonment and a maximum sentence of life. Community outrage followed, and so too did some "striking and unusual"[321] legislative activity. That activity culminated in the NSW Parliament's enactment of s 154A of the *Crimes (Administration of Sentences) Act 1999* (NSW) – the "purpose and practical effect"[322] of which was (as indicated above) to deprive all "non-release recommendation" prisoners (two of whom were aged, respectively, 14 and 16 when they offended[323]) of the realistic possibility of parole.

In *Crump v State of New South Wales*,[324] Crump challenged s 154A on separation of powers grounds. But the HCA rejected his argument that the section had substituted a legislative sentence for a judicial one. "On any view",[325] it was said, McInerney J's sentence was left "untouched and unaltered – penal servitude for life".[326] All that *had* been altered, their Honours continued, were the conditions that Crump had to satisfy before he could be granted parole.[327] Moreover, this formalistic reasoning – surely s 154A did change McInerney J's sentence from a life *with* parole sentence to a life *without* parole sentence[328] – was then repeated by the Court in two cases

317 Ibid. 527–8 [27]–[29] (McHugh, Gummow, Hayne and Heydon JJ).

318 As noted, e.g., in: *R v Jamieson* (1992) 60 A Crim R 69, 80 (Gleeson CJ, with whom Lee AJ and Hope AJA agreed at 80) ("*Jamieson*").

319 *Re Application of Crump* (Unreported, Supreme Court of NSW, McInerney J, 24 April 1997).

320 *R v Crump* (Unreported, Supreme Court of NSW, 20 June 1974).

321 *Elliott v The Queen* (2007) 234 CLR 38, 50 [42] (The Court).

322 *Minogue 2019* (2019) 268 CLR 1, 20 [31] (Gageler J).

323 *Jamieson* (1992) 60 A Crim R 69, 69.

324 (2012) 247 CLR 1.

325 Ibid. 18 [34] (French CJ). This would most certainly not have been the view of Kirby J: *Baker* (2004) 223 CLR 513, 549 [104] (Kirby J).

326 *Crump* (2012) 247 CLR 1, 29 [74] (Heydon J).

327 Ibid. 19 [35] (French CJ), 26–7 [60] (Gummow, Hayne, Crennan, Kieel and Bell JJ), 29 [72] (Heydon J).

328 Andrew Dyer, "Irreducible Life Sentences, Craig Minogue and the Capacity of Human Rights Charters to Make a Difference" (2020) 43(2) *UNSW Law Journal* 484, 500–505; Andrew Dyer, "*Minister for Home Affairs v Benbrika* and the Capacity of Chapter III of the *Commonwealth Constitution* to Protect Prisoners' Rights" (2022) 45(1) *UNSW Law Journal* 209, 243–4. See too Andrew Dyer, "Irreducible Life Sentences: What Difference have the European Convention on Human Rights and the United Kingdom Human Rights Act Made?" (2016) 16(3) *Human Rights Law Review* 541, 564–5.

that came to it from Victoria.[329] In those cases, their Honours upheld ss 74AA and 74AB of the *Corrections Act 1986* (Vic), which, respectively, apply to Julian Knight and Craig William Minogue alone, and provide that they may be released from their life sentences only when, among other things, they are "imminent danger of dying" or are "seriously incapacitated". As indicated above, Parliament has expressly disapplied the Victorian Charter for the purposes of these sections.[330] And while Knight's sentencing judge imposed on him a non-parole period of 27 years' imprisonment, and Minogue's sentencing judge imposed on him a non-parole period of 28 years' imprisonment, the HCA has held that neither s 74AA nor s 74AB contradict those minimum terms.[331] "The non-parole period", the plurality observed in *Minogue*, "remain[s] […] 28 years".[332]

We are back where we began. The amendment referred to above could validly be made in all Australian jurisdictions. Indeed, it is perfectly open to an Australian Parliament to impose such a sentence on any life-sentence prisoner whose sentencing judge was unable to punish, or refrained[333] from punishing, in this way.

---

329 *Knight v State of Victoria* (2017) 261 CLR 306 ("*Knight*"); *Minogue 2019* (2019) 268 CLR 1.

330 *Corrections Act 1986* (Vic) ss 74AA(4) and 74AB(4).

331 *Knight* (2017) 261 CLR 306, 323–4 [29] (The Court); *Minogue 2019* (2019) 268 CLR 1, 17–18 [20] (Kiefel CJ, Bell, Keane, Nettle and Gordon JJ).

332 *Minogue 2019* (2019) 268 CLR 1, 18 [20] (Kiefel CJ, Bell, Keane, Nettle and Gordon JJ).

333 *R v Knight* [1989] VR 705, 711; *R v Taylor* (Unreported, Supreme Court of Victoria, Vincent J, 24 August 1988). Note that, in *Knight*, the Crown did not even request the sentencing judge to impose a life without parole sentence on the offender.

2. Belgium*

By** *Frank Verbruggen**** and *Pieter Van Rooij*****

Vignette 1: Trolley Problem – Killing one Person to Save Many

Five young children are playing on railway tracks. An express train is approaching, and it is too late to stop the train before it hits the children, probably killing them. Operator D recognizes the emergency situation. He electronically flips a switch and thus deflects the train from its regular track to a little-used sidetrack. However, the lone repairman V is busy on the sidetrack, and the deflected train kills V, as D had anticipated. Is D criminally responsible for murder of V?

It seems implausible that D will be punishable for flipping the switch and the resulting death of V. Although D's conduct qualifies as homicide, he will be able to rely on the justification of necessity (lesser evil), which neutralises the wrongfulness of the conduct and thereby renders the offence unpunishable. As a backup defence, he could rely on duress (moral compulsion), which would not be a justification, but an excuse.

D can state that he lacked the intent to kill V and only had the intention to avoid the death of the children. However, indirect intent is sufficient, i. e. not wanting the consequence but knowing it is very likely to occur and going ahead with your action regardless, taking the unwanted consequence for granted.

D wanted his action (flipping the switch) and accepted the death of V as a possible consequence thereof although he did not directly want V to die. Under Belgian criminal law this qualifies as an indirect (eventual) intent, which is according to a substantial part of legal doctrine equated to a direct intent.[1] The subjective element (*mens rea*) of the offence of homicide is present.

Even though D's conduct corresponds to a statutory offence description, it must be verified whether the further conditions for punishability are met. The conduct must also be wrongful (unlawful) *in concreto.* A legally recognised ground for justification can neutralise the abstractly formulated criminal nature of behaviour, and then there is no criminal offence.[2]

The justification of necessity seems to apply, as there was an acute and serious conflict of interests, a situation in which a person has to weigh several competing needs

---

* State of Belgian law in 2024.

** The authors thank Tiele Allaert, student of the research master law 2024 for his research support.

*** Professor of criminal law at the Faculty of Law and Criminology.

**** PhD candidate and Research and Teaching Assistant at the Institute of Criminal Law at KU Leuven.

1 Cass. 2 October 2018, *RABG* 2019, afl. 1, 22; V. Vereecke, "Het eventueel opzet bij de beoordeling van het oogmerk om te doden", *RABG* 2019, afl. 1, (25) 26, nr. 6.

2 H. Fransen, "Rechtvaardiging", in: X., *Postal Memorialis. Lexicon strafrecht, strafvordering en bijzondere wetten*, 2001, 280; R. Verstraeten and F. Verbruggen, *Inleiding tot het Belgische strafrecht en strafprocesrecht*, Intersentia, Antwerpen, 2023, 80, nr. 210.

and can only safeguard the interest with the highest value by sacrificing the other through the commission of a criminal offence.[3] Necessity as a ground of justification does not yet have an explicit base in the BeCC, but has been accepted and applied without any controversy by case law for almost forty years,[4] and implicitly sanctioned by parliament, e. g., in the parliamentary debates on abortion, the offence of revealing matters covered by professional privilege or on the ban on justifications for torture.

The *first condition* for necessity is an acute, certain, and significant danger to a good or interest. There is no doubt that the approaching train put the five children on the first track in imminent danger, as it was too late to stop. The case mentions "probably killing them", indicating that the danger was virtually certain and not merely imaginary. As a *second condition*, the criminal offence must have been the only way to safeguard that interest. Changing the track (and the subsequent fatal collision with V) was the only and last resort by which D could save the children, as it was too late to stop the train. As a *third condition*, there is a proportionality test. The safeguarded interest must be of (equal or) greater value than the interest sacrificed by committing of the crime. This will always be evaluated by the judge that tries the facts, mindful of hindsight bias,[5] under the supervision of the Court of Cassation. It seems reasonable that saving five lives rather than a single life would be proportionate. This is further reinforced by the fact that it involves five children's lives, making this condition too seem fulfilled. As a *fourth condition*, the perpetrator must not have knowingly and voluntarily placed himself in a situation that foreseeably led to the tragical conflict of interest.[6] This does not seem to be the case.

Once a defendant invokes a ground of justification which is not entirely implausible, it is up to the opposing party (the prosecution or victim) to prove that the relevant conditions of application are not met.[7] Doubt as to the existence of necessity would therefore favour D as well.

---

3 Cass. 28 April 1999, *AC* 1999, 581; A. Dierickx, "Over de (putatieve) noodtoestand", *NC* 2007, afl. 6, (395) 395–397; F. Van Volsem, "De onoverwinnelijke rechtsdwaling en de noodtoestand in het bijzonder met betrekking tot milieumisdrijven", *TMR* 2012, afl. 1, (4) 19; F. Verbruggen and R. Verstraeten, *Inleiding tot het Belgische strafrecht en strafprocesrecht*, Intersentia, Antwerpen, 2023, 87–89.

4 For the first time in Cass. 13 May 1987, *Arr.Cass.* 1986–1987, 1203. More recently: Cass. 22 May 2012, *Arr.Cass.* 2012, 1353; Cass. 4 March 2014, *Arr.Cass.* 2014, 594; Cass. 5 April 2023, AR P.22.1589.F.

5 A. Verheylesonne, "Les causes de justification", in: P. Chomé, A. Lorent, F. Roggen and J. P. Collin (eds.), *Droit pénal et procédure pénale*, Mechelen, Kluwer, 2011, 82.

6 Cass. 4 March 2014, AR P.13 1775.N.

7 Regarding the burden of proof, it was initially the prevailing position that the defendant relying on a justification had to present satisfying evidence of that justification. However, it is now settled case-law of the Court of Cassation that this is no longer the case: Cass. 4 January 1994, *Arr.Cass.* 1994, 10; Cass. 24 March 1999, P.98 1127.F; Cass. 14 December 2001, *JLMB* 2002, afl. 13, 532; Cass. 24 February 2010, AR P.09 1614.F; Cass. 5 January 2016, AR P.15.1203.N; H. Fransen, "Rechtvaardiging", in: X., *Postal Memorialis. Lexicon strafrecht, strafvordering en bijzondere wetten*, 2001, 280; A. Verheylesonne, "Les causes de justification", in: P. Chomé, A. Lorent, F. Roggen and J. P. Collin (eds.), *Droit pénal et procédure pénale*, Mechelen, Kluwer, 2011, 18–19.

In the new Belgian Criminal Code, which should enter into force by 2026, necessity as a ground of justification is explicitly listed and defined for the first time. (Art. 1.13 New BeCC).[8] Regarding this justification, the fourth requirement becomes somewhat narrower: the offender must not have deliberately provoked the emergency situation.[9]

Vignette 2: Attribution of Death

D intends to kill his neighbour V. Hidden near V's house, D waits for V and stabs him several times with a knife. V is taken to the hospital, where his wounds are treated. His injuries are not life-threatening and V is kept overnight for observation. During the night, a technical defect in the hospital kitchen leads to the outbreak of a fire, which kills V and other persons. Can D be held criminally responsible for V's death?

Causality has always played a central role in criminal law, since many important offences are so-called consequential crimes: a specific consequence is either a constitutive component or an aggravating circumstance.[10] D has intentionally inflicted knife wounds on victim V with the specific intent to kill and with premeditation. Even though the injuries he inflicted were not life-threatening, they did lead to the hospitalisation of V. The death of V in the hospital was not the direct result of the stabbing, but due to a fire at the hospital with no relation to D's actions.

The choice of causality theory in this case will decide whether V's conduct qualifies as an intentional homicide (murder, Art. 394 BeCC) or as a mere attempted murder (Art. 51 and Art. 394 BeCC). The stabbing itself did not result in an immediate life-threatening condition of the victim. If the fire had not taken place, V's conduct would therefore be qualified as a punishable attempted murder. The punishment of attempted murder is (3 to) 30 years of imprisonment, murder carries (3 years to) a life sentence. Attempted murder can be dealt with by ordinary criminal courts (reducing the maximum sentence to 20 years), murder can only be handled by a jury in the assizes court.

As the fire resulted in the death of V, the question is therefore whether D has committed murder or whether the causal chain has been "interrupted" by the fire as an "independent" cause of death.

In the absence of a legal definition, the causality issue has been decided by case law. Traditionally Belgian courts and doctrine have insisted in applying the same causality theories in tort law and criminal law.[11] Belgian case law is usually said[12]

---

8 Bill of 23 May 2023, House of Representatives, 2022–23, DOC 55 nr. 3374/001, 842–843.

9 Article 13, 2 New BeCC.

10 R. Verstraeten and F. Verbruggen, *Inleiding tot het Belgisch strafrecht en strafprocesrecht*, Antwerpen-Gent-Cambridge, Intersentia, 2023, 55.

11 L. Dupont and R. Verstraeten, *Handboek Belgisch Strafrecht*, Leuven, Acco, 1990, 190; R. Verstraeten and F. Verbruggen, *Inleiding tot het Belgisch strafrecht en strafprocesrecht*, Antwerpen-Gent-Cambridge, Intersentia, 2023, 55–56.

12 Cases in which judges apply other, more restrictive causation theories may be decided without the case ending up in criminal courts and definitely not in the Court of Cassation. That

to apply the "doctrine of equivalent causes". Any cause without which the damage would not have occurred as it did (in concrete terms), is designated as a cause of the consequence.[13] The effect may result from several (interacting) causes, if they are equally necessary.[14]

To determine whether a particular act was a necessary cause, the court conducts a thought experiment: would the consequence have occurred, as it occurred in the specific circumstances, if that act (and only[15] this act) is removed from the chain of events? If the answer to this question turns out to be negative, then there is a causal link.[16] Since there can be multiple equally necessary causes, this thought experiment should be conducted for each alleged criminal act separately.[17] Each one has to be a *conditio sine qua non.*

Many legal systems take a more measured approach and filter out some causes to avoid unduly extending the causal chain.[18] The doctrine of equivalent causes does not. All necessary causes remain intact in the causal chain, including faults that only had a limited contribution to the outcome.[19] Indirect causes are also included,

Court would not scrutinize the factual appreciation of the trial court as to whether an action was necessary for a consequence to ensue.

13 R. Verstraeten and F. Verbruggen, *Inleiding tot het Belgisch strafrecht en strafprocesrecht*, Antwerpen-Gent-Cambridge, Intersentia, 2023, 56–57; J. Rozie and T. Vansweevelt, "Causaliteit in het Belgische strafrecht. Over de kruisbestuiving tussen het buitencontractueel aansprakelijkheidsrecht en het Strafrecht", *NC* 2014, 436.

14 J. Rozie and T. Vansweevelt, "Causaliteit in het Belgische strafrecht. Over de kruisbestuiving tussen het buitencontractueel aansprakelijkheidsrecht en het Strafrecht", *NC* 2014, 436; H. De Page, *Traité élémentaire de droit civil belge*, II, Brussel, Bruylant, 1964, 962.

15 J. Rozie and T. Vansweevelt, "Causaliteit in het Belgische strafrecht. Over de kruisbestuiving tussen het buitencontractueel aansprakelijkheidsrecht en het Strafrecht", *NC* 2014, 437.

16 R. Verstraeten and F. Verbruggen, *Inleiding tot het Belgisch strafrecht en strafprocesrecht*, Antwerpen-Gent-Cambridge, Intersentia, 2023, 56–57; N. Blaise, "La suspension du prononcé octroyée au médecin, auteur d'un homicide involontaire, déjà sanctionné par la presse", *T.Gez.* 2011, afl. 4, (327) 328; H. Bocken, I. Boone and M. Kruithof, *Inleiding tot het schadevergoedingsrecht. Buitencontractueel aansprakelijkheidsrecht en andere schadevergoedingsstelsels*, Brugge, die Keure, 2014, 64; S. Stijns and I. Samoy, *Leerboek Verbintenissenrecht – Boek 1bis*, Brugge, die Keure, 2020, 140.

17 R. Verstraeten and F. Verbruggen, *Inleiding tot het Belgisch strafrecht en strafprocesrecht*, Antwerpen-Gent-Cambridge, Intersentia, 2023, 56–57.

18 H. Bocken and I. Boone, "Causaliteit in het Belgische recht", *TPR* 2002, 1632; J.-L. Fagnart, La causalité, Waterloo, Kluwer, 2009, 51; H. Bocken, I. Boone and M. Kruithof, *Inleiding tot het schadevergoedingsrecht. Buitencontractueel aansprakelijkheidsrecht en andere schadevergoedingsstelsels*, Brugge, die Keure, 65; J.-L. Fagnart, *La causalité*, Waterloo, Kluwer, 2009, 22.

19 H. Bocken, I. Boone and M. Kruithof, *Inleiding tot het schadevergoedingsrecht. Buitencontractueel aansprakelijkheidsrecht en andere schadevergoedingsstelsels*, Brugge, die Keure, 2014, 65; J. Rozie and T. Vansweevelt, "Causaliteit in het Belgische strafrecht. Over de kruisbestuiving tussen het buitencontractueel aansprakelijkheidsrecht en hetstrafrecht", *NC* 2014, (433) 436.

even if the damage was not foreseeable or probable.[20] An intervening error also does not break the causal relation.[21] On several occasions, courts have accepted that the suicide[22] of a crime victim was the consequence of the offence (death of the victim as aggravating circumstance). The judge accepts this causal link if he, based on his inner conviction, believes beyond all reasonable doubt that the consequence would not have occurred without the antecedent, the way it did occur in the particular circumstances. To establish a causal link, there need not be absolute certainty, only sufficient certainty.[23]

There seems to be no doubt about the causal link between D's conduct and V's death. After all, if D had not stabbed V, V would not have ended up in the hospital, and therefore V would not have died in the fire. The consequence as it occurred in the specific circumstances of the case (death) would not have occurred if the stabbing were filtered out of the chain of events.

The doctrine of equivalent causes is very victim-friendly, which is mainly important for the recognition of civil liability. Since a causal link can be established rather easily, this doctrine increases the prospects of the victim to recover damages.[24]

Critics regard the theory of equivalent causes as contrary to essential characteristics of criminal law, such as the requirement of *mens rea* (guilty mind) with regard to the *actus reus*. They argue that the *mens rea* can only relate to reasonably foreseeable consequences, that it should not simply be adopted from tort law.[25]

Moreover, the radical choice of the victim-friendly causation theory is unfair, as in some cases its results can be disproportionately detrimental to "offenders" who were minor contributors to the consequence.

---

20 Cass. 17 April 1975, *Arr.Cass.* 1975, 908, *Pas.* 1975, 820; J. Rozie and T. Vansweevelt, "Causaliteit in het Belgische strafrecht. Over de kruisbestuiving tussen het buitencontractueel aansprakelijkheidsrecht en het Strafrecht", *NC* 2014, 436.

21 J. Rozie and T. Vansweevelt, "Causaliteit in het Belgische strafrecht. Over de kruisbestuiving tussen het buitencontractueel aansprakelijkheidsrecht en het Strafrecht", *NC* 2014, 446; J. De Codt, "L'appréciation de la causalité dans le jugement des actions publique et civile", in: M. Mandoux and O. Klees (eds.), *Actualités de droit penal et de procédure pénale*, Editions du Jeune Barreau de Bruxelles 2001, 72.

22 Or, for one of the victims of Brussels Airport terrorist bombings of 2016, euthanasia because of intolerable mental suffering. (Court of assizes Brussels 25 July 2023).

23 J. Rozie and T. Vansweevelt, "Causaliteit in het Belgische strafrecht. Over de kruisbestuiving tussen het buitencontractueel aansprakelijkheidsrecht en het Strafrecht", *NC* 2014, 444–445.

24 Since the res judicata of a criminal judgment affects the related torts procedure, the application of the theory of equivalent causes in criminal law seems especially important for a subsequent civil case. In practice, almost all civil (tort) claims for damages resulting from an offence are first decided by the criminal courts.

25 A. Delannay, "Les homicides et lésions corporelles volontaires", in: M.-A. Beernaert, H. Bosly, C.-E. Clesse, A. Delannay, I. De la Serna, M. De Rue, C. De Valkeneer, F. Lugentz, P. Magnien, N. Van Der Eecken, D. Vandermeersch and I. Wattier (eds.), *Les infractions. Volume 2. Les infractions contre les personnes*, Brussel, Larcier, 2010, (85) 155.

Proponents of the theory of equivalent causes argue that it ensures legal certainty, [26] by avoiding that judges filter out causes using subjective criteria such as "foreseeability". Opponents retort that by linking completely unforeseeable consequences to indirect causes, it actually undermines legal certainty. They believe that the broad extension of the causal chain and the disregard for intervening factors is unfair.[27]

Belgian legal doctrine puts forward some alternatives to address these allegedly unfair consequences, often referring to theories used in neighbouring countries. The doctrine of efficient causes only accepts a causal link if the damage was reasonably foreseeable.[28] In turn, the doctrine of adequate causes accepts a causal link if the damage was "probable".[29] Application of both theories to the case at hand would probably lead to a different conclusion: V's death *as it occurred in the specific circumstances* (i. e. by fire) was, at the moment of the stabbing, neither foreseeable nor probable. D would only be liable for attempted murder.

As mentioned above, Belgian case law still sticks to the doctrine of equivalent causes for the time being. One must, however, take into account that prosecutors and judges may in practice have applied other, more restrictive causation theories without stating this explicitly or without being challenged in the Court of Cassation. The matter is too technical to have resulted in a debate in society, even though the "sacrificing one person to save more other" always pops up as an example in the debate on ethical programming of AI-driven robots and vehicles.

Recently, both Belgian tort law and criminal law have undergone major reforms which will enter into force in the years to come. At least in the new tort law, there seems to be a slight change of direction. The new Civil Code introduces a fairness test, where the probability of damage in light of the antecedent must be considered as a correction criterion. Such correction, the law immediately adds, may only be applied in exceptional cases, though.[30] The intention is thus not to abandon the equivalence theory, but to exclude the most unjust excesses. It remains to be seen what this will mean for criminal cases in the future. Since the new Belgian Criminal Code does not discuss the causality problem in detail, future changes will have to originate from new case law.

---

26 J. Rozie and T. Vansweevelt, "Causaliteit in het Belgische strafrecht. Over de kruisbestuiving tussen het buitencontractueel aansprakelijkheidsrecht en het Strafrecht", *NC* 2014, 437.

27 J. Rozie and T. Vansweevelt, "Causaliteit in het Belgische strafrecht. Over de kruisbestuiving tussen het buitencontractueel aansprakelijkheidsrecht en het strafrecht", *NC* 2014, afl. 6, (433) 437; R. Pirson and A. De Ville, *Traité de la responsabilité civile extra-contractuelle*, Brussel, Bruylant, 1935, 30; H. Brocken, "Enkele hoofdthema's van de causaliteitsproblematiek", *TBBR* 1988, 270.

28 J. Rozie and T. Vansweevelt, "Causaliteit in het Belgische strafrecht. Over de kruisbestuiving tussen het buitencontractueel aansprakelijkheidsrecht en het strafrecht", *NC* 2014, afl. 6, (433) 438.

29 J. Rozie and T. Vansweevelt, "Causaliteit in het Belgische strafrecht. Over de kruisbestuiving tussen het buitencontractueel aansprakelijkheidsrecht en het strafrecht", *NC* 2014, afl. 6, (433) 437.

30 Article 10 Bill of 1 February 2024, House of Representatives, 2023–2024, DOC 55 nr. 3213/012, 10.

The unfairness of the equivalent causes doctrine seems more obvious in the case of unintentional offences (e. g. negligent manslaughter) than in the case of D, who had the intent to kill. For intentional offences where there was no intent to kill, the Belgian Criminal Code considers the unintended death as a consequence as an aggravating circumstance, but in most cases, the punishment is less severe than the one for murder (e. g., Art. 401 for battery, Arts. 402 and 404 for poisoning, Art. 417/12 for sexual offences resulting in the death of the victim).

Vignette 3: Torture to Save a Life

Kidnapper K has abducted an 8-year-old girl G and hidden her in a small cave in the woods. K is trying to extort money from G's parents for her release. The police manage to arrest K. Although being questioned for 24 hours, K steadfastly refuses to disclose where he hid G. Police officer D correctly assumes that G may soon die of thirst if she cannot be found. He therefore severely beats K to make him tell the truth. Fearing even more violence, K eventually leads the police to the cave, where they find G still barely alive. Should D be punished for torturing K?

The acts committed by police officer D are in principle punishable under the Belgian Criminal Code (BeCC). As a state party to the European Convention of Human Rights, Belgium must comply with the Strasbourg standards. Article 3 ECHR prohibits torture, inhuman and degrading treatment or punishment. Belgium is also party to the European Convention for the Prevention of Torture and Inhuman or Degrading Treatment or Punishment and the UN Convention against Torture and Other Cruel, Inhuman or Degrading Treatment or Punishment.

The prohibition on torture protects one of the fundamental values of our constitutional order and does not allow for exceptions, not even in times of emergency. It is perhaps even a peremptory norm (*jus cogens*). It is settled case-law of the ECtHR that the Article 3 contains an absolute prohibition, which cannot be derogated from, even in the most extreme circumstances, such as the fight against terror and organised crime, regardless of the behaviour of the individual or the nature of the crime committed.

Belgium introduced specific criminal offences for torture and inhuman or degrading treatment to implement its international obligations.[31] The only debate will be whether the severity of the beatings amounts to torture or to inhuman treatment.[32] D has intentionally caused serious mental or physical harm to a person to obtain information from the victim, so it must be qualified as inhuman treatment.[33] To be qual-

31 Law of 14 June 2002 on the conformity of Belgian law with the Convention against Torture and Other Cruel, Inhuman or Degrading Treatment or Punishment, adopted in New York on 10 December 1984, *BS* 14 August 2002.

32 Less severe beating can be degrading treatment: in the *Bouyid* case, the Grand Chamber of the ECtHR found Belgium guilty of a violation of Art. 3 ECHR, after police officers had slapped suspects, one of them being a minor (ECtHR 28 September 2015, nr. 23380/09, ECLI: CE:ECHR:2015:0928JUD002338009, Bouyid/Belgium, https://hudoc.echr.coe.int/eng?i=001-157670.).

33 Art. 417/1, 2°BeCC: "any treatment which intentionally causes serious mental or physical suffering to a person, including to obtain information from him or to extract confessions or to punish him, or to put pressure on him or third parties, or to intimidate him or third parties".

ified as torture, the judge must consider it to be the deliberate infliction of "*a serious and heinous suffering*" (Art. 417/1, 1°BeCC). The difference is the amount of punishment. For both offences, it is an aggravating circumstance that it has been committed by a police officer in the exercise of his duty.[34] In the *Gäfgen* case, very similar to D's, the ECtHR ruled that a credible threat of violence constitutes inhuman treatment.[35] A fortiori, the effective administration of severe beatings should therefore be considered inhuman treatment under Art. 3 ECHR.

In case of a possible violation of Art. 3 ECHR, the ECtHR imposes several positive obligations on the State party concerned. Among them is the *obligation* to conduct a thorough and effective independent investigation of the facts in question capable of leading to the *identification* and *punishment* of those responsible.[36]

D will of course argue that his behaviour was justified by necessity or the legitimate defence of another person. If the beatings are considered torture, Art. 417/2, 5 BeCC, adopted following a recommendation of the CPT[37], explicitly provides that there can be no justification on the grounds of necessity.[38] The consequence is that D will not be able to profit from necessity or legitimate defence as grounds of justification. The law expressly provides that a superior's order can never justify torture or inhuman treatment.[39]

In the explanatory note to the Bill and in the consultative opinion of the Council of State, there seems to be a mix-up between the concepts of *emergency* (as an overall situation in society) and *necessity* (as a criminal law ground of justification for individuals choosing to commit a specific offence because they consider that the lesser evil).

The government stressed, however, that it had made the deliberate choice not to introduce a similar "irrelevance of necessity clause" in the article on inhuman treatment.[40] That would allow D to invoke it, if the beatings are qualified as inhuman treatment short of torture: he could claim that he chose the lesser evil, as the beatings were the only way to save G's life which was in immediate and serious danger.

He cannot be sure to be successful, though. Because the government, somewhat confusingly, also stated that the fact that it prohibited the recourse to necessity in cases of torture, did not mean it could not also be unavailable for other offences.[41] That would run afoul of the ban in criminal law on the use of *analogia ad malam partem*, unless there is a prohibition under international law with direct effect. But for inhu-

34 Arts. 417/2, 2, 1°a) and 417/3, 2, 1°a) BeCC.

35 ECtHR 1 June 2010, nr. 22978/05, ECLI:CE:ECHR:2010:0601JUD002297805, *Gäfgen v. Germany.*

36 Arts. 1 and 3 ECHR; ECtHR 1 June 2010, nr. 22978/05, ECLI:CE:ECHR:2010:0601-JUD002297805, *Gäfgen v. Germany*, §§ 116–117.

37 Bill of 12 April 2006, House of Representatives, 2005–06, DOC 51 2193/001, p. 4.

38 Art. 417/2, 5 BeCC.

39 Arts. 417/2, 4 (torture) and 417/3, 4 BeCC (inhuman treatment).

40 Bill of 12 April 2006, House of Representatives, 2005–06, DOC 51 2193/001, p. 8.

41 Bill of 12 April 2006, House of Representatives, 2005–06, DOC 51 2193/001, p. 8.

man treatment outside of the context of armed conflict, that does not seem to be the case.

Still, the Grand Chamber judgment in *Gäfgen*, which is very clear about the absolute prohibition to use inhuman treatment, even for those who want to save an abducted child's life[42], came a few years after the Belgian law. Ever since, the duty to have ECHR-conform interpretation of Belgian law makes it hard to see how any Belgian court could grant D the benefit of a justification on the basis of necessity without entering in conflict with Belgian obligations under ECtHR case law.

While public sentiment might be less straightforward on this issue, the principled position of the ECtHR (which on the other hand was also pragmatic as it left the conviction of the kidnapper-murderer untouched) has not received any public criticism from Belgian authorities or observers.

D would, most likely, have to rely on the excuse of duress, as the mental strain on him was such as to lose control and commit the offence. As some judges or juries might sympathise, this could be successful and lead to an acquittal, although it might be a problem for Belgium at the ECtHR. More likely is that the situation and the strain on the officer would be seen as a mitigating circumstance, which under Belgian law would allow courts to reduce the amount of punishment substantially.

Vignette 4: Lethal Self-Defence

R, a well-trained young man armed with a knife, accosts 50-year-old D, who is on her way home from a party in the early morning hours. R threatens her with the knife and takes away her purse filled with 500 € and her wristwatch worth 1,000 €. As R turns to run away, D draws a pistol she is secretly carrying in her jacket, and shoots and kills R in order to retrieve her property. Is D guilty of murder?

D had the – direct or indirect[43] – intent to kill V and will be punishable for homicide[44] (Art. 393 BeCC), as she does not meet the requirements necessary under Belgian law to rely on legitimate defence as a ground for justification.

Legitimate defence[45] can justify behaviour that would otherwise amount to homicide (Art. 416 BeCC).[46] That said, there are strict conditions for a person committing

42 ECtHR 1 June 2010, nr. 22978/05, ECLI:CE:ECHR:2010:0601JUD002297805, *Gäfgen v. Germany*, § 107.

43 Cass. 2 October 2018, *RABG* 2019, afl. 1, 22; V. Vereecke, "Het eventueel opzet bij de beoordeling van het oogmerk om te doden", *RABG* 2019, afl. 1, (25) 26, nr. 6.

44 Unlike English law, the Belgian legal vocabulary (Art. 394 BeCC). limits the concept of "assassinat/moord" to killings with malice aforethought (premeditation), which was absent in D's case.

45 Thus, in exceptional cases it may be, legally speaking, "justified" to e.g. harm or kill someone. H. Fransen, "Rechtvaardiging", in: *Postal Memorialis. Lexicon strafrecht, strafvordering en bijzondere wetten*, 2001, 280; F. Verbruggen and R. Verstraeten, *Inleiding tot het Belgische strafrecht en strafprocesrecht*, Intersentia, Antwerpen, 2023, 83–87.

46 In the BeCC, it is only foreseen for homicide and battery, but case law and jurisprudence have extended this scope to other offences, rendering it a quasi-general justification, which is not questioned by anyone. J. De Herdt, *Fysiek interpersoonlijk geweld. Een onderzoek naar de*

an offence to successfully invoke it.[47] Legitimate defence is strictly construed, as it is an exception to the prohibition of taking the law into one's own hands, a general principle of law.[48]

The situation is simple. If D had used the deadly violence during R's attack on her, she would most likely have profited from the justification of legitimate (self-)defence. She did however shoot R in the back while he was fleeing the scene of the crime, in order to retrieve her property. That is not justified.

Belgian law does not allow for violence merely to safeguard goods from an attack, it will only be legitimate to safeguard the freedom to come and go[49], physical and sexual integrity of *persons*. This will remain so under the upcoming new Criminal Code.

D could profit from the explicit legal presumption that an armed robbery is not considered an attack only on property but also on persons, which creates an immediate need for self-defence (Art. 417, (3) BeCC). It is a – rebuttable[50] – presumption that there is no possibility to flee or to notify the authorities to avert the danger.[51] That is why defensive violence from D during the robbery would have been justified, at least if it was proportionate. "Proportionate" means no more than necessary to avert the illegal attack, taking into account the strain under which the person acted and the limited time and information on which the assessment had to be based. In specific situations, it may have sufficed to threaten to use a firearm or to fire warning shots rather than shooting at the assailant without warning. In general, however, prosecutors

---

accuraatheid en coherentie van de strafrechtelijke kwalificaties en instrumenten aangewend als reactie op fysiek interpersoonlijk geweld, Antwerpen, Intersentia, 2014, 648; A. Verheylesonne, "Les causes de justification", in: P. Chomé, A. Lorent, F. Roggen and J. P. Collin (eds.), *Droit pénal et procédure pénale*, Mechelen, Kluwer, 2011, 55–56. The New BeCC acknowledges this explicitly (Art. 1.14 New BeCC).

47 Cass. 7 December 1977, *Arr.Cass.* 1978, 417; Cass. 28 February 1989, *Arr. Cass.* 1989, 738; Cass. 5 October 2016, AR P.16.0698.F; Cass. 5 September 2018, AR P.18.0242.F; Cass. 28 May 2019, AR P.19.0130.N; T. Ongena, "Wettige verdediging of noodweer", in: *Strafrecht en strafvordering. Artikelsgewijze commentaar met overzicht van rechtspraak en rechtsleer*, 2000, afl. 35, (181) 185–198; B. Spriet, "Noodweer of wettige verdediging als rechtvaardigingsgrond in het strafrecht", *RW* 1990–91, (546) 546–547; C. Van Den Wyngaert and S. Vandromme, *Strafrecht en Strafprocesrecht in hoofdlijnen*, 2019, Oud-Turnhout, Gompel&Svacina, 246–250.

48 Cass. 24 May 1976, *Arr.Cass.* 1976, 1053.

49 In the sense that it can be used to avoid or escape from kidnap situations.

50 The Court of Cassation, under increasing pressure from legal doctrine, has recently stated that this presumption is rebuttable, meaning that the conditions for legitimate defence must always be examined. Cass 13 February 2018, *JLMB* 2018, afl. 12, 536; J. De Herdt, "Recente cassatierechtspraak betreffende de vermoedens van wettige verdediging", *NC* 2018, afl. 5, (475) 478. This presumption was long considered irrebuttable: Cass. 3 March 1941, *Arr.Cass.* 1941, 43; J. De Herdt, *Fysiek interpersoonlijk geweld. Een onderzoek naar de accuraatheid en coherentie van de strafrechtelijke kwalificaties en instrumenten aangewend als reactie op fysiek interpersoonlijk geweld*, Antwerpen, Intersentia, 2014, 744; J. Simon, *Handboek van het Belgisch Strafrecht*, Brussel, Bruylant, 1948, 167.

51 T. Ongena, "Wettige verdediging of noodweer", in: *Strafrecht en strafvordering. Artikelsgewijze commentaar met overzicht van rechtspraak en rechtsleer*, 2000, afl. 35, (181) 196; C. Van Den Wyngaert and S. Vandromme, *Strafrecht en Strafprocesrecht in hoofdlijnen*, 2019, Oud-Turnhout, Gompel&Svacina, 248.

and courts seem rather sympathetic with persons relying on self-defence and grant them some leeway on the proportionality of the violence used.[52]

In D's situation, the attack on her by R was over. There was no immediate need for defensive violent action to preserve her physical integrity anymore. She shot R "in order to retrieve her property". That is clearly not an act in defence of personal integrity, but a prohibited form of taking the law into one's own hands.

D will therefore have to rely on duress (temporary mental incapacity) as an excuse. This has been invoked – sometimes, but very rarely with success – by jewellers and shopkeepers who had already been victimised several times before, to such an extent that they had been suffering from anxiety, sleeplessness and use of pharmaceuticals and because of that, lost control over their behaviour in the extreme situation.

While in the media the debate surges every time an offender is killed by the victim of an offence, only the extreme right-wing party seems to want to change the law, without being very clear on which violence would be justified and when. The New Criminal Code will nevertheless retain the existing system, making only technical changes.

The empathy or even sympathy that society might have with persons like D will most likely be expressed in sentencing. First and foremost, she can rely on Arts. 411 and 414 BeCC, which reduce the sentence to a maximum of five years (instead of thirty) if the homicide had been directly provoked by serious violence against persons. That reduction can be combined with other mitigating circumstances (such as the lack of previous convictions). That is why in practice most situations of killings that exceeded legitimate defence end with symbolic and at any rate suspended sanctions, also in view of the unlikelihood of recidivism of the perpetrator.

R's next of kin will be able to bring a civil claim for damages in tort. Even excused criminal behaviour still qualifies as a civil wrong. Judges will however take account of R's own share of the responsibility for the damage.

The new Belgian Criminal Code, due to enter into force in 2026, enshrines legitimate defence in Art. 1.14 New BeCC Sw. as a general ground for justification applicable to all criminal offences.[53] It also introduces as a new requirement that the defensive acts be made with a defensive intent, which means that people who join in the violence without knowing about the legitimacy of the defence can no longer profit from the justification.[54] Furthermore, the new law abolishes the specific presumptions of the current Art. 417 Sw.[55], but only because the rebuttable presumption of

[52] This is a personal impression, because there will be no prosecution or at least not a referral to trial procedure. Only the more exceptional and controversial cases (often on the initiative of the family of the deceased assailant) make it to the trial stage.

[53] With the exception of certain offences, such as genocide, crimes against humanity, war crimes, rape and terrorist acts. The latter seem inherently incapable of meeting the conditions for legitimate defence to be accepted anyway.

[54] Under the current system, participants profit from the successful claim of legitimate defence by the main perpetrator, regardless of their knowledge or intentions.

[55] Bill 22 February 2024, House of Representatives, 2023–2024, DOC 55 nr. 3374/001, 75–76.

legitimate defence has become the general rule. Someone who invokes a justification only has to make this credible, then it will be up to the prosecution to prove that the relevant conditions are not met.[56] Another novelty is that the prohibition of taking the law into one's own hands is, for the first time, expressly put into statute.[57]

Art. 34 New BeCC defines excessive self-defence: "when a person reacts in a disproportionate or unnecessary manner to an illegitimate, serious and present attack on their person or the person of a third party, and this reaction was in a direct causal relationship with the intense emotion caused by the aggression" and prescribes a reduction of punishment.

Vignette 5: Responsibility of Subordinates for Systemic Offences

D is a soldier in the army of a country ruled by a junta of generals who have come to power through a violent coup. When an opposition group demands the return to a democratic system, the government orders the soldiers to shoot and kill any person who resists arrest. Following this order, D kills three young men who take part in a protest demonstration and hit a police officer who tries to arrest them. When D is tried after a change of regime, he says that he did not like to shoot the protesters but that he thought that he had to obey his commanders' orders. D knew that if he had refused to shoot, he might have been demoted, but no physical harm would have occurred to him. Should D be convicted of murder? If so, should his sentence be mitigated because of his situation?

The context, a dictatorial regime, might be relevant for the qualification, *murder* (Arts. 393, 393 bis or 394 BeCC) or *murder as a crime against humanity* (Art. 136 ter BeCC), depending on the systemic nature of crimes committed by the regime and on D's knowledge of whether the actions are part of a pattern of attacks. If it is a single or isolated event, Belgian law on homicide or murder would apply.

As far as the regime change is concerned, as a state party to the European Convention on Human Rights, Belgium would be able to refer to the case law of the Court (ECtHR, 22 March 2001 *Streletz, Kessler and Krenz v. Germany*[58]) to apply the post-regime-change law. In the absence of contemporary domestic Belgian criminal law on crimes against humanity at the time of the offences (1980–82), the court of assizes of Leuven in 2024 directly applied international criminal law to convict (in absentia) four Guatemalans for offences against Belgian nationals in Guatemala.

The question here is whether D could rely on the ground of justification of "legal order or permission" of Art. 70 BeCC. The article itself excludes its application in

56 Cass. 4 January 1994, *Arr.Cass.* 1994, 10; Cass. 24 March 1999, P.98 1127.F; Cass. 14 December 2001, *JLMB* 2002, afl. 13, 532; Cass. 24 February 2010, AR P.09 1614.F; Cass. 5 January 2016, AR P.15.1203.N; H. Fransen, "Rechtvaardiging", in: X., *Postal Memorialis. Lexicon strafrecht, strafvordering en bijzondere wetten*, 2001, 280; A. Verheylesonne, "Les causes de justification", in: P. Chomé, A. Lorent, F. Roggen and J. P. Collin (eds.), *Droit pénal et procédure pénale*, Mechelen, Kluwer, 2011, 18–19.

57 Bill 22 February 2024, House of Representatives, 2023–2024, DOC 55 nr. 3374/001, 76.

58 Applications nos. 34044/96, 35532/97 and 44801/98, see also ECtHR 21 June 2001, *K.-H. W. v. Germany*, application no. 37201/97.

case of international crimes (Book II, chapter Ibis BeCC). If D's actions amount to murder as a crime against humanity, no justification can be sustained.

Art. 136 octies BeCC repeats explicitly that

> No interest, no necessity of a political, military or national nature can justify [a crime against humanity] even committed in reprisal.

D will have to face Art. 136 octies, § 2 BeCC:

> The fact that the accused acted on the orders of his government or a superior does not relieve him of his responsibility if, in the circumstances, the order could clearly have resulted in the commission of [an international crime].

If the action were not an international crime, the rules on the use of deadly violence by the police would apply. Art. 2 ECHR states that a

> Deprivation of life shall not be regarded as inflicted in contravention of this article when it results from the use of force which is no more than absolutely necessary: (a) in defence of any person from unlawful violence; (b) in order to effect a lawful arrest or to prevent the escape of a person lawfully detained; (c) in action lawfully taken for the purpose of quelling a riot or insurrection.

In this case, probably all three grounds could be invoked. It is not clear whether the "hitting" of the officer was life threatening. If so, the shooting might be justified as legitimate defence of others (Art. 416 BeCC). If not, and that seems more likely, D's action will be deemed "*more than absolutely necessary*", especially in the light of the ECtHR's strict construction of this criterion (ECtHR, *McCann and others v. UK*, § 147) and the obligation of states to apply a test of strictly proportionate use of force excluding any margin of appreciation for deprivation of life by state authorities (see also ECtHR, *Ribcheva and others v. Bulgaria*, § 165).

This is important, as for a superior order under Belgian law to justify criminal behaviour, it must not only have been issued in advance and executed in conformity with the order. The order must also have been within the limits of the superior's authority and must be legitimate. The latter condition does not seem to be met in D's case.

D could rely on a mistake of law, claiming that he could not know that the order was illegal, especially taking into account the junta-ruled system. As a soldier, for whom Art. 28 BeMilitary CC punishes insubordination with three or five years of imprisonment, he could rely on Arts. 152 and 260 BeCC, which state that if an illegal order was not manifestly illegal, only the official issuing the order, not the officials executing the order can be punished. While traditionally listed as a ground of justification, Verstraeten and Verbruggen believe it is rather a rebuttable presumption of error of law in the mind of the subordinate official. In view of the incompatibility of the government's order with Art. 2 ECHR, it will be difficult for the soldier to sustain that it was not manifestly illegal.

The conditions for duress (Art. 71 BeCC) do not seem to be met, as there was no real threat to D's life or limb if he had not killed the victims.

Under Belgian law, mitigating circumstances (Art. 81 BeCC) are an open category and D could definitely invoke them. It would offer judges and juries the possibility to reduce the sentence to three years imprisonment (and suspend its execution). Alternative sanctions are not possible for murder, even if there is mitigation (Art. 37 ter, § 1, second indent, 3; Art. 37 quinquies, § 1, second indent, 4°and Art. 37 octies, § 1, fourth indent, 4°BeCC).

Vignette 6: Limits of Consent

V is a 21-year-old ambitious athlete and short-distance runner. He has learned that certain artificial limbs can enhance a runner's speed. He decides that he would rather have an artificial limb instead of his right lower leg. He approaches D, a surgeon in private practice, and asks him to amputate his leg below the knee and replace it with an artificial limb. D complies with V's request. Should D be punished for mayhem?

The victim's consent is not accepted by jurisprudence or most of the legal doctrine as a justification for what is in principle criminal behaviour.[59] Since criminal law has an *ordre public* character, parties cannot impinge on it by agreement. The legislature deprives citizens of the free disposal of certain legal rights (such as the right to life, physical integrity, and sexual integrity under the age of 16).[60] However, the absence of consent is (sometimes implicitly) a material component of numerous criminal offences, such as theft.[61]

A medical intervention which interferes with the physical integrity of the patient, such as the one in the present case, meets the description of the offence of battery under Art. 398 Sw.[62] Strictly speaking, the doctor injures the patient (*actus reus*) and performs the intervention knowingly and intentionally (*mens rea*). The doctor's motive and the victim's consent are of no importance.[63] Therefore, to explain why medical practices are nevertheless generally not punishable, it is necessary to appeal to another ground of justification which removes the unlawfulness of the offence.

It is currently generally accepted in case law and legal doctrine that doctors can rely on the justification of permission by law (Art. 70 Sw.).[64] Indeed, by regulating the

---

59 Regarding battery: Cass. 6 December 2005, AR P.05.0576.N; Brussel (corr.) 12 February 2014, *JLMB* 2014, 996. In general: F. Deruyck, A. De Nauw, *Inleiding tot het bijzonder strafrecht*, Wolters Kluwer Belgium, Mechelen, 2020, 274–275; B. Meganck, "Opzettelijk doden en opzettelijk toebrengen van lichamelijk letsel", in: *Postal Memorialis. Lexicon strafrecht, strafvordering en bijzondere wetten*, 2013, (141) 160; C. Trouet, *De bewijslast van de geïnformeerde toestemming tot een medische ingreep*, *TBBR* 2002, afl. 6, (335) 338–339; C. Van Den Wyngaert and S. Vandromme, *Strafrecht en Strafprocesrecht in hoofdlijnen*, 2019, Oud-Turnhout, Gompel&Svacina, 265–266.

60 F. Verbruggen and R. Verstraeten, *Inleiding tot het Belgische strafrecht en strafprocesrecht*, Intersentia, Antwerpen, 2023, 90.

61 Ibid.

62 E. Verjans, "Het recht op informatie en toestemming van de patiënt herbekeken", *T.Gez.* 2019–20, afl. 1, (4) 20–21.

63 Cass. 6 December 2005, AR P.05.0576.N; B. Meganck, "Opzettelijk doden en opzettelijk toebrengen van lichamelijk letsel", in: *Postal Memorialis. Lexicon strafrecht, strafvordering en bijzondere wetten*, 2013, (141) 160.

64 Charleroi (corr.), 29 March 1983, *RRD*, 1983, 248; F. Deruyck and A. De Nauw, *Inleiding tot het bijzonder strafrecht*, Wolters Kluwer Belgium, Mechelen, 2020, 274–275;

exercise of the health professions by Royal Decree[65], the law implicitly allows doctors to interfere with the physical integrity of patients through acts of diagnosis and treatment.[66]

Doctors can only benefit from this justification if their interventions meet certain conditions. These include having the informed consent of the patient, the intervention having a curative or preventive therapeutic purpose,[67] a reasonable relationship between the dangers for the patient and the intended benefits of the treatment, and the treatment carried out respecting both the scientific state of the art and deontological rules.[68] Only if all these elements are cumulatively present will the doctor not be punishable. However, even if these conditions are fulfilled, the doctor can still be punishable for (un)intentional blows and injuries when errors are committed during the medical intervention.[69] In the present case, the condition of curative or preventive therapeutic intent seems to be particularly relevant.

The notions "curative" and "preventive" are, of course, evolving concepts strongly driven by societal views of what contributes to restoring or promoting a person's health. For example, unlike in the past, it is accepted today that transsexual surgery and sterilisation also fit into this category.[70] Provisions were added to the aforementioned Royal Decree, so that aesthetic surgery now also enjoys protection. The terms "curative" and "preventive" can clearly be contrasted with purely experimental medical activities which do not benefit the patient. A doctor who had performed brain biopsies on patients purely for purposes of research and observation was found guilty of intentional blows and injuries.[71] In the present case, there is (arguably) a benefit for the patient (being able to run slightly faster), but this benefit does not relate to the pa-

---

R. D'Haese, "Medische contracten in het licht van het recht op eerbied voor de fysieke integriteit. De informed consent-vereiste als raakpunt", *TBBR* 2010, afl. 9, (430) 449–450; C. Van Den Wyngaert and S. Vandromme, *Strafrecht en Strafprocesrecht in hoofdlijnen*, 2019, Oud-Turnhout, Gompel&Svacina, 265–266. The ground for justification of necessity also remains relevant, mainly in cases where the patient has not (anymore) been able to give prior consent for an intervention to the doctor. The justification of permission by law is now contained in Art. 1.11 New BeCC.

65 Royal Decree No 78 of 10 November 1967.

66 C. Trouet, "De bewijslast van de geïnformeerde toestemming tot een medische ingreep", *TBBR* 2002, afl. 6, (335) 338–339; R. D'Haese, "Medische contracten in het licht van het recht op eerbied voor de fysieke integriteit. De informed consent-vereiste als raakpunt", *TBBR* 2010, afl. 9, (430) 449–450.

67 Cass. 14 December 2001, *JLMB* 2002, afl. 13, 532.

68 Brussel (corr.) 12 February 2014, *JLMB* 2014, 996; R. D'Haese, "Medische contracten in het licht van het recht op eerbied voor de fysieke integriteit. De informed consent-vereiste als raakpunt", *TBBR* 2010, afl. 9, (430) 449–450; G. Genicot, *Droit médical et biomédical*, 2016, Brussel, Larcier, 114–121; C. Van Den Wyngaert and S. Vandromme, *Strafrecht en Strafprocesrecht in hoofdlijnen*, 2019, Oud-Turnhout, Gompel&Svacina, 265–266.

69 C. Van Den Wyngaert and S. Vandromme, *Strafrecht en Strafprocesrecht in hoofdlijnen*, 2019, Oud-Turnhout, Gompel&Svacina, 265–266.

70 G. Genicot, *Droit médical et biomédical*, 2016, Brussel, Larcier, 118; C. Van Den Wyngaert and S. Vandromme, *Strafrecht en Strafprocesrecht in hoofdlijnen*, 2019, Oud-Turnhout, Gompel&Svacina, 265–266.

71 Charleroi (corr.), 29 March 1983, *RRD*, 1983, 248.

tient's health. This distinguishes the instant case from, for example, the practice in breast cancer treatment of preventively amputating a breast in certain cases.

Some authors suggest that the recognition of transsexual surgery, for example, indicates an extension of the therapeutic purpose beyond the improvement of the patient's medical health towards the promotion of his mental and social well-being.[72] In this way, patients can decide for themselves whether they are "sick", regardless of prevailing societal attitudes.[73] In the present case, however, it seems difficult to assert that the amputation was aimed at improving the patient's psychological or social well-being. Questions also arise as to the social acceptability of a doctor amputating a healthy functional leg just to enable the patient to run a little faster with a prothesis, whether the risk-benefit ratio is proportionate and, moreover, whether the intervention is reconcilable with a doctor's deontology. It therefore seems plausible that the conditions for justification are not met. If the doctor were to face criminal charges, he could only invoke the justification of permission by law with some credibility. It would then be up to the prosecution to show that the relevant conditions are not met.[74]

Vignette 7: Withdrawal from an Attempt

25-year-old D is deeply upset with her former boyfriend V, who had ended their relationship to be with another woman. To punish V, D plans to stab him with a large knife. D knows that the stab wounds can be fatal and accepts V's death as a possible outcome. When V goes jogging, D attacks him from behind and stabs him in the back three times. V breaks down. D realises that she has injured him but that the injuries will not cause his death. She realises that she could kill him by stabbing him again but decides to leave him alone. Should D be punished for attempted murder?

Murder is a felony, which means that an attempt is always punishable. For a punishable attempt, Art. 51 BeCC requires that

The intention to commit a crime has manifested itself by outward acts that constitute a beginning of the execution of that crime and have ceased or failed to produce their effects only as a result of circumstances independent of the will of the perpetrator.

Case law is rather strict with regard to "only". It has indeed decided that external circumstances (such as the unexpected reaction of the victim or a bystander) influencing the will of the perpetrator and leading to a withdrawal before the actual completion may take away the spontaneity of the withdrawal. It would be considered a failure as the result of external circumstances. Even though the withdrawal was partially a choice of the offender, it would not entail impunity of the attempted offence.

---

72 F. Swennen, "Juridische grondslagen voor de strafrechtelijke immuniteit van de geneesheer i.h.b. de vereiste van het therapeutisch oogmerk", *T.Gez.* 1997–98, (3) 14–15.

73 Ibid.

74 Cass. 4 January 1994, *Arr.Cass.* 1994, 10; Cass. 24 March 1999, P.98 1127.F; Cass. 14 December 2001, *JLMB* 2002, afl. 13, 532; Cass. 24 February 2010, AR P.09 1614.F; Cass. 5 January 2016, AR P.15.1203.N; A. Verheylesonne, "Les causes de justification", in: P. Chomé, A. Lorent, F. Roggen and J. P. Collin (eds.), *Droit pénal et procédure pénale*, Mechelen, Kluwer, 2011, 18–19; E. Verjans, "Het recht op informatie en toestemming van de patiënt herbekeken", *T.Gez.* 2019–20, afl. 1, (4) 20–21.

In this case, however, at a moment when it was clear that V would not die without further stabbing, D indeed desisted spontaneously. Therefore, there would not be an attempted murder[75], which carries a sentence of thirty years. D would be liable for battery, most likely aggravated battery depending on the seriousness and long-term effects of the injuries suffered by V. She would also be liable for failure to assist a person in danger by abandoning the victim instead of helping (by calling an ambulance, for example), but that carries a maximum sentence of two years (Art. 422 bis BeCC) and will be absorbed by the punishment for aggravated battery (Art. 65 BeCC).

The New BeCC, adopted on 28 February 2024 but not yet in force, would limit the effects of spontaneous withdrawal to the individual person withdrawing and not extend the benefit to other participants, but as D is a sole perpetrator, it will make no difference.

Vignette 8: Criminal Responsibility of Minors

D is a 13-year-old boy. He abducts and rapes V, a girl of the same age. Should D be punished for a criminal offence?

In the 20th and early 21st centuries, Belgian law underwent major changes in the way it addressed deviant behaviour of young people. Between 1830 and 1912, minors were subject to the general criminal law and in principle treated the same as adults. Consequently, no absolute legal ground existed that excluded guilt by setting a certain age limit, nor were children considered too young to be punished.[76] However, if the child did not yet have sufficient intellectual maturity, judges could acquit the child and refer it to the prosecutor's office, which could impose other measures if the child's family did not provide an adequate environment to grow up in.[77]

Gradually, the focus in legal doctrine and the case law, influenced by developments in criminological science, shifted from repression to re-education, heralding a legal shift.[78] At the beginning of the 20th century, the repressive approach of criminal law in general[79] and the non-existence of a separate system for minors[80] were heavily crit-

---

75 Cass. 29 July 2003, *Pas.* 2003, 1321.

76 J. Put, *Handboek Jeugdbeschermingsrecht*, Brugge, die Keure, 2021, 21.

77 B. Brouwers, "Jeugdsanctierecht in Europa: is uithandengeving een evidentie?", *Jura Falconis* 2007–08, 3–4; J. Christiaens, "De geboorte van de jeugddelinquent", *Belgisch tijdschrift voor nieuwste geschiedenis* 2000, 305; M. S. Dupont-Bouchat, J. Christiaens and C. Vanneste, "Jeugd en Justitie (I). Modellen, praktijken en hervormingen van het jeugdrechtsysteem (1830–2014)", in: M. De Koster, D. Heirbaut and X. Rousseau, *Tweehonderd jaar justitie. Historische encyclopedie van de Belgische justitie*, Brugge-Brussel, die Keure, 252; E. Goedseels, "Het eeuwenoude spanningsveld tussen straffen en heropvoeden", in: F. Cova, T. Daems, K. Geens et al., *Justitie 2020. Straffen: waarom? Hoe?*, Antwerpen-Apeldoorn, Maklu, 2017, 129; J. Put, *Handboek Jeugdbeschermingsrecht*, Brugge, die Keure, 2021, 21.

78 E. Goedseels, "Het eeuwenoude spanningsveld tussen straffen en heropvoeden", in: F. Cova, T. Daems, K. Geens et al., *Justitie 2020. Straffen: waarom? Hoe?*, Antwerpen-Apeldoorn, Maklu, 2017, 129.

79 B. Brouwers, "Jeugdsanctierecht in Europa: is uithandengeving een evidentie?", *Jura Falconis* 2007–08, 5–6; E. Goedseels, "Het eeuwenoude spanningsveld tussen straffen en

icised. Instead of considering the perpetrator to be a rational person completely responsible for his own actions, the focus shifted to a more sociological approach according to which the act of a perpetrator cannot be separated from the biological and social influences in his life. Hence, not retribution for a morally wrongful act, but protection of society against dangerous individuals legitimated a response with criminal sanctions.[81] This meant a shift from repression to prevention. Moreover, prevention was thought to have maximum effect in cases of minors. Already in the midst of the 19th century, a penitentiary institution for minors was constructed to separate them from adults and to introduce a regime more focused on rehabilitation and education.[82] With regard to children, the Child Protection Act of 1912 set the criminal age of majority at 16 years[83] and introduced a special legal regime for young offenders who committed "*an act defined by law as a criminal offence*[84]". The double objective was to install social control over the child and to provide him or her with therapeutic assistance.[85] Younger people were henceforth considered guiltless by definition and removed from the scope of the criminal law. "Youth protection measures" could now be imposed without first considering the guilt or the intellectual maturity of the child.[86] In 1965 the legislature raised the age of criminal majority to 18, but with the possibility to refer minors above the age of 16 to the criminal courts in serious cases.[87] The focus shifted from punishment to treatment, rehabilitation, and education.

The sixth state reform of the Belgian federal state shifted juvenile délinquency law from the federal level to the three Communities (Flanders, the French(-speaking) Community and the Germanophone community). This new competence led to a

---

heropvoeden", in: F. Cova, T. Daems, K. Geens et al., *Justitie 2020. Straffen: waarom? Hoe?*, Antwerpen-Apeldoorn, Maklu, 2017, 129.

80 J. Put, *Handboek Jeugdbeschermingsrecht*, Brugge, die Keure, 2021, 21.

81 J. Christiaens, "De geboorte van de jeugddelinquent", *Belgisch tijdschrift voor nieuwste geschiedenis* 2000, 305–306; E. Goedseels, "Het eeuwenoude spanningsveld tussen straffen en heropvoeden", in: F. Cova, T. Daems, K. Geens et al., *Justitie 2020. Straffen: waarom? Hoe?*, Antwerpen-Apeldoorn, Maklu, 2017, 130.

82 M. S. Dupont-Bouchat, J. Christiaens and C. Vanneste, "Jeugd en Justitie (I). Modellen, praktijken en hervormingen van het jeugdrechtsysteem (1830–2014) in M. De Koster, D. Heirbaut and X. Rousseau, *Tweehonderd jaar justitie. Historische encyclopedie van de Belgische justitie*, Brugge/Brussel, die Keure, 252; E. Goedseels, "Het eeuwenoude spanningsveld tussen straffen en heropvoeden", in: F. Cova, T. Daems, K. Geens et al., *Justitie 2020. Straffen: waarom? Hoe?*, Antwerpen-Apeldoorn, Maklu, 2017, 129.

83 J. Put, *Handboek Jeugdbeschermingsrecht*, Brugge, die Keure, 2021, 22; R. Verstraeten and F. Verbruggen, *Inleiding tot het Belgische Strafrecht en strafprocesrecht*, Brussel, Intersentia, 2023, 101.

84 Article 16 Law 15 May 1912.

85 Ch. Eliaerts, "De toekomst van het jeugdbeschermingssysteem. Naar een jeugdsanctierecht in lijn met internationale normen", *T.Straf.* 2013, 215; E. Goedseels, "Het eeuwenoude spanningsveld tussen straffen en heropvoeden", in: F. Cova, T. Daems, K. Geens et al., *Justitie 2020. Straffen: waarom? Hoe?*, Antwerpen-Apeldoorn, Maklu, 2017, 130–131.

86 R. Verstraeten and F. Verbruggen, *Inleiding tot het Belgische Strafrecht en strafprocesrecht*, Brussel, Intersentia, 2023, 101.

87 Art. 57 bis Youth Law of 8 April 1965; J. Put, *Handboek Jeugdbeschermingsrecht*, Brugge, die Keure, 2021, 25.

new decree (legislation of communities, the equivalent to a federal law) on juvenile delinquency in Flanders in 2019.[88] Since then, only children under 12 are always considered guiltless or blameless.[89] Young people between 12 and 18 years of age, like 13-year-old D, are, in principle capable of guilt. However, because they are considered too young to be criminally punished with general sanctions meant for adults, the decree provides for specific measures.[90] Minors between the age of 16 and 18 are usually tried in a normal court in case of traffic crimes[91] and exceptionally, after a specific procedure, in case of a limited list of serious offences[92]. That was already the case under the federal law before the introduction of the Flemish decree.[93] Moreover, capability of guilt in case of elder minors was also already accepted in case of some administrative punitive sanctions for minors above the age of 14, for public nuisance or for misbehaviour at sports events or on public transport.[94]

Thus, a 13-year-old boy can only be "sanctioned" with specific "juvenile measures" and never with "general" criminal sanctions, regardless of the seriousness of the offence committed. The juvenile court has a diverse choice of measures at its disposal, including a simple reprimand[95], the imposition of a "positive project"[96] or the imposition of certain conditions[97]. In case of more serious offences, the juvenile court may also revert to more serious measures that can indeed be considered to be sanctions given the nature of the measure and the impact on the young person.[98] Of particular importance here is the closed supervision via placement in a ward of a community institution, which can be imposed for three, six or nine months.[99] This measure, preceded by a short observational stay[100], is possible for children under the age of 14 only if the offence is punishable under the general criminal law as a crime by at least five to ten years of imprisonment and if there are urgent, serious and exceptional circumstances relating to the protection of public safety.[101] Given that the BeCC provides for a sentence of five to ten years' imprisonment for the ab-

88 Decree of 15 February 2019, Flemish Parliament, 2017–18, nr. 1670/12.

89 Art. 4 § 2 Decree of 15 February 2019; R. Verstraeten and F. Verbruggen, *Inleiding tot het Belgische Strafrecht en strafprocesrecht*, Brussel, Intersentia, 2023, 101.

90 R. Verstraeten and F. Verbruggen, *Inleiding tot het Belgische Strafrecht en strafprocesrecht*, Brussel, Intersentia, 2023, 101.

91 Art. 5 Decree of 15 February 2019.

92 Art. 38 Decree of 15 February 2019.

93 Art. 36, 4°Youth Law of 8 April 1965.

94 Art. 38 bis Youth Law of 8 April 1965.

95 Art. 31 Decree of 15 February 2019.

96 Art. 32 Decree of 15 February 2019.

97 Art- 34 Decree of 15 February 2019.

98 R. Verstraeten and F. Verbruggen, *Inleiding tot het Belgische Strafrecht en strafprocesrecht*, Brussel, Intersentia, 2023, 101.

99 Art. 36, first section Decree of 15 February 2019.

100 Art. 26 Decree of 15 February 2019.

101 Art. 26 § 3, 2 and 3, Art. 27 § 2, first section and Art. 36, second section Decree of 15 February 2019.

duction of a minor[102] and a sentence of 20 to 30 years' imprisonment for the rape of a minor[103], this first condition is fulfilled in the present case. In addition, this deprivation of liberty is considered to serve as a last resort. [104]

Initially, the intention of the Flemish legislature in 2019 was to focus on restorative measures. In 2024, the legislature implemented some reforms in the juvenile delinquency decree.[105]

Some politicians believed that the approach was too focused on education and rehabilitation and that too little attention went to the repressive aspect. Some stakeholders and legal scholars criticised the new provisions. According to them, the reform has departed from its initial restorative mindset. They deplore that under the guise of an alleged rise of the rate of juvenile crime[106], it has opted for an increased repressive mindset. Under the new rules, the system of electronic surveillance will be extended and a system of short stays in a closed community institution will be introduced by decree after a pilot project that lasted for several years.[107] The stakeholders fear that judges and prosecutors will resort to electronic surveillance too quickly, with little attention for therapeutic treatment, and that young people will too often be deprived of their freedom for short periods of time.[108]

In society and the media, discussions on criminal sanctions for juveniles tends to flare up following especially shocking offences (and wane after a short while), but they would usually only concern "older" minors, from fifteen or sixteen years onwards. Few people suggest applying the criminal law to thirteen-year-olds. Belgium's obligations under the Convention on Children's Rights (and perhaps even under the ECHR) would probably stand in the way of any such change.

Conversely, Belgian lawmakers could have considered the introduction of a special regime for young adults (up to the age of 25), based on scientific knowledge on the development of the juvenile brain and on the effects of existing adult prisons on young offenders. So far, they have failed to make any impact. During the debate on the New BeCC, adopted in 2024, it was never really an issue.

A new Decree also came into force in Wallonia[109] and the Brussels Capital Region[110]. There are some differences in their approach compared to Flanders. Whereas

102 Art. 428 BeCC.

103 Arts. 417/11 and 417/16 BeCC.

104 Art. 26 § 3, 1 and 4, Art. 27 § 2, first section and Art. 36, second section Decree of 15 February 2019.

105 Draft Decree of 8 February 2024, Flemish Parliament, 2023–24, nr. 2013/01.

106 Juvenile crime has fluctuated quite significantly over the last ten years, partly due to the corona crisis. In general, the number of juvenile delinquency cases has hardly decreased compared to ten years ago. See https://stat.om-mp.be/jeu/n/index.html (consulted on 12 April 2024).

107 Art. 8 Draft Decree of 8 February 2024, Flemish Parliament, 2023–24, nr. 2013/01, 208.

108 https://www.nieuwsblad.be/cnt/dmf20230926_97578323.

109 Decree of 18 January 2018, *Parliament of the French community*, 2017–2018, nr. 467.

in Flanders there is a separate trajectory between the response to the offence on the one hand and the response to the underlying social problem on the other, in Wallonia these matters are at least in principle not treated as completely separate on a procedural level.[111] Moreover, the Walloon Decree seems to adhere more explicitly to the classic youth protection logic, while Flanders deliberately chose to depart from it.[112] The Walloon Decree speaks of "educational measures" instead of "sanctions". While the ideological differences reflected in the choice of concepts seem clear, the difference in practice might not be that big. It cannot be denied that many juvenile offenders being subjected to educational measures, especially those depriving them of their freedom, may perceive them as sanctions.

Vignette 9: Statute of Limitations

> In 1995, D violently raped V, a 35-year-old woman, using a knife. D managed to escape and was not apprehended until 2023. Traces of his DNA taken from the victim's body leave no doubt that D is the perpetrator. Should D be convicted despite the long delay?

The question is whether a statute of limitations (prescription) would bar prosecution and criminal conviction of D in 2023, 28 years after the crime.

Prescription is a ground for extinction of criminal prosecution.[113] The system rests on several considerations. One argument is that through the passage of time social peace is restored to a degree where public order no longer requires punishment and, moreover, such punishment would no longer be appropriate or effective.[114] The second argument is that in the long period of time, evidence will disappear or weaken, which compromises legal certainty and the rights of defence, increasing the risk of miscarriages of justice.[115]

The situation under Belgian law is very complex, because of a long series of changes to both the laws on sexual offences and statutes of limitation. The length of "prescription term"' depends on the seriousness of the offence.

---

110 Ordonnance of 24 April 2018, Common Commission, 2018–19, nr. B–175/2; in the (bilingual) Brussels Capital Region the so-called Common Commission (of the Flemish and French Communities) regulates measures that impose rights and duties on natural persons. See E. Goedseels and I. Ravier, Recente Ontwikkelingen in het Belgische Jeugdrecht, *Justitie en veiligheid*, April 2020, 16.

111 E. Goedseels and I. Ravier, "Recente Ontwikkelingen in het Belgische Jeugdrecht", *Justitie en veiligheid*, April 2020, 21.

112 Ibid. 8.

113 Meaning that there will never be a verdict on guilt or innocence. F. Verbruggen and R. Verstraeten, *Inleiding tot het Belgische strafrecht en strafprocesrecht*, Intersentia, Antwerpen, 2023, 679, nr. 2204.

114 I. Delbrouck, "Niet-consensuele seksuele misdrijven – Bijzondere strafrechtelijke en strafprocesrechtelijke aspecten", in: *Postal Memorialis. Lexicon strafrecht, strafvordering en bijzondere wetten*, 2023, (N31/01) N31/32, nr. 40; F. Kuty, *Justice pénale et procès équitable. Essai de systématisation*, II, Brussel, Larcier, 2023, 1421, nr. 1399.

115 O. Michiels and G. Falque, *Principes de procédure pénale*, Brussel, Larcier, 2023, 79–80, nr. 178.

Until 2024, that length was affected by the standardized practice of so-called "correctionalization" (Art. 21, 2 Preliminary Title Belgian Code of Criminal Procedure (BeCCP)) of offences such as rape by pre-trial courts or prosecutors, i. e., the referral of cases that would normally go to jury trial in the assizes court to ordinary criminal courts by anticipatory acceptance of mitigation.[116]

On the other hand, the nominal term of prescription provided by law was always prolonged in practice. Almost inevitably, there would be grounds of interruption[117]: acts of investigation or prosecution[118] by authorized persons, which reset the term, but only if they occurred within the initial term[119]. The term could also be extended by suspension: a standstill because of a temporary legal obstacle to investigation or prosecution, after which it resumes, but without causing a new timespan to begin. Unlike interruption, suspension could also occur outside of the original period (if there had been interruption within that initial term).[120] The rationale is that suspects should not benefit from temporary impediments to criminal prosecution.[121] Grounds for suspension were provided by both statute and case law.[122]

Even taking into account interruptions and suspension,[123] it does not seem plausible that conviction of D would still be possible 28 years after the rape took place. Rape under threat of a weapon was, in 1995, punishable based on the now replaced

---

116 A crime (felony) can become a misdemeanor and a misdemeanor can become an infraction (Art. 80 BeCC).

117 E. Baeyens, "Stuiting van de verjaring van de strafvordering", *T.Strafr.* 2019, afl. 5, (291) 291.

118 E.g., the order and serving of a summons before the trial court, a guilty verdict at first instance, and the service of a judgement in default. O. Michiels and G. Falque, *Principes de procédure pénale*, Brussel, Larcier, 2023, 86, nr. 193. They are unlikely is this case, given the unknown identity of the perpetrator during the relevant period.

119 Art. 22 Preliminary Title BeCCP. This means that, based on interruption alone, a prescription period can at most be almost doubled in length.

120 In turn, a temporary suspension within the original period is relevant for interruption, since it prolongs this original period, during which interruption is possible. In case an interruption occurs during a suspension, the new timespan will start to run at the moment the suspension ends, insofar as this interruption takes place during the original period. R. Verstraeten and F. Verbruggen, *Inleiding tot het Belgische strafrecht en strafprocesrecht*, Intersentia, Antwerpen, 2023, 682, nr. 2220 and 685, nr. 2236.

121 However, not all grounds of suspension meet this logic; some were used as a sanction for the use of defence rights regarded as dilatory. See Art. 24, 3 Preliminary Title BeCCP.

122 They include, among others, the situation in which incompetence, inadmissibility or nullity is invoked before the trial court (unless it is invoked by the Public Prosecutor's Office or declared well-founded by the judge), when the suspect asks the investigating judge for an additional investigation, in the phase in which the council chamber determines whether there is enough evidence to refer the case to the trial court (suspension for a maximum of one year), referral for decision on a preliminary ruling, from the request of one of the parties for an amicable settlement until it is established that it will not happen or has failed, during the procedure in cassation against a final decision. O. Michiels and G. Falque, *Principes de procédure pénale*, Brussel, Larcier, 2023, 87–92, nrs. 197–210.

123 However, since D was not identified for 28 years, it seems unlikely that any ground of suspension would apply.

Art. 376 BeCC.[124] From 1995 until 2024, the prescription period for this type of crime was 10 years (Art. 21, 3°Preliminary Title BeCCP). Interruptions could extend that to a maximum of 20 years. Since correctionalisation of rape cases was a standard procedure, however, the term would become five years (Art. 21, 4°Preliminary Title BeCCP), extendable by interruptions to ten years.

If D kept committing other rapes (or linked offences), the whole series could be considered a continued offence. It that case, the prescription term (also that for the rape in 1995) would only start at the time of the last offence in the series that has been proven, on the condition that no full prescription term had elapsed between two successive offences.[125]

The Belgian system of prescription had clearly become unnecessarily complex. In 2024, parliament drastically overhauled and simplified the system.[126] The limitation periods were extended, but they are no longer affected by "correctionalisation" based on mitigating circumstances. The grounds for suspension are strictly limited to those that really impede the criminal procedure[127]. Interruption has been abolished altogether.[128] Moreover, due to a new general rule, limitation periods will stop running as soon as the procedure reaches the trial stage.[129] The prescription term for rape has been brought to a fixed term of 15 years, regardless of investigative actions. It suffices that the case is brought to trial, from the moment it reaches the trial stage, statutes of limitation no longer bar conviction. If an offence is not yet time-barred, the new regime applies, but offences that became time-barred under the old legislation, stay time-barred and cannot be prosecuted, regardless of the new regime. It seems unlikely that these changes would have led to a different outcome in the present case.

Prescription of sexual offences has become a more controversial issue over the last few years, but mainly with regard to offences against minors. After some intermediate steps (such as only starting the term when the victim turns 18 and not reducing the term in spite of correctionalisation), a drastic change was implemented in 2019. For

---

124 Since the reform of sexual criminal law in 2022, rape under threat of a weapon is treated by Art. 417/14 BeCC, where it is carries imprisonment of 15 to 20 years.

125 R. Verstraeten and F. Verbruggen, *Inleiding tot het Belgische strafrecht en strafprocesrecht*, Intersentia, Antwerpen, 2023, 682–683, nr. 2216.

126 Laws changing the statute of limitations immediately apply to all pending proceedings which were not yet time-barred at the time of its entry into force, unless the law itself provides otherwise. Cass. 23 May 2000, *Arr.Cass.* 2000, 968. Art. 7.1 ECHR does not oppose this retroactivity, as it only concerns the introduction of more stringent substantive criminal laws. R. Verstraeten and F. Verbruggen, *Inleiding tot het Belgische strafrecht en strafprocesrecht*, Intersentia, Antwerpen, 2023, 683, nr. 2221.

127 Bill of 20 July 2023, House of Representatives, 2023–24, DOC 55 nr. 3514/004, 50–51. The ground for suspension based on the request by the suspect for an additional investigation during the criminal investigation phase has been abolished.

128 Art. 21, 3 Preliminary Title BeCCP.

129 Bill of 20 July 2023, House of Representatives, 2023–24, DOC 55 nr. 3514/004, 46–50. As a result, the reasonable timeframe requirement is given a more prominent role in the trial phase. The reform even provides the judge with the possibility of pronouncing the extinction of the criminal prosecution based on this requirement, in case of a very serious disregard thereof. Another consequence is that the suspension of the prescription period remains only relevant in the criminal investigation phase.

some sexual offences against a minor[130], the criminal prosecution is now exempt from prescription Art. 21 bis, 2 Preliminary Title BeCCP). Until then, that exemption had only concerned genocide, crimes against humanity and war crimes. Murder of a minor however can still be statute-barred. If a rapist kills the minor after the sexual abuse, that may have as a consequence that the murder is statute barred, but the abuse is not. That apparent lack of logic was not deemed unconstitutional by the Constitutional Court.[131] Some politicians wanted to expand the list of offences, but in the 2024 reform only murders which strongly affect society (such as terrorist murders) have been added to the list of offences that can never be statute barred.

In the unlikely event that prosecution would not be time-barred in 2023, it would be necessary to consider whether a "reasonable period" has been exceeded. This seems improbable.

Under the influence of European law, and in particular the case law on Art. 6 § 1 ECHR, Belgium has adopted Art. 21 ter Preliminary Title BeCCP, which states that any criminal prosecution must be completed within a reasonable time.[132] Unlike the prescription terms, this reasonable time has no fixed length. It will in every case be up to the judges to decide whether it has been exceeded.[133] If the delay has been excessive, the judge can impose a sentence below the legal minimum and can even opt for a simple declaration of guilt.[134] It is generally accepted that the period starts to run when the suspect is officially notified that there is a criminal investigation against him.[135] According to the facts, D (presumably) only got involved in criminal proceedings in 2023, which renders the question of a trial within a reasonable amount of time rather irrelevant in this case.

---

130 Under 18 years of age.

131 Constitutional Court 9 June 2022 nr. 76/2022, ECLI:BE:GHCC:2022:ARR.076.

132 This rule is to prevent the suspect from being left in uncertainty for too long and to safeguard his rights of defense (for example if evidence may disappear). F. Kuty, *Justice pénale et procès équitable. Essai de systématisation*, II, Brussel, Larcier, 2023, 1421–1422, nr. 1400.

133 I. Delbrouck, "Niet-consensuele seksuele misdrijven – Bijzondere strafrechtelijke en strafprocesrechtelijke aspecten", in: *Postal Memorialis. Lexicon strafrecht, strafvordering en bijzondere wetten*, 2023, (N31/01) N31/34–N31/35, nr. 41.

134 Depending on what is appropriate in proportion to the exceeding of the reasonable period; R. Verstraeten and F. Verbruggen, *Inleiding tot het Belgische strafrecht en strafprocesrecht*, Intersentia, Antwerpen, 2023, 378, nr. 1319. The judge even has an obligation to impose a lower sentence than would have been the case without violation of the reasonable period requirement: Cass. 28 January 2004, *Arr.Cass.* 2004, afl. 1, 147; Cass. 11 June 2013, *RABG* 2014, afl. 1, 18. This is of course difficult to check in practice.

135 This can be done, for example in the course of an interrogation, arrest or seizure. In this regard, it is often stated that the period begins to run when the person concerned is accused. I. Delbrouck, "Niet-consensuele seksuele misdrijven – Bijzondere strafrechtelijke en strafprocesrechtelijke aspecten", in: *Postal Memorialis. Lexicon strafrecht, strafvordering en bijzondere wetten*, 2023, (N31/01) N31/35, nr. 41; J. Reniers, "Het sanctioneren van de te lange duur van het strafproces: waarom en op welke wijze? Een vernieuwende kijk op de verjaring en redelijke termijn als sanctioneringsprincipes- en mechanismen in rechtsvergelijkend perspectief", *Jura Falc.* 2020–21, afl. 2, (391) 470, nr. 57. The period ends as soon as a final decision removes the uncertainty about the fate of the suspect.

The prosecution of D would most likely have been time-barred by 2023 and he cannot be prosecuted or convicted.

Vignette 10: Life Imprisonment without Parole

The Penal Code of State S provides for imprisonment for life as the maximum penalty for murder, but also authorises the court to order an offender's early release after a minimum of 15 years if the offender is no longer dangerous. Reacting to cases of particularly heinous murders, the legislature of S wishes to introduce a penalty of life imprisonment without any possibility of early release, regardless of the offender's continued dangerousness. Would this amendment be acceptable?

Early release in case of life imprisonment has always been at least theoretically possible under Belgian law, first as a favour by the King and nowadays as a right if certain conditions, such as a minimum amount of time served in prison, are met. The Belgian legislature has however gradually increased that time period in the course of history. Before 1888, a prisoner could ask for a conditional favour by the King to be released after seven years of imprisonment in case of a life sentence.[136] In 1888, the system based on royal pardon was replaced by a system in which the Minister of Justice decided on the conditional early release (parole).[137] The time period for life imprisonment was set to ten years of time served in prison or 14 years in case of a repeated offence. Early release was not a conditional right, but still a favour heavily influenced by the positive advice of the prison director.[138]

Nowadays, decisions on early release are taken by the sentence enforcement court, which makes it an impartial judicial decision. If the prisoner fulfils all the conditions set by law, the release should be approved. It is therefore not a favour, but a conditional right.[139] Under current Belgian law, a convict who serves a sentence of life imprisonment can apply for an early conditional release after 15 years of the sentence have been served.[140] The time limit is set to 19[141] or 23[142] years if there was a conviction for some serious offences by a regular criminal court or an assize court respectively. In case of some serious crimes, the legislature introduced a "security period", which gives the judge the possibility to further increase the time period for an early conditional release.[143] One of the crimes for which this has been made possible is murder of a police officer.[144] If the jury imposes a life sentence on a perpetrator of

---

136 E. Maes, "Het wettelijk kader, korte historiek, inhoud en commentaren", in: J. Goethals and M. Bouverne-De Bie (eds.), *De voorwaardelijke invrijheidstelling: wetgeving, predictie en begeleiding*, Gent, Academia Press, 2000, 4; V. Scheirs, *De strafuitvoeringsrechtbank aan het werk*, Antwerpen-Apeldoorn, Maklu, 2014, 38.

137 Art. 1 Law of 31 May 1888.

138 V. Scheirs, *De strafuitvoeringsrechtbank aan het werk*, Antwerpen-Apeldoorn, Maklu, 2014, 39.

139 Art. 25 Law of 4 May 2006 on the external legal position, *BS* 15 June 2006, 30449.

140 Art. 25, § 2, c) Law of 4 May 2006.

141 Art. 25, § 2, d) Law of 4 May 2006.

142 Art. 25, § 2, e) Law of 4 May 2006.

143 Law of 21 December 2017 on the security period, *BS* 11 January 2018, 1177.

144 Art. 195, section 7 and 8 Code of Criminal Procedure.

that crime, the jury and the court can decide to not allow an early conditional release before 25 years in prison have been served.[145]

In 2023 Belgium was convicted by the ECtHR (and subsequently by Belgian courts) for failing to provide an institution and the necessary care for a prisoner who had been imprisoned for 44 years.[146] Already in 2017, a panel of psychiatric experts had told the sentence execution court that prolonging the detention of this person in prison was no longer appropriate, "*in terms of public safety and with a view to his resocialisation and reintegration into society.*" A return to society without any preparation would however create a "moderate risk of reoffending", so they suggested his transfer to a forensic psychiatric unit to "*mitigate the risks and provide the applicant with an appropriate living environment that would serve as a transition between prison and society.*" However, the two existing Psychiatric Forensic Centres only accept persons detained as a security measure, not offenders serving criminal punishment. So far, the government has failed to provide a solution and has not yet complied with the judicial orders. The man is still detained in prison.

In 2024, parliament introduced a new criminal sanction, the "security measure to protect society". Unlike "detention", the long-lasting security measure for offenders who are "criminally insane and dangerous", the new sanction concerns offenders who have a mental disturbance which cannot be remedied under the current medical state of the art (but is not one that would make them criminally insane) and remain dangerous after having served the complete criminal sentence. This sanction has to be imposed by the criminal court at the same time as the initial punishment, and the sentencing execution court has to decide on its execution (Law 29 February 2024 on the introduction of a security measure to protect society[147]). To guarantee compatibility with the exigencies of the ECHR, this measure cannot be executed in regular prisons but has to be served in a special institution.

The Belgian constitution does not prohibit life imprisonment or the exclusion of early release. If Belgium were not bound by international treaties, the proposed amendment would be possible. There are currently no proposals in that regard, but strangely enough, not only the extreme right-wing party, but also right-wing nationalists, Christian democrats and social democrats included "life should be full life" in their election proposals.[148] However, Art. 3 ECHR limits the possibility for Belgium to amend the legislation in that way and installs strong guardrails if political or legal opinion changes. Indeed, life imprisonment with no possibility of an early conditional release violates the prohibition of torture and inhuman and degrading treatment in Art. 3 ECHR.[149] For a change of course in Belgium, it would therefore be necessary

---

145 Art. 195, section 8 Code of Criminal Procedure.

146 ECtHR, 9 August 2023, *Horion v. Belgium*, https://hudoc.echr.coe.int/eng?i=001-224563, ECLI:CE:ECHR:2023:0509JUD003792820.

147 http://www.ejustice.just.fgov.be/eli/wet/2024/02/29/2024002089/staatsblad.

148 Scientifically supported "voter orientation module", approved by the parties, which was based on statements. One of them was: "Someone convicted with a life sentence should never be released" (https://www.vrt.be/vrtnws/nl/kies24/stemtest/).

149 ECtHR, 9 July 2013, nr. 66069/9, 130/10 and 3896/10, *Vinter and Others v. the United Kingdom*, § 121.

to leave the Council of Europe, for which there is not a clear majority in the Federal Parliament, or wait for the ECtHR to overturn its case law on life sentences.

The ECtHR has ruled that there must be at least a theoretical possibility of reducing a life sentence at the execution stage and that there must be a possibility of a review of the sentence. More specifically, this implies that it should be possible to consider significant evolutions in the convicted person's behaviour as well as progress in the rehabilitation process. If, based on these changes, a further deprivation of liberty cannot be justified, it must be possible in theory to release the convict.[150]

How this human rights obligation is to be implemented in concrete terms is left by the ECtHR to the Member States, which have broad discretion. The monitoring required at the implementation stage may take the form of judicial review, although this is not mandatory. Member States are also free to determine when such a check takes place, although the Court notes a certain consensus in the legislation of the states parties that such a check takes place no later than 25 years after the start of the execution of life imprisonment, with periodic follow-up checks.[151] Moreover, in case of a life sentence the prisoner is entitled to know, at the outset of his sentence, how, when and under what conditions he will be able to apply for an early release.[152] The Belgian legislation is in conformity with all these requirements, since 25 years is the maximum period before which such an assessment is excluded in exceptional cases.

No statistical data are available yet, but it is remarkable that ever since the threshold for early release has been raised for convictions of 30 years and life sentences, popular juries (who deliberate on sentencing together with the professional judges) often impose 27, 28 or 29 years. Ordinary people called on jury duty and deciding on an individual defendant may therefore be less repressive and punitive (and more favourable towards parole) than the political world assumes.

150 Ibid. § 119.

151 Ibid. § 120.

152 Ibid. § 122.

3. Chile

By *Carla Sepúlveda Penna**

Vignette 1: Trolley Problem – Killing one Person to Save Many

Five young children are playing on railway tracks. An express train is approaching, and it is too late to stop the train before it hits the children, probably killing them. Operator D recognizes the emergency situation. He electronically flips a switch and thus deflects the train from its regular track to a little-used sidetrack. However, the lone repairman V is busy on the sidetrack, and the deflected train kills V, as D had anticipated. Is D criminally responsible for murder of V?

There is little doubt that D has indeed caused the death of V while foreseeing the result. Consequently, the attribution of both the *actus reus* and the *mens rea* does not present any significant difficulties. The central issue, therefore, lies in the possible defences available to D.

Necessity is recognised under the Chilean Penal Code in Article 10 No. 7 (a permissive norm allowing to cause harm to someone else's property in cases of so-called aggressive justifying necessity) and Article 10 No. 11, which was introduced as part of a legal reform aimed at providing a defence for battered women in domestic violence cases. The provision states:

Article 10.

The following are exempt from criminal liability: [...]

11. Anyone who acts to avoid serious harm to his or her person or rights or those of a third party, provided that the following circumstances exist:
    1. The harm to be avoided is current or imminent.
    2. There is no other practicable and less harmful means of avoiding it.
    3. The harm caused is not substantially greater than that avoided.
    4. The sacrifice of the good threatened by the harm cannot be reasonably demanded of the person who removes it from himself or, where appropriate, of the person from whom it is removed, provided that this was or could be known to the person acting.

A key debate concerns the question whether this provision contains a justification or an excuse, or both.[1] This distinction is crucial because, if no justification is recognized, D's best legal recourse under Chilean law would be an excuse.

While circumstances 1, 2 and 4 seem unproblematic for the Vignette case, circumstance 3 lies at the heart of the issue. Unlike Article 10 No. 7 of the Chilean Penal Code, which requires that a lesser evil be caused, this defence merely stipulates that the harm inflicted must not be *substantially greater* than the harm avoided.

---

* Assistant Professor of Law at Universidad Adolfo Ibáñez, Chile.

1 See Juan Pablo Castillo Morales, "El estado de necesidad del artículo 10 n°11 del Código penal chileno: ¿Una norma bifronte? Elementos para una respuesta negativa", (2016) 11 Política criminal 340.

Even under this lower threshold, the law necessitates an assessment of whether the death of five young children can be said to constitute a (substantially) greater harm than the death of one repairman.

When different legal goods are at stake, scholars have traditionally evaluated the relative severity of harms by interpreting the legislative will and conducting a systematic analysis of the law (e. g., by contrasting the statutory penalties for offences involving those harms). Human life, however, is often treated separately. In cases where life is the relevant legal good, "a significant part of jurists is inclined to consider it (the conflict between two human lives threatened by the same danger) as an unlawful fact (*hecho antijuridico*) which will not ensue in criminal liability for subjective reasons, namely a lack of culpability (blameworthiness)."[2]

According to Novoa, an influential author of the early second half of the twentieth century, "the difficulty is compounded when the conflict is between one human life and several others which could be saved at the price of the former. By remembering that utility is not the same as justice, that no norm authorises the sacrifice of the innocent and that respect for human life is not modified by the number of individuals whose life is endangered, we must maintain that even in such an extreme case the death of one to save many cannot be deemed right (*justo*), albeit the perpetrator may be exempt from criminal liability for the aforementioned reasons."[3]

More recent scholarship has sometimes challenged this position. One contemporary Chilean author has advanced a non-consequentialist argument in favour of considering the number of lives at stake as a morally relevant criterion, provided that no absolute prohibition applies to the case. "On par with other arguments, the agent has a moral duty to choose the course of action causing fewer deaths."[4] This leads to the conclusion that "[s]ince saving the greatest number is a requirement of justice deriving from the equal value of human life, the relevance of numbers must be taken into account by the law in cases where the agent has a positive duty to act. In this way, it must be judged that he who, having a positive duty to save, chooses, in equal circumstances, to save the greatest number is covered by a justification."[5] This raises the question of whether D has a duty to save the lives of any person in danger of being run over by the train. This view probably remains a minority position.

A deontological approach has also found support in terms of the moral dilemma from the point of view of normative ethics: "The right thing to do is not to kill another, even if the good thing would be to try to kill in order to save as many lives as possible."[6]

---

2 Eduardo Novoa, *Curso de Derecho Penal Chileno, Tomo 1* (2010) 358.

3 Ibid. 360–361 note 2.

4 Alejandro Miranda, "La relevancia del número de vidas en situaciones de necesidad" (2023) 29 Ius et Praxis 109, 120.

5 Ibid. 121.

6 Gustavo A Beade, "¿Derribar un avión actuando en estado de necesidad? Los límites de la dogmática penal y la necesidad de analizar dilemas morales mediante la ética normativa", (2022) 58 Revista de Derecho – Pontificia Universidad Católica de Valparaíso 93.

An alternative perspective could frame the problem as a clash of duties. In this case, the question is whether D, as a railway operator, has any legal duties that would result in compelling him to cause the death of V. Drawing from Judith Jarvis Thomson's variations of the trolley problem, Wilenmann argues that even appealing to a collision of duties is unlikely to succeed. He illustrates this by considering the alternative scenario: instead of diverting the train to a little-used sidetrack, the agent pushes a heavy man off a bridge to stop the train. This clearly is a killing that qualifies as homicide and is not justified. Therefore, "as long as the action can be construed as an interference with another's autonomy, a collision of duties has no applicability".[7]

If Article 10 No. 11 Chilean Penal Code contains a justification, it seems that it would most likely not permit the sacrifice of a human life, since such an act cannot be considered a "lesser evil". Therefore, the only viable alternative to benefit D appears to be an exculpatory necessity. If Article 10 No. 11 contains such an excuse, D may benefit from it. If it does not, traditional legal doctrine suggests that D would not be held criminally liable due to a lack of blameworthiness, even though his actions would be deemed unlawful – a form of supra-legal necessity defence.

Vignette 2: Attribution of Death

> D intends to kill his neighbour V. Hidden near V's house, D waits for V and stabs him several times with a knife. V is taken to the hospital, where his wounds are treated. His injuries are not life-threatening and V is kept overnight for observation. During the night, a technical defect in the hospital kitchen leads to the outbreak of a fire, which kills V and other persons. Can D be held criminally responsible for V's death?

Scholarship often operates in these cases by a two-fold analysis of liability, which is then united through the rules regulating the concurrence of offences for the purpose of sentencing.[8] This is not, however, the path usually followed by courts, which only consider the liability for one title of attribution.[9] I will develop both ways of proceeding, in that order.

The fact that the knife wounds in the Vignette are not life-threatening leads to the conclusion that D did not do all that was required of him to consummate the offence of murder and also not enough to complete such an attempt, despite having the required *mens rea*. Under Chilean law (Art. 7 Código Penal (CP)), a complete attempt (*delito frustrado*) occurs if the offender does everything in his power (*pone todo de su parte*) to consummate the offence, but this does not happen for causes independent of his will. In the case at hand, D stops stabbing before the wounds have become lethal.

---

7 Javier Wilenmann, *La Justificación de Un Delito En Situaciones de Necesidad* (Marcial Pons 2017) 662–663.

8 For a comparative overview on this concept, see Antonio Cuerda Riezu, "Concurrence of Offences", *Elgar Encyclopedia of Crime and Criminal Justice* (Edward Elgar Publishing 2024), https://www.elgaronline.com/display/book/9781789902990/b-9781789902990.concurrence.of.offences.xml, accessed 11 April 2024.

9 Sebastián Salinero Echeverría, "El concurso de delitos en la práctica de la judicatura chilena. Una aproximación empírica desde el estudio de casos simulados" (2021) 16 Política criminal 30.

An incomplete attempt (*tentativa*) occurs when the offender begins with the execution of the offence by direct actions, but one or more acts are missing to complete them. This latter term matches the description of the facts. Therefore, D can be held criminally responsible for the incomplete attempt of murder. The wounding as an independent offence description is "absorbed" by the reference to the offence of murder.

The more relevant question is whether V's death can also be concurrently attributed to D. The leading strand of scholarship holds that the solution is offered by the "objective attribution/imputation" doctrine. According to this view, a result may not be attributed to a defendant if the naturalistic *conditio sine qua non* is normatively defeated. This normative assessment is based on the notion of "legally prohibited risk", and a series of specific applications have been developed by doctrine to exclude the attribution of certain results falling outside this kind of risk.

One mechanism that may account for the exclusion of the attribution of a result is the so-called "prohibition of regress", due to third-party intervention and extraordinary natural events. If the independent action of third parties is the last relevant cause to lead to a death, one ought not to "go back" beyond it.[10] The textbook example concerns an ambulance car being driven fast to the hospital and colliding with a tree, resulting in the death of the patient. Here, the driver's intervention excludes the objective attribution of the result to the person who had shot the victim and caused a deadly wound, which did not materialise. Under this interpretation, in the case of our Vignette, where the wounds were not fatal, the attribution of the result would be foreclosed even more clearly, whether the fire was caused due to negligence or by a spontaneous natural event.[11]

Other scholars would classify a case like this as one where the risk created is legally relevant, in that serious although not life-threatening wounds have been caused, but the fire represents a "general risk of everyday life" which materialised in the result. In these cases, there is no concurrence of risks generating competing alternative explanations for the result.[12] The death result in our Vignette is not attributable to the initial risk, as it is not a prevalent explanation for the result since the injuries were not life-threatening. As the result is not objectively attributable under these doctrines, there would only be liability for the attempt.

Courts have long relied on the notion of "co-causal homicides" for cases like this. This kind of homicide has been defined as cases where the agent, with an intention to kill, performs an act itself insufficient to cause the death, which nevertheless occurs due to pre-existent, concomitant or supervenient causes, which are alien to the will of the agent or unknown by her. If the agent's causal contribution was apt to cause the death but nevertheless did not do so, she is considered the perpetrator of a complete

---

10 Mario Garrido, *Derecho Penal, Parte Especial, Tomo III* (Editorial Jurídica de Chile 2002) 42.

11 Sergio Politoff, Juan Bustos and Francisco Grisolía, *Derecho Penal Chileno. Parte Especial* (Editorial Jurídica de Chile 1992) 64.

12 Alex van Weezel, *Curso de Derecho Penal – Parte General* (Universidad Católica 2023) 217–218.

attempt (*delito frustrado*).[13] However, if the wound was not deadly, the accused did not do all he needed to consummate the offence and thus the offence would be punishable as an incomplete attempt (*tentativa*).[14] The death result would thus not be attributed to D.

Vignette 3: Torture to Save a Life

Kidnapper K has abducted an 8-year-old girl G and hidden her in a small cave in the woods. K is trying to extort money from G's parents for her release. The police manage to arrest K. Although being questioned for 24 hours, K steadfastly refuses to disclose where he hid G. Police officer D correctly assumes that G may soon die of thirst if she cannot be found. He therefore severely beats K to make him tell the truth. Fearing even more violence, K eventually leads the police to the cave, where they find G still barely alive. Should D be punished for torturing K?

The criminal offence of torture was introduced in 2016 (Law 20968, creating Art. 150 A CP). This comparatively belated adoption of the Convention against Torture and Other Cruel, Inhuman or Degrading Treatment or Punishment of 1984 and the Statute of Rome of 1998 was affected by the aftermath of the Chilean dictatorship and the discussions about how to deal with the perpetrators of torture and forced disappearances.[15] The difficulties in generating a consensus to criminalise torture were the object of several reports from the UN's Committee Against Torture.[16]

In its short life, there have been scant opportunities for either judicial or doctrinal discussion of the issue of justification and, in particular, the study of cases such as the "ticking bomb" or the defence of a third party. There have been no comparable cases. Not even for the earlier and less severe form of "illegal coercion" (*apremios ilegítimos*) are there substantive pronouncements of the courts.[17] However, these constellations have been dealt with by scholarship, and three broad approaches have been adopted.

The respect for the person and human dignity frames an approach anchored on a view of the constitutional values and the content of international treaties on human rights. Carnevali adheres to what he considers to be the view of "the large majority" of academics (although probably not of public opinion) who oppose not only torture

---

13 SCA Santiago, 06.07.2007, Repertorio, 352; Gustavo Labatut, *Derecho Penal, Parte Especial* (Editorial Jurídica de Chile) 229.

14 CA Rancagua, 09.04.2020, 155–2020 c 23.

15 *Mensaje* at Historia de la ley 20.968 and *passim* along the legislative debate contained in that document.

16 Asamblea General de Naciones Unidas. Informe del Comité contra la Tortura. Suplemento No. 44 (A/50/44), 1995: párr. 60 letra (d) http://bcn.cl/1p9pz; Comité contra la Tortura. Examen de los Informes presentados por los Estados partes en virtud del artículo 19 de la Convención. Conclusiones y recomendaciones del Comité contra la Tortura. Chile, 14 de junio de 2004. CAT/C/CR/32/5: párr. 6 letra (c). http://bcn.cl/1pbfa; Comité contra la Tortura. Examen de los Informes presentados por los Estados partes en virtud del artículo 19 de la Convención. Observaciones finales del Comité contra la Tortura. Chile, 23 de junio de 2009. CAT/C/CHL/CO/5: párr. 10. http://bcn.cl/1p9pz.

17 Nevertheless, courts have sometimes mentioned *obiter* the possibility of both justification and exculpation in these cases, for instance TJOP Viña del Mar O–445–2022.

but also the possibility of any kind of justification within the criminal law.[18] According to this view, justification would lead to the recognition of torture as a socially accepted activity, which instrumentalises a person.[19] Carnevali, however, recognises the possibility of an exculpatory defence (especially through a German-style "supra-legal necessity", *übergesetzlicher Notstand*).[20] Under this reasoning, the permissive norm contained in grounds of justification would mean that both for the state and for individuals it is possible to torture given the right (or wrong) circumstances. However, exculpation can only benefit persons at the individual level. This mechanism may help contain the otherwise expansive wave that a justification would create.

Others, however, question the appropriateness of exculpation in these cases, while also considering a justification inadequate. "It is not easy to admit an excuse even when the innocent character (of the agent) is in doubt, such as in the case of an individual accused of terrorist acts and who might be tortured to avoid conduct of that sort that could affect many lives."[21] Vargas and Henríquez consider the applicability of the defence contained in Art. 10 No. 11 CP, which debatably contains a justificatory as well as an exculpatory version of necessity.[22] It requires (1) an actual or imminent harm which is to be avoided; (2) the absence of any other practicable and less harmful means to avoid the harm; (3) that the harm caused is not substantially greater than the one avoided; (4) that the sacrifice of the threatened good cannot reasonably be demanded of the person affected provided that the agent knew or could have known that.

As this provision necessarily requires the weighing of benefits and evils, these authors argue that the exercise is frustrated and the defences will not succeed. "This is what happens with the torture of one to save many lives [and other cases]. The superiority of the saved legal goods does not seem to suffice. The substantive or natural weighing of evils is discarded, because the only evil caused is always greater than the other, which in the end does not materialise. A comparison of this sort impedes defences of justification based on the lesser evil."[23] A provision requiring weighing will not be able to capture this situation.

The most extensive treatment in the literature is provided by Wilenmann. In his view, the crucial point about the absolute prohibition of torture is an institutional one: it represents a limitation to the functioning of the state in normal situations. If torture were considered exceptionally permissible in exceptional cases, the risk would be that it is condoned for the normal operation of police investigations. Ac-

---

18 Raúl Carnevali, "El Derecho penal frente al terrorismo: Hacia un modelo punitivo particular y sobre el tratamiento de la tortura" [2010] Revista de derecho (Valparaíso) 109, 132.

19 Ibid. 137.

20 Following Kai Ambos and Carnevali, Matus and Ramírez adhere to this solution, Jean Pierre Matus and Cecilia Ramírez, *Manual de Derecho Penal Chileno. Parte Especial* (4th edn, Tirant 2021) 177.

21 Tatiana Vargas and Ian Henríquez, "La defensa de necesidad en la regulación penal chilena. Aproximación dogmática a partir de una reforma" 22.

22 Ibid. 19.

23 Ibid. 22–23.

cording to Wilenmann, the German *Daschner* case (and, I would argue, this Vignette) is within such a context of normality and thus does not provide an exception.[24]

This does not mean that in his view the prohibition of torture is absolute,[25] but that it is inadequate to allow for an exception in these cases due to the significant symbolic dimension of the prohibition of torture. One ought not to fall for the simplistic but tempting alternative of assuming that any exception will lead us to an overmighty and totalitarian state, Wilenmann says. Also, the assumption that our moral development has reached a stage where torture seems completely outside of the accepted practices is unconvincing. Rather,

> Torture is too valuable in a world governed by means-to-end rationality, and where the obtention of information is as relevant as in ours. The problem is not that torture is incompatible with our ways of life and thought and that, therefore, its reintroduction could alter them or make them recede, but rather that torture is *compatible* with them. The prohibition of torture is not, so to say, a rule intending to avoid a regress from modernity to brutal premodern or totalitarian forms of action. Rather it is a limit imposed on an institution which is immediately understandable in modern logic. This is the reason why its *exaggeratedly broad* institutional recognition makes sense.[26]

More recently, in one of the few works analysing the description of the offence, Durán has held the view that the "rigid and impenetrable" framework provided by the Chilean constitution (Art. 19 No. 1 III and Art. 5 II) does not allow for any conceivable grounds of justification in cases of torture. He highlights the deontological limit of human dignity and the utilitarian argument of the slippery slope as both contributing to this interpretation. No single case of torture can be permitted.[27] He does not, however, analyse the applicability of exculpatory defences.

Thus, despite arriving at the conclusion from very different paths, which in circumstances different from those described in the Vignette may lead to different outcomes, for this particular set of facts all positions seem to agree that D should be punished for torturing K.

Vignette 4: Lethal Self-Defence

> R, a well-trained young man armed with a knife, accosts 50-year-old D, who is on her way home from a party in the early morning hours. R threatens her with the knife and takes away her purse filled with 500 € and her wristwatch worth 1,000 €. As R turns to run away, D draws a pistol she is secretly carrying in her jacket, and shoots and kills R in order to retrieve her property. Is D guilty of murder?

Self-defence is regulated in Art. 10 No. 4 of the Penal Code. This provision allows self-defence to be used in cases of an illegitimate aggression, that is, a current or im-

---

24 Javier Wilenmann, *La Justificación de un Delito en Situaciones de Necesidad* (Marcial Pons 2017) 417.

25 The example provided is the hypothetical case of a nuclear bomb just about to explode.

26 Wilenmann (n 24) 413–414.

27 Mario Durán Migliardi, "Propuestas para la delimitación típica e interpretación sistemática del nuevo delito de tortura y su bien jurídico protegido" (2019) 14 Política criminal 202, 235–236.

minent aggression[28] against the person or her rights, including property. The other two requirements are the rational need of the means employed and the lack of sufficient provocation of the victim.

Two elements seem to be at stake in the case of this Vignette: the persistence of the aggression at the time of the defensive act by R and the proportionality of that response.

a) Persistent Aggression

The timeframe for the defence starts just before the actual aggression, with its imminence. The endpoint, however, is less clearly captured in a concept. The requirement of the aggression being current or imminent is interpreted, for cases like our Vignette, as also covering "persistent" aggressions. Here, an aggression may be persistent after the offence has been consummated but while it is still "unfinished" (*no agotada*). Defining the point in time where an offence is finished requires some reference to the specific offence at stake. For the case of theft, the limit is usually drawn considering the particular structure of the offence as a "cut result" offence: it is consummated by the taking of control of the good, but it continues further due to the *mens rea* requiring an "aim to take ownership" (*ánimo de apropiación*). In order for such a *mens rea* to materialize, the thief needs to secure that possession, and thus the aggression persists until she has abandoned the scene of the crime and reached a safe position.

The question is about the implications for the norm permitting the owner to attempt to recover the goods. Arguably, a systematic interpretation solves the issue in Chilean law.[29] The owner is not entitled to recover the goods "by her own hand" when control has been secured by the thief. At that point, the state's monopoly of force is the only alternative for recovery. But before that point, the owner may still reach out to retrieve her property. Like in Germany, it is said, that this securing of control only occurs when there has been a spatial or temporal distancing between the owner and the thief. "A theft would not be finished, for example, when a burglar has not yet left the property where he committed the offence."[30]

The victim's right to use force does not end with the "formal consummation" of the offence, but the "material one".[31] As a consequence, R would in this case still be within the timeframe set by this requirement for her reaction.[32]

---

28 Sergio Politoff, Jean Pierre Matus and Cecilia Ramírez, *Lecciones de Derecho Penal Chileno Parte General* (Editorial Jurídica de Chile 2003) 217.

29 Wilenmann (n 24) 278.

30 Ibid., citing BGHSt 19, 324.

31 Juan Pablo Mañalich, "El 'hurto-robo' frente a la autotutela y la legítima defensa de la posesión" (2006) 7 Revista de Estudios de la Justicia 90.

32 If it were otherwise, one could consider "vindicating a proximate offense" as a mitigating factor (Art. 11 No. 4). Some authors also consider that a defensive reaction outside of this timeframe may be covered by the exculpatory defence of "unsurmountable fear", "such as in the case where a woman has suffered reiterated and humiliating violations and attacks the aggressor when he is leaving the place, already with her back towards her", Politoff, Matus and Ramírez (n 28) 218.

b) Proportionality Requirement: Rational Need of the Means Employed

This test has usually been understood as the requirement to "not use excessive means, but only those required for protection".[33] This is not a proportionality test *stricto sensu* but rather a prohibition of excess.[34] It is generally rejected that this requirement entails a "mathematical equivalence" between the aggressive and the defensive action, but "reasonableness considering the particularities of the case".[35] The defensive act should be assessed objectively, by asking whether the means available and used by the attacked person were necessary to repel the attack, in the concrete circumstances, according to that person's *ex-ante* perspective.[36] Some scholars and court decisions add that the means selected should be the least harmful one possible.[37]

Once R has turned away and is intending to leave the scene, there is no longer any aggression to the life and limb of D. "The aggression refers now exclusively to the property, to which a shot to the back to impede the flight and recover the object ought to be considered disproportionate."[38]

Chilean law contains no differentiated regulation concerning more or less valuable property, and there is no clarity as to whether the courts would consider the case of large sums of money to be any different from smaller amounts.

Having rejected the resort to self-defence, we may point out that what is known as "excessive self-defence" may amount to an "incomplete exemption of criminal liability", which allows for a significant reduction of the sentence (Art. 73).

A final possibility to exclude liability for murder is the defence of "duress or unsurmountable fear" (Art. 10 No. 9). "Imagine the case of a woman who pursues a robber and picks up a gun, shooting at his head or heart, while it would have sufficed to aim at his legs".[39] This is an exculpatory defence. However, from the facts of the case, we can see that (despite the difference in sex, age and training) the act was not a fearful reaction of D to protect herself, but in order to retrieve her property. Therefore, the reaction would not be covered by this defence.

Vignette 5: Criminal Responsibility of Subordinates for Systemic Offences

D is a soldier in the army of a country ruled by a junta of generals who have come to power through a violent coup. When an opposition group demands the return to a democratic system, the government orders the soldiers to shoot and kill any person who resists arrest. Following this order, D kills three young men who take part

33 Luis Cousiño, *Derecho penal chileno*, vol. 2 (Editorial Jurídica de Chile 1979) 267.

34 Juan Pablo Mañalich, "El Desistimiento de La Tentativa Como Evitación o Impedimento Imputable de La Consumación" (2020) 15 Política Criminal 82.

35 SCS Rol N.°6466–05, 03/05/2007.

36 Jean Pierre Matus and Cecilia Ramírez, *Manual de Derecho Penal Chileno. Parte General* (22nd edn, Tirant 2021) 335; Mario Garrido, *Derecho Penal, Parte General, Tomo I* (Editorial Jurídica de Chile 1997) 133. Eduardo Novoa, Curso de derecho penal chileno: parte general (Editorial Jurídica 2005) 343.

37 Politoff, Matus and Ramírez (n 28) 220.

38 Wilenmann (n 24) 339.

39 Politoff, Matus and Ramírez (n 28) 221.

in a protest demonstration and hit a police officer who tries to arrest them. When D is tried after a change of regime, he says that he did not like to shoot the protesters but that he thought that he had to obey his commanders' orders. D knew that if he had refused to shoot, he might have been demoted, but no physical harm would have occurred to him. Should D be convicted of murder? If so, should his sentence be mitigated because of his situation?

Under the general framework of defences in Chilean law, D's allegations seem to indicate an act in compliance with a duty, often used in cases of subordinates who are following their superior's orders. It may seem from the mere text of Art. 10 No. 10 CP that acting "in compliance with a duty" may free D from liability. However, it has been considered that if the order is unlawful (*ilícita*), the conduct is not justified.[40] For unlawful orders, the general rule that applies for public servants is the so-called "reflexive obedience" rule (Art. 62 Estatuto Administrativo).[41] An official who considers that a direct order from a superior is unlawful ought to document this in writing. If the superior insists (equally in writing), the subordinate is liberated from any responsibility (be it administrative, civil or criminal), while the superior is to be held responsible. It is debated whether this is a justification or an exculpatory defence.[42]

For military personnel, however, there are specific rules. The regulation is contained in Arts. 334 and 335 of the Military Code. Military personnel are under a duty to obey any order "given by their superior in the use of their legitimate authority" and may not suspend compliance with that order or avoid it by the general "reflexive obedience" mechanism. The subordinate may however suspend it or, in urgent cases, modify it, but only if the subordinate knows that the superior has not been able to properly assess the situation; if the facts have changed before the order was given; if it seems that the order has been the result of deceit; if he fears that execution of the order may lead to grave harm that the superior could not foresee; and finally, if the order evidently leads to the perpetration of a crime. If the superior insists, the order must nevertheless be obeyed.

As has been highlighted, all this presupposes that the order has been given by the superior "in the use of legitimate authority" (*atribuciones legítimas*). *A contrario*, this means that for orders by which the superior exceeded his legitimate authority, the rule does not establish a duty of due obedience. But this requires, in turn, to recognize that "legitimate authority" needs to be understood in a sense broad enough so that such an order may at the same time lead to the perpetration of a crime. Otherwise, at least this part of Art. 335 would be meaningless.[43]

In line with this interpretation, Art. 214 declares that the commission of a crime in the execution of an order will lead to responsibility only for the superior. The subor-

40 "La causal de justificación consistente en obrar en cumplimiento de un deber, cuando se refiere específicamente al deber de obediencia que se debe a un superior jerárquico, supone que la orden de ese superior sea legítima", CS 2894–2000, 29/03/2000.

41 Etcheberry I 243, CA Santiago 13447–2006, see *obiter* CS 6308–2007, c. 33.

42 Cf. Enrique Cury, *Derecho Penal Parte General* (Universidad Católica 2005) 92; Juan Pablo Mañalich, "Miedo insuperable y obediencia jerárquica" 68.

43 Mañalich, "Miedo insuperable y obediencia jerárquica" (n 42) 69.

dinate, if he has not complied with the formality contained in Art. 335, is to be punished, with a mandatory mitigation. Therefore, if the subordinate has used the mechanism, he will be covered by the defence of Art. 10 No. 10 Penal Code, and the superior would be a principal by proxy.[44]

Consequently, even in normal times, D could not benefit from this defence, since he did not use the prescribed mechanism to protect himself. He can however benefit from the mitigation contained in Art. 214.

The Penal Code also contains a general defence of "unsurmountable fear" in Art. 10 No. 9, a form of exculpation based on the unreasonableness of demanding a behaviour "motivated by a loyalty to the law".[45] However, the fear of being demoted is not suitable to constitute this defence. Not even in a subjective sense does it seem to amount to a fear that would exonerate the soldier from criminal liability. The fear of demotion is even less suitable according to an objective assessment requiring that "the degree of fidelity to the law to be expected [of a member of the armed forces] surpasses greatly the one expected of a common citizen".[46]

The specific context narrated in the Vignette introduces a further set of legal rules relevant to the case. The systematic violation of human rights and the violent rule by the junta highlight the possible applicability of the regulations on crimes against humanity. The circumstances required to elicit these crimes are 1. that the act is committed as part of a widespread or systematic attack against a civilian population, and 2. that such an attack is based on a policy of the state or another organised group as described in the law (Art. 1). The facts described in the case fit smoothly within this description. The sentence for homicide as a crime against humanity encompasses the range of common murder and aggravated murder (Art. 4).

In Chilean law, the introduction of the catalogue of offenses contained in the Rome Statute[47] has reshaped to some extent the understanding of the role of defences in this context.[48] Art. 38 contains specific defences applicable in this context. In principle, the provision excludes due obedience both as a justification and as a ground of exculpation.[49] Exceptionally, if obeying the illicit order of a superior, one may avoid punishment if acting under duress (*coaccionado*) or as a consequence of a mistake. The final sentence of the provision excludes mistakes as to the illicit character of the order in cases of genocide or crimes against humanity, thus allowing this defence to operate only for war crimes. For war crimes, then, both the erroneous understanding of D's obligation to obey his commander's orders (a mistake over the existence of an exculpatory defence) and debatably a mistaken idea of the personal consequences that

---

44 Ibid. 71.

45 Ibid. 66.

46 Ibid. 67.

47 Law 20.357.

48 Jean Pierre Matus, "El Error En La Ley N° 20.357 a La Luz Del Estatuto de La Corte Penal Internacional y Sus Efectos En La Regulación General Del Error En Chile" (2014) 9 Política Criminal.

49 Juan Pablo Mañalich, "La responsabilidad del superior bajo la ley 20.357" (2021) 1 Revista de Ciencias Sociales 58.

could arise out of his disobedience (a mistake on the objective requirements of an exculpatory defence) could have been discussed as mistakes excluding liability.[50] But none of these applies to crimes against humanity.

Thus, D should be convicted of murder and his sentence will not be reduced.

Vignette 6: Limits of Consent

> V is a 21-year-old ambitious athlete and short-distance runner. He has learned that certain artificial limbs can enhance a runner's speed. He decides that he would rather have an artificial limb instead of his right lower leg. He approaches D, a surgeon in private practice, and asks him to amputate his leg below the knee and replace it with an artificial limb. D complies with V's request. Should D be punished for mayhem?

Consent is a little-developed subject in Chile. The Penal Code does not contain a regulation of consent in the general part. Scattered mentions of the will or acquiescence of the victim in the special part may determine a specific justificatory defence or, rather, a lack of *actus reus* for those offences.[51] For all other crimes, the traditional approach distinguishes between "disposable" and "non-disposable" legal goods. The former may be "sacrificed" by the right-holder. Thus, collective goods cannot be "disposed of", while property paradigmatically can. Life, bodily integrity and health are, under the traditional view, non-disposable.[52] In an old case, the Supreme Court convicted as perpetrators of mayhem the mining workers who reciprocally cut their fingers in order to obtain undue social benefits and payments.[53]

The extent to which individuals are permitted to waive protection of certain goods is considered a deeply political matter. A more liberal legal framework would give more space to consent, while a more conservative view would restrict such powers of the individual. It is noteworthy that the concept of human dignity is used by either side as a bedrock of their principled positions.[54]

Medical interventions, however, are generally considered lawful. The doctrinal device operating is not consent but a "lack of *actus reus* due to social adequacy of the behaviour" (*atipicidad por adecuación social*).[55] A justification may also be grounded in the legitimate exercise of the medical profession, covered by Art. 10 No. 10 CP, requiring that the intervention is done in accordance with the *lex artis*.

For therapeutic interventions, the wounding is not constitutive of a criminal offence if the previous and informed consent has been given before their execution. Un-

50 Matus (n 48) 260.

51 Etcheberry 240–241, Héctor Hernández, "Consentimiento informado y responsabilidad penal médica: una relación ambigua y problemática" (2010) VI Cuadernos de Análisis Jurídico 168. This author highlights that these hypotheses are more precisely cases of agreement, rather than consent, as has been developed in other jurisdictions.

52 Etcheberry 241. With many references, ibid. 169, note 3.

53 Etcheberry DPG II, 360.

54 As highlighted by Ignacio Ackermann and María Fernanda Ovalle, "La disponibilidad en los bienes jurídicos" [2020] Revista de Ciencias Sociales 42–45.

55 Politoff, Bustos and Grisolía (n 11) 187; Hernández (n 51) 169 note 5.

der the new prevailing trends in scholarship, the permissibility of such an intervention does not derive from an external assessment of the best interest of the patient. Rather it is the self-determination of the patient which defines the lawfulness of the action.[56] This has not always been the case. Arguably, this change was institutionally introduced with the Law on Rights and Duties of Patients (Law 20.584) of 2012 and since the previous regime relied on an assessment of the objectively indicated treatment to define the permissibility of an intervention, most of the literature before that date will not give consent a recognisable role.[57]

Medical interventions with no actual therapeutic purpose were also considered not covered by a consent justification, under traditional approaches.[58] "The reasons, as we see it, do not have to do with abstract moral principles but with the risks entailed in the generalisation of methods made viable by modern science, not serving need or solidarity, but abusing the weak, whose consent might be 'snatched' or bought."[59] Recent criticism highlights the paternalistic attitude of this position, which disregards the citizens' capacity to decide about what conduct ought or not to be consented to.[60]

One could question what ought to be considered therapeutic. Authors writing at the end of the last century expressed the view that "under a modern and broad concept of health like the one we propose an intervention may be considered therapeutic if it is undertaken to produce psychic wellbeing and a better adaptation of an individual to his environment".[61] A more recent textbook highlights that, except for one classical author, this is now a shared position for aesthetic interventions, which are all, in principle, therapeutic.[62]

There are no criminal court decisions to guide us in determining whether the facts in the Vignette would be classified as therapeutic under this broader definition. If considering solely V's consent, D should be punished for mayhem. However, if the intervention is considered therapeutic, the defence of Art. 10 No. 10 together with acting within the *lex artis* and with the consent of V will free him from liability.

Currently, a bill for a new criminal code contains consent as a cause for the exclusion of unlawfulness:

> Art. 18. No unlawful act or omission is committed by a person who has the consent of the person concerned [...].

---

56 Wilenman, Consentimiento informado 209–210.

57 For an overview of positions claiming absolute independence of the consent of the patient, see Hernández (n 51), 171.

58 Politoff, Bustos and Grisolía (n 11) 185.

59 Ibid. 187.

60 Mauricio Rettig, *Análisis comparativo del tipo básico del delito de lesiones en España y en Chile. Bases para una reforma*, Barcelona: Tesis Doctoral, Universitat de Barcelona, 2010, 391 ss.

61 Politoff, Bustos and Grisolía (n 11) 190.

62 Jean Pierre Matus and Cecilia Ramírez, *Manual de derecho penal chileno. Parte especial* (2nd edn, Tirant 2018) 122.

The more liberal spirit of this regulation may indeed be read as an extension of consent *per se* as a defence to any individual right or interest, with the exclusion of consented homicide (Art. 215).

Vignette 7: Withdrawal from an Attempt

> 25-year-old D is deeply upset with her former boyfriend V, who had ended their relationship to be with another woman. To punish V, D plans to stab him with a large knife. D knows that the stab wounds can be fatal and accepts V's death as a possible outcome. When V goes jogging, D attacks him from behind and stabs him in the back three times. V breaks down. D realizes that she has injured him but that the injuries will not cause his death. She realizes that she could kill him by stabbing him again but decides to leave him alone. Should D be punished for attempted murder?

Article 7 of the Penal Code regulates attempts.[63] It distinguishes incomplete (*tentativa*) from complete attempts (*delito frustrado*).

a) Attempts and Dolus Eventualis

The traditional position of Chile's Supreme Court has been to negate the possibility of perpetrating an attempt with *dolus eventualis.*

> The person who acts with *dolus eventualis* forecloses the possibility to stop during the commission and avoiding the foreseeable and foreseen harm to the endangered object, the agent does not care about the harmful consequences of her actions, accepting their occurrence.[64]

Scholarship, however, favours the compatibility between *dolus eventualis* and either form of attempt.[65] And so have also several recent decisions of the Supreme Court:

> One ought to consider that *dolus* in attempts is the same *dolus* of consummated offences, since an attempt is not an offence in itself but an imperfect form of a specified offence, a dependent kind from an autonomous offence contained in the Special Part. As a consequence, if the consummated offence requires *dolus directus* or any other *mens rea*, the [incomplete] attempt (and even more, the complete attempt) will have to be undertaken with the same [*mens rea*]. [66]

Therefore, even if this is a highly contested and current issue, we can continue the analysis in terms of analysing the withdrawal.

---

63 In a literal translation: "Article 7. Punishable is not only the consummated crime or simple offence, but also the frustrated crime or simple offence and the attempt. There is a frustrated crime or simple offence when the offender does everything necessary for the crime or simple offence to be consummated and this does not occur for reasons independent of his will."

64 Corte Suprema, 02/07/2009, Rol 3970–2008, c. 4.

65 With references, Juan Pablo Mañalich Raffo and Alejandra Olave Albertini, "Tentativa y dolo eventual: una crítica de la jurisprudencia reciente de la Corte Suprema chilena" (2021) 27 Discusiones 165, n 11.

66 Corte Suprema, Rol 40.795–2022.

b) General Efficacy of the Withdrawal

Withdrawals from attempts are not explicitly regulated. Nevertheless, there is almost unanimous agreement in the acceptance of withdrawal as a circumstance excluding the "punishability" of the act.

Art. 7 CP expresses a favourable legislative decision to acknowledge the complete exclusion of punishment for a timely and effective withdrawal.[67] This may be seen in the fact that the rule recognises *voluntary* impediment of the consummation of the offence as excluding the punishability of completed attempts. This implies, *a fortiori*, that there is even more reason to recognise voluntary impediment as blocking the finding of criminal liability for incomplete attempts.

Withdrawal from an incomplete attempt thus does not require D to prevent the consummation of the offence, it merely requires a retreat expressing his compliance with the general duty which the attempt had violated. To gain impunity for a complete attempt, D is obliged to voluntarily prevent the consummation of the offence. Because the offence has materialised to different extents, the law makes different demands of the actor to express his "taking the side of the norm" (*toma de posición a favor de la norma*). Once he has taken this position, the offender benefits from the "golden bridge".[68]

These doctrinal developments can be synthesised in the proposed text for a new Penal Code, currently being debated in Congress:

> Proyecto CP: Art. 32.
>
> Desistimiento de la tentativa. No es punible la tentativa para quien voluntariamente abandona la realización del hecho o impide su consumación. Si el delito no se consuma con independencia de su actuar, tampoco es punible la tentativa si se hubiere esforzado seriamente por impedir la consumación.
>
> Siendo dos o más los intervinientes en el hecho, no es punible la tentativa para aquel que voluntariamente impide su consumación. Si el delito no se consuma con independencia de su actuar, tampoco es punible para el interviniente que se hubiere esforzado seriamente por impedir la consumación.
>
> Lo dispuesto en los incisos anteriores no obsta a la responsabilidad por cualquier delito distinto de la tentativa de la cual el hechor o interviniente se hubiera desistido.

c) "Extra-Legal Intentions"

However, the case presents one more feature that requires attention. In the Vignette, the motive of the attack is the aim to punish V. The infliction of punishment on the former boyfriend may be considered an "extra-legal intention" (*intención ex-*

---

67 Mañalich, "El Desistimiento de La Tentativa Como Evitación o Impedimento Imputable de La Consumación" (n 34) 781.

68 For a synthesis of the various positions held by scholarship and the Chilean courts on the justification for this institution see Felipe Belmar Todorovic, "El desistimiento de la tentativa en la doctrina y la jurisprudencia chilenas" (Tesis de licenciatura, Universidad de Chile 2017).

tra-típica), as it is separate from the offence-relevant *mens rea.*[69] But this extra-legal intention changes at the time when D abandons V, stopping the wounding.

Juan Pablo Mañalich has discussed this possibility by way of introducing the concept of conditional intent in the analysis. He explains that the extra-legal intention may play a role in determining a conditional intention: D will continue inflicting harm on V as long as it is needed for punishing him; if D assumes that harming V is not necessary to punish him, D will not form the (unconditional) intention to continue stabbing him.[70] This solution is built upon a construction of the obligation of a person undertaking an attempt: for an incomplete attempt, the duty is the one contained in the behaviour norm expressed in the offence, while for a complete attempt, it is the offender's duty to prevent the consummation.[71]

The consequence of this reasoning is that once in D's eyes V has suffered enough, she has lost the intention to continue stabbing him. Therefore, she cannot take a position in favour of the norm by abandoning the commission of the offence. She has already lost the resolve to offend (*resolución-al-hecho*) and therefore she cannot give up the commission of the offence.[72]

The Vignette does not clarify the reasoning behind D's decision to "leave him alone". If it is because he has been punished enough already, Mañalich's solution would mean that it is no longer possible for D to withdraw from the attempt. If D's decision is based on "taking a stance favourable to the norm", then the traditional doctrine allowing for an exoneration of criminal liability would succeed. At the time of writing, I have not been able to find any other author referring to this constellation of facts from this or any comparable perspective.

Vignette 8: Criminal Responsibility of Minors

D is a 13-year-old boy. He abducts and rapes V, a girl of the same age. Should D be punished for a criminal offence?

A three-tier system regulates criminal liability according to age in Chile (Art. 10 No. 2 CP). There is no criminal liability for children under 14 years of age. Children and adolescents between 14 and 18 years old are subject to the youth criminal liability regime,[73] while the general regime applies to adults. The answer to the question posed in the Vignette is thus univocally answered in the negative.

Before the introduction of this system, in force since 2007, the general rule for adolescents under the age of 18 was the lack of criminal responsibility, notwithstanding the possibility of judicial assessment of discernment for persons older than 16 and

69 The discussion in Mañalich addresses the German *Denkzettel* case and is in dialogue with the German literature.

70 Mañalich, "El Desistimiento de La Tentativa Como Evitación o Impedimento Imputable de La Consumación" (n 34) 795; facts adapted.

71 Ibid. 783–784.

72 Ibid. 796.

73 This regime is regulated in Law 20.084. A sub-division is drawn at the age of 16, under which adolescents are not generally liable for less serious offences (*faltas*). These are then dealt with directly by Family Courts under a procedure regulated in Law 19.968.

younger than 18. Under that age, children may have been subject to protection measures imposed by a civil judge, but no criminal liability would have arisen. These measures were criticised as often implying covert punishment without the protection of criminal due process.[74]

The discernment test was criticised for being excessively discretionary.[75] Chilean law did not contain a definition of discernment or any guidance for the judge. This rejection led to the establishment of a clear-cut border between 14 and 18. The upper limit was commended as "offering greater legal certainty and, in consequence, guaranteeing greater equality between all adolescents".[76] In fact, a case similar to our Vignette was brought up during the legislative debate, where a young man of 14 years of age raped a 4-year-old girl and was declared of insufficient discernment and thus acquitted.[77]

The lower limit was seen as complying with Article 40.3 of the Convention on the Rights of the Child, "excluding, at least in the normative realm, the extension of the formal punitive system under the age of fourteen".[78] However, the intervention of Family Courts through protection measures was retained, and it was warned that "if not adequately delimited, these measures could allow the informal application of penal sanctions for persons under the age of 14".[79]

The decision to set the minimum age for criminal responsibility at 14 is sustained on various grounds.

In terms of development, a frequent argument distinguishes stages in a child's process in developing their cognitive functions, their identity, their moral reasoning, their physical and biological growth and their competences. In this sense, early adolescence (10 to 13 years of age) is separated from median or full adolescence (14 to 18) and late adolescence (18 to 20).[80] This position is in line with Rule 4 of the Beijing Rules, which recommends that the minimum age for criminal liability should not be set at too early an age, considering the emotional, mental and intellectual maturity of children.

---

74 María Elena Santibáñez and Claudia Alarcón, "Análisis crítico de la aplicación práctica de la Ley de Responsabilidad Penal Juvenil y propuestas de mejoramiento" (2009) 4 Temas de la Agenda Pública PUC 1.

75 Mensaje Ley 20.084, 5 ("[A]bandonado por la mayor parte de los ordenamientos jurídicos del mundo, debido a que es un concepto impreciso y de muy difícil determinación provocando decisiones jurisdiccionales excesivamente discrecionales. Es de notar que la legislación chilena carece de una definición de discernimiento de una indicación acerca de cuáles son los elementos que el juez de menores debe considerar para fundar su pronunciamiento").

76 Miguel Cillero Bruñol, "Ley N° 20.084 sobre Responsabilidad Penal de Adolescentes" [2006] Anuario de Derechos Humanos 191.

77 Historia de la ley N° 20.084, 168, Sr Leal.

78 Cillero Bruñol (n 76) 191.

79 Ibid.

80 Defensoría Penal Pública, "Principales Aspectos de la Teoría del Desarrollo Adolescente: Guía para Defensores Penales Juveniles" [2006] Documento de trabajo.

One author adds that "it's not just a psychological or "maturity" issue, but the material conditions for effectively making use of the protections and minimum rights that children need to access in case of facing a legal procedure, which cannot be guaranteed below that age [of 14]".[81]

Legislators seemed to have believed that 14 was a common age limit in OECD countries, while most Latin-American jurisdictions set it at 12. The opinion of the Interamerican Committee for Human Rights, which promotes the progressive elevation of the minimum age of juvenile criminal liability to an age closer to 18 years, also was significant for the legislature.[82]

The Interamerican Committee for Human Rights also expressed concern about regulations in certain countries of the region setting different rules for serious crime.

> In the opinion of the Committee, if the State determines that boys and girls under a certain age have no capacity to infringe the criminal law, it is inadmissible to make them subject of liability when they have broken a law specifying an especially serious offence.[83]

Chile, however, has stayed away from a regime like this. Although such a move has not been supported by scholars in Chile, the adoption of more intensive child protection interventions has gained some traction. Some scholars have justified the detention of children between 12 and 14 for "serious" offences, described as those causing "great social alarm", when the aim is to prevent the development of "criminal careers".[84]

Around the same time as the introduction of the youth criminal justice regime, the family courts were also reformed. Since 2004, the procedure for dealing with these situations has been amended. The new Family Law regime mentions the commission of offences by children but contemplates a single hearing where the judge may remind the parents of their power to correct their children or order a provisional measure for the protection of the child's rights (Arts. 8 no. 9, 102 N of Law 19.968, and Art. 234 Civil Code).

These provisional measures include turning over the child to their parent or legal guardian; the determination of a different carer; the inclusion in a programme of foster families or residences; the obligation of the child, the parents or carers to attend support, reparation or orientation programmes; and the placement in a health, psychiatric or treatment facility. The norm explicitly prohibits the detention of a child or adolescent in an adult detainment facility as a protection measure (Art. 71 Law 19.968).

Permanent measures can also be imposed under the procedure to protect children whose rights are endangered or violated (Art. 30 Law 16.618). These include requir-

---

81 Sergio Henríquez, "Justificación de la intervención estatal por hechos que revisten caracteres de delito bajo los catorce años" [2022] Revista Derecho Aplicado – LLM UC 30.

82 Comisión Interamericana de Derechos Humanos Relatoría sobre los Derechos de la Niñez, "Justicia Juvenil y Derechos Humanos En Las Américas" [2011] OEA documentos oficiales 17.

83 Ibid. 15.

84 The term is derived from the national victimisation survey and is often used in criminal policy debates. See Henríquez (n 82) 26.

ing the child, the parents or carers to attend support, reparation or orientation programmes and placing the child in a residence or foster home. Scholars have criticised that some courts impose intensive measures in circumstances that for an adult would not have carried any sanction or a much lower one. Since these measures are based on the irregular family situation of a child, they disproportionately affect poorer and more vulnerable children.[85] Thus, this new procedure does not avoid the problems of previous one, as it allows for the imposition of punitive measures through a protective framework.

Thus, D should not be punished.

Vignette 9: Statute of Limitations

In 1995, D violently raped V, a 35-year-old woman, using a knife. D managed to escape and was not apprehended until 2023. Traces of his DNA taken from the victim's body leave no doubt that D is the perpetrator. Should D be convicted despite the long delay?

According to Article 93 No. 6 of the Chilean Penal Code, criminal liability is extinguished due to the expiry of the limitation period for the prosecution of crimes (*prescripción de la acción penal*). The length of this period is defined in Article 94, consisting in a laddered scale of 6 months for minor infractions, 5 years for simple offences, 10 years for serious crimes and 15 years for crimes carrying a life sentence. The concepts of infractions, simple offences and crimes must be interpreted by reference to the scale of sentences established in Articles 3 and 21. In 1995, the sentence range for rape was from 3 years and a day to 5 years of imprisonment, making it a simple offence. Thus, the limitation period was 5 years. The counting of the period begins on the day the offence is committed (Art. 95). Therefore, a prosecution for rape could have been initiated until the year 2000. As this date is long past and no factors suspending or restarting the counting have occurred,[86] D should not be convicted.

In 2022, the limitation period for rape was extended to 10 years (Art. 94 bis II). Even if this rule applied to the Vignette case, the time limit would already have expired at the time of writing. In any case, it does not apply. Generally, limitation periods have been understood to be subject to the prohibition of retroactivity of criminal laws (Art. 18 I).[87] This is in line with the majority view in Chilean scholarship, according to which limitation periods are substantive in nature.[88] But even if it was considered a procedural device, this would have led to the same result: although changes in procedural law apply to any new procedure from the time of their entering into

---

85 Nel Greeven, "Análisis crítico de la regulación del procedimiento contravencional ante los tribunales de familia" [2016] Revista de estudios judicialese 2–3.

86 Chilean law contains two such mechanisms, Art. 96.

87 Art. 18. No crime will be sanctioned with a punishment other than the one provided by law promulgated before its commission.

88 Gustavo Balmaceda, "Prescripcion Penal Chile" (2016) 43 Revista de Ciencias Penales 110, with further references in note 28. The Supreme Court has also adhered to this view, but in some decisions seems to consider that limitation periods have a mixed substantive-procedural nature; Corte Suprema, 10/08/2010, Rol N° 514–2010.

force, if the previous norms are more favourable to the accused the court will apply those (Art. 11 Code of Criminal Procedure).

The situation in the Vignette needs to be distinguished from the case of underaged victims of sexual crimes. Concerns about the incapacity of children to appreciate their victimization have led to the exclusion of all limitation periods for a list of offences, which include the rape of a minor (Article 94 bis I). Yet, the same rules on retroactivity apply.

a) General Justification for the Existence of Limitation Periods for the Prosecution of Crimes

aa) Traditional Debate

Concerning the reasons for establishing a categorical time limit to the possibility of convicting D in light of the long delay, the literature proposes theories similar to those present in many civil law jurisdictions: the loss of evidence, the reduced capacity of a criminal sanction to rehabilitate the offender or to deter the commission of crimes, the disappearing need for retribution.[89]

The idea of legal security (*seguridad jurídica*) has been a cornerstone of the discussion.[90] This argument conflates two perspectives. One looks at the social peace achieved by consolidating a *de facto* situation (the non-prosecution) into a legal one: disturbing the waters that have settled back on their own due to the time elapsed. The other looks at the peace of mind of potential suspects (thus, in theory, all members of society).

Because the Chilean regulation on limitation periods contains a norm interrupting the running of the period and restarting it anew every time a new offence has been committed by the accused (Art. 96), a justification based on the apparent rehabilitation of the offender has been raised.[91] This comparatively uncommon norm makes this latter argument more solid here than in other jurisdictions.

bb) Recent Approaches

In recent years, a new strand of literature has emerged. The exclusion of the possibility to prosecute and convict D has been justified by an appeal to the principle of humanity.[92] According to this view,

> The state declares that, after a certain amount of time, it is not justified anymore to seek an individual's liability, not because the need for punishment has become stale, but merely because, in a legal system centred on the individual and her protection, the existence of a power

[89] Cury (n 42) 797–798.

[90] Balmaceda (n 86) n 9. With references to Cury, Guzmán Dalbora and Etcheberry.

[91] Garrido (n 36) 388.

[92] See recently Carlos Cabezas, *Prescripción de La Acción Penal* (Der 2021) 82–95; Agustina Alvarado Urízar, "The Criminal Statute of Limitations in Chile" (2022) 49 DPCE Online. Earlier also José Luis Guzmán Dalbora, "Crímenes internacionales y prescripción", in: Kai Ambos, Ezequiel Malarino and Jan Woischnik (eds.), *Temas actuales del derecho penal internacional: contribuciones de América Latina, Alemania y España* (Konrad-Adenauer Stiftung 2005).

which may unleash (legitimate) violence against her, without any limit, would be contrary to the individual's protection. Therefore, time becomes an important limitation.[93]

Together with the modern historical origins of generally applicable limitation periods and the movement for the humanisation of the criminal law, the liberal ethos of time limits is highlighted: "Criminal limitation is proof of the superlative position occupied in liberal legal systems of the unabated nature of the law, the security of its subjects and, especially, human dignity, even when dealing with the most abominable misdeeds and the most impious criminals."[94]

b) Special Justification for the Extended Period to Prosecute Rape

When introducing the new more extensive period of limitation for rape, the legislature expressed the concern that because of "the nature itself of these crimes [rape], victims take several years to come to the criminal justice system, and it is reasonable for this to be taken into consideration when defining the limitation period".[95] Although some legislators considered this extension as insufficient and proposed to include rape in the narrow catalogue of imprescriptible crimes,[96] the final decision was to establish a 10-year period.

There was some resistance to this solution, especially because it entailed an exceptional position of rape when compared to all other "simple crimes" with adult victims.[97] This unsystematic result was seen as undesirable, and one possible solution would have been to simply increase the punishment for the offence so as to make it a "serious crime". This would have had the same practical result. Nevertheless, because other legislative initiatives were being discussed in parallel to change the legal definition of the offence, it was preferred to restrict the content of this modification to the limitation period.

Vignette 10: Life Imprisonment without Parole

The Penal Code of State S provides for imprisonment for life as the maximum penalty for murder, but also authorizes the court to order an offender's early release after a minimum of 15 years if the offender is no longer dangerous. Reacting to cases of particularly heinous murders, the legislature of S wishes to introduce a penalty of life imprisonment without any possibility of early release, regardless of the offender's continued dangerousness. Would this amendment be acceptable?

There is little certainty about the extent to which there are limits to the capacity of the legislator to create forms of punishment and to legally determine sentences in Chile.[98]

---

93 Cabezas (n 92) 83.

94 Guzmán Dalbora (n 92) 77.

95 HdL 17, and similarly 74, 87, 96, 154.

96 HdL 26, 30.

97 HdL 32.

98 In the region, contrast Chilean law with Art. 34 of the Colombian Constitution of 1991, which prohibits "banishment, life imprisonment and confiscation".

Specific punishments are explicitly excluded or restricted. Illegal coercion by public officers *(apremios ilegítimos)*, seizures of property *(confiscación de bienes* 19 n 7 letter g) or the loss of social security rights (*perdida de derechos previsionales*, 19 n 7 letter h) are banned by the Constitution. International treaties also contain a few clear boundaries, such as limits to the death penalty (Art. 6 PIDCP, Art. 4 CAADDHH), and the prohibition of imprisonment as a consequence of a person's inability to fulfil a contractual obligation (Art. 11 PIDCP and Art. 7 CADDHH). There is no constitutional prohibition for establishing or expanding the death penalty, only a restriction as to the formal requirements.[99]

The highest currently existing sentence in Chile is "qualified life imprisonment" (*presidio perpetuo calificado*), providing for the possibility of early release only after 40 years of effective imprisonment (Art. 32 bis CP). This severe form of imprisonment at the top of the scale of punishments was introduced in 2001 in the Act abolishing the death sentence for common crimes. The existence or applicability of this sentence has not been legally challenged, although it has been criticised by scholars.[100]

The introduction of an even more severe sentence – such as the one proposed in this Vignette – excluding any possibility of early release could be doctrinally assessed through three possible roads: (a) the aims of punishment; (b) the principle of proportionality; and (c) fundamental rights and the principle of humanity.

a) The Aims of Punishment

There is no constitutional regulation on the purposes of punishment. Thus, compared to other jurisdictions, there is no supra-legal duty of promoting any of these aims in particular or of using them as limits to permissible modes of punishment. Nevertheless, the Constitutional Court and scholarship have developed some reflections on the matter.

In terms of the forward-looking aims of punishment, a life sentence without the possibility of parole has been severely questioned. In terms of general deterrence, it has been argued that the perpetrators of such grave offences are not easily intimidated, as is demonstrated by the fact that crimes with high penalties are still being committed.[101] Special deterrence might indeed justify perpetual deprivation of liberty, at least to avoid recidivism for the same offence, which does not, however, impede the commission of crimes from within prison.[102]

Rehabilitation understood as reintegration, however, would be conceptually foreclosed, as there will not be a re-entry into society. Even though the Constitutional

---

99 Art. 19 n 1 III of the Chilean constitution requires a law with "qualified quorum" (i. e. an absolute majority) to be passed.

100 Raúl Carnevali, "Un Examen a La Constitucionalidad de La Pena de Presidio Perpetuo Calificado", *Hacia un Derecho Penal liberal* (2023); Nicolás Oxman and Claudio González, "La Pena de Presidio Perpetuo Calificado En Chile y Los Derechos Humanos" (2014), https://congresos.adeituv.es/imgdb/archivo_dpo15371.pdf, accessed 26 February 2024.

101 Silvio Cuneo Nash, "Prisión perpetua y dignidad humana: Una reflexión tras la muerte de Manuel Contreras" (2016) 11 Política criminal 1, 6–7.

102 Ibid. 8.

Court has not declared any proposed punishment to be excessively long contrary to the Chilean Constitution, it has highlighted that "the legislature cannot forego the aim of reintegration of those convicted when establishing the rules on punishing crimes. This necessitates the rational use of deprivations of liberty."[103] Thus, any punishment making rehabilitation and reintegration impossible is by definition dubious as it cannot meet this standard.

The argument against a retributive justification of this kind of sentence is built upon the notion of identity change: from a certain point onwards, we will not be able to continue attributing guilt to an individual for a crime perpetrated very long ago. "Guilt, understood as the part of oneself, determined by her own will, by her Self, who in a specific moment has decided to commit a crime, which is now not the same anymore."[104]

b) The Principle of Proportionality

Under the doctrinal framework most used by criminal lawyers, the acceptability of an amendment like this would be analysed in terms of the principle of proportionality. Even though this principle is not explicitly enshrined in legislation or the Constitution, it serves as the analytical framework for the Constitutional Court's assessment.[105]

There has been no use of the *ex-ante* constitutional control to foreclose the establishment of punishments, and thus there is no point of reference or case law on the matter. There has been an ever-growing use of the *ex-post* mechanism.[106] In practice, the Constitutional Court has excluded the possibility of applying punishments excessively (*crasamente*) or especially (*especialmente*) disproportionate to the offence.[107]

The principle of proportionality may therefore be insufficient to prevent a law permitting life sentences without the possibility of parole, at least as long as they are not a single mandatory sentence but rather an option among other less intense sanctions. The Chilean system for the imposition of sentences usually defines the minimum as well as the maximum possible sentence. The current maximum sentence (*presidio perpetuo calificado*) is always provided as the upper limit of a range.[108]

---

103 STC Rol N° 3991–2017–INA, c. 6.

104 Cuneo Nash (n 101) 15.

105 For an account of the anchoring and interpretations of current constitutional norms on the issue see Guillermo Silva, "La proporcionalidad de las penas. Un comentario sobre el principio de proporcionalidad en la propuesta de Constitución chilena de 2022", in: Kai Ambos and José Luis Guzmán Dalbora, *Constitución y Derecho penal en Chile* (Der 2023) 137–139.

106 Pablo Grez Hidalgo and Javier Wilenmann Von Bernath, "Un desarrollo preocupante: sobre una tendencia reciente en el control constitucional de leyes penales" (2019) 26 Revista de Derecho (Coquimbo) e3859.

107 Matus and Ramírez, *Manual de Derecho Penal Chileno. Parte General* (n 36) 115–118.

108 See for example the offences contained in Articles 150 B, 268 ter, 372 bis, 390 bis, and 433, in addition to some crimes defined outside of the Criminal Code (Law No. 20.357; Law No. 18.314), and the possibility of reaching this sentence as a consequence of aggravating circumstances (Art. 77), or in case of reoffending during the time of serving the sentence (Art. 91).

It is worth mentioning that Chile underwent a series of failed constitutional processes during the last few years. An innovation in one of the drafts incorporated an explicit provision about the necessary proportionality between the punishment and the infraction committed (Art. 111 Constitutional Proposal 2022). Although it is difficult to conclude if the rejection of this proposal by popular vote means a rejection of the idea (as the whole proposed text was voted *en bloc*), at least it shows that the commissioners proposing the text considered this a relevant constitutional norm that would be a meaningful addition to the current normative landscape.

c) Fundamental Rights, the Prohibition of Cruel, Inhuman or Degrading Punishments, and the Principle of Humanity

Another potential constitutional limit on the proposed sentence is the protection of "essential rights" contained in international treaties ratified by Chile, through Art. 5 CPR. For example, Art. 5.2. of the American Convention on Human Rights proscribes cruel, inhuman, or degrading punishments. According to Guzmán, "cruel" punishments are those that are intolerable or excessive. In this second group, he includes the death penalty and corporal punishment, "perpetual punishments, independently of the kind of legal good which they affect", "temporal penalties which deprive the convicted person of a whole stage in adult life" and all those which even if bearable, are disproportionate to the intrinsic gravity of the offence. Cruelty belongs to a form of inhumanity *lato sensu*, characterised by "the absence of sensibility against the pain or misfortune" of another. With regards to life sentences he argues: "Infinite punishment, particularly when it deprives the convicted person of their liberty of movement, is doubly cruel, as it is so in itself and because it is disproportionate to the gravity of any offence, including heinous crimes."[109]

In this author's view, the positive implementation of this principle in Chile, both at a constitutional and at a legal level, has regressed.[110] In very broad terms, the Constitutional Court tends to mention the principle of humanity as a limit and a mandate to avoid excessive punishment, and in certain cases it makes reference to the issue of the length of those sentences.[111] However, the Court does not make it an operative principle or explain where the boundaries should be set.

Within these limits, the Constitutional Court has in general shown a deferential attitude toward the legislature:

> The prohibition of torture and inhuman or degrading punishment or treatments, as well as the dignity standards in which those convicted ought to serve their sentences represent sharp boundaries within which the criminal policy of any country or civilised community may act. Within that framework, it is tolerable to define sanctions in accordance with the ends

109 José Luis Guzmán Dalbora, "Constitución y penas prohibidas", in: Kai Ambos and José Luis Guzmán Dalbora, *Constitución y Derecho penal en Chile* (Der 2023) 165. Although as constitutive of retributive aims of punishment, Cuneo also mentions the dehumanisation entailed in perpetual punishment, Cuneo Nash (n 101) 9.

110 For a historical overview see Guzmán Dalbora (n 109) 159–164.

111 See for instance Rol N° 3062–16–INA, c. 25.

of coexistence, as determined by the legitimate organs as to their greater severity or leniency, whichever is more effective to the achievement of the proposed aims.[112]

112 STC Rol N° 2045–11–INA, c. X; STC Rol N° 787–07–INA, c. 9.

4. China

By *Zhiwei Tang**

Introduction

A country's approach to criminal justice is shaped by both predetermined and contingent factors, rooted in a country's history, culture, political system, and philosophical foundations. This approach may also be influenced by various individual events, making the task of describing a country's view of criminal justice particularly challenging. This is especially true for a society like China, with its long history, vast population, and a modern society that blends both traditional and forward-looking elements. To some extent, the principles of criminal justice in Chinese criminal law resemble a patchwork, with few clear patterns. However, by examining these ten controversial issues, we may be able to take a more holistic view in a condensed form, gaining insights into the concept of criminal justice underlying Chinese law. In fact, a country's concept of criminal justice is also an aspect of its national or societal identity, but this identity is always relative. In other words, it is only by comparing with other countries' identities that one can define the specific characteristics of one's own. In this regard, the purpose of this comparative law project is not only to explore the possibility of a "universal criminal justice" that transcends national boundaries but also to foster a deeper understanding of each country's criminal justice among scholars worldwide.

Vignette 1: Trolley Problem – Killing one Person to Save Many

> Five young children are playing on railway tracks. An express train is approaching, and it is too late to stop the train before it hits the children, probably killing them. Operator D recognizes the emergency situation. He electronically flips a switch and thus deflects the train from its regular track to a little-used sidetrack. However, the lone repairman V is busy on the sidetrack, and the deflected train kills V, as D had anticipated. Is D criminally responsible for murder of V?

The trolley problem is a well-known issue in China.[1] In the context of criminal law, it raises questions about necessity. Unlike the criminal laws of countries like Germany, Chinese criminal law does not distinguish between justificatory necessity (*rechtfertigender Notstand*) and excusatory necessity (*entschuldigender Notstand*). Instead, it only stipulates that acts of necessity meeting the requirements of Article 21 of the Chinese Criminal Code "shall not bear criminal responsibility". According to Article 21 of the Chinese Criminal Code:

---

* Prof. Dr. *Zhiwei Tang*, LL.M. (Augsburg), is an Assistant Professor at Wuhan University School of Law.

1 See Chinese version of *Thomas Cathcart*, The Trolley Problem, or Would You Throw the Fat Guy Off the Bridge? A Philosophical Conundrum, translated by *Chenzhi Zhu*, 2014; *Xiang Luo*, The Details of the Rule of Law, 2021, 16.

> If a person is compelled to commit an act in an emergency to avert an immediate danger to the interests of the State or the public, or his own or another person's rights of the person, property or other rights, thus causing damage, he shall not bear criminal responsibility.
>
> If the act committed by a person in an emergency to avert danger exceeds the limits of necessity and causes undue damage, he shall bear criminal responsibility; however, he shall be given a mitigated punishment or be exempted from punishment.

Although Chinese criminal law does not explicitly distinguish between justificatory and excusatory necessity in statutory law, over the past twenty years, under the influence of German and Japanese criminal law, Chinese scholars have begun to attempt to differentiate between the two. Based on this distinction, some scholars argue that Article 21 of the Chinese Criminal Code only regulates justificatory necessity.[2]

Specifically, regarding necessity acts involving killing, as stated in the second paragraph of Article 21, necessity in the Chinese Criminal Code is premised on not exceeding what is necessary. Therefore, conflicting interests must be weighed. According to the prevailing view, human life is the highest-ranking interest, meaning that necessity acts using killing as a means cannot be deemed legal based on the first paragraph of Article 21 and thus do not eliminate criminal responsibility.[3] However, an increasing number of scholars believe that in cases of defensive necessity (*Defensivnotstand*), if the party causing the emergency is also in a state of emergency, the value of the life to be protected will be considered less significant. In such cases, necessity acts using killing can also be justified.[4] Meanwhile, a minority of utilitarian scholars propose that in specific situations sacrificing one life to save many others can be justified and should not incur criminal liability.[5]

However, many scholars in the Chinese criminal law community invoke the theory of "lack of expectation to act in accordance with the norm" (*Unzumutbarkeit normgemäßen Verhaltens*) and argue for supra-legal necessity (*übergesetzlicher entschuldigender Notstand*).[6] They recognize that necessity acts involving killing to eliminate an imminent danger to human life may be permissible and could exempt the individuals from criminal responsibility. However, due to the lack of explicit legal provisions, there remains considerable controversy over the prerequisites for supra-legal necessity.[7] The core issue remains whether it is permissible to weigh lives or

---

2 See *Guangquan Zhou*, Criminal Law General Part, 4th ed. 2021, 227; *Xuan Chen*, Conflict of Life, Necessity and Exemption of Guilt, Chinese Journal of Law 2016, Issue 5, 133.

3 See *Mingxuan Gao* and *Kechang Ma* (eds.), Criminal Law, 10th ed. 2022, 138.

4 See *Hong Li*, A Study on the Legal Nature of Necessity, Tsinghua University Law Journal 2007, Issue 1, 49–50; *Xuan Chen*, Conflict of Life, Necessity and Exemption of Guilt, Chinese Journal of Law 2016, Issue 5, 135–139.

5 See *Mingkai Zhang*, Criminal Law, 6th ed. 2021, 294; *Mingkai Zhang*, Utilitarian View of Unlawfulness, China Legal Science 2011, Issue 5, 125.

6 It is worth noting that, unlike the discussion in Germany, the main issues discussed in the context of supra-legal necessity in Chinese criminal law involve the circumstances of excusatory necessity under Article 35 of the German Criminal Code.

7 In the literature, there is an argument that, similar to the provisions of Article 35(1) of the German Criminal Code, the establishment of supra-legal excusatory necessity requires that the person rescued should be the actor himself, a relative, or close person, or another person with a special identity. See *Mingkai Zhang*, The Grounds for Exemption from Criminal Responsi-

sacrifice one life to save many. With the development and application of autonomous driving technology, the trolley problem has gained practical significance, re-introducing the discussion in criminal law.

Since cases similar to the trolley problem have not yet occurred, Chinese judicial authorities have not made a clear statement on this issue. In Chinese criminal law academia, the prevailing view supports the doctrine that life is immeasurable and unquantifiable, arguing that (justificatory) necessity under Article 21 of the Chinese Criminal Code cannot exempt individuals from criminal responsibility. This stance is based on the idea that if necessity is justified by social solidarity obligations, and considering that the value of life is irreplaceable and the foundation of survival, a rational person would never willingly sacrifice their own life to save others under normal circumstances. Therefore, in Vignette 1, the actions of D do not meet the requirements for necessity under Article 21 of the Chinese Criminal Code.[8]

While opposing such a justification, some Chinese scholars nevertheless argue that acts sacrificing one life to save many may be exempt from criminal responsibility under the doctrine of necessity. They believe that this approach avoids the controversy of "whether it is permissible to quantify human life" and demonstrates respect for human life. For example, in a scenario analogous to the trolley problem, A is driving a vehicle that suddenly malfunctions and is about to collide with five people. To avoid killing multiple individuals, A intentionally steers toward B, a person not among the five in danger, thereby resulting in B's death. Some scholars in China view A's action as excusatory necessity, arguing that five persons coincidentally encountered danger and engaged in a survival competition under conditions of mutual equality. Even if it appears that A used B as a means to save multiple lives, they argue that A's acts are difficult to justify but should still be considered excusatory and thus exempt from condemnation.[9] However, this viewpoint may assess the facts inaccurately. This case resembles the trolley problem, where B was not initially in danger. A's decision caused the danger to B's life. Had A decided not to turn the steering wheel, staying with the original trajectory, even with the foreseeable result of five people's deaths, A's inaction would still be lawful. Under these circumstances, the true ethical dilemma is whether supra-legal necessity could be recognized.[10] Clearly, the discussion in Chinese criminal law largely attempts to avoid answering this question.

Furthermore, in discussions involving cases where terrorists hijack airplanes to crash them into buildings, some Chinese scholars argue that excusatory necessity can be established under Chinese criminal law based on the theory of lack of expec-

---

bility in Cases of Abused Women Killing, Legal Forum 2022, Issue 2, 25; *Xuan Chen*, Conflict of Life, Necessity and Exemption of Guilt, Chinese Journal of Law 2016, Issue 5, 146–147.

8 See *Gang Wang*, A New Theory of Necessity Involving Killing Life, Political Science and Law 2016, Issue 10, 101–102.

9 See *Guangquan Zhou*, Criminal Law General Part, 4th ed. 2021, 228.

10 See, e.g., *Liane Wörner*, Der Weichensteller 4.0 – Zur strafrechtlichen Verantwortlichkeit des Programmierers im Notstand für Vorgaben an autonome Fahrzeuge, Zeitschrift für Internationale Strafrechtsdogmatik (ZIS) 2019, 44; *Claus Roxin* and *Luis Greco*, Strafrecht Allgemeiner Teil, Vol. 1, 5th ed. 2020, § 22 marginal note 165; *Ulfrid Neumann*, in: Urs Kindhäuser, Ulfrid Neumann, Hans-Ullrich Paeffgen and Frank Saliger (eds.), NomosKommentar, Strafgesetzbuch, Vol. 1, 6th ed. 2023, § 35 marginal notes 61–62.

tation to act in accordance with the norm (*Unzumutbarkeit normgemäßen Verhaltens*).[11] However, unlike in the terrorist hijacking case, in the trolley problem (or the "*Weichensteller-Fall*" devised by Hans Welzel), the sacrificed party (V) was also not initially in danger. Therefore, the conclusion of negating guilt in the terrorist hijacking case may not apply to the trolley problem. Based on the prevailing view in Chinese criminal law, in Vignette 1, D's acts constitute intentional homicide under Article 232 of the Chinese Criminal Code.

Vignette 2: Attribution of Death

D intends to kill his neighbor V. Hidden near V's house, D waits for V and stabs him several times with a knife. V is taken to the hospital, where his wounds are treated. His injuries are not life-threatening and V is kept overnight for observation. During the night, a technical defect in the hospital kitchen leads to the outbreak of a fire, which kills V and other persons. Can D be held criminally responsible for V's death?

Causality is one of the fundamental issues in criminal law theory, and this is also true in China. Vignette 2 addresses the problem of abnormal causation, or, to put it another way, causation interruption. In Chinese criminal law discussions, there is near-consensus on the outcome in this case: since V's death was ultimately caused by the fire, D is not held responsible for V's death and is only guilty of attempted homicide under Article 232 and Article 23 of the Chinese Criminal Code.

However, Chinese scholars struggle to reach a consensus on the systematic location of abnormal causation within criminal law.

a) Objective Aspect

First, the mainstream view in Chinese literature attempts to analyze the interruption of causation from an objective perspective. However, scholars' interpretations are influenced by their educational backgrounds, leading to differing concepts and theories.

aa) Theory of Adequate Causation

The first approach is the theory of adequate causation (*Adäquanztheorie*). According to this theory, only conditions that are adequate to the result are considered causally significant in criminal law. A cause is deemed legally adequate only if the act significantly increases the probability of the result, as determined by general societal experience. The adequacy of causation is negated only when the causal process entirely deviates from the ordinary and foreseeable course of events. In Vignette 2, it is generally believed that the development of the causal process deviates from the ordinary course of events as understood by general societal experience, thereby negating the adequacy of causation.[12]

---

11 See *Chencheng Chu*, The Legitimacy of Criminal Law in Solving the Trolley Problem in Automated Vehicle Programming, Global Law Review 2018, Issue 3, 89.

12 See, e.g., *Liqing Fu*, Criminal Law General Part, 2020, 146–147; *Yanhong Liu*, The Theory of Objective Attribution: Questioning and Reflection, Peking University Law Journal 2011, Issue 6, 1220.

bb) Theory of Objective Attribution

Influenced by German criminal law, Chinese criminal law has increasingly emphasized the theory of objective attribution (*Lehre von der objektiven Zurechnung*) in discussions on causation issues.[13] Chinese scholars understand that the purpose of criminal law is to attribute responsibility for infringing upon legal interests. For an infringement to be deemed a "work" of the perpetrator, objective attribution must be analyzed only after factual causation (cause in fact) has been established. The formula for objective attribution is "creating and realizing a legally relevant risk", which includes both the creation of a legally relevant risk and its realization.[14] In Vignette 2, proponents of objective attribution believe that although the perpetrator created a legally relevant risk, that risk was not realized in the result. However, some scholars point out that a retrospective perspective should be taken to determine whether the risk created by the act continued to play a substantial role in the causation process and directly contributed to the result, thereby affirming the realization of the risk.[15]

cc) Theory of Realization of Behavioral Risk

In addition to the theory of objective attribution from Germany, some Chinese scholars use the "theory of realization of behavioral risk" from Japan to address the problem of abnormal causation.[16] Influenced by Japanese criminal law theory, many scholars emphasize the concept of "execution act (*Ausführungshandlung*)".[17] An execution act refers to an act that contains specific risks capable of causing a result. The causal process between the execution act and the result is the realization of the risks contained in the execution act, essentially a process of manifesting the behavioral risk. Therefore, the criterion for determining causation is whether the risks associated with a particular execution act actually transform into results, including judging whether the execution act contains risks that could lead to the result and whether those risks have been realized.[18] In the context of the theory of realization of behavioral risk, it is generally believed in Vignette 2 that the intervening causes are unrelated to the execution act, and the risk of the execution act is not considered to have been realized, thus excluding causation.

---

13 See, e. g., *Guangquan Zhou*, Criminal Law General Part, 4th ed. 2021, 128; *Yunliang Sun*, Introduction of Objective Imputation Theory and Reconsideration of Functions of Causality, Modern Law Science 2013, Issue 1, 148.

14 See *Xingliang Chen*, From Causality to Attribution: A Study on the Theory of Objective Attribution, Chinese Journal of Law 2006, Issue 2, 75–81.

15 See *Xuan Chen*, On the Boundary between Objective and Subjective Attribution and the Deviation of Causal Process, The Jurist 2014, Issue 6, 109–110.

16 See, e. g., *Mingkai Zhang*, Criminal Law, 6th ed. 2021, 240; *Hong Li*, Criminal Law General Part, 2nd ed. 2016, 99.

17 See *Mingkai Zhang*, Criminal Law, 6th ed. 2021, 233.

18 See, e. g., *Yeliu Qian*, Important Developments and Positional Choices in the Theory of Criminal Law Causation, Criminal Science 2022, Issue 4, 104; *Hong Li*, The Problem of Mistake of Causation and Its Response: With a Reinterpretation of the Theory of Realization of Behavioral Risk as the Center, Chinese Journal of Law 2022, Issue 1, 110.

b) Subjective Aspect

In contrast to the mainstream view that advocates reasoning from an objective aspect, a few scholars in China propose to address the problem of abnormal causation from a subjective perspective. Some scholars directly proclaim the existence of only attempted homicide based on the determination of intent, while others advocate for the introduction of the concept of "subjective attribution (*subjektive Zurechnung*)" from Germany.

aa) Determination of Intent

Before Chinese criminal law adopted theories from German and Japanese criminal law, the traditional view typically reasoned from the perspective of intent determination, especially in cases involving a mistake about causation. This means that the perpetrator misunderstands the causation between their conduct and the resulting outcome.[19] Specifically, in Vignette 2, it is considered that the result pursued by perpetrator D was caused by other reasons, which leads to the conclusion that it constitutes only attempted intentional homicide.

bb) Subjective Attribution

In recent years, many Chinese scholars have focused on the concept of subjective attribution in German criminal law. However, interpretations vary regarding the relationship between subjective and objective attributions theory.

(1) Subjective Attribution as a Supplement to Objective Attribution

One view suggests that subjective attribution complements objective attribution theory.[20] Proponents of this view consider subjective attribution as a negative review process, arguing that it is only necessary after positive findings on objective attribution and intent have been established. The focus is on determining whether there is an inconsistency between subjective intent and objective result.[21] Some scholars believe that both objective and subjective unlawfulness should be examined together, initially by determining whether there exists intentional or negligent behavioral risk, followed by assessing whether the result is the consequence of this risk.[22] In Vignette 2, the actual causal process differs from the actor's anticipated one, and the resulting death does not reflect his behavioral risk, so it does not constitute a completed homicide.

---

19 See *Mingxuan Gao* and *Kechang Ma* (eds.), Criminal Law, 10th ed. 2022, 121–122.

20 See, e. g., *Benqi Ouyang*, On the Subjective Attribution of Deviation of Causal Process, Law Review 2015, Issue 6, 110.

21 See *Erpen Yan*, Deviation of Causal Process and the Realization of Intentional Attribution: On the Restatement of the Principle of Unity of Objective and Subjective, Tribune of Political Science and Law 2022, Issue 4, 103.

22 See *Langtao Bai*, The Essence of Mistake of Fact: Deviation of Intentional Behavioral Danger, Chinese Journal of Law 2018, Issue 3, 148.

(2) *Subjective Attribution Replacing Objective Attribution*

Some scholars have recently attempted to introduce the concept of impermissible risk – a concept reflected in objective attribution theory – at the level of subjective attribution. Based on this, they propose a reconstruction of the concepts of intent and negligence. Regarding intent, it is argued that it includes the actor's awareness that he is taking an impermissible risk and that the result lies within the scope of that risk.[23] Scholars advocating for the replacement of objective attribution theory by subjective attribution theory, and for applying subjective attribution theory to result attribution, argue that result attribution requires an examination of the completeness of the actor's unlawful conduct. Objective unlawfulness is viewed as the realization of the actor's subjective will, which exerts an "unlawful directing effect" on objective facts. For intentional offenses, the core of result attribution lies in the dominance of subjective content over objective risk. The judgement in result attribution is based on the concurrence of the actor's subjective understanding, the objective harm, and the scope of impermissible risk.[24]

Due to space limitations, the author cannot take a stance on the doctrinal controversies discussed above. However, it is worth mentioning that not all results of causation cases in Chinese criminal law, are free from controversy like the "Hospital Fire Case". On the contrary, in cases involving missing the target (*aberratio ictus*) or cases where results occur prematurely or belatedly, such as the "Jauchegruben-Fall" and the "Bridge Pier Case", reaching a consensus in Chinese criminal law discussions remains difficult.

Vignette 3: Torture to Save a Life

Kidnapper K has abducted an 8-year-old girl G and hidden her in a small cave in the woods. K is trying to extort money from G's parents for her release. The police manage to arrest K. Although being questioned for 24 hours, K steadfastly refuses to disclose where he hid G. Police officer D correctly assumes that G may soon die of thirst if she cannot be found. He therefore severely beats K to make him tell the truth. Fearing even more violence, K eventually leads the police to the cave, where they find G still barely alive. Should D be punished for torturing K?

Compared to the trolley problem in Vignette 1, the problem of torture to save lives is rarely discussed in Chinese criminal law. One possible reason is the lack of high-profile cases, such as the well-known German "*Fall Daschner*"[25], which received significant media attention. Additionally, the absence of pronouncements on the criminal evaluation of torture to save lives by Chinese judicial authorities has further limited discussion on this matter. Therefore, this paper will primarily present the academic viewpoints within Chinese criminal law regarding this issue and the related controversies.

---

23 See *Jin Zhuang*, Objective Attribution or Subjective Attribution? Rediscovering an "Outdated" Approach to Result Attribution, The Jurist 2015, Issue 3, 68.

24 See *Yingwen Gao*, Analysis of Result Attribution in Deviation of Causal Process, Peking University Law Journal 2023, Issue 2, 535.

25 LG Frankfurt a. M. NJW 2005, 692; OLG Frankfurt a. M. NJW 2013, 75.

Firstly, the violent acts of Police Officer D in Vignette 3 satisfy the elements of intentional injury under Article 234 of the Chinese Criminal Code. Furthermore, Article 247 of the Chinese Criminal Code specifically addresses the crime of extracting confessions through torture. According to this provision,

> Any judicial officer who extorts a confession from a criminal suspect or defendant by torture, or extorts testimony from a witness by violence, shall be sentenced to fixed-term imprisonment of not more than three years or criminal detention. If the victim suffers injury, disability or death, the officer shall be convicted and given a heavier punishment in accordance with the provisions of Article 234 or 232 of this Law.

Therefore, in Vignette 3, Police Officer D's act of beating K fulfills the requirements of both Article 234 and Article 247 of the Chinese Criminal Code, constituting the concurrence of offences (*Idealkonkurrenz*). The controversy concerns whether Police Officer D's use of torture to extract a confession can be justified or excused. In this regard, Chinese criminal law presents both supporting and opposing arguments based on different rationales.

a) Not Punishable

Within Chinese literature, many scholars advocate for the non-punishment of torture to save lives, proposing either a justification or an excuse. The first view is based on justificatory self-defense, followed by the view suggesting an excuse.

aa) Justification Based on Self-Defense

The first view argues that torture to save a life meets the prerequisites of self-defense under Article 20(1) and (3) of the Chinese Criminal Code and thus can be justified.[26] The rationale behind this perspective is that the principles of personal protection and maintenance of legal order – fundamental to self-defense – both aim to safeguard citizens' freedom and rights. These principles share a common theoretical foundation, constituting a coherent and unified whole. From this standpoint, law enforcement officers, such as police officers, who use torture to obtain necessary information and protect legal interests, can be justified through self-defense. However, it is crucial that the objective of torture to save lives is strictly limited to eliminating the risk of harm to legal interests, rather than using it to gather evidence against the criminal suspect or defendant.[27]

bb) Justification Based on (Defensive) Necessity

Some scholars argue that torture to save a life fulfills the prerequisites of necessity under Article 21(1) of the Chinese Criminal Code.[28] This perspective justifies the act

---

26 See, e. g., *Long Cheng*, Torture to Save Lives in Terrorism Crimes: Justification and Its Limitations, Tribune of Political Science and Law 2020, Issue 5, 125; *Mingkai Zhang*, Criminal Law, 6th ed. 2021, 1185; *Gang Wang*, Justification and Limits of Justifiable Self-Defense: A Discussion on the Legality of Torture to Save Lives, 2019, 315.

27 See *Long Cheng*, Torture to Save Lives in Terrorism Crimes: Justification and Its Limitations, Tribune of Political Science and Law 2020, Issue 5, 130.

28 See *Huanji Li*, Torture to save lives and Defensive Necessity, Renmin University Law Review, Vol. 35 (2022), 347–348.

of police officers inflicting torture in order to rescue hostages based on (defensive) necessity. According to this viewpoint, defensive necessity is grounded in the need to protect the person at risk. Since criminal suspects are the creators of the danger, they bear the obligation to provide rescue information. Therefore, the use of torture to save lives aligns with the conditions of defensive necessity. Moreover, the "no other alternative" requirement – essential for establishing defensive necessity – restricts the use of torture to situations where law enforcement officers have exhausted all other measures to obtain rescue information and the victim's life is in imminent danger.

cc) Excuse Based on Supra-Legal Necessity

Lastly, some scholars argue that torture to save a life should be exempted from criminal liability based on supra-legal necessity. The advantage of this exemption is that it functions as a post-factum defense, providing an individual exclusion of criminal responsibility, without general applicability. Consequently, law enforcement officers who employ torture may still face criminal liability and could also be subject to civil liability.[29]

b) Punishable

Some scholars propose opposing views. They contend that torture to save a life constitutes a violation of Article 234 and Article 247 of the Chinese Criminal Code, for the following reasons:

Firstly, from an international treaty perspective, scholars argue that the obligation to prohibit torture, as established by relevant international treaties, is non-negotiable.[30] China signed the Convention against Torture and Other Cruel, Inhuman or Degrading Treatment or Punishment on December 12, 1986, deposited the instrument of ratification with the United Nations on October 4, 1988, and the Convention officially came into effect in China on November 3 of the same year. Article 2(2) and (3) of the "Convention against Torture" stipulate that "No exceptional circumstances whatsoever, whether a state of war, or a threat of war, internal political instability or any other public emergency, may be invoked as a justification for torture. An order from a superior officer or a public authority may not be invoked as a justification for torture."

Furthermore, some scholars argue that from the perspective of domestic law, there is no legal basis for the application of torture to save a life under Article 36 on the Chinese Constitution, Article 50 of the Chinese Criminal Procedure Law, and Article 22 of the Chinese Police Law.[31]

---

29 See *Chunran Yang* and *Peiliang Ren*, Preventive Torture: Preventing Illegal Acts or Preventing Liability? – A Discussion on the Fate of Torture, Criminal Science 2013, Issue 3, 38–40.

30 See *Shanshan Zhao*, The Theory of Absolute Prohibition of Torture in International Perspective, Journal of Comparative Law 2013, Issue 1, 96–100.

31 See *Ming Ai*, The Legal Effects of Coercive Interrogation Conducted for the Purpose of Rescue: Taking the Judgment of Gäfgen v. Germany by the European Court of Human Rights as an Example, Journal of Comparative Law 2014, Issue 2, 186; *Chencheng Chu*, Exploration of the Legitimacy of Torture to save lives in Terrorism Crimes with the Purpose of Disruption, Journal of Southeast University (Philosophy and Social Science) 2019, Issue 2, 69.

Lastly, some scholars contend that the justifications for legitimizing torture to save a life are unfounded. If the State were allowed to violate fundamental rights without explicit legal basis and justify such actions through defenses like justification, it would grant the State organs the power to exceed legal boundaries and undermine the principle of legality. Moreover, regarding the view that torture to save a life could be justified as a defense, current perspectives on the legitimacy of self-defense generally agree that self-defense is a private right and cannot be exercised by State organs. Therefore, since torture to save a life is fundamentally an act performed in the line of duty, it cannot be justified.[32]

Considering the aforementioned pro and contra arguments, it could be argued that the view favoring non-punishment for torture to save a life holds a slight majority. However, regardless of the number of supporters, this issue remains worthy of further in-depth discussion within Chinese criminal law.

Vignette 4: Lethal Self-Defense

> R, a well-trained young man armed with a knife, accosts 50-year-old D, who is on her way home from a party in the early morning hours. R threatens her with the knife and takes away her purse filled with 500 € and her wristwatch worth 1,000 €. As R turns to run away, D draws a pistol she is secretly carrying in her jacket, and shoots and kills R in order to retrieve her property. Is D guilty of murder?

The grounds and limits of self-defense law[33] have been among the most discussed issues in Chinese criminal law in recent years.[34] The movie "Article 20", released during the 2024 Spring Festival, centers around this controversy, sparking widespread discussions in Chinese society.[35] The title "Article 20" refers to the section of Chinese Criminal Code governing self-defense.

Article 20 of the Chinese Criminal Code consists of three paragraphs. The first paragraph defines the elements and legal consequences of legitimate defense:

---

32 See *Chencheng Chu*, Exploration of the Legitimacy of Torture to Save Lives in Terrorism Crimes with the Purpose of Disruption, Journal of Southeast University (Philosophy and Social Science) 2019, Issue 2, 69.

33 See only *Mingkai Zhang*, The Principle and Application of Self-Defense: A Critical Examination of Dualism Theory, Global Law Review 2018, Issue 2, 51–76; *Gang Wang*, The Legitimacy Basis and Limitations of Self-Defense, Peking University Law Journal 2018, Issue 6, 1589–1613; *Cheng Xu*, Weighing Interests in the Determination of Self-Defense Limits, Chinese Journal of Law 2019, Issue 3, 148–166; *Su Jiang*, Systematic Development of Self-Defense Limit Determination Rules, Science of Law 2022, Issue 1, 142–157; *Wanlong Xu*, Reconstruction of the Legal Basis of Self-Defense, Global Law Review 2024, Issue 1, 141–156.

34 For an overview of the development of the discussion on self-defence in China see *Daniel Sprick*, Entwicklungslinien der Notwehr in China, in: Urs Kindhäuser and Michael Pawlik (eds.), Notwehr in Deutschland und China: Weltanschaulicher Hintergrund und dogmatische Grundfragen, 2020, 53 et seq.

35 See *Arash Nahandian*, Article 20 Review: The Dilemma of Self-Defense Against Injustice – When Systems Fail: Zhang Yimou's Dark Morality Tale Questions Strict Self-Defense Laws, Gazettely (March 5, 2024), https://gazettely.com/2024/03/entertainment/article-20-review/.

> Where a person, in order to protect the interests of the state or the public, or his own or another person's personal rights, property rights or other rights from a present unlawful attack, takes action to stop such an unlawful attack and therefore causes harm to the attacker, this person shall be considered acting in justifiable defense and shall not bear criminal liability.

The second paragraph of Article 20 stipulates the circumstances of excessive self-defense:

> Where a person acting in justifiable defense obviously exceeds the necessary limit and therefore causes major harm, he shall bear criminal liability, but shall be given a mitigated punishment or be exempted from punishment.

In judicial practice, when excessive self-defense is established, the defender is often found to have committed a negligent crime. Although the Chinese Criminal Code does not have specific provisions regarding the recognition of mistakes by the actor, the final conclusion is consistent with German criminal law, which states that culpability of an intentional crime is excluded when there is a mistake regarding the prerequisites of a justificatory defense (*Erlaubnistatbestandsirrtum*).

The third paragraph of Article 20 of the Chinese Criminal Code outlines situations where the limits of defense do not need to be considered. This provision is also known as the "unlimited self-defense" clause:

> Where a person takes action against present physical assault, murder, robbery, rape, kidnapping, or any other violent crime that seriously endangers personal safety and therefore causes injury to or the death of the attacker, his action shall not be considered excessive defense and he shall not bear criminal liability.

Overall, starting from the "Yu Huan Case",[36] there has been a "shift in values" regarding lethal self-defense in Chinese criminal law. Prior to the "Yu Huan Case", Article 20 of the Chinese Criminal Code, which explicitly defined the right to justifiable self-defense, was considered a "zombie clause",[37] and this was reflected in the "Yu Huan Case". The first-instance court held that Yu Huan's self-defense act did not meet the requirement of urgency and therefore did not even qualify as self-defense. The second-instance court, however, reversed this decision, acknowledging that Yu

---

36 The "Yu Huan Case" refers to a Supreme Court Guidance Case (No. 93) in China. In this case, Yu Huan's parents became involved with a private lender who instructed henchmen to collect debts, including a 10% monthly interest rate. On April 14, 2016, a group of 11 debt collectors held Yu Huan and his mother captive for an extended period, subjected them to physical and verbal abuse, and severely humiliated his mother. Although the police were called, they failed to fully resolve the situation, and the collectors prevented Yu Huan from leaving. In a moment of desperation, Yu Huan retrieved a knife and stabbed four collectors, resulting in one death and injuries to three others, two of them serious. In the first instance, Yu Huan was found guilty of intentional injury and sentenced to life imprisonment. On appeal, the Shandong Higher People's Court overturned the first instance ruling and reduced the sentence to five years, ruling that Yu Huan's actions constituted self-defense, though "obviously excessive". On the facts and controversial points of the "Yu Huan Case" see *Daniel Sprick*, Entwicklungslinien der Notwehr in China, in: Urs Kindhäuser and Michael Pawlik (eds.), Notwehr in Deutschland und China: Weltanschaulicher Hintergrund und dogmatische Grundfragen, 2020, 76 et seq.

37 See *Xingliang Chen*, How Can Self-Defense Avoid Becoming a Zombie Clause, The Jurist 2017, Issue 5, 98.

Huan's act met the requirements for self-defense but was excessive, thus constituting excessive self-defense.

According to traditional theory in China, although the literal meaning of Article 20(1) of the Chinese Criminal Code does not specify the extent of self-defense, it can be inferred from the provision regarding "unlimited self-defense" in Article 20(3) that the self-defense against acts not listed in Article 20(3) must consider the hierarchical relationship between the legal interests infringed by the unlawful act and the interests that may be harmed by the act of self-defense.[38] In judicial practice, even in cases of rape, there are instances where justifiable self-defense is not recognized, such as the famous "Deng Yujiao Case".[39] This illustrates that, in China's judicial practice, the judgment of justifiable self-defense is often based on the harm caused by the defensive act.[40] This approach to limiting self-defense is largely rooted in China's unique view of life and pragmatism.[41]

The "Yu Huan Case" has attracted significant media attention and sparked public debate. The general public largely disagreed with the trial court's conclusion. Chinese criminal law scholars also began to critically examine the application of Article 20(1) of the Chinese Criminal Code.[42] Some argue that the judgment on the limits of justificatory self-defense should shift from a result-oriented approach to an action-oriented one. Additionally, there is growing support for a new interpretation of Article 20(3). According to this view, the provision on "unlimited self-defense" in Article 20(3) is seen as a cautionary provision, meaning that self-defense under Article 20(1) does not need to fulfill a proportionality requirement.[43]

On August 28, 2020, the Supreme People's Court, the Supreme People's Procuratorate, and the Ministry of Public Security issued the "Guiding Opinions on the Ap-

---

38 See only *Genlin Liang*, Position, Standards, and Logic of Excessive Defense Unlawfulness Judgment, Law Science, 2019, Issue 2, 11–12; *Xingliang Chen*, Analysis and Development of the Doctrine of Self-Defense, Criminal Science 2021, Issue 2, 26.

39 On May 10, 2009, three government officials from a town government in Hubei Province were playing in a hotel in the town. They requested the female attendant Deng Yujiao to accompany them for a bath. After Deng Yujiao refused, the three individuals multiple times forcibly prevented Deng Yujiao from leaving the room. As a result, Deng Yujiao used a fruit knife to stab them, causing one of them to die. In this case, the court determined that Deng Yujiao's defense exceeded the limits of self-defense and constituted intentional injury under Article 234 of the Chinese Criminal Code. However, she was exempted from criminal punishment. For an introduction and evaluation of the Deng Yujiao Case, see *Xingliang Chen*, Dogmatic Criminal Law, 3rd 2017, 386–387.

40 See *Xuan Chen*, Notwehrexzess: von einer Erfolgs- zu einer Handlungsperspektive, in: Martin Böse, Kay H. Schumann and Friedrich Toepel (eds.), Festschrift für Urs Kindhäuser, 604 et seq.

41 See *Xuan Chen*, Self-Defense, Stability Maintenance Priority and Result Orientation: Legal Thinking Triggered by the "Yu Huan Case", Science of Law 2018, Issue 3, 81–82.

42 See *Xuan Chen*, Notwehrexzess: von einer Erfolgs- zu einer Handlungsperspektive, in: Martin Böse, Kay H. Schumann and Friedrich Toepel (eds.), Festschrift für Urs Kindhäuser, 606 et seq.

43 See only *Gang Wang*, Basis and Limits of the Legitimacy of Self-Defense, Peking University Law Journal 2018, Issue 6, 1608; *Mingkai Zhang*, Excessive Defense: Judgment Standards and Types of Excessiveness, Law Science 2019, Issue 1, 6.

plication of the Justifiable Self-Defense System in accordance with the Law".[44] The Guiding Opinions quoted the famous statement by German scholar Albert Berner regarding the right to self-defense: "The law cannot yield to lawlessness."[45] However, China's highest judicial authorities still require, in principle, a certain degree of proportionality between the self-defensive act and the infringement. For example, Article 10 of these Guiding Opinions states:

> In cases of significantly minor unlawful infringements, if the person, under identifiable circumstances, directly uses means that are sufficient to cause serious injury or death to stop the infringement, it should not be deemed an act of self-defense.

The release of the movie "Article 20" in February 2024 further brought the issue of the right to justifiable self-defense into the public spotlight. This sparked widespread social discussion, which in turn influenced academic debates. The Supreme People's Court, in its work report, stated: "The phrase 'The law cannot yield to lawlessness' is not just a slogan. Article 20 of the Chinese Criminal Code has been awakened and will continue to be implemented." This statement suggests the potential for further expansion of the scope of justifiable self-defense under Article 20(1) of the Chinese Criminal Code.

If the scenario described in Vignette 4 were to occur today, it is highly likely that Chinese judges would consider D's act as justificatory self-defense rather than intentional homicide under Article 232 of the Chinese Criminal Code.

From the "Deng Yujiao Case" in 2009 to the "Yu Huan Case" in 2016 and the discussions surrounding the movie "Article 20" in early 2024, the evolution in criminal law theory and judicial practice is striking. These shifts illustrate that, despite a country's legal order being deeply influenced by a particular cultural framework, social changes and developments can still trigger a shift in citizens' understanding of "criminal justice" or, more precisely, a deeper reflection on their own concept of "justice".

> **Vignette 5: Criminal Responsibility of Subordinates for Systemic Offenses**
> D is a soldier in the army of a country ruled by a junta of generals who have come to power through a violent coup. When an opposition group demands the return to a democratic system, the government orders the soldiers to shoot and kill any person who resists arrest. Following this order, D kills three young men who take part in a protest demonstration and hit a police officer who tries to arrest them. When D is tried after a change of regime, he says that he did not like to shoot the protesters but that he thought that he had to obey his commanders' orders. D knew that if he had refused to shoot, he might have been demoted, but no physical harm would have occurred to him. Should D be convicted of murder? If so, should his sentence be mitigated because of his situation?

In the Chinese context, the issue of criminal responsibility of subordinates involved in systemic offenses, as described in Vignette 5, is more of a "textbook problem" since such cases have not yet appeared in judicial practice.

---

44 https://www.spp.gov.cn/spp/xwfbh/wsfbt/202009/t20200903_478676.shtml#1.

45 *Albert Berner*, Die Notwehrtheorie, Archiv des Criminalrechts, N.F., 19 (1848), 557, 562.

Firstly, the criminal responsibility of subordinates who follow orders largely depends on the role of the commander in the joint crime of systemic offenses. This issue remains highly controversial in Chinese criminal law discussions. The first viewpoint argues that the commander, as order-giver, qualifies as an indirect perpetrator (*mittelbare Täterschaft*), while the subordinate who executes the order remains a direct perpetrator (*unmittelbare Täterschaft*). While there is a consensus that the order-giver's control is a form of volitional control, some scholars invoke the concept of "perpetration through an organization" (*Organisationsherrschaft*) to explain this relationship. Proponents of this view argue that, as a mastermind with command authority, the order-giver can establish indirect perpetration by ordering criminal acts through the organizational power structure. This type of domination or control typically applies in cases of state power abuse or systemic offenses, where the front-line perpetrator is a direct perpetrator and the commander is an indirect perpetrator.[46] Some scholars argue that the concept of "coerced accomplice", as stipulated in Article 28 of the Chinese Criminal Code, supports the idea of perpetration through an organization.[47] In terms of criminal intent, the subordinate executing the order is coerced but retains control over his body and will. Thus, the punishment for the subordinate should be mitigated.[48] Similarly to the view of perpetration through an organization, some scholars argue that the relationship between the commander and the subordinate can be understood as a form of compulsion. This view suggests that control achieved through a power organization can be classified as control through compulsion. Specifically, the order-giver forces the subordinate to commit acts that meet the *actus reus* of the crime, thereby gaining control over the conduct (*Tatherrschaft*).[49]

The theory of perpetration through an organization has, however, been criticized in China. According to some authors, the order-giver should be classified as an "instigator" under Article 29 of the Chinese Criminal Code.[50] They argue that subordinates in cases of organized crimes usually possess awareness of law-abiding and criminal responsibility. They may also have personal motives that prevent the commission of illegal acts, known as "normative obstacles". Therefore, the commission of the crime is seen as the result of the subordinates' free will rather than the commander's control.

---

46 See *Bo Li* and *Jianhang Zhou*, Organizational Control and the Basis of Attribution of Organizational Crimes, Journal of Soochow University (Law Edition) 2018, Issue 4, 48–51.

47 According to Article 28 of the Chinese Criminal Code, "Anyone who is coerced to participate in a crime shall be given a mitigated punishment or be exempted from punishment in the light of the circumstances of the crime he commits."

48 See *Yijian Chen*, The Dominant Co-perpetrator as the Direct Perpetrator of Organizational Control: Understanding in Germany and Issues in China, Northern Legal Science 2010, Issue 4, 45–46.

49 See *Mingkai Zhang*, Criminal Law, 6th ed. 2021, 527.

50 See only *Xiaotian Zhou*, Reconstruction of the Criminal Qualification of Crimes Committed with "Intention but without Identity Tools", Law Review 2015, Issue 3, 90; *Guohe Yuan*, Logic and Reflection on the Theory of Organizational Control in Criminal Law, The Jurist, 2020, Issue 6, 96.

Lastly, some scholars propose applying the concept of "conspirative co-perpetrators" from Japanese criminal law, considering the commander a co-perpetrator.[51] The term "conspirative co-perpetrator" refers to the commander, as the order-giver, who, though not directly involved in the act, plays an important role in inducing criminal intent, guiding the criminal process, providing criminal direction, and exerting strong psychological control over the actual execution of the order. Regarding the punishment of the executor, some scholars argue that their punishment should be based on their role in the joint crime, without requiring an increased sentence compared to the order-giver.[52]

On the other hand, Chinese criminal law literature also discusses whether a subordinate's execution of a commander's order can be justified. The mainstream viewpoint holds that in cases where a commander's order is procedurally legal the subordinate is justified in executing it. However, if the order has obvious and significant defects, the subordinate cannot use the execution of the order as a justification and instead becomes a joint perpetrator of the crime with the commander.[53]

At the same time, a minority viewpoint argues that when a subordinate is aware of the unlawfulness of a command but still carries it out, they can be excused based on the theory of lack of expectation to act in accordance with the norm (*Unzumutbarkeit normgemäßen Verhaltens*). Due to the unequal power relationship between commanders and subordinates, it is often difficult to expect subordinates to resist unlawful orders, especially in the military, where personnel have the right to dissent but not to refuse orders. Therefore, the defense of lack of expectation to act in accordance with the norm (*Unzumutbarkeit normgemäßen Verhaltens*), a supra-legal excusatory defense, could be invoked to mitigate the subordinate's criminal responsibility.[54]

Summing up, according to the majority view in China, D should be convicted of intentional homicide under Article 232 of the Chinese Criminal Code and held jointly responsible with the commander who issued the order. However, there is controversy regarding whether the order-giver qualifies as an indirect perpetrator, co-perpetrator, or instigator under Article 28 of the Chinese Criminal Code. Since D can be regarded as a coerced accomplice under Article 28 of the Chinese Criminal Code, his punishment should be mitigated or withheld altogether, depending on the circumstances of the crime.

---

51 See only *Yanhong Liu*, Theory of Joint Responsibility as Co-perpetrators, China Legal Science 2012, Issue 6, 123; *Hongyan Meng*, Development of the Theory of Joint Responsibility as Co-perpetrators in China, Journal of Chinese Academy of Social Sciences University, 2022, Issue 8, 133; *Zhibo Yang*, Criminal Responsibility of "Conspiring" Organizers and Leaders in Organized Crime, Journal of Political Science and Law 2020, Issue 1, 62–64.

52 See *Yanhong Liu*, Theory of Joint Responsibility as Co-perpetrators, China Legal Science 2012, 2012, Issue 6, 120.

53 See only *Guangquan Zhou*, Criminal Law General Part, 4th ed. 2021, 228–229; *Xingliang Chen*, Dogmatic Criminal Law, 3rd 2017, 412.

54 See *Huaying Liu*, Criminal Responsibility for Soldiers' Execution of Illegal Orders, Law Science Magazine 2009, Issue 7, 24; *Yeliu Qian*, Introduction and Limited Application of the Theory of Zumutbarkeit, Chinese Journal of Law 2015, Issue 6, 131.

Vignette 6: Limits of Consent

V is a 21-year-old ambitious athlete and short-distance runner. He has learned that certain artificial limbs can enhance a runner's speed. He decides that he would rather have an artificial limb instead of his right lower leg. He approaches D, a surgeon in private practice, and asks him to amputate his leg below the knee and replace it with an artificial limb. D complies with V's request. Should D be punished for mayhem?

With the turn of Chinese criminal law toward the German and Japanese paradigms of criminal law doctrine, the issue of consent has become a controversial topic among Chinese legal scholars.[55] Although Chinese criminal law does not explicitly stipulate consent as a ground for excluding criminal liability, as is the case in the criminal laws of Sweden, Italy, South Korea, and the Macau Special Administrative Region of China, traditional Chinese legal thought has given to the victim's consent the effect of excluding criminal liability. According to this view, "when the rights holder requests or agrees to the perpetrator's infringement of their legitimate rights, that indicates that he has waived those rights. As a result, the law does not need to punish the person who has infringed upon them."[56] Based on this, some scholars consider the victim's consent as an "extra-legal defense" in Chinese criminal law.[57]Some scholars advocate for the full implementation of the principle of self-responsibility, believing that individuals should have the freedom to dispose of all their personal legal interests, including the right to life.[58] In contrast, the prevailing view argues that criminal law should set limits to the recognition of a victim's consent, based on considerations of social and public interest. It is generally accepted that consent does not exclude criminal liability in cases involving the victim's life. There is also broad agreement that Chinese criminal law does not impose restrictions on consent regarding the disposal of property rights. The focus of the debate in Chinese criminal law theory and judicial practice concerns the question whether consent should remove the actor's criminal responsibility in cases of serious bodily harm or the infringement on bodily health interests.

Three main views have emerged in the discussion:

The first view argues that the victim's freedom to voluntarily waive their interests should take precedence under criminal law, and that therefore the validity of the victim's consent to serious bodily harm should be fully recognized.[59] Scholars who sup-

---

55 In recent years, in addition to the issue of the limits of consent, Chinese criminal law has also debated the legal basis of victim's consent and its position in the criminal law system. See *Hong Li*, A Study on the Issue of Victim Consent, Chinese Journal of Law 2007, Issue 1, 86–89; *Hao Che*, The Systematic Position of Victim Consent: A "German Problem" in the Chinese Context, China Legal Science 2008, Issue 4, 109–118; *Gang Wang*, The Systematic Position of Victim Consent, Journal of Comparative Law 2019, Issue 4, 29–46.

56 *Mingxuan Gao* and *Kechang Ma* (eds.), Criminal Law, Vol. 1, 1999, 253.

57 See *Xingliang Chen*, Dogmatic Criminal Law, 3rd ed. 2017, 413.

58 See *Gang Wang*, Denial of the Illegality of Suicide Behavior: A Discussion with Dr. Yeliu Qian, Tsinghua University Law Journal 2013, Issue 3, 143; *Jun Feng*, Self-Responsibility in Criminal Law, Chinese Journal of Law 2006, Issue 3, 95–96.

59 See, e. g., *Hong Li*, A Study on the Issue of Victim Consent, Chinese Journal of Law 2007, Issue 1, 94; *Yicheng Deng* and *Min Shen*, A Study on the Allocation of Interests in Victim Consent, Legal Science, Science of Law 2014, Issue 4, 178; *Jun Fang*, Victim Consent: Basis,

port the "validity of consent to serious bodily harm"[60] principle emphasize the significance of individual autonomy. Since criminal law protects legal interests to ensure individual freedom and self-realization, individual autonomy should also be safeguarded. Except in rare cases where individuals lack the capacity to dispose of their rights, such as in cases involving authorized killings that relate to the material basis of the right to life, i. e., the freedom to make decisions, the victim's autonomy should be fully respected.[61]

The second view argues that only consent to minor bodily harm can exempt the actor from punishment. Once the harm reaches the threshold of serious bodily harm, as defined by Article 95 of the Chinese Criminal Code,[62] consent becomes invalid.[63] An exception exists only when the victim consents to serious bodily harm in order to protect another significant legal interest, such as for the transplantation of organs to a patient.[64] This view is mainly based on the connection between serious bodily harm and the right to life.[65] It argues that serious bodily harm poses a direct threat to the victim's life and therefore should not be allowed. Moreover, although life and significant health interests belong to the individual, they also involve social and public interests. The disappearance of individuals from society or the occurrence of severe physical disabilities can cause social unrest and additional burdens on the victim's family.[66] This view is consistent with judicial practice, where the determination of serious bodily harm is based on the legislative definition in Article 95 of the Chinese Criminal Code, which includes injuries resulting in permanent disability, disfigurement, loss of hearing, vision, other organ functions, or any other significant harm to personal health.

The third view builds on the second, emphasizing that the offense of intentional injury under Article 234 of the Chinese Criminal Code protects not only individual

Position, and Limits, Contemporary Law Review 2015, Issue 5, 48. Based on the principle of supporting the validity of consent to serious bodily harm, some scholars, in accordance with the provisions of Chinese criminal law, believe that "acts causing serious bodily harm that seriously endanger life" should be the limit of victim consent in the crime of intentional injury. See *Zhongjun Huang*, The Normative Limit of Victim Consent in the Crime of Intentional Injury, Nanjing University Law Journal 2022, Issue 1, 82–86.

60 See *Zhengxun Wang*, Theory of Justified Conduct, 2000, 458.

61 See *Hong Li*, A Study on the Issue of Victim Consent, Chinese Journal of Law 2007, Issue 1, 94.

62 Article 95 of the Chinese Criminal Code stipulates: "For purposes of this Law, a 'serious injury' refers to any of the following injuries: (1) an injury that results in disability or disfigurement to a person; (2) an injury that results in the loss of a person's hearing, sight, or the function of any other organ; or (3) any other injury that causes serious harm to a person's physical health."

63 See *Mingkai Zhang*, Criminal Law, 6th ed. 2021, 1119; *Hongjie Tian*, Justified Conduct in Criminal Law, 2004, 390.

64 See *Mingkai Zhang*, Criminal Law, 6th ed. 2021, 1118.

65 See *Mingkai Zhang*, Criminal Law, 6th ed. 2021, 1119.

66 See *Guangquan Zhou*, Criminal Law General Part, 4th ed. 2021, 231.

bodily health but also the super-individual legal interest of "good social customs".[67] Scholars taking this view argue that, from the perspective of safeguarding the normal social ethical order, consent to serious bodily harm should be considered invalid when it violates good social customs. Specifically, "good social customs" can be understood as "causing serious bodily harm through especially cruel means", a standard derived from the aggravating circumstances of intentional injury under Article 234(2) of the Chinese Criminal Code.[68] In Vignette 6, the different doctrinal views would lead to vastly different conclusions. If we follow the interpretation of judicial practice, which is also the majority view among scholars, and apply the standard of "serious bodily harm", V's request to amputate his leg below the knee would be invalid. In this case, D would be guilty of intentional injury under Article 234 of the Chinese Criminal Code, with the aggravating circumstance of causing serious bodily harm, resulting in a sentence of three to ten years in prison. By contrast, if we accept the principle of "validity of consent to serious bodily harm" and the "good social customs" argument, it could be concluded that V's consent is valid and D would not be guilty of any offense. Additionally, there is a factual factor in Chinese judicial practice that could affect whether D is guilty of an offense. In Chinese judicial practice, medical acts are generally not considered to infringe on legal interests and to meet the *actus reus* of a crime. According to the prevailing view, medical acts are deemed beneficial, and acts that benefit the body are not seen as infringing on legal interests. Therefore, if an act is classified as a medical procedure, it may not be necessary to discuss its justification under criminal law.

Vignette 7: Withdrawal from an Attempt

25-year-old D is deeply upset with her former boyfriend V, who had ended their relationship to be with another woman. To punish V, D plans to stab him with a large knife. D knows that the stab wounds can be fatal and accepts V's death as a possible outcome. When V goes jogging, D attacks him from behind and stabs him in the back three times. V breaks down. D realizes that she has injured him but that the injuries will not cause his death. She realizes that she could kill him by stabbing him again but decides to leave him alone. Should D be punished for attempted murder?

67 See *Hao Che*, The Limits of Victim Consent in Intentional Injury: Focusing on the Second Paragraph of Article 234 of the Chinese Criminal Code, Peking University Law Journal 2008, Issue 5, 723.

68 Article 234(1) of the Chinese Criminal Code stipulates: "Whoever intentionally inflicts bodily harm on another shall be sentenced to fixed-term imprisonment of not more than three years, short-term custody, or non-custodial correction." Article 234(2) of the Chinese Criminal Code states: "Whoever commits a crime as prescribed in the preceding paragraph, thereby causing serious injuries to another, shall be sentenced to fixed-term imprisonment of not less than three years but not more than 10 years. If the offender causes the death of another or, by resorting to especially cruel means, causes serious injuries to another to the extent of severely disabling that person, the offender shall be sentenced to fixed-term imprisonment of not less than 10 years, life imprisonment or death. Where it is provided otherwise in other provisions of this Law, such provisions shall prevail."

Like the criminal law of many countries, such as § 24(1) of the German Criminal Code[69], Chinese criminal law provides for a functional equivalent of withdrawal from an attempted offense, referred to as the discontinuation of a crime. According to Article 24(1) of the Chinese Criminal Code,

> Discontinuation of a crime refers to a situation where, during the commission of a crime, the offender voluntarily discontinues the crime or voluntarily and effectively prevents the crime's intended consequences from occurring.

Article 24(2) of the Chinese Criminal Code then stipulates the legal consequences of discontinuation:

> An offender who discontinues a crime shall be exempted from punishment if no damage occurs, or, if damage is caused, shall receive a mitigated punishment.

Regarding Vignette 7, discussions in Chinese criminal law mainly focus on the situation of voluntarily abandoning possible further harmful acts. A minority view argues that this should not be considered discontinuation of a crime as defined in Article 24(1) of the Chinese Criminal Code.[70] Instead, it should be regarded as an attempted crime under Article 23(1) of the Chinese Criminal Code. The reason is that the initial harmful acts undertaken by the perpetrator and the potential further acts he has refrained from performing, while independent, are of the same kind. If the perpetrator undertook preliminary acts but failed to achieve the intended result due to circumstances beyond his control, this constitutes an attempted crime rather than a withdrawal from an attempt.[71] Some scholars further argue that, based on the mitigating punishment provisions for discontinued crimes in Chinese criminal law, even if the perpetrator fails to complete the crime due to unforeseen circumstances, the danger posed by the perpetrator is already apparent. Therefore, even if he voluntarily refrained from committing further harmful acts, his acts should be considered an attempted crime rather than a withdrawal.[72]

A larger number of scholars, however, hold the view that voluntarily refraining from committing additional harmful acts meets the requirements of Article 23(1) of the Chinese Criminal Code for discontinuation of a crime.[73] Proponents of this view believe that discontinuation should be assessed from the perspective of the entire criminal activity, rather than solely be based on whether the perpetrator completed an act sufficient to achieve the result. If the perpetrator has not finished his crim-

69 See *Michael Bohlander*, Principles of German Criminal Law, 2009, 146–152.

70 See, e.g., *Jian Cai*, Abandonment of Repeated Harmful Acts Should Be Considered Attempted Crime, Modern Law Science 1985, Issue 1, 26; *Wangyuan Xie*, On the Basis of Reducing Punishment for Discontinuation of a Crime: From the Perspective of Comparative Criminal Law, ECUPL Journal 2012, Issue 2, 27.

71 See *Jian Cai*, Abandonment of Repeated Harmful Acts Should Be Considered Attempted Crime, Modern Law Science 1985, Issue 1, 26.

72 See *Wangyuan Xie*, On the Basis of Reducing Punishment for Discontinuation of a Crime: From the Perspective of Comparative Criminal Law, ECUPL Journal 2012, Issue 2, 27.

73 See only *Mingxuan Gao* and *Kechang Ma* (eds.), Criminal Law, 10th ed. 2022, 158; *Hong Li*, Criminal Law General Part, 2nd ed. 2016, 252; *Xingliang Chen*, Normative Criminal Law, 5th ed. 2023, 304; *Bingzhi Zhao*, Abandonment of Repeated Harmful Acts Should Be Considered Discontinuation of a Crime, Modern Law Science 1984, Issue 1, 22–23.

inal conduct and can still carry out further harmful acts, his voluntary abandonment of those acts should be considered a discontinuation of the crime.[74] In addition, scholars who support this perspective argue that recognizing the cessation of repeated harmful acts as discontinuation of a crime encourages offenders to stop their criminal acts.[75]

The Chinese courts[76] and some legal authors tend to adopt a compromise view. Under this approach, discontinuation of a crime may be recognized in specific cases, while criminal liability for attempt may still apply. Supporters of this view believe that if the perpetrator's partial acts are sufficient to complete the execution of the crime, discontinuation is no longer possible.[77] In addition, Chinese courts pay more attention to the voluntariness of the perpetrator's abandonment of further harm. If the abandonment is driven by external factors, an attempted crime can be established.[78]

In Vignette 7, since D realized that one more stab could kill V but decided to leave him alone, this should be considered as voluntary abandonment of the crime. Therefore, D meets the prerequisites for discontinuation of a crime under Article 24(1) of the Chinese Criminal Code. Since D has already inflicted serious injury on V, according to Article 24(2) of the Chinese Criminal Code, her punishment should be mitigated based on the statutory penalty for intentional homicide under Article 232 of the Chinese Criminal Code.

Vignette 8: Criminal Responsibility of Minors

D is a 13-year-old boy. He abducts and rapes V, a girl of the same age. Should D be punished for a criminal offence?

Recently, the age of criminal responsibility has become a highly debated issue in Chinese media, and public opinion on serious cases has influenced legislative action. Prior to the implementation of the 11th Amendment to the Chinese Criminal Code on March 1, 2021, the age of criminal responsibility for minors in China was set at 14 years. If the conduct in Vignette 8 occurred before 2021,[79] then a 13-year-old

---

74 See *Mingxuan Gao* and *Kechang Ma* (eds.), Criminal Law, 10th ed. 2022, 158; *Hong Li*, Criminal Law General Part, 2nd ed. 2016, 252.

75 See *Xingliang Chen*, Normative Criminal Law, 5th ed. 2023, 304.

76 See Guiding Case No. 611 (Li Guanrong Robbery and Intentional Homicide Case), Criminal Trial Reference, Vol. 73, 2010, 17–24.

77 See *Guangquan Zhou*, Criminal Law General Part, 4th ed. 2021, 313; *Mingkai Zhang*, On the Nature of Abandonment of Repeated Harmful Acts, Peking University Law Journal 2017, Issue 6, 1475–1476.

78 See Guiding Case No. 611 (Li Guanrong Robbery and Intentional Homicide Case), Criminal Trial Reference, Vol. 73, 2010, 23.

79 According to Article 17 of the old version of the Chinese Criminal Code: "If a person who has reached the age of 16 commits a crime, he shall bear criminal responsibility.

If a person who has reached the age of 14 but not the age of 16 commits intentional homicide, intentionally hurts another person so as to cause serious injury or the death of the person, or commits rape, robbery, drug-trafficking, arson, explosion or poisoning, he shall bear criminal responsibility.

If a person who has reached the age of 14 but not the age of 18 commits a crime, he shall be given a lighter or mitigated punishment.

like D would not be subject to criminal punishment, even if they committed serious crimes such as murder.

However, the Chinese criminal law underwent a significant policy shift in 2021. According to the amended Article 17 of the Chinese Criminal Code:

> A person who has reached the age of 16 shall assume criminal liability if they commit a crime.
>
> A person who has reached the age of 14 but is under the age of 16 and commits a crime such as intentional homicide, intentional infliction of bodily harm resulting in a serious injury or death, rape, robbery, drug trafficking, arson, explosion, or the addition or release of hazardous substances, shall assume criminal liability.
>
> A person who has reached the age of 12 but is under the age of 14 and commits a crime such as intentional homicide or intentional infliction of bodily harm, resulting in the death or the serious disability of another person due to especially cruel means, and where the circumstances are execrable, shall assume criminal liability, subject to the Supreme People's Procuratorate's approval for prosecution.
>
> A person under the age of 18 who is held criminally liable in accordance with the provisions of the preceding three paragraphs shall receive a lighter or mitigated punishment.
>
> If a person is not subject to criminal punishment because they have not reached the age of 16, their parents or guardian shall be ordered to provide discipline. If necessary, the person shall be subjected to specialized correctional education in accordance with the law.

The 11th Amendment to the Chinese Criminal Code increased the possibility of criminal punishment of offenders aged 12 to 14 years in cases of serious crimes. According to the legislative reasons, "In recent years, there has been growing concern over serious crimes committed by young minors, sparking widespread social debate. The consensus is that this issue must be addressed. This is aimed not only at correcting criminal behavior but also at protecting the rights and interests of victims. However, opinions differ on how to address this issue, particularly whether to lower the age of criminal responsibility and send minors to prison or to improve the custody and education system based on the characteristics of juvenile crime. Overall, for minors, the focus remains on education, reform, and rescue, with education as the main focus and punishment as a supplementary measure. This policy has not changed. For young minors who commit crimes, we should neither simply 'close the case' nor 'let them go'."[80] In line with such guidance, the Chinese Criminal Code draws on the principle *Malitia supplet aetatem* (malice supplements age) of Anglo-American law, allowing criminal responsibility for minors aged 12 to 14 who "commit intentional homicide or intentional injury, causing death or serious disability through particularly cruel means, in cases with extremely malicious circumstances". In addition, Article 17(3) of the Chinese Criminal Code stipulates a procedural requirement: criminal prosecution of minors aged 12 to 14 can only be initiated with the approval of the Supreme People's Procuratorate.

If a person is not given criminal punishment because he has not reached the age of 16, the head of his family or his guardian shall be ordered to discipline him. When necessary, he may be taken in by the government for rehabilitation."

80 See *Aili Wang* (eds.), Explanation of the Criminal Code of the People's Republic of China: Legislative Reasons and Relevant Provisions, 2021, 40–41.

If the events in Vignette 8 occurred after March 1, 2021, according to the current version of the Chinese Criminal Code, D's robbery and rape would not meet the prerequisites for criminal prosecution unless they resulted in the victim V's death, serious injury, or severe disability.

Overall, opinions from the public, media, and literature welcome the lowering of the age of criminal responsibility. The main reasons for supporting this view include:

Firstly, from the perspective of psychological development, minors aged 12 to 14 generally possess sufficient insight and self-control to understand the nature of serious violent crimes and to refrain from committing them.[81] Secondly, lowering the age of criminal responsibility can have a positive deterrent effect, addressing numerous highly violent incidents that have attracted widespread public attention.[82] Thirdly, it can also help prevent judicial corruption.[83]

However, the practice of lowering the age of criminal responsibility remains a controversial topic in academic circles, and China is no exception.[84] For example, scholars who oppose the addition of exceptional provisions argue that there is insufficient scientific evidence in developmental psychology to justify such changes. They suggest that if we followed the perspective of developmental psychology, the concept of a minimum age for criminal responsibility might be completely abandoned.[85] In addition, some scholars propose from the perspective of general deterrence that restoring public trust in the legal order does not solely rely on punishment. Instead, they propose alternative sanction systems that focus on education, which can be applied to minors below the age of criminal responsibility to address public concerns.[86] Finally, they argue that preventing judicial corruption cannot be solved by simply lowering the age of criminal responsibility, as the system of criminal responsibility itself is not the root cause of judicial corruption.

---

81 See *Tao Man*, The Best Interests of Minors and the Lowering of the Age of Criminal Responsibility: A Commentary on Article 1 of the 11th Amendment to the Chinese Criminal Code, Hebei Law Science 2021, Issue 1, 97.

82 See *Tao Man*, The Best Interests of Minors and the Lowering of the Age of Criminal Responsibility: A Commentary on Article 1 of the 11th Amendment to the Chinese Criminal Code, Hebei Law Science 2021, Issue 1, 97; *Wenhua Peng* and *Liang Fu*, On the Provisions of the 11th Amendment to the Chinese Criminal Code Regarding the Age of Criminal Responsibility, Issues on Juvenile Crimes and Delinquency 2021, Issue 1, 28.

83 See *Enhai Wang*, Lowering the Age of Criminal Responsibility without Hesitation, Issues on Juvenile Crimes and Delinquency 2020, Issue 2, 65.

84 See *Ying Wang*, Zur Gegenwart und Zukunft des Jugendstrafrechts in China vor dem Hintergrund der Herabsetzung des *Strafmündigkeitsalters*, in: Horst Beisel et al. (eds.), Festschrift für Dieter Dölling, 610 et seq.; *He Liu*, Die Herabsetzung der Strafmündigkeit in China: Ein Scheitern zwischen Jugend und Kriminalpolitik?, Kriminalpolitische Zeitschrift (KriPoZ) 2024, 441 et seq.

85 See *Moulin Xiong*, The Legal Basis for the Age of Criminal Responsibility, Issues on Juvenile Crimes and Delinquency 2023, Issue 5, 132.

86 See *Jianlong Yao*, Punishment without Education: Legislative Reflections on Lowering the Age of Criminal Responsibility, Peking University Law Journal 2023, Issue 5, 1215; *Junjie Liu*, The Impracticability of Lowering the Starting Age of Criminal Responsibility, Law Science Magazine 2020, Issue 7, 125; *Jiusheng Xu*, Denial of Lowering the Age of Criminal Responsibility, Contemporary Youth Research 2020, Issue 2, 117.

Nevertheless, with the implementation of the 11th Amendment to the Chinese Criminal Code, lowering the age of criminal responsibility has become a reality in some cases. In a recent case, three individuals aged 12 to 14 were accused of intentionally killing a 13-year-old student and burying the body. In this case, for the first time, the Supreme People's Court approved the criminal prosecution of the three individuals based on the provisions of Article 17(3) of the Chinese Criminal Code.[87]

Vignette 9: Statute of Limitations

> In 1995, D violently raped V, a 35-year-old woman, using a knife. D managed to escape and was not apprehended until 2023. Traces of his DNA taken from the victim's body leave no doubt that D is the perpetrator. Should D be convicted despite the long delay?

Like the criminal laws of most countries in the world, the Chinese criminal law also includes a statute of limitations for prosecution. According to Article 87 of the Chinese Criminal Code:

> Crimes shall not be prosecuted if the following periods have elapsed: (1) five years, when the maximum punishment prescribed is fixed-term imprisonment of less than five years; (2) 10 years, when the maximum punishment prescribed is fixed-term imprisonment of not less than five years but less than 10 years; (3) 15 years, when the maximum punishment prescribed is fixed-term imprisonment of not less than 10 years; and (4) 20 years, when the maximum punishment prescribed is life imprisonment or the death penalty. If after 20 years it is considered necessary to prosecute a crime, the matter shall be submitted to the Supreme People's Procuratorate for examination and approval.

The prevailing view in Chinese criminal law is that the statute of limitations for prosecution is established to effectively achieve the objectives of criminal law.[88] The statute of limitations reflects the purpose of punishment, embodies a balanced criminal policy, and supports the reintegration of offenders into society. In addition, the Chinese legislature emphasized positive general prevention in their legislative reasons.[89]

The statute of limitations for prosecution is also seen as beneficial for the judicial authorities, allowing them to focus on prosecuting current criminal cases and conserving social resources.[90] Recently, scholars have further explored the rationale for time limits on criminal prosecution from the perspective of the philosophy of time. This view suggests that the statute of limitations marks the temporal limit of

---

87 See Hebei Provincial Procuratorate WeChat Official Account (April 8, 2024), https://www.spp.gov.cn/zdgz/202404/t20240408_651102.shtml.

88 See *Mingkai Zhang*, Criminal Law, 6th ed. 2021, 830.

89 See *Aili Wang* (eds.), Explanation of the Criminal Code of the People's Republic of China: Legislative Reasons, and Relevant Provisions, 2021, 262: "From the perspective of repairing social relationships, the social relationships harmed by the crime tend to stabilize after a certain period of time. The emotions of the victims gradually calm down, and the criminals have new social lives and social relationships. In this situation, not prosecuting cases that meet the conditions may be more conducive to reducing social conflicts."

90 See *Mingxuan Gao* and *Kechang Ma* (eds.), Criminal Law, 10th ed. 2022, 305.

a crime's relevance as an unlawful act, suggesting that once this period has expired, the offense no longer constitutes a criminal act.[91]

In Vignette 9, the offense committed by D falls under Article 236 of the Chinese Criminal Code on rape. The basic offense of rape under Article 236(1) of the Chinese Criminal Code carries a maximum statutory penalty of less than ten years of fixed-term imprisonment, establishing a statute of limitations of 10 years. If it is determined that D's conduct constitutes the offense under Article 236(1) of the Chinese Criminal Code, there is no dispute that D should not be convicted.

By contrast, if it is established that the act of rape in the case contains one of the aggravated circumstances specified in Article 236(3) of the Chinese Criminal Code, D may be sentenced to more than ten years of fixed-term imprisonment, life imprisonment, or the death penalty.[92] In this case, the statute of limitations under Article 87(1) No.4 of the Chinese Criminal Code would apply, making the issue more complex.

For cases where "the maximum punishment prescribed is life imprisonment or the death penalty", Chinese criminal law adopts a model of principle with exceptions. In principle, prosecution is not allowed after 20 years. However, exceptions can be made by seeking approval from the Supreme People's Procuratorate for prosecution. According to the literal meaning of the provision, the exception provision in the second sentence of Article 87(1) No.4 of the Chinese Criminal Code is referred to as "approval of prosecution".

According to the official legislative reasons, the provision allowing "prosecution approval for cases where the maximum statutory penalty is life imprisonment or the death penalty, even if the statute of limitations has expired" plays a significant role in addressing deficiencies in the statute of limitations in special circumstances: "On the one hand, it adheres to the basic principles of the statute of limitations for prosecution, and on the other hand, it allows flexibility for practice. The Supreme People's Procuratorate can decide on approval based on factors such as the circumstances of the case and its social impact, thereby maximizing the criminal law's role in punishing crimes, balancing fairness and justice, and maintaining social stability."[93] According to prevailing interpretations, the situations in which the second sentence of Article 87(1) No.4 of the Chinese Criminal Code applies are limited to cases that are extremely socially harmful, where the offender poses a particularly high danger to society, where the social impact of the crime is extremely negative, and where

91 See *Gang Wang*, Systematic Interpretation of the Statute of Limitations in Criminal Proceedings, The Jurist 2021, Issue 4, 50–53.

92 According to Article 236(3) of the Chinese Criminal Code: "Whoever rapes a woman or has sexual intercourse with a girl under the age of 14 shall, in any of the following circumstances, be sentenced to fixed-term imprisonment of not less than 10 years, life imprisonment or death: (1) the circumstances being flagrant; (2) raping a number of women or girls under the age of 14; (3) raping a woman before the public in a public place; (4) raping a woman with one or more persons in succession; or (5) causing serious injury or death to the victim or any other serious consequences."

93 See *Aili Wang* (eds.), Explanation of the Criminal Code of the People's Republic of China: Legislative Reasons, and Relevant Provisions, 2021, 261.

the major crimes have not faded from public memory even after 20 years.[94] In practice, the Supreme People's Procuratorate considers only a very small number of cases as meeting the requirement for prosecution. Therefore, the exception provision in the second sentence of Article 87(1) No.4 of the Chinese Criminal Code should be regarded as a strict exception.[95]

Therefore, in Vignette 9, if D's conduct is determined to constitute aggravated rape under Article 236(3) of the Chinese Criminal Code, according to Article 87(1) No. 4 of the Chinese Criminal Code, D's offense committed in 1995 should not result in a conviction after 28 years. However, if the prosecuting authority deems it necessary to prosecute, an exception may be made to allow prosecution, provided that approval is obtained from the Supreme People's Procuratorate. However, this is highly unlikely in practice.

Vignette 10: Life Imprisonment without Parole

The Penal Code of State S provides for imprisonment for life as the maximum penalty for murder, but also authorizes the court to order an offender's early release after a minimum of 15 years if the offender is no longer dangerous. Reacting to cases of particularly heinous murders, the legislature of S wishes to introduce a penalty of life imprisonment without any possibility of early release, regardless of the offender's continued dangerousness. Would this amendment be acceptable?

Life imprisonment without parole was introduced by the 9th Amendment to the Chinese Criminal Code, which came into effect on November 1, 2015. Currently, life imprisonment without parole applies only to the crimes of embezzlement under Article 382 and bribery under Article 385 of the Chinese Criminal Code. According to Article 383(4) of the Chinese Criminal Code,

> If a convict sentenced to death with a reprieve under paragraph 1 falls under any circumstance listed in item (3) is sentenced to death with a reprieve, the people's court may, in light of the circumstances of the crime, commute the sentence to life imprisonment after the two-year period expires. In such cases, the convict shall not be eligible for commutation or parole.

According to the Chinese legislature, life imprisonment without parole is not an independent type of punishment, but rather a measure applied when a death penalty is warranted but not carried out. In this sense, life imprisonment without parole serves as an alternative measure to the death penalty.[96]

Although Chinese criminal law has explicitly introduced life imprisonment without parole, its legitimacy remains a subject of significant academic debate. Supporters of its introduction generally present two main arguments:

Firstly, life imprisonment without parole is beneficial in limiting the application of the death penalty. Scholars who support life imprisonment argue that those convicted of embezzlement and bribery, who are sentenced to a two-year suspension of execu-

94 See *Mingxuan Gao* and *Kechang Ma* (eds.), Criminal Law, 10th ed. 2022, 306.

95 See *Weizhong Shi et al.*, Investigation of Several Practical Issues in the Approval for Prosecution, People's Procuratorial Semimonthly 2016, Issue 10, 13.

96 See *Aili Wang* (eds.), Explanation of the Criminal Code of the People's Republic of China: Legislative Reasons, and Relevant Provisions, 2021, 1486.

tion followed by life imprisonment without parole, are offenders who might previously have been subject to immediate execution. Therefore, life imprisonment serves to restrict the use of the death penalty.[97] Additionally, including life imprisonment without parole as a substitute for the death penalty, along with a suspension of execution, can garner broad public support and acceptance, ultimately leading to the reduction, control, and even abolition of the death penalty.[98]

Furthermore, some scholars emphasize that life imprisonment without parole can fill a gap in the types of punishment. Life imprisonment with a suspension of execution is considered more severe than ordinary suspension of execution. For cases where a sentence of ordinary suspension of execution does not suffice to meet the principle of proportionality between crime and punishment, but where immediate execution of the death penalty is not appropriate, life imprisonment without parole effectively bridges the gap between suspension of execution and immediate execution of the death penalty.[99]

However, many scholars in the literature have criticized the introduction of life imprisonment without parole:

Firstly, some scholars criticize life imprisonment from a constitutional perspective. They argue that the establishment of life imprisonment without parole is contrary to the Constitution. Article 38 of the Chinese Constitution states, "The personal dignity of citizens shall not be infringed upon." Based on this, the state must respect individuals. However, life imprisonment without parole treats criminals merely as instruments of negative general deterrence. This approach not only deprives criminals of the humane treatment they deserve, which contradicts the trend toward more humane punishment, but also violates their inherent dignity.[100]

Secondly, scholars have also expressed negative opinions regarding the purpose of punishment. They point out that life imprisonment without parole contradicts this purpose. In terms of special prevention, since life imprisonment in China is only applicable to embezzlement and bribery crimes, it lacks the incentive for rehabilitation and deprives criminals of the possibility of reintegrating into society, thus diminishing its educational or corrective value. Moreover, in terms of recidivism, embezzlement and bribery criminals generally do not pose a risk of reoffending in these areas, nor are they likely to commit other serious crimes.[101] From the perspective of general

---

97 See *Xingliang Chen*, Judicial Interpretation of Embezzlement and Bribery Crimes: Interpretation of Criminal Law Doctrine, Law Science 2016, Issue 5, 77; *Bingzhi Zhao*, Legislative Control and Abolition of the Death Penalty for Embezzlement and Bribery Crimes in China: From the Perspective of the 9th Amendment to the Chinese Criminal Code, Modern Law Science 2016, Issue 1, 4.

98 See *Genlin Liang* and *Huawei Wang*, The Fate of Substitutes for the Death Penalty in China: Concepts, Models, and Practices, China Law Review 2020, Issue 5, 76.

99 See *Zhixiang Wang*, The Significance of the Introduction of Life Imprisonment System into Criminal Law, China Review of Administration of Justice 2019, Issue 3, 28.

100 See *Mingkai Zhang*, Circular Interpretation of the Constitution and Criminal Law, Law Review 2019, Issue 1, 25; *Guoxiang Sun*, Research on Embezzlement and Bribery Crimes, Vol. 2, 2018, 1219.

101 See *Hao Che*, Reflection on the Doctrine of Criminal Legislation: Analysis Based on the 9th Amendment to the Chinese Criminal Code, Law Science 2015, Issue 10, 8.

prevention, life imprisonment without parole represents a severe punishment. Whether making corrupt officials devise more sophisticated plans to evade prosecution or the existence of criminal networks, it reduces the certainty of punishment, ultimately leading to a counterproductive effect.[102]

Thirdly, scholars argue that those sentenced to life imprisonment without parole are completely deprived of the possibility of sentence reduction and parole. This will render the existing quantitative assessment and incentive mechanisms in Chinese prisons ineffective for these prisoners, greatly increasing the difficulty and burden of prison management.[103]

Finally, concerning its relationship with the death penalty, some scholars have pointed out that life imprisonment without parole cannot fulfill the intended role as a substitute for the death penalty, as expected by the Chinese legislature.[104] On the one hand, the application of life imprisonment is premised on the two-year suspension of execution for those convicted of serious embezzlement and bribery crimes. However, regardless of the criteria for application or its punitive effect, a two-year suspension of execution differs fundamentally from the immediate execution of the death penalty. Therefore, life imprisonment does not have a normative basis to serve as a substitute for the death penalty, including the suspension of execution, within the death penalty system. On the other hand, life imprisonment is attached to the suspension of execution of the death penalty and depends on the existence of the death penalty system. Logically, if the death penalty were abolished, life imprisonment without parole would no longer fulfill its intended role as a substitute for the death penalty. Without the death penalty, life imprisonment without parole would have no function.

Returning to Vignette 10, the introduction of life imprisonment without parole in the Chinese criminal law aims to reduce the application of the death penalty. Considering that the maximum punishment for murder under the Penal Code of State S is life imprisonment, this reasoning is not applicable to S. As a result, this amendment would likely be unacceptable to the majority of the Chinese criminal law academic community.

Conclusion

In summary, the responses to the ten "hard cases" in Chinese criminal law reveal significant variations in the evaluation of issues, even within a single country. This is particularly evident in matters such as lethal self-defense, the criminal responsibility of minors, and life imprisonment without parole. In terms of the temporal dimension, discussions on certain issues tend to lean towards liberalism, while others are more conservative. Some issues, however, are difficult to categorize within these frame-

---

102 See *Yuping Wu*, Review of the Legitimacy of Life Imprisonment, Law Science 2020, Issue 1, 80–81.

103 See *Yuhao Wu*, On Life Imprisonment as a Substitute for the Death Penalty, Global Law Review 2017, Issue 1, 144.

104 See *Yongqiang Zhang*, Legislative Reflection on the Substitute Function of Life Imprisonment for the Death Penalty, Modern Law Science 2020, Issue 2, 200–201.

works. As a result, it is difficult to determine the developmental trajectory of China's idea of criminal justice. Additionally, ongoing discussions on issues like the trolley problem, the use of torture for rescue to save a life, and the limits of consent have yet to produce definitive conclusions. In practice, the Chinese criminal law does not offer clear-cut answers to these questions, making it difficult to anticipate the criminal justice principles held by the legal system. Even within a single country, it is challenging to find a genuine concept of criminal justice, let alone a "universal criminal justice" on a global scale.

5. England and Wales

By *Sam J Cole**, *Steven Cammiss*** and *John J Child****

Vignette 1: Trolley Problem – Killing one Person to Save Many

Five young children are playing on railway tracks. An express train is approaching, and it is too late to stop the train before it hits the children, probably killing them. Operator D recognizes the emergency situation. He electronically flips a switch and thus deflects the train from its regular track to a little-used sidetrack. However, the lone repairman V is busy on the sidetrack, and the deflected train kills V, as D had anticipated. Is D criminally responsible for murder of V?

The so-called Trolley Problem is one that has exercised the minds of philosophers and legal theorists for many decades, having originated in the work of Philippa Foot in 1967.[1] The Vignette facts engage the classic version of that problem – in line with Foot's hypothetical – where D is the operator of the trolley.[2]

The theoretical context to the problem explores the difference between positive and negative duties, between acts and omissions. Foot claims that redirecting the trolley to kill the single person is morally permissible because *killing* one person is better than *killing* multiple people. This is referred to as the doctrine of double effect, where the lesser harm becomes permissible as a known side-effect of avoiding the greater evil. This can be contrasted with the hypothetical surgeon (D2), deciding whether to kill one innocent person in order to harvest his organs and save the life of multiple others who will die without a transplant. Such actions would not be permissible. The difference is that D2's choice is between *killing* one person and *letting* multiple others die: D2's negative duty not to do harm takes precedence. A central debate, therefore, is whether we should place such moral weight on the difference between positive and negative duties.[3]

The Trolley Problem has clear relevance to the substantive criminal law. This is most obvious in analogous medical cases, where doctors provide treatment that will necessarily shorten the life of their patient (and/or the removal of treatment, leading to death). In this medical context, something like a doctrine of double effect argument has been accepted by the courts, though uncertainty remains as to whether it

---

* Dr Sam J Cole, Assistant Professor in Criminal Justice, University of Birmingham.

** Dr Steven Cammiss, Associate Professor in Law, University of Birmingham.

*** Professor John J Child, Professor of Criminal Law, University of Birmingham.

1 P Foot, "The Problem with Abortion and the Doctrine of Double Effect" (1967) 5 *Oxford Review* 5.

2 For variations of the problem, see G Andrade, "Medical ethics and the trolley Problem" (2019) *J Med Ethics Hist Med* 12.

3 See J Rachels, "Killing and Letting Die", in: Lawrence C et al. (eds.) *Encyclopaedia of Ethics* (2nd ed., Routledge, 2001) 947.

should be understood as a denial of offending or as a new specific supervening defence.[4] As Lord Goff set out in *Bland*,

> It is this principle too which, in my opinion, underlies the established rule that a doctor may, when caring for a patient who is, for example, dying of cancer, lawfully administer painkilling drugs despite the fact that he knows that an incidental effect of that application will be to abbreviate the patient's life. Such a decision may properly be made as part of the care of the living patient, in his best interests; and, on this basis, the treatment will be lawful. Moreover, where the doctor's treatment of his patient is lawful, the patient's death will be regarded in law as exclusively caused by the injury or disease to which his condition is attributable.

The issue is whether, and to what extent, legal protections of this kind are available outside of the medical context.

a) Doctrinal Application

The first question is whether D commits the offence of murder. Liability for murder requires D's conduct to have caused V's death (actus reus), and for D to have acted with intent to kill or to cause grievous bodily harm (mens rea).[5] It is clear on the facts that D's action (flipping the switch) causes V's death in the relevant manner. Mens rea, however, may be more debatable. D does not directly intend V's death or grievous bodily harm in the sense of acting in order to bring it about;[6] though he may intend it obliquely. Oblique intention, as defined in *Woollin*, requires (i) the result to be virtually certain; (ii) D to foresee the result as virtually certain; and (iii) for the jury to find intention.[7] The first two limbs of this test are satisfied, but the final limb provides a form of "moral elbow room" for the jury choosing whether or not to find intention.[8] Note that this is a question of fact for the jury, and so we are not discussing the legal application of the doctrine of double effect. However, in deciding to find intention (or not) this form of moral reasoning is open to the jury.

On the basis that intention might be found, and thus murder committed, the next stage is to consider potential defences. There are three main options here, including duress, self-defence, and necessity, of which the defence of necessity is most promising for D.

Both duress and self-defence (otherwise known as the public and private defence) are unlikely on the facts. Duress of circumstances provides an excusatory defence where D offends to avoid circumstantial threats to life or of serious injury:[9] duress of circumstances would be an attractive option were V to have suffered non-fatal harms, but does not provide a defence to murder.[10] Self-defence provides a justifica-

---

4 See *Airedale NHS Trust v Bland* [1993] AC 789; note by Finnis, "*Bland:* Crossing the Rubicon?" (1993) 109 *LQR* 329.

5 *Cunningham* [1982] AC 566.

6 *Moloney* [1985] AC 905.

7 [1998] 4 All ER 103.

8 J Horder, "Intention in the Criminal Law – A Rejoinder" (1995) 58 *MLR* 678, 688.

9 *Willer* (1986) 83 Cr App R 225.

10 *Howe* [1987] 1 All ER 771.

tory defence where D uses force to protect her private or public interests:[11] self-defence may be arguable, as it can be used exceptionally to justify force on innocent parties; and a broad analogy could be drawn with the case of *Re A*,[12] where self-defence was discussed as a possible basis for defence in separating conjoined twins (i. e. where one twin would inevitably be killed in separation). However, it is difficult to see how the Trolley Problem can be modelled as an attack (in any sense) from V, such as to justify lethal force.

The defence of necessity applies (in theory at least) as a balance of evils defence at common law,[13] such that it may apply to the facts of the Trolley Problem. There remains some doubt whether necessity can apply as a defence to murder, though the better view is that it may do so in exceptional cases.[14] The difficulty is predicting which cases will be seen as sufficiently exceptional for the application of a defence that exists as something of an imperfect safety-net. The defence has the potential to apply expansively on a balance of evils test, but is one that is rarely applied (and with great reluctance) in practice.[15] There are few certainties with the English law of necessity, though it is likely to be D's best option in defence.

b) Widening Debate

The central debates at issue concern the meaning of oblique intention; the potential application of duress as a defence to murder; and the understanding of necessity. Each one has a long academic pedigree, and has remained somewhat intractable. One recent development has been a debate on the legal status of autonomous vehicles, including questions on how such vehicles should respond to Trolley Problem-style dilemmas.[16]

Vignette 2: Attribution of Death

> D intends to kill his neighbour V. Hidden near V's house, D waits for V and stabs him several times with a knife. V is taken to the hospital, where his wounds are treated. His injuries are not life-threatening and V is kept overnight for observation. During the night, a technical defect in the hospital kitchen leads to the outbreak of a fire, which kills V and other persons. Can D be held criminally responsible for V's death?

This Vignette focuses on questions of causation in the criminal law:[17] to be criminally responsible for V's death, the prosecution must prove that D *caused* V's death in the relevant way. Unfortunately, despite the centrality of causation to the application of all result crimes, its precise meaning remains contested and (varyingly) uncer-

---

11 Criminal Justice and Immigration Act 2008, s76.

12 [2000] 4 All ER 961.

13 See JJ Child et al., *Simester and Sullivan's Criminal Law* (8th ed., Hart, 2022) Ch 21.4.

14 See *Re A* [2000] 4 All ER 961.

15 See I Dennis, "On Necessity as a Defence to Crime" (2009) 3 *Crim L & Phil* 29.

16 See, e. g., R Jenkins et al. (eds.), *Autonomous Vehicle Ethics: The Trolley Problem and Beyond* (OUP, 2022).

17 See JJ Child et al., *Simester and Sullivan's Criminal Law* (8th ed., Hart, 2022) Ch 4.2.

tain.[18] This is particularly true for cases – such as that set out in the Vignette – where D's causal role may have been interrupted or usurped by a subsequent causal event (i. e. a so-called *novus actus interveniens*).

Where a potential *novus actus* arises, courts will typically focus on principles of foreseeability and voluntariness. In this way, the more foreseeable the intervention was, the more likely that it will *not* break the causal chain; and, where the intervention was involuntary or uninformed, again, the more likely that it will *not* break the causal chain. Despite the presence of causal principles however, their application is far from scientific, with considerable margin left to the jury in making a determination of causation. It is also notable that we see significant variation in the application of causal principles depending on the source of the intervention. The law will distinguish potential *novus actus* arising from (i) natural events; (ii) third-part interventions; (iii) victim's own interventions; and (iv) the defendant's own interventions.

In recent years, we have seen a series of challenging appeal cases engaging with third party and victim interventions. These include *Wallace*,[19] a case of euthanasia (in Belgium) following an acid attack by D, where it was held that D may be liable for V's death despite a very clear and voluntary intervention by doctors; and the case of *Field*,[20] where V's belief that he was drinking in the company of someone who loved him, when in fact D intended his death, was held by the court (when he drank himself to death) to indicate that V's drinking was not an informed choice. It is arguable that both cases were wrongly decided,[21] and they certainly add to the sense that policy reasons may be applied ahead of legal principle in the application of causation. Our present Vignette involves a "natural event", or at least a non-agential intervention, and so avoids many of the more problematic precedents. However, as we will see, there remains a degree of uncertainty.

a) Doctrinal Application

Focusing on D's potential responsibility for the death of V, we apply the offence of murder. It is highly likely that when stabbing V several times, D did so with an intention to kill or at least to cause grievous bodily harm (i. e. the mens rea for murder).[22] However, whilst mens rea is clear on the facts, it is less certain whether D's act (stabbing V) caused V's death in the manner required to fulfil the actus reus of the offence.

Causation is traditionally analysed across two limbs, factual and legal. Factual causation requires a mechanical connection between D's conduct and the result, often characterised as a "but for" test (i. e. but for D's conduct, would the result have come about).[23] In our Vignette, it is clear that *but for* D's conduct V would not have been in the hospital during the fire, and so D's conduct is a factual cause of V's death. Legal causation requires D's conduct to have played a significant role (un-

---

18 See, generally, HLA Hart and T Honoré, *Causation in the Law* (2nd ed., OUP, 1985).

19 [2018] EWCA Crim 690.

20 [2021] EWCA Crim 380.

21 See GR Sullivan and AP Simester, "Deadly Whisky" (2022) 138 *LQR* 11.

22 *Cunningham* [1982] AC 566.

23 *White* [1910] 2 KB 124.

derstood simply as more than *de minimis*);[24] and that D's conduct must have been independently blameworthy.[25] Both are straightforwardly satisfied on our facts. Beyond this, legal causation requires D's conduct to be an operative cause, meaning that it must be continuing at the time the result arises. It is here that we engage with potential *novus actus interveniens.*

D would argue that his conduct was not an operative cause of V's death, which was caused by the hospital fire as a (natural event) *novus actus.* There is much to be said for this argument. Although there is limited case law exploring natural event interventions, the lack of human agency allows us to focus on the causal principle of foreseeability without the complicating factor of additional voluntary/involuntary actors. And, on this basis, although courts have been willing to interpret the foreseeability principle broadly (particularly in medical intervention cases[26]) it is likely that a hospital fire would be found to be unforeseeable. This would mean that D is not causally responsible for V's death. This is supported by the case of *Bush v Commonwealth,*[27] where D was held not to have caused V's death following an infection V contracted in hospital. V was in hospital following an attack from D, but the risk of the particular infection (like the risk of fire in our Vignette) was not increased by V's presence in hospital.

For the prosecution, the task will be to prove that fires of this kind are more likely – and therefore more foreseeable – in hospital buildings. This seems unlikely to succeed. Alternatively, the prosecution may focus on an exception to the general rule, which suggests that even unforeseeable natural events may not be a *novus actus* when the ultimate result was *intended* by D.[28] Thus, for example, where D shoots to kill V in the mountains and misses, but the noise of the shot triggers an avalanche that kills V, D will be liable for causing death.[29] This rule may apply on our facts, but it will depend (i) on whether D intended the result (i. e. to kill V, beyond an intention to cause serious non-fatal injuries); and (ii) on whether the fire in the hospital is viewed as too remote from D's initial attack (i. e. the fire (unlike the avalanche) is not triggered by D's conduct, but occurs independently at a later point). The second of these concerns – we believe – is likely to undermine causation.

Where D does not cause V's death, he will be alternatively liable for attempted murder (if his intention was to kill),[30] or for causing grievous bodily harm with intent.[31]

24 *Cato* [1976] 1 All ER 260.

25 *Dalloway* (1847) 2 Cox CC 273.

26 See, e. g. *Cheshire* [1991] 3 All ER 670.

27 78 Ky 268 (1880).

28 *Michael* (1840) 9 C&P 356; *Demirian* [1989] VR 97, 113–114.

29 Example from JJ Child et al., *Simester and Sullivan's Criminal Law* (8th ed., Hart, 2022) 99–100.

30 Criminal Attempts Act, s1.

31 Offences Against the Person Act 1861, s18.

b) Widening Debate

The Vignette engages with a broad debate about theoretical and legal understandings of causation. In this regard, the Criminal Law Team within Law Commission of England and Wales produced a useful Working Paper in 2002, setting out options for the codification (and clarification) of principles of causation. The project, however, has not been taken forward since. More novel options for reform also appear periodically within the literature, with a particularly notable contribution more recently from Andrew Simester.[32]

Vignette 3: Torture to Save a Life

Kidnapper K has abducted an 8-year-old girl G and hidden her in a small cave in the woods. K is trying to extort money from G's parents for her release. The police manage to arrest K. Although being questioned for 24 hours, K steadfastly refuses to disclose where he hid G. Police officer D correctly assumes that G may soon die of thirst if she cannot be found. He therefore severely beats K to make him tell the truth. Fearing even more violence, K eventually leads the police to the cave, where they find G still barely alive. Should D be punished for torturing K?

The relevant offences here are straightforward and depend upon the extent of the injuries B sustains. If we assume that a severe beating encompasses serious bodily harm, then the relevant offence will likely be causing grievous bodily harm with intent.[33] The much more interesting question here concerns any likely defence available to D. Arguments could be made that the circumstances call into play the private defence of self-defence (where D uses force to defend himself *or another*)[34] and/or the public defence (where D uses force in the *prevention of crime*, or in effecting lawful arrest).[35] However, the more likely defence would be "duress of circumstances".[36] This defence has parallels with necessity, but has developed from the defence of duress by threats; as a consequence, the elements of the defence closely align with that of duress by threats and do not strictly follow the "balancing of harms" approach that is typically found in necessity defences.

For the defence of duress of circumstances to apply, the defendant needs to act to avert an imminent risk of death or serious injury[37] to herself or another for whom she can be expected to be responsible.[38] The risk of death or serious injury does not have

---

32 AP Simester, "Causation in (Criminal) Law" (2017) 133 *LQR* 416.

33 Offences against the Person Act 1861, s18.

34 This is a common law defence, but codified in section 76 of the Criminal Justice and Immigration Act 2008.

35 Criminal Law Act 1967, s3(1).

36 The courts regularly conflate these defences together given their similarities (see S Cammiss, G Hayes and B Doherty, "Necessity, Non-Violent Direct Activism, and the Stansted 15: Reasserting 'Hoffmann's Bargain'" 85(6) *Modern Law Review* 1515) – in that they are all based on versions of "self-help" – which, as we will see, is problematic, but it does mean that focusing upon one defence here – duress of circumstances – is realistic given the likely approach in practice.

37 *Hasan* [2005] UKHL 22; *Graham* [1982]1 WLR 294; *Conway* [1989] QB 290.

38 *Shayler* [2001] EWCA Crim 1977.

to be proven in fact; all that is required is that the defendant reasonably believes there is a risk of that kind.[39] Also, the actions of the defendant, in averting this risk, have to be such that a person of reasonable steadfastness, in the defendant's circumstances, might have similarly acted.[40] Under the heading of imminence, the courts have withdrawn the defence when alternative methods exist which regulate the defendant's activity. For instance, the courts have denied duress of circumstances in protest cases, arguing that the risks the defendant claims to avert are not imminent, in part because there are legal and political avenues open to protesters.[41] Similarly, the Court of Appeal ruled that duress of circumstances was not available as a defence to the possession of controlled substances when used for pain relief, *inter alia*, because the possession of these substances is subject to a legal regime.[42]

a) Doctrinal Application

As noted above, the offence here is straightforward; if serious injury has been caused, it will be difficult for D to claim this was not intentional, given the controlled circumstances of the beating and the motive for doing so. What matters is whether the defence of duress of circumstances or of self-defence applies.

There is little doubt that D acts due to a reasonable belief that G is at risk of death or serious injury. Similarly, following *Shayler*,[43] we can say that D acts to avert the risk from someone for whom he is expected to be responsible; G is an identified individual and D's law enforcement role means he has a duty, under Article 2 of the ECHR, to take positive steps to ensure her safety.[44] One could question whether the reasonably steadfast person would respond to this threat as D does, if we ask the question, is it ever reasonable to respond to a threat with torture, given this is a clear violation of Article 3 of the ECHR? However, as this defence grew out of duress, which is regarded as a concession to human frailty,[45] then the question of reasonableness will take into account the unenviable position that D is in. Ultimately, however, this is a question for the jury.

The difficult question for assessing the applicability of the defence is imminence. For the defence of duress by threats, the courts have tightened this requirement in more recent decisions.[46] While some commentators have suggested that the imminence requirement for duress of circumstances is applied more flexibly,[47] as noted above, the courts are prone to withdraw duress of circumstances when there is a legal

---

39 *Safi and others* [2003] EWCA Crim 1809.

40 *Graham* [1982]1 WLR 294.

41 *Thacker and ors* [2021] EWCA Crim 97. For commentary, see S Cammiss, G Hayes and B Doherty, "Necessity, Non-Violent Direct Activism, and the Stansted 15: Reasserting 'Hoffmann's Bargain'" 85(6) *Modern Law Review* 1515.

42 *Quayle* [2005] EWCA Crim 1415.

43 [2001] EWCA Crim 1977.

44 *LCB v UK* (1998) 27 EHRR 212.

45 *Howe* [1987] 1 All ER 771; *Hasan* [2005] UKHL 22.

46 See *Hasan* [2005] UKHL 22.

47 S Kyd et al., *Clarkson and Keating: Criminal Law* (10th ed., Sweet and Maxwell, 2020) 456.

regime which regulates the defendant's activities (in the case of the possession of controlled drugs for pain relief) or there is an alternative means of averting the risk (legal and democratic means of complaint in protest cases). Here, police custody and the questioning of suspects is subject to legal regulation under the Police and Criminal Evidence Act 1984 and numerous associated and detailed Codes of Practice. Furthermore, as already indicated, the prohibition of torture is an absolute right under Article 3 of the ECHR and the courts have clearly ruled that torture is not permissible.[48] As a consequence, it is likely that the risk will be held to not be imminent.

Self-defence is similarly likely to not apply due to the reasons advanced above; the clear breach of the suspect's rights under the Police and Criminal Evidence Act 1984 and the prohibition of torture under Article 3 are such that the amount of force used was unreasonable.

b) Widening Debate

This Vignette displays the problems with the conflation of the defences of necessity, duress of circumstances and public defence noted above. This is regarded as problematic as these defences have different underlying rationales: duress of circumstances takes an excusatory form, while the public defence and necessity are justificatory in nature. This has implications for how these defences develop. For instance, the essence of necessity is not imminent threats, but rather a situation of emergency.[49] In drawing upon an excusatory framework from duress, the courts have restricted the full development of a necessity type defence. We see this in the Vignette (and elsewhere) in the problem of finding "imminence", but in other cases the restriction of averting a risk of death or serious injury could lead to a lack of a defence where one is normatively justified.

But this Vignette also evidences the courts' reluctance to expand the reach of necessity defences. As was stated by Edmund Davis LJ in *Southwark LBC v Williams*:[50]

> The law regards with the deepest suspicion any remedies of self-help, and permits those remedies to be resorted to only in very special circumstances. The reason for such circumspection is clear – necessity can very easily become simply a mask for anarchy.

In this Vignette, to allow a necessity defence would be to allow the defendant to ignore the absolute prohibition on torture which would conflict with judicial practice in areas such as the exclusion of improperly obtained evidence.

Vignette 4: Lethal Self-Defence

R, a well-trained young man armed with a knife, accosts 50-year-old D, who is on her way home from a party in the early morning hours. R threatens her with the knife and takes away her purse filled with 500 € and her wristwatch worth 1,000 €. As R turns to run away, D draws a pistol she is secretly carrying in her

---

48 See *A v Secretary of State for the Home Department (No 2)* [2005] UKHL 71 on the exclusion of evidence obtained by torture, whether obtained within the UK or overseas by agents of other states.

49 See *Re A (Children)* [2000] 4 All ER 961.

50 [1971] Ch 734, 745–746.

jacket, and shoots and kills R in order to retrieve her property. Is D guilty of murder?

The Vignette is concerned with the public and private defence, commonly referred to as self-defence, and particularly the thresholds for excessive force in defence. The public and private defence provides a complete defence to any charge where D uses otherwise unlawful force to protect her public or private interests. Although often treated as a single defence, it is useful to recognise that it comes from the amalgamation of two overlapping defences: the private defence developed at common law, providing a defence where D uses force to protect herself or another from physical harm,[51] or in the protection of property;[52] and the public defence, set out in section 3 of the Criminal Law Act 1967, providing a defence where D uses force to prevent a crime, or in effecting or assisting a lawful arrest.

There will be cases where only one of the two applies. However, in the majority of cases, both defences will apply simultaneously, as with the Vignette facts. The upshot of this has been a progressive alignment of the defence requirements, to the extent now that the defences are best analysed as a single public and private defence. This alignment has been ongoing for many years within the common law, and has been codified within section 76 of the Criminal Justice and Immigration Act 2008 (CJIA).

76. Reasonable Force for Purposes of Self-Defence etc.

(1) This section applies where in proceedings for an offence –

(a) an issue arises as to whether a person charged with the offence ("D") is entitled to rely on a defence within subsection (2), and

(b) the question arises whether the degree of force used by D against a person ("V") was reasonable in the circumstances.

(2) The defences are –

(a) the common law defence of self-defence; and

(aa) the common law defence of defence of property; and

(b) the defences provided by section 3(1) of the Criminal Law Act 1967 [...] (use of force in prevention of crime or making arrest).

(3) The question whether the degree of force used by D was reasonable in the circumstances is to be decided by reference to the circumstances as D believed them to be [...]

(4) If D claims to have held a particular belief as regards the existence of any circumstances –

(a) the reasonableness or otherwise of that belief is relevant to the question whether D genuinely held it; but

(b) if it is determined that D did genuinely hold it, D is entitled to rely on it for the purposes of subsection (3), whether or not –

---

51 *Duffy* [1967] 1 QB 63.

52 Note that where D damages property to protect other property, this is governed by the Criminal Damage Act 1971, s5(2)(b).

(i) it was mistaken, or

(ii) (if it was mistaken) the mistake was a reasonable one to have made.

[...]

Where no exclusion applies, the public and private defence requires the satisfaction of two core elements, usefully characterised as trigger and response. (i) Trigger: D must have believed (subjective) that force was immediately required in order to protect her public or private interests; and (ii) Response: the amount of force used by D must have been reasonable (objective) on the facts as she believed them to be. After D has raised the defence, the legal burden is on the prosecution to prove beyond reasonable doubt that the elements of the defence are not satisfied.[53]

a) Doctrinal Application

It is likely that D commits the offence of murder on the facts of the Vignette. The actus reus of murder is clear, with D's conduct (shooting) the cause of V's death. The mens rea of murder requires D to have acted with intent to cause death or grievous bodily harm.[54] Such an intention is not stated categorically in the facts of the Vignette, though it is extremely likely that when shooting V in a manner that caused death, D was acting with *at least* the intention to cause grievous bodily harm. The fact that D's primary aim was to retrieve her property will not undermine this mens rea, as long as causing serious harm was perceived as a means to that end or as a virtually certain consequence of it.[55]

Moving to the application of the public and private defence, it is clear that D uses force to protect her public and private interests (i. e. both protection of property and effecting arrest). In this manner, the subjective trigger limb of the public and private defence is likely to be satisfied. Having established that the use of *some force* may be necessary however, we must now consider whether the degree of force used by D in response was objectively reasonable. This is ultimately a question of fact for the jury.[56] But, in making that determination, the law is clear that the objective assessment should be made on the basis of the facts as D subjectively believed them to be, and that a margin of appreciation should be acknowledged where D (as in our facts) is acting in a pressured and stressful situation.[57] It is also important to note that we are assessing the degree of *force* employed by D and not the degree of *harm* caused; so a reasonable level of force in defence does not become unreasonable simply because it results in unforeseeable levels of harm to V.[58]

Despite these caveats, it is likely that D's response (shooting and killing V) will be judged as excessive, undermining the defence. Where D is acting in defence of property – as we are told in the Vignette – it will rarely, if ever, be reasonable to employ

---

53 *O'Brian* [2004] EWCA Crim 2900.

54 *Cunningham* [1982] AC 566.

55 *Woollin* [1998] 4 All ER 103.

56 *AG's Reference (No 1 of 1975)* [1976] 2 All ER 937, 947.

57 *Palmer* [1971] AC 814; codified within the CJIA, s76(7).

58 *Keane* [2010] EWCA Crim 2514; *Noye* [2011] EWCA Crim 650, [9] and [55].

deadly force. Indeed, to allow the defence in these circumstances would likely contravene Article 2 of the European Convention on Human Rights, even if the property preserved was priceless in terms of culture and heritage. Although Article 2 allows certain derogations from V's right to life in circumstances of self-defence, there is no provision for the protection of property. Thus, on the facts of the Vignette, the protection of personal property will not suffice.[59]

Where D's use of force is found to be excessive (i. e. not reasonable) the public and private defence will not be available. From here, D may wish to raise one of the partial defences to murder (Loss of Self-Control or Diminished Responsibility), but neither are likely on the facts. English law does not recognise a defence – complete or partial – of excessive self-defence.[60]

b) Widening Debate

Debates about excessive self-defence are perennial, both as a potential complete and/or a partial defence.[61] Interestingly, where this has gained most traction has been in the context of (at least partial) defence of property, where homeowners use excessive force to repel a home invasion. The so-called householder defence was added to English law as an amendment to the CJIA in 2013,[62] allowing the public and private defence in this context where D uses disproportionate force (i.e. as long as force was not grossly disproportionate).[63] The merits of this reform however, including its relationship with Article 2 ECHR rights, remain contested.[64]

Vignette 5: Criminal Responsibility of Subordinates for Systemic Offences

D is a soldier in the army of a country ruled by a junta of generals who have come to power through a violent coup. When an opposition group demands the return to a democratic system, the government orders the soldiers to shoot and kill any person who resists arrest. Following this order, D kills three young men who take part in a protest demonstration and hit a police officer who tries to arrest them. When D is tried after a change of regime, he says that he did not like to shoot the protesters but that he thought that he had to obey his commanders' orders. D knew that if he had refused to shoot, he might have been demoted, but no physical harm would have occurred to him. Should D be convicted of murder? If so, should his sentence be mitigated because of his situation?

---

59 The only potential route to acquittal via the public and private defence, it seems, will be if D's use of force (shooting V) caused death unintentionally, and in unforeseeable circumstances. E. g. where D shot V in the leg to prevent his escape only, but V died unexpectedly. This possibility is not implied however in the Vignette.

60 *Clegg* [1995] 1 All ER 334.

61 See J Stannard, "In the Spirit of Compromise: The Irish Doctrine of Excessive Defence", in: A Reed and M Bohlander (eds.), *General Defences in Criminal Law* (Routledge, 2014) 171.

62 CJIA 2008, s75(5 A).

63 *Ray* [2017] EWCA Crim 1391.

64 See M Dsouza, "Understanding the 'Householder Defence': Proportionality and Reasonableness in Defensive Force" (2016) 75 *CLJ* 192.

The offence of murder in England and Wales is to kill another with either an intention to kill or to cause grievous bodily harm. The only possible defences available here would be the defence of superior orders, the prevention of crime, or duress.

While likely *obiter*, the House of Lords in *Clegg* confirmed that no defence of superior orders exists in the law of England and Wales.[65]

The defence of prevention of crime is a statutory defence in England and Wales,[66] which overlaps with the law on self-defence.[67] The prevention of crime defence allows for the use of "such force as is reasonable in the circumstances in the prevention of crime, or in effecting or assisting in the lawful arrest of offenders or suspected offenders".[68] Self-defence applies where the defendant acts to defend himself *or another* and the use of force is both subjectively necessary and reasonably proportionate.

Duress applies where the defendant reasonably believes that she has been threatened by another with death or serious injury (i.e. to herself, or to another for whom she is expected to be responsible), unless she commits a specified offence; and D's actions in committing the offence are reasonable in the circumstances.

a) Doctrinal Application

The attribution of criminal liability in this Vignette is relatively straightforward: the defendant kills the protester and, as was ordered, likely did so with an intention to kill; but even if this was not present, it would be difficult for the defendant to argue that there was no intention to cause grievous bodily harm. There is also no likely defence. There is no defence of superior orders; prevention of crime and self-defence will not be available as the use of force was clearly disproportionate and therefore unreasonable in the circumstances; and duress does not apply as a defence to murder. As there is no applicable defence, this would be a straightforward case of murder.

b) Widening Debate

The House of Lords in *Clegg*[69] provided no justification for the denial of a defence of superior orders, other than to point to historic[70] and commonwealth precedents.[71] In *Hayden*, the High Court of Australia justified as the denial of a superior orders defence on the ground that:[72]

> It is fundamental to our legal system that the executive has no power to authorise a breach of the law and that it is no excuse for an offender to say that he acted under the orders of a superior [...]

---

65 [1995] 1 AC 482.

66 Criminal Law Act 1967, s3.

67 Criminal Justice and Immigration Act 2008, s76.

68 Criminal Law Act 1967, s3(1).

69 [1995] 1 AC 482.

70 *Thomas* (1816) 4 M&S 448.

71 *Hayden (No 2)* (1984) 156 CLR 532; *Yip Chiu-Cheung* [1995] 1 AC 111.

72 Ibid, 540.

This approach has been referenced as an important and longstanding[73] constitutional principle, holding that public officials are not able to authorise or excuse any acts which are unlawful.[74] Consequently, in *Yip Chiu-Cheung*, the Privy Council held that this would even apply to an undercover drugs officer who participated in a criminal conspiracy to export controlled drugs, who would only evade liability due to the exercise of prosecutorial discretion.

The denial of a superior orders defence has raised little debate in England and Wales. It has been claimed that the law currently places junior soldiers in an unenviable position of having to decide between obeying what could be an unlawful order or being court-marshalled for refusing to obey what could be a lawful order.[75] But these arguments have little traction on the facts of the Vignette, for two reasons: the defendant does not fear physical harm, only demotion, which would not place the defendant in an overly difficult position; and the order, given its disproportionality, as discussed above, could not be regarded as "arguably" lawful.

The defences of duress, self-defence and prevention of crime have been examined for completeness. For self-defence and the prevention of crime, there is some debate as to whether disproportionate actions should be covered by the defence; the law has been amended in a manner that suggests that disproportionate, but not grossly disproportionate, self-defence in householder cases would not necessarily lead to conviction.[76] But this has been described as a controversial reform.[77]

Vignette 6: Limits of Consent

> V is a 21-year-old ambitious athlete and short-distance runner. He has learned that certain artificial limbs can enhance a runner's speed. He decides that he would rather have an artificial limb instead of his right lower leg. He approaches D, a surgeon in private practice, and asks him to amputate his leg below the knee and replace it with an artificial limb. D complies with V's request. Should D be punished for mayhem?

Mayhem is a common law offence, applicable where D mutilates himself or another person in a manner that would make V unfit to fight for his country.[78] It was applied, historically, where D "a young strong and lustie rogue, to make himself impotent, thereby to have the more colour to begge or to be relieved without putting himself to any labour, caused his companion to strike off his left hand";[79] and in Victorian times, where D (a soldier) had a dentist remove his front teeth to avoid a drill in which soldiers were required to bite cartridges.[80] The status of mayhem within the current law is unclear, and the Law Commission has recommended that it should

73 Stretching back to *Entick v Carrington* (1765) 19 St Tr 1029.

74 JJ Child et al., *Simester and Sullivan's Criminal Law* (8th ed., Hart, 2022).

75 Ibid.

76 Criminal Justice and Immigration Act 2008, s76(5 A) and s76(6).

77 JJ Child et al., *Simester and Sullivan's Criminal Law* (8th ed., Hart, 2022).

78 W Blackstone, *Commentaries on the Laws of England* (1st ed. 1765–1769) vol. 4, 205.

79 E Coke, 1604, Co 1 Inst, 127a and b.

80 J Stephen, *A Digest of the Criminal Law* (3rd ed., Macmillan, 1883) 142.

be expressly abolished.[81] In its place, prosecutors will apply the common law offences of assault and battery; and the statutory offences contained within the Offences Against the Person Act 1861 (OAPA).

The current law recognises a ladder of offences, with increasing harms and culpability. The principal offences are: assault and battery, where D intentionally or recklessly applies any unlawful force, or causes V to apprehend imminent application of such force; section 47 OAPA, where D's assault or battery results in actual bodily harm; section 20 OAPA, where D causes grievous bodily harm or a wound, intending or being reckless as to causing some harm to V; and section 18 OAPA, where D causes grievous bodily harm or a wound, intending to cause grievous bodily harm.[82] It is the last of these – section 18, causing grievous bodily harm with intent – that is most relevant to the Vignette.

Regarding consent, there is an ongoing debate whether consent should be understood as a defence to offences within the ladder, or whether non-consent should be understood as an element of each offence.[83] The dominant view however, echoed by a bare majority of the Lords in *Brown*, is that consent should be applied as a defence.[84] To establish consent, it must be demonstrated (i) that V agreed to the harm/ risk of harm in fact;[85] (ii) that V's consent was effective, in the sense that it was informed, made freely, and V had capacity to consent; and (iii) that, where actual or grievous harm was caused, the conduct consented to fell within one of the permissible categories identified in *Brown*. Those categories include surgery; certain forms of body modification; religious flagellation; sports; horseplay; and (in extremely limited circumstances) sexual gratification. Where consent is established, D will be acquitted.

a) Doctrinal Application

It is clear that D commits a section 18 offence, causing grievous bodily harm or wounding with intent. Amputating V's leg below the knee would certainly constitute grievous bodily harm (as well as wounding); and there is no question regarding D's intention to do so. The central issue for liability is whether V consents and is permitted to consent in law.

The first two requirements for consent appear to be met: V has expressly communicated consent to D, and V is acting (apparently) with full knowledge and understanding of what he is consenting to. The third requirement however – that the activity falls within a permitted category – is less certain.

---

81 Law Commission, *Reforming Offences Against the Person* (Law Com No 361, 2015), clause 23 of the draft bill.

82 See, generally, JJ Child et al., *Simester and Sullivan's Criminal Law* (8th ed., Hart, 2022) Ch 11.

83 See S Shute, "Something Old, Something New, Something Borrowed: Three Aspects of the Project" [1996] *Crim LR* 684.

84 [1994] AC 212. Lord Jauncey, Lord Lowry, and Lord Templeman analysed consent as a defence; Lord Mustill and Lord Slynn considered non-consent as part of the offence.

85 I.e., that consent was expressly or implicitly communicated to D.

Perhaps the most obvious category would be body modification, akin to lawful activities such as tattooing and piercing. However, case law within this category suggests that more extreme forms of modification, akin to surgery, will not be covered. In *BM*,[86] D (a professional piercer and tattooist) began performing more extreme forms of body modification, including the removal of an ear, the removal of a nipple, and tongue splitting. It was not disputed that each V (customer) consented in fact to the procedures, but nevertheless, D's convictions for section 18 offences were upheld on appeal.

D would therefore look to justify his conduct within the surgical category for consent. This was not possible in *BM*, in part because the defendant in that case was not medically qualified. D within the Vignette, in contrast, is a surgeon in private practice. It is clear, within the surgical category, that non-essential forms of surgery (i. e. cosmetic surgeries) may be permissible.[87] However, the limits to this – if there are limits – are far from clear. It is notable, for example, that the Court of Appeal in *BM* highlighted both D's lack of medical expertise *as well as* the status of the modifications as "extreme cosmetic surgery".[88] The implication here is that certain forms of cosmetic surgery, even if performed by a medical professional, may fall outside permitted categories of consent. The degree of legal uncertainty here is, of course, entirely unsatisfactory.[89]

b) Widening Debate

Despite being governed by a statute from 1861, the prospect of reform to the non-fatal offences remains a distant one. This is not for want of trying. Since 1980, there have been no fewer than six law reform documents on non-fatal offending published by various government bodies, culminating with the most recent Law Commission report in 2015.[90] However, despite wide ranging critique of the current law – on grounds of fairness, coherence, clarity, and language – successive governments have chosen (for now at least) not to take recommendations for reform forward into legislation.

The Law Commission's 2015 report is notable also because, in an effort to make its recommendations more attractive, the Commission chose to focus on offences only (i. e. severing the issue of consent). This was an understandable, but equally regrettable move. The defence of consent, as we have seen above, represents one of the most complex and problematic aspects of the current law, and so reform and clarification here should be a priority. For the Commission, this is now left within a separate project exploring consent more generally, which has been stalled since 1995.[91]

---

86 [2018] EWCA Crim 560.

87 Discussed in *Corbett v Corbett* [1971] P 83.

88 *BM* [2018] EWCA Crim 560, [37].

89 See S Pegg, "Not So Clear Cut: The Lawfulness of Body Modifications" [2019] *Crim LR* 579; R Williams, "Body Modification and the Limits of Consent to Injury" (2019) 135 *LQR* 19; R Clement, "Consent to Body Modification in Criminal Law" (2018) *CLJ* 451.

90 Law Commission, *Reforming Offences Against the Person* (Law Com No 361, 2015).

91 Law Commission, *Consent and Offences Against the Person* (Consultation No 134, 1995).

Vignette 7: Withdrawal from an Attempt

25-year-old D is deeply upset with her former boyfriend V, who had ended their relationship to be with another woman. To punish V, D plans to stab him with a large knife. D knows that the stab wounds can be fatal and accepts V's death as a possible outcome. When V goes jogging, D attacks him from behind and stabs him in the back three times. V breaks down. D realises that she has injured him but that the injuries will not cause his death. She realises that she could kill him by stabbing him again but decides to leave him alone. Should D be punished for attempted murder?

Liability for attempts within England and Wales is governed by the Criminal Attempts Act 1981, which provides that a person is guilty of an attempt "if, with intent to commit an offence [...] a person does an act which is more than merely preparatory to the commission of an offence".[92] The courts have interpreted the actus reus to require that the defendant must have "embarked on the crime proper",[93] while the state of mind required is to intend the full substantive offence, with intention bearing the same meaning as elsewhere in the criminal law.[94] There is no stand-alone definition of intent for attempts; intention is, therefore, defined as the defendant's purpose in acting, or where the consequence is foreseen by the defendant as virtually certain to result from her actions the jury are entitled to find intention.[95]

In England and Wales, there is no "defence" of abandonment or renunciation of a criminal purpose for attempts liability.[96] Once the defendant has committed, with the required intention, an act which is more than merely preparatory to the commission of the principal offence, the elements of the attempt offence have been satisfied and any renunciation of a criminal purpose is only relevant in mitigation.

To summarise, to be guilty of attempted murder, D must, while intending to kill, complete an act which is more than merely preparatory to the commission of murder; and any renunciation of criminal purpose, if these elements are satisfied, will not provide for a "defence".

a) Doctrinal Application

While the question of whether the defendant has committed "an act which is more than merely preparatory" is a question for the jury, on the facts of the Vignette it seems likely that D has satisfied the actus reus, given she has stabbed V three times; this is clearly, "embarking on the crime proper". Similarly, her decision to "leave him alone", whilst evidence of a renunciation of an intention to kill, can be dealt with simply: it is not relevant to her completion of the actus reus, or her corresponding mens rea at that point in time. Essentially, if she "embarked on the crime proper" with an intention to kill, she will be liable for attempted murder.

---

92 Section 1(1).

93 *Gullefer* (1990) 91 Cr App R 356. The court rejected previous common law "tests" such as a "proximity" test or a "last act" requirement and held that the Act was a substantive reform of the common law.

94 *Walker and Hayles* (1990) 90 Cr App R 226; *Hayles* [2005] EWCA Crim 1118.

95 *Woollin* [1999] 1 AC 82. Cf. JJ Child and A Hunt, "Beyond the Present-Fault Paradigm: Expanding Mens Rea Definitions in the General Part" (2022) 42(2) *OJLS* 438.

96 *Haughton v Smith* [1975] AC 476.

Liability, therefore, falls on whether she has an intention to kill. As noted, intention for attempts bears the same meaning as it does elsewhere in the criminal law; a jury can find a defendant guilty of attempted murder if causing death was her purpose or if she foresaw death as a virtually certain outcome of her actions. Here, the defendant knows "that stab wounds *can* be fatal" and she "accepts V's death as a *possible* outcome".[97] This suggests that death is not her purpose and that her foresight of death as a possible outcome falls short of the requirement of a *virtual certainty.* As a result, she is unlikely to be convicted of attempted murder. Liability will, however, likely fall within wounding with an intent to cause grievous bodily harm,[98] which carries a maximum sentence of life imprisonment.

b) Widening Debate

Largely in response to conflicting decisions of the Court of Appeal in *Khan*[99] and *Pace and Rogers*,[100] recent academic commentary on the law of attempt in England and Wales has focused upon the requirement that the defendant intend the substantive offence when this offence includes a state of mind requirement less than intention (such as recklessness) for relevant circumstances.[101] In contrast, there has been relatively little commentary on the two issues raised in this Vignette: the state of mind requirement for criminal attempts and the lack of a defence for abandonment or renunciation of criminal purpose.

On the state of mind requirement for attempts, the current law is uncontroversial. Reform proposals have called for narrowing the definition of intention to purpose only, as this fits with a semantic interpretation of attempting as it being the actor's purpose. The Law Commission, however, has rejected this proposed reform, stating that it is satisfied with the current state of the law and noting that it would be inappropriate for intention to be interpreted differently for attempts, and that "consultees were in broad agreement".[102] Child and Hunt have challenged that position, arguing that mens rea definitions cannot be applied to ulterior (future) offence elements in the same way that they are applied to present circumstances and results, and calling for definitional reform wherever mens rea terms are applied to future conduct events (e.g. in the context of incomplete attempts; conspiracy; assisting and encouraging; complicity; and so on).[103] This argument does not, however, engage with complete attempts (such as the facts of the Vignette).

---

97 Emphasis added.

98 Offences against the Person Act, 1861, s18.

99 [1990] 1 WLR 813.

100 [2014] EWCA Crim 186. See, for example, JJ Child and A Hunt, "*Pace and Rogers* and the *Mens Rea* of Criminal Attempt: *Khan* on the Scrapheap?" (2014) *JCL* 220.

101 See, for instance, the offence of rape, which requires (simplifying somewhat) an intention to have sexual intercourse (the relevant act) while lacking a reasonable belief that the complainant consents (relevant circumstances).

102 Law Commission, *Conspiracy and Attempts* (Law Com No 318, 2009) [8.92].

103 JJ Child and A Hunt, "Beyond the Present-Fault Paradigm: Expanding Mens Rea Definitions in the General Part" (2022) 42(2) *OJLS* 438.

On the question of whether withdrawal should be a defence for attempts, the Law Commission considered this in its report which led to the enactment of the Criminal Attempts Act 1981.[104] A defence of withdrawal was rejected by the Commission, as the offence provides for an opportunity for the police to intervene in an early stage of criminal actions. This rationale was reasserted by the Law Commission in 2009, although only when discussing conspiracy and not attempts liability.[105] Other authors have also pointed out that a renunciation of a criminal purpose can only truly excuse when the defendant has engaged in a voluntary abandonment, and that this raises important questions on how to prove voluntariness.[106] Duff provides an account of attempts that should aim to criminalise those attempts where the defendant's acts constitute a direct attack upon the interests of the victim; in those instances, a withdrawal after a "complete" attempt, even though short of the substantive offence, still constitutes an attack on the victim.[107] In these circumstances, punishment is still justified. The case for reform here – creating a defence of withdrawal – continues to arise in the literature,[108] but remains unlikely to succeed.

Vignette 8: Criminal Responsibility of Minors

D is a 13-year-old boy. He abducts and rapes V, a girl of the same age. Should D be punished for a criminal offence?

The age of criminal responsibility in England and Wales is 10.[109] Therefore, all children from the age of 10 are *prima facie* ascribed criminal capacity.[110] The vast majority of sexual offences in English criminal law are contained within the Sexual Offences Act 2003 (SOA 2003). Certain offences within the Act can only be committed against victims, or by defendants, of a certain age. However, owing to the comparatively low age of criminal responsibility in England and Wales, a number of very serious offences, such as Rape (section 1), and rape of a child under 13 (section 5), can be committed by defendants aged 10 and over.

The offence of rape requires (i) intentional penile penetration of the vagina, anus or mouth of another person (V); (ii) that person (V) does not consent to the penetration; and (iii) that the defendant (D) does not reasonably believe that V consents. The complainant's non-consent is defined across three sections. Section 76 sets out "conclusive presumptions" of non-consent;[111] where these are proven by the prosecution, this

---

104 Law Commission, *Attempt, and Impossibility in Relation to Attempt, Conspiracy and Incitement* (Law Com No 102, 1980) [2.133].

105 Law Commission, *Conspiracy and Attempts* (Law Com No 318, 2009).

106 M Wasik, "Abandoning Criminal Intent" [1980] *Crim LR* 785.

107 RA Duff, *Criminal Attempts* (OUP, 1997).

108 E.g. S Eldar, "Reforming the Law of Criminal Attempt: Take Two", in: JJ Child and RA Duff (eds.), *Criminal Law Reform Now* (Hart, 2021) Ch3.

109 Children and Young Persons Act 1933, s50, as substituted by s16(1) Children and Young Persons Act 1963.

110 D Hamer and T Crofts, "The Logic and Value of the Presumption of *Doli Incapax* (Failing That, an Incapacity Defence)" (2023) 43(3) *OJLS* 546.

111 See SOA 2003, s76(2).

will establish non-consent, and that D did not reasonably believe that V consented.[112] Section 75 sets out "evidential presumptions"; these presumptions can be rebutted by D where they adduce "evidence beyond the fanciful or speculative"[113] that could create a reasonable doubt about the prosecution's claim. Finally, section 74 sets out the general definition of consent, stating that "a person consents if they agree by choice and have the freedom and capacity to make that choice". The general definition is useful, but the concepts contained within the section (i. e. choice; freedom; capacity) are not further defined in the statute.[114]

The SOA 2003 also contains several separate offences which can apply to victims and defendants of certain ages. These include:

- *Sections 5–8:* Sexual offences against complainants aged 12 and under. These offences do not require the prosecution to prove non-consent, nor that D reasonably believed that V consented, creating a form of strict liability based upon V's age.[115]
- *Sections 9–12:* Offences by adults (aged 18 and over) who offend against children under 16 – currently the age of sexual consent. This includes a broader range of criminalised conduct, including "sexual activity with a child", encompassing intentional sexual touching.[116] Again, the age of the complainant shapes the structure of the offence – if the relevant offence elements are present, and the complainant is under 13, the offence is complete; however, if V is aged 13–15, the prosecution must then prove that D did not reasonably believe V was 16 or over.
- *Section 13:* Criminalises the same conduct as sections 9–12, but for defendants aged 17 and under. The main difference here is the maximum sentence which can be handed down.

All criminal cases involving those under the age of 18 begin in the youth court, where there is a legal presumption in favour of the court retaining the case.[117] However, if the case constitutes a grave crime, and there is a realistic prospect that the defendant would be handed a custodial sentence substantially exceeding two years if convicted, then the case can be committed to the Crown Court for trial.[118] Both offences under section 1 and section 13 SOA 2003 constitute grave crimes and may therefore be referred to the Crown Court – in essence, an adult court with trial by jury.[119] If committed to the Crown Court, children are entitled to a number of modifi-

---

112 SOA 2003, s76(1).

113 *Ciccarelli* [2011] EWCA Crim 2665.

114 P Rook and R Ward, *Rook and Ward on Sexual Offences Law & Practice* (5th ed., Sweet & Maxwell 2016) 81.

115 J Spencer, "The Sexual Offences Act 2003: (2) Child and family offences" [2004] *Crim LR* 347, 348.

116 SOA 2003, s9.

117 Magistrates' Courts Act 1980, s24(1).

118 G Branston and H Norton, *Youth Defendants in the Crown Court* (Judicial College, 2023) 44.

119 Now consolidated in the Sentencing Act 2020, s249.

cations, such as the removal of wigs and gowns by barristers and judges, regular breaks and time taken to explain court proceedings to the child defendant.[120]

a) Doctrinal Application

Owing to the legislative overlap across the SOA 2003, a number of possible charges may be brought simultaneously. The most serious possible charge could be rape (section 1). As the victim in the scenario is 13 years old, a rape of a child offence (section 5) would not apply; thus, V's non-consent and D's lack of a reasonable belief in consent need to be established. Owing to the abduction being a relevant circumstance under section 75(2)(c), there would be an evidential presumption that V did not consent and that D did not have a reasonable belief in consent.[121] The Vignette facts indicate that D rapes V, so we will assume that all actus reus and mens rea elements are satisfied.

As D is under 18, a section 13 charge may be brought in the alternative – this is because D appears to fulfil the offence requirements of section 9, therefore satisfying section 13(1) of the SOA 2003. In the scenario, D's intentional sexual touching involved penetration.[122] As the victim is under 16, but over 12, it must be further proved that D did not reasonably believe that V was 16 or over. Such a charge is typically easier to apply and prove beyond reasonable doubt as compared to a section 1 rape charge.

As section 1 and section 13 offences are both listed as "grave crimes", the case may be committed to the Crown Court. The youth court can, however, retain jurisdiction of a case involving penetration if committed by a very young defendant,[123] and/or if there is not a real likelihood that the final sentence would be beyond the youth court's jurisdiction.[124] If tried in the youth court, as the scenario involves penetrative activity it would be heard by an "authorised district judge" – a judge who has received training in dealing with serious sexual offences.[125] If committed to the Crown Court for trial, it would be heard in front of a jury. Penetrative activity involving coercion and prolonged detention would constitute levels of harm and culpability crossing the sentencing custody threshold or that of a detention and training order; the victim's age (vulnerability) would also constitute an aggravating factor, increasing the likely length of sentence.[126]

---

120 Criminal Practice Directions [2015] EWCA Crim 1567, 3G.

121 SOA 2003, s75(1).

122 SOA 2003, s9(1) and s9(2)(a).

123 M Ashford and N Redhouse, *Blackstone's Youth Court Handbook 2014–2015* (OUP, 2013) 37.

124 *W and M* [2010] EWCA Crim 1926.

125 G Branston and H Norton, *Youth Defendants in the Crown Court* (Judicial College, 2023) 264.

126 Sentencing Council, "Sexual offences – Sentencing children and young people" (1 June 2017).

b) Widening Debate

England and Wales is regularly criticised by the United Nations for its comparatively low age of criminal responsibility, and for trying those under 18 in adult courts.[127] Despite the age of criminal responsibility rising from 8 to 12 in neighbouring Scotland,[128] consecutive UK governments have signalled that the age will not rise in England and Wales.[129] Academic critics note how this low age of criminal responsibility contrasts starkly with legal conceptions of responsibility in family law, where considerations around the child's age, level of maturity and mental capacity must be considered.[130] Others argue that rather than considering such psychological or behavioural grounds, leniency in attributing criminal responsibility and punishment to children should be based upon the fact that they are denied the vote – those who have no voice in how the law is formed having less reason to adhere to it.[131]

Whilst previous common law presumptions served to mitigate this comparatively low age of criminal responsibility, since the early 1990s these accommodations have been abolished by Acts of Parliament. For example, prior to 1993, there was an irrebuttable common law presumption that a boy under the age of 14 was incapable of vaginal or anal intercourse. However, the Sexual Offences Act 1993 abolished this presumption.[132] Furthermore, section 34 of the Crime and Disorder Act 1998 abolished the rebuttable presumption of *Doli Incapax* – that a child between the ages of 10 and 14 was incapable of committing a criminal offence. This common law presumption was only rebuttable where the prosecution proved beyond reasonable doubt that the offence elements were completed by the child, and also that the child knew that the act was "seriously wrong" – not simply naughty or mischievous.[133]

Decisions by the youth court to either retain jurisdiction or commit rape cases to the Crown Court have been frequently challenged via judicial review.[134] Despite the challenges, decisions to commit defendants as young as 11 years to the Crown Court for a rape trial have been upheld.[135]

---

127 United Nations Committee on the Rights of the Child, *Concluding observations on the fifth periodic report of the United Kingdom of Great Britain and Northern Ireland*, (CRC/C/GBR/CO/5, 2016) 22.

128 Age of Criminal Responsibility (Scotland) Act 2019.

129 K Fraser, "Speech: What next for the youth justice system?", (Youth Justice Board for England and Wales, June 2023).

130 H Keating, "The 'responsibility' of children in the criminal law" (2007) *Child & Fam LQ* 19(2) 183.

131 G Yaffe, *The Age of Culpability: Children and the Nature of Criminal Responsibility* (OUP, 2018).

132 Sexual Offences Act 1993, s1.

133 P Rook and R Ward, *Rook and Ward on Sexual Offences Law & Practice* (5th ed., Sweet & Maxwell 2016) 66.

134 Ibid, 1734.

135 *R (on the application of W) v Oldham Crown Court* [2010] EWHC 661 (Admin).

Vignette 9: Statute of Limitations

In 1995, D violently raped V, a 35-year-old woman, using a knife. D managed to escape and was not apprehended until 2023. Traces of his DNA taken from the victim's body leave no doubt that D is the perpetrator. Should D be convicted despite the long delay?

The general principle under English common law is that there is no time limit on the commencement of a criminal prosecution, unless the UK Parliament has legislated otherwise.[136] There is no specified time limit for the more serious "indictable offences", or "triable either way offences" tried at the Crown Court. Over the past 15 years, an increasing number of historic indictable sexual offence cases have been reported, investigated and prosecuted in England and Wales. However, for minor "summary offences" heard in the Magistrates' Court, section 127(1) of the Magistrates' Courts Act 1980 specifies that the court shall not hear a complaint unless it was made within 6 months of the offence being committed.

Despite no defined time limit for prosecutions of indictable offences, it is well established that a delay *may* prejudice D's right to a fair trial, potentially halting proceedings as an "abuse of process".[137] An application to "stay" on grounds of abuse of process is considered on a case by case basis, alongside criminal evidence considerations.[138] As such, the length of a delay does not necessarily mean that an abuse of process is more likely, with convictions for sexual offences committed 63 years ago upheld by the Court of Appeal.[139] Statutory reforms have served to further the principle – for example, section 112 of the Coroners and Justice Act 2009 abolished a previous requirement that a complaint "be made as soon as could reasonably be expected after the alleged conduct".

Where specimen evidence such as DNA has been preserved, there is no time bar on its possible use at trial – in fact, advances in forensic science have secured convictions for serious sexual offences many years after the offence was committed.[140] The CPS in England and Wales operate under the discretionary principle, meaning that for a prosecution to be brought it must satisfy the Code of Crown Prosecutors' Test: (i) that there is sufficient evidence to provide a realistic prospect of conviction; and (ii) that it is in the public interest to prosecute the case.[141]

It is a well-established principle that the criminal law does not have retroactive effect. As such, any historic charge must be based on the criminal law at the time the alleged offence was committed. The offence of rape was previously defined under section 1(1) of the Sexual Offences Act 1956, as amended by the Sexual Offences (Amendment) Act 1976, as follows:

---

136 R Vogler, "Why is There No Statute of Limitations for Criminal Cases in England and Wales?" *DPCE Online* [2022] 49(4) 3907, 3914.

137 Ibid, 3918.

138 P Rook and R Ward, *Rook and Ward on Sexual Offences Law &Practice* (5th ed., Sweet & Maxwell 2016) 1644–1662.

139 *R v RD* [2013] EWCA Crim 1592.

140 P Rook and R Ward, *Rook and Ward on Sexual Offences Law &Practice* (5th ed., Sweet & Maxwell 2016) 1638.

141 Crown Prosecution Service, *The Code for Crown Prosecutors* (8th ed., 2018).

1 (1) For the purposes of section 1 of the Sexual Offences Act 1956 (which relates to rape) a man commits rape if –

(a) he has unlawful sexual intercourse with a woman who at the time of the intercourse does not consent to it; and

(b) at that time he knows that she does not consent to the intercourse or he is reckless as to whether she consents to it

[…]

This was amended further in 1994, removing the term "unlawful" and including both vaginal and anal penetration of a man or a woman.[142]

a) Doctrinal Application

The fact the offence occurred 29 years ago would not automatically bar it from prosecution. In applying the CPS' two-part test, DNA evidence "leaving no doubt" (a "one in a million" match probability, perhaps) as to the profile of the perpetrator would likely pass the sufficient evidence test; the prosecution of a historic violent sexual offence would also likely be deemed in the public interest. It would be for the jury to decide if D deposited the DNA trace during the course of the violent offence, alongside other evidence.[143]

If the rape involved penile penetration of the victim's vagina or anus, and the knife was used as a coercive threat of violence, then the offence would be charged under section 1(1) of the Sexual Offences Act 1956, as substituted by section 142 of the Criminal Justice and Public Order Act 1994. Prior to 2003, no statutory definition of consent existed; the issue of consent was left to the jury to decide upon on the basis of its "ordinary meaning".[144] As discussed in the case of *Olugboja*[145] – the leading authority on consent at the time – where the allegation was that the intercourse was by force or fear of force (such as the knife), then the absence of consent would be clear.[146] It would also need to be proven that D knew that V was not consenting or was reckless as to whether she was consenting – highly likely to be satisfied on the facts.

b) Widening Debate

There are no proposals to introduce a general statute of limitations for indictable criminal offences. Where Parliament has legislated to limit historic criminal investigations, this has been in relation to specific crimes or circumstances. Recently, the Northern Ireland Troubles (Legacy and Reconciliation) Act 2023 received royal assent, providing forms of immunity from criminal prosecution for those who cooperate with an Independent Commission for Reconciliation and Information Recovery

142 Criminal Justice and Public Order Act 1994, s142.

143 P Rook and R Ward, *Rook and Ward on Sexual Offences Law & Practice* (5th ed., Sweet & Maxwell 2016) 1388.

144 *Olugboja* [1981] 3 All ER 443.

145 Ibid.

146 If the scenario occurred post 2004, the facts would fit within the evidential presumptions of non-consent under s75(2)(a).

(ICRIR) in relation to offences committed during "the troubles" conflicts in Northern Ireland. Following this, the High Court in Belfast declared the immunity from prosecution provisions to be incompatible with Article 2 (right to life) and Article 3 (prohibition against torture) of the European Convention on Human Rights.[147]

Proponents of a lack of limitation point to discretion within English and Welsh criminal procedures – such as with the police, CPS, and the judiciary's option to stay proceedings – as being able to filter cases which may lead to an unfair trial.[148] One issue, however, is with regard to how juries interpret and apply legal concepts without breaching the rule of law principle of non-retroactive criminalisation. In historic sexual offence cases, the CPS have argued that both contemporary notions of "indecency"[149] and post-2003 legal conceptions of "consent"[150] should apply. Such arguments have not found favour in the courts – either being rejected outright, or through perhaps generous interpretations as to what constituted consent in law pre-2003.[151] The challenge for a jury hearing a historic sexual offence case today, therefore, is to what extent they can meaningfully apply previous legal notions of concepts such as consent and indecency, especially since such concepts previously afforded wider bandwidths of jury discretion.[152] It is evident that jurors today will have their own interpretations of what constitutes a free agreement, by choice, in any case.[153]

Vignette 10: Life Imprisonment without Parole

The Penal Code of State S provides for imprisonment for life as the maximum penalty for murder, but also authorises the court to order an offender's early release after a minimum of 15 years if the offender is no longer dangerous. Reacting to cases of particularly heinous murders, the legislature of S wishes to introduce a penalty of life imprisonment without any possibility of early release, regardless of the offender's continued dangerousness. Would this amendment be acceptable?

In response to proposals from the Law Commission, the Sentencing Act 2020 was enacted to consolidate existing sentencing legislation and reduce complexity in sentencing law.[154] The Act is therefore referred to as "The Sentencing Code", and is intended to serve as a single, updatable source of sentencing law. The Sentencing Code sits alongside specific sentencing guidelines available for most offences, produced by the Sentencing Council; courts must follow these guidelines, unless it would be contrary to the interests of justice to do so.[155]

---

147 *Re Dillion and others v Secretary of Stage for Northern Ireland* [2024] NIKB 11.

148 R Vogler, "Why is There No Statute of Limitations for Criminal Cases in England and Wales?" *DPCE Online* [2022] 49(4) 3907, 3913.

149 *CPS v Fox*, Westminster Magistrates' Court, 15 December 2015.

150 *R(Monica) v DPP* [2018] EWHC 3508 (Admin).

151 As stated by the Court of Appeal in *Lawrance* [2020] EWCA Crim 971: "There is no sign that Parliament intended a sea change in the meaning of consent when it legislated in 2003."

152 JJ Child et al. *Simester and Sullivan's Criminal Law* (8th ed., Hart, 2022) 23.

153 E Finch and V Munro, "Sexual Consent in the Jury Room" *LS* (2006) 26(3) 303.

154 Law Commission, *The Sentencing Code. Volume 1: Report* (Law Com No 382, 2018).

155 Sentencing Act 2020, s59(1).

A whole life sentence for murder, without the possibility of parole, has existed for some time in England and Wales. The powers for judges to issue such a sentence are now consolidated in section 321 and Schedule 21 of the Sentencing Act 2020. Section 2(1) of Schedule 21 states:

> If –
>
> (a) the court considers that the seriousness of the offence (or the combination of the offence and one or more offences associated with it) is exceptionally high, and
>
> (b) the offender was aged 21 or over when the offence was committed,
>
> the appropriate starting point is a whole life order.

The schedule goes on to list murder cases that would fall within those parameters, including, but not limited to: the murder of two or more people with either a substantial degree of planning, involving abductions of victims, or sexual or sadistic conduct; the murder of a police or prison officer in the course of their duty; a murder done to advance a political, religious, racial or ideological cause.[156] The Court of Appeal has endorsed "the line of authority which does not shut the door to a whole life tariff in a case not involving murder".[157] Nonetheless, it held that the whole-life order did not apply to a non-fatal case where the defendant was convicted of 136 rape offences, instead submitting that a determinate sentence of 60 years' imprisonment be appropriate.[158]

Those sentenced to a whole life order do not have the opportunity to be released: formally, early release provisions do not apply, regardless of the offender's ongoing dangerousness.[159] Whole life prisoners can only be released by the Secretary of State if they are satisfied that there are exceptional circumstances which justify release on compassionate grounds.[160] This compassionate release option means that whole life tariffs have been ruled to not be incompatible with Article 3 ECHR, on the basis that (i) those serving such sentences have the possibility of release in exceptional circumstances; and that (ii) in reaching such a decision, the Secretary of State is bound to consider such exceptional circumstances in compatibility with the ECHR.[161] However, whether these "exceptional circumstances" include penological grounds, as the ECtHR perceived, is highly questionable.[162]

---

156 See Sentencing Act 2020, Schedule 21, s2(2).

157 *McCann, Sinaga, Shah* [2020] EWCA Crim 1676, [89].

158 Ibid, [94].

159 Sentencing Act 2020, s321(5).

160 Crime (Sentences) Act 1997, s30(1).

161 *Hutchinson v the United Kingdom* [2016] ECHR 021. In a departure from a previous ECHR decision, where the Grand Chamber concluded the whole life sentence was incompatible with Article 3. See *Vinter and other v United Kingdom*, Apps Nos. 66069/09, 130/10 and 3896/10 (9 July 2023).

162 N Padfield, "Justifying indefinite detention – on what grounds?" [2016] 117 *Crim LR* 797, 803; A Blick, "'An Obligation of Means, Not one of Result': A Historical Overview and Theoretical Assessment of the Whole Life Order Sentencing Regime in England and Wales" [2023] *JCL* 87(5–6) 355.

Governments may amend the Sentencing Code through either primary legislation (i.e., an Act of Parliament) or secondary, delegated legislation (i.e., regulations, known as statutory instruments) through specific means set out in Schedule 23 of the Sentencing Act 2020. This includes amending provisions dealing with whole life tariffs. For example, section 125 of the Police, Crime, Sentencing and Courts Act 2022 amended Schedule 21 of the Sentencing Act by inserting "the murder of a child involving a substantial degree of premeditation or planning" to the list of likely cases requiring a whole life order to be the starting point of sentencing; and section 126 permitting whole life orders to be imposed on offenders aged 18–21. Section 19(1) Schedule 23 of the Sentencing Act 2020 confers powers on the Lord Chancellor,[163] in consultation with the Sentencing Council, to amend Schedule 21 by regulations made through the affirmative procedure. Whilst delegated legislation made through this procedure requires the approval of both Houses in the UK Parliament, the level of parliamentary scrutiny afforded to such measures is limited in practice.[164]

a) Doctrinal Application

As outlined above, for heinous murders in England and Wales, a sentence of life imprisonment without any possibility of early release is permitted under the current Sentencing Code. The Government, and/or the Lord Chancellor in consultation with the Sentencing Council, can amend provisions under Schedule 21 of the Code, provided appropriate and specified parliamentary processes are followed. As such, legislators are permitted to expand the circumstances in which a court could consider murder of an "exceptionally high" seriousness permitting a whole life order. In doing so, however, the legislature would need to retain the compassionate release option in order to maintain perceived Article 3 ECHR compatibility.

b) Widening Debate

In 2023, there were 65 whole-life prisoners in the English and Welsh prison estate.[165] It is currently a sentence that is handed down in exceptional circumstances.[166] Legislative proposals by the previous Conservative government were set to expand these exceptional circumstances further: for example, Clause 1 of the Sentencing Bill 2023–24, if ratified, would have made it mandatory for a judge to impose a whole life order in cases where the whole life order would currently be a sentencing "starting point", and for *a* murder (rather than of two or more persons) involving sexual or sadistic conduct.[167] Whilst a change of government in July 2024 meant that this Bill did not make it into law, the point remains that the UK Parliament has the power to expand the reach of the whole life order.

163 A Government Minister who heads the Ministry of Justice.

164 House of Commons Library, *Acts and Statutory Instruments: the volume of UK legislation 1850 to 2019* (CBP 7438, 4 November 2019) 23–24.

165 MOJ, "Offender management statistics quarterly: July to September 2023" (National statistics, 25 January 2024).

166 *McCann, Sinaga, Shah* [2020] EWCA Crim 1676.

167 House of Commons Library, *Sentencing Bill 2023–24* (Number 9907, 4 December 2023).

Despite the perceived Article 3 ECHR compatibility, the sentence is broadly criticised by academics and criminal justice charities. It is unclear whether the government would consider progress on rehabilitative grounds as an exceptional, compassionate ground for release, rather than a prisoner's ill-health alone.[168] As such, an expectation that such prisoners progress in their rehabilitation is considered unfair without a mechanism for parole.[169] Academic reform proposals have suggested that a 25 year "backstop" for sentence review, and an express inclusion of 'exceptional progress to rehabilitation' in the compassionate release circumstances, is required for full Convention compliance.[170]

168 N Padfield, "Justifying indefinite detention – on what grounds?" [2016] 117 *Crim LR* 797, 803.

169 Ibid.

170 A Blick, "'An Obligation of Means, Not one of Result': A Historical Overview and Theoretical Assessment of the Whole Life Order Sentencing Regime in England and Wales" [2023] *JCL* 87(5–6) 355.

6. Finland

By *Kimmo Nuotio**

Vignette 1: Trolley Problem – Killing one Person to Save Many

Five young children are playing on railway tracks. An express train is approaching, and it is too late to stop the train before it hits the children, probably killing them. Operator D recognizes the emergency situation. He electronically flips a switch and thus deflects the train from its regular track to a little-used sidetrack. However, the lone repairman V is busy on the sidetrack, and the deflected train kills V, as D had anticipated. Is D criminally responsible for murder of V?

In Finnish criminal law, this question has not been analysed in great detail, and we do not find case law which would be very helpful in answering it. Today's textbooks do not deal with constellations like that directly.[1] Where older criminal law textbooks, which more often discuss abstract examples of this kind, are concerned, they are somewhat out of date in their views on doctrinal issues and conceptualization.

The textbooks by Brynolf Honkasalo from the 1960s (first editions in the 1940s) that dealt with criminal law were built on the idea of sharply distinguishing between self-defence and necessity as grounds of justification and similar grounds of excuse. The Finnish Penal Code of today since the reform of the general part in 2004 has a more flexible approach. Chapter 4 on grounds for exemption from liability includes the provisions on self-defence and necessity.

The most relevant ground for exemption from liability in this type of case is necessity. The statute states the following:

Section 5 (515/2003). Necessity

An act necessary to ward off an immediate, compelling and imminent danger to a legally protected interest [other than one referred to in section 4 above] is permissible as an act of necessity if the act is justifiable when assessed as a whole, taking into consideration the nature and extent of the interest to be defended and the damage and harm caused by the act, the origin of the danger, and the other circumstances.

If the act committed to defend a legally protected interest is not to be deemed permissible under subsection 1, the perpetrator is, nonetheless, exempt from criminal liability, if the perpetrator could not have reasonably been expected to act otherwise, taking into consideration the importance of the interest to be defended, the unexpected and compelling nature of the situation, and the other circumstances.

---

* Professor of Criminal Law, University of Helsinki.

1 Concerning the so-called general doctrines of criminal law, the leading Finnish textbooks are: Sakari Melander, *Rikosvastuun* yleiset edellytykset (General prerequisites of criminal liability), Tietosanoma 2016; Jussi Tapani, Matti Tolvanen, Tatu Hyttinen, *Rikosoikeuden yleinen osa. Vastuuoppi* (General Part of Criminal Law. Doctrines on liability), 3. Painos, Alma Talent 2019; Heli Korkka-Knuts, Dan Helenius, Dan Frände, *Yleinen rikosoikeus* (The General Criminal Law), 3. uudistettu painos Edita 2020.

The statutory text on necessity is rather open to interpretation. Section 4 is about self-defence, and our situation cannot be self-defence since we are not talking about an unlawful attack. Self-defence also needs to be directed against the attacker.

In our vignette case, the act was indeed necessary to ward of an immediate, compelling and imminent danger since the express train, without any intervention in the course of events, would have run over the children. The lives of the children are an important legal interest and deserve protection. Any intervention to save a life or lives of human beings might be justified and lead to exemption from penal liability, if the damage and harm caused by the intervention remains moderate. The origin of the danger also needs to be taken into account. When the act of necessity is directed against the source of danger, we speak about defensive necessity. As regards this kind of necessity, we would allow for a greater harm to be caused than in a case of offensive necessity, in which the harm will be caused to an outsider and to the interests of a person who is not the originator of the danger.

Our situation deals with offensive necessity. Balancing life against life is very difficult and problematic for reasons of principle. The repairman V has no role in the creation of the dangerous situation. Human beings are not expected to play God and decide who may live and who should die.

Honkasalo's textbook, mentioned above, is full of references to earlier Nordic criminal law literature. It summarizes the views of scholars and also of Norwegian and Danish Penal Codes that an act can only be justified on grounds of necessity if the harm caused by it is significantly smaller than the harm that was avoided.[2] Honkasalo maintains that this principle can only give us partial guidance. Usually, loss of property to save a life would count as justified, as would the loss of a smaller amount of property to save a bigger one. Honkasalo also refers to a situation in which a climber in an impossible situation might need to save his own life by cutting a rope and sacrificing the life of his fellow climber. This is manslaughter in the eyes of the legal order, says Honkasalo, but society sees here instead the aim to limit the harm since without this action both lives would have been lost. He mentions, however, that we need to distinguish situations in which no single interest has already been destined for loss, and where loss only follows after a choice is made. Our Vignette situation is precisely this. In such a case, says Honkasalo, punishability can only be negated on subjective grounds (meaning on grounds concerning culpability). In the travaux préparatoires of 2002, these problems are mentioned, but no single quick fix could be offered (see GB 44/2002 at p. 118).

Our case is obviously a hard one since we have a combination of life against life and a significant number of saved lives against one sacrificed life. The legal order has for obvious reasons tried to avoid quantifying interests of life since every life should be protected and every life counts. Whether a person is young or old in principle makes no difference either. The value of human life is not quantifiable, and it is not a lesser crime to kill a person who will soon die anyway.

---

2 Brynolf Honkasalo, *Suomen rikosoikeus. Yleiset opit*, Ensimmäinen osa, toinen painos (The Criminal Law of Finland. General Doctrines. 1st Part, 2nd Edition), SLY 1965, p. 168.

It has been claimed that the prevailing view in criminal law doctrine today is that killing a person can never be fully justified on the grounds of necessity, not even when many people are saved. Necessity could thus only operate in such cases as a ground of excuse.[3]

In our case, we can observe that the children made a mistake in playing in such a dangerous place, but at least if they are small children they should not be blamed for that. If it had been a group of adults, we might see this as relevant in that they themselves contributed to the emergency situation. However, as life matters, in this constellation we would not pay much attention to such aspects. D has a simple choice to make and does not have to reason through all aspects.

But what if the operator had done nothing? Is it clear that he would go unpunished? He would not have caused the fatal accident by action, that is sure. But we might discuss the issue from the point of view of a crime of omission. He might theoretically be in charge of the safety of persons around him. If this is the case, he would face a collision of interests since he can only save the children by allowing an outsider to die. We will not, however, follow this line of thinking further here.

Thus, we would conclude that operator D obviously seeks to save a worthy interest and could be exempted from penal liability on subjective grounds alone, or on the basis of taking into consideration all relevant factors. Regarding subjective factors, it is problematic that the operator knows quite well what the outcome will be so that the subjective constituent elements of manslaughter are present. Under Finnish law, a conviction of murder would be excluded since no aggravating elements are present. In fact, D would be convicted of involuntary manslaughter, which is a less serious form of manslaughter.[4]

A Finnish court would most likely not see this as a case of justified necessity, but rather as a case of exemption from penal liability, due to the fact that the perpetrator could not have reasonably been expected to act otherwise. This verdict would involve taking into consideration the importance of the interest to be defended, the unexpected and compelling nature of the situation, as well as other circumstances. We would deem the act of the perpetrator to be understandable in this exceptional situation. In real life, the court would most likely solve the case by convicting D of killing but waiving punishment.[5]

Vignette 2: Attribution of Death

D intends to kill his neighbour V. Hidden near V's house, D waits for V and stabs him several times with a knife. V is taken to the hospital, where his wounds are treated. His injuries are not life-threatening and V is kept overnight for observa-

[3] Eero Backman, *Pakkotila ja velvollisuuksien kollisio rikosoikeudessa* (Necessity and collision of interests in criminal law), *Lakimies* 3/2004 pp. 395–403, p. 401.

[4] FPC 21:3. On case law, see, FSC 2021:90. The main perpetrator had acted in circumstances close to necessity.

[5] As regards the so-called special part of Finnish criminal law, the leading general commentators would be Tapio Lappi-Seppälä et al., Rikosoikeus (Criminal Law), 5th edition, Alma Talent 2022, and Dan Frände et al., Keskeiset rikokset (The Most Central Offences), Edita 2023.

tion. During the night, a technical defect in the hospital kitchen leads to the outbreak of a fire, which kills V and other persons. Can D be held criminally responsible for V's death?

In Finnish (and Swedish) criminal law, this situation would be dealt with as a case of excessive reach of culpability, especially criminal intent. Thus, the intent of the perpetrator covers more than what in fact happened. The stabbings intending to kill the victim would – should the intended outcome have occurred – constitute either murder or manslaughter according to Finnish penal law; but in the Vignette case, death occurs as a result of an unusual course of events. V had been taken to the hospital and treated there, and his injuries were not life-threatening. He was kept in the hospital for observation. V's death was the result of a technical defect that caused fire. D had no control over the fire and had not foreseen it.

In the early days, so-called theories of causation were developed to handle this kind of situation.[6] Typical questions asked might be whether the acts taken were a necessary condition of the death, or whether the concrete chain of events leading to the death was foreseeable at the time of the act, in this case the stabbing. Foreseeability or adequate causation was regarded as a decisive criterion.[7] As theorizing along these lines was somewhat unsatisfactory and could be challenged on several grounds, attempts were made to develop better normative principles for such cases.[8] Finnish criminal law scholarship, which began to develop in the 1990s, received influences from German, Nordic, British and American sources.[9]

Finnish criminal law scholarship on these issues has not generally been built on the famous German doctrine of "objective imputation", developed by Claus Roxin and others. According to this doctrine, one would ask whether the risk caused by the stabbings materialized in the outcome, that is, the death of the victim. This doctrine has sometimes been discussed in criminal law literature, but it has not been widely endorsed. The Supreme Court of Finland has not even elaborated on it, much less approved of it. The Swedish version of objective imputation developed by Nils Jareborg instead looks at the objective features of carelessness and negligence and understands unlawful risk-taking as the ground for penal liability in objective terms. This doctrine has also found only moderate support in Finland, and the Supreme Court of Finland

---

6 See, Brynolf Honkasalo, *Suomen rikosoikeus. Yleiset opit*, Ensimmäinen osa, toinen painos (The Criminal Law of Finland. General Doctrines, 1st Part, 2nd Edition), SLY 1965, p. 109 ff. (The Criminal Law of Finland. General Doctrines, 1st Part, 2nd Edition); Kimmo Nuotio, *Ennalta arvattavuuden merkityksestä Brynolf Honkasalon kausaalisuus- ja rikosopin kannalta* (On the Significance of Foreseeability in the Doctrines of Causation Penal Liability as Developed by Brynolf Honkasalo), in: *Rikosoikeudellisia kirjoitelmia VI.* Rikosoikeuden juhlavuonna 1989, Suomalainen lakimiesyhdistys 1989, pp. 309–341.

7 Brynolf Honkasalo, *Suomen rikosoikeus. Yleiset opit*, Toinen osa, Toinen painos (The Criminal Law of Finland. General Doctrines, 2nd Part, 2nd Edition), SLY 1967, pp. 98–104.

8 Regarding Finnish scholarship, see, for instance, Ari-Matti Nuutila, *Rikosoikeudellinen huolimattomuus* (Criminal Negligence), Lakimiesliiton kustannus 1996; Kimmo Nuotio, *Teko, vaara, seuraus. Rikosvastuun rikosvastuun filosofisista, kriminaalipoliittisista ja lainopillisista perusteista* (Act, danger, outcome. On the philosophical, criminal policy and doctrinal grounds of penal liability), Suomalainen lakimiesyhdistys 1998, pp. 133–328.

9 Ari-Matti Nuutila, *Rikoslain yleinen osa* (The General Part of the Penal Code), Kauppakaari 1997, p. 16.

has not used this vocabulary either. It would seem that Finnish legal scholarship these days is a pragmatic exercise developing its own grounds.[10]

It is apparent that related theoretical debates were taken into account when the new penal law norm concerning negligence was drafted: [11]

Section 7 (515/2003). Negligence

The conduct of a perpetrator is negligent if he or she breaches the duty of care called for in the circumstances and required of him or her, even though he or she would have been able to comply with it (negligence).

Whether negligence is to be deemed gross (gross negligence) is decided on the basis of an overall assessment. In the assessment, the significance of the duty of care breached, the importance of the interests jeopardised, the probability of the violation, the deliberateness of risk-taking and the other circumstances related to the act and the perpetrator shall be taken into consideration.

An act that is deemed to have occurred more by accident than through negligence is not punishable.

Not all aspects of normative blameworthiness, however, were covered by these definitions. Put simply: the danger and the breach of duty that the stabbing meant could not be linked to the outcome due to intervening factors. The overall policy in reforming the law on the general prerequisites of penal responsibility was to avoid theoretical commitments that were not necessary. A neutral stance was thus adopted.[12]

A short answer would be that D would only be held accountable for the aggravated assault and be sentenced to imprisonment or for attempted murder or attempted manslaughter, if the requirements for this are present. Due to the intervening factor, not even a penal liability for negligent causing of death would be fair and grounded.

He would thus not be convicted of manslaughter or murder since he cannot be held liable for that. The penalty scale for aggravated assault goes as far as imprisonment for ten years, but the punishment is not likely to be high since the wounds were not life-threatening.

Vignette 3: Torture to Save a Life

Kidnapper K has abducted an 8-year-old girl G and hidden her in a small cave in the woods. K is trying to extort money from G's parents for her release. The police manage to arrest K. Although being questioned for 24 hours, K steadfastly refuses to disclose where he hid G. Police officer D correctly assumes that G may soon die

10 See, e. g., the remarks in Kimmo Nuotio, Criminal Law Scholarship – Should It Be Able to Present Itself as Science?, in: Shin Matsuzawa, Kimmo Nuotio, *Methodology of Criminal Law Theory: Art, Politics or Science?* Nomos 2021, pp. 77–103.

11 Raimo Lahti, *Moderni rikosoppi ja tuottamus rikosoikeudessa, rikoslakiuudistus ja Korkein oikeus* (Modern doctrine of penal liability and negligence in criminal law, criminal law reform and the Supreme Court), in: Kimmo Nuotio, Esko Yli-Hemminki, *Kotimaisen rikosoikeustieteen tila ja tulevaisuus*, SLY 2023, pp. 63–81.

12 On the difference between the German doctrine often linked to *Roxin* and the Swedish version worked out by *Jareborg*, see Dan Frände, Gärningsculpa och "objektive Zurechning" – några jämförelser, in: Flores juris et legum Nils Jareborg, Iustus Förlag 2002, pp. 237–250.

of thirst if she cannot be found. He therefore severely beats K to make him tell the truth. Fearing even more violence, K eventually leads the police to the cave, where they find G still barely alive. Should D be punished for torturing K?

The Finnish criminal law is relatively clear on this type of question. The prohibition against torture is regarded as absolute, and not even the benevolent purpose of saving an abducted child's life can justify such action.

Finnish criminal law has a long history in this area. The Penal Code contained an offence of torture for confession. This offence did not require a special capacity but could be committed by anyone. The old provision was, however, regarded as outdated and was therefore abolished in 1995 as part of a comprehensive criminal law reform.[13]

A few years later it had become clear that a specific criminalization concerning torture would still be needed as the UN Torture Convention required this, and a new provision was subsequently adopted. In the preparatory work, the UN Convention was taken as the main model as can be seen in the formulation of Section 11:9a of the Finnish Penal Code:

Section 9a (990/2009). Torture

If a public official causes another person strong physical or mental suffering

1) to get him or her or another person to confess or to provide information,
2) to punish him or her for something that he or she or some other person has done or is suspected of having done,
3) to intimidate or coerce him or her or another person, or
4) on the basis of race, national or ethnic origin, colour, language, sex, age, family relations, sexual orientation, genetic inheritance, disability, state of health, religion, societal opinion, political or vocational activities or other comparable factors,

the public official shall be sentenced for torture to imprisonment for at least two and at most twelve years and, in addition, to be removed from office.

The debate concerning whether a more flexible attitude was needed when the stakes are especially high, as in the US war on terror measures as a response to the 9/11 attacks, were taken into account in the Finnish law drafting procedure. In the travaux préparatoires, specific mention was made that the prohibition of torture is absolute in practical life situations. Not even when interrogating a suspected terrorist may the interrogating authority rely on the usual grounds of justification, such as self-defence or necessity, in order to justify the use of harsh interrogation methods that would otherwise constitute torture.[14]

In real life, it is important to look at the way police interrogation powers are regulated. When the police apply interrogation methods within the limits of law, this cannot be regarded as torture. We should also be mindful of the fact that the suspect has

13 Regarding the discussion in Finnish criminal law on the offence of torture, just before the adoption of the new penal provision, see Kimmo Nuotio, Zur Kriminalisierung der Folter im finnischen Strafrecht (On Criminalizing Torture in Finnish Criminal Law), in: *Nullum Ius Sine Scientia, Festschrift für Jaan Sootak zum 60. Geburtstag am 16 Juli 2008.* Juura, pp. 193–223.

14 See Gov Bill 76/2009, p. 24.

the right to remain silent. In the Vignette case, the police acted on the basis of preventive powers since they aimed at saving a victim from of an ongoing crime. The powers of the police for that purpose are less strictly regulated, but the general police powers cannot be interpreted to include powers to torture anyone. The case setting is in a way a classical one. If we follow the Kantian line, the prohibition of torture should be taken as absolute. If we add a more utilitarian approach, the prohibition becomes more flexible. The reason for being cautious and not admitting utilitarian reasoning is that we may end up going down a slippery slope. State authorities should not be granted the right to go down that slope since we all deserve protection vis-á-vis the state.

The final test would require that a case would be brought before a court. The Finnish Police Act, 17 §, regulates the use of force by the police for preventing crime. The use of force in a concrete situation must be both necessary and defensible (justifiable), and human rights need to be respected. A police officer even has the right to self-defence, which covers the right to defend another person. The prohibition of torture is more absolute than the regulation adopted in the Police Act. Our view, in any case, is that a Finnish court would not hold that the use of force in beating the kidnapper excludes the applicability of the prohibition of torture. The particular circumstances would, however, be taken into account. As the police officer acted in his official capacity, the provisions on crimes in office would apply as well.

Vignette 4: Lethal Self-Defence

R, a well-trained young man armed with a knife, accosts 50-year-old D, who is on her way home from a party in the early morning hours. R threatens her with the knife and takes away her purse filled with 500 € and her wristwatch worth 1,000 €. As R turns to run away, D draws a pistol she is secretly carrying in her jacket, and shoots and kills R in order to retrieve her property. Is D guilty of murder?

The previous view of Finnish law on excessive self-defence was stricter than the current one. It was considered that an excess in self-defence when committed too early or too late was not self-defence at all, and excess could not be relevant. In the 2004 reform, more flexibility regarding the time limits was introduced.

Section 4 (515/2003). Self-defence

An act that is necessary to defend against an ongoing or imminent unlawful attack is permissible as self-defence, unless the act manifestly exceeds what is to be deemed justifiable when assessed as a whole, taking into consideration the nature and strength of the attack, the personal characteristics of the defender and the attacker, and other circumstances.

If the defence exceeds the limits of self-defence (excessive self-defence), the perpetrator is nonetheless exempt from criminal liability if the circumstances were such that the perpetrator could not have reasonably been expected to act otherwise, taking into consideration the dangerousness and unexpected nature of the attack and the situation also in other respects.

The provision above includes two grounds, the first being a ground of justification, the other one being a ground of excuse.

It is worth noting that a criterion of justifiability has been introduced in the first part. Even though the robbery has been frightening as a knife was used, not all actions of a victim when fighting back can be deemed justifiable. Killing the aggressor after the facts is absolutely beyond what is justifiable. It is clear that as the robbery was completed and the robber went away, the imminent threat to life was no longer present. Shooting a robber lethally in the back was no longer necessary as a measure of self-defence against that attack. The attack was motivated by other concerns, such as getting back the robbed items, or it may have been simply revenge.

The idea of a justifiability requirement is precisely that a kind of proportionality needs to be maintained. Even the interests of the aggressor must be taken into account. One could say that for socio-ethical reasons the legal order cannot accept a total exclusion of the protection of the rights and interests of the original offender even when he committed a serious violent crime.

It is for this reason slightly doubtful whether even the second part of the section, that of excessive self-defence, would be applied here. We could say that the lady might simply have called the police and trusted the authorities to bring the offender to justice. A Finnish court would most probably not accept the use of lethal violence just for the purpose of stopping a robber. A rather cautious attitude of the Finnish Supreme Court concerning the use of lethal violence as part of self-defence can be seen in the judgement of SC 2020:88, to give just one example.[15] Even if the perpetrator is not fully exempted from criminal liability on relevant grounds, the circumstances may nonetheless be taken into account as mitigating factors in sentencing.

Vignette 5: Criminal Responsibility of Subordinates for Systemic Offences

D is a soldier in the army of a country ruled by a junta of generals who have come to power through a violent coup. When an opposition group demands the return to a democratic system, the government orders the soldiers to shoot and kill any person who resists arrest. Following this order, D kills three young men who take part in a protest demonstration and hit a police officer who tries to arrest them. When D is tried after a change of regime, he says that he did not like to shoot the protesters but that he thought that he had to obey his commanders' orders. D knew that if he had refused to shoot, he might have been demoted, but no physical harm would have occurred to him. Should D be convicted of murder? If so, should his sentence be mitigated because of his situation?

This constellation has not really been actualized in Finnish criminal law recently. Therefore, we cannot give a definite answer, but instead we can discuss relevant matters for dealing with this situation. In the Finnish Penal Code, the significance of a superior's order has been regulated not in the General Part but in Chapter 11 on war crimes and crimes against humanity:

FPC Chapter 45 on Military Offences, Section 26b (515/2003). Order of a superior

A subordinate soldier shall be sentenced to a punishment for an act that he or she has committed by order of a superior officer only if

---

[15] See, https://www.finlex.fi/fi/oikeus/kko/kko/2020/20200088, visited 27 January 2025 (in Finnish only).

1) the soldier has understood that by carrying out the order he or she would be violating the law or his or her official duty or service duty, or

2) the soldier should have understood the unlawfulness of the order and of the act it requires, taking into consideration the manifestly illegal nature of the act ordered.

If, however, the act has occurred under circumstances in which the subordinate could not have reasonably been expected not to carry out the order, the perpetrator shall be exempt from criminal liability.

Government Bill 44/2002 deals extensively with different constellations concerning the impact of a superior's order on the penal liability of the person obliged by the order. In a military setting, the obligation to follow orders is the strictest, whereas in administration, for instance, there normally is time to make sure whether an order is unlawful. Certain types of activities, such as police or border guard work, may constitute a grey zone in which a relevant situation may occur faster than in office work but still more slowly than in conditions of war.

The provision cited above creates the structure for reasoning in cases of illegal superior orders. I would draw the conclusion that the order given by the government in the Vignette case is indeed manifestly illegal since it demands a completely disproportionate reaction to demonstrators. It amounts to state terror. The soldier should thus have understood the unlawfulness of the order and of the act ordered. The order is so manifestly unlawful that even the circumstances do not give any reason for an exemption of liability as might be granted according to the second part of the section.

The shooting of the civilians would be regarded as manslaughter, but the specific circumstance of the killings would be taken into account as factors mitigating the punishment. Chapter 6 of the Finnish Penal Code regulates this, and the provision on mitigating factors expressly states that significant pressure, threat or another similar factor that has affected the commission of the offence will be taken into account in sentencing.

Vignette 6: Limits of Consent

V is a 21-year-old ambitious athlete and short-distance runner. He has learned that certain artificial limbs can enhance a runner's speed. He decides that he would rather have an artificial limb instead of his right lower leg. He approaches D, a surgeon in private practice, and asks him to amputate his leg below the knee and replace it with an artificial limb. D complies with V's request. Should D be punished for mayhem?

Finnish criminal law does not know the offence of mayhem. Only if a soldier harms his health for the purpose of rendering himself unfit for service would this constitute a criminal service offence of the soldier. Our case is different from this, however.

Theoretically we could also discuss here the act in terms of fraud if the motive is to gain economic benefits by unlawful means. We will not, however, pursue this line of investigation further here.

The more challenging question which has to be discussed concerns performing a limb operation without a medical indication. Even though people enjoy a high level of (medical) self-determination, undergoing such a treatment without a medical indication does not automatically fall into the sphere of that right. The criminal law protection of bodily integrity does not, however, cover harm to oneself, but only harm to others.

The surgeon, however, might be regarded as having wilfully harmed the health and bodily integrity of the "patient". The question then in fact concerns the role of consent. Here the athlete not only consented but even requested this operation. The doctrine of consent has not been expressly regulated in Finnish Criminal law. It is, however, clear that one cannot consent to such in-depth bodily harms as described in our example.[16] Such operations are irreversible and there is a risk of regret since the surgery cannot be undone.

The surgeon would thus risk conviction for having committed an offence. Since consent has been given, he might only be convicted of ordinary assault, not its aggravated form, and consent would certainly be taken into account in sentencing. The surgeon would also risk losing his licence.

Vignette 7: Withdrawal from an Attempt

25-year-old D is deeply upset with her former boyfriend V, who had ended their relationship to be with another woman. To punish V, D plans to stab him with a large knife. D knows that the stab wounds can be fatal and accepts V's death as a possible outcome. When V goes jogging, D attacks him from behind and stabs him in the back three times. V breaks down. D realises that she has injured him but that the injuries will not cause his death. She realises that she could kill him by stabbing him again but decides to leave him alone. Should D be punished for attempted murder?

The described course of events indicates that the attack with a large knife has been premeditated and that D has even accepted the death of her former boyfriend as a possible outcome. The Finnish Penal Code includes rules on the punishability of a criminal attempt as well as a rule on withdrawal from an attempt.

According to Finnish criminal law, punishability of a criminal attempt requires a specific legal provision in the context of the substantive rule on the completed offence. Attempted murder is clearly an offence. The attempt is punishable only when intentional. There seems to be no doubt about intentionality since the intent of the perpetrator would have covered even the death of the victim, should it have occurred.

The general legal rules on attempt are given in Chapter 5 of the Finnish Penal Code. The doctrines on criminal attempts have evolved over time. Two lines of thought may be distinguished, one emphasizing the subjective element and the other one emphasizing the objective element. Due to the original influence of Franz von Liszt's view, the idea that an objective element of danger is the decisive criterion for criminal attempt gained the upper hand. Thus, a concrete danger that a criminal outcome would have emerged was regarded as crucial. This view has been supported throughout the

---

16 For a discussion, see, for example, Vilja Hahto, *Uhrin myötävaikutus ja rikoksentekijän vastuu* (The contribution of a victim and the criminal liability of the offender), Edilex 2004, pp. 271–276.

years, but with the modification that if a harmful consequence was avoided only due to accidental factors, this does not exclude the fact that a concrete danger has been present. In one case, for instance, a person was convicted of breaking into cars attempting to steal car radios, even though only some cars in fact had a radio.[17] From the point of view of the offender, it was a random fact whether there was a radio or not. Thus, the existence of a concrete object is not being required since this would lead to counterintuitive legal outcomes.

In our case, the situation is somewhat different since the stabbings were immediately directed at a human body, and we would presume that the stabbings were as such highly dangerous. This excludes the application of the doctrine concerning "impossible" attempts, which covers cases in which the means used could not have succeeded in resulting in harm to the protected interest.

In objective terms, a punishable attempt requires the beginning of concrete actions which might lead to an outcome, such as death in our example. Stabbing someone in the back with a large knife would certainly count as having begun the act. Moreover, a concrete danger must have been caused. Since the victim was seriously stabbed, the concrete danger of loss of life was present. The victim must have been lucky that the stabbings did not immediately lead to his death.

Now that we have preliminarily established criminal liability for attempted murder (or at least for attempted manslaughter), we will have to look at the rules concerning withdrawal. As stated by Chapter 5 Section 2.1, an attempt is not punishable if the perpetrator has voluntarily withdrawn from the completion of the offence or otherwise prevented the consequence referred to in the statutory definition of the offence from occurring.

The question concerns the first part of the sentence. The perpetrator did not rescue the victim by means of active actions but merely did not continue with stabbings that would have led to the death of the victim. D did not intend to kill her ex-boyfriend but realized that this might happen and took it into account. If one actively removes the risk of further harmful consequences, we call this effective repentance. An attempted murder may thus go unpunished if the perpetrator at a stage when this is still possible takes action and succeeds in helping the victim save his or her life.

Withdrawal from an attempt must be voluntary. If, for instance, the perpetrator sees the police coming and decides to escape before the murder has been completed, this withdrawal is not voluntary. The idea is to create an incentive for the perpetrator not to complete the offence and thus gain a reward for so deciding.

In our case, it seems that there was no external reason to stop proceeding towards killing V. Thus, it seems that the withdrawal was voluntary.

We will find some case law of the Supreme Court of Finland on the relevant issues which may be helpful in further assessing how the vignette case would be solved according to Finnish law. The case law on effective repentance is richer than the one on discontinuing the attempt. In SC 1990: 9 the perpetrator had tried to kill the victim by

---

17 SC 1988:109. A comment by Raimo Lahti in Korkeimmasta oikeudesta, *Defensor Legis* 1989 (70), pp. 1–11. A constant case law of the FSC follows this line.

hitting him in the neck and in the flank. Immediately after that he had asked the neighbour to call an ambulance. The life of the victim was hence rescued. In SC 2009: 48, the stabber had himself called an ambulance.

The doctrine differentiates between attempts which have been completed and those which have not yet been completed. The distinction also fits our intuition. When you have already done everything you believe is needed to reach the expected outcome, it is not enough just to stop further actions. If you set up an explosive device which would detonate and kill someone when he arrives, it is not enough simply to stop wishing that this would happen. One must intervene and remove the risk of the outcome in order to gain the benefit of a more lenient disposition.

In our case the three stabbings constituted a concrete danger to life, but for some reason they did not lead to life-threatening consequences. Thus, we might have to come back to the issue of whether a real risk to life occurred. Maybe a risk occurred on a general level, but the precise points where the knife entered the body were luckily not where life-threatening damage might be caused. Be that as it may, if we discover that a real danger to life was not present at all, D cannot be punished for attempted murder.

If the deadly outcome was avoided only due to luck, punishability of the attempt would be presumed. In our case, this might be relevant since if the stabbings were serious, one might have expected that after the stabbings the victim would still have been in danger and would have needed medical care in order for the risk of death to be excluded.

In our case the interpretation remains slightly difficult. It would seem that the case description is also somewhat unusual. If we conclude that the actions constituting the attempted killing had not been completed yet, a withdrawal from attempt would be possible by simply deciding not to pursue the attempt further. If the actions constituting the attempt were completed, the stabber would have needed to take active measures to save the life of the victim in order to deserve the benefit of withdrawal from an attempt. Our case stands somewhat in the middle. D may well have already thought that the three stabbings were all that was needed but then realized that the victim was not going to die. It would make sense to reward D for not having continued. Thus, it seems that this withdrawal should be given legal weight. We might, however, as well reason that the danger of dying had been real and that it was only due to good fortune that loss of life was avoided. If we follow that line, the attempt could be regarded as punishable. Intuitively, we would say that the courts would rather follow the second line of thought since for the perpetrator the risks of death were difficult to assess, and the risks were so obvious. It is simply highly difficult to decide whether the risk of dying is still imminent.

In any case, the attacker would be held accountable for the aggravated assault which had been completed in any case. A withdrawal may only concern offences which have not yet been completed.

Vignette 8: Criminal Responsibility of Minors

D is a 13-year-old boy. He abducts and rapes V, a girl of the same age. Should D be punished for a criminal offence?

According to Finnish law, children under the age of 15 years cannot be held responsible for a criminal offence. Therefore, the issue of punishment is not relevant. FPC 3:4.1 states:

Prerequisites for criminal liability are that the perpetrator had reached the age of fifteen years at the time of the act and has criminal capacity.

A police hearing, however, is possible and such a serious offence would certainly result in measures taken by the childcare authorities. Victim-offender mediation is also possible, but in practice it only applies to smaller scale offences, not rape.

According to the Finnish and Nordic approach, these two sectors work basically separately and even for children in the 15–17 age group the two sectors would act in parallel.

Vignette 9: Statute of Limitations

In 1995, D violently raped V, a 35-year-old woman, using a knife. D managed to escape and was not apprehended until 2023. Traces of his DNA taken from the victim's body leave no doubt that D is the perpetrator. Should D be convicted despite the long delay?

According to the law in force in 1995, the described violent rape would basically fall under the offence description of forced sexual intercourse (väkisinmakaaminen), the predecessor of the later offence entitled rape. The upper end of the penalty scale provided for that former offence was, however, identical to the provision on aggravated rape, that is, ten years of imprisonment. The new statutory law entered into force in 1998. As the offence has been described as including a threat of severe violence, it would basically be categorized as an aggravated rape.

In the 1998 reform, the understanding of sexual offence was modernized so that the self-determination of the individual was highlighted as the protected legal interest. The previous understanding was coloured by the historical view of sexual offences as a matter of social morality ("*Sittlichkeit*").

This development in the substantive law on rape is, however, irrelevant as regards the question concerning prescription, that is, statutory limitation. In 1995, the prescription time for the forced sexual intercourse was twenty years. For certain sexual violence cases in which the victim is under 18, the later amended law provides that the prescription time only begins to run when the victim turns 18. This amendment has been adopted after 1995 and cannot be applied retroactively. As in our case the victim was an adult woman, we need not go into this matter in more detail.

The answer is clear that charges cannot be raised any longer since more than twenty years have passed after the events.

Vignette 10: Life Imprisonment without Parole

> The Penal Code of State S provides for imprisonment for life as the maximum penalty for murder, but also authorises the court to order an offender's early release after a minimum of 15 years if the offender is no longer dangerous. Reacting to cases of particularly heinous murders, the legislature of S wishes to introduce a penalty of life imprisonment without any possibility of early release, regardless of the offender's continued dangerousness. Would this amendment be acceptable?

Finland resembles State S in that it has adopted a procedure that permits release from a life sentence either based on a pardon granted by the President of Finland or on a decision of the Appeal Court of Helsinki, as the result of a request by the prisoner. A prisoner with a life sentence may file such a request and be released after twelve years of the sentence have been served. A person sentenced to life imprisonment for an offence committed under the age of 21 may be conditionally released at the earliest once he or she has served ten years.[18]

In practice, the regular procedure only runs through the Appeals Court. The release procedure has been regulated in detail. The crime or crimes for which the life sentence has been imposed still count as one of the relevant factors. The dangerousness of the offender, that is, the risk of re-offending, will also be considered and a risk assessment will be prepared as part of the procedure. There is a practice that the seriousness of the previous offence or offences may lead to a prolonging of the sentence, but approximately after 20 years of serving a sentence every prisoner will be released. Finnish criminal law does not at present include any indeterminate sentence which would be solely based on the continued dangerousness of the offender. One might say that the principle of act proportionality also applies here, even though an elevated risk for serious re-offending may increase the length of the time served, as indicated above:

Finish Penal Code Chapter 2c:10.2

> When considering conditional release, attention shall be paid to the nature of the offence or offences that had led to the sentence of life imprisonment, other punishments that were incorporated into the sentence of life imprisonment or that have been served during the period to be served in prison referred to in section 10a, other possible subsequent criminality of the sentenced person, and the circumstances referred to in section 9, subsection 2. When considering the release, account shall be taken of the implementation of the sentence plan referred to in chapter 4, section 6 of the Imprisonment Act and of the behaviour of the prisoner while in prison also in other respects. The commitment of the prisoner to complying with the conditions of medical treatment referred to in section 4 of the Act on Probationary Liberty under Supervision (629/2013) and of other possible related treatment and support may also be taken into account in the consideration. (628/2013)

---

18 FPC Chapter 2c, Section 10.1. On the historical background of life sentences in Finland, see, e.g., Raimo Lahti, Life Imprisonment and Other Long-Term Sentences in the Finnish Criminal Justice System: Fluctuations in Penal Policy, in: K. Ghanayim, Y. Shany (eds.), *The Quest for Core Values in the Application of Legal Norms*. Springer, Cham. https://doi.org/10.1007/978-3-030-78953-4_12. See also Tapio Lappi-Seppälä, Life Imprisonment and related institutions in the Nordic Countries, in: Dirk Val Zyl Smit, Catherine Appleton (eds.), *Life Imprisonment and Human Rights.* (Oñati International Series in Law and Society) Hart Publishing 2016, pp. 461–505.

In 2005 the procedure to be followed in release proceedings has been regulated.[19] Before that, a life sentence could be terminated only by a pardon.

Introducing a life sentence without parole would go against the basic principles of Finnish criminal law. It might in principle be within the margin of appreciation of the legislature if a pressing social need would require this. It is, however, relevant that the Finnish Constitution creates a system of fundamental rights, and in order for such an amendment to be compatible with the Constitution, it would have to pass a check on its constitutionality. This would require an examination of the compatibility of the proposed amendment with the protection of fundamental rights provided by the Constitution as well as human rights law binding on Finland. If such a governmental bill were prepared and passed to the Parliament, the Constitutional Law Committee of the Parliament would carry out this scrutiny and would also hear constitutional law experts.[20]

The European Court of Human Rights has case law on this matter. The Grand Chamber judgement in the case of *Vinter and Others v. The United Kingdom* deals with this issue.[21] The court held that a life sentence without any chance of release would constitute a violation of Art. 3 of the European Convention on Human Rights. It would be regarded as cruel and unusual treatment as prohibited by that article. Although the complaint arose from the UK, the judgement contains a broad set of comparative information on this topic as well as relevant soft law from, among others, the Council of Europe.

Since the Finnish ex-ante scrutiny of the compatibility of proposed amendments carried out by the Constitutional Law Committee includes a check on the relevant human rights law, since the Committee also hears relevant experts before issuing its statement, and since the statement of the Constitutional Law Committee will be regarded as de facto legally binding on the other bodies of the Parliament, we can confidently say that in Finland such an amendment would be rejected should it be proposed by a government.

The Finnish legal order builds its constitutionality review mainly on the ex-ante review by the Constitutional Law Committee of the Parliament. There is some minor room for an ex-post review by the Supreme Court, but this is not relevant in our case.

Finland had abolished the former system of coercive detention, which was meant to address the issue of recidivism among seriously violent offenders. That problematic sanction was replaced by a sentence of imprisonment of a determined length which is to be served to the end, without parole. This sanction was in 2016 replaced by a new form of punishment, i.e., a combined sentence, in which the sentence of, e.g., eight years would be extended by one year of electronic supervision. In this context, the

---

19 *Laki elinkautisvankien vapauttamismenettelystä (781/2005).*

20 On the Finnish system of constitutional review, see Juha Lavapuro, Constitutional Review in Finland, in: Kimmo Nuotio, Sakari Melander, Merita Huomo-Kettunen (eds.), *Introduction to Finnish Law and legal Culture*, Forum Iuris 2012, pp. 127–140.

21 ECHR, Case of Vinter and Others v. The United Kingdom, 9 July 2013, Applications nos. 66069/09, 130/10 and 3896/10. On the case law of the European Court of Human Rights, see, e.g., the factsheet on life sentences, https://www.echr.coe.int/documents/d/echr/FS_Life_sentences_ENG.

Constitutional Law Committee of the Parliament has dealt with the issue of determining sentences on the basis of an assessed risk of repeated violent offences. The Committee stressed the need to present strong grounds for a loss of liberty for such reasons.[22]

As a last point, the current government is planning to introduce a new type of sanction, preventive detention, which will be used for dangerous recidivists of serious offences.[23] The principles of release from life sentence may also be reviewed. It is, however, rather unlikely that the current government would propose that release on parole for life prisoners would be completely abolished.

Recently, a working group of the Ministry of Justice has also scrutinized the system of release on parole of the most dangerous offenders. It did not, however, propose any significant legislative amendments to the current system.[24]

---

22 See, for instance, the Constitutional Committee Report 10/2017 on the Gov. Bill 268/2016.

23 Programme of Prime Minister Petteri Orpo's Government. Publications of the Finnish Government 2023:60, p. 218: "The Government will immediately seek solutions to ensure that prisoners who are the most dangerous to society and to the safety of other people are not released. Preventive detention will be introduced. The assessment of the risk of violence will be developed and its significance as part of the consideration of the release of a prisoner will be substantially increased."

24 Vaarallisimpien väkivaltarikollisten vapauttamisen edellytykset: Vapauttamista koskevien säännösten ja käytäntöjen arviointi (Release on parole of the most dangerous offenders: an assessment of the legal provisions and of the practices of their application), Oikeusministeriön julkaisuja 2023:11.

7. Germany

By *Thomas Weigend** and *Elisa Hoven***

Vignette 1: Trolley Problem – Killing one Person to Save Many

Five young children are playing on railway tracks. An express train is approaching, and it is too late to stop the train before it hits the children, probably killing them. Operator D recognizes the emergency situation. He electronically flips a switch and thus deflects the train from its regular track to a little-used sidetrack. However, the lone repairman V is busy on the sidetrack, and the deflected train kills V, as D had anticipated. Is D criminally responsible for murder of V?

Since D's act of flipping the switch was a cause of V's death and D anticipated V's death, he intentionally killed V.[1]

But D's act might be justifiable under one of the grounds of justification recognized in German law. One possible ground of justification could be defense of others (*Notwehr*, § 32 Penal Code[2]). But since the train had not been instrumentalized by anyone to kill the children, there was no unlawful attack on them as required for a justification by defense of others. And even if an unlawful attack existed, V was not the source of that attack on the children, hence § 32 Penal Code does not permit D to take V's life in defense of the children.

Justification is also possible in cases of necessity, as defined in § 34 Penal Code:

> Whoever, when faced with a present danger to life, limb, liberty, honor, property or another legal interest which cannot otherwise be averted, commits an act to avert that danger from himself or another person does not act unlawfully if, upon balancing the conflicting interests, in particular the affected legal goods and the degree of danger to each of them, the protected interest substantially outweighs the one interfered with. [...]

In the present case, there was an imminent danger to the lives of five children, and D has averted that danger by killing one person (V), which was the only possible means of saving the children. One could well argue that five human lives weigh substantially more than the life of a single person. But according to the great majority of German legal writers, human life cannot be quantified; it is therefore largely accepted that the active killing of a single person to save several others from death cannot be

---

* Professor of Criminal Law (retired), University of Cologne.

** Professor of German and Foreign Criminal Law, Criminal Procedure Law, Economic and Media Criminal Law, University of Leipzig.

1 D would probably be charged with aggravated homicide (*Mord*, § 211 Penal Code). Since V did not expect any attack on his life, the killing could be termed "treacherous" (*heimtückisch*), which is an aggravating circumstance giving rise to a possible conviction of *Mord.*

2 § 32 Penal Code: "(1) Whoever commits an act demanded by self-defense does not act unlawfully. (2) Self-defense is the defense which is necessary to avert a present unlawful attack from oneself or another person."

Duncker & Humblot · Berlin | https://doi.org/10.3790/978-3-428-59449-8.2025.416256

justified.[3] The main argument in favor of this view is that the law cannot demand that an innocent person sacrifice his life for saving others.[4]

The view that lives must not be counted in an emergency situation has gained additional support by a 2006 decision of the Federal Constitutional Court.[5] The decision concerned a statute[6] passed in the aftermath of the events of September 11, 2001, which authorized the German Minister of Defense to order the shooting down of a hijacked aircraft which terrorists intend to use as a weapon to kill people on the ground. The Federal Constitutional Court ruled that this statute permitted the state-ordered killing of innocent crew members and passengers and thereby violated the human dignity of these individuals, who were used as mere objects to stop the terrorists. Since human dignity is absolutely protected under Art. 1 subsec. 1 of the Federal constitution (*Grundgesetz*), the statute in question was held to be unconstitutional.[7] Although the Federal Constitutional Court explicitly left open the question of whether a person ordering the shooting down of a highjacked airplane would be criminally liable,[8] the judgment has been understood as a clear statement against regarding the intentional killing of innocent persons as justified even in emergency situations. The judgment was however criticized by some scholars who pointed out that the Court seemed to neglect the human dignity of the persons on the ground, who were left to be killed by the terrorists although the state could have saved them.[9]

If § 34 Penal Code does not provide a ground of justification for killing V, D might still be excused under § 35 Penal Code, which provides:

> Whoever, when faced with a present danger to life, health or liberty which cannot otherwise be averted, commits an unlawful act to avert the danger from himself, a relative or another person close to him acts without guilt. […]

This provision provides an excuse for persons in immediate danger of losing their most important legal interests, based on the notion that the law cannot expect heroism in a situation of extreme danger. But the effect of § 35 Penal Code is limited to avert-

---

3 See, e. g., Federal Court of Justice (*Bundesgerichtshof*, hereafter BGH) Neue Juristische Wochenschrift (NJW) 1989, 912, 913; *Erb*, in: von Heintschel-Heinegg (ed.), Strafgesetzbuch. Münchener Kommentar, 4th ed. 2020, § 34 marginal number (hereafter MN) 148; *Heinrich*, Strafrecht Allgemeiner Teil, 4th ed. 2014, MN 425; *Pawlik*, Der rechtfertigende Notstand, 2002, 251–257; *Perron*, in: Schönke/Schröder, Strafgesetzbuch. Kommentar, 30th ed. 2019, § 34 MN 23–24; *Roxin/Greco*, Strafrecht Allgemeiner Teil, vol. 1, 5th ed. 2020, § 16 MN 88.

4 *Neumann*, in: Kindhäuser et al. (eds.), Strafgesetzbuch. Nomos-Kommentar, 6th ed. 2023, § 34 MN 73, 74. Some authors would allow the killing of a person from whom the danger for others emanates, as in the case where a truck driver suddenly loses consciousness with his foot stuck on the gas pedal, so that the truck would run into a group of school children unless the driver was killed immediately. See on this so-called „defensive necessity" (*Defensivnotstand*) *Erb* (note 3), § 34 MN 205–206; *Perron* (note 3), § 34 MN 31 with further references: *Roxin*, in: Vogler (ed.), Festschrift für Hans-Heinrich Jescheck, vol. 1, 1985, 457, 470–471.

5 Entscheidungen des Bundesverfassungsgerichts (hereafter BVerfGE) 115, 118.

6 § 14 subsec. 3 Law on the Safety of Air Traffic (*Luftsicherheitsgesetz*).

7 BVerfGE 115, 118 MN 119 et seq.

8 BVerfGE 115, 118 MN 130.

9 See, e. g., *Erb* (note 3), § 34 MN 156; *Hörnle*, in: Putzke et al. (eds.), Strafrecht zwischen System und Telos, 2008, 555, 567; *Merkel*, Juristenzeitung (JZ) 2007, 373, 379.

ing dangers to the actor or to persons close to him; D therefore cannot rely on this excuse.

German criminal courts so far did not have to resolve "tragic choice" cases as described in the vignette. A similar situation presented itself, however, when doctors who were involved in the "euthanasia" action of the NS regime in the early 1940s, in the course of which more than 700,000 disabled persons were killed, were tried before the courts of the British occupation zone after the war. Some of the defendants who had selected the patients to be killed claimed that they had participated in the action only in order to avoid being replaced by more radical National-Socialists who would have had all patients killed. There was evidence that the defendants had done their best to stall and sabotage the "euthanasia" killings. The High Court of the British occupation zone nevertheless ruled that the doctors could not be excused but might be granted a personal ground of non-punishment (*persönlicher Strafausschließungsgrund*) if their claim was found to be true.[10]

In the present debate on this issue, some scholars would deny D an excuse, insisting on the principle that no one can be tolerated to intentionally kill a person who has not been involved in the creation of the danger to others.[11] Those holding the opposite view argue that D in the hypothetical case found himself in the particularly difficult situation of a tragic choice, without being responsible for that situation. Although the Penal Code does not provide an excuse, they would grant D a "supra-statutory" excuse (*übergesetzlicher entschuldigender Notstand*) if he takes action to save the greater number of lives rather than remaining passive and – in the hypothetical – letting the children be smashed by the train.[12] Both views marshal strong theoretical arguments. As a matter of fairness it seems overly harsh to punish D for murder of V although he did what he could to save lives.

Vignette 2: Attribution of Death

D intends to kill his neighbor V. Hidden near V's house, D waits for V and stabs him several times with a knife. V is taken to the hospital, where his wounds are treated. His injuries are not life-threatening and V is kept overnight for observation. During the night, a technical defect in the hospital kitchen leads to the out-

---

10 Entscheidungen des Obersten Gerichtshofs für die Britische Zone, vol. 1, 321; vol. 2, 117. Accord, *Neumann* (note 4), § 35 MN 60, 62. See also *Otto*, Jura 2005, 470, 477 (favoring justification of the doctors). These cases differ from the "Trolley" problem in that the patients selected by the defendants for being killed would have been lost in any event, whereas V in the hypothetical case would have survived without D's interference.

11 *Frister*, Strafrecht Allgemeiner Teil, 9th ed. 2020, 20/28 (with exceptions); *Mitsch*, Goltdammers Archiv für Strafrecht (GA) 2006, 11, 13; *Neumann* (note 4), § 35 MN 61; *Roxin/Greco* (note 3), § 22 MN 161–163; *Stübinger*, Zeitschrift für die gesamte Strafrechtswissenschaft (ZStW) 123 (2011), 403, 438 et seq.

12 See, e.g., Baumann/Weber/Mitsch/*Eisele*, Strafrecht Allgemeiner Teil, 13th ed. 2021, § 18 MN 49; *Hoven*, in: Bublitz et al. (eds.), Recht – Philosophie – Literatur, 2020, 857, 883; *Jescheck/Weigend*, Lehrbuch des Strafrechts Allgemeiner Teil, 5th ed. 1996, 502–503; *Paeffgen/Zabel*, in: Kindhäuser et al. (eds.), Strafgesetzbuch. Nomos-Kommentar, 6th ed. 2023, Vor § 32 MN 294 with further references; *Rönnau*, in: Cirener et al. (eds.), Strafgesetzbuch. Leipziger Kommentar, vol. 2, 13th ed. 2019, Vor § 32 MN 359.

break of a fire, which kills V and other persons. Can D be held criminally responsible for V's death?

D intended V's death, he stabbed V, and V died. D might therefore be criminally liable for intentionally killing V (*Totschlag*, § 212 Penal Code, or, if an aggravating circumstance exists, *Mord*, § 211 Penal Code). In view of the unusual sequence of events, however, it is doubtful whether V's death can legally be attributed to D. The German Penal Code does not contain any provision on the issue of attribution, which is hence left to scholarly debate and case law.[13]

The primary requirement for attributing a result (in this case: V's death) to an individual is a causal connection between the individual's act or omission and the result. German courts use the *conditio sine qua non* ("but for") test to establish causation. According to this formula, act A is causal for result R if R would not have occurred but for A; in other words, if we contra-factually posit that A was not done, R would not exist. This sounds logical, but at closer inspection it becomes clear that the required thought operation is based on a fiction ("A was not done") and thus remains subject to speculation; moreover, we are unable to say whether R would have occurred without A unless we know that acts of the type A regularly bring about results of the type R.[14] If it is not evident that A is, according to the laws of science, a sufficient cause of R, the court would need experts to explain what is the probability of A in fact leading to R. Leaving these theoretical complications aside and employing everyday reasoning, we can say that in our case D caused V's death: If D had not stabbed V, V would not have been in the hospital; if he had not been in the hospital in the night when the fire broke out, V would not have died.

Causation along these lines forms the basis for attribution of an outcome to the actor. But there are several exceptional situations in which the law negates attribution even though causation can be proved. This is the case, for example, when an independent actor (or the victim himself) interfered autonomously and created a new risk which superseded the original risk created by the defendant.[15] In a variant of the case Vignette discussed here, assume that V is in the hospital waiting to be released when a nurse N in a sudden rage attacks V and kills him. In that case, V's death would solely be attributed to N, because her attack "overtook" the causal chain initiated by D. V's death is attributed to N even if D's attack might later have caused V's death.

---

13 For an overview, see *Weigend*, in: Hilgendorf (ed.), Aktuelle Herausforderungen des chinesischen und deutschen Strafrechts, 2015, 117. In-depth discussions of the requirements of attribution can be found in Baumann/Weber/Mitsch/*Eisele* (note 12), § 10 MN 76 et seq.; *Frisch*, Tatbestandsmäßiges Verhalten und Zurechnung des Erfolgs, 1988; *Frisch*, GA 2018, 533; *Frister* (note 11), ch. 10; *Jakobs*, System der strafrechtlichen Zurechnung, 2012; *Puppe*, Die Erfolgszurechnung im Strafrecht, 2000; *Roxin/Greco* (note 3), § 11 MN 44 et seq.; *Walter*, in: Cirener et al. (eds.), Strafgesetzbuch. Leipziger Kommentar, 13th ed. 2020, Vor § 13 MN 89 et seq.

14 For an extensive critical discussion of the concept of causation in criminal law see *Puppe/Grosse-Wilde*, in: Kindhäuser et al. (eds.), Strafgesetzbuch. Nomos-Kommentar, 6th ed. 2023, Vor §§ 13–15, MN 80–110a.

15 *Eisele*, in: Schönke/Schröder, Strafgesetzbuch. Kommentar, 30th ed. 2019, Vor § 13 MN 100, 101a.

Attribution of a result to the initiator of a causal chain is also negated if the legal prohibition of the initiator's act does not have the purpose of averting the type of risk that eventually led to the fatal result.[16] Take this example: A is the owner of a gun. In violation of legal rules, A does not store the gun in a locked container but leaves it in his open bedroom closet, along with ammunition. Burglar B breaks into A's house and takes the gun with him. When B is leaving the house, he is stopped by police officer P. B hits P on the head with the gun, seriously injuring him. Can A be found guilty of negligent wounding of P? A's act of leaving the gun easily accessible to anyone who entered the house caused P's injury, because B could not have used the gun against P if it had been securely locked away. But the purpose of the rule violated by A was to protect people from the specific danger associated with a loaded gun, that is, from being shot. This specific risk did not materialize when B assaulted P: B could have used any piece of metal or wood to hit P on the head. Therefore, P's injury cannot be attributed to A.

Finally, German doctrine recognizes an exception to the attribution of results caused by an actor where the chain of causation was "extraordinary" or "totally atypical" (*völlig atypisch*).[17] Consider this hypothetical: A knocks B to the ground, which results in a small bleeding wound on B's arm. B wraps a dirty cloth around his arm to stop the bleeding. The wound gets infected. Although he suffers great pain, B refuses to seek medical assistance. B eventually dies of sepsis. In this case, B would not have died but for A knocking him to the ground. But two unusual circumstances interfered with the "normal" chain of causation: B used a dirty cloth for covering the open wound, and he refused to seek medical assistance when the wound got infected. B's death would therefore probably not be attributed to A.[18]

Returning to the instant hypothetical, several arguments can be advanced against attributing V's death to D: First, the causal chain between the stabbing and V's death was quite atypical. Second, the prohibition of stabbing persons is not meant to protect anyone from burning to death in a hospital blaze. Third, V's risk of being killed by a fire was not increased significantly by being in a hospital; fires are not more likely to break out in hospitals than in private homes. V's death can thus not be attributed to D's act but is part of the "general life risk" (*allgemeines Lebensrisiko*) that a fire can break out and kill persons near the fire. One counterargument could be that D had *intended* to kill V. But even D's intention cannot provide a sufficient link for the necessary "objective" attribution of V's death to D's act. D can therefore only be convicted of *attempted* murder of V.

Vignette 3: Torture to Save a Life

Kidnapper K has abducted an 8-year-old girl G and hidden her in a small cave in the woods. K is trying to extort money from G's parents for her release. The police manage to arrest K. Although being questioned for 24 hours, K steadfastly refuses to disclose where he hid G. Police officer D correctly assumes that G may soon die

---

16 See *Puppe/Grosse-Wilde* (note 14), Vor §§ 13–15 MN 228–254.

17 Baumann/Weber/Mitsch/*Eisele* (note 12), § 10 MN 77–87.

18 For a discussion of a similar (but less extreme) case, see *Weigend*, in: Hecker/Weißer/Brand (eds.), Festschrift für Rudolf Rengier zum 70. Geburtstag, 2018, 135.

of thirst if she cannot be found. He therefore severely beats K to make him tell the truth. Fearing even more violence, K eventually leads the police to the cave, where they find G still barely alive. Should D be punished for torturing K?

D could be liable for inflicting bodily harm (*Körperverletzung*) committed by a public official (§ 340 Penal Code[19]) and coercion (*Nötigung*; § 240 Penal Code[20]). It is beyond doubt that D carried out the *actus reus* of each offense. But his act could possibly be justifiable or excusable given that he tortured K in order to save G's life.

The most likely ground of justification would be defense of others, a variant of self-defense. According to § 32 subsec. 1 Penal Code, a person does not act unlawfully if his act was demanded by self-defense. Self-defense is defined as the defense which is necessary to avert a present unlawful attack from oneself or another person (§ 32 subsec. 2 Penal Code). In principle, one could argue that kidnapping G and holding her captive in a remote location was a continuing unlawful assault on her health, freedom and eventually her life. Since K did not respond to questioning, it is difficult to see what other means beyond using physical force could have been available to the police to make him disclose G's location.

There are, however, two arguments that can be raised against justifying D's act on the grounds of defense of others. The first argument relates to his position as a public official. Generally, any person may come to the aid of another who is being unlawfully attacked and can use any necessary means to avert the attack. Thus, if G's parents had gotten hold of K and had beaten him until he disclosed G's whereabouts, there would hardly be any doubt that they could be justified under § 32 Penal Code. But as a member of the police force, D is subject to special legal rules concerning whether and to what extent he may use force against citizens. For example, according to § 55 subsec. 2 of the Police Law of the State of Northrhine-Westphalia[21] the police may not use physical force to coerce a person to make any statement.

The relationship between the rules of police law and of criminal law are contested, especially with regard to acts of self-defense and defense of others. At least three approaches can be distinguished.[22] The courts and the majority of legal writers give pri-

---

19 § 340 Penal Code: "A public official who commits or permits someone to commit a bodily assault in the course of or in relation with his public function shall be punished with imprisonment between three months and five years [...]". Note that German Penal Law does not have a special provision on torture.

20 § 240 Penal Code: "(1) Whoever, by force or by threat with a serious harm, unlawfully compels another person to do any act, to acquiesce in any act, or to desist from doing any act shall be punished by imprisonment of up to three years or a fine [...] (4) In especially serious cases, the penalty shall be imprisonment between six months and five years. A case is deemed especially serious, as a rule, where the perpetrator [...] abuses his powers or position as a public official."

21 In Germany, police authority to avert crime is regulated not by Federal law but by State law of each of the 16 *Länder*. See, for example, Polizeigesetz (Police Law) des Landes Nordrhein-Westfalen of 25 July 2003 (https://recht.nrw.de/lmi/owa/br_text_anzeigen?v_id=3120071121100036031).

22 For in-depth discussions, see *Erb* (note 3), § 32 MN 186–200; *Rönnau/Hohn*, in: Cirener et al. (eds.), Strafgesetzbuch. Leipziger Kommentar, 13th ed. 2019, § 32 MN 216–224.

ority to the general rules of criminal law;[23] they would thus deem D justified by defense of others. One argument in favor of this solution is that many – but not all – State police laws explicitly declare that their provisions leave § 32 (self-defense) and § 34 (necessity) of the Penal Code undisturbed.[24] It is argued, further, that it would undermine the subsidiary character of individual self-defense if the police were more restrained than a private individual in using force against an unlawful attack.[25]

The opposite solution – police cannot rely on the grounds of justification in the Penal Code – has been based on the argument that the differentiated limitations of police law on the use of force by police officers would be obsolete and useless if any police officer could base the use of deadly force on the loose standard of "necessity" provided by § 32 Penal Code.[26]

There have also been suggestions for intermediary solutions. One proposition is to apply the rules of the Penal Code with regard to police officers' criminal liability but to hold them responsible for any breach of the rules of police law under internal disciplinary law.[27] Another group of scholars argue in favor of differentiating between defense of self and defense of others: Whereas a police officer should be able to make full use of the right to self-defense when he is attacked, the defense of others against attacks is a main part of his official function and should therefore be subject to the limitations imposed by police law, for example, concerning the use of firearms.[28] The latter distinction appears plausible, although it would lead to different treatment of instances mentioned together in § 32 Penal Code.[29]

Even if one applied the standard of "regular" self-defense under § 32 Penal Code to D's conduct, he might not be justified because he may have violated the prohibition of torture and maltreatment as provided in several international instruments, for example, in Art. 3 of the European Convention on Human Rights (ECHR). Although the prohibition of torture is not mentioned explicitly in the German constitution (*Grundgesetz*, hereafter: GG), the infliction of serious physical pain by a public officer in the context of his official function, especially in order to obtain a statement from the person affected, is regarded as a violation of Art. 1 subsec. 1 GG. This Ar-

---

23 BGH Neue Zeitschrift für Strafrecht (NStZ) 2005, 31; Oberlandesgericht (OLG) Frankfurt, Neue Zeitschrift für Strafrecht Rechtsprechungsreport (NStZ-RR) 2013, 107; *Herzberg*, JZ 2005, 321; *Perron/Eisele*, in: Schönke/Schröder, Strafgesetzbuch. Kommentar, 30th ed. 2019, § 32 MN 42b–42c with further references.

24 See, e.g., § 57 subsec. 2 Police Law Northrhine-Westphalia (note 21). Such a clause is absent, however, in the Police Laws of Bremen, Hamburg and Saarland.

25 Bayerisches Oberstes Landesgericht (BayObLG) JZ 1991, 936; *Perron/Eisele* (note 23), § 32 MN 42c.

26 *Kunz*, Zeitschrift für die gesamte Strafrechtswissenschaft (ZStW) 95 (1983), 973, 981 et seq.; *Rönnau/Höhn* (note 22), § 32 MN 220.

27 *Erb* (note 3), § 32 MN 189–194; *Frister* (note 11), § 16 MN 37; *Hoven* Zeitschrift für internationale Strafrechtsdogmatik (ZIS) 2021, 115, 121; *Rogall*, Juristische Schulung (JuS) 1992, 551, 559; *Schmidhäuser*, GA 1991, 97, 137.

28 See, e.g., *Amelung*, NJW 1977, 833, 839; *Ostendorf* JZ 1981, 165, 172; *Zieschang*, in: Cirener et al. (eds.), Strafgesetzbuch. Leipziger Kommentar, 13th ed. 2019, § 34 MN 43.

29 *Erb* (note 3), § 32 MN 188.

ticle provides: "Human dignity is inviolable. To respect and protect it is the obligation of all state authority." The German Federal Constitutional Court has left no doubt that Art. 1 GG is a "fundamental constitutional principle and supreme constitutional value"[30] and therefore cannot be compromised in favor of other constitutionally protected interests.[31]

According to the majority view, the right to self-defense is inherently limited by the protection of human dignity. If the attacked person would have to violate someone's human dignity to protect the legal interest under attack, self-defense is said not to be "demanded" (*geboten*) as required by § 32 Penal Code.[32] And there can be no doubt that torturing a person violates that person's human dignity, because this act reduces the victim to his animalistic instincts of self-preservation.[33]

There is no consensus, however, as to whether this rule also applies if the attacked person's life is at stake. Some scholars argue that human dignity, being "inviolable" and absolutely protected by the constitution, cannot be balanced even against a human life, hence torture is not a means of legitimate defense of others.[34] In that vein, the Federal Constitutional Court ruled unconstitutional a statute that would have permitted the Minister of Defense to have an airplane shot down when it was abducted by terrorists who planned to use the plane to kill a large number of civilians.[35] And in a case similar to the one discussed here, a high-ranking police officer was convicted of coercion for threatening an arrested child-abductor with inflicting severe pain if he did not reveal the location of the child.[36]

The opposite view[37] argues that human life and human dignity are closely interrelated, hence the impending killing of a human being also violates the victim's human dignity. In that situation, the state would actively contribute to a violation of the victim's human dignity by prohibiting the use of force against the abductor. It is also counter-intuitive to permit a police officer to kill a kidnapper if that is necessary to save his victim from being killed but to deny the officer the option of using non-lethal "torture" in the same situation. If at all, the absolute prohibition of torture can be justified by the high risk of abuses if it were made legal in exceptional cases.[38] But if the

30 Entscheidungen des Bundesverfassungsgerichts (BVerfGE) 109, 279, 311; BVerfGE 115, 118, 152.

31 BVerfGE 93, 266, 293; BVerfGE 107, 275, 284.

32 *Kargl*, in: Paeffgen et al. (eds.), Strafrechtswissenschaft als Analyse und Konstruktion, 2011, 1163, 1178; *Hilgendorf*, JZ 2004, 331, 336, 339.

33 Cf. *Saliger*, ZStW 116 (2004), 35, 47.

34 See, e. g., *Perron/Eisele* (note 23), § 32 MN 62a; *Rönnau/Hohn* (note 22), § 32 MN 224; *Roxin*, in: Arnold et al. (eds.), Menschengerechtes Strafrecht, 2005, 461, 465; *Roxin/Greco* (note 3), § 15 MN 106; *Saliger*, ZStW 116 (2004), 35, 46 et seq.

35 BVerfGE 115, 118. For a discussion of this decision see text at note 5 (Vignette 1, supra).

36 Landgericht Frankfurt a. M. NJW 2005, 692. On this case, see also European Court of Human Rights, Gäfgen v. Germany, no. 22978/05, Judgment of 1 June 2010.

37 Baumann/Weber/*Mitsch*/Eisele, Strafrecht Allgemeiner Teil, 13th ed. 2021, § 15 MN 62–64; *Engländer*, Grund und Grenzen der Nothilfe, 2008, 331 et seq.; *Erb*, NStZ 2005, 593, 596; *Erb* (note 3), § 32 MN 8; *Merkel*, in: Pawlik/Zaczyk (eds.), Festschrift für Günter Jakobs, 2007, 375.

38 *Hoven*, ZIS 2021, 115, 120.

general prohibition is a safety measure against abuse, a police officer who violates the rule to save a life cannot be held responsible for harming the abductor but only for disregarding a rule of caution – which means that he should only be responsible under disciplinary law.[39]

Summing up, one can say that according to the majority of courts and legal scholars D should not be convicted of bodily assault on K, although the reasons given for this outcome differ.

Vignette 4: Lethal Self-Defense

> R, a well-trained young man armed with a knife, accosts 50-year-old D, who is on her way home from a party in the early morning hours. R threatens her with the knife and takes away her purse filled with 500 € and her wristwatch worth 1,000 €. As R turns to run away, D draws a pistol she is secretly carrying in her jacket, and shoots and kills R in order to retrieve her property. Is D guilty of murder?

It may be assumed that D knew that a gun shot from a short distance was likely to kill R and that she was not averse to that outcome. She therefore killed R intentionally, because *dolus eventualis* is a sufficient form of intention under German law. Since R was not aware that D carried a pistol and therefore did not expect an assault on his life when he turned to run away, one can say that he was shot while unaware of a risk to his life, so that the killing was "treacherous" (*heimtückisch*). It would then be punishable as an aggravated homicide (*Mord*, § 211 Penal Code), which carries a mandatory life sentence. In line with a recent judgment of the Federal Court of Justice,[40] one could however argue that R *should* have expected some violent reaction of D to the robbery of her property, which would render him suspicious and would thus exclude a "treacherous" killing. In that case, the killing would be regarded as intentional manslaughter (*Totschlag*, § 212 Penal Code) and would carry a lesser penalty.

The main question is whether D's shooting can be justified as an act of self-defense. According to § 32 subsec. 1 Penal Code, a person does not act unlawfully if his act was demanded by self-defense. Self-defense is defined as the defense which is necessary to avert a present unlawful attack from oneself or another person (§ 32 subsec. 2 Penal Code).

The first issue to be discussed concerns the "presence" of R's attack on D. Since R had turned and started to run away, one could argue that the attack on D's property was already terminated when she shot at R. But German courts maintain that in cases of theft and robbery the "attack", for purposes of § 32 Penal Code, persists until the thief has brought the loot into safety, for example, in his car or his home.[41]

If there was a present attack on D, the next question is whether shooting to kill R was "necessary" to avert the attack. An act is necessary for self-defense if it is the

---

39 *Hoven*, ZIS 2021, 115, 120.

40 Entscheidungen des Bundesgerichtshofes in Strafsachen (BGHSt) 48, 207.

41 BGH Monatsschrift für deutsches Recht (MDR) 1979, 985; for further references see *Perron/Eisele* (note 23), § 32 MN 15; *Rönnau/Hohn* (note 22), § 32 MN 148.

least intrusive effective means for averting the attack in the situation at hand.[42] In assessing the necessity of an act, the court must consider the concrete circumstances and the means available to the defender and the aggressor. If the aggressor is physically stronger, the defender may use a weapon available to him. It may however be an effective means of defense to just show the weapon to the aggressor and warn him that it will be used, or to use the weapon in a non-lethal manner.[43] If that is the case, the defender must use these less intrusive means rather than, e. g., immediately firing a fatal shot to the head. In a recent case, the Federal Court of Justice affirmed the conviction of a defendant who had fatally shot at the upper body of a man who was running away with 4,000 Euro in cash stolen from the defendant. The Court argued that the defendant, who was a trained shooter, should first have fired a warning shot or should have aimed at the victim's legs. This could have been an effective means of defense since the victim was running just three meters ahead of the defendant.[44]

In the hypothetical case posited here, D is not experienced in using a firearm and it is thus not clear whether she would have been able to stop R by aiming at his legs. This would also depend on the speed at which R ran away and on how far he had advanced when D fired the shot.

Assuming that D's act is regarded as "necessary" for the defense of her property, the question arises whether the right of self-defense permits her to kill a robber in order to retrieve objects worth 1,500 Euro. German law generally favors the position of the attacked person, based on the general idea that that person not only defends his own legal interests but also the interest of society in upholding the law against violations.[45] German law therefore does not require that the harm inflicted in self-defense is proportional to the harm defended against. In the same vein, the courts generally allow the use of a deadly weapon if the attacked person has no other effective way of defending his property.[46] Some scholars would, however, limit the right to defend one's property to using means that do not seriously risk the life of the attacker,[47] and the Federal Court of Justice has recently shown some inclination to adopt that view.[48]

There are some exceptions to the general rule that self-defense does not have to be proportionate. For example, a defensive act is not "demanded" by self-defense if the

---

42 BGH NJW 2003, 1955, 1957; NStZ 2006, 152, 154; NStZ 2012, 272, 274. It should be noted that German law does not demand the attacked person to retreat or flee, even if that would avoid harm.

43 BGHSt 26, 143, 147; BGHSt 26, 256, 258; BGH NStZ 1996, 29, 30.

44 BGH NStZ 2023, 222.

45 *Erb* (note 3), § 32 MN 12; *Roxin/Greco* (note 3), 767–770.

46 Entscheidungen des Reichsgerichts in Strafsachen (RGSt) 69, 308; BGH NJW 2013, 2133, 2135.

47 See *Erb* (note 3), § 32 MN 218; *Frister* (note 11), 228; *Perron/Eisele* (note 23), § 32 MN 49.

48 BGH NStZ 2016, 333 (*dictum*). In that case, the defendant had not realized that intruders into his home had in fact taken some of his money; his act of shooting one of them in the back and killing him therefore lacked the subjective element of self-defense.

defender had himself unlawfully provoked the attack.[49] Another exception, which may be relevant here, concerns situations in which the legal interest protected is of extremely low value compared to the harm done by defending it. The hornbook example of such a situation concerns a disabled man sitting in a wheelchair on the porch of his house and observing a boy climbing a tree in his orchard and stealing apples from the tree. When the boy does not listen to his protest, the man grabs the gun standing next to him and shoots the boy. In this case, the owner of the tree may not have had any alternative means of defense available; but he still is not deemed justified because of the extreme difference in value between a few apples and the health or life of the boy.[50] In such a case, it is said that self-defense is not "demanded" (*geboten*) as required by § 32 subsec. 2 Penal Code.[51]

In the instant case, the amount of property D wished to defend against the robber was not trivial, hence an act of self-defense was "demanded". On the other hand, shooting R in the back clearly presented a serious risk to his life. Those writers who would rule out potentially fatal acts of self-defense if only a property right is at stake[52] would therefore conclude that D was not justified by self-defense. The courts, which generally take a more generous view of the rights of an unlawfully attacked person, might however acquit D.

Vignette 5: Criminal Responsibility of Subordinates for Systemic Offenses

> D is a soldier in the army of a country ruled by a junta of generals who have come to power through a violent coup. When an opposition group demands the return to a democratic system, the government orders the soldiers to shoot and kill any person who resists arrest. Following this order, D kills three young men who take part in a protest demonstration and hit a police officer who tries to arrest them. When D is tried after a change of regime, he says that he did not like to shoot the protesters but that he thought that he had to obey his commanders' orders. D knew that if he had refused to shoot, he might have been demoted, but no physical harm would have occurred to him. Should D be convicted of murder? If so, should his sentence be mitigated because of his situation?

D intentionally killed the protesters and can thus, in principle, be convicted of intentional manslaughter (*Totschlag*, § 212 Penal Code) or, if one of the aggravating circumstances listed in § 211 Penal Code is applicable, of murder (*Mord*, § 211 Penal Code). The fact that D did not "like" to shoot the protesters does not negate his intention to kill them.

---

49 See *Perron/Eisele* (note 23), § 32 MN 54–60 with further references.

50 See, e.g. Baumann/Weber/*Mitsch*/Eisele (note 37), § 15 MN 52; *Jäger*, Examens-Repetitorium Strafrecht Allgemeiner Teil, 10th ed. 2021, MN 123. For a court decision along these lines see OLG Braunschweig MDR 1947, 205 (securing a peach tree against thieves by using an electric fence potentially causing death). For further cases see *Perron/Eisele* (note 23), § 32 MN 51.

51 BGH NJW 2003, 1955, 1957.

52 See notes 47 and 48.

D's position as a soldier subject to sanctions for refusing to carry out an order[53] might give rise to the excuse of necessity. According to § 35 Penal Code, "Whoever, when faced with a present danger to life, health or liberty which cannot otherwise be averted, commits an unlawful act to avert the danger from himself, a relative or another person close to him acts without guilt. [...]". This provision might lead to the excuse of soldiers who would be executed or imprisoned if they refused to carry out an order to shoot protesters. But the mere risk of a demotion is not onerous enough to present an excuse under § 35 Penal Code, which has intentionally been limited to dangers to the three most important legal interests of a person.[54]

Although a soldier is obliged to carry out binding orders of his superiors, the mere fact that he was ordered to commit a criminal offense does not by itself justify or excuse his act. Under German military law, an order is not binding (which means that it must not be carried out) if the order implies the commission of a criminal offense (§ 11 subsec. 2 Soldiers Law (*Soldatengesetz*)[55]). Since the conduct of the protesters, even if they injured a policeman, does not justify killing them, the order given to D implied that he was expected to commit manslaughter or murder. The order was therefore not binding and did not provide a legal justification for D to shoot the protesters.

D may however be excused if he did not realize that his act violated the criminal law, unless it was evident, under the circumstances that the act was criminal (§ 5 subsec. 1 *Wehrstrafgesetz* (Military criminal law).[56] D declared that he thought that he had to obey his commander's order. He can therefore be found guilty only if it was evident that the act he was ordered to perform was a criminal offense (§ 5 subsec. 1 Military Criminal Law[57]). Even in a state under authoritarian rule, it is evident that persons must not be shot just because they are resisting arrest.[58] It was thus obvious even to an ordinary soldier that he was ordered to commit an intentional homicide for

---

53 See § 20 Military Criminal Law *(Wehrstrafgesetz*): "Whoever refuses to carry out an order by insurgence in word or deed, or whoever insists on refusing to carry out an order after it has been repeated, shall be punished by imprisonment of up to three years."

54 See *Zieschang* (note 28), § 35 MN 23.

55 § 11 subsec. 2, 1st sent. Soldiers Law (*Soldatengesetz*): "An order must not be carried out if that would mean that a criminal offense is committed." A soldier also need not obey an order that implies the violation of his human dignity (§ 11 subsec. 1 Soldiers Law).

56 With regard to the commission of war crimes in the context of an international or non-international armed conflict, § 3 of the Law on crimes under international law (*Völkerstrafgesetzbuch*) similarly provides that a subordinate acts without guilt if he carries out an order and does not recognize that the order is unlawful, unless its unlawfulness is evident. The term "unlawful" here refers to orders that are not binding in the sense of § 11 subsec. 2 *Soldatengesetz* (see note 55); *Weigend/Kuhli*, in: Safferling (ed.), Münchener Kommentar zum Strafgesetzbuch, vol. 9, 4th ed. 2022, § 3 VStGB MN 15.

57 § 5 subsec. 1 *Wehrstrafgesetz:* "If a subordinate, in carrying out an order, commits an unlawful act which meets the definition of a criminal offense, he is guilty only if he recognizes that the act is unlawful or if that fact is evident under the circumstances known to him."

58 See BGHSt 39, 1, 34–35 denying an unavoidable mistake of law of former GDR soldiers who shot and killed fugitives who tried to climb over the fence separating the German Democratic Republic and the Federal Republic of Germany.

which there existed no military necessity or justification. § 5 subsec. 1 Military Criminal Law thus does not provide an excuse for D.

According to § 5 subsec. 2 Military Criminal Law, the court may reduce the sentence of a soldier who committed a crime he was ordered to commit if his culpability is minor, given the special situation in which he found himself when carrying out the order. Depending on the exact circumstances and the pressure exerted on the soldiers by their superiors, it is quite possible that a court will grant a reduction of sentence to D.

Vignette 6: Limits of Consent

V is a 21-year-old ambitious athlete and short-distance runner. He has learned that certain artificial limbs can enhance a runner's speed. He decides that he would rather have an artificial limb instead of his right lower leg. He approaches D, a surgeon in private practice, and asks him to amputate his leg below the knee and replace it with an artificial limb. D complies with V's request. Should D be punished for mayhem?

Amputating a person's lower leg meets the definition of intentionally causing grievous bodily harm *(schwere Körperverletzung*, § 226 subsec. 1 no. 2 Penal Code).[59] The definition of this crime includes causing the loss of an important member of the body. The lower leg, which is needed for walking, undoubtedly is an important member.[60]

D's act may have been justified by V's consent. There has been some debate in Germany as to whether the victim's consent negates the *actus reus* of an offense or provides a justification. Most legal writers and the courts have accepted the following distinction: If the definition of the offense refers to acting against the victim's will (as, for example, sexual coercion, which is defined in § 177 subsec. 1 Penal Code as performing a sexual act "against the recognizable will of the other person"), the assent of the person involved negates the *actus reus*; if the offense definition does not contain an element of overcoming the will of the victim, the *actus reus* is completed even if the person consents, but the act can be justified if valid consent has been given. The offense of inflicting grievous bodily harm belongs to the second category.

The German Penal Code does not provide any definition of the requirements of a valid consent. There is general agreement, however, that consent to the commission of an otherwise criminal act requires that the person giving the consent can legally dispose of the legal interest involved,[61] that he or she is mature enough and has the necessary information to understand the consequences of giving consent, that the

---

59 Intentionally causing grievous bodily harm carries a penalty between three and 15 years of imprisonment (§ 226 subsec. 2 Penal Code).

60 See *Hardtung*, in: Sander (ed.), Strafgesetzbuch. Münchener Kommentar, vol. 4, 4th ed. 2021, § 226 MN 27.

61 § 216 Penal Code defines the killing of a person with that person's consent as a criminal offense. As a consequence, a person is legally precluded from disposing of his life except by suicide (which is not punishable in Germany). A person can also not validly dispose of communal interests, such as the safety of road traffic.

consent is given without duress or threats, and that the consent is expressed (verbally or non-verbally) before the act is carried out.[62]

The only specific provision of the Penal Code which relates to consent concerns consent to the infliction of bodily harm. § 228 Penal Code provides:

> Whoever inflicts bodily harm with the victim's consent acts unlawfully only if, despite the consent, the act offends common morality (*die guten Sitten*).

This provision, which was introduced in 1933, evidently presupposes that the victim's valid consent in suffering bodily harm normally provides a ground of justification. The exception for instances in which the act violates "common morality" was originally understood as referring to the infliction of pain or bodily harm for immoral purposes, such as sexual arousal (in sado-masochistic practices) or the alteration of the person's appearance to enable him to escape from justice.[63] This interpretation was criticized as punishing not a criminal impairment of someone's health but the violation of public mores. In the early 2000s, the Federal Court of Justice abandoned its earlier reference to "public morals" and equated the violation of "common morality" in § 228 Penal Code with the infliction of injuries that carry the risk of the victim's death.[64] According to this view, "common morality" is violated only if the act in question places the consenting party in a concrete danger of death.[65] This limitation is linked to the fact that a person cannot validly consent to being killed (§ 216 Penal Code). Consequently, the Federal Court of Justice upheld the acquittal of a man who had used a knife to carve his initials into the lower back of his girlfriend, with the woman's consent.[66]

There remains the question, relevant to the case under discussion here, whether the infliction of injuries below the level of a risk to life can be regarded as violating the standard of common morality set in § 228 Penal Code. The amputation of the lower part of a person's leg evidently not only has the effect of disfiguring the person but also severely inhibits his ability to walk.[67] The lack of a medical necessity to perform the amputation does not foreclose its justifiability by the patient's consent; if it were otherwise, aesthetic surgery would generally be impermissible. Since the surgery, if performed *lege artis*, is not life-threatening, the criterion for violations of "common morality" as established by modern case law is not met. A different result could be reached only if "common morality" could be said to be offended by the loss of an im-

---

62 For a discussion of the requirements of valid consent, see *Rönnau* (note 12), Vor § 32 MN 157–210.

63 See BGHSt 4, 24 (granting a justification for injuries inflicted in the course of fencing in student fraternities); OLG Düsseldorf NStZ-RR 1997, 325, 327 (denying a justification for consensual "car surfing").

64 BGHSt 49, 34 (sale of heroin); BGHSt 49, 166, 169 (sadomasochistic practices). For an in-depth discussion of the case law and scholarly debate, see *Grünewald*, in: Cirener et al. (eds.), Strafgesetzbuch. Leipziger Kommentar, vol. 11, 13th ed. 2023, § 228 MN 4–7, 15–29.

65 See, e.g., BayObLG NJW 1999, 372; BGH NJW 2015, 1540, 1542.

66 BGH NStZ-RR 2018, 314, 315.

67 In determining the lawfulness of the surgery, the fact that later a prosthesis is attached to the knee should not be considered, because the surgery itself is the potentially criminal act, and any later activities are subject to various imponderables.

portant part of the body.[68] It is debatable whether persons suffering from a rare mental impairment called Body Integrity Identity Disorder (BIID), which consists in the afflicted person's wish to "get rid" of a member of the body,[69] might interfere with the voluntariness of the person's consent in the surgery.[70] But V in our hypothetical case did not suffer from that impairment. V's wish to gain an advantage over his opponents in running might be considered a violation of fairness in sports; but even if that were the case, it would not affect the justifiability of the surgery as such.[71]

Consequently, D should not be found guilty of inflicting grievous bodily harm.

Vignette 7: Withdrawal from an Attempt

25-year-old D is deeply upset with her former boyfriend V, who had ended their relationship to be with another woman. To punish V, D plans to stab him with a large knife. D knows that the stab wounds can be fatal and accepts V's death as a possible outcome. When V goes jogging, D attacks him from behind and stabs him in the back three times. V breaks down. D realizes that she has injured him but that the injuries will not cause his death. She realizes that she could kill him by stabbing him again but decides to leave him alone. Should D be punished for attempted murder?

D committed attempted murder. She had *dolus eventualis* as to V's death and set out to put her plan into action by stabbing him (cf. § 22 Penal Code: "Whoever sets out to immediately perpetrate the actus reus of an offense according to his concept of the act commits an attempt."). D attacked V from behind while he did not expect any assault on his life; she hence acted treacherously (*heimtückisch*), which means that her intended killing was aggravated and would be regarded as *Mord* (§ 211 Penal Code).

D may however be free from punishment due to her abandoning the attempt, in accordance with § 24 subsec. 1, 1st sent. Penal Code, which reads: "Whoever voluntarily abandons the further commission of the offence or prevents its completion will not be punished for attempt."

In scholarly debate, different rationales have been put forward for the generous absolution from punishment in § 24 Penal Code. According to one traditional explanation, § 24 Penal Code is meant to build a "golden bridge" for the perpetrator to encourage him to give up his criminal plan and to return to lawfulness, thus sparing

---

68 This has been advocated by *Engländer*, in: Matt/Renzikowski, Strafgesetzbuch. Kommentar, 2nd ed. 2020, § 228 MN 4 (consent valid only if the amputation was medically indicated).

69 *Noll/Kasten*, Psychology and Behavioral Sciences 2014, 222.

70 See the discussion in *Grünewald* (note 64), § 228 MN 29 (affirming valid consent). On the other hand, if BIID is recognized as a mental disease, amputation could be termed medical treatment; cf. *Nitschmann*, ZStW 119 (2007), 547, 590; *Sternberg-Lieben*, in: Schönke/Schröder, Strafgesetzbuch. Kommentar, 30th ed. 2019, § 228 MN 21.

71 Applying prohibited chemicals to consenting athletes for doping is not punishable as inflicting bodily injury; *Grünewald* (note 64), § 228 MN 34; *contra*, Sternberg-Lieben (note 70), § 228 MN 30. But such practices are punishable under §§ 2 and 4 *Gesetz gegen Doping im Sport.*

the victim.[72] Although it makes sense to create an incentive for giving up the attempt by offering the perpetrator impunity, it is unlikely that many offenders are aware of the existence of this provision and let their conduct be determined by it.

Another approach refers to the preventive functions of punishment.[73] As regards rehabilitation, one can argue that a person who has voluntarily abandoned his criminal design although it was still possible to carry it out has already shown that he is willing to conduct himself in accordance with the law and therefore need not be rehabilitated through criminal sanctions. Similarly, the need to confirm the validity of legal norms after an offense has been committed is reduced where the offender himself refrained from completing his act of violating the norm. In relation to the retributive purpose of punishment, § 24 Penal Code can be interpreted as a reward for the perpetrator's positive attitude in voluntarily abandoning the attempt.[74] It is probably a combination of these considerations that explains the generous treatment of persons who abandon an attempt before the crime is completed.

A perpetrator can voluntarily "give up" a criminal plan only if he thinks that he would be able to bring about the intended result; if he thinks that he has failed, there is nothing for him to give up.[75] The issue of possible failure is determined on the basis not of the objective facts but of the perpetrator's perception of the situation. According to the Federal Court of Justice, an attempt has failed if the perpetrator does not believe that his criminal plan can still be completed by the means he has available in the given situation.[76] Conversely, withdrawal is still possible if the attempt has failed but the perpetrator is not aware of it. If, for example, the perpetrator tries to kill his enemy with a gun and has fired so many shots that there are no bullets left, but thinks that there are additional bullets in the magazine, and at this point gives up his plan, § 24 Penal Code is applicable because the perpetrator was not aware of the failure.

In the hypothetical case discussed here, D's attempt to kill V had not failed because she could have continued stabbing V with the knife and was aware of that option.

Regarding the requirements for an exonerating withdrawal, § 24 Penal Code inherently distinguishes between two situations: (1) The perpetrator still needs to take action to bring about the intended result (unfinished attempt); (2) the intended result will come about without any further action on the part of the perpetrator but can still be averted by counter-action (finished attempt). In situation (1), withdrawal demands no more than an abstention from further activity, whereas in situation (2) the law requires that the perpetrator, to benefit from the rules on withdrawal, takes some action

---

[72] RGSt 73, 60; BGHSt 39, 221, 232; *Kudlich*, JuS 1999, 241; *Weinhold*, Rettungsverhalten und Rettungsvorsatz beim Rücktritt vom Versuch, 1990, 38.

[73] BGHSt 9, 48, 52; Baumann/Weber/*Mitsch*/Eisele (note 37), § 23 MN 11; *Roxin*, in: Lüttger (ed.), Festschrift für Ernst Heinitz, 1972, 251, 270.

[74] *Heger* Strafverteidiger (StV) 2010, 320; *Murmann*, Versuchsunrecht und Rücktritt, 1999, 28.

[75] Baumann/Weber/*Mitsch*/Eisele (note 37), § 23 MN 18; *Eser/Bosch*, in: Schönke/Schröder, Strafgesetzbuch. Kommentar, 30th ed. 2019, § 24 MN 7–11; *Murmann*, in: Cirener et al. (eds.), Strafgesetzbuch. Leipziger Kommentar, vol. 2, 13th ed. 2019, § 24 MN 71–76.

[76] BGHSt 39, 221, 228; BGH NStZ 2010, 690.

and thereby averts the completion of the offense.[77] Again, it is the perpetrator's subjective perception of the situation that determines how he needs to conduct himself to gain impunity: If the perpetrator *believes* that he still needs to take some action to bring about the intended result, the attempt is deemed unfinished and he can withdraw by mere inaction.[78] Conversely, an attempt is deemed finished if the perpetrator thinks that the result may come about without further action on his part. In that situation, the perpetrator can gain impunity only by making an honest (albeit objectively unnecessary) effort to save the victim.[79]

In the hypothetical case posed here, D's attempt to kill V is unfinished: D realizes that V's death will not come about unless she continues stabbing him. According to the first alternative of § 24 subsec. 1, 1st sent. Penal Code, it is sufficient for withdrawal that D abstains from further assaults on V. D will therefore not be convicted of attempted murder (but is criminally liable for the completed assault with a dangerous weapon, § 224 Penal Code).

Vignette 8: Criminal Responsibility of Minors

D is a 13-year-old boy. He abducts and rapes V, a girl of the same age. Should D be punished for a criminal offence?

§ 19 Penal Code declares that persons who are not yet 14 years old when committing a crime cannot be guilty. Under that rule, D could not be prosecuted or convicted of rape. § 19 Penal Code provides an absolute lower limit for criminal responsibility; the rule applies irrespectively of the young person's individual stage of maturity. The law assumes irrefutably that persons younger than 14 years are not capable of appreciating the unlawfulness of their acts or of acting in accordance with any such appreciation.[80] Acts of children also do not trigger a general-preventive need for confirm-

---

77 If the completion of the offense is averted by an independent cause (example: D stabs V to kill him, and V lies on the ground bleeding. D realizes that V would die unless he receives medical emergency treatment. D calls a doctor by phone, but before that doctor arrives, an ambulance happens to pass by and takes V to a hospital where he is saved), the perpetrator will not be punished if he has honestly and voluntarily tried to avert the completion of the offense (§ 24 subsec. 1, 2nd sent. Penal Code). In the example case, D will hence not be convicted of attempted murder.

78 BGHSt 35, 90; *Hoffmann-Holland*, in: Heintschel-Heinegg (ed.), Strafgesetzbuch. Münchener Kommentar, vol. 1, 4th ed. 2020, § 24 MN 72. Note, however, that D in this case will only remain unpunished if V's life has indeed been saved. The rules on withdrawal from an attempt do not apply if the *actus reus* of the offense has in fact been completed: If V stabs D, and V dies of the injuries suffered, D will be convicted of murder regardless of any efforts he made to save V.

79 It is not necessary (and will often be impracticable) that the perpetrator himself averts the result; it is sufficient, for example, that a person who has seriously wounded the victim calls an ambulance.

80 See *Perron/Weißer*, in: Schönke/Schröder, Strafgesetzbuch. Kommentar, 30th ed. 2019, § 19 MN 1; *Verrel/Linke/Koranyi*, in: Cirener et al. (eds.), Strafgesetzbuch. Leipziger Kommentar, vol. 2, 13th ed. 2020, § 19 MN 1.

ing the validity of the social norm the child has violated.[81] Since a conviction of the child is legally impossible, no criminal process against him can be initiated.[82]

In the original Imperial Penal Code of 1871, the age limit for criminal responsibility was set at 12 years. The limit was raised to 14 years by the Juvenile Courts Law (*Jugendgerichtsgesetz*) of 1923. In 1943, an exception for the responsibility of 12- and 13-year-olds was introduced for cases in which "the protection of the people requires a criminal sanction in view of the seriousness of the offense".[83] In 1953, a new Juvenile Courts Law again set the absolute limit at 14 years. As this checkered history indicates, there are no empirically based fixed limits for the criminal responsibility of young persons.

Spectacular cases of murder and rape committed by children aged 12 or 13 have in recent years re-ignited the debate about lowering the age limit.[84] The majority of legal writers have however so far rejected this idea.[85] They argue that the formal criminal adjudication in a criminal trial and the labelling as a "criminal" would do more harm than good to a child, and that the means available in family law and youth welfare law (*Jugendhilferecht*) are more appropriate than criminal sanctions for persons younger than 14.[86] However, the instruments of family and youth welfare law are generally designed as mere support measures for families willing to accept help. If the offender's parents reject the support that is offered, little can be done by state agencies.[87]

On the other hand, the Juvenile Court Law, applicable to young offenders between 14 and 21 years, generally follows the idea of educating, not just punishing offenders.[88] In line with this general idea, juvenile criminal law provides for special measures designed to meet the offender's individual needs, including educative and disciplinary measures such as warnings, directives to live with his family or in a juvenile shelter, and directives to do community service or to seek reconciliation with the victim.[89] Custodial sanctions are reserved for the most serious cases.[90] There does not appear to exist a principled argument against applying this panoply of youth-specific measures to offenders who were younger than 14 years when they commit-

---

81 *Roxin/Greco* (note 3), § 20 MN 3; *Streng*, in: von Heintschel-Heinegg (ed.), Münchener Kommentar zum Strafgesetzbuch, 4th ed. 2020, § 19 MN 1.

82 For details of procedural law, see *Streng* (note 81), § 19 MN 11–13; *Verrel/Linke/Koranyi* (note 80), § 19 MN 1.

83 § 3 subsec. 2, 2nd sent. Juvenile Court Law 1943.

84 See *Hinz*, ZRP 2000, 107; *Hinz* NJW 2023, 3138; *Paul*, ZRP 2003, 294.

85 See, e.g., *Heinz*, ZStW 114 (2002), 519, 582; *Laubenthal* JZ 2002, 807, 811–812; *Neubacher* ZRP 1998, 121, 123; *Streng*, in: Dölling/Erb (eds.), Festschrift für Karl Heinz Gössel zum 70. Geburtstag, 2002, 501, 507–508.

86 *Streng* (note 81), § 19 MN 17.

87 *Hefendehl*, JZ 2000, 600, 601.

88 See § 2 subsec. 1 Juvenile Court Law (*Jugendgerichtsgesetz*): "The application of juvenile criminal law shall primarily serve to prevent further criminal acts of the juvenile or adolescent. To reach that goal, the legal consequences […] are primarily to be shaped in accordance with the concept of education."

89 For details, see §§ 9–16 Juvenile Court Law.

90 § 17 subsec. 2 Juvenile Court Law.

ted (serious) offenses. Withholding an official reaction to a serious crime may also not be in the interest of the offender, who may feel that he and his acts are not taken seriously by society. Older children may also benefit from sanctions as an incentive to conduct themselves better in the future. Finally, victims of serious crime committed by young persons who are very likely to understand the wrongfulness of acts like murder, rape or robbery may feel wronged if state agencies just send the offender home and refrain from taking any action. The state should therefore investigate the matter and by its reaction convey to the offender, the victim, and society that a crime has been committed and that it does not remain without consequences.

Any finding of guilt should of course be conditioned on a determination that the young person in question was in fact able to recognize the wrongfulness of his conduct and was able to act in accordance with this insight. § 3 Juvenile Court Law already establishes that requirement for any offender younger than 18 years. Lowering the age of criminal responsibility (for certain violent crimes) to 12 years would thus not mean that every 12- or 13-year-old would automatically be punished for such an offense. Rather, an expert would have to determine in each individual case whether the young person, at the time when he committed the offense, was able to understand the wrongfulness of the act and to conduct himself in accordance with this understanding.

Vignette 9: Statute of Limitations

In 1995, D violently raped V, a 35-year-old woman, using a knife. D managed to escape and was not apprehended until 2023. Traces of his DNA taken from the victim's body leave no doubt that D is the perpetrator. Should D be convicted despite the long delay?

Under German law, D could not be convicted of rape. Only aggravated intentional homicide (*Mord*, § 211 Penal Code), genocide, crimes against humanity, and serious war crimes are not subject to temporal limitation.[91] For all other offenses, the limitation period depends on the sentence range provided for the offense.

§ 78 subsec. 3 Penal Code provides:

(3) Where prosecution is subject to limitation, the limitation period is

1. 30 years if the offense is punishable by imprisonment for life,
2. 20 years if the offense is punishable by a maximum sentence of imprisonment of more than 10 years,
3. 10 years if the offense is punishable by a maximum sentence of imprisonment of more than 5 years but not more than 10 years,
4. 5 years if the offense is punishable by a maximum sentence of imprisonment of more than one year but not more than 5 years,
5. 3 years for all other offenses.

---

91 See § 78 subsec. 2 Penal Code (murder), § 5 Law of Crimes against International Criminal Law (*Völkerstrafgesetzbuch*) (genocide and other serious crimes against international law).

Rape[92] (§ 177 subsec. 5 Penal Code) is punishable by imprisonment between one and 15 years. According to § 78 subsec. 3 no. 2 Penal Code, the limitation period for this offense is 20 years. The limitation period begins to run as soon as the offense has been completed (§ 78a Penal Code). For sexual offenses, the limitation period is stayed until the victim of the offense has reached the age of 30 years (§ 78b Penal Code). Since V was 35 years old when the crime was committed, there is no stay of the period of limitation. The running of the period of limitation can be interrupted by certain judicial acts, among them an interrogation of a suspect, the issuance of an arrest warrant, and any request for the undertaking of a judicial act of investigation in a foreign country (§ 78c subsec. 1 nos. 2, 5, 12 Penal Code).[93] But none of these acts was undertaken in D's case, hence limitation occurred in 2015, precluding any further act of prosecution.

The majority view in German doctrine regards the completion of a period of limitation as a procedural bar to prosecution, not as an extinction of the offender's substantive criminal responsibility.[94]

One may question whether it is good criminal policy to abstain from prosecution after several years even if there is clear evidence of the criminal responsibility of a person known to criminal justice agencies. Two main reasons have been suggested for the barring of prosecution after the period of limitation has run. It has been argued, first, that evidence is likely to have deteriorated after a long time, especially testimonial evidence may have become unreliable.[95] But this argument hardly applies to real evidence, as the instant hypothetical case demonstrates; and even testimonial evidence can have been preserved on video tape shortly after the discovery of the offense.[96] A further policy argument in favor of limitation is that it encourages police and prosecutors to investigate cases quickly.[97]

Another strand of argument maintains that the purposes of punishment can no longer be achieved – or need not be achieved – after a long delay. The relevance of a long-past offense for society will have diminished,[98] and the offender – if he has led a law-abiding life since the offense – does not need to be rehabilitated. On the oth-

---

92 For this Vignette, "rape" is defined as a sexual act performed against the will of the victim by force or threats with a present danger to life or health, or by exploiting a helpless situation of the victim.

93 Interruption of the period of limitation means that the period starts again after the act in question (§ 78b subsec. 3 Penal Code). Thus, if a judge had in 2014 issued a warrant to arrest D, the limitation period would end only in 2034.

94 See BVerfGE 25, 269, 287; BGHSt 62, 184, 195; *Bosch*, in: Schönke/Schröder, Strafgesetzbuch. Kommentar, 30th ed. 2019, Vor § 78 MN 3; *Greger/Weingarten*, in: Cirener et al. (eds.), Strafgesetzbuch. Leipziger Kommentar, vol. 6, 13th ed. 2020, Vor § 78 MN 7–9, with further references.

95 See, e. g., *Heinrich*, wistra 2009, 10, 11; *Satzger* Jura 2012, 433, 435; *Wolter* GA 2016, 316, 324.

96 For further counterarguments see *Greger/Weingarten* (note 94), Vor § 78 MN 1b; *Mitsch*, in: von Heintschel-Heinegg (ed.), Strafgesetzbuch. Münchener Kommentar, 4th ed. 2020, § 78 MN 2.

97 BGHSt 62, 184, 195; *Mitsch* (note 96), § 78 MN 4; *Satzger*, Jura 2012, 433, 435.

98 *Greger/Weingarten* (note 94), Vor § 78 MN 1a; *Mitsch* (note 96), § 78 MN 3.

er hand, the weight of the offense does not change over time, hence in a system based on retribution periods of limitation do not make much difference, especially where the offender has managed to hide from justice. In the end, it is a policy decision to what extent a temporal limitation of prosecution should be granted; the need to do justice needs to be weighed against a social interest in letting past events rest.[99]

Vignette 10: Life Imprisonment without Parole

The Penal Code of State S provides for imprisonment for life as the maximum penalty for murder, but also authorizes the court to order an offender's early release after a minimum of 15 years if the offender is no longer dangerous. Reacting to cases of particularly heinous murders, the legislature of S wishes to introduce a penalty of life imprisonment without any possibility of early release, regardless of the offender's continued dangerousness. Would this amendment be acceptable?

In 1949, Germany abolished the death penalty by adopting Article 102 of the Constitution (*Grundgesetz*). Since that time, the most severe sanction provided by the German Penal Code is imprisonment for life (§ 38 subsec. 1 Penal Code), which is the sole penalty for aggravated intentional homicide (*Mord*, § 211 Penal Code). Life imprisonment can also be imposed for some other crimes causing the death of the victim, such as rape, robbery and arson resulting in death (§§ 178, 251, 306c Penal Code), as well as for certain cases of genocide, crimes against humanity, and war crimes under the Code of Crimes Against International Law (*Völkerstrafgesetzbuch*).

Although § 38 Penal Code provides for "imprisonment for life", an amendment as described in the Vignette would not be acceptable under German law. The German Federal Constitutional Court held in 1977 that life imprisonment without any possibility of early release, regardless of the offender's continued dangerousness, violates human dignity enshrined in Article 1 subsec. 1 *Grundgesetz*.[100]

Respect for and protection of human dignity is the highest-ranking and unchangeable principle of the German constitution.[101] In its 1977 decision, the Federal Constitutional Court interpreted the meaning of human dignity in the context of imprisonment in these words (citations omitted):

> The offender must not be turned into a mere object of the state's fight against crime in violation of his constitutionally protected right to social value and respect [...]. The fundamental prerequisites of the individual and social existence of man must be preserved. From Article 1 subsec. 1 Basic Law, in conjunction with the principle of a social state, one can – and this is particularly true in the execution of criminal punishments – derive the obligation of the state to grant everyone at least that minimum level of existence at which human dignity can be maintained. It would be inconsistent with human dignity perceived in this way if the state were to claim the right to forcefully strip a human being of his freedom without the person having at least the possibility of regaining freedom.[102]

---

99 *Hörnle*, in: Fahl et al. (eds.), Ein menschengerechtes Strafrecht als Lebensaufgabe. Festschrift für Werner Beulke, 2015, 115.

100 BVerfGE 45, 187.

101 BVerfGE 6, 32, 41; BVerfGE 27, 1, 6; BVerfGE 30, 173, 193; BVerfGE 32, 98, 108.

102 BVerfGE 45, 187, 246.

The Court thus held that human dignity requires that the prisoner be given a concrete and realistically attainable chance of regaining freedom. The possibility of obtaining a pardon as an act of grace – the conditions of which were not regulated by law and were not subject to judicial review – was deemed insufficient in that regard.

In the aftermath of the Federal Constitutional Court's judgment, the legislature in 1981 introduced § 57a Penal Code:

Suspension of the remainder of imprisonment for life

(1) The court conditionally suspends enforcement of the remainder of a sentence of imprisonment for life where

1. 15 years of the sentence have been served,
2. the particular gravity of the convicted person's guilt does not require its continued enforcement and
3. the conditions of § 57 subsec. 1, 1st sent., nos. 2 and 3 are met.

[...]

When an offender has served 15 years of his life sentence, he must thus be released, with his consent, if his release can be granted without violating security interests of the public, that is, if there is no risk of his committing further serious offenses (§ 57 subsec. 1, nos. 2 and 3 Penal Code), unless the trial court[103] had entered a finding that his blameworthiness was particularly grave (*besondere Schwere der Schuld*). The trial court must base such a finding on an assessment of all circumstances of the case and a comparison with "regular" murder cases.[104] Aggravating circumstances can be, for example, a particularly reprehensible way of killing the victim or the killing of more than one victim.[105]

The decision on early release is made not by the trial court but by the correctional court (*Vollstreckungsgericht*), which has jurisdiction on all decisions on corrections and early release. If the offender applies for early release – which normally happens after 13 years in prison – the correctional court must independently decide, on the basis of an expert's testimony, whether the requirements for early release have been fulfilled (§ 454 Code of Criminal Procedure). If the trial court had made a finding that the offender's guilt was particularly grave, the correctional court decides how many more years the prisoner must serve before he can be released unless he still poses a risk to public security.[106]

It should be noted that German law provides for a special measure to keep dangerous offenders in custody even after they have served their prison sentences. If an of-

103 The Federal Constitutional Court ruled in 1992 that this decision must be made by the trial court; BVerfGE 86, 288.

104 BGH NStZ 2018, 652, 653.

105 For details, see *Ceffinato/Hubrach*, in: Cirener et al. (eds.), Strafgesetzbuch. Leipziger Kommentar, vol. 5, 13th ed. 2022, § 57a MN 13–16.

106 See Meyer-Goßner/*Schmitt*, Strafprozessordnung, 67th ed. 2024, § 454 MN 41a. Most of the prisoners whose sentence is suspended according to § 57a Penal Code had previously spent about 17 years in prison, and only a few had served more than 20 years; *Dünkel/Pruin*, in: Kindhäuser et al. (eds.), Strafgesetzbuch. Nomos-Kommentar, 6th ed. 2023, § 57a MN 57, 60.

fender has committed more than one serious crime, the trial court can order security detention (*Sicherungsverwahrung*) in addition to a prison sentence (§ 66 Penal Code). Security detention is not a punishment for crimes committed but a measure of rehabilitation and security (*Maßregel der Besserung und Sicherung*). It is intended to prevent the commission of further serious offenses by the offender. Security detention must therefore be served *after* the offender has served the prison sentence. Security detention can also be ordered to be served after a sentence of life imprisonment, in case the prison sentence has been shortened according to § 57a Penal Code (see above).

Normally, imposition of security detention requires that the offender has twice been sentenced to imprisonment for a term of at least one year for a serious offense listed in the statute and has served a sentence of at least two years of imprisonment before the present conviction.[107] The trial court can then order security detention if an overall evaluation of the offender and the offenses he committed justifies a finding that the offender possesses a continuing propensity to commit serious crimes and thus poses a danger to the general public.[108]

The duration of detention is not linked to the seriousness of the prior offenses but depends on the continuing dangerousness of the offender. Its duration is not limited by a statutory maximum period. Normally, security detention shall be terminated at the latest after ten years (§ 67d subsec. 3 Penal Code). But if the offender remains dangerous, security detention can last until death.

Since security detention is not "punishment", the Federal Constitutional Court has emphasized that this measure can only be justified if the law ensures that the offender is not burdened beyond the indispensable deprivation of liberty.[109] Enforcement of security detention must therefore focus on rehabilitation. Detainees must be offered suitable therapeutic measures, and the conditions of security detention must perceptibly differ from those of imprisonment. For example, security detainees must be placed in buildings or wards separate from prisoners, have the possibility to move freely within designated spaces, and must be given more opportunities for outside contact and furloughs (§ 66c subsec. 1 Penal Code).

---

107 According to § 66 subsec. 2 Penal Code, an offender can be placed in security detention even without previously having served a prison term if he stands convicted of at least three serious offenses against life, health, or sexual autonomy.

108 If the trial court cannot make a safe prognosis about the offender's future dangerousness, it can sentence him to a prison term and declare that a decision on security detention will be made later. If the court later finds that the offender continues to be dangerous, it must order his placement in security detention (§ 66a subsec. 3 Penal Code). On the other hand, the correctional court can suspend the enforcement of security detention if it appears, after the offender has served the prison sentence, that detention is no longer necessary (§ 67c subsec. 1 Penal Code).

109 BVerfGE 109, 133, 166; BVerfG NStZ 2011, 450.

8. Israel

By *Mordechai Kremnitzer**

Vignette 1: Trolley Problem – Killing one Person to Save Many

Five young children are playing on railway tracks. An express train is approaching, and it is too late to stop the train before it hits the children, probably killing them. Operator D recognizes the emergency situation. He electronically flips a switch and thus deflects the train from its regular track to a little-used sidetrack. However, the lone repairman V is busy on the sidetrack, and the deflected train kills V, as D had anticipated. Is D criminally responsible for murder of V?

There is no direct reference to a case of this type in the Israeli case law. The following discussion is therefore highly speculative. Yet the Vignette bears a structural resemblance to the "Torture Case", which permits an analogous analysis.[1]

On the first level of examination, it is a case of murder (carrying a maximum sentence of life imprisonment) committed with oblique intention (indirect intention), treated by law like direct intention. D expected the fatal result of his act with near certainty. The case is not aggravated murder since there was no prior planning or premeditation.[2]

The case raises the possibility of the defense of necessity. The law does not distinguish between different types of necessity. The prevailing view is that the defense covers both types. Professor Feller limits the defense to justification only.[3]

Article 34k of the Penal Law states:

A person shall bear no criminal liability for an act required to have been done immediately by him to save his or another's life, freedom, body or property from a concrete danger of serious injury deriving from the circumstances at the time of the act, and he had no other alternative but to do it.[4]

According to section 34P, this provision (as well as self-defense and duress) shall not apply where, in the circumstances of the case, the act is not a reasonable means to prevent the injury.[5]

On the first look, it seems that the elements of necessity, namely the immediacy of the required act, the need to save others' lives from a concrete danger to life, are met in the case, except that reasonableness must be discussed.

---

* Professor (emeritus) of Law, The Hebrew University of Jerusalem, senior fellow at the Israel Democracy Institute.

1 HCJ 5100/94 Public Committee Against Torture in Israel and others v. Government of Israel, The General Security Services and other, 53(4) PD 817 (1999) (hereinafter, The Public committee Against Torture judgment).

2 § 20(b), 300(a), 301a(a), Penal Law, 5737–1977 (Isr.).

3 2 S.Z. Feller, Elements of Criminal Law 387–393, 503–511 (1987) (in Hebrew).

4 Ibid. Penal Law § 34K.

5 Ibid. § 34P.

On a second look, there is a slight doubt concerning the element of "danger". It seems that it is not a case of averting a certain danger, since the children may have noticed the approaching train and gotten off the track. Yet, it seems that the danger to their lives was concrete, and this is sufficient.

There is also an issue of doubt whether there was no other way but to do what was done. It boils down to the question of the feasibility of warning the children (and not deflecting the train) or warning V, while deflecting the train. If one of these alternatives had a real chance to be effective, then D had to opt for it.

For the sake of brevity, I assume that these options were not feasible alternatives.

The real question is whether D's action was not reasonable, in the circumstances of the case, for preventing the death of five children. In such a case the defense is inapplicable. If the legal system follows a strict/pure utilitarian approach, it is reasonable (or at least not unreasonable) to save the lives of five children at the price of one person's life. Moreover, D was probably under official duty to prevent or minimize loss of lives related to the train traffic. What this duty meant in the circumstances of the case is not clear and begs the issue of our case. It stands to reason that subjectively D was convinced that he was fulfilling his duty.

There are two related objections to this analysis, stemming from a deontological approach. First, one can argue that the value of one person's life is infinite and cannot be quantified. Even the mere act of quantification in this context diminishes the value of human life. It degrades humans to objects serving an ulterior purpose and denies their inherent dignity and human character.

The second objection is that it is absolutely forbidden to injure (let alone kill) an innocent person – one who is not attacking another person or putting him at risk.[6] It can be debated whether this rule applies only to intentional acts or also to cases of indirect/oblique intention as in the case discussed here.[7]

Since the law equates oblique intention with intention (article 20 (b) of the Penal Law), the rule should probably apply in this case as well. It follows that the law should not allow/give license to such an attack on an innocent person. If this view is accepted, it has a clear bearing on D's duties as a public official who even has a special duty to abide by the law.

This does not rule out the possibility of recognizing an excuse covering such a case, similar to the approach of the Israeli Supreme Court in the torture case.[8] Some scholars would however deny public officials this excuse because of their special duty to act only within the framework of law.[9]

---

6 Miriam Gur-Arye, *Legitimating Official Brutality: Can the War Against Terror Justify Torture?* 38–42 (HUJI. Leg. Stud. Working Paper Series, 2003), https://ssrn.com/abstract=391580.

7 The quality of the standard or the act is arguable and can be formulated in less negative terms, more sympathetic to the perpetrator.

8 The Public Committee Against Torture judgment, *supra* note 1.

9 Mordechai Kremnitzer, *The Landau Commission Report – Was the Security Service Subordinated to the Law, or the Law to the "Needs" of the Security Service?*, 23 Isr. L. R. 216, 229 (1989); Gur-Arye, *supra* note 6, at 36–37.

This view was not accepted by the Supreme Court. It seems that the general approach of Israeli Law is utilitarian and that it is reluctant, in general, to fully recognize absolute principles. This could in principle open the possibility to treat the case as justified necessity.[10]

On the other hand, it will be difficult to accept that D's act is fully justified, thus depriving V of the right of self-defense, if it was feasible for him to violently repel the attack. Regarding D's action as excused makes it easier, since it honors the sanctity of life of the innocent, and this view could also rely on the Torture Case.[11] This suggested solution leaves intact the wrongfulness of the act and emphasizes, on the other hand, the unique and exceptional nature of the case, characterized by the difficulty of the situation, the mental distress, the scarcity of time, the positive motivation, the lack of clarity as to the content of the official duty, D's subjective sense of fulfilling his duty. If, because of all these factors, it could not have been expected of D to act legally, then he should be excused as a matter of principle because he is not to be blamed. Imposing criminal responsibility on a person who is not culpable contradicts the principle of culpability and violates human dignity.

If this view is not accepted, there are still the possibilities of refraining from prosecution, based on considerations of public interest,[12] or charging D with manslaughter, which would lead to a reduced responsibility.[13]

Vignette 2: Attribution of Death

D intends to kill his neighbor V. Hidden near V's house, D waits for V and stabs him several times with a knife. V is taken to the hospital, where his wounds are treated. His injuries are not life-threatening and V is kept overnight for observation. During the night, a technical defect in the hospital kitchen leads to the outbreak of a fire, which kills V and other persons. Can D be held criminally responsible for V's death?

There are four approaches:

According to S. Z. Feller, when the act is intentional, the result has to be attributed to the person who intentionally created the danger.[14]

---

10 See HCJ 9018/17 Tabish v. The Attorney General, 53 Nevo Legal Database (Nov. 26, 2018), https://www-nevo-co-il.eu1.proxy.openathens.net/search/Highlighter2.aspx?id=7e90a9f4-90ac-4d2f-98a4-fbe7045c92ed#0, where the nature of necessity as justification was suggested and discussed in the context of the use of physical means in Israeli National Security Service interrogations. However, the judge's statement on this matter was made as a side note, and is therefore an *obiter dictum.*

11 In The Public Committee Against Torture judgment, there was no direct discussion of the reasonableness requirement. The terms "justification" and "excuse" were not mentioned. Instead a distinction was made between an authorization or a permission, applying ex-ante (that matches the character of justification), and an acquittal of criminal responsibility, that is applied ex-post factum (that matches the character of an excuse).

12 § 62(a), Criminal Procedure Law, 5725–1965 (Isr.).

13 § 301b(b)(3), Penal Law, 5737–1977 (Isr.).

14 1 S.Z. Feller, Elements of Criminal Law 434–454 (1984).

The case law[15] and part of the literature pose the question whether the course of events that took place, based on a relatively high level of generalization (in contrast to the concrete course of events with all its details), was reasonably foreseen/predicted by D.

The critical questions are the level of abstraction being applied, and concretely what is included within reasonable prediction. The rule is that most courses of events are considered to be reasonably foreseen. It is only a course of events that is extremely exceptional that would be considered beyond foreseeability.

Kugler suggests to adopt directly and expressly the test of an extreme deviation as the basis for non-imputation of the result.[16]

It seems that the course of events in this case falls under the exception to the reasonable prediction test and under the extreme deviation test.

The same result is reached by my own approach, following German Law: Was the result within the risk created by D?[17] I think it was not, since although V's hospitalization is inside the created risk-zone, a hospital is not a dangerous place in this sense – suffering from fires initiated by technical defects. Normally, a hospital is safer from accidental fire than a normal lodging. If the defect had occurred at V's home, V being under observation at home, the death would clearly be considered an accident. The case is not different from the situation of a wounded person being killed in a car accident on the way to the hospital or from the hospital back home.

It is easier to reach this result when the direct result is caused by an intervening agent who acted with mens rea. Still, it seems that the result is basically a result of an accident and it is not, therefore, just to impute it to the person who started the chain of events. The result would be probably different if the injuries were life-threatening.

Vignette 3: Torture to Save a Life

Kidnapper K has abducted an 8-year-old girl G and hidden her in a small cave in the woods. K is trying to extort money from G's parents for her release. The police manage to arrest K. Although being questioned for 24 hours, K steadfastly refuses to disclose where he hid G. Police officer D correctly assumes that G may soon die of thirst if she cannot be found. He therefore severely beats K to make him tell the truth. Fearing even more violence, K eventually leads the police to the cave, where they find G still barely alive. Should D be punished for torturing K?

According to the first level of examination, D committed the offence of oppression by a public employee, according to article 277 to the Penal Law[18]. Depending on the level of injuries caused to K, other more serious offences may have been committed[19].

---

15 See CrimA 18/66 Kornik v. The Attorney General 20(2) PD 163, 167 (1966) and CrimA 402/75 Elgavish v. State of Israel 30(2) PD 561, 574 (1975).

16 Itzhak Kugler, Theory and Practice of Criminal Law: an Introduction and the Actus Reus 359–581(2020) (in Hebrew).

17 Mordechai Kremnitzer, *Some Features of the German Criminal Law*, in: Essays in Honor of Shimon Agranat 325 (Ruth Gavison, Mordechai Kremnitzer, eds., 1986) (in Hebrew).

18 Penal Law § 277.

19 § 333, 339(a)(1).

This case immediately rings a bell – the Torture Case and the *Daschner* Case.[20] The Israeli Supreme Court stated that international treaties, to which Israel is a signatory, prohibit the use of "torture and other cruel inhuman and degrading treatment"[21]."These prohibitions are 'absolute'. There are no exceptions to them and there is no room for balancing"[22]. The court also mentions the specific criminal offence applying to such conduct – article 277 of the Penal Law[23]. This prevents a-priori authorization of such acts. Nevertheless, the Court left open/opened the door for the defense of necessity as a defense (not using the term excuse) applicable ex-post factum. The Court even invited the Attorney General to instruct himself as to the instances falling under this exemption. The Attorney General did so, entirely ruling out torture.

Our case differs from the "ticking bomb case" in several aspects:

The concern that illegal pressure would be applied by mistake to an innocent person or one that does not have the relevant information does not exist here.

The concern that the pressure will not be effective and fruitful is also not relevant here.

The case here is more a concrete dilemma than a systemic issue (interrogation of suspected terrorists). On the other hand, ticking bomb scenarios involve typically the effort to save many innocent lives, while in our case it is one life that is at stake.

Most elements of necessity as an excuse are fulfilled. I will deal with the less obvious.

Wasn't there another way to act that had to be preferred? At first glance, it was possible to offer K immunity from prosecution for the information he had, he could have been offered money, or both. In fact, the rule of law does not allow these alternatives that require the law to surrender to the criminal's will and deeds.

For the sake of brevity, I will assume that a warning preceded the use of force, a threat to use force came before force had been used and the use of force was applied in a gradual way.

As to reasonableness – human dignity is not an absolute value in Israeli law. From the point of view of reasonableness, it seems that the interest of one innocent life weighs more than the interests of bodily integrity and dignity, especially under the circumstances of this case (the elements of self-defense (discussed below), D's perception that he acts within his official duty to save the life of a child, his positive motivation, the tension and mental distress in which he operated): "He who saved one life is deemed to have saved the entire world"[24].

---

20 Gäfgen v. Germany, app. No. 22978/05 (Eur. Ct. H.R. June 1, 2010).

21 The Convention Against Torture and Other Cruel, Inhuman or Degrading Treatment or Punishment, Dec. 10, 1984, 1465 U.N.T.S 85.

22 The Public committee Against Torture judgment, *supra* note 1, at 830.

23 Penal Law § 277.

24 Mishnah Sanhedrin 4:5.

Even if the weighing of interests should lead to a different outcome, necessity as an excuse is not excluded. It is difficult to see D as culpable, and hence the recognition of an excuse, derived from the principle of blameworthiness as part of human dignity.

The unspoken reality: it is probably difficult, perhaps impossible, to ignore the fact that D will enjoy strong public support. Imposing criminal responsibility or even administrative or disciplinary responsibility on him may harm the public trust in the legal system. In these circumstances the Attorney General may change his view and remove the ban on torture which prevents the recognition of an excuse. She might also, more convincingly, adopt a narrow interpretation of torture, limiting it to extreme suffering. In that case, D could be excused,[25] because K had control of his situation and was not helpless[26].

Another possibility is to treat the case as one of self-defense, as suggested by Gur-Arye.[27] K's conduct can be regarded as continuous possession of a kidnapped person (hiding a kidnapped person – article 375[28]) or neglect of the duty to provide necessaries when under a duty to provide them created by the kidnapping (responsibility for a helpless person – article 322[29], and violation of obligation by a parent or a responsible person – article 337[30]). It is true that pressuring a person to provide information is not the typical way of defense, but it still keeps its quality as a means to repel an unlawful attack. Other elements of self-defense are fulfilled.[31]

The problem is that self-defense is granting too much here, since it provides a license, a permission to do what is absolutely forbidden and cannot be justified according to customary international law. Whether self-defense is used per se, or its elements are included in necessity, the legal effect must be limited to an excuse, and both necessity and self-defense are opening the door for including both a justification and an excuse.

If the Attorney General (A-G) thinks that all these roads are blocked, she may still decide not to press charges because of considerations of public interest.[32]

It can be assumed that an opposing opinion will be voiced, arguing that the norm against torture turns severe beatings into an unreasonable measure for all kinds of defenses. In hierarchical organizations, it is unfeasible to keep the distinction between

25 See Gur-Arye, *supra* note 6, at 6–9.

26 Ibid. at 42.

27 Ibid. at 43–49.

28 Penal Law § 375.

29 Penal Law § 322.

30 Penal Law § 337.

31 See Penal Law § 34 J ("No person shall bear criminal responsibility for an act that was immediately necessary in order to repel an unlawful attack, which posed real danger to his own or another person's life, freedom, body or property; however, a person is not acting in self-defence when his own improper conduct brought about the attack whilst he foresaw the possibility of such development.").

32 See The Public Committee Against Torture judgment, *supra* note 1, at 846; Elyakim Rubinstein, *National Security and Law: trends*, 44 Hapraklit L. J. 409, attach. no. 1 – "The general security service interrogations and the defense of necessity" – Guidelines for the Attorney General decision (1999) (Isr.).

justification and excuse, especially in systems in which this distinction is not deeply entrenched. What enters the system as an excuse in time turns into a justification. At the beginning, the scope of what is permitted only de facto is narrow, but gradually it will be broadened for less clear-cut cases. The permanent pressure on the door dilutes the protection against torture.

But this will be a voice crying in the desert.

Vignette 4: Lethal Self-Defense

R, a well-trained young man armed with a knife, accosts 50-year-old D, who is on her way home from a party in the early morning hours. R threatens her with the knife and takes away her purse filled with 500 € and her wristwatch worth 1,000 €. As R turns to run away, D draws a pistol she is secretly carrying in her jacket, and shoots and kills R in order to retrieve her property. Is D guilty of murder?

It is unclear whether the shooting was done with a direct intention to kill or indifference to the possibility of causing death. If it was, then it is, at the first stage, a case of murder. If D aimed at the legs, with an intention to only cause serious bodily harm, then we are dealing with that crime.[33]

It is a situation that could fall under self-defense, since property is one of the interests that can be protected by self-defense. But there are three problems as to the applicability of self-defense.

Firstly, is the robbery – the unlawful attack – still present? Since R is just turning to run, the attack was not finished. This view has support in the case law,[34] in the writings of those who distinguish between "Vollendung" and "Beendigung" of an offence,[35] and those who delay the completion of the offence to its material conclusion.[36]

Secondly, there is the question whether the shooting was necessary or whether a less dangerous course of action was a reasonable option. As mentioned, it is unclear whether the shot was aimed to kill or created a high probability of being fatal (aiming at the upper part of the body). If the shot was aimed to be fatal, the alternatives include a warning shot and a shot aimed at the legs. A warning shot should be ruled out since its estimated results are that R is running even quicker or that he turns back on D. Shooting at the legs was an alternative capable of stopping R and enabling D to take back her belongings. On the other hand, it could have required a struggle with a wounded and enraged R, who was physically stronger. Such a confrontation could have endangered D's life. In the case law, the view has been expressed that in cases of using lethal force the requirement of necessity is stronger, which would perhaps deny

33 Penal Law § 333.

34 See CrimA (DC BS) 1010/07 Dromi v. State of Israel, 53 Nevo Legal Database (July 15, 2009), https://www-nevo-co-il.eu1.proxy.openathens.net/search/Highlighter2.aspx?id=f4c042af-4d8d-419a-8f96-99e2d91e34c4#0.

35 See Mordechai Kremnitzer, *Additional Reference to the Timing of Completion of Theft*, 18 Mishpatim L. Rev. 487 (1989) (Isr.).

36 According to Feller, *supra* note 14, 499–504, at that moment, the robbery is not complete.

D justification by self-defense, because she did more than necessary.[37] It is expected that different judges will differ on this point. Assuming that D acted under mental stress and needed to act without time to reflect, it would be fair to regard her act as necessary. It can be labeled as a case of an excuse within self-defense.

The third question is whether her action was reasonable in the sense of proportionality. If she had aimed at the legs, it would be easier to regard her act as proportional than in the case of shooting at the upper body. It is also an open question whether legal analysis should focus only on the final stage and her subjective purpose to retrieve her non-negligible property, or whether the last stage should be examined as part of the attack as a whole. On the one hand, there is a difference between this case and a case in which resistance takes place during the first stage (the threat with the knife). On the other hand, it is artificial to split the robbery into two parts and regard the second stage as if it were a case of theft. The nature of the offender's conduct must be seen in its entirety, that is, as parts of a robbery. D's subjective purpose of retrieving her property does not exhaust what is at stake here – it is a robbery, which involves much more than mere property. It is also an attack on D's bodily integrity and on her liberty from coercion. More important, it is an attack on the victim's sense of security. It also involves a danger to life in the case of resistance. Therefore, it is justified to assess her conduct from the aspect of defending her safety.

This is an in-between case, between protecting against a simple theft and protecting against rape or serious bodily injury. In the first case, lethal protection would probably be considered as disproportional and therefore unreasonable.[38] The opposite assessment will probably be applied in the second case. It seems that, based on the analysis above, armed robbery belongs to or at least is closer to the second group.[39]

This result will not be approved by all, or even many, in the case of a lethal shot; it would be generally accepted if she aimed at the legs.

From the perspective of the legal order, it should be noted that unless the crime scene was under camera surveillance, if R had succeeded to escape with his prey, the chances that he would be captured are low and that he will continue robbing rather high.

According to S.Z. Feller, it is possible to deny D self-defense in case of a lethal shot since she lacked the defensive spirit that is required as part of the subjective element. Instead, she acted with a combative spirit, which falls outside of self-defense.[40] Others contest this view as superfluous.[41]

---

37 See CrimC 4784/13 Somech v. State of Israel, 184 Nevo Legal Database (Feb. 18, 2016), https://www-nevo-co-il.eu1.proxy.openathens.net/search/Highlighter2.aspx?id=19c0eeda-8c50-4a70-b0eb-18d0d944928f#0.

38 Boaz Sangero, Self Defence in Criminal Law 216–224 (2000) (in Hebrew).

39 For instance, see § 402(a), 402(b), 403, Penal Law, 5737–1977 (Isr.) in comparison with §§ 329, 380, 381. The penalty for robbery is close to penalties for grievous bodily harm crimes. On the contrary, see the penalty for theft, § 384.

40 Feller, *supra* note 14, at 433–434.

41 See Sangero, *supra* note 38, at 178–179.

Vignette 5: Criminal Responsibility of Subordinates for Systemic Offenses

D is a soldier in the army of a country ruled by a junta of generals who have come to power through a violent coup. When an opposition group demands the return to a democratic system, the government orders the soldiers to shoot and kill any person who resists arrest. Following this order, D kills three young men who take part in a protest demonstration and hit a police officer who tries to arrest them. When D is tried after a change of regime, he says that he did not like to shoot the protesters but that he thought that he had to obey his commanders' orders. D knew that if he had refused to shoot, he might have been demoted, but no physical harm would have occurred to him. Should D be convicted of murder? If so, should his sentence be mitigated because of his situation?

There is no similar case in Israeli jurisprudence.

On the first level of examination, the killing of the three demonstrators is aggravated murder, since it can be assumed that it was carried out with premeditation.

The examination of the wrongfulness of the shooting at the last stage requires going back and checking the whole series of events, including the fact that the ruling junta came to power through a violent coup. A government of this type rules under the shadow of illegality of its acts, especially repressive acts against opposition to the regime. This rules out the binding effect of its orders – to forbid demonstrations (implied in the case) and to kill demonstrators resisting arrest. The content of the order – to use unnecessary, excessive lethal force – and the lack of a competent authority (a law enacted by an elected parliament) deprive the order of any color, facade, or pretension of legality. Even if a formal basis for such orders had been established, the ultimate and extreme divorce of the content of the orders from an aspiration to justice makes them null and void.[42]

The demonstrators acted to exercise their fundamental rights of speech, protest, and demonstration – an area of liberty that deserves special and enhanced protection. There was no valid reason and legal basis to violate their rights and to arrest them. The steps taken to arrest them were therefore unlawful attacks. Being unlawfully attacked, the demonstrators acted under self-defense as they resisted and tried to repel these attacks. These acts of the demonstrators were justified and permitted, devoid of any wrongfulness. It follows that any act done in order to suppress them by force was unlawful and criminal. Using lethal force against them was also extremely excessive and blatantly unjustified. It is possible that D was aware of the transparent illegality of the orders (he stated that he did not like to shoot the demonstrators). But even if he was not aware, he does not enjoy the defense of obedience to orders since the order was manifestly illegal.[43]

If D volunteered to join the army knowing the kind of orders he will have to execute, this is another (not really needed) reason to deny him any kind of defense.

---

42 Gustav Radbruch, *Statutory Lawlessness and Supra-Statutory Law (1946)*, in: 26 Oxf. J. Leg. Stud. 1 – 11 (Bonnie Litschewski Paulson and Stanley L. Paulson trans., 2006).

43 Penal Law § 34M.

D is not entitled to leniency. He would have deserved leniency if he had tried to act in a way that would minimize the use of lethal force – trying to disperse the demonstration by milder means. Also, his statement is lukewarm and does not express a real and deep resistance and distancing from his deeds, not even remorse. Demotion is a kind of consequence that he was reasonably expected to be ready to "pay" in order to avoid killing innocent persons.

The treatment of cases of this type should express a state's commitment to democracy and its readiness to protect it. This should be done, inter alia, by refusing to recognize acts of dictatorship (including what was done in its name and for preserving and protecting it) as legal.

Democracies willing to survive should make it difficult for a dictatorship to function, create incentives against cooperation with such a regime, make it easier to turn back to democracy, and uproot any legacy of the dictatorship.

Vignette 6: Limits of Consent

> V is a 21-year-old ambitious athlete and short-distance runner. He has learned that certain artificial limbs can enhance a runner's speed. He decides that he would rather have an artificial limb instead of his right lower leg. He approaches D, a surgeon in private practice, and asks him to amputate his leg below the knee and replace it with an artificial limb. D complies with V's request. Should D be punished for mayhem?

Israeli Law distinguishes between several offences against the body:

1. Assault, a conduct offence that is conditioned upon lack of consent of the victim.[44]
2. Causing serious injury and aggravated cases of causing serious injury.

These are result crimes that do not include an element of lack of consent. These crimes require that the perpetrator acted "unlawfully"; but this term is not meant as demanding lack of consent.[45]

Israeli law did not develop a general doctrine of consent as negating criminal responsibility, mainly because of an emphasis of the public nature of all protected interests.[46] Is there a chance that the courts would develop such a defense in this case? According to one view, the principle of legality precludes the judiciary from shaping defenses.[47] But even if the competence of courts for creating defenses were acknowledged in principle, it is very doubtful whether this case would serve as a good trigger, especially since it involves the permanent loss of a limb. A court would probably leave it to the legislature to decide on this value-laden, complex issue rather than taking the decision upon itself.

---

44 Penal Law §§ 378, 379, 380.

45 Penal Law §§ 333, 334, 335.

46 Life, freedom, health or property, as detailed in the defenses to criminal liability in Penal Law §§ 34 J, 34 J1, 34K, 34 L.

47 Feller, *supra* note 14, at 20–21.

The law regards as justified an act done with the lawful consent of a person in the context of a medical intervention or treatment designed to benefit the patient or another person.[48] But the amputation of a leg will not be considered a benefit for the patient.

The reasons for reservations in this case are numerous:

First, it is not clear that V's wish expresses a serious, well-considered, permanent decision. He may regret it deeply after a short or long while. Life is more than sports, and running races loses relevance with age.

Second, Israeli Law prefers long-term autonomy to short-term autonomy, permitting medical treatment of a non-consenting or even resisting patient under specific circumstances.[49]

Third, the operation desired may give V an unfair advantage over other runners and also create an incentive for them to follow his example.

Fourth, it devalues bodily integrity, one of the most important protected interests.

Fifth, it has negative implications for the role of medicine as well as medical doctors and their perception by the public.

Sixth, there is a risk that V will in the future need public support.

According to a religious approach, life and body do not belong to the individual person but to the Lord, who entrusted them to persons to keep – not to harm or destroy.[50] According to Amnon Rubinstein, a secular-liberal legal scholar, maiming the body infringes on the sanctity of life.[51]

Vignette 7: Withdrawal from an Attempt

> 25-year-old D is deeply upset with her former boyfriend V, who had ended their relationship to be with another woman. To punish V, D plans to stab him with a large knife. D knows that the stab wounds can be fatal and accepts V's death as a possible outcome. When V goes jogging, D attacks him from behind and stabs him in the back three times. V breaks down. D realizes that she has injured him but that the injuries will not cause his death. She realizes that she could kill him by stabbing him again but decides to leave him alone. Should D be punished for attempted murder?

Article 28 of the Penal Law states that a person who attempts to commit an offence shall not bear criminal liability for the attempt if he proves that he, solely of his own accord and repentance, refrained from completing the act or substantially contributed to preventing the consequences on which the completion of the offence depended. However, abandoning the attempt shall not extinguish his criminal liability for any other completed offence deriving from his act.

---

48 Penal Law § 34M.

49 § 15(2) Patient Rights Act, 5768–1996 (Isr.).

50 See Genesis 9, 6.

51 See Ruth Kanai, *The Victim's Consent in Criminal law*, 29 Mishpatim L. Rev. 389, 400 (1997) (Isr.).

It can be assumed that D refrained from further stabbing solely of her own accord since no external factor is mentioned that could have influenced her.

Is the element of repentance fulfilled? In this point there has been a change in Israeli case law. At first, the Supreme Court declared that the repentance should be emotional-moral. Later, the Court ruled that repentance does not have to be emotional-moral[52] but can be rooted in other considerations – economic, social or otherwise.

The Court explained that this approach serves the purpose of the provision to give the perpetrator an incentive to abandon his original plan, which is the main rationale of the excuse. The Court also mentioned the difficulty of finding out what is hidden in the perpetrator's soul and supported its conclusion by referring to other legal systems. It is sufficient, wrote the Court, that the perpetrator retreats from his intention to complete the offence upon his own initiative and with no influence of external factors. It seems that D fulfilled this requirement.

Feller holds a different view. According to him, repentance stemming from the depth of the heart is required, expressing a mental impossibility to continue and to complete what the perpetrator had started[53].

The difficulty with the Supreme Court's position is that it nullifies the requirement of repentance and does not ensure that the perpetrator will not try again. Its advantage is that it provides a stronger incentive for desisting and increases the possibility that the crime will not be completed. D may have repented her intention to kill V on this occasion, but she did not repent what she had already done. Her refraining from calling an ambulance proves this point. She should have considered that her lay assessment of the danger to V's life could be too optimistic and that his situation will worsen with no medical care. It is true that if she had to call an ambulance, she might have decided to continue what she had started out of fear of being detected. On the other hand, it is extremely doubtful that she had such a change of heart that makes her deserve an excuse.

It is also not entirely clear that V will in the future be safe from another attack by D.

According to the position of the Israeli Supreme Court, D should be excused. But the Vignette case might make the Court reconsider its position, perhaps even abandon it.

Vignette 8: Criminal Responsibility of Minors

D is a 13-year-old boy. He abducts and rapes V, a girl of the same age. Should D be punished for a criminal offence?

This case falls under kidnapping to commit a sexual offence (article 374)[54] and aggravated rape (article 345(b)(1))[55] – both with a maximum imprisonment of 20 years.

---

52 CrimA 5767/14 Ploni v. The State of Israel, § 56–69 Nevo Legal Database (Jun. 16, 2015), https://www-nevo-co-il.eu1.proxy.openathens.net/search/Highlighter2.aspx?id=88839b32-e1f9-47ad-9113-680636a7945c#0.

53 Feller, *supra* note 3, at 132.

54 Penal Law § 374.

The fact that D is 13 years old does not provide him with immunity from punishment. According to article 34F,[56] the age threshold is 12 years.

It is not legally relevant that he was the same age as the victim. It could have exculpated the offender only if the victim was 14–16 years old, had consented to the act and the act had been done in the course of normal friendly relations and with no abuse of status.[57]

Vignette 9: Statute of Limitations

In 1995, D violently raped V, a 35-year-old woman, using a knife. D managed to escape and was not apprehended until 2023. Traces of his DNA taken from the victim's body leave no doubt that D is the perpetrator. Should D be convicted despite the long delay?

In such a case, the period of limitation is extended if the suspect was not found within 15 years after the crime had been perpetrated, the investigative authority has a piece of evidence that consists of a means of biometric identification, and there is a reasonable ground to expect that it can prove the identity of the suspect.

But even after the extension, the period is limited to 23 years after the crime was perpetrated. In our case, the period that had passed since the commission of the crime is 28 years; the crime therefore falls under the statute of limitation, and D cannot be charged and convicted.[58]

Vignette 10: Life Imprisonment without Parole

The Penal Code of State S provides for imprisonment for life as the maximum penalty for murder, but also authorizes the court to order an offender's early release after a minimum of 15 years if the offender is no longer dangerous. Reacting to cases of particularly heinous murders, the legislature of S wishes to introduce a penalty of life imprisonment without any possibility of early release, regardless of the offender's continued dangerousness. Would this amendment be acceptable?

The Israeli system does not have a constitutional rule according to which (in principle) a life prisoner is entitled to an examination of the possibility of early release.[59] But the system in fact provides such a review.

According to the law on conditional release,[60] a special release committee may recommend to the President to fix the sentence, on the condition that the prisoner has served 7 years of imprisonment. The committee's recommendation will be to fix

55 Penal Law § 345(b)(1).

56 Penal Law § 34F.

57 Penal Law § 353.

58 § 9(a1)(1) Criminal Procedure Law, 5725–1965 (Isr.).

59 Bundesverfassungsgericht [BVerfG] [Federal Constitutional Court] Jun. 21, 1977, 45 Entscheidungen des Bundesverfassungsgerichts [BVerfGE] 187 (1977) (Ger.).

60 § 29(a) Parole Law, 5762–2001 (Isr.).

the sentence for a term of no less than 30 years. In case of rejection, it may consider it again after two years or less.[61]

The parole committee may decide, after two thirds of the period have been served, to release the prisoner on parole for the rest of the sentence, provided that it is convinced that his conditional release will not endanger public peace.[62] If the parole committee's decision was negative, it does not have to re-consider its decision, except if one of the situations enumerated in the law exists.[63]

The vignette case raises two related issues:

Firstly, is dangerousness the ultimate criterion in sentencing, so that it dictates the shortening of imprisonment because of a lack of dangerousness?

Secondly, is it acceptable to determine that under specific circumstances of the crime there should be life imprisonment stricto sensu with no possibility of release (locking the door and throwing away the key)?

Clearly the answer to the first issue is "no". The main criterion in sentencing is retribution.[64] There are cases (including genocide) in which retribution requires a very heavy penalty although the offender is not dangerous or is not considered to be dangerous. His early release based on his lack of dangerousness is out of the question.

On the other hand, it is wrong to entirely preclude the examination of the propriety and necessity of imprisonment as long as the imprisonment and the life of the prisoner continue, especially when the term is very long, and the offender committed his crime when he was young.

If the purpose of a law providing for life imprisonment is said to be deterrence, it can be doubted whether it is effective if most offenders trust that they will not be caught. It is also questionable whether there exists an added net value of deterrence in the difference between 30 or 40 years of imprisonment and life imprisonment. Only extreme retributionists will support ignoring all other considerations.

The passing of a very long period since the crime may even change society's reaction to the crime. The impact of the crime on society as a whole and of those who were personally affected by the crime may be reduced with time.

---

61 § 29(c) Parole Law.

62 § 5 Parole Law

63 Such situations are, for example:The Prisoner Rehabilitation State's Authority submitted a pleading to re-consider a case, as the parole, if granted, will be termed by the prisoner's participation in a rehabilitation program; the Attorney General requested to re-consider a case for reasons of public interest; the prisoner requested to re-consider his case, at least a year after the committee decided not to parole him, and now, the committee is convinced that the circumstances have changed in a manner that justifies re-consideration. See the list of exceptions in Parole Law § 19.

64 See § 40B Penal Law, 5737–1977: "The guiding principle in sentencing is proportionality between the seriousness of the offence committed by the offender and the degree of his culpability, and the type and severity of his punishment."; Parole Law § 5: "[...] the committee is convinced that the *prisoner is deserving release* and his release would not endanger the public." (Italicization added).

Throwing away the key turns the life sentence into an extremely harsh ordeal, allowing release from prison only after death and thereby depriving the prisoner of any glimpse of hope to regain liberty. Hope is needed to make life worth living. A sentence of life imprisonment without a prospect of parole makes the convict's rehabilitation difficult to achieve. It also cannot be reconciled with a dignified perception of human beings in two aspects:

Firstly, human beings should not be reduced to one deed, heinous and horrible as it may be.

Secondly, persons should not be considered as monolithic, unchangeable entities.

A sentence of life imprisonment without parole expresses disbelief in the capacity of people to change radically for the better, a capacity underlying the concept of human beings and their dignity. This is degrading and perhaps even cruel.

9. Italy

By *Gian Marco Caletti** and *Paolo Beccari***

Vignette 1: Trolley Problem – Killing one Person to Save Many

Five young children are playing on railway tracks. An express train is approaching, and it is too late to stop the train before it hits the children, probably killing them. Operator D recognizes the emergency situation. He electronically flips a switch and thus deflects the train from its regular track to a little-used sidetrack. However, the lone repairman V is busy on the sidetrack, and the deflected train kills V, as D had anticipated. Is D criminally responsible for murder of V?

The first Vignette – and the conduct of D – is to be placed within the issue of grounds of justification and the related balancing of interests. The legal system justifies certain human acts that appears criminally relevant, exempting them from punishment as they are not considered – under concrete circumstances – to be contrary to the legal system. Within this framework, the present case is based on the ground of justification named state of necessity. Article 54 of the Italian Criminal Code (ICC) regulates this case, excluding punishment when there is a need to save oneself or others from the present danger of serious personal injury.[1] One prerequisite is an ongoing danger – here: children playing on railway tracks and an express train approaching – which Art. 54 ICC defines as "not voluntarily caused by the agent" and "not otherwise avoidable". In the present case, it must obviously be ruled out that the agent (D) caused the danger for the children, which was instead an "unfortunate coincidence of circumstances". And it is equally clear that such danger is not otherwise avoidable, as it is "too late to stop the train before it hits the children". D's action therefore appears mandatory given his possibilities in his position as operator, in which he could not act otherwise (*ad impossibilia nemo tenetur*). His choice – electronically flipping a switch and thus deflecting the train from its regular track to a little-used sidetrack – results in the death of V, a lone repairman busy on the sidetrack and thus a "blameless third party".

The balancing of interests in this case is not a foregone conclusion. On both sides, the supreme interest in life is at stake, and both contemplate innocent persons. On the one hand, certainly the lives on the main track appear to be greater in number – five to one. If one therefore considered V's life as "qualitatively less", that would be an ethically unacceptable conclusion. However, Art. 54 ICC requires a judgement of proportionality between the harmful conduct and the danger, in other words, between conflicting interests, thus deeming one life inferior to another life. It is precisely for this reason that the state of necessity has been called an "amoral" ground of justification, because it places in the hands of an individual the choice to kill one inno-

---

* Senior Researcher of Criminal law at the Department of Legal Studies of the University of Bologna.

** PhD Candidate in Criminal Law at the Department of Legal Studies of the University of Bologna.

1 On Art. 54 ICC see, *ex multis*, M. Romano, *Commentario sistematico del codice penale*, Milano, 1995 (2nd ed.), *sub art. 54 c.p.*, § 25.

cent person in order to save another one, a situation that the legal system somehow "disregards".[2] And the choice of operator D – who clearly "had anticipated" V's death – can be said to proportionately benefit the interest to be safeguarded: the lives of the children, greater in number and younger in age than hapless V. Nevertheless, it is by no means certain that D's conduct can be considered justified under Italian law. In the absence of case law on cases involving a balancing of lives, the prevailing scholarship holds that the law cannot justify killing an innocent person, not even to save more lives, considering a mathematical calculation aberrant.

Precisely for this reason, according to some scholars the state of necessity would not configure a cause of justification but an exclusion of culpability due to the lack of a lawful alternative behavior and the unavoidability of an injurious outcome.[3] Following this approach, D should be excused for his tragic choice of deflecting the train from its regular track to a little-used sidetrack.

Vignette 2: Attribution of Death

> D intends to kill his neighbor V. Hidden near V's house, D waits for V and stabs him several times with a knife. V is taken to the hospital, where his wounds are treated. His injuries are not life-threatening and V is kept overnight for observation. During the night, a technical defect in the hospital kitchen leads to the outbreak of a fire, which kills V and other persons. Can D be held criminally responsible for V's death?

The second Vignette focuses on the issue of contributing factors, i.e., situations that are part of the causal link between a course of conduct and its result. The ICC distinguishes between pre-existing, concomitant and supervening contributing factors, affirming by Art. 41 the rule of equivalence of such causes with respect to the original contribution.[4] Therefore, a conduct's criminal relevance is not diminished by factors occurring before or at the same time or subsequently to the conduct itself – even if the contributing factor consists in the unlawful act of a third party. Art. 41 ICC, however, introduces an exception in its para. 2, whereby superseding factors exclude causation if they were per se sufficient to produce the injurious result. Without this specification, any subject could be charged with regard to factors exceeding and deflecting an ordinary causal link, but also to any element outside his *mens rea.* This would run against the principle of culpability in Art. 27, para. 1 of the Italian Constitution,[5] which requires the existence of a minimal subjective connection between a crime and its perpetrator. In the present case, the superseding factor – a technical defect in the hospital kitchen leading to the outbreak of a fire, then

---

2 On this issue, see O. Di Giovine, *Dilemmi morali e diritto penale: istruzioni per un uso giuridico delle emozioni*, Bologna, 2022.

3 See, e.g., F. Viganò, *Stato di necessità e conflitto di doveri*, Milano, 2000, pp. 551 ff. On inexigibility and state of necessity, see G. Fornasari, *Il principio di inesigibilità nel diritto penale*, Padova, 1990, p. 352.

4 See G. Fiandaca/E. Musco, *Manuale di diritto penale. Parte Generale*, Bologna, 2019 (8th ed.), pp. 266 ff.; A. Vallini, "*Cause sopravvenute da sole sufficienti*" *e nessi tra condotte*, in: *Diritto Penale Contemporaneo*, 2011.

5 As interpreted by the Italian Constitutional Court, sent. no. 364/1998 and no. 1085/1988.

killing V – clearly represents the beginning of a new causal link, totally independent of the first action, without which the result would still come about.[6]

In addition, even if one considered the contributing factor here to be a later development of the initial conduct, it would still appear exceptional within the theory of human causation. On this issue, the Italian Supreme Court has spoken of a "new and immeasurable risk, totally incongruous with the original risk activated by the initial conduct",[7] describing the character of exceptionality as an "exorbitant risk". The fire in the hospital where V is housed can be considered an "exorbitant impact factor" and therefore certainly not foreseeable by D. The latter could at most be held liable for the injuries caused to V according to Art. 41 para. 2 ICC, but certainly not for the death of his neighbor.

Vignette 3: Torture to Save a Life

Kidnapper K has abducted an 8-year-old girl G and hidden her in a small cave in the woods. K is trying to extort money from G's parents for her release. The police manage to arrest K. Although being questioned for 24 hours, K steadfastly refuses to disclose where he hid G. Police officer D correctly assumes that G may soon die of thirst if she cannot be found. He therefore severely beats K to make him tell the truth. Fearing even more violence, K eventually leads the police to the cave, where they find G still barely alive. Should D be punished for torturing K?

The Vignette addresses the issue of torture, on which Italy has recently introduced a new provision in Art. 613-bis ICC (by Law no. 110/2017),[8] implementing the Convention against Torture adopted by the UN in 1984.[9] The definition of torture consists in producing, by "severe violence or threats" or by "acting with cruelty", "mental suffering or severe psychological trauma to a person deprived of his/her liberty or held in custody, or in a position to be cared for or assisted by the actor or otherwise being in a

6 On causation and the laws of science, see, e.g., F. Stella, *Leggi scientifiche e spiegazione causale nel diritto penale*, Milano, 1990, p. 97; C. De Maglie/S. Seminara (eds.), *Scienza e causalità*, Padova, 2006; M. Romano, *Nesso causale e concretizzazione delle leggi scientifiche in diritto penale*, in: *Scritti per Federico Stella*, Napoli, 2007, I, pp. 891 ff.; R. Bartoli, *Il problema della causalità penale. Dai modelli unitari al modello differenziato*, Torino, 2010, pp. 55 ff.; K. Summerer, *Causalità ed evitabilità*, Pisa, 2013, pp. 29 ff., 45 ff.

7 See, e.g., Cass., sect. IV, 06.06.2017, no. 28010.

8 On Art. 613-bis ICC and its genesis see, among others, F. Viganò, *Sui progetti di introduzione del delitto di tortura in discussione presso la Camera dei deputati*, in: *Diritto penale contemporaneo*, 2014; A. Colella, *La repressione penale della tortura: riflessioni* de jure condendo, in: *Diritto penale contemporaneo*, 2014; G. Lanza, *Verso l'introduzione del delitto di tortura nel codice penale italiano: una fatica di Sisifo. Un'analisi dei "lavori in corso" anche alla luce della pronuncia della Corte EDU sul caso Cestaro c. Italia*, in: *Diritto penale contemporaneo*, 2016; M. Botto, *Il reato di tortura*, in: A. Cadoppi/S. Canestrari/A. Manna/M. Papa, *Diritto penale*, Milano, 2022, pp. 6585 ff.

9 The implementation of this crime occurred after decades of silence of the Italian legislature on this issue and several convictions of Italy by the ECtHR. See C. Fioravanti, *Divieto di tortura e ordinamento italiano: sempre in contrasto con gli obblighi internazionali?* in *Quaderni Costituzionali*, 2004, pp. 555 ff.; A. Pugiotto, *Repressione penale della tortura e Costituzione: anatomia di un reato che non c'è*, in: *Diritto penale contemporaneo*, 2014; F.S. Cassibba, *Violato il divieto di tortura: condannata l'Italia per i fatti della scuola "Diaz-Pertini"*, in: *Diritto penale contemporaneo*, 2015.

condition of diminished defense". The Vignette case, which also invokes the concept of inhuman and degrading treatment (often linked to penal institutions), describes the presence of a "dominant position" on the part of D and a position of diminished defense on K's part.[10] The penalty, 4 to 10 years imprisonment, is aggravated if the public servant commits the act with abuse of power or in violation of the duties linked to his office or service. In the present case, such a qualification exists with regard to D, a police officer, who repeatedly beats K, who is deprived of personal freedom and entrusted to the custody of the police officers, thus in a position of "diminished defense".

Despite the purpose of obtaining information for rescuing the girl, D must not harm the mental and physical integrity of a confined person or eventually endanger his life. Therefore, since beatings clearly fall under the concept of violence, D would be punished – with an aggravated penalty – for torturing K.[11]

It should be added that the statements provided by K, due to the public official's conduct, would not be usable in the criminal proceedings against K for kidnapping the young girl: Law no. 110/2017, in fact, also amended the Italian Criminal Procedure Code, providing for the exclusion of statements obtained by torture. But these statements could be used in another criminal proceeding against D to prove his criminal liability for torture.

Vignette 4: Lethal Self-Defense

> R, a well-trained young man armed with a knife, accosts 50-year-old D, who is on her way home from a party in the early morning hours. R threatens her with the knife and takes away her purse filled with 500 € and her wristwatch worth 1,000 €. As R turns to run away, D draws a pistol she is secretly carrying in her jacket, and shoots and kills R in order to retrieve her property. Is D guilty of murder?

This Vignette turns on the justification of self-defense, based on the balancing of interests and particularly on the prevalence of the interest of the attacked person over the aggressor's interest. Art. 52 ICC excludes punishment if there was a need to save a right of the actor or another person threatened by the present danger of an unlawful attack, if the defense was proportionate to the threatened harm.[12] The starting point of

---

10 On the conduct and the concept of inhuman and degrading treatment, see T. Padovani, *Tortura: adempimento apparentemente tardivo, inadempimento effettivamente persistente*, in: *Criminalia*, 2018, pp. 32 ff.

11 A stir was caused by the case of torture inflicted on brigatists by Carabinieri special units (NOCS) following the kidnapping of James Dozier, NATO commander for southern Europe, who was kidnapped in Verona in 1981. Four officers were later convicted of this torture (including so-called waterboarding). See Judgment of the Court of Padua (Pres. Aliprandi), issued July 15, 1983, in: *Il Foro Italiano*, May 1984, vol. 107, no. 5, with commentary by Domenico Pulitanò. On the Dozier case, see also C. Beccalossi, *La memoria riannodata. Il sequestro Dozier. 17 dicembre 1981–28 gennaio 1982*, Lucca (Italy), 2023.

12 On this topic, see G. Fiandaca/E. Musco, *Diritto penale. Parte generale*, Bologna, 2019, pp. 298 ff.; S. Canestrari/L. Cornacchia/G. De Simone, *Diritto penale. Parte Generale*, Bologna, 2017, pp. 607 ff.; see also, above all others, T. Padovani, *Legittima difesa* (voce), in:

the norm is a legally protected interest threatened by an attack in violation of the legal system (an attack "contra ius"). The attack must give rise to a present danger which the attacked person cannot avoid by early defense or by other means (such as escape). The defensive reaction must thus be necessary for the person attacked according to the concrete circumstances of time, place, person and means. For an elderly or disabled person, for example, escape from a physical attack would be far more difficult than for a healthy 50-year-old person. Additionally, as the law expressly states, a proportional relationship between the assets involved is required, with the consequence that the person defending himself must not harm an asset of the attacker that is markedly greater than that endangered by the initial unlawful assault. This requirement is rather easy to verify when the balancing of interests involves different legal interests, but it must still be checked and the intensity compared between the attack and the defense. In recent years (2006 and 2019), reforms have greatly expanded the scope of self-defense in the home, introducing a presumption of proportionality between defense and attack when the dangerous situation occurs in the home of the attacked person.[13] However, this was "symbolic legislation", since the Courts have stated that proportionality still has to be ascertained, along with the present danger and the necessity of the defensive reaction; if proportionality were always taken for granted, this would create an internal "short circuit" in Art. 52 ICC.

In addition, Art. 55 ICC regulates cases of negligent excess, in which the attacked person negligently exceeds the limits established by law, authority or necessity. If that is the case, the actor can be punished for a negligent crime if the Code provides for a crime of negligence covering the defensive reaction.

In the present case, it is very difficult to argue for proportionate self-defense, not only because of the heterogeneity of the interests involved (life of the aggressor vs. D's money and wristwatch) and the disproportionate means (gun in response to knife), but also because of the requirement of a present danger. In fact, the threat from R with the knife had already ended "as R turns to run away" (so D's life is not endangered anymore), but she still chooses to draw a gun (not exactly an item to secretly carry in your pocket every day!) and shoot the robber from behind. The act represents more than negligent excess in self-defense, amounting to voluntary murder (albeit impetuous), for which D can be held guilty. This solution is also in line with case law on the subject. The Court of Asti sentenced M.R., a jeweler from the area of Cuneo, to 17 years imprisonment for voluntary double murder and attempted murder. M.R., in April 2021 shot and killed two robbers and wounded a third. Shots were fired from an illegally possessed weapon when the three robbers were already outside the shop and getting back into their car. The court not only held this to be a disproportionate reaction but even denied a situation of self-defense.

Dig. Disc. Pen., Torino, 1989, pp. 496 ff.; C.F. Grosso, *Legittima difesa (dir. pen.)*, in: *Enc. Dir.*, Milano, 1974, pp. 27 ff.

13 See, e.g., G.L. Gatta, *La nuova legittima difesa nel domicilio: un primo commento*, in: *Diritto penale contemporaneo*, 2019, and D. Notaro, *La legittima difesa domiciliare. Dalla giustificazione alla scusa fra modelli presuntivi e tensioni soggettive*, Torino, 2020.

Vignette 5: Criminal Responsibility of Subordinates for Systemic Offenses

D is a soldier in the army of a country ruled by a junta of generals who have come to power through a violent coup. When an opposition group demands the return to a democratic system, the government orders the soldiers to shoot and kill any person who resists arrest. Following this order, D kills three young men who take part in a protest demonstration and hit a police officer who tries to arrest them. When D is tried after a change of regime, he says that he did not like to shoot the protesters but that he thought that he had to obey his commanders' orders. D knew that if he had refused to shoot, he might have been demoted, but no physical harm would have occurred to him. Should D be convicted of murder? If so, should his sentence be mitigated because of his situation?

This Vignette deals with the framework of military subordination and a possible justification related to the performance of a duty.[14] Art. 51 ICC excludes punishment when the performance of a duty is required by law or by order of an authority.[15] These are situations in which the legal system not only permits but obliges an action that constitutes an offence. Particularly, in the case of military subordination, the law or the order requires the strictest and most prompt obedience, without which (at least) disciplinary liability of the subordinate will ensue. It may therefore happen that the latter finds himself/herself carrying out an order of his/her superior that constitutes an offence; Art. 51 ICC lays down express rules on this point: The superior who gave the order is always guilty of the offence committed; the person who carried out the order is punished unless he/she mistakenly believed that he/she was carrying out a lawful order. However, the law also specifies that a person who carries out an order over which he/she has no say (an "unquestionable order")[16] is not punished. The concept of an unquestionable order (for which the Italian Constitutional Court[17] has recognized an excuse and a related exclusion of culpability rather than a ground of justification) has long constituted a barrier to the liability of public officials. Later, scholars and case law have recognized a limit to unquestionable orders in case the order is evidently unlawful.[18] Art. 4 of the Military Order Act of 1979 (Law No. 382/1979) already provided for this limitation.[19] Hence every public official, although subordinate and therefore bound to obedience, has the right and duty to refuse such an order and to inform other superiors as soon as possible; otherwise, he is jointly guilty of the offence committed by executing the order.

---

14 See D. Pulitanò, *Esercizio di un diritto e adempimento di un dovere* (voce), in: Dig. Disc. Pen., Torino, 1990, pp. 320 ff.; G. Delitalia, *Adempimento di un dovere* (voce), in: *Enc. Dir.*, 1958, 567 ff.

15 On this topic, see G. Bettiol, *L'ordine dell'autorità nel diritto penale*, Milano, 1934; S. Vinciguerra, *Profili sistematici dell'adempimento del dovere imposto da una norma giuridica*, Milano, 1971.

16 On unquestionable orders, see S. Messina, *L'ordine insindacabile dell'autorità come causa di esclusione del reato*, Torino, 1942.

17 Sentence no. 123/1972.

18 See, e.g., Cass., sect. V, judgment no. 9424/1983.

19 See F. Bellagamba, *Sui limiti della responsabilità penale dell'esecutore di un ordine illegittimo insindacabile*, in: *Dir. pen. e proc.*, 2009, pp. 192 ff.

In the present case, therefore, soldier D cannot invoke the performance of a duty to excuse his conduct: shooting a group of demonstrators during a protest is evidently unlawful, so the killing of three of these will make D guilty of murder. Nor may D invoke the general rules on error under Art. 59 para. 4 ICC regarding an order allegedly received from superiors (for which the cause of justification would in any case occur objectively). D still had to assess for himself its clear unlawfulness and disregard the order. Some indication of D's personal knowledge of the unlawfulness can be found in his own *Kulturnormen*, since he declared that he did not like to shoot the protesters.

Vignette 6: Limits of Consent

V is a 21-year-old ambitious athlete and short-distance runner. He has learned that certain artificial limbs can enhance a runner's speed. He decides that he would rather have an artificial limb instead of his right lower leg. He approaches D, a surgeon in private practice, and asks him to amputate his leg below the knee and replace it with an artificial limb. D complies with V's request. Should D be punished for mayhem?

The topic of consent is central in Italian criminal law, as it appears in various forms, one of which being a ground of justification under Art. 50 ICC.[20] Here it takes the shape of a legal act whereby the holder of a right confers on the addressee the power to interfere with that right – a free and always revocable consent, which does not require any specific form and can be given by the holder on all rights that he may validly dispose of. As to the latter, it is debated whether only material rights (for the disposition of which legal limits must in any case be observed) or also personality rights are included. While it is common opinion that harm to property can be permitted, this is not the case for higher-ranking legal interests, such as life and bodily integrity. In stating that "one who infringes on a right with the consent of the person who can validly dispose of it is not punishable", Art. 50 ICC seems to exclude non-transferable rights. Moreover, Art. 5 of the Italian Civil Code prohibits acts of disposing of one's body when they cause a permanent impairment of physical integrity or when they are contrary to law, public order, or morality.[21] This principle is tempered with regard to some surgical operations usually and lawfully carried out in practice, such as skin transplantation, kidney donation and blood transfusions, since these operations are functional in improving the general health of the disposer. According to some authors, the new form of living wills (introduced in Italy by Law No. 219/2017[22]) are a way of expressing consent with regard to the supreme interest of life, in ordering "*pro futuro*" the interruption of (or totally refusing) life-saving treatment. Otherwise, life is protected from any dispositive act under Art. 579 and

20 See F. Grispigni, *Il consenso dell'offeso*, Roma, 1924; C. Pedrazzi, *Consenso dell'avente diritto* (voce), in: *Enc. Dir.*, Milano, 1961, pp. 140ff.; more recently, S. Cagli, *Principio di autodeterminazione e consenso dell'avente diritto*, Bologna, 2008.

21 On Art. 50 ICC and Art. 5 of Italian Civil Code, see S. Seminara, *La dimensione del corpo nel diritto penale*, in: S. Rodotà-P. Zatti (eds.), *Trattato di biodiritto. Il governo del corpo*, I, Milano, 2011, pp. 209ff.

22 On Italian Law No. 219/2017, see, e.g., S. Canestrari, *La legge n. 219 del 2017 in materia di consenso informato e disposizioni anticipate di trattamento*, in: *Leg. Pen.*, 2018, pp. 1ff.

Art. 580 ICC, which incriminate killing of a consenting person and inciting someone or helping to commit suicide.[23] Similarly, the interest of physical integrity is protected by the criminal provision on personal injury (Art. 582 ICC).

In the present case, although V had approached D asking him to amputate his leg *de lege artis*, thus giving consent to the permanent amputation, it must be considered prohibited by law. Under this very paternalistic civil law, the agreement would be null and void because of the illegality of the object. Therefore, D will be punishable for personal injury, qualified as very serious (and therefore aggravated) as "mutilation that renders a limb useless" (Art. 583 ICC), with the penalty of imprisonment between six and twelve years.

Vignette 7: Withdrawal from an Attempt

25-year-old D is deeply upset with her former boyfriend V, who had ended their relationship to be with another woman. To punish V, D plans to stab him with a large knife. D knows that the stab wounds can be fatal and accepts V's death as a possible outcome. When V goes jogging, D attacks him from behind and stabs him in the back three times. V breaks down. D realizes that she has injured him but that the injuries will not cause his death. She realizes that she could kill him by stabbing him again but decides to leave him alone. Should D be punished for attempted murder?

The Vignette raises the issue of attempted crime and withdrawal from attempt. In the Italian Penal Code, the criminal liability for attempts is based on the objective notion of punishable acts, i. e., acts toward committing the offense during the "*iter criminis*" even if the perpetrator does not achieve the completion of the offense.[24] Circumstances external to the agent's will are, in fact, interposed between his acts and the completion of the crime, so the act is not fully performed or the result does not occur. To justify the extension of punishment to a stage prior to the completion of the crime, the acts must fulfill two specific requirements, set forth in Art. 56 ICC. These are the suitability of the acts for the commission of the crime, i. e., their capacity to infringe upon a legal interest protected by the criminal law, and unequivocality, that is, the finalistic direction of those acts, supported by the offender's specific will. An attempted crime, therefore, requires the psychological element of intent.

In the present case, the attempt is supported by the intent of injury and murder (D "plans to stab him with a large knife […] and accepts V's death as a possible outcome").[25] In establishing the objective requirement of suitable and unequivocal

[23] See S. Canestrari, *Ferite dell'anima e corpi prigionieri. Suicidio e aiuto al suicidio nella prospettiva di un diritto liberale e solidale*, Bologna, 2021.

[24] See E. Gallo, *Il delitto di attentato nella teoria generale del reato*, Padova, 1966; Morselli, *Il tentativo*, in: *Giust. pen.*, 1988, II, pp. 129 ff.; S. Seminara, *Il delitto tentato*, Milano, 2012; G.A. De Francesco, *L'enigma del tentativo: vicende sistematiche ed interrogativi politico-criminali*, in: *Leg. Pen.*, 2002, pp. 927 ff.; F. Palazzo, *Il tentativo: un problema ancora aperto? (tipicità e offesa tra passato e futuro)*, in: *Riv. it. dir. e proc. pen.*, 2011, pp. 38 ff.; G. Marinucci, *A proposito di tentativo e "atti immediatamente antecedenti l'inizio dell'esecuzione"*, in: *Riv. it. dir. e proc. pen.*, 2012, pp. 1542 ff.

[25] Some scholars opine that *dolus eventualis* – here at issue – is not sufficient for an attempted crime. On that basis, the solution proposed here would *a fortiori* be preferred.

acts, the Penal Code precisely marks the beginning of a punishable activity to avoid a premature onset of criminal liability. It may happen, however, that the act is not completed because the agent voluntarily decides to desist from the act. This is the case of voluntary desistance, in which the acting party is not punishable for the acts so far performed, unless these in themselves constitute a different offense.[26] Although one step away from killing V, D finally decides to leave him alone, stopping the action by her own will. She therefore will not be punished for attempted murder but only for injuries to the person, having stabbed V in the back three times.

Vignette 8: Criminal Responsibility of Minors

> D is a 13-year-old boy. He abducts and rapes V, a girl of the same age. Should D be punished for a criminal offence?

The Vignette presents the issue of the imputability of minors, a prerequisite of their criminal liability. Art. 85 ICC defines imputability as the capacity of intending and willing. The law further defines this capacity "by exclusion", i. e., by establishing a number of circumstances that exclude or diminish it. Art. 97 ICC states that a person who was under the age of 14 when he/she committed a criminal act is not imputable; this means that the young person cannot be criminally punished. This is an absolute legislative presumption of non-imputability.[27] In the present case, therefore, although the actions of 13-year-old D are repugnant, he cannot be found guilty and punished. However, according to Article 224 ICC the judge may even for a minor like D order the application of a security measure, such as admission to a judicial reformatory or probation, if he is deemed dangerous, as the seriousness of the crime suggests.

Vignette 9: Statute of Limitations

> In 1995, D violently raped V, a 35-year-old woman, using a knife. D managed to escape and was not apprehended until 2023. Traces of his DNA taken from the victim's body leave no doubt that D is the perpetrator. Should D be convicted despite the long delay?

The Vignette case is a useful cue for the topic of statutes of limitation on crime. The passage of time, in fact, determines the extinction of the crime – and consequently of punishment and further consequences – according to the legal system's loss of interest in the crime. It is thus necessary to assess how long the interest of the legal system in prosecuting a particular crime persists.[28] The time required for the statute of limitations was once set according to classes of progressive severity into which the var-

---

[26] See G. Fornasari, *Il recesso dal tentativo negli ordinamenti tedesco e italiano*, in: *Dir. Pen. e proc.*, 1995, pp. 499 ff.; D. Falcinelli, *L'attualità dell'offesa. Desistenza volontaria e genesi del disvalore penale*, Torino, 2009.

[27] See A. Franchini/F. Introna, *Delinquenza minorile*, Padova, 1972; G. Ponti-P. Gallina Fiorentini, *Imputabilità e immaturità nel procedimento penale minorile*, in: *Riv. It. Med. Leg.*, 1983, pp. 873 ff.

[28] See A. Molari, *Prescrizione del reato e della pena (diritto penale)* (voce), in: *Noviss. Dig. It.*, Torino, 1966; F. Giunta/D. Micheletti, Tempori cedere. *Prescrizione del reato e funzioni della pena nello scenario della ragionevole durata del processo*, Torino, 2003; S. Silvani, *Il giudizio del tempo. Uno studio sulla prescrizione del reato*, Bologna, 2009.

ious crimes were grouped. In 2005, a major reform introduced a different system of calculation, which is still basically in force today: the maximum sentence for each offense is considered, and in any case a minimum threshold of 6 years for felonies and 4 years for misdemeanors. This means that an offence of theft, punishable by a sentence of six months to three years, will ordinarily be prescribed in six years after its commission. To this time frame, the maximum time for interrupting the statute of limitations is usually added, which may not exceed ¼ of the ordinary time: a theft will thus have a maximum statute of limitations of 7 years and 6 months (6 years + ¼ of 6 years = 7 years and 6 months).

There are, however, some exceptions. Firstly, crimes punishable by life imprisonment (such as a massacre or causing an epidemic) are never time-barred, as the interest of the legal system in their prosecution is always valid. For other particularly serious crimes, such as terrorism, organized crime, ill-treatment and sexual violence, the time limits have been doubled by two reforms in 2008 and 2012. Sexual violence, being punishable by imprisonment between 6 and 12 years (Article 609-bis ICC), is thus ordinarily prescribed after 24 years.

In the case described in the Vignette, it is irrelevant that conclusive evidence of the perpetrator's DNA was found: the limitation period has already expired. The aggravating circumstance of the use of a knife is not relevant for the length of the limitation period. While it is true that the law (Art. 157 ICC para. 2) takes into account circumstances of special consequences, the Supreme Court has ruled on this very aggravating circumstance that it is not taken into account for the increase of the statute of limitation for the crime of sexual assault.[29] It follows that, due to the long delay, D cannot be convicted.

Vignette 10: Life Imprisonment without Parole

> The Penal Code of State S provides for imprisonment for life as the maximum penalty for murder, but also authorizes the court to order an offender's early release after a minimum of 15 years if the offender is no longer dangerous. Reacting to cases of particularly heinous murders, the legislature of S wishes to introduce a penalty of life imprisonment without any possibility of early release, regardless of the offender's continued dangerousness. Would this amendment be acceptable?

The last Vignette focuses on the problematic issue of so-called "hostile life imprisonment" or life imprisonment without parole.[30] In Italy, the current rules absolutely preclude a person who has not cooperated effectively with the justice system from applying for conditional release, even if his/her rehabilitation is certain. After numerous appeals, the Italian Constitutional Court has decided on the issue in May 2022

---

29 See Cass., United sections, sentence no. 28953/2017, rule of law: "For the purposes of determining the time necessary to prescribe, the so-called independent circumstances entailing an increase in the penalty of not more than one third (in this case, that provided for in Article 609-ter(1) of the Criminal Code) do not fall within the category of special effect circumstances".

30 See C. Musumeci/A. Pugiotto, *Gli ergastolani senza scampo. Fenomenologia e criticità costituzionali*, Napoli, 2016; E. Dolcini, *Fine pena: 31/12/9999. Il punto sulla questione ergastolo*, in: *Sist. pen.*, 2021.

(see order no. 227/2022). Recalling its jurisprudence, the Constitutional Court pointed out that punishment for life is compatible with the Constitution precisely by virtue of the effective possibility of parole. Consequently, if this possibility were absolutely precluded, life imprisonment would be contrary to the rehabilitative purpose of punishment (as stated in Art. 27 para. 3 of the Italian Constitution). The Court, however, referred the documents back to the Supreme Court, as the legislature was at that time considering several bills on the subject, which were then merged at the end of the year into Decree-Law No. 162/2022. This Law contains, *inter alia*, urgent measures in the matter under consideration. These measures do not weaken the regime of life imprisonment without parole, as it can be necessary, even after a prisoner serving 30 years of imprisonment, to impose certain measures to neutralize his continuing dangerousness. For a determination of the constitutional compatibility of the newly introduced rules (which did not in fact defeat life imprisonment without parole), a new referral to the Constitutional Court will be needed. In the meantime, however, the court's warning and the constitutional-ranking principle of rehabilitation remain in place. That is why in Italy an amendment such as the one proposed in the present Vignette, albeit focused on particularly heinous murders, cannot be considered acceptable.

10. Japan

By *Tomoko Utsumi**

Vignette 1: Trolley Problem – Killing one Person to Save Many

Five young children are playing on railway tracks. An express train is approaching, and it is too late to stop the train before it hits the children, probably killing them. Operator D recognizes the emergency situation. He electronically flips a switch and thus deflects the train from its regular track to a little-used sidetrack. However, the lone repairman V is busy on the sidetrack, and the deflected train kills V, as D had anticipated. Is D criminally responsible for murder of V?

The so-called trolley problem is being actively discussed in Japan in relation to AI-automated driving. It is therefore necessary to answer this question from the view of criminal law.

Article 37 of the Japanese Penal Code (JPC) permits to harm another to avert a present danger to the life, body, liberty or property of oneself or any other person.

Article 37 (1) Japanese Penal Code[1]

An act a person was compelled to take to avert a present danger to the life, body, liberty or property of oneself or any other person is not punishable only when the harm produced by such act does not exceed the harm to be averted; provided, however, that an act causing excessive harm may lead to the punishment being reduced or may exculpate the offender in light of the circumstances.

The requirement of a present danger means that there must exist a present or imminent danger to legally protected interests, including dangers caused by natural phenomena. The necessity requirement implies that no other means are available to protect the legal interest and that committing the actus reus of a crime is the only option. Additionally, the harm resulting from the act must not exceed the harm intended to be avoided (balance of legal interests).

Concerning the legal character of an act of necessity, it is commonly held that it constitutes a ground of justification. If it is necessary to protect one legal interest at the expense of another, according to the common view, it is permissible to sacrifice the less important legal interests in order to safeguard more significant ones. However, some scholars argue that necessity can be considered only a defense negating personal responsibility, because transferring harm to unrelated third parties cannot be legitimized. A prominent view named dualistic theory[2] suggests that necessity is generally considered to be a ground of justification. However, necessity only negates responsibility if the protected and the infringed legal interests are equivalent or cannot be compared.

---

* Professor, Graduate School of International Social Sciences, Yokohama National University.

1 https://www.japaneselawtranslation.go.jp/ja/laws/view/3581#je_pt1ch7at3.

2 Kazushige Asada, Keiho Soron, 3rd ed., 2024, p. 261.

According to the prevailing view, if it is necessary to sacrifice one life to save five lives, this act is not illegal. In this case, there is an immediate danger to the lives of five individuals so that D's action can be considered necessary. Therefore, the act is not unlawful due to necessity, and D cannot be convicted.

However, scholars have examined the trolley problem from various perspectives. Behind the prevailing view that sacrificing less important legal interests to protect more significant ones is permissible, there lies a utilitarian way of thinking. In the example, where pushing a person standing next to you off a bridge to stop a trolley, according to a utilitarian standpoint, there would be no illegality. If this conclusion seems inappropriate, it suggests a need to modify utilitarianism. Therefore, another theory suggests that different treatment is possible in cases where a sort of "community of danger" exists between the person rescued and the victim, such as the worker on the tracks. On the other hand, in cases where only general citizen relationships between them exist there is no duty for someone standing on the bridge to rescue the workers on the tracks, so that it is not allowed to push the man down from the bridge.[3] The acceptance of justification by necessity depends on what duty of accepting the transfer of danger exists for the person affected by the act. The existence of such a duty is influenced by the principle of "social solidarity" to enhance the chances of mutual survival among citizens. Thus, acts of necessity may be permissible in cases where the principle of social solidarity is applicable.

From a liberal point of view, individuals are not obliged to intervene or request assistance from others, but on the contrary, intervening in others persons' affairs, especially by transferring burdens to others, is not permitted. However, thinking in this way does not maximize the overall societal benefit. Therefore, it may be necessary to permit the transfer of burdens to significantly less valuable interests in order to protect more important legal interests. Members of society would be likely to agree to maximizing the protection of legal interests in this way, and such a societal agreement must be accepted by the law. The theory of necessity would transfer this agreement into law.

Kaoru Endo has conducted surveys on the trolley problem in Japan, China, and the United States.[4] According to his results, 90 % of Japanese respondents agreed that it was legitimate to switch tracks in response to the question whether it is allowed to sacrifice one worker on the track to rescue five other workers. However, in the scenario involving pushing a man off a bridge, nearly 80 % of respondents were opposed to doing so. This study also included a question with additional conditions added to the first question, such as the five workers being elderly and the single worker on the alternative track being younger. The percentage willing to accept the deaths of the five elderly people in this alternative jumped to approximately 36 %, roughly 3.6 times higher than in the original scenario.

---

3 Takaaki Matsumiya, Sentan Keiho Soron, 1st ed., 2019, pp. 90–96.

4 Endo Kaoru, AI ka suru Shakai to rinriteki Jirenma Torokko Mondai no Nichibeichu Bunka Hikaku kara kanngaeru ("Discussion: AI-dominated Society and Ethical Dilemmas – Considerations from a Cultural Comparison of the Trolley Problem in Japan, the United States, and China"), in: Gakushuin Homukenkyu 14, 2020, p. 1.

Vignette 2: Attribution of Death

D intends to kill his neighbor V. Hidden near V's house, D waits for V and stabs him several times with a knife. V is taken to the hospital, where his wounds are treated. His injuries are not life-threatening and V is kept overnight for observation. During the night, a technical defect in the hospital kitchen leads to the outbreak of a fire, which kills V and other persons. Can D be held criminally responsible for V's death?

In Japan, a causal connection between the act of an offender and the harm is determined as follows. According to the common view, first the "but for" test (conditio sine qua non) between the offender's act and the harm is required. A causal relationship is said to exist when the result (harm) B would not have occurred without the act A of the actor. However, as is well known, the scope of attribution would be too large if attribution required only a causal relationship, because causal chains are endless. Therefore, to limit the scope of attribution, the formerly common view considered that a "usual" relationship must exist between the offender's act and the result. In other words, a causal connection is affirmed when it is normal for such an act to produce such a result, and denied when it is unusual that the act causes such a result (adequate relationship theory).

How to determine whether a normal or an abnormal relationship exists between the act and the harm? The distinction between normal and abnormal is judged by the criterion of "reasonableness", but what should be the content of this criterion? The conclusion may vary depending on how the criterion is considered. There are three answers to this question.

According to the first view, we must consider only the facts that the offender knows. But this approach could be too narrow, because it is difficult to determine which facts the offender knows about, so that one needs to fall back on the objective facts. The other two views have broad support in the legal literature. One of them is named objective theory, the other is the compromise theory. They differ from each other with regard to which factual circumstances existing at the time of the act should be taken into consideration. Let me explain the difference with the following case 1:

Case 1:

X strikes A on the head once with a stick with the intention to injure A. The stick was covered with a highly virulent pathogen, and the pathogen entered A's body through the wound on A's head, resulting in A's death.

There is a causal relationship, because if X had not struck A, the pathogen would not have entered A's body and A would not have died. If we ignore the fact that there was the pathogen covering the stick, because it is very rare that there are pathogens on a stick and people cannot recognize this fact, it is extraordinary that a person would die when being struck on the head with a stick. For this reason, we should conclude that it is not to be expected that the act of striking a person once with a stick would result in the death of the person struck. On the other hand, it is not surprising that the act of striking a person once with a stick *covered with a virulent pathogen* would result in the death of the person struck. Therefore, reasonableness of the causal chain is affirmed.

The theory of adequate causation has long been the prevailing theory in academic writing. But the Japanese Supreme Court did not follow the prevailing theory but responded to each case by adopting variable theories as to the causal relationship. For example, in the Osaka Nanko case,[5] the Supreme Court did not use the adequate causation theory in determining the causal relationship. The facts of the case are as follows:

Case 2: Osaka Nanko Case

X struck A's head, and after A lost consciousness, he was carried to a storage yard at the port and left by himself. Then someone struck A's head again. The Supreme Court held that the injury that caused A's death was formed mainly by X's beating and that there was a causal relationship between X's beating and the victim's death, even if the death was hastened somewhat by a subsequent assault by a third party.

In the Osaka Nanko case, the Supreme Court recognized a causal connection between X's beating and the victim's death. However, it would be unusual for someone to approach a person who was left unconscious in a materials yard at a port at night and beat him further. Therefore, if we adopt the adequate causal relationship theory, the causal relationship between X's act and A's death must be denied. This theory conventionally assumes that when a third party intervenes with an intentional act, the link of adequate causation disappears. The unjust result of this case led to questioning the arguments in favor of the adequate causal relationship theory.

As seen in the Osaka Nanko case, there are cases in which the relationship should be affirmed even if the causal course after the act is abnormal. To solve this problem, the objective attribution theory has gradually gained support among scholars. The objective attribution theory favors the attribution of harm to an act if the danger inherent in the act has been realized in the result. Attribution is affirmed on the basis of assessments of the creation and the realization of danger. The objective attribution theory in Japan was advanced following the development of the German objective attribution theory, but it has been shaped in a unique form in Japan.

It has been remarked that Japanese case law has traditionally kept a distance from the commonly accepted theory of adequate causation. In recent years, courts have adopted a position closer to the objective attribution theory. This theory differs from the adequate causation theory in that the risk of the act is considered based on circumstances that objectively existed at the time of the act rather than the expectations of ordinary people; and even if unusual circumstances intervene after the act, attribution is not necessarily denied. Still, the influence of the act and the intervening circumstances on the result are considered in determining whether attribution is required. This theory differs from the theory of adequate causation in the influence of the intervening circumstances on the outcome of the act.

In Vignette 2, according to the theory of adequate causation conventionally supported in Japan, the intervening circumstance of "fire caused by a technical defect in the kitchen of the hospital" can occur in daily life. The outcome is therefore regarded as reasonably to be expected, and V's death is attributed to D. Another view would,

---

[5] Supreme Court decision of November 20, 1990.

however, deny the attribution of V's death to D's act because the breaking out of a fire is a risk of daily life that could cause harm to V even without D's prior act.

Vignette 3: Torture to Save a Life

Kidnapper K has abducted an 8-year-old girl G and hidden her in a small cave in the woods. K is trying to extort money from G's parents for her release. The police manage to arrest K. Although being questioned for 24 hours, K steadfastly refuses to disclose where he hid G. Police officer D correctly assumes that G may soon die of thirst if she cannot be found. He therefore severely beats K to make him tell the truth. Fearing even more violence, K eventually leads the police to the cave, where they find G still barely alive. Should D be punished for torturing K?

The question of whether torture by public authorities is permissible for the purpose of saving lives has often been discussed in Japan with regard to German case law and doctrine.[6] Fukamachi[7], for example, has introduced the German arguments on the justification of police violence to rescue an illegally detained person and has analyzed them as follows:

With regard to the criminal investigation agency concerned, the problem is whether justification under § 32 (self-defense) or § 34 (necessity) German Criminal Code is accepted. The majority view in Germany admits the application of § 32 or § 34 Criminal Code to the acts of state authorities. However, Article 1 sec. 1 of the German Basic Law on human dignity absolutely prohibits torture, and the common view in Germany holds that a person subjected to torture is treated as a mere object for gaining information, denying his/her personality. But Fukamachi insists that respect for human dignity is not a suitable reason for an absolute prohibition of torture by public agents, because torture can be applied not only by public agents but also by private persons. Fukamachi also suggests that it remains unclear to what extent exoneration by §§ 32 or 34 German Criminal Code is granted according to the majority view.

Iijima has also considered the discussion in Germany related to torture to save a crime victim.[8] He asserts that

> Torture for the purpose of rescuing a person's life is permissible as long as it is legitimate legal coercion. To determine which coercion is legitimate, different criteria (objective retrospective judgment or ex-ante judgment based on the perspective of an ordinary person) are required, depending on the difference between the entities exercising coercion (public officials or private individuals). The fundamental aspects of the satisfaction of the requirements of justificatory necessity, although derived from discussions in Germany, should apply to the legal situation in our country.

Iijima further states,

---

6 In 2014, a Japanese translation of an essay written by Christian Jäger (Das Verbot der Folter als Ausdruck der Würde des Staates, in: Strafecht zwischen System und Telos, Festschrift für Rolf Dietrich Herzberg, 2008, pp. 539–553) was published in: Hosei Kenkyu, Nr. 81–1/2, 2014, pp. 85–108 (Mitsuru Nozawa, translator).

7 Shinya Fukamachi, Doitsu ni okeru Gomon ni yoru Kujo wo meguru Shomondai, in: Riron Keihogaku Nr. 6, 2013, pp. 243.

8 Mitsuru Iijima, Kyuujo no tameno Gomon no Keihojo no Seitoka ni tsuite, in: Kagawa Hogaku 29–3/4, 2010, p. 45.

Even to rescue the victim, torture by police officers should not be easily tolerated.[9] But I cannot agree with the commonly held view in Germany, which unconditionally prioritizes the protection of the dignity of criminals and seeks to establish an absolute prohibition of torture on that basis. To prevent abuse, it is necessary to carefully determine the fulfilment of the requirements for necessity while rigorously excluding any torture acts that cannot be justified as legitimate legal coercion.

Let us now take a look at the situation of legislation in Japan. In cases such as Vignette 3, there is the possibility that legitimate self-defense under Article 36 of the Japanese Penal Code (JPC) may apply.

Article 36 Japanese Penal Code[10]

(1) An act a person was compelled to take to protect the rights of oneself or any other person against imminent and unlawful infringement is not punishable.

(2) An act exceeding the limits of self-defense may lead to the punishment being reduced or may exculpate the offender in light of the circumstances.

In modern states, it is generally prohibited to protect or enforce one's rights through force. If individuals were allowed to enforce their rights by force, society would descend into chaos, resembling the law of the jungle, which is why protecting rights is considered the task of the state. However, in emergencies without time to wait for state intervention, private individuals may exceptionally protect their rights by using force. Thus, as an exceptional measure, the criminal law recognizes acts of legitimate self-defense (Article 36, paragraph 1 JPC) and necessity (Article 37, paragraph 1 JPC) for the protection of rights by individuals.

Legitimate self-defense can be employed to defend one's own rights or the rights of others, such as life, body, liberty, honor, and property. The requirements for legitimate self-defense are as follows.

a) Urgency

The concept of urgency refers to the imminent or present character of the infringement. Urgency does not apply to past infringements that have already ended or future infringements that are only anticipated. However, if there is a situation where it is likely that further infringements will occur even after the initial infringement has stopped, urgency can still be regarded as present. Even if an infringement was anticipated in advance, urgency is not necessarily lacking if an immediate attack occurs. For example, a woman carrying a knife for self-defense while walking alone at night may be justified in using the knife if attacked. It was traditionally believed that self-defense is not legitimate if the counterattack is made with an aggressive intent to do harm. Regarding this point, the Supreme Court decision of April 26, 2017 emphasized the need to consider all circumstances, including not only the intention of the defender, but also the situation preceding the interaction.

---

9 Article 36 of Japan's Constitutional Law states: "Torture by public officials and cruel punishments shall absolutely not be permitted".

10 https://www.japaneselawtranslation.go.jp/ja/laws/view/3581#je_pt2ch28at4.

b) Wrongfulness of the Attack

The infringement subject to legitimate defense must be "wrongful", which has the same meaning as "illegal". Even if the act is committed by someone who lacks legal responsibility, it is considered a legitimate reason for self-defense if it is illegal.

c) Reasonableness of the Defensive Act

An act of self-defense must be unavoidable for the defense of one's rights. The attacked person is, however, not obliged to flee from the attacker but may confront him to some extent in defense. This differs significantly from the case of necessity. As to whether the act of defense was unavoidable, the criteria of necessity and reasonableness are used: the act must be necessary and reasonable for the defense. That is the case if an ordinary person would consider the act necessary and reasonable to eliminate the infringement at the time of the act. Even if an attempt to protect the body results in taking the life of the other person, self-defense may be affirmed.

An act of self-defense can be justified even if there would have been other ways to avoid the attack. The defense is deemed reasonable even if the consequences of the counterattack are more serious than the legal interest to be protected, unless there exists a significant imbalance.

d) Intent to Defend

The general view among scholars as well as the case law requires an intent to defend as a subjective requirement for legitimate self-defense. However, this intent does not necessarily require a purely defensive motivation; it is sufficient for the defender to act with a mental state corresponding to the defense situation while recognizing it. The intent to defend exists even if the action is almost unconscious or reflexive based on self-preservation instincts, if it is carried out in anger or rage in response to a sudden attack, or even if there is a simultaneous intent to hurt the attacker. However, the intent to defend cannot be recognized if the act is carried out only with the purpose to harm the opponent.

In the Vignette case, if the four requirements mentioned above are met, D's action can be justified under Article 36 JPC.

Vignette 4: Lethal Self-Defense

R, a well-trained young man armed with a knife, accosts 50-year-old D, who is on her way home from a party in the early morning hours. R threatens her with the knife and takes away her purse filled with 500 € and her wristwatch worth 1,000 €. As R turns to run away, D draws a pistol she is secretly carrying in her jacket, and shoots and kills R in order to retrieve her property. Is D guilty of murder?

The Act on Prevention and Disposition of Thefts and Other Related Offenses can apply in this case. In Article 1, Paragraph 1, this Act extends the application of Article 36 of the Japanese Penal Code, which justifies self-defense, to the following cases: (1) Preventing a thief from stealing or recovering stolen property, (2) attempting to prevent a person from entering another person's residence etc., if that person carries a deadly weapon or climbs over or damages a gate or barrier, and (3) attempting to exclude a person who has entered a residence etc. illegally or refuses to leave that residence.

In these three situations cases it is permissible to kill or injure the offender if there is a present danger to the life, body or chastity of the actor or another person. The defender must act with the intention to eliminate the danger. Under Article 1(2) of the Act, even if there is no present danger to one's own or another's life, body, or chastity, one is not guilty of a crime if one kills or injures the offender out of fear, astonishment, excitement or dismay.

In the Vignette case, D killed R to get back what R had stolen from D. The question is whether there is a present danger to D's life, body, or chastity. Since R is trying to escape, the attack on D's person has already ended, and a "present danger" cannot be said to exist. Thus, Article 1(1) does not apply. However, if D killed R in fear, astonishment, excitement or dismay caused by the attack, Article 1(2) of the Act would apply, and D would not be punished.

If the Act on Prevention and Disposition of Thefts and Other Related Offenses is not applicable, how would the case be decided? First, the question arises whether it is permissible to take a person's life to recover property. Second, since the act of committing the robbery had already been completed and R was about to flee, the issue could be whether the urgency requirement is met. We shall examine these two issues in turn.

An act of self-defense can be justified even if there would have been other ways to avoid the attack. The defense is deemed reasonable even if the consequences of the counterattack are more serious than the legal interest to be protected, unless there exists a significant imbalance. Therefore, if an attempt to protect the body results in taking the life of the attacker, it may be justified by self-defense.

If the attacked person acts in self-defense but exceeds the bounds of reasonableness, the penalty may be reduced or waived according to the circumstances under Article 36 sec. 2 Japanese Penal Code (excessive defense). The courts and the majority of scholars base the reduction on the actor's diminished responsibility on the consideration that a person who is suddenly attacked will often be in a psychological state of surprise, fear or excitement and will be upset. In such an emergency situation, it is more difficult to maintain one's normal composure, and the person may thus act excessively in fighting back. The attacked person therefore cannot be blamed strongly for his or her excessive counterattack, so that his or her responsibility is diminished. The concurring theory of diminished illegality argues that the state need not go out of its way to protect the legal interests of an attacker and that even if the defensive act goes too far, its illegality is reduced because there exists only a diminished need to protect the legal interests of the attacker.

The concept of excessive defense includes not only cases in which the defensive act is excessive but also cases where the act of defense continues after the wrongful attack has ended. According to the case law and the majority opinion, the reason for the reduction of responsibility continues even when the attack is over, if the attacked person is left in panic, which prevents him or her from immediately terminating the defensive act. The continuation of the counterattack is therefore evaluated as a kind of excessive defense (quantitative excessive defense).

If the actor is so excited that he chases after the person who committed the wrongful attack and attacks him further although he is running away, this may be said to constitute an excessive defense. However, there are cases in which a diminished responsibility on the grounds of excessive defense has not been found: If the attacked person was not surprised or excited but responded by calmly attacking the former aggressor, the application of Article 36 sec. 2 Penal Code should be denied. The difference can be shown in the following case, decided by the Japanese Supreme Court on June 25, 2008:

Aluminum Ashtray Case

X, who had been attacked by A, struck A's face. In response, A threw an aluminum ashtray toward X. X avoided the ashtray and struck A. A fell, hit his head on the ground and became immobile (first assault of X). X then inflicted further violence such as kicking A's abdomen (second assault of X). The first assault of X led to injuries resulting in A's death due to subdural hematoma.

In this case, A's imminent illegal act had finished when the ashtray missed X. The Court nevertheless did not acknowledge an excessive defensive action of X because X, having toppled A with a legitimate act of defense ("first assault"), subsequently continued with a series of assaults ("second assault") in temporal and spatial continuity, although he recognized that A was unable to engage in further attacks. Since the second assault was based not on defensive but solely on aggressive intentions, there existed a discontinuity between the first and the second assault. When considering the overall context of both assaults, the court did not consider them to be a single instance of excessive defense.

In the Vignette case, D took R's life to protect her property while R was running away. If D was still upset because of R's attack, one can say that D acted in excessive defense.

Vignette 5: Criminal Responsibility of Subordinates for Systemic Offenses

D is a soldier in the army of a country ruled by a junta of generals who have come to power through a violent coup. When an opposition group demands the return to a democratic system, the government orders the soldiers to shoot and kill any person who resists arrest. Following this order, D kills three young men who take part in a protest demonstration and hit a police officer who tries to arrest them. When D is tried after a change of regime, he says that he did not like to shoot the protesters but that he thought that he had to obey his commanders' orders. D knew that if he had refused to shoot, he might have been demoted, but no physical harm would have occurred to him. Should D be convicted of murder? If so, should his sentence be mitigated because of his situation?

D's actions were carried out in compliance with government orders. His actions could have been legal under the political system at that time. Would it be permissible to apply the laws valid under the new regime to D's actions after a change of government?

In Japan, the principle of legality in criminal law, also known as "nulla poena sine lege", is not included in the Penal Code but is based on Article 31 of the Constitution, which provides that the principle of legality applies when the state exercises its power to impose penalties.

Article 31 of the Japanese Constitution[11]

No person shall be deprived of life or liberty, nor shall any other criminal penalty be imposed, except according to procedure established by law.

The principle of legality in punishment requires that the content of crimes and punishments must be predetermined by law. The principle of legality in punishment is necessary from the perspectives of democracy and liberalism. One of the principles derived from legality in punishment is the prohibition of retroactive punishment. This principle asserts that penal legislation shall not be applied retroactively to acts committed before its enactment, a requirement stemming from liberal principles. Punishing acts that were not punishable at the time when they were committed poses the risk of catching individuals off guard.

Therefore, retroactively evaluating and punishing an act that was legal at the time when it was committed may violate the prohibition of retroactive punishment. Hence, in Vignette 5, punishing D according to the laws of the new regime is not permissible if shooting protesters was considered legal when D acted.

Even if the application of the law under the new regime is not considered retroactive punishment, D may have believed that his actions were legal because he was following orders of his superiors. It is true D was not obliged to obey his superiors without question, but he acted in accordance with the judgment of the government at the time. Since the state considered D's actions legal, that is a sufficient reason for D to believe that his actions were legal. Therefore, D lacks awareness of illegality and is not punishable.

It may be questionable whether a military regime established by a coup d'état constitutes an unlawful state and whether the so-called Radbruch formula can be applied. However, it is difficult to determine how Japanese legal scholars would consider the application of laws under the new regime to acts taken under the previous political system. While cases involving the Radbruch formula or trials of the East German border guards have been discussed extensively in Japan, there is a lack of discussion on how to address such situations if they were to arise in Japan. One reason for this may be that the trials of war criminals by the Allied occupation Powers after World War II (Tokyo Trials) did not lead the Japanese people to believe that the regime before and during World War II was an unlawful state.

It is questionable whether the order to shoot protesters was illegal. Assuming that the order was illegal, even though it was supported by the government, how could D be punished? Japan has no army, no military penal code and no regulation on crimes against humanity; D therefore cannot be charged with a crime against humanity. In the field of international criminal law, a defense of superior orders has been discussed, but this discussion cannot be applied directly to the field of civilian criminal

---

11 https://www.japaneselawtranslation.go.jp/ja/laws/view/174#je_ch3at26.

law. In Japan, D would only be subject to the Penal Code, and the charge might be murder. The court might consider that D, being ordered by his superiors to shoot, could not be expected to obey the law. But disobeying the order would not have had serious consequences for D, hence he could not be excused. D could only hope to be pardoned like many Japanese soldiers after World War II.

Vignette 6: Limits of Consent

V is a 21-year-old ambitious athlete and short-distance runner. He has learned that certain artificial limbs can enhance a runner's speed. He decides that he would rather have an artificial limb instead of his right lower leg. He approaches D, a surgeon in private practice, and asks him to amputate his leg below the knee and replace it with an artificial limb. D complies with V's request. Should D be punished for mayhem?

If the victim decides to waive his or her legal interest, that decision must be respected as an exercise of the victim's self-determination. However, it depends on the nature of the crime how consent is evaluated under criminal law. In crimes such as home invasion and rape, which can only occur contrary to the victim's will, the constitutive elements of the offense are negated by the victim's consent. For example, under Article 130 of the Japanese Penal Code entering someone's home without a valid agreement of the resident is punishable, but entering with consent is not considered a home invasion. Similarly, receiving an item from the owner does not constitute theft under Article 235 JPC. On the other hand, when it comes to life, which is the most important legal interest and, once relinquished, cannot be reclaimed, the right to self-determination is restricted. Article 202 JPC provides for the crime of consented killing. According to that provision, even if the victim consents to being killed, the illegality of the act of killing is only diminished, not negated.

Article 202 Japanese Penal Code

(Participation in Assisted Suicide; Consensual Homicide)

A person who induces or aids another person to commit suicide, or kills another person at the other's request or with the other's consent, is punished by imprisonment for not less than 6 months but not more than 7 years.

In cases of bodily injury, the affected person's consent is generally regarded as an extralegal justification, although there is no explicit provision on the subject in the Criminal Code. But some writers hold the view that the illegality is not negated by the victim's consent when the act causes serious harm and puts his life into danger. The requirements for valid consent include (1) capacity to consent, that is, the victim must understand the content and meaning of consent, and (2) voluntariness, that is, consent must be given voluntarily and in good faith. Consent is considered invalid if given under coercion, including not only physical but also psychological coercion.

Case 1: Judgment of Fukuoka District Court, Miyazaki Branch, of March 24, 1989

X had gained almost blind trust from A, a 66-year-old woman living alone, and within a short period obtained from her an amount of money totaling 7.5 million yen through fraudulent means. When it became apparent that repayment was almost impossible for X, X conceived a plan to induce A to commit suicide. X deceived A into believing that the police were pur-

> suing her as a perpetrator of violations of investment laws. Ultimately, X convinced A that suicide was the only way for her to escape the police investigation. X misled A into ingesting approximately 100 milliliters of a liquid pesticide, leading to her death.

The Court made it clear that where the offender induces the victim to commit suicide through physical or psychological coercion resulting in a significant defect in the victim's decision-making process, so that the decision to commit suicide cannot be considered as stemming from the victim's free will, the offense is no longer incitement to suicide but murder. In this case, X was punished for the crime of robbery-murder.

There is controversy over whether consent is invalid if the victim gives it under a mistaken belief. The prevailing doctrine and case law hold that consent is invalidated if a mistake has significantly influenced the victim's decision-making process. However, another prominent theory distinguishes between mistakes regarding the content of the legal interest being waived and other mistakes. According to this theory, consent remains valid despite the mistake if the victim recognizes what legal interest he or she is giving up. Consent is deemed invalid if there is a mistake regarding the type or scope of the legal interest being waived. However, if the victim is deceived into consenting under a mistaken belief that waiving the legal interest will provide certain benefits, such as being deceived into consenting to an injury in exchange for money, the consent is considered valid. In this context, the following case is notable:

> *Case 2: Supreme Court Judgment of November 21, 1958 (Double Suicide Incident)*
>
> X (man) and A (woman) entered into a love relationship, but X's parents were against their getting married, and A became pessimistic about the future. Therefore, A suggested to X that they commit double suicide. X was pushed by A's enthusiasm and prepared for the suicide. He went for a drive with A to an isolated area. X gave poison to A, and she drank it up in one stretch and died. But X had already given up the intent to die together with A and drove back home.

The Supreme Court decided that X had utilized A's belief that he would die alongside her out of affection for A. X deceived A into believing this and caused A's death by poisoning. The court determined that A decided to die alongside X due to X's deception. Therefore, A's decision had a significant flaw and did not align with her genuine intent. X's act was therefore held to constitute murder.

In the Vignette case, V is 21 years old and should be capable of understanding the consequences of the leg amputation, thus possessing the capacity to consent. His consent appears genuine and voluntary and was given without coercion or deception. Therefore, it may be argued that the consent is valid, and D's actions could be considered lawful. However, it is necessary to discuss the limitations of consent. In Japanese law, consented killings are punishable, and serious acts of bodily harm may be treated similarly, even with the victim's consent. It is doubtful whether D's act can be justified as a medical procedure, raising the possibility of punishment for the offense of bodily injury.

Vignette 7: Withdrawal from an Attempt

25-year-old D is deeply upset with her former boyfriend V, who had ended their relationship to be with another woman. To punish V, D plans to stab him with a large knife. D knows that the stab wounds can be fatal and accepts V's death as a possible outcome. When V goes jogging, D attacks him from behind and stabs him in the back three times. V breaks down. D realizes that she has injured him but that the injuries will not cause his death. She realizes that she could kill him by stabbing him again but decides to leave him alone. Should D be punished for attempted murder?

D's act, carried out with intent to kill V by stabbing him with a large knife, posed a risk of causing V's death and thus constituted attempted murder. The issue at hand is whether the provisions on abandonment apply. Article 43 JPC deals with both incomplete attempts, where an obstacle prevents the completion of the crime, and abandonment, where the actor voluntarily gives up the commission of the offence.

Article 43 Japanese Penal Code[12] *(Reduction or Exculpation of Punishment for Attempts)*

The punishment of a person who commences a crime without completing it may be reduced; provided, however, that voluntary abandonment of commission of the crime leads to the punishment being reduced or the offender being exculpated.

Article 44 Japanese Penal Code[13] *(Attempts)*

An attempt is punishable only when so provided in the Article concerned.

In the Vignette case, the second sentence of Article 43 JPC may apply. As the offender initiated the commission of the crime but the results did not yet occur, it falls into the category of an attempted crime. While in regular attempts (incomplete attempts) the punishment can be mitigated by the judge, the legal consequence of abandonment is more favorable to the offender because it necessarily leads to either a reduction of the sentence or to his complete exemption from punishment.

Various theories, such as the criminal policy theory, the illegality reduction theory, and the responsibility reduction theory compete with regard to the legal character of abandonment. The criminal policy theory regards abandonment provisions as a "golden bridge for retreat". The Penal Code discourages people from committing crimes by informing them that they will be punished if they engage in the prohibited conduct. However, once an offender has decided to commit a crime and initiated its execution, conventional deterrents lose their effectiveness. Therefore, to avoid the infringement of legally protected interests, it becomes necessary to persuade the offender to abandon the act. Consequently, a reward in the form of a reduced sentence or an exemption from punishment is given to offenders who abandon their criminal acts, the law aiming to prevent the occurrence of the intended outcome.

By contrast, the illegality reduction theory posits that as the offender has abandoned the intent to commit the crime, the element of intent, i. e., mens rea, is absent, reducing the illegality of his act. The responsibility reduction theory suggests that despite committing the criminal act, condemnation of the offender should be dimin-

---

12 https://www.japaneselawtranslation.go.jp/ja/laws/view/3581#je_pt1ch8at1.

13 https://www.japaneselawtranslation.go.jp/ja/laws/view/3581#je_pt1ch8at2.

ished due to his voluntary abandonment of the intended act. Some legal writers argue for a combination of these theories (combination theory).

To establish the elements of abandonment, three factors are necessary: the act of abandonment, a sincere effort, and voluntariness. With regard to the act of abandonment, the common view regards it as sufficient for the offender to cease the execution of the act if he has not yet completed it. On the other hand, if the criminal act has already been completed but the result has not yet occurred, active measures to prevent the outcome are deemed necessary. However, there are situations where further action is required to achieve the intended result, even after the intended dangerous act has already been completed. The commonly held view was weakened by the existence of such situations. If the offender voluntarily refrains from such actions despite being aware of such circumstances, the existence of abandonment should be recognized.[14] The question of whether further action is necessary for preventing the harm or whether it is enough to simply abandon the continuation of the offense should be determined at the point in time at which the act of abandonment becomes an issue. According to this theory, if the result can be avoided by inaction, abandonment can be established by inaction alone. However, active measures are required if there is a risk that the result occurs if the causal chain is not interrupted.

As for the requirement of a sincere effort, according to precedent, the offender's act of preventing the occurrence of the result must be a sincere effort to avoid the result. Regarding voluntariness, the offender must engage in the act of abandonment voluntarily without coercion.

In the Vignette case, assuming that the second and third criteria are satisfied, the issue revolves around the presence of an act of abandonment. According to conventional standards, since the criminal act has already been completed, active measures to prevent the outcome are deemed necessary. Therefore, D would be punished for an attempt if she did not perform actions such as transporting V to the hospital. However, according to the new theory, if D voluntarily leaves the scene without further action, knowing that V will not die, abandonment can be established. Consequently, although an attempted crime is established for D, she should either be exempted from punishment or receive a reduction of sentence.

Vignette 8: Criminal Responsibility of Minors

D is a 13-year-old boy. He abducts and rapes V, a girl of the same age. Should D be punished for a criminal offence?

According to Article 41 of the Japanese Penal Code, children less than 14 years of age are not held criminally responsible for their actions and thus are not subject to punishment.

Article 41 Japanese Penal Code[15] *(Punishable Age)*

An act of a person less than 14 years of age is not punishable.

---

14 Makoto Ida, Kogi Keihogaku Soron, 2nd ed. 2018, p. 469.

15 https://www.japaneselawtranslation.go.jp/ja/laws/view/3581#je_pt1ch7at7.

Special procedures are established by the Juveniles Act for cases where individuals of less than 20 years of age commit acts constituting a crime. The Juveniles Act is based on the principle of providing treatment from a welfare and educational perspective rather than condemnation when dealing with juveniles. Recognizing that children are different from adults, the Juveniles Act prefers to provide educational measures rather than subject young persons to harsh punishment through criminal sanctions.

According to the Juveniles Act, family courts conduct hearings to determine the most appropriate treatment for juveniles aged 14 and above who commit crimes (juvenile offenders) and for children under 14 who engage in acts violating penal regulations (delinquent juveniles). Cases of individuals aged 14 and above are initially referred to family courts, and only if the family court deems it appropriate to impose punishment will the case be returned to the prosecutor's office. The prosecutor may then prosecute juvenile offenders in an ordinary court (district court). However, individuals less than 20 years of age are granted special treatment under the Juveniles Act.

Juveniles Act[16]

Article 1 (Purpose of the Act)

The purpose of this Act is to promote the sound development of juveniles, while correcting character flaws and modifying the environment of delinquent juveniles through disposition for rehabilitation of adjudicated delinquents and implementing special measures for juvenile criminal cases.

Article 2(1) (Definitions)[17]

In this Act, the term "Juvenile" refers to a person less than 20 years of age.

Article 3(1)[18]

A juvenile to whom any of the following items applies is subject to trial and decision of the family court:

(i) A juvenile who has committed a crime;

(ii) a juvenile under 14 years of age whose actions violate criminal laws or regulations;

(iii) a juvenile who, due to any of the following reasons and taking into consideration the juvenile's character or environment, is likely to commit a crime or violate criminal laws or regulations:

(a) has a tendency not to abide by their parents' or guardian's proper supervision;

(b) stays away from home without just cause;

(c) associates with persons of a criminal nature or who are immoral, or frequents questionable places;

(d) has a tendency to act in way that harms his own moral character or that of others.

16 https://www.japaneselawtranslation.go.jp/ja/laws/view/4827#je_ch1.

17 https://www.japaneselawtranslation.go.jp/ja/laws/view/4827#je_ch1.

18 https://www.japaneselawtranslation.go.jp/ja/laws/view/4827#je_ch1.

In 2021, significant amendments were made to the Juveniles Act. The age of legal adulthood in the Japanese Civil Code and the age of suffrage were lowered from 20 to 18 years, leading to discussions about treating individuals aged 18 and 19 as responsible under criminal law. By an amendment of the Juveniles Act, individuals aged 18 and 19 have been named "specified juveniles", who are treated differently from those aged 17 and below in criminal procedure.

As a consequence of this reform, more crimes committed by individuals aged 18 and 19 years should be returned from family courts to the prosecutor's office. This reform also had an influence on the mass media. They had previously been prohibited from reporting the details of a criminal case against a juvenile, including the name, age, occupation, residence, or appearance of the young person. This prohibition has been abolished for individuals aged 18 and 19 years, so that now mass media can, for example, publish pictures of the offender in newspapers or on TV.

D's act in the Vignette case constitutes kidnapping (Article 224 JPC) and forcible sexual intercourse (Article 177 JPC).

Article 224 Penal Code[19] *(Kidnapping of Minors)*

A person who kidnaps a minor using force or through enticement is punished by imprisonment for not less than three months but not more than seven years.

Article 177 Penal Code

A person who has engaged in sexual intercourse, anal intercourse, oral cavity intercourse, or inserting a part of the body (excluding the penis) or object into the vagina or anus (hereinafter referred to as "sexual intercourse, etc." in this Article and Article 179 para. 2) by causing a person to be in a state where it is difficult to form, express, or fully compose his or her intention not to consent due to the acts or the reasons listed in Article 176 para. 1 or other similar acts or reasons, or by taking advantage of such state, shall be punished by imprisonment with work for not less than five years, regardless of marital status.

(2) The same article is applied to a person who has sexual intercourse with another person by misleading that person into believing that the act is not indecent or by misleading that person about the person committing the act or by taking advantage of such person's wrong belief or misidentification.

(3) The previous article is applied as in Paragraph 1 to a person who has sexual intercourse with another person under 16 years of age (in case said person under 16 years of age is 13 years of age or older, limited to a person who was born five years or more before the date of birth of said person).

However, since D is under 14 years of age, he is not criminally responsible and cannot be found guilty; the family court will try D under the Juveniles Act, and as a result he may be placed in a juvenile training school or be placed on probation.

Vignette 9: Statute of Limitations

In 1995, D violently raped V, a 35-year-old woman, using a knife. D managed to escape and was not apprehended until 2023. Traces of his DNA taken from the victim's body leave no doubt that D is the perpetrator. Should D be convicted despite the long delay?

---

19 https://www.japaneselawtranslation.go.jp/ja/laws/view/3581#je_pt2ch35at1.

Article 337 Japanese Criminal Procedure Code stipulates that when a period of limitation for public prosecution has been completed, the court shall render a judgment of dismissal. Several reasons are put forward for introducing a statute of limitations for public prosecution:

1. the weakening of the societal impact of crimes over time, leading to the expiry of punitive authority;
2. from a procedural standpoint, the difficulty of achieving fair trials due to the disappearance of evidence;
3. the unjustifiability of holding a trial due to the decrease in punishability and the disappearance of evidence; and
4. the fact that the state had for a certain time refrained from exercising its right to prosecution.

Article 337 Criminal Procedure Code[20]

(1) The court must bar further prosecution through a judgment if:
- (i) a final and binding judgment has been reached in a case;
- (ii) the punishment is repealed by laws and regulations established after the crime;
- (iii) there is a general pardon;
- (iv) the statute of limitations has expired.

The statute of limitations for public prosecution is stipulated in Article 250 Criminal Procedure Code. In 2004, Article 250 was amended and some of the periods of limitation were extended: from 15 to 25 years for crimes punishable by the death penalty, from 10 to 15 years for crimes punishable by unlimited imprisonment, and from 7 to 10 years for crimes punishable by imprisonment of 15 years or more. The reasons for the amendments were the ageing population and advancements in investigative technology, making possible the acquisition of new evidence even after the passage of much time.[21]

In 2010, the temporal limitation for crimes punishable by death was abolished and the periods for other crimes were extended further. Supplementary provisions of the amended law provide that the new laws concerning the extension or abolition of limitation periods shall apply to cases in which the period of limitation was running before the revision of the law came into force. The Supreme Court has affirmed the constitutionality of these changes.

According to Article 253(1) Criminal Procedure Code, the statute of limitations begins to run when the criminal act is completed. The running of the period is suspended when the public prosecutor files charges, and recommences when jurisdiction is transferred or a dismissal of the public prosecution becomes final (Article 254 Criminal Procedure Code). This means that the running of the statute of limitations is suspended when the prosecutor indicates to the court his or her intention to prosecute for specific criminal acts, regardless of whether the prosecution is lawful or

20 https://www.japaneselawtranslation.go.jp/ja/laws/view/3739#je_pt2ch1at51.

21 Takeshi Matsuda, Kouso Jikou, in: Keiji Sosho no Souten, 2013, p. 114.

not. Even in case of an unlawful prosecution, the Supreme Court believes that suspending the period of limitation is permissible. The running of the period of limitation is also suspended while the offender is abroad or is hiding so that the indictment or a notification of a summary order cannot be served on him (Article 255 Criminal Procedure Code).

In 2023, there were amendments in the field of sexual crimes. The period of limitation under Article 177 Penal Code is now governed by Article 250(3) Criminal Procedure Code, which was added by these amendments und specifies a period of limitation of 15 years. Article 250(4) Criminal Procedure Code further stipulates that if the victim was under 18 years old when the crime was committed, the time between the end of the crime and the victim's 18th birthday is added to the period of limitation (15 years).

In the Vignette case, D is guilty of raping V, an offense under Article 177 Penal Code. Since the victim in this case was over 18 years old, Article 250(4) Criminal Procedure Code does not apply. Therefore, the period of limitation is 15 years, and it expired in 2010, if there were no grounds for suspension. D should therefore not be prosecuted; if D is prosecuted, the court must render a judgment of dismissal.

Vignette 10: Life Imprisonment without Parole

> The Penal Code of State S provides for imprisonment for life as the maximum penalty for murder, but also authorizes the court to order an offender's early release after a minimum of 15 years if the offender is no longer dangerous. Reacting to cases of particularly heinous murders, the legislature of S wishes to introduce a penalty of life imprisonment without any possibility of early release, regardless of the offender's continued dangerousness. Would this amendment be acceptable?

In Japan, the maximum penalty for murder is the death penalty. The abolition of capital punishment has not yet been realized. To fix the maximum penalty of murder at imprisonment for life is hard to imagine in Japan. Therefore, I first examine the situation of the death penalty.

In Japan, there is at present a tendency toward a more and more severe system of punishment, which makes the abolition of capital punishment difficult. It has been pointed out that Japan's tendency to limit the use of the death penalty was strong from the 1970s through the 1980s.[22] However, after the 1990s, revisions of the criminal law were mostly in the direction of toughening penalties. In 2004, the upper limit of the term for freedom-restricting punishments (imprisonment with work and imprisonment without work[23]) was raised from 15 to 20 years, and the lower limit of imprisonment with work for murder was raised from 3 years to 5 years. In the time that followed, several new driving-related crimes were introduced as a reaction to a series of cases of killing through dangerous driving. Some new sexual crimes were also introduced in the Japanese Penal Code.

It has been said that the trend toward harsher penalties is not unique to Japan but is a global phenomenon. In such a climate of increasing penalties, advocating for the abo-

22 Makoto Ida, Shikei Seido to Keibatsu Riron, 2022, p. 66.

23 This distinction between these two kinds of imprisonment has been abolished.

lition of the death penalty will hardly have the backing of public opinion. In judicial practice, the criteria for applying the death penalty have been based on the standards set forth by the Supreme Court in the Nagayama case.[24] These criteria are as follows: the gravity of the crime, the offender's motive, the manner of committing the crime (especially the persistence or cruelty of the method of killing), the seriousness of the consequences (especially the number of victims killed), the feelings of the victim's family, the social impact of the offense, the age of the offender, the offender's criminal record, and his conduct after the crime. The Supreme Court declared that imposition of the death penalty (carried out by hanging) is permissible if the offender's culpability is deemed exceptionally serious and if the balance between guilt and punishment and also considerations of general deterrence make the death penalty unavoidable.

However, in a mother and child murder case in Hikari City, the Supreme Court issued a judgment that deviated from the conventional criteria.[25] In this case, there were two victims, but on the other hand the murders were not planned. The offender strangled the mother during a rape because the mother resisted intensely. The 11-month-old daughter was nearby, and she began to cry. To stop her crying he also killed the baby. The offender was just over 18 years old at the time of the crime. If he had been younger than 18, the death penalty could not have been imposed, because Article 51 Juveniles Act stipulates that juveniles under 18 years of age should receive life imprisonment instead of the death penalty. The Supreme Court confirmed the death penalty,[26] although it would have been difficult to justify imposing capital punishment according to the conventional criteria. This case highlights the trend toward harsher penalties in judicial practice.

This trend has been attributed to the decline of the notion that individual behavior is decisively conditioned by social factors and the increasing emphasis on individual decisions by persons who commit crimes.[27] Additionally, in Japan the prevailing theory holds that the purpose of punishment is retribution, whereas general and specific deterrence are only secondary purposes of punishment. In retributive thinking, the notion that "taking a life should be repaid with death" is justified. There is also a growing emphasis on the protection of victims' interests. The retention of the death penalty is based on the idea of "death as redemption", meeting the emotional needs of victims and their families. The death penalty is also said to be necessary for the deterrence of crime.

Abolitionists, on the other hand, argue that the death penalty is inherently inhuman and that there exists an international trend towards abolition. They also point out the irreversible nature of wrongful death sentences. The topic of wrongful convictions has gained renewed attention in the wake of the Hakamada case. That case concerned the murder of the family of an executive director of a Miso making company. In the director's house, a fire broke out at midnight, and all family members were found

24 Supreme Court decision of July 8, 1983.

25 Supreme Court decision of June 20, 2006.

26 Supreme Court decision of February 20, 2012.

27 Ida, Shikei Seido to Keibatsu Riron, p. 86.

dead in the building. Mr. Hakamada, who was a boxer and a worker at the company, was suspected of the murder. In 1980, the Supreme Court confirmed his conviction and the imposition of the death penalty. However, the suspicion of a miscarriage of justice grew. After the first request for a retrial had been denied, a second request in 2014 led to a retrial, and a decision was made to suspend the execution of the death penalty and the detention of Mr. Hakamada. He was subsequently released. At the end of the retrial in Shizuoka District Court, Mr. Hakamada was acquitted in 2024. The Prosecution Service did not file an appeal so that the judgment of acquittal became final. This case once again brought attention to the abolitionist argument against the death penalty.

It is not yet clear whether the death penalty will be abolished in the near future. If that should happen, the next question would be what kind of penalty should be the alternative to the death penalty. Some members of the Japanese Lawyers Society, who aim to abolish the death penalty, suggest that a life sentence without the possibility of parole would be a suitable alternative.

So let us look at the situation of life imprisonment. In Japan, even for offenders sentenced to life imprisonment, parole may be granted after ten years of serving the sentence.

Article 28 Penal Code[28]

When a person sentenced to imprisonment or imprisonment without work evinces signs of substantial reformation, the person may be paroled by a disposition of a government agency after that person has served one-third of the definite term sentenced or 10 years in the case of life imprisonment.

However, as mentioned above, due to the increasing severity of punishment in Japan, decisions to grant parole to individuals serving life imprisonment have become increasingly rare. In the 1970s, it was common for individuals to be eligible for parole after serving 14 to 18 years of their sentence. However, by the 2010s, it became more common for parole to be granted only after serving over 30 years of the sentence. This trend has effectively turned life imprisonment into a de facto "life sentence", as the likelihood of early parole for those serving life imprisonment has diminished. Considering this situation, if the death penalty were indeed abolished in Japan, the introduction of life imprisonment without the possibility of parole would probably be readily accepted.

---

28 https://www.japaneselawtranslation.go.jp/ja/laws/view/3581#je_pt1ch5at1.

11. Namibia

By *Pilisano Masake** and *Inonge Mainga***

Vignette 1: Trolley Problem – Killing one Person to Save Many

Five young children are playing on railway tracks. An express train is approaching, and it is too late to stop the train before it hits the children, probably killing them. Operator D recognizes the emergency situation. He electronically flips a switch and thus deflects the train from its regular track to a little-used sidetrack. However, the lone repairman V is busy on the sidetrack, and the deflected train kills V, as D had anticipated. Is D criminally responsible for murder of V?

The scenario deals with the question of murder and the defence of sudden emergency. D would be held liable for murder with *dolus eventualis.* In *S v Valombola*[1] the court found that the assumption that undergirds *dolus eventualis* is that the offender is deemed to have a reduced level of blameworthiness because of the sudden event that occurred. *Dolus eventualis* as explained in the matter of *S v Simon*[2] refers to a situation where:

> An accused does foresee (as distinct from ought to have foreseen) the possibility of such resultant death and persists in his conduct with indifference to fatal consequence (or if he actually intends to kill), the crime would be that of murder. Having regard to the requirements of foresight and persistence, the dividing line between (a), murder with *dolus eventualis* and (b), culpable homicide, is sometimes rather thin.

In *S v Roelf*, the court elucidated that the

> Distinguishing feature of dolus eventualis is the volitional component: the agent (the perpetrator) "consents" to the consequence foreseen as a possibility; he reconciles himself to it, and he takes it into the bargain.[3]

It follows that the question in the present scenario is whether D (because of his action of deflecting the train) had foreseen the possibility that V may be killed on the rail track and reconciled himself with the possibility that V would be killed.

In the scenario, D was faced with a sudden emergency with two foreseeable possibilities, that is (i) if the train is not deflected the five children would likely be killed, and (ii) if the train is deflected the lone repair man V would be killed. Either way, the possibility of a negative consequence was foreseeable. Thus, to elect one course of action over the other, implies that D was consciously aware and did foresee the possibility of the resultant consequences of his action and elected to deflect the train, which resulted in V's death. Therefore, D may be held liable for murder with *dolus eventualis.*

---

* Namibia University of Science and Technology.

** Inonge Mainga Attorneys, Namibia.

1 CC18/2019 [2021] NAHCMD 562 (2 December 2021).

2 2007 (2) NR 500 (HC).

3 CC 5/2019 [2020] NAHCMD 222 (12 June 2020), § 27.

D would escape liability for the murder of V, if D only ought to have foreseen the possibility that deflecting the train would cause V's death. In that case, D's conduct would have qualified as negligence, and he would be liable for culpable homicide. The test of negligence is whether a reasonable person ought to have acted in a manner that is consistent with the conduct of D.

In either situation – *dolus eventualis* or negligence – D may raise the defence of sudden emergency. This defence entails that

> An "operator" [person] who finds himself in a position of imminent danger, cannot be held guilty of negligence merely because in that emergency he does not act in the best way to avoid the danger.[4]

D may seem to have acted in Deity-like manner, deciding whether the children or V should die. This leads to the question whether extrajudicial killing is acceptable in Namibia. Article 6 of the Namibian Constitution provides for the right to life, and there is no law that permits any form of extrajudicial killing or self-help kind of justice. Therefore, causing the death of another person without justification may amount to the common law crime of murder or culpable homicide. However, it is comprehensible that D was faced with a sudden emergency in which he ought not to be expected to act in the best way to avoid danger, because all the options that were available were evil options.

Vignette 2: Attribution of Death

> D intends to kill his neighbour V. Hidden near V's house, D waits for V and stabs him several times with a knife. V is taken to the hospital, where his wounds are treated. His injuries are not life-threatening and V is kept overnight for observation. During the night, a technical defect in the hospital kitchen leads to the outbreak of a fire, which kills V and other persons. Can D be held criminally responsible for V's death?

Snyman[5] states that there are five requirements for criminal liability, namely, "(a) legality; (b) an act (c) the requirement that the act must correspond to the definition of the proscription; (d) unlawfulness and (e) *mens rea* (culpability)". The elements of a crime will not be discussed here as the crux of the issue is whether the stabbing of V by D was the cause of V's death, which falls within the ambit of (b) and (c), as the questions focuses solely on criminal responsibility. This is premised on the assumption that, according to Snyman, an act "forms the basis of liability" and at the same time limits "the scope of liability".

The generally accepted test on causation is whether the act, to the exclusion of any other factor, led to the result or whether the act of the accused was the *sine qua non* (cause) of the result. The question in the current scenario is whether there was a break in the causal link between D stabbing V and V's death. Put differently, was there a new intervening event that severed the act from the result? Such an event is known as a *novus actus interveniens.* This is where usually a distinction is drawn between

---

4 See *Booysen v S* (HC–MD–CRI–APP–CAL–2022/00041) [2023] NAHCMD 143 (27 March 2023), § 35.

5 C R Snyman, Criminal Law, 5th Edition, Lexis Nexis, 2008, p. 33.

factual causation and legal causation, as there are instances where an act is the factual cause but not the legal cause of the result.[6]

In order for an intervening event to qualify as such, it has to be an abnormal one and should not be foreseeable by the perpetrator. In the matter of *S v Haileka*[7], it was held as follows:

> Normally the intervening incident that breaks the chain of causation and constitutes a *novus actus interveniens* has to be an abnormal one and not one foreseen by the person injuring another.

The defence of *novus actus interveniens* found application in the matter of *S v Louw*,[8] the facts of which were briefly that the accused was arraigned for the murder of his sister. He had stabbed his sister once on the shoulder and subsequently she was admitted to a hospital in a stable condition. She remained stable during the day following admission, but evidence was that she underwent some other medical procedure prior to her demise, the details of which were not presented to the Court. The Accused raised the defence of *novus actus interveniens*, which defence succeeded. At paragraphs 93 and 94, Claasen, J held as follows:

> [93] At the end of the day the issues for a conviction of murder were unsurmountable and the State's evidence did not constitute a cogent account. The court cannot ignore that somewhere between the deceased being stable at the Swakopmund State Hospital and then succumbing to death, there was medical intervention, but the details and treatment thereof remain a secret […].
>
> [94] It should have been clarified by the State what caused the change in the condition of the deceased, whether it was related to the shoulder stab wound or what precisely caused her death. This court cannot blindly follow a flawed post mortem report. In addition, it is not known whether the correct procedures were followed and proper treatment was given at the Swakopmund State Hospital. If the State has nothing to hide, why not bring the patient's file. If it was so that the patient file was missing, why not call a staff member who bears knowledge of the case to fill in the gaps as to what happened at the Hospital? In conclusion, the defence managed to create reasonable doubt and successfully raised the defence of *novus actus interveniens* in respect of the murder charge.

The defence succeeded on the basis that the details of the medical procedure were not known and, as a result, the death of the deceased could not be linked to the initial stabbing. In the matter of *S v Ananias*[9], which was an application brought by the State for leave to appeal the discharge of the accused/respondent in the court *a quo* at the close of the State's case in terms of Section 174 of the Criminal Procedure Act,[10] the Court explored the general application of *novus actus interveniens.* The facts of the case were briefly that the accused had hit the deceased with a glass on the deceased's cheek and as a direct result of that attack the deceased sustained serious injuries, and he subsequently died from them. The accused had raised the defence of *novus actus interveniens* on the basis that the deceased had refused to go to the hospital after he

6 Snyman, *id.*

7 CA–2006/92 [2006] NAHC 62 (30 November 2006).

8 [2021] NAHMCMD 268.

9 [2013] NAHCMD (6 August 2013).

10 Act 51 of 1977.

was struck by the accused. In discharging the accused, the court *a quo* found that the deceased's refusal to go to the hospital was a *novus actus interveniens.* In granting the leave to appeal in favour of the State, the Court found that the Magistrate in the *court a quo* had misdirected herself in the application of the *novus actus interveniens* defence in that there was irrefutable evidence that the injuries inflicted on the deceased were lethal and would have inevitably led to the death of the deceased; and that in such circumstances the refusal by the deceased to go to the hospital does not amount to a *novus actus interveniens.*

In the matter of *Shekunyenge v S,*[11] in dismissing an application seeking leave to appeal and condonation for the late filing of the application for leave to appeal, the Court reiterated its position on the application of *novus actus interveniens.* The facts thereof were briefly that the applicant had assaulted his then girlfriend. Subsequent to the assault, she was hospitalized, but her condition deteriorated to such an extent that she needed to be transferred to a hospital with ICU facilities as the hospital she was in initially did not have such facilities. The applicant, during the trial, had raised the defence of *novus actus interveniens*, which was dismissed by the trial court on the basis that the causal link between the assault on the deceased and her death had not been broken by the failure to transfer her to another facility. Liebenberg, J stated as follows at paragraph 16:

> [16] To this end, the court found as per the judgment on conviction, that the applicant's actions were a sine qua non of the deceased being hospitalized following the assault on her by the applicant. It was the conclusion of the court that there was no evidence showing that the deceased should have been treated differently, or that the causal relationship had been broken. Further that, from the assessment of the medical evidence, there were strong indicators showing that the deceased's condition was deteriorating as a result of her injuries and no evidence to show that, had the deceased been transferred to Windhoek sooner for whatever reason, that she would have survived. The trial court after this evaluation found that there is no basis to find that the causal relationship between the accused's actions and the deceased's subsequent death had been broken by the alleged lack of proper medical care. The applicant thus enjoys no prospects of success in this regard.

If one applies the criteria laid out above on what constitutes a *novus actus interveniens* and how it has found application by the Courts to the current scenario, it can be concluded that D cannot be held criminally responsible for V's death. Although D's actions are the *sine qua non* of V's death (in that V would not have been admitted to the hospital had D not stabbed him) it is not a legal cause of V's death, as the event of the fire breaking out at a hospital and killing V is abnormal and could not have been foreseen by D.

Vignette 3: Torture to Save a Life

> Kidnapper K has abducted an 8-year-old girl G and hidden her in a small cave in the woods. K is trying to extort money from G's parents for her release. The police manage to arrest K. Although being questioned for 24 hours, K steadfastly refuses to disclose where he hid G. Police officer D correctly assumes that G may soon die of thirst if she cannot be found. He therefore severely beats K to make him tell the

[11] [2023] NAHCMD 789.

truth. Fearing even more violence, K eventually leads the police to the cave, where they find G still barely alive. Should D be punished for torturing K?

In the Namibian context at a domestic level, torture is prohibited. However, it has not yet been criminalised. Therefore, consistent with the legality principle, it is possible that D may not be punished for a crime of torture but may be punished for assault as the circumstances may require, or may be subjected to civil proceedings for damages. However, currently there is a 2019 Bill on Torture. This Bill defined torture consistent with the definition provided under the United Nations Convention Against Torture and Other Cruel, Inhuman or Degrading Treatment or Punishment (CAT). CAT Article 1(1) defines "torture" as:

> Any act by which severe pain or suffering, whether physical or mental, is intentionally inflicted on a person for such purposes as obtaining from him or a third person information or a confession, punishing him for an act he or a third person has committed or is suspected of having committed, or intimidating or coercing him or a third person, or for any reason based on discrimination of any kind, when such pain or suffering is inflicted by or at the instigation of or with the consent or acquiescence of a public official or other person acting in an official capacity.

This definition has been incorporated verbatim into the Namibian Bill on Prevention and Combating of Torture of 2019. The Bill is yet to be passed into law. But for all intents and purposes this definition retains its relevance at the domestic level.

Although torture has not been criminalised, it is however prohibited. The fundamental principle against torture is provided for in Article 8 of the Namibian Constitution, which enshrines the right to dignity, and specifically in Article 8(2)(b), which provides that "no persons shall be subject to torture or to cruel, inhuman or degrading treatment or punishment." In the absence of a domestic law that criminalises torture, the practice has been that when an official commits torture, instead of charging such an official for a crime of torture, an alternative and lesser charge of assault (either by threat, common, or with intent to do bodily harm) may be raised against the offending official.

The charge of assault is then artificially linked to the right to dignity and the prohibition against inhuman and cruel treatment. The relevance of linking assault to Article 8 of the Namibian Constitution resonates well when victims of torture (here disguised as assault) sue for damages in civil litigation against the offending official or government. Civil proceedings against a state official for violating Article 8 of the Constitution are common and prevalent in Namibia. Therefore, D may not in a strict sense be punished for an offence of torture but may be punished for the lesser charge of assault.

Vignette 4: Lethal Self-Defence

R, a well-trained young man armed with a knife, accosts 50-year-old D, who is on her way home from a party in the early morning hours. R threatens her with the knife and takes away her purse filled with 500 € and her wristwatch worth 1,000 €. As R turns to run away, D draws a pistol she is secretly carrying in her jacket, and shoots and kills R in order to retrieve her property. Is D guilty of murder?

D will not be found guilty of murder. But the Court will most likely convict her of culpable homicide, if the defence of private defence fails. R committed the crime of robbery with aggravating circumstances as defined in Section 1 (b) (i) and (iii) of the Criminal Procedure Act 51 of 1977 (as amended) that reads:

> (b) robbery or attempted robbery, means –
>
> (i) the wielding of a firearm or any other dangerous weapon;
>
> (ii) the infliction of grievous bodily harm; or
>
> (iii) a threat to inflict grievous bodily harm,
>
> by the offender or an accomplice on the occasion when the offence is committed, whether before or during or after the commission of the offence.

Robbery with aggravating circumstances is a schedule 1 offence (serious crimes) in Namibia, and a knife is construed as a dangerous weapon. To first sketch the offence committed by R was necessary to provide the context as to why D may not be found guilty of murder.

Murder is a common law crime that is defined as unlawful and intentional causing the death of another human being. Thus, the elements of murder are (i) unlawfulness, (ii) intention, (iii) causing the death, (iv) another human being. From the scenario, it is clear that D acted unlawfully as she brought about a prohibited result (R's death). However, D lacked the necessary intention to cause R's death.

To vitiate the requirement of unlawfulness, D may rely on private defence. Private defence is treated as a ground that justifies the unlawful conduct on the part of D. In the matter of *S v Thomas*,[12] the High Court determined the legal requirements of private defence:

> A person acts in private defence, and her act in therefore lawful, if she uses force to repel an unlawful attack which has commenced, or is imminently threatening, upon her or somebody else's life, bodily integrity, property or other interest which deserves to be protected, provided the defensive act is necessary to protect the interest threatened, is directed against the attacker, and is reasonably proportionate to the attack.

R's conduct at the time when R was fleeing from D ceased to constitute a threat to D's bodily integrity. But the elderly D lacked the physical power to prevent R from fleeing. Thus, the threat of appropriation of D's property continued and was still imminent while R was fleeing with D's property. Thus, D had to use force to recover her property.

The question may arise whether the force that was used by D was proportional to the attack. The courts' approach to the question of proportionality of force is well elaborated and explained in the matter of *S v Naftali*[13] and in *S v Thomas*,[14] where the court explained that:

> [29] The requirements of private defence can be summarized as follows; (a) The attack: To give rise to a situation warranting action in defence there must be an unlawful attack upon a

12 CC 5/2019 [2021] NAHCNLD 46 (17 May 2021), § 28.

13 1992 NR 299 HC, §§ 303–4.

14 CC 5/2019 [2021] NAHCNLD 46 (17 May 2021, §§ 29–30.

> legal interest which had commenced or was imminent. (b) The defence must be directed against the attacker and necessary to avert the attack and the means used must be necessary in the circumstances. When the defence of self-defence is raised or apparent, the enquiry is actually twofold. The first leg of the enquiry is whether the conditions and/or requirements of self-defence have been met, which includes the question whether the bounds of self-defense were exceeded. The test here is objective but the onus is on the State to prove beyond reasonable doubt that the conditions or requirements for self-defense did not exist or that the bounds of self-defense have been exceeded.
>
> [30] […] The second leg of the enquiry is then whether the State has proven beyond reasonable doubt that the accused did not genuinely believe that he was acting in self-defence and that he was not exceeding the bounds of self-defence. Here the test is purely subjective and the reasonableness or otherwise of such belief, whether or not it is based on or amounts to a mistake of fact or of law or both, is only relevant as one of the factors in the determination of whether or not the accused held the aforesaid genuine belief. […] Culpable homicide will be a competent verdict where, for example, the accused, although he genuinely believed that he acted in self-defence and within the bounds of self-defence, was not, objectively speaking, acting reasonably in holding the aforesaid belief.

D's conduct under these circumstances may be construed to be proportional to the attack that was warded off. Therefore, D may succeed with the defence of private defence.

There is another dimension that comes to light, namely the fleeing aspect. It is difficult to separate the act of robbing and the act of fleeing in this scenario, because they happened contemporaneously as the fleeing was used to complete the robbery.

R after robbing commenced fleeing. The fact that R was now fleeing implies that there was no longer an imminent threat to the bodily integrity of D, therefore there was no reason for D to use force, thus rendering self-defence in respect of D's bodily integrity obsolete. However, R was fleeing with D's property and D had no ability to apprehend (confine) R. Therefore, D had no option available to prevent R from fleeing, other than using lethal force.

Since D is not a peace officer, D may rely on the defences listed in Section 49 of the Criminal Procedure Act (CPA) 51 of 1977 read together with Section 42 of CPA. Section 42 empowers a private person to arrest a suspect who commits a crime in his or her presence. In order for D to rely on this section, there should be a shift from the aspect of private defence (warding off the attack), which may not necessarily lead to an arrest, to D using force to arrest R or to prevent R from fleeing and to recover the robbed property.

CPA Section 49 provides:

> *Use of Force in Effecting Arrest*
>
> (1) If any person authorized under this Act to arrest or to assist in arresting another, attempts to arrest such person and such person –
>
> (a) resists the attempt and cannot be arrested without the use of force; or
>
> (b) flees when it is clear that an attempt to arrest him is being made, or resists such attempt and flees,

the person so authorized may, in order to effect the arrest, use such force as may in the circumstances be reasonably necessary to overcome the resistance or to prevent the person concerned from fleeing.

(2) Where the person concerned is to be arrested for an offence referred to in Schedule 1 or is to be arrested on the ground that he is reasonably suspected of having committed such an offence, and the person authorized under this Act to arrest or to assist in arresting him cannot arrest him or prevent him from fleeing by other means than by killing him, the killing shall be deemed to be justifiable homicide.

In the matter of *S v Coetzee*,[15] the court determined that where the suspect is fleeing without a prospect of being successfully apprehended, the private person may use force. The court further held that "the accused at that stage was entitled to prevent the deceased from fleeing and he was also entitled to use force to prevent the deceased from fleeing." Therefore, in the context of Section 49(2) of CPA, it follows that if R dies as a result of D's action, R's death may be deemed justifiable. Thus, D may not be found liable neither for murder nor for culpable homicide.

Vignette 5: Criminal Responsibility of Subordinates for Systemic Offences

D is a soldier in the army of a country ruled by a junta of generals who have come to power through a violent coup. When an opposition group demands the return to a democratic system, the government orders the soldiers to shoot and kill any person who resists arrest. Following this order, D kills three young men who take part in a protest demonstration and hit a police officer who tries to arrest them. When D is tried after a change of regime, he says that he did not like to shoot the protesters but that he thought that he had to obey his commanders' orders. D knew that if he had refused to shoot, he might have been demoted, but no physical harm would have occurred to him. Should D be convicted of murder? If so, should his sentence be mitigated because of his situation?

In a scenario as the one sketched herein, it is of utmost importance to first determine whether the order given constitutes a lawful order.[16] Emphasis is placed on "lawful", as obedience to orders is available as a defence in our law. Prior to making the requisite determination, it is prudent to first explore the different laws, including public international law, that contain the defence. International law finds application in the Namibian context through Article 144 of the Namibian Constitution, which provides that "the general rules of public international law and international agreements binding upon Namibia shall form part of the law of Namibia" unless otherwise provided by the Constitution or by an Act of Parliament. Namibia is a State Party to the Rome Statute which establishes the International Criminal Court.

Article 33 of the Rome Statute provides as follows:

---

15 1993 NR 313 (HC), p. 315 §§ C–D.

16 See generally Visser and Vorster, General Principles of Criminal Law Through the Cases (1982), pp. 182–189.

Superior Orders and Prescription of Law

1. The fact that a crime within the jurisdiction of the Court has been committed by a person pursuant to an order of a Government or of a superior, whether military or civilian, shall not relieve that person of criminal responsibility unless:

   (a) The person was under a legal obligation to obey orders of the Government or the superior in question;

   (b) The person did not know that the order was unlawful; and

   (c) The order was not manifestly unlawful.

2. For the purposes of this article, orders to commit genocide or crimes against humanity are manifestly unlawful.

It is evident that although the defence is available, the order should not be manifestly unlawful, even if a subordinate is under legal obligation to obey orders of his superior.

The defence has previously found application in our courts through interpretation of the legislation governing the armed forces. Burchell and Hunt[17] are of the opinion that this defence ordinarily arises in the military context: "The recognition of this defence flows from the strict discipline enforced in military and paramilitary forces that, among other things, demands absolute and unquestioning obedience to the orders of a superior officer. A subordinate who fails or refuses to obey an order is liable to severe sanctions which may include death."

In the matter of *R v Smith*,[18] the accused had shot and killed a person after an unlawful order by his superior. He was charged with murder. In the discussion of the obedience to orders, Solomon, JP explored two extreme scenarios, namely, on the one hand that "absolute, implicit and unquestioning obedience" is expected of a soldier in complying with orders of his superiors, and on the other hand that a soldier should only obey lawful orders of his superiors, and where such orders are not lawful the soldier should be held liable for his acts in carrying them out. In rejecting both scenarios and opting for a scenario that can be said to be a blend of the two extreme scenarios, he held as follows:[19]

> [...] After looking at authorities quoted from the bar and such other authorities as have been accessible, it seems to me that the rule laid down in the Manual of Military Law is a reasonable and proper rule to apply in such a case as this.
>
> This states that if the commands are obviously illegal, an inferior would be justified in questioning or even refusing to execute such commands, but as long as the superior orders are not obviously and decidedly in opposition to the law of the land, or to the well-known established custom of the army, so long must they meet with complete and unhesitating obedience. There is an opinion of Mr Justice Wills to the effect that an officer or soldier acting under orders from his superior which are not necessarily or manifestly illegal would be justified. I think the rule is a reasonable one, and one which has become a well-established principle of law. The well-known principle of criminal law demands that there must be some blameworthy

17 South African Criminal Law and Procedure, Volume 1 (1997), 3rd Edition, pp. 108–109.

18 (1900) 17 SC 561.

19 Ibid. at 566–568.

> condition of mind, some guilty knowledge shown to the Court to justify finding a person guilty of a crime. [...] I think it is a safe rule to lay down that if a soldier honestly believes he is doing his duty in obeying the commands of his superior and if the orders are not so manifestly illegal that he must or ought to have known that they were unlawful, the private soldier would be protected by the orders of his superior officer [...].

In utilizing this approach, the Court found that the accused was not guilty as the order was carried out during a war.

In the matter of *R v Van Vuuren*[20], the accused, who was a staff sergeant in the Defence Force, had been involved in a car accident and was charged with failing to render assistance to an individual who was injured in the accident. His defence was that his superior had ordered him to stay in the vehicle. The Court found the accused guilty on the basis that the command was outside the scope of military duty. Some scholars have criticized this judgment as it does not take into account the requisite *mens rea*.

In Namibia, the Defence Act[21] defines an order as an order made under the Act. The Military Discipline Code, passed in terms of Section 39 of the Defence Act, makes it an offence for a soldier to be in wilful defiance of authority by disobeying any lawful command given personally by the soldier's superior officer in the execution of his or her duty, whether orally, in writing or by signal. The soldier is susceptible to imprisonment not exceeding five years if the disobedience was done whilst the soldier was in service. It is evident from the sanction that disobedience of a lawful order is deemed to be serious as there is no option of a fine, only direct imprisonment.

Applying these principles to the current scenario, Article 33 of the Rome Statute lays out the basis on which a person would be excused from liability when carrying out orders of his or her superior. The soldier can be excused if there was an obligation to obey the Government or superior in question, he or she did not know that the order was unlawful, and the order was not manifestly unlawful. In the present scenario, D was under a legal obligation to obey the Government as he was a soldier of the Government; and it was his contention that he was of the belief that he had to obey his commander's orders. The third requirement gives rise to the enquiry of whether the order falls within the ambit of lawfulness. If one takes into account that the Government that was in power at the time was a Junta, which Government was obviously opposed to democratic rule but nevertheless the recognized Government, and that its orders were only specific to persons who resisted arrest, it could be concluded that the order was not manifestly unlawful, under the circumstances prevailing at the time.

If one further applies the principles laid out in *R v Smith*,[22] there needs to be some form of blameworthy conduct and knowledge of wrongdoing on the part of the perpetrator to justify a guilty verdict. In this instance, D's contention is that he was under the belief that he should obey his superiors. Therefore, it can be concluded that he lacked the requisite intent or *mens rea* to commit murder. The question of whether D ought to have known that the order was unlawful becomes mute by the conclusion

---

20 1944 OPD 35.

21 Act 1 of 2002.

22 (1900) 17 SC 561. For details, see text at note 19, *supra*.

that the order was not manifestly unlawful. Sight should also not be lost of the fact that the three persons who were shot and killed were hitting a police officer who was trying to arrest them. It could be that the situation was so dire for the police officer that D had to use minimum force to defray the attack on the police officer, albeit the minimum force was fatal. Under this premise, D should not be convicted of murder.

Vignette 6: Limits of Consent

V is a 21-year-old ambitious athlete and short-distance runner. He has learned that certain artificial limbs can enhance a runner's speed. He decides that he would rather have an artificial limb instead of his right lower leg. He approaches D, a surgeon in private practice, and asks him to amputate his leg below the knee and replace it with an artificial limb. D complies with V's request. Should D be punished for mayhem?

The scenario deals with limits of consent to commit an unlawful act that is contrary to public policy. D may be punished for mayhem or assault. Mayhem is a common law crime consisting of maiming another person. In the Namibian context, the approach is to recognise individual choices that include the decision to injure oneself; for example, suicide is not criminalised. In the matter of *LM et al. v Government Republic of Namibia*,[23] the Court declared that where a victim consents to any injury, the accused or defendant may rely on the defence of *volenti non fit iniuria*. Thus, consent is accepted as a ground of justification. However, the court explained that consent alone is not enough, rather it must be informed consent. For informed consent to be successfully used as a defence, the Court at § 11 stated that:

> The law should recognise that a doctor has a duty to warn a patient of a material risk inherent in the proposed treatment; a risk is material if, in the circumstances of the particular case, a reasonable person in the patient's position, if warned of the risk, would be likely to attach significance to it or if the medical practitioner is or should reasonably be aware that the particular patient, if warned of the risk, would be likely to attach significance to it. This duty is subject to the therapeutic privilege.

Under this interpretation, there are acts where the person committing them may be held criminally responsible, notwithstanding the fact that there was assumably prior consent. For example, sexual intercourse with a child under the age of 14 is treated as rape if the offender was at least three years older. Possession of drugs, bigamy, and sodomy are a few other examples. Equally, in the present case consent to commit mayhem may not suffice since mayhem is contrary to public policy or public interest. In V's case, amputating the leg is not based on any medical condition but rather on the desire to enhance competitiveness. However, the effect of such amputation causes permanent self-imposed disability. This is contrary to public policy, and the condemnation of such an act is based on the assumption that an individual is not free to grant the impairment of these interests. There are exceptions to this rule, for example if there are health concerns or adjustments that are not detrimental, i.e., breast, nose, ear, or hip enhancement, to mention a few.

---

23 Case No. I 1603/2008, § 9.

Vignette 7: Withdrawal from an Attempt

> 25-year-old D is deeply upset with her former boyfriend V, who had ended their relationship to be with another woman. To punish V, D plans to stab him with a large knife. D knows that the stab wounds can be fatal and accepts V's death as a possible outcome. When V goes jogging, D attacks him from behind and stabs him in the back three times. V breaks down. D realises that she has injured him but that the injuries will not cause his death. She realises that she could kill him by stabbing him again but decides to leave him alone. Should D be punished for attempted murder?

The question to be determined is whether D can be convicted of attempted murder even though she voluntarily withdrew her intent after consummation or commencement of the execution of the crime. It should be emphasized that D had reconciled herself to the fact that the stab wounds she would inflict could be fatal and thus had accepted the possibility of that outcome. In other words, she foresaw that her actions could lead to V's death and she reconciled herself thereto. It can therefore be concluded that she had the requisite *mens rea.*

The court in the matter of *S v Amukoto*[24] succinctly dealt with a case of attempted robbery. The accused had intended to take possession of cash under the control of the complainant through violent means, but he was unable to carry out his plans because he was unable to gain access to the safe where the money was kept. In stating the applicable principles in such circumstances, Liebenberg, J held as follows:

> [6] The accused in the present instance intended through violent means to take possession of cash under control of the complainant, but his endeavours were unsuccessful only because he could not obtain access to the safe where the money was kept. Thus, except for the act of appropriation, all the remaining elements were present. In *S v Agliotti* the court as per Kgomo, J said the following on attempting to commit a crime:
>
> A person is guilty of attempting to commit a crime if he/she, intending to do so, unlawfully engages in conduct that is not merely preparatory but has also reached at least the commencement of the execution of the intended crime. A person is equally guilty of attempting to commit a crime even though the commission of the crime is impossible, if it would have been possible in the factual circumstances which he/she believes exist or will exist at the relevant time. A person will also be guilty of an attempt even when he/she voluntarily withdraws from its commission after his/her conduct has reached the commencement of the execution of the intended crime. The stage of commencement of execution is also called the stage of consummation. Once this stage is reached, 'attempt' at a crime is complete.[25]

It is evident that in order for a person to be convicted of an attempt of a crime, even where the perpetrator has voluntarily withdrawn from the commission of the offence, there has to be commencement of the execution of the intended crime.

If one applies the approach in *S v Amukoto*[26], it can safely be concluded that D should be punished for attempted murder on the premise of her reconciliation to

24 (CR 01-2016) [2016] NAHCMD 6 (21 January 2016).

25 (CR 01-2016) [2016] NAHCMD 6 (21 January 2016), § 6.

26 (CR 01-2016) [2016] NAHCMD 6 (21 January 2016). For details, see text at note 25 *supra.*

the possible outcome of her actions and the fact that she had stabbed V, which amounts to commencement of the intended crime.

Vignette 8: Criminal Responsibility of Minors

D is a 13-year-old boy. He abducts and rapes V, a girl of the same age. Should D be punished for a criminal offence?

The scenario focuses on capacity to commit an offence. In Namibia, the question of capacity in general is regulated by common law (for criminal liability) and statutory law. In terms of common law, the presumption is that a person's capacity to commit offences falls into three categories, namely: (i) persons aged below 7 years are irrebuttably presumed to lack capacity to commit any crime; (ii) juvenile persons aged 7–14 are rebuttably presumed to have (limited) criminal capacity; and (iii) persons aged 14 and above are presumed to have full criminal capacity and are criminally accountable.

D, who was 13 years at the time of committing the crime of abduction and rape, falls under category 2, namely a person aged 7–14, who is presumed to have limited capacity to commit an offence. The presumption is rebuttable. It follows that to determine the criminal liability of a minor of this age group, a two-stage inquiry is undertaken. In *S v Basson and Another*,[27] the court formulated the two-stage inquiry as follows:

> *A two-stage enquiry:* (i) did the child possess criminal capacity and if so, (ii) did the child possess the *mens rea* required for a conviction of the crime for which the child is charged. The preliminary investigation into capacity precedes the enquiry into fault (or *mens rea*) whether the fault required is intention or negligence.

With regard to stage 2, a child above the age of 7 but below 14 can be liable for conviction of an offence only if the prosecution proved beyond reasonable doubt that the child committed the alleged offence knowingly or intended to commit the wrongful act, and further that the child appreciated the wrongfulness of the act. In relation to capacity, it is commonly accepted that the closer the minor is to the age of 14 the weaker the rebuttable presumption, and when the offender's age is far from the age of 14 the stronger the presumption. In the present scenario, D is 13 years old, an age that is near to the age of 14, therefore the presumption that D is incapable of committing crimes is weaker. Therefore, in the present scenario, D may be punished if it is proved that he had the necessary *mens rea* to commit the abduction and rape.

It is worth noting that when a minor is prosecuted for a crime, the interests of the minor are fully protected. For instance, Section 153 of the CPA 51 of 1977 makes it an offence to publish the particulars of a minor that may reveal his or her identity, and the court may be closed for the public when a minor is prosecuted.

With respect to criminal law and procedure, the common law presumption on capacity of minors subsists and has not been repealed by legislation. This presumption

---

[27] Criminal 177 of 2007 [2007] NAHC 143 (13 December 2007), § 9.

operates alongside various statutes that deal with the litigation capacity of minors under civil law.

Previously, the Age of Majority Act 57 of 1972 did not define a child – however, it set the parameters as per Section 1, stating that "all persons, whether males or females, attain the age of majority when they attain the age of twenty-one years." Thus, in practice any person below the age of 21 was deemed to be a minor, and any person above the age of 21 was accepted as major. The consequences of this statutory demarcation included that a person below the age of 21 was presumed to lack capacity in civil matters. In addition, a person who has reached the age of 18 may apply to the court for a declaration of majority as contemplated in Section 2 of the Age of Majority Act 57 of 1972. The Child Care and Protection Act 3 of 2015 repealed portions of the Age of Majority Act 57 of 1972. The Child Care and Protection Act 3 of 2015 Section 1 introduced the definition of "child" to "mean a person who has not attained the age of 18 years". In addition, the age of majority, as per Section 10(1), was reduced from the age of 21 to that of 18. Thus, in the new legislation a person who attains the age of 18 equally reaches the age of majority.

Vignette 9: Statute of Limitations

In 1995, D violently raped V, a 35-year-old woman, using a knife. D managed to escape and was not apprehended until 2023. Traces of his DNA taken from the victim's body leave no doubt that D is the perpetrator. Should D be convicted despite the long delay?

The scenario deals with prescription of offences, stay of proceedings and in part with withdrawal of charges. In the Namibia context, the Criminal Procedure Act (CPA) 51 of 1977 is instructive on prescription of offences, and in Section 18 it provides as follows:

Prescription of right to institute prosecution

(1) The right to institute a prosecution for any offence, other than an offence in respect of which the sentence of death may be imposed, shall, unless some other period is expressly provided by law, lapse after the expiration of a period of twenty years from the time when the offence was committed.

(2) The right to institute a prosecution for an offence in respect of which the sentence of death may be imposed shall not be barred by lapse of time.

According to Section 18(1) of CPA 51 of 1977, ordinarily all offences that are not classified as schedule 1 offences may be prescribed (if no proceedings have been instituted) at the expiration of the period of 20 years from the date when the offence was committed. But if the crime in question falls under schedule 1, the lapse of 20 years does not lead to prescription.

D may be convicted and punished under the common law crime of rape (Section 261 of CPA 51 of 1977 as amended). This is because at the time when D committed the rape, the legal regime was based on common law. This is consistent with the legality principle of *nullum crimen sine lege.* The common law crime of rape was replaced by the Combating of Rape Act 8 of 2000. Therefore, any allegations of rape that occurred before the coming into force of the Combating of Rape Act 8 of 2000 are dealt with under the common law.

Under the common law, rape was construed as a serious offence falling under the category of schedule 1 offences, which were ordinarily punishable by death or life imprisonment as contemplated in Section 277(1)(b) of CPA 51 of 1977, which provided that the "death sentence may be passed upon a person convicted of treason, kidnapping, child-stealing or rape." In this context, since the death sentence was available for rape, the crime of rape is not subject to the prescription period of 20 years as stated in Section 18 of CPA 51 of 1977. Simply put, rape does not prescribe.

It is important to note that the sentence of death is no longer constitutional under Article 6 of the Namibian Constitution, which prohibits the death penalty. Rapists can however be sentenced to imprisonment for life. The substitution of the death penalty by a life sentence is consistent with the constitutional value of the right to life.

Having clarified the issue of prescription, the constitutional question may arise whether D, due to the long period that passed from 1995 to 2023, may bring an application for a stay of proceedings concerning the rape committed against V. The test that needs to be satisfied before a person may be granted a permanent stay of criminal proceedings was fully explored in the matter of *Mostert v Prosecutor-General and Others.*[28] In that judgment, the Court stated:

> It is necessary to reiterate that the remedy of a permanent stay of prosecution will only be granted if the applicant has proved that the trial has not taken place within a reasonable time and that there is irreparable trial prejudice as a result or other exceptional circumstances justifying such a remedy.

In the matter of *S v Myburgh,*[29] the court determined two approaches for computing the period of delay. Delay can be counted from (i) the date of arrest, or (ii) the time when the offender was officially informed about the charges by the police or prosecution (if the offender was not arrested). The Court in *S v Myburgh*, explained that:

> When the issue of whether or not Art. 12(1)(b) has been complied with must be decided, time begins to run from the time a person has been arrested on a particular charge or when not arrested, from the time that he is officially informed by the police or prosecutor of the charge against him and some official action is taken against him in regard to the charge, such as a summons served upon him to appear in court on a specified charge or given a warning to appear in court on a specified date on a specified charge.[30]

When interpreting Article 12(1)(b) of the Constitution with reference to the concept of the right to trial within a reasonable time, the Court in the matter of *S v Heidenreich*[31] found that:

> Reasonable is of course a relative term and what constitutes a reasonable time for the purposes of Art. 12(1)(b) must be determined according to the facts of each individual case. The

---

28 (HC-MD-CIV-MOT-GEN-2022/00210) [2023] NAHCMD 237 (28 April 2023), § 103.

29 2008 (2) NR 592 (SC).

30 2008 (2) NR 592 (SC), § 600.

31 1995 NR 234 (HC) (1996 (2) SACR 171), § 241D.

> courts must endeavour to balance the fundamental right of an accused to be tried within a reasonable time against the public interest in the attainment of justice in the context of the prevailing social, economic, and cultural conditions to be found in Namibia. What is required at the end of the day is a value judgment.

In the present scenario, it is doubtful that D may succeed, because he partly had caused the delay in that he escaped and managed to evade prosecution until 2023, when he was apprehended. In *Mostert v Prosecutor-General and Others*,[32] the Court held that:

> The evidence on record is that the applicant (offender) escaped and was outside the jurisdiction of the Republic. He was residing in the Republic of South Africa. This led to the authorities in Namibia to initiate extradition proceedings against the applicant. An extradition request to which the said warrant of arrest was annexed was sent to South Africa for execution. In the interim, the applicant (offender) returned to the Republic and was arrested upon his return on 1 May 2021. The delay for the trial not to have taken place between September 2015 and May 2021, therefore, cannot be attributed to the respondents (state) alone but also to the applicant (offender). In my considered view, such delay, preceding 1 May 2021, does not constitute actionable delay for purposes of Art. 12(1)(b) of the Constitution.

It is clear from this matter that where the offender escapes and manages to evade arrest and prosecution, he may not succeed with his claim for a permanent stay of criminal proceedings for the period when he was on the run, since he caused the factors that contributed to the delay. Other factors to consider when adjudicating on the question of a stay of criminal proceedings include the length of the delay, a waiver of the periods, prejudice to the accused, and reasonable delays such as the time required for adjudicating the case, actions by the accused, actions by the state, and resources, to state but a few.

Vignette 10: Life Imprisonment without Parole

The Penal Code of State S provides for imprisonment for life as the maximum penalty for murder, but also authorises the court to order an offender's early release after a minimum of 15 years if the offender is no longer dangerous. Reacting to cases of particularly heinous murders, the legislature of S wishes to introduce a penalty of life imprisonment without any possibility of early release, regardless of the offender's continued dangerousness. Would this amendment be acceptable?

In order to determine whether the envisaged amendment would be acceptable, it is imperative to explore different pieces of legislation including the Namibian Constitution and applicable legal principles as developed by the Superior Courts of Namibia. This in essence requires one to explore the purpose of punishment and its intended outcome on the one hand and on the other hand, the powers vested in the legislature. It is further required to explore the Court's interpretation of life imprisonment. The Correctional Services Act,[33] which establishes the Namibian Correctional Services, provides in Section 3 that the functions of the Correctional Services are, *inter alia*, as far as practicable, to apply such rehabilitation programmes and other meaningful and constructive activities to sentenced offenders that contribute to their rehabilita-

---

32 (HC-MD-CIV-MOT-GEN-2022/00210) [2023] NAHCMD 237 (28 April 2023), § 128.

33 Act 9 of 2012.

tion and successful reintegration into community as law-abiding citizens.[34] The Courts have time and again stated that punishment should aim at rehabilitation, deterrence, prevention and retribution. In the matter of *S v Gothard*,[35] Salionga, J held as follows:

> At the same time the sentence to be imposed must satisfy the objectives of punishment which are: (i) the prevention of crime; (ii) deterrence of the offender from re-offending and would-be offenders from committing crimes; (iii) rehabilitation of the offender and (iv) retribution. A sentence to be considered should equally be blended with a measure of mercy."[36]

The relevant provisions of the Namibian Constitution are Articles 25 and 44. Article 44 confers legislative powers on the National Assembly, and Article 25 provides that the legislature may not pass any legislation that infringes upon the fundamental rights and freedoms contained in Chapter 3 of the Constitution.[37]

The Constitution guarantees various entrenched fundamental rights and freedoms. An entrenched right has been defined as a right that cannot be easily amended and would thus require extraordinary circumstances to be amended. Article 8 of the Constitution provides as follows:

> (1) The dignity of all persons shall be inviolable.
>
> (2) (a) In any judicial proceedings or in other proceedings before any organ of the State, and during the enforcement of a penalty, respect for human dignity shall be guaranteed.
>
> (b) No persons shall be subject to torture or to cruel, inhuman or degrading treatment or punishment.

In the matter of *S v Gaingob and Others*,[38] the crux of the appeal was whether excessively long fixed terms of imprisonment, which have the possibility of depriving an offender of the hope of release during his or her lifetime, constitute cruel, inhuman, or degrading treatment or punishment in conflict with Article 8. In its discussion, the Court referred to its earlier judgment of *S v Tcoeib*,[39] where it had dismissed a challenge to the constitutionality of life imprisonment because the then applicable statutory provisions allowed for parole. In arriving at its conclusion in *Tcoeib*, the Court held that life imprisonment is the most severe and onerous sentence to be imposed and should therefore only be imposed in extreme cases, where the public needs protection from the offender. It further highlighted that there is room in a democratic society for sentences that effectively mean that an offender has no chance of release from in-

---

34 Section 3(c).

35 (CC 15/2019) [2022] NAHCNLD 5 (25 January 2022), § 3.

36 See generally the matters of *S v Zinn* 1969 (2) SA 537 (A) and *S v Rabie* 1975 (4) SA 855.

37 Article 25(1) provides that "(1) Save in so far as it may be authorised to do so by this Constitution, Parliament or any subordinate legislative authority shall not make any law, and the Executive and the agencies of Government shall not take any action which abolishes or abridges the fundamental rights and freedoms conferred by this Chapter, and any law or action in contravention thereof shall to the extent of the contravention be invalid."

38 (SA 7 of 2008) [2018] NASC 4 (6 February 2018).

39 1999 NR 24 (SC).

carceration. In essence, the conclusion was that a type of life imprisonment where the sentencer throws away the key for the offender's prison cell cannot be constitutionally sustained in Namibia.

Mahomad CJ, in *Tcoeib* further stated:

> There is no escape from the conclusion that an order deliberately incarcerating a citizen for the rest of his or her natural life severely impacts upon much of what is central to the enjoyment of life itself in any civilised community and can therefore only be upheld if it is demonstrably justified. In my view, it cannot be justified if it effectively amounts to a sentence which locks the gates of the prison irreversibly for the offender without any prospect whatever of any lawful escape from that condition for the rest of his or her natural life and regardless of any circumstances which might subsequently arise.

In the matter of *S v Njuluwa*,[40] the court in its discussion of Section 276 of the Criminal Procedure Act[41] held that a sentence may not include an order that a convicted person may not be paroled.

In sum, under a proper analysis of the applicable legislation and legal principles, the proposed amendment would not be acceptable as its effect would translate to mean that the offender has no hope of release during his or her lifetime, which according to the cases discussed herein amounts to cruel and inhuman punishment in violation of Article 8 of the Namibian Constitution.

---

40 2000 NR 97 (HC).

41 Act 51 of 1977.

12. Norway

By *Johan Boucht**

Vignette 1: Trolley Problem – Killing one Person to Save Many

Five young children are playing on railway tracks. An express train is approaching, and it is too late to stop the train before it hits the children, probably killing them. Operator D recognizes the emergency situation. He electronically flips a switch and thus deflects the train from its regular track to a little-used sidetrack. However, the lone repairman V is busy on the sidetrack, and the deflected train kills V, as D had anticipated. Is D criminally responsible for murder of V?

Under Norwegian law, this case would most likely be dealt with under the rules on necessity. Under section 17 of the Norwegian Criminal Code, an act which would otherwise be punishable is lawful when it is committed to protect life, health, property or another relevant interest from a risk of harm which cannot be averted in any other reasonable way, and this risk of harm is far greater than the risk of harm associated with the act. It is not required that the averted danger has originated in unlawful conduct caused by another; in fact, the dangerous situation may have been caused by the defendant's own hand.

To be justified, the defensive act must be both necessary and proportionate. The availability of alternative avenues of averting the danger is essential for assessing the necessity requirement: there must not have been any reasonable alternative way of preventing the danger. The act must be a means of last resort. The Supreme Court has interpreted this requirement rather strictly, particularly where alternative lawful measures would have been available. For example, in the case HR-2018-1458-A the defendant had driven her car 35 km while intoxicated in order to escape from her violent partner. The court found that this could not be justified under section 17. As she had passed a road-toll station where she could have requested assistance but failed to do so, the act was not necessary in the sense required by the provision. It is also required that the risk is of a certain urgency (cf. Supreme Court case HR-2020-955-A).

The proportionality requirement demands that the risk of harm which was averted must be far greater than the risk of harm associated with the act. Therefore, the less valuable interest must yield to the more valuable interest.[1] This assessment is objective. The proportionality requirement under section 17 is stricter than that which applies to self-defence under section 18 of the Criminal Code. In assessing whether the act was proportionate, the court needs to consider not only the nature of the endangered interest, but also the intensity of the danger, the probability that the act was capable of averting the danger, and the magnitude of the damage caused by the act.[2]

---

* Professor of Criminal Law, BI Norwegian Business School in Oslo.

1 Bill Ot.prp. nr. 90 (2003–04), p. 425.

2 Bill Ot.prp. nr. 90 (2003–04), p. 425.

Whether the danger was caused by the defendant's own hand is also a relevant consideration.[3]

Under section 93 of the Norwegian Constitution, everyone has the right to life. In accordance with this, life is regarded as the highest value protected by the Norwegian legal system.[4] Therefore, life can never be justifiably sacrificed to save another life, not even when one's own life is at stake. In this case, the protected interest will not be far greater than the sacrificed interest.

This was considered by the Supreme Court in the case Rt. 1950 s. 377. In this case, two Norwegian police officers were required to participate in the execution of a Norwegian man who had been sentenced to death by a special nazi court in 1944 during the German occupation of Norway. After the war had ended, the two police officers were charged with murder and assisting the enemy. The Supreme Court held that while it is likely that the police officers would have been executed had they refused to participate in the execution, this could not justify their actions. The court observed that sacrificing the life of another person to save one's own cannot be justified.[5] This principle is considered to apply also where one life is sacrificed for the purpose of saving several lives.[6]

However, while killing another in a state of necessity cannot be justified, the court may nevertheless either mitigate the sentence under section 78(a), or set the punishment below the prescribed minimum or impose a less severe form of punishment, under section 80(d) of the Criminal Code. Ultimately, where the defendant cannot be blamed because of extraordinary circumstances, the court may acquit him or her under section 81(2). Commentators have suggested that acquittal might be a reasonable outcome in extreme situations where one person's life has been sacrificed to save one or several other lives.[7]

In the present case, there was no lawful alternative that D could have reverted to. The option was to refrain from flipping the switch, which would have resulted in the probable death of the children. The answer to the conundrum should therefore be sought in the proportionality assessment. In view of the case law referred to above, it would seem quite clear that D's actions, however understandable, cannot be justified under section 17. Each life is unique, and the protected interest will therefore not be far greater than the sacrificed interests, not even where five lives are potentially saved. It is therefore likely that D would be held to have committed murder. However, the extreme circumstances of this case would be likely to give rise to either a heavily

---

3 See, e.g., Supreme Court case Rt. 1948 s. 957.

4 See, e.g., Linda Gröning, Erling Johannes Husabø and Jørn Jacobsen, *Frihet, forbrytelse og straff. En systematisk fremstilling av norsk strafferett*, 3rd ed. (Fagbokforlaget 2023), 451.

5 For this view, see also Francis Hagerup, *Strafferettens almindelige del* (Aschehoug & Co 1911), p. 253 and Johs. Andenæs, Georg Fredrik Rieber-Mohn and Knut Erik Sæther, *Alminnelig strafferett*, 6th ed. (Universitetsforlaget 2016), p. 191 and Bill Ot.prp. nr. 90 (2003–04), p. 205.

6 Jon Skeie, *Den norske strafferett I*, 2nd ed. (Olaf Norlis Forlag 1946), p. 154, Andenæs (note 5), p. 191, Gröning et al. (note 4), 451, Bill Ot.prp. nr. 90 (2003–04), p. 205.

7 Erling Johannes Husabø, Straffeloven, *Karnov Lovkommentar*, § 17(4).

mitigated sentence or full acquittal, on the grounds of excuse under sections 78(a), 80(d) or 81(b)(1) of the Criminal Code.

Vignette 2: Attribution of Death

D intends to kill his neighbour V. Hidden near V's house, D waits for V and stabs him several times with a knife. V is taken to the hospital, where his wounds are treated. His injuries are not life-threatening and V is kept overnight for observation. During the night, a technical defect in the hospital kitchen leads to the outbreak of a fire, which kills V and other persons. Can D be held criminally responsible for V's death?

This is a classic example of causality and superseding effects. In Norwegian law, causality has traditionally been understood in terms of *conditio sine qua non*, i. e. that every necessary condition constitutes a relevant cause.[8] On this view, the causality requirement is not satisfied where effect B would have arisen even if cause A would not have occurred. The theory has been criticized by commentators as being flawed, inter alia, because of the problems it gives rise to in cases of multiple causes. Some writers have suggested that it should be abandoned.[9]

In the case HR-2022-1271-A, the Supreme Court went some way toward depreciating the position of the *conditio* theory in Norwegian criminal law. The Court held that the question whether there is a requirement of causation, and what it entails, must be resolved by interpreting the relevant penal provision, and that this conclusion ought not to be based on a universally applicable doctrine of causation. However, it is still likely that a court would use the *conditio* theory as a starting point in many instances.

In cases with a single cause, the *conditio* theory, as traditionally understood in Norwegian criminal law, suggests that any significant change in terms of time, place, or manner of occurrence of the effect caused by the act is sufficient to establish causation.[10] Where several causes are involved, the assessment varies depending on the causal constellation as the *conditio* requirement cannot be fully maintained in these cases.[11]

For the purposes of criminal law, the causal relationship also has to be adequate.[12] This means, first, that the act in question was capable of causing the relevant risk and thus contributed to the way in which the harm occurred. The act must, in other words, have been relevant for the effect. Secondly, the effect must have resulted from a reasonably normal, or foreseeable, realisation of that risk, i. e., the effect must be connected to the dangerous nature of the act in question in a relevant way.

With regard to superseding causes, the relevant inquiry relates to whether it can reasonably be said that the responsibility for the effect has shifted from the first

---

8 Hagerup (note 5), pp. 153–154, Andenæs (note 5), p. 128.

9 See Erling Johannes Husabø, *Rett til sjølvvalt livsavslutning?* (Gyldendal 1994), pp. 182–196, Gröning et al. (note 4), p. 165–167.

10 Andenæs (note 5), p. 129.

11 Andenæs (note 5), p. 130.

12 See Andenæs (note 5), pp. 132–133.

cause (A) to the second (B).[13] The starting point is that where A causes a danger to the life of victim V, he is responsible unless the ensuing chain of events leads to a conclusion that the relevant effect must be considered to have been removed from A's natural or foreseeable sphere of responsibility. In view of the *conditio* theory, A's act will, as a starting point, be regarded as causally relevant where the effect of A's act forms part of the factual premise for B's act.

In the present case, the question is whether D ought to be held responsible for V's death, i. e., whether V's death lies within D's natural or foreseeable sphere of responsibility. For D to be responsible, his act must have been capable of causing V's death. The vignette does not say where V was stabbed but indicates that the injury was not life-threatening. When the fire broke out, V's wounds were already treated, and V remained at the hospital merely for observation. As the initial cause was not life-threatening, and V would appear to have recovered when the fire broke out, it cannot be said that his death occurred in a foreseeable way connected to the dangerous nature of D's act. D's intent to kill V relates to the effect, not to the means of achieving that effect and should therefore not necessarily be relevant for the causality assessment. The effect of D's act was in any case neutralised by the time that the fire broke out. D can therefore not be held responsible for causing D's death, merely for his attempt to do so.

Vignette 3: Torture to Save a Life

Kidnapper K has abducted an 8-year-old girl G and hidden her in a small cave in the woods. K is trying to extort money from G's parents for her release. The police manage to arrest K. Although being questioned for 24 hours, K steadfastly refuses to disclose where he hid G. Police officer D correctly assumes that G may soon die of thirst if she cannot be found. He therefore severely beats K to make him tell the truth. Fearing even more violence, K eventually leads the police to the cave, where they find G still barely alive. Should D be punished for torturing K?

This is a hard case for which the solution under Norwegian law is not clear. It follows that it is not possible to provide a clear answer, only to point in the direction of possible outcomes.

The starting point is the prohibition against torture under Art. 3 of the European Convention on Human Rights (ECHR): no one shall be subjected to torture or to inhuman or degrading treatment or punishment. The protection against torture and inhuman treatment is absolute.[14]

In *Gäfgen v Germany*, the European Court of Human Rights (ECtHR) found, in a scenario which is reminiscent of the vignette, that a threat to cause the applicant intolerable pain in order to extract a statement from him during an interrogation, constituted a violation of Art. 3 ECHR.[15] According to the Grand Chamber (at para. 107), the prohibition against ill-treatment of a person applies irrespective of the conduct of the victim or the motivation of the authorities:

---

13 Husabø (note 9), p. 208.

14 Harris, O'Boyle and Warbrick, *Law of the Convention on Human Rights*, 5th ed. (OUP 2023), 242.

15 Gäfgen v Germany, No. 22987/05 (ECtHR, 1.6.2010).

> Article 3 recognises that every human being has an absolute, inalienable right not to be subjected to torture or to inhuman or degrading treatment under any circumstances, even the most difficult.

In Norway, torture or inhuman treatment is prohibited under section 93(2) of the Norwegian Constitution. The prohibition against the use of violence during police interviews in custody is found in the Norwegian prosecutorial regulation (28.06.1985 nr. 1679), section 8–2(4).[16]

Under section 1 of the Norwegian Human Rights Act, the ECHR applies as law in Norway. As the ECHR has a very strong position in Norwegian law, one possible outcome of the Vignette is that the Norwegian court would abide strictly by the ruling of the ECtHR in the *Gäfgen* case and establish a violation of Art. 3 ECHR. D would hence be convicted of inflicting bodily harm on K under section 271 or 273 of the Norwegian Criminal Code. However, in view of the relatively pragmatic approach that the Norwegian Supreme Court has traditionally adopted also in cases relating to criminal law, it is not ruled out that it would seek to find a solution where D's action would not be punishable, particularly considering that G's life was in fact saved. There would seem to be three possible approaches to achieve this.

The first would be to interpret Art. 3 ECHR in light of the context, that is, G's competing right not to be subjected to inhuman or degrading treatment and her right to life, as well as D's aim to liberate G and prevent her death.[17]

The ECtHR has in a number of cases pointed at the relative nature of the minimum level of ill-treatment that must be reached in order for Art. 3 ECHR to apply. In *V v. the United Kingdom*, the Court explained:

> Ill-treatment must attain a minimum level of severity if it is to fall within the scope of Article 3. The assessment of this minimum is, in the nature of things, relative; it depends on all the circumstances of the case, such as the nature and context of the treatment or punishment, the manner and method of its execution, its duration, its physical or mental effects and, in some instances, the sex, age and state of health of the victim.[18]

In line with this statement, the ECtHR has accepted relatively far-reaching and intrusive treatment from state officials where it was applied while carrying out official duties. In *Wainwright v. the United Kingdom*, a case which concerned intimate body searches of visitors to a prison which caused considerable long-term psychological damage to the individuals concerned, the Court held that such a search could be compatible with Art. 3 ECHR when "carried out in an appropriate manner with due respect for human dignity and for a legitimate purpose".[19]

The rules on self-defence under section 18 of the Norwegian Criminal Code would seem to apply to the scenario played out in the vignette. According to this provision, an act which would otherwise be punishable is lawful when it is committed to avert an

---

16 Ørnulf Øyen, *Straffeprosess*, 3rd ed. (Fagbokforlaget 2022), p. 171.

17 In Z and others v the United Kingdom, No. 29392/95 (ECtHR, 10.5.2001), para. 73, the Court held that the obligation to prevent such treatment of children is stronger than with adults.

18 *V v the United Kingdom*, No. 24888/94 (ECtHR, 16.12.1999), para. 70. See also Jalloh v Germany, No. 54810/00 (ECtHR, 11.7.2006), para. 67.

19 *Wainwright v the United Kingdom*, No. 12350/04 (ECtHR, 26.9.2006), para. 42.

unlawful attack, provided that it is necessary and does not clearly go beyond what is proportionate. The right to self-defence, both of one's own interests and those of others, applies to all citizens, including police officers.[20]

To be justified under section 18, the defence must, first, be necessary, both temporally and in terms of intensity.[21] The defender must therefore resort to the least intrusive means of averting the attack. The defence must also not be clearly disproportionate in view of the dangerousness of the attack, the type of interest the attack violates, and the culpability of the assailant. In the context of self-defence, the defender is traditionally awarded a wide margin of appreciation.[22]

When someone is deprived of his or her liberty, the attack is considered to continue until the person is liberated. Consequently, self-defence can be used during the entirety of this period. In the present case, the assessment of whether D's act was necessary and proportionate would have to consider not only K's attack on G's liberty, but also the imminent risk for G's life. It could be argued that D's act was not necessary as other means would have been available, such as modern techniques of interrogation. However, a contrasting conclusion also appears plausible: other measures would simply not have been equally effective, considering the seriousness of the situation and the imminent risk of G's death. In contrast to the risk to G's life, D's act was limited to physical violence for a short period of time. Moreover, the use of force directly targeted the main perpetrator K. It is therefore not ruled out that the force used by D would be considered acceptable under section 18 of the Criminal Code in view of the circumstances.

A possible outcome of this approach would be that D's action would be held not to have reached the minimum threshold required for Art. 3 ECHR to apply, and that the act would thus be justified under the rules on self-defence.[23] It follows that the normative conflict that arises would be removed by a narrow interpretation of Art. 3 ECHR.

An alternative approach would be to differentiate between state and individual responsibility, and to apportion blame utilising the dogmatic device in criminal law of distinguishing between justification and excuse.[24] If this approach were to be applied in the present scenario, the court could follow the first option above and establish a violation of Art. 3 ECHR as D's act, D being a representative of the state, could not be justified. However, as regards D's individual responsibility, the court could apply section 18 (self-defence) in combination with section 81(2) of the Criminal Code not as a defence, but as a ground of excuse. Section 81(2) enables the court to acquit a

20 Supreme Court case Rt. 2007 s. 1172.

21 Andenæs (note 5), pp. 166–167.

22 Andenæs (note 5), p. 167.

23 A reasoning in this direction would seem to be favoured by some Norwegian commentators, although not explicitly suggested. See Ørnulf Øyen and Gert Johan Kjelby, "Saken Gäfgen mot Tyskland – noen synspunkt på absolutte og relative sider ved EMK art. 3", *Tidsskrift for strafferett* (2008), p. 296.

24 For a solution along these lines in the international debate, see Kai Ambos, "May a State Torture Suspects to Save the Life of Innocents?", *Journal of International Criminal Justice* (2008), pp. 285–286.

defendant who has exceeded the normative limits of self-defence where the perpetrator, in view of the circumstances, cannot be blamed. Considering that D acted to liberate G and prevent her death, this might not be an unreasonable result. If D were not acquitted, his sentence could still be (heavily) mitigated under sections 78(1) and 80(4) of the Criminal Code. A solution of this kind might draw the delicate balance of upholding the prohibition of torture and inhuman treatment while duly considering the pressing circumstances of the case and the premise for D's action. A benefit of this approach is that the outcome respects the interests of both norms by accepting the existence of a normative conflict and by distinguishing between the state and individual levels in terms of its consequences.

Under the third approach, which probably is the least plausible, the court could justify an acquittal utilising the distinction between the state's positive and negative obligations under Art. 3 ECHR in conjunction with the right to self-defence in the present case. Had D not been a police officer but a private individual, and the beating would not have taken place in police custody, it is, as suggested above, not implausible that D's acts could be considered to be justified by self-defence under the present circumstances. Such a conclusion is unlikely to constitute a violation of Norway's positive obligation under Art. 3 ECHR.

In the vignette, D is a police officer, and his actions were carried out while K was in police custody. However, it is not unequivocally clear that D's actions in self-defence should be equated with those of the state.[25] It might therefore be arguable that D ought not to be identified with the Norwegian state when acting in self-defence. Consequently, the court could argue that D's act should be assessed in view of the state's positive rather than its negative obligation under Art. 3 ECHR. In line with this reasoning, D's act in self-defence would therefore not constitute a violation of the state's negative duty to refrain from actions which amount to torture of inhuman treatment.

Vignette 4: Lethal Self-Defence

> R, a well-trained young man armed with a knife, accosts 50-year-old D, who is on her way home from a party in the early morning hours. R threatens her with the knife and takes away her purse filled with 500 € and her wristwatch worth 1,000 €. As R turns to run away, D draws a pistol she is secretly carrying in her jacket, and shoots and kills R in order to retrieve her property. Is D guilty of murder?

Under section 18 of the Norwegian Criminal Code, an act which would otherwise be punishable is lawful as self-defence when it is committed to avert an unlawful attack provided that it is necessary and does not clearly go beyond what is proportionate, taking into account the dangerousness of the attack, the type of interest the attack

25 This has been unclear also in the other Nordic countries. In Finnish law, the Supreme Court ruled in judgment 2004:75 that when a police officer acts in self-defence, even if this occurs in the line of duty, he is to be considered to have acted as a private individual. This position was reversed when the new Police Act entered into force in 2014. Under Swedish law, the position remains unclear, although commentators have argued that a police officer acting in self-defence should be considered a representative of the state (see Johan Boucht, *Polisiär våldsanvändning. En straff- och offentligrättslig undersökning* (Iustus förlag 2011), pp. 335–339).

violates, and the culpability of the assailant. Self-defence constitutes a justification under Norwegian law, which makes the act lawful.[26]

For section 18 to apply, the unlawful attack must either be imminent or already have been initiated. The meaning of imminence is not defined in law, but the Supreme Court has held that the necessity requirement, and particularly the assessment of available options to avert the attack, will be stricter in regard to impending attacks.[27] When the attack has ended, self-defence is no longer permitted.[28] However, this may be different where the immediate attack has ended but a further attack can still be expected. For example, if A hits B once in the face, B can defend himself provided that a further blow is likely to occur.

The necessity requirement implies that the least intrusive means of averting the attack must be used.[29] The defender's options are essential in this assessment. The more violent the attack, the more generous the assessment of necessary force will be. In assessing the proportionality of the defence, the defendant is granted a generous "margin of appreciation".[30] However, the courts have traditionally been restrictive in accepting the use of weapons.[31] For example, in the case HR-2019-642-A the Supreme Court held that the defendant, who had stabbed an unarmed attacker four times in the thigh, had gone too far as other options were available to him.

In the present case, D uses a pistol to retrieve her property subsequent to a violent robbery involving a knife attack. As R had the already taken possession of the property when D used her firearm killing R, the attack had already ended according to Norwegian law. As noted above, self-defence requires that the unlawful attack is either imminent or has already begun, but it is not permitted when the attack has ended. An exception might apply if D suspected that R's attack would continue, but there are no indications in the vignette that this was the case here; in fact, R is about to turn around to run away when D fires her pistol. It follows that self-defence is not available in this case.

However, D's act could be assessed under section 19 of the Criminal Code, which regulates so-called "self-enforcement", i.e., to justifiably take "the law into one's own hands" in certain situations. According to this provision, an act which would otherwise be criminal is lawful when an entitled person acts to restore an unlawfully altered position, and it would be unreasonable for him to wait for assistance from the authorities.

This rule is connected to the rules on self-defence: while self-defence may be used during an attack, "self-enforcement" enables the victim to restore the situation and recover what is hers after the attack has ended. For example, if the owner of a bicycle discovers that a thief is in the process of stealing his bike, he may invoke self-defence

26 Cf. Andenæs (note 5), p. 161.

27 Supreme Court case Rt. 2006 s. 141.

28 Bill Ot.prp. nr. 90 (2003–04), p. 420. See also Supreme Court judgment Rt. 2014 s. 605, para. 13.

29 Bill Ot.prp. nr. 90 (2003–04), p. 420.

30 Bill Ot.prp. nr. 90 (2003–04), p. 421, Andenæs (note 5), p. 167.

31 See, e.g., Supreme Court case HR–2017–1784.

to protect his property. However, when the thief has taken possession of the bike, the owner may invoke section 19 to recover the bike from the thief. Self-enforcement is a justification, making the act lawful.[32]

For the defence to apply, the position of the entitled person must have been unlawfully altered, for example as a consequence of a criminal offence. A subsidiarity requirement also applies: it must be unreasonable for the defendant to wait for assistance from the authorities. The more time the defender has at his or her disposal, the stronger the expectation is to first consult with the authorities. However, self-enforcement can be invoked where time is of the essence and it is necessary to act fast.[33]

Proportionate force may be resorted to provided that the violation is apparent.[34] The normative limits that apply are relatively strict and less generous than those which apply to self-defence. Some commentators have suggested that only force that does not result in severe and protracted consequences for the attacker can be accepted under this rule.[35]

If the normative limit of justified self-enforcement is exceeded, the act is unlawful.[36] However, the circumstances of the case may be considered in sentencing. Sections 78(a) and 80(d) of the Criminal Code enable the court to mitigate the sentence, and if the defendant cannot be blamed for his actions because of particular circumstances, the court may acquit him or her under section 81.

D has been the object of an unlawful attack in which her property rights to the cash and wristwatch were unlawfully altered. It would probably be unreasonable to expect D to rely on assistance by the police as this would permit K to escape and potentially thwart the recovery of her property. Section 19 would therefore seem to apply. D may resort to proportionate force as the violation is evident. Although D's options were limited, shooting R to death would seem to be neither necessary nor proportionate. D had been attacked with a knife, but the object of the attack was D's personal affects, not her life and limb. It might be justifiable to threaten R with the firearm, possibly even to fire a warning shot, but certainly not to kill R (probably not even to shoot him in the leg). However, in view of the circumstances, D's punishment might be somewhat mitigated (cf. section 78 and 80 of the Criminal Code). There would not seem to be any grounds for excusing D under section 81.

Vignette 5: Criminal Responsibility of Subordinates for Systemic Offences

D is a soldier in the army of a country ruled by a junta of generals who have come to power through a violent coup. When an opposition group demands the return to a democratic system, the government orders the soldiers to shoot and kill any person who resists arrest. Following this order, D kills three young men who take part in a protest demonstration and hit a police officer who tries to arrest them. When D

32 Erling Johannes Husabø, Straffeloven, *Karnov Lovkommentar*, § 19(1).

33 Bill Ot.prp. nr. 90 (2003–04), p. 423.

34 Bill Ot.prp. nr. 90 (2003–04), p. 423.

35 Husabø, *Karnov Lovkommentar*, § 19(1).

36 Gröning et al. (note 4), 451.

> is tried after a change of regime, he says that he did not like to shoot the protesters but that he thought that he had to obey his commanders' orders. D knew that if he had refused to shoot, he might have been demoted, but no physical harm would have occurred to him. Should D be convicted of murder? If so, should his sentence be mitigated because of his situation?

D is charged with the murder of three protesters. Murder is punishable under section 275 of the Norwegian Criminal Code. The question is whether any justifications might apply. D objects that he did not like to shoot the protesters, but that he would have been demoted if he had resisted the order.

Under section 24 of the Military Criminal Code (1904), a subordinate is exempted from punishment when carrying out a superior officer's order, provided that he or she neither exceeded the order, nor realised nor ought to have realised, that by carrying out the order he or she contributed to an unlawful act. In any case, the court can mitigate the punishment below the prescribed minimum or impose a less severe form of punishment. Under section 3 of the Military Criminal Code, this provision only applies in times of war, that is after a declaration of war because of an armed attack from a foreign power. In this case, no such declaration would seem to exist. It follows that section 24 is not applicable to D.

D's objection is therefore likely to be assessed under the rules of necessity in section 17 of the Norwegian Criminal Code. For D's act to be justified, his act must be committed to save life, health, property or another legally protected interest from a risk of harm which cannot be averted in any other reasonable manner, and that interest must be clearly greater than that which is sacrificed.

Under Norwegian law, the sacrifice of the life of another person to save one's own life can never be justified. In the Supreme Court case Rt. 1950 s. 377, three Norwegian police officers were forced in 1944 to participate in the execution of a Norwegian man under the German occupation. The police officers were tried for murder and assisting the enemy after the war had ended. The Supreme Court held that although they would most likely have been executed themselves if they had refused to carry out the order, this did not make their action justified.

Under the facts of the vignette, it is clear that no physical harm would have come to D had he refused to carry out the orders, only a risk of demotion. As the interest of not being demoted is unlikely to be considered a legally protected interest, the first criterion of section 17 would not appear to be satisfied. The rules on necessity would therefore not apply. However, even if they did apply, it is clear that the value of the sacrificed interests, the lives of three protestors, is far greater than the value of those which are saved. D's actions can therefore not in any case be justified.

Sections 78(a) and 80(d) enable the court to mitigate the sentence where the normative limits of necessity have been exceeded. Section 81(2) also enables the court to acquit the defendant if particular circumstances prevailed so that the defendant should not be blamed for his actions.[37] However, for these provisions to be applicable, section 17 must apply. This would not seem to be the case here. D will therefore probably be held responsible for murder.

---

37 Erling Johannes Husabø, "Straffeloven", *Karnov Lovkommentar*, § 81(4).

Vignette 6: Limits of Consent

> V is a 21-year-old ambitious athlete and short-distance runner. He has learned that certain artificial limbs can enhance a runner's speed. He decides that he would rather have an artificial limb instead of his right lower leg. He approaches D, a surgeon in private practice, and asks him to amputate his leg below the knee and replace it with an artificial limb. D complies with V's request. Should D be punished for mayhem?

Under Norwegian law, consenting to a violation of one's physical integrity is traditionally seen as a justification which makes the act lawful (*volenti non fit injuria*).[38] For the consent to be valid, it has to satisfy certain conditions.[39] The interest which is harmed must be such that the individual can dispose of it, i. e., it must be of a private rather than public nature. The person who consents must have the capacity to do so, that is, to be of sound mind and understand what it is that he or she consents to. The consent must be voluntary and given at the latest at the time when the act is performed. Lastly, the consent must not exceed the substantive scope of valid consent.

The scope of valid consent to the infliction of bodily harm is limited by section 276 of the Criminal Code. Under this provision, criminal responsibility for the consensual infliction of bodily harm (according to sections 271–274(1) of the Criminal Code) will not arise unless the harm is "grievous". Grievous bodily harm is defined in section 11 as "the loss or substantial impairment of a sense, an important organ or an important body part, serious disfigurement, deadly or protracted disease, or serious mental harm". Where consent will not justify the act, the defendant will be held responsible for causing grievous bodily harm under section 274(2) of the Criminal Code. The maximum penalty for this offence is 15 years imprisonment. However, the sentence may be mitigated under section 276(2), either by imposing punishment below the prescribed minimum or by imposing a less severe form of punishment.

In this case, V asks a surgeon to amputate his leg below the knee and replace it with an artificial limb. The interest involved is clearly of a private nature, and V is capable of disposing of it. There is nothing in the vignette suggesting that V was not of a sound mind or that he would have possessed insufficient information about what he was consenting to. The consent was also given voluntarily before the amputation. Thus, the crucial question is whether D's act exceeded the scope of justifiable consent under section 276(1) and section 11 of the Criminal Code.

A leg amounts to a "body part" under section 11.[40] The fact that the harm in this case is inflicted only on a part of V's leg is likely to be irrelevant. The body part must also be "important", but considering that a leg for most people is an integral bodily part it is unlikely that this criterion would lead to a different conclusion. A likely conclusion would therefore be that D's act exceeds the lawful scope of consensual infliction of bodily harm and is therefore not justified. However, D's sentence may be mitigated in accordance with section 276(2) of the Criminal Code.

---

38 Andenæs (note 5), p. 194. Cf. Thomas Frøberg, *Alminnelig strafferett i et nøtteskall*, 2th ed. (Gyldendal 2020), pp. 92–95 who sees it as an element of whether an unlawful act has been committed.

39 See Andenæs (note 5), pp. 203–206.

40 Jørn Jacobsen and Linda Gröning, "Straffelov", *Karnov Lovkommentar*, § 11(3).

One qualification should be made to this analysis. For the act to be punishable under Norwegian law, it has to be normatively "unlawful" in view of its "socio-ethical acceptability".[41] As a consequence, the wording of a criminal provision will in certain situations be interpreted narrowly so as to exclude a particular act from its scope. For example, if D's leg were to be consensually amputated for a medical reason, the amputation is likely to be justified because of the concurrent effects of consent and medical necessity.[42] Where the surgery has no medical purpose, such as in this case, it would seem to be more doubtful whether the amputation could be considered lawful.[43] However, it might still be argued that V's consent in conjunction with the outcome, which was a de facto improvement of the functionality of V's leg, ought nevertheless to justify an acquittal.

If the amputation were to be considered unlawful under section 276(2), the question arises whether the fact that the functionality of V's leg was restored by replacing the leg with an artificial limb should be given any relevance. As the criminal law seeks to protect the individual from being harmed, this would seem irrelevant for the question of D's criminal responsibility. However, it may be relevant as a mitigating circumstance in sentencing. Sections 78(b) and 80(1) allow the court to mitigate the sentence where "the offender has prevented, reversed or limited the harm or loss of welfare caused by the offence, or sought to do so" and where he "without knowing he/she was under suspicion has to a significant degree prevented or reversed the harm caused by the offence". Replacing the original leg with an artificial limb has limited the harm, restored its functionality, and, indeed, quite possibly even improved it from V's perspective. As the mitigating rule in section 276(2) relates to a different interest (the existence of consent) compared to section 78(b) and 80(1) (the limitation of harm), both grounds for mitigation might apply in this case.

Vignette 7: Withdrawal from an Attempt

25-year-old D is deeply upset with her former boyfriend V, who had ended their relationship to be with another woman. To punish V, D plans to stab him with a large knife. D knows that the stab wounds can be fatal and accepts V's death as a possible outcome. When V goes jogging, D attacks him from behind and stabs him in the back three times. V breaks down. D realises that she has injured him but that the injuries will not cause his death. She realises that she could kill him by stabbing him again but decides to leave him alone. Should D be punished for attempted murder?

Attempts are punishable under section 16 of the Norwegian Criminal Code. According to this provision, "anyone who intends to commit an offence which is punishable by imprisonment for a term of one year or more, and acts in a way which leads directly to the commission of that offence, shall be liable for attempt, unless otherwise provided".

41 NOU 1983:57, s. 122.

42 Johs. Andenæs and Anders Bratholm, *Spesiell strafferett. Utvalgte emner* 2nd ed. (Universitetsforlaget 1990), p. 77.

43 Andenæs and Bratholm (note 42), p. 77.

Liability for attempt requires that both the subjective and objective elements of section 16 are satisfied. The subjective element is fulfilled if the person has the requisite intent to commit a criminal offence. For the objective requirement to be satisfied, the perpetrator must have taken steps to realise his or her intent. Thus, the objective element must be assessed in view of the perspective of the perpetrator's intent. Whether the objective criteria under section 16 are fulfilled is determined in the light of three parameters: 1) proximity in time, i. e., how distant in time is the completion of the criminal offence; 2) proximity to completion, i. e., how much remains to be done before the offence is completed, and 3) the nature of the act, for example, whether the steps taken to realise the intent involved other criminal acts.[44]

In the present case, the subjective element appears to be clear enough. D has planned to stab V and accepts that V's death is a possible outcome of this act. As regards the objective side of the attempt, D has taken steps towards realising her criminal intention by stabbing V three times in the back. It follows that the requirements for criminal responsibility for attempted murder under section 275 and section 16 are in place.

The question is whether her conduct qualifies as a withdrawal under section 16(2) of the Criminal Code. Under this provision, "anyone who voluntarily desists from completing the offence or prevents its commission, shall not be punished for attempt." Under Norwegian law, withdrawal from attempt is viewed not as an excuse but as a separate ground of acquittal.[45]

Section 16(2) distinguishes between incomplete and complete attempts. An attempt is incomplete when the perpetrator has set out to commit an offence, but one or several acts required to bring about the offence have not yet been realised. The robber has, for example, threatened the victim, but not yet taken his wallet. A complete attempt means that the perpetrator has done all that he intended to do to bring about the effect, but that effect has not yet materialised. Whether the attempt is complete is assessed subjectively from the perspective of the perpetrator's own understanding of what is required to bring the offence to completion.[46] If, for example, A has administered what she believes to be a lethal dose of poison to her husband, but the effect has not yet come about, the attempt is complete. In contrast, if A believes that further doses must be administered for the poison to be lethal, the attempt is incomplete.

In the case of incomplete attempts, section 16(2) specifies that where the perpetrator voluntarily desists from bringing about the intended offence, i. e., where he or she desists from carrying out the acts required to complete the intended offence, he will only be punished for the harm actually caused, but not for the harm that he intended to cause. Similarly, in the case of complete attempts, if the perpetrator prevents the effect from occurring, he or she will only be punished for the harm already caused. In this case, section 16(2) requires that the defendant successfully prevents the effect from occurring for the withdrawal to be effective.

---

44 See Supreme Court case Rt. 2008 s. 867.

45 Andenæs (note 5), p. 364 and Gröning et al. (note 4), p. 559.

46 See Supreme Court case HR-2019-47-A, para. 21.

Withdrawal must be voluntary. This means that the perpetrator must decide to withdraw from the attempt although there are, from his perspective, plausible alternative avenues of action that would realise the goal of committing the offence.[47] If, for example, he desists because he believes that the offence cannot be brought to completion without him being discovered the withdrawal is involuntary. If, in contrast, the perpetrator withdraws when he or she believes that the offence can be successfully completed, the withdrawal is voluntary.

In the present case, V stabs D three times, but she is aware that this is not enough to kill V. D desists from further stabbing. It follows that this is an incomplete attempt to commit murder. D desists from killing V not because she is fearful, for example, of being found out, but for other undisclosed reasons. Her withdrawal would thus seem to be voluntary. D would therefore not be convicted of attempted murder and would be held responsible for inflicting bodily harm on V.

Vignette 8: Criminal Responsibility of Minors

D is a 13-year-old boy. He abducts and rapes V, a girl of the same age. Should D be punished for a criminal offence?

The minimum age of criminal responsibility in Norway has varied over time. Under the Criminal Code of 1842 the general age limit was 10 years. However, if the perpetrator was between 10 and 15 years of age, responsibility was relative: while the perpetrator was to be acquitted of minor offences, his or her responsibility for more serious offences was contingent on his or her comprehension of the criminal nature of the conduct. The Criminal Code of 1902 set the minimum age at 14 years (section 46). In 1987 this was raised to 15 years. The reasons for increasing the minimum age were partly that the age limit in the other Nordic countries was 15 years, partly the wish to avoid custodial sentences for children.[48] It was considered that not only would it lead to unforeseeable results to let criminal responsibility be contingent on the child's individual level of maturity, but it would also be problematic in practice.[49]

The age limit for criminal responsibility under section 20(1) of the current Norwegian Criminal Code (2005), is 15 years. Where the child was under 15 years of age at the time of committing the offence, he or she is not criminally responsible and cannot be the subject to criminal proceedings in court. The cut-off point is at 24:00 hours on the day before the child turns 15.

It follows that D cannot be the object of criminal proceedings in court under Norwegian law.

Despite the rules on criminal responsibility, section 224(2) of the Criminal Procedural Code 1981 enables the police to initiate a criminal investigation in cases where there are reasons to believe that a criminal offence has been committed, even where the potential perpetrator was a child between 12 and 15 years of age at the time of

---

47 Supreme Court case HR-2019-47-A.

48 See Bill Ot.prp. nr. 8 (1986–87), pp. 9–10.

49 The Criminal Law Commission report NOU 1983:57, p. 159.

committing the offence. It follows that D can be made the object of a criminal investigation into the abduction and rape of V.

Vignette 9: Statute of Limitations

In 1995, D violently raped V, a 35-year-old woman, using a knife. D managed to escape and was not apprehended until 2023. Traces of his DNA taken from the victim's body leave no doubt that D is the perpetrator. Should D be convicted despite the long delay?

According to section 96 of the Norwegian Criminal Code, criminal conduct cannot be punished when the prosecution is time barred. When this happens is contingent on the severity of the offence in question. The period during which a perpetrator can be criminally charged varies according to a sliding scale from 2 years in cases where the maximum penalty for the criminal conduct is a fine or one year imprisonment, to 25 years where the maximum penalty is imprisonment of 21 years. According to section 87 of the Criminal Code, the relevant date is the day when the offence was committed or when the effect occurred. In regard to some offences, such as people trafficking of persons, conversion therapy and rape of a minor under 16 years of age, the relevant date is the day when the victim turned 18.

Under section 91, some offences are never statute barred. These include genocide, crimes against humanity, war crimes and terrorist crimes, provided that they can be punished by imprisonment of 15 years or more. The offences of murder, rape, rape of a person under 14 years of age, and sexual conduct with a person between 14 and 16 years of age are also never statute barred.

D's conduct amounts to rape under section 291 of the Criminal Code. This offence is never statute barred according to the current provision. However, under section 3(1) of the Criminal Code, the criminal law of the time when the act was committed should be applied unless the law at the time of the judgment leads to a more lenient result for the defendant. In 1995, rape was punishable under section 192 of the former Norwegian Criminal Code (1902), which provided for a penalty of up to 10 years imprisonment for ordinary rape (section 192(1), and a maximum of 21 years imprisonment for aggravated rape (section 192(3)). The facts as indicated in the vignette do not seem to warrant application of section 192(3). At the time, rape followed the ordinary statute of limitations in the 1902 Code. Under those rules, ordinary rape was statute barred 10 years after the act was committed. It follows, that the rape of V was statute barred in 2005. As the old rules lead to a more lenient result, they should be applied. D can therefore no longer be punished for the offence in 2023.

Vignette 10: Life Imprisonment without Parole

The Penal Code of State S provides for imprisonment for life as the maximum penalty for murder, but also authorises the court to order an offender's early release after a minimum of 15 years if the offender is no longer dangerous. Reacting to cases of particularly heinous murders, the legislature of S wishes to introduce a penalty of life imprisonment without any possibility of early release, regardless of the offender's continued dangerousness. Would this amendment be acceptable?

Under section 275 of the Norwegian Criminal Code, the maximum punishment for murder is 21 years imprisonment. Early release can be ordered when the offender has served two thirds of the sentence, and at least 60 days.[50] In addition to ordinary imprisonment, section 40 of the Criminal Code enables the court to order preventive detention in some cases. This is available where imprisonment is deemed to be insufficient to protect the life, health or freedom of other individuals and where the offender is found guilty of having committed, or attempted to commit, a violent offence, including murder, a sexual offence, unlawful imprisonment, arson or another offence that has violated or endangered the life, health or freedom of another individual. It is a prerequisite for preventive detention that there is a considerable risk that the offender will return to serious criminality in the future. Preventive detention may be extended for five years at a time if the offender remains dangerous. Early release from preventive detention may be ordered when the minimum time of detention has elapsed.

It is mainly an issue for each state to decide on criminal policy and the severity of sentences to be imposed by its courts for violations of the criminal law. Therefore, a state remains free to impose life sentences on adult offenders for especially serious crimes.[51] However, certain limits may be established by international law, mainly the ECHR. In the case of *Vinter v. the United Kingdom*, the Grand Chamber of the ECtHR held that a grossly disproportionate sentence would violate Art. 3 of the Convention, although this test would, according to the court, only be met on rare and unique occasions.[52] The *Vinter* case concerned the compatibility of a whole life order scheme under English law with Art. 3 of the Convention.

In *Vinter*, the Grand chamber interpreted Art. 3 ECHR as requiring the possibility of a review of life sentences by the domestic authorities for the purpose of a potential mitigation by considering whether any changes in the life prisoner are so significant, and such progress towards rehabilitation has been made in the course of serving the sentence, that continued detention can no longer be justified on legitimate penological grounds. According to the Court, such grounds include punishment, deterrence, public protection and rehabilitation (*Vinter*, para. 111). A whole life sentence would not measure up to the standards of Art. 3 ECHR where the domestic law does not provide for the possibility of such a review.

Under Norwegian law, the ECtHR's finding in *Vinter* would constitute an outer limit to the type of the sentence that it would be possible to impose, not only for the courts but also for the legislature. Therefore, the proposed scheme would be unlikely to be passed by the Norwegian legislature.

In addition, several other considerations speak against accepting the proposed amendment. In recent years, the Norwegian Supreme Court has more explicitly than previously referred to proportionality as a cornerstone both in criminal legislation and sentencing. In the case HR-2022-731-A (para. 43), the Court held:

---

50 Section 42(1) of the Execution of Sentences Act.

51 Vinter v the United Kingdom, No. 66069/09 (ECtHR, 9.7.2013), para. 102.

52 Vinter v the United Kingdom, No. 66069/09 (ECtHR, 9.7.2013), para. 102.

> The punishment should be fair and proportionate. The perception of what constitutes an appropriate punishment is influenced by general legal and moral perceptions in society and may change over time. Value perspectives expressed by the Parliament must be considered as an authoritative expression of the general sense of justice.

Indeed, proportionality does not in itself express or clearly delineate the accurate cardinal level of punishment. However, the Supreme Court judgment expresses that not only should the punishment be proportionate, but it should also be fair. The reference to proportionality can thus be understood as meaning that there has to be a reasonable and fair balance between the unlawful conduct and the punishment to be imposed.

Consequentialist considerations have traditionally been given relevance in the Norwegian debate on punishment levels. These considerations do not necessarily relate to the deterrent effect of punishment as such (which could be used in advocating harsher punishments), but rather to the functionality of harsher penalties as vehicles for achieving the objectives of punishment. It has been argued that the decrease over time in achieving the intended objective of punishment supports moderation as regards punishment levels.[53] In this context, it has also been emphasised that longer custodial sentences will increase the likelihood of unintended negative effects on the prisoners, such as an impairing their resocialisation into society.

Lastly, the legal culture in Norway, and indeed in the Nordic countries, speaks against very severe punishments. Traditionally, Nordic criminal policy has been characterised as being both humane and rational, with moderate punishment levels, low imprisonment rates, and a focus on rehabilitation.[54] Even if these features of the criminal justice system have been challenged in recent years, arguably they still contribute to tempering the political pressure to severely increase punishments.

In view of these additional considerations, it would seem unlikely that the amendment referred to in the vignette would be acceptable in a Norwegian context.

---

[53] See consultation response by the Director of Public Prosecutions (*Riksadvokaten*), 2016/02130-025 RT0006151, 21.3.2017, p. 3 regarding a government bill to severely increase punishment levels in Norway in cases of multiple crime.

[54] See, e.g., Tapio Lappi-Seppälä, "Crime, Criminal Justice, and Criminology in the Nordic Countries", in: Michael Tonry and Tapio Lappi-Seppälä (eds.), *Crime and Justice in Scandinavia*. Vol. 40 (The University of Chicago Press 2011), p. 1–29. See also Johan Boucht, "Nordisk kriminalpolitik: Finns den längre, och i så fall, vart är den på väg?", *Tidskrift, utgiven av Juridiska Föreningen i Finland* (2020), pp. 216–223.

13. Poland

By *Alicja Limburska** and *Konrad Lipiński***

Vignette 1: Trolley Problem – Killing one Person to Save Many

Five young children are playing on railway tracks. An express train is approaching, and it is too late to stop the train before it hits the children, probably killing them. Operator D recognizes the emergency situation. He electronically flips a switch and thus deflects the train from its regular track to a little-used sidetrack. However, the lone repairman V is busy on the sidetrack, and the deflected train kills V, as D had anticipated. Is D criminally responsible for murder of V?

It is obvious that D acted under some kind of necessity. In Polish criminal law "a state of necessity" (art. 26 Criminal Code of 1997) requires that (a) a perpetrator acts with the purpose of averting an immediate danger to any legally protected interest while (b) the danger cannot be otherwise avoided. Necessity has a dual legal characteristic. On the one hand, if the sacrificed interest represents a lower value than the interest that is being saved, necessity results in lawfulness of the act question, i. e., it works as a justification. On the other hand, if the sacrificed interest does not represent an obviously higher value than the interest that is being saved, necessity results in the exclusion of culpability, i. e., it works as an excuse.

According to the Polish Supreme Court, human life always has the same value, regardless of age, health, level of knowledge, education, family status, or usefulness for society.[1] The problem of comparing the value of one person's life with the lives of a larger number of people has been discussed in the legal literature. It is usually assumed that in such situations the compared legal interests (one life versus several lives) also are equal in value. In other words, sacrificing the life of one person to save the lives of several people should be perceived as sacrificing a legal interest of the same value as the legal interest that is being saved.

In the described situation, D acted with the purpose of averting an immediate danger to a legally protected interest (the lives of five children), and there was no other way to avert the danger (it was too late to stop the train). D sacrificed a legal interest (the life of V) of the same value as the legal interest that was saved (the lives of five children). As a result, D should be found to have acted under necessity, resulting in the exclusion of culpability. It means that D's act – although unlawful – did not constitute a crime and he/she would not be punished. The admissibility of undertaking self-defence against D's behaviour is a tangible effect of excluding only culpability and not unlawfulness of the act in question.

---

* Assistant Professor, Department of Substantive Criminal Law, Faculty of Law, Administration and Economics, University of Wrocław, and attorney-at-law, Bar Council in Wrocław, Poland; ORCID: https://orcid.org/0000-0002-6722-0249.

** Assistant Professor, Department of Substantive Criminal Law, Faculty of Law, Administration and Economics, University of Wrocław, and attorney-at-law, Bar Council in Wrocław, Poland; ORCID: https://orcid.org/0000-0001-5342-4905.

[1] Judgment of 17. 02. 1989, IV KR 15/89.

Vignette 2: Attribution of Death

> D intends to kill his neighbour V. Hidden near V's house, D waits for V and stabs him several times with a knife. V is taken to the hospital, where his wounds are treated. His injuries are not life-threatening and V is kept overnight for observation. During the night, a technical defect in the hospital kitchen leads to the outbreak of a fire, which kills V and other persons. Can D be held criminally responsible for V's death?

In the Polish legal system, it would not be possible to convict D of killing V; it would however be possible to convict him of attempted murder. This is due to the fact that we commonly use the objective attribution (*obiektywne przypisanie*, *objektive Zurechnung*) theory. Starting in the early 2000s, this theory has been widely accepted by the Supreme Court. It is said[2] that the first sign of change in this field was the Supreme Court's judgment of 4 November 1997,[3] stating that in cases of result crimes (in this case: a road accident) it is crucial not only to establish a causal link between events (their temporal and local relation) but also to examine whether the result was connected with the inadvertence of the defendant. The milestone judgment was issued by the Supreme Court on 8 March 2000.[4] Here, the Court explicitly used the term "objective attribution", stating:

> Causing a consequence can only be objectively attributed to the perpetrator if the danger that the breach of required caution was intended to prevent materializes in it. A person shall not be held criminally liable for committing a result crime if their behavior did not create or significantly increase the risk to the legal interest.

Since that time, objective attribution has become a permanent feature of the Supreme Court's jurisprudence.[5] In fact, recent judgments have specified that non-use of the criteria of objective attribution in a judgment should be regarded as a substantive violation of the law.[6]

In the Vignette case, exclusion of liability would happen on a quite basic level, i.e., regarding the so-called normative connection between D's action and its consequence – V's death. That is because – using the theory of objective attribution – in order to attribute the negative result as an element of the criminal offense to D, we have to determine that there exists both a causal (natural, ontological) and a normative link between his act and the negative result. For example, the Supreme Court specified that "in addition to the need to demonstrate the relationship between the perpetrator's behaviour and the result, it is also necessary to demonstrate the normative connection."[7] This is a commonly accepted requirement of attribution that can be

2 D. Czerwińska, *Nauka o obiektywnym przypisaniu skutku w orzecznictwie Sądu Najwyższego i Sądu Apelacyjnego we Wrocławiu*, „Prokuratura i Prawo" 2/2016, p. 158.

3 V KKN 303/97.

4 III KKN 231/98.

5 S. Zabłocki, *Zagadnienie przypisywalności skutku w najnowszym orzecznictwie Sądu Najwyższego*, "Kwartalnik Prawa Publicznego" 4/2004, pp. 33–48.

6 See, for example, Supreme Court judgment of 19 May 2015, V KK 85/15.

7 Judgment of 12 October 2016 (V KK 153/16).

found in most (if not all) criminal law textbooks in Poland. Jacek Giezek addresses this problem as follows:[8]

> There should be a causal connection corresponding to a specific regularity between the occurrence of phenomenon A (i. e., the behavior of a possible perpetrator) and the occurrence of phenomenon B (a state of affairs specified in the provision of law as a negative result), and then the normative relations should be examined, determining the criminal law attribution of the result to a possible perpetrator, whose behavior turned out to be inappropriate (excessively risky). The second phase therefore leads to the elimination of cases in which – despite the presence of a causal connection – normative considerations do not allow the assumption of causation.

We can say that in the Vignette case it would be possible to agree that the first kind of connection is present – that there is in fact a causal link between stabbing V and his death, since there is a general rule that stabbing somebody may lead to his or her death.[9] On the other hand, there is no normative connection because V's death is not an effect of D's breaching of a safety rule. In other words, the risk resulting in V's death is not the one created by D's action. There was another, separate source of danger to the legal interest which was in fact connected with V's death. Therefore, D cannot be held criminally responsible for V's death – only for attempted murder.

Depending on further circumstances of the case, it might be possible to find D guilty of an offense being simultaneously an attempted murder and grievous bodily harm. Art. 11 § 2 Criminal Code establishes the rule of so-called concurrent application of provisions:

> If an act fulfils the elements provided for in two or more provisions of a criminal statute, the court imposes the conviction for a single crime based on all concurring provisions.

Cases in which an attempted offense happens also to be a "full" offense under a different provision of the Criminal Code are sometimes called aggravated attempts.

Having in mind the circumstances of the case presented in the Vignette, it seems important to emphasise that the theory of objective attribution can be applied specifically in medical cases – for instance, in the case of medical negligence. This kind of negligence may constitute an instance of so-called "transfer to someone else's scope of responsibility",[10] excluding the possibility of attributing a negative result to the actor.

---

8 J. Giezek, *Teorie związku przyczynowego oraz koncepcje obiektywnego przypisania*, in: *System prawa karnego (The System of Criminal Law), Tom 3. Nauka o przestępstwie. Zasady odpowiedzialności*, ed. R. Dębski, Warszawa 2013, pp. 521–522.

9 This conclusion is the effect of using the so-called "appropriate condition" test of causality. If we used the *sine qua non* ("but for") test – which is not consistent with recent judgments of Supreme Court – we would probably achieve the same result: If V had not been stabbed, he would not have died (because he would not have been taken to the hospital).

10 This idea was introduced to the Polish doctrine by C. Roxin in his text *Problematyka obiektywnego przypisania (The Issue of Objective Attribution)*, published in 1990 in Wrocław in the collection of studies edited by T. Kaczmarek, *Teoretyczne i praktyczne problemy odpowiedzialności karnej w polskim oraz niemieckim prawie karnym (Theoretical and practical problems of criminal responsibility in Polish and German criminal law).*

Vignette 3: Torture to Save a Life

> Kidnapper K has abducted an 8-year-old girl G and hidden her in a small cave in the woods. K is trying to extort money from G's parents for her release. The police manage to arrest K. Although being questioned for 24 hours, K steadfastly refuses to disclose where he hid G. Police officer D correctly assumes that G may soon die of thirst if she cannot be found. He therefore severely beats K to make him tell the truth. Fearing even more violence, K eventually leads the police to the cave, where they find G still barely alive. Should D be punished for torturing K?

The prohibition of torture stems from international law (for example Art. 3 of the European Convention on Human Rights) and is directly applicable in the Polish legal system. There are no exceptions to this prohibition. For this reason alone, the policeman's conduct should be considered unlawful.

However, in the case of D, one could claim that he acted under some kind of necessity. As mentioned above (Vignette 1), in Polish criminal law "a state of necessity" (art. 26 Criminal Code of 1997) requires that (a) a perpetrator acts with the purpose of averting an immediate danger to any legally protected interest while (b) the danger cannot be otherwise avoided. If a sacrificed interest represents a lower value than the interest that is being saved, necessity results in the lawfulness of the act; it works as a justification. If, however, the sacrificed interest does not represent an obviously higher value than the interest that is being saved, necessity results in the exclusion of culpability, operating as an excuse.

As a rule, necessity cannot be invoked by a police officer – or any other public official – as a ground for justifying his or her actions. It is widely accepted by scholars that a state of necessity cannot justify actions of public officials taken without a proper legal basis.[11] Art. 7 of the Polish Constitution requires public authorities to operate on the basis and within the limits of the law (principle of legality). Therefore, necessity cannot be used to extend the authority of public officials and "fill a gap" in the legal basis of their actions. In the literature on the subject, it is however noted that the inability of a public official to invoke necessity is subject to exceptions.[12] To be precise, in relation to a particular unlawful act of a state official, necessity may be considered an excuse and thus exclude the culpability of the perpetrator. This point of view has also been expressed by the Polish Constitutional Tribunal in a judgment concerning the illegality of shooting down a civilian plane due to necessity:[13]

> The law may exceptionally decriminalize the effects of such behavior, recognizing the lack of guilt of the actor, but cannot legalize (deny unlawfulness) an action consisting in intentionally taking the life of innocent people by specifying the formal and legal conditions for its correctness.

---

[11] P. Daniluk, *Stan wyższej konieczności jako podstawa legalności działań funkcjonariuszy organów władzy publicznej*, "Wojskowy Przegląd Prawniczy" 1/2007, p. 41 i n.; A. Zoll, in: *Kodeks karny. Część ogólna. Komentarz*, t. I, cz. I, ed. W. Wróbel, A. Zoll, Warszawa 2016, art. 26; J. Lachowski, in: *Kodeks karny. Komentarz*, ed. V. Konarska-Wrzosek, Warszawa 2023, art. 26. An opposing view was presented in the judgment of the Supreme Court of 17.01.2013 (V KK 99/12, OSNKW 2013, nr 5, poz. 44).

[12] A. Zoll (note 11).

[13] Judgment of 30.09.2008 r., K 44/07.

Under the Polish Criminal Code (PCC), the use of torture is not defined autonomously as a separate type of offense (except for war crimes and crimes against humanity); however, maltreating a person deprived of liberty is penalized under art. 246 PCC:

> A public officer or a person acting upon his command who, with the purpose of obtaining specific testimony, explanations, information or a statement, uses force, an unlawful threat or in another manner physically or mentally maltreats another person, is subject to the penalty of deprivation of liberty for between one year and ten years.

The conduct of a policeman who seriously beats a detainee thus potentially constitutes the crime defined in art. 246 PCC. Yet, police officer D acted with the purpose of averting an immediate danger to a legally protected interest (the life of G) and there was no other way to avert the danger (K was the only source of information about the location of G and he would not share it voluntarily). The use of torture violates human dignity and health, but in this case, it served to protect G's life. In our opinion, it may be reasonably claimed that in such a scenario the sacrificed interest did not represent an obviously higher value than the interest saved. As a result, it is possible that police officer D would be found to have acted under necessity, resulting in the exclusion of culpability. The policeman's act – although unlawful – would then not constitute a crime, and he would not be punished. Since only D's guilt, not the unlawfulness of the act is excluded, K would retain the right to use self-defence.

Vignette 4: Lethal Self-Defence

> R, a well-trained young man armed with a knife, accosts 50-year-old D, who is on her way home from a party in the early morning hours. R threatens her with the knife and takes away her purse filled with 500 € and her wristwatch worth 1,000 €. As R turns to run away, D draws a pistol she is secretly carrying in her jacket, and shoots and kills R in order to retrieve her property. Is D guilty of murder?

The Polish Criminal Code addresses self-defence and defence of others in art. 25 § 1 and 2:

§ 1 Whoever in necessary defence repels a direct, unlawful attack on any legally protected interest does not commit a crime.

§ 2 In case of exceeding the limits of necessary defence, especially by employment of means of defence that are disproportionate to the danger of the attack, the court may apply extraordinary mitigation of the penalty or even waive its imposition.

Self-defence is a substantive defence (ground of justification) that negates the unlawfulness of the act. It requires the attack to be unlawful, direct, imminent, and real, and the defence – as a reaction to this attack – to be proportionate to the act's dangerousness. In order for the defendant to act within the limits of necessary defence, he or she must act with the intention to repel the attack.

There is no doubt that there was an unlawful attack by R against D's legally protected interests, both her health and her property. Given the fact that the attacker used a knife to threaten her, it can be assumed that using a firearm in order to repel that attack – given the potential close-combat situation – would be appropriate. It is said that the person defending himself or herself from the attacker is allowed to use an implement that gives him or her a fair (sufficient) advantage to repel the attack.[14] The Appellate Court of Kraków stated that

> A person defending himself against an attack has the right to use a dangerous tool that can repel the attack, even if the attacker uses his bare hands. It is permissible to use a dangerous tool even if the attacker uses only physical force, if the attacked person has no other means of defence

and that

> When attacking a legal interest, and especially when attacking the health or life of another person, the attacker must take into account the defence on the part of the attacked person, which will be necessary to repel the attack, therefore the attacker should take into account every consequence that may result from such an attack, with the risk of bodily harm or even loss of life.[15]

Nevertheless, even in these circumstances, the means of defence need to be proportionate.

The assessment that D's defence fell within the scope of application of art. 25 § 1 PCC would be valid only if we examined the situation statically, simply weighing the dangerousness of the attack (coming from a well-trained young man with a knife) and the effectiveness of the defence. The situation presented in the Vignette was, in fact, a bit more complex, since D used her pistol when R turned to run away, and she did so in order to retrieve her property. That means that she shot R after the robbery; therefore, at this moment her health wasn't threatened anymore. The attack undertaken by R was finished. That means that D exceeded the limits of self-defence in the form of so-called "extensive excess", occurring if the victim undertakes a defensive action before the attack of the offender (when the attack is not yet imminent) or after it has already been finished. For example, the Appellate Court of Szczecin stated that[16]

> Exceeding the limits of necessary defence may take the form of an extensive excess, i. e., a situation where the defensive action has been extended for a period of time when the attacker has already given up on continuing the attack.

Since D exceeded the limits of self-defence, she is guilty of murder. The court, however, may grant an extraordinary mitigation of the penalty. Since murder is punishable by a minimum of ten years of imprisonment (art. 148 § 1 PCC), that means that in this case the minimum possible penalty would be three years and four months of imprisonment (i. e., one third of the penalty as specified in the special part of the Code, according to art. 60 § 6 no. 2 PCC).

Even though they are not applicable in this situation, it is important to emphasise that there are two more grounds of impunity relating to self-defence and defence of

---

14 Zoll (note 11), art. 25.

15 Judgment of 31 August 2005 (II AKa 168/05).

16 Judgment of 26 May 2022 (II AKa 225/21).

others, negating – respectively – guilt and punishability elements of the offense. According to art. 25 § 3 PCC,

> Whoever exceeds the limits of necessary defence due to fear or agitation excusable in the circumstances of an attack is not subject to a penalty.

Even though the wording of the provision suggests that it provides only a ground for not being subject to a penalty, it is established that these circumstances in fact constitute an excuse.[17] In 2018, art. 25 PCC was amended by adding § 2a, stating that

> Whoever exceeds the limits of necessary defence while repealing an attack consisting in an intrusion into an apartment, premises, house, or adjoining fenced area, or while repealing an attack that has been preceded by an intrusion into these places, is not subject to a penalty, unless the limits of necessary defence have been flagrantly exceeded.

Vignette 5: Criminal Responsibility of Subordinates for Systemic Offences

D is a soldier in the army of a country ruled by a junta of generals who have come to power through a violent coup. When an opposition group demands the return to a democratic system, the government orders the soldiers to shoot and kill any person who resists arrest. Following this order, D kills three young men who take part in a protest demonstration and hit a police officer who tries to arrest them. When D is tried after a change of regime, he says that he did not like to shoot the protesters but that he thought that he had to obey his commanders' orders. D knew that if he had refused to shoot, he might have been demoted, but no physical harm would have occurred to him. Should D be convicted of murder? If so, should his sentence be mitigated because of his situation?

The Vignette addresses the problem of military orders, which has been defined in art. 115 § 18 PCC:

> A military order is a command to perform or omit to perform a specified action, issued to a soldier by a superior or an authorised soldier of superior rank.

As a general rule, a military order might provide an excuse, negating the guilt of the perpetrator. Art. 318 PCC, located in the military part of the Criminal Code, states that

> A soldier who commits a prohibited act as a result of carrying out an order does not commit a crime, unless he intentionally commits a crime while carrying out an order.

This provision does not specify the boundaries of a binding order; it only specifies when obeying it will or will not exclude criminal liability.

D's situation perfectly reflects the final part of art. 318, i. e., a situation when being given an order does not provide an excuse. D was ordered to shoot and kill anyone who resists arrest, and he did so, knowing that his action will lead to a loss of a human life and wanting this to happen. In other words, he intentionally killed three young men. The fact that he did not desire to kill them but did so only because he was given an order does not change the fact that his action was intended, as defined in art. 9 § 1 PCC:

---

17 W. Wróbel, A. Zoll, *Polskie prawo karne. Część ogólna*, Kraków 2014, p. 361.

> A prohibited act is committed intentionally if the perpetrator intends its commission, i.e., wants to commit it or, foreseeing the possibility of its commission, accepts it.

D wanted it even though he did not desire or long for it – and that is sufficient for establishing intent.

That means that, in accordance with the Polish Criminal Code, D should be convicted of murder. There is no separate legal basis for mitigating his sentence; specifically, there are no grounds for a so-called extraordinary mitigation of penalty. The court may, however, take into account the fact that D was a subordinate, therefore his guilt was diminished due to the pressure he was subjected to by his superior. But it would only be possible to include this factor in the process of imposing a penalty within its statutory (not mitigated) range.

There are two additional problems connected with the responsibility of subordinates. The first is the responsibility of superiors. Art. 18 § 1 PCC defines several forms of perpetration. One of them – fitting perfectly for this situation – involves ordering to commit an offense. In this specific part, art. 18 § 1 PCC states that

> Not only a person committing a prohibited act alone or jointly and upon mutual agreement with another person is liable for perpetration, but also a person who (…) orders another person to commit such an act by exploiting this person's dependence of him.

Secondly, there is a separate regulation for systemic offenses in Chapter XVI of the Criminal Code – Crimes against peace, crimes against humanity, and war crimes. This provision is broader than art. 18 § 1 PCC. According to art. 126b PCC, whoever, by failing to perform a duty of due supervision, permits the commission of these acts by a person under his effective authority or supervision, is subject to the penalty provided for a perpetrator of this offense. Even unintentionally failing to supervise is subject to deprivation of liberty between three months and five years.

Vignette 6: Limits of Consent

> V is a 21-year-old ambitious athlete and short-distance runner. He has learned that certain artificial limbs can enhance a runner's speed. He decides that he would rather have an artificial limb instead of his right lower leg. He approaches D, a surgeon in private practice, and asks him to amputate his leg below the knee and replace it with an artificial limb. D complies with V's request. Should D be punished for mayhem?

In Polish criminal law, consent of a (potentially) aggrieved party appears in different contexts:

a) in some cases, lack of consent is an element – express or implied – of the actus reus (e.g., abortion without the woman's consent, theft, trespassing);

b) in other cases, consent is an element of the actus reus (e.g., consensual illegal adoption or abortion with the woman's consent);

c) consent of a participant is one of the conditions for the legality of an experiment (e.g., a medical experiment);

d) some scholars perceive consent as an autonomous ground for the lawfulness of the act in question.

The legal meaning of consent in the sense of (d) has never been expressly regulated by the Polish Criminal Code, but it has always been a subject of doctrinal debate. Currently – at least to our knowledge – there are no plans to regulate this issue in the Code. To simplify the matter, one could say that consent in the sense of items (a) and (d) plays a similar role: an act committed with the consent of the potentially injured party is not unlawful, and thus it is not criminal. Therefore, it is often said that consent has a legalizing function. To be more precise, one should say that consent not so much legalises (in the sense of a ground of justification), but makes it impossible to consider unlawful the act that was done with the consent of the affected person.

As for the prerequisites of a legally valid consent, there is no doubt that consent must be expressed *knowingly* and *voluntarily.* The first requirement means that the person must be aware that he or she is consenting to a certain behaviour as well as of the risk associated with it. Consent must also be voluntary, meaning that it is a free expression of the person's actual will. Consent cannot be deemed voluntary if it was coerced or obtained by fraud. Consent is deemed involuntary if the person expressing it is unable to control his or her behaviour or to recognize the relevance of the decision being made, caused either by an insufficient degree of mental development or by certain mental disorders (e. g., disability, mental illness). According to the dominant view, consent must be *externalized* (expressed externally) in some way; however, no specific form of this manifestation is required, and consent may even be implied. Consent must be expressed prior to the act in question or at the latest during the act.

In Polish criminal law, the scope of possible consent is *limited*, in the sense that not all legal interests may be disposed of by consent. Although there is no general agreement as to what legal interests an individual may have at his or her disposal, it is usually claimed that consent may only apply to legal interests that are closely related to the individual. In such cases, the need to protect the individual's interest outweighs the social interest in preserving it, and thus if an individual gives up the protection of such interests (by consenting to a behaviour that endangers them), there is no social need to protect them against the will of their disposer. Legal interests subject to an effective consent usually include: physical integrity, health (to a limited extent), freedom (including sexual freedom), good name, domestic privacy, confidentiality of correspondence, and property.

In V's case, the consent concerned an act of D that resulted in bodily harm (i. e., amputation of the leg). Polish criminal law distinguishes between a "grievous" bodily harm (in the form of deprivation of sight, hearing, speech, or the ability to procreate, another severe disability, a severe, incurable illness or a protracted illness, a life-threatening illness, a permanent mental illness, a permanent total or substantial incapacity to work in a profession or a permanent, substantive disfigurement or deformation of a body, excision, infibulation, or other permanent and substantial mutilation of a female genital organ), a "medium" bodily harm (duration exceeding seven days, other forms than listed above), and a "light" bodily harm (duration up to seven days). The amputation of a leg without a medical justification is considered a "grievous" bodily harm in the form of severe disability. It is widely accepted that consent concerning an act resulting in "medium" and "grievous" bodily harm is not legally valid, meaning that it does not negate the unlawfulness of the act in question (it seems that the only major exception is *ex vivo* transplantation). As a result, D will be punished for intentionally causing "grievous" bodily harm in the form of severe disability. The fact that V has consented to the surgery may, however, be seen as a factor reducing the culpability of the surgeon and be reflected in the severity of the punishment imposed.

Vignette 7: Withdrawal from an Attempt

25-year-old D is deeply upset with her former boyfriend V, who had ended their relationship to be with another woman. To punish V, D plans to stab him with a large knife. D knows that the stab wounds can be fatal and accepts V's death as a possible outcome. When V goes jogging, D attacks him from behind and stabs him in the back three times. V breaks down. D realises that she has injured him but that the injuries will not cause his death. She realises that she could kill him by stabbing him again but decides to leave him alone. Should D be punished for attempted murder?

According to art. 15 § 1 PCC,

> Whoever has voluntarily withdrawn from the commission of a prohibited act or has prevented the consequence constituting an element of a prohibited act, is not subject to a penalty for the attempt.

The quoted provision contains a so-called "active repentance" clause, which covers two variants: (a) withdrawal from an attempt and (b) preventing a result from occurring. According to the Supreme Court, voluntary withdrawal from an attempt exists if the perpetrator voluntarily gives up committing the prohibited act during the phase of an incomplete attempt. If the conduct directly intended to commit a crime reaches the stage of a completed attempt (i. e., when the perpetrator has performed all the activities intended to bring about the actus reus), the perpetrator needs to prevent the result of his/her action from happening in order to achieve impunity for the attempted crime. Voluntary withdrawal from committing a prohibited act (a) must be an expression of the perpetrator's will, (b) must take place when the perpetrator still has the opportunity to commit the prohibited act, and (c) must not have been "coerced" by a change of circumstances beyond the perpetrator's control. It is worth noting that the condition of voluntariness is not met if the perpetrator is mistakenly convinced that it is impossible to commit the previously intended crime.

As a result of "active repentance", the perpetrator cannot be punished for the attempted crime. However, he or she will be punished for the offense he or she successfully committed during the attempt. The court may apply extraordinary mitigation of the penalty if the perpetrator voluntarily made efforts to prevent the consequence constituting an element of a prohibited act but did not succeed.

In the case of D stabbing V, D clearly has voluntarily withdrawn from killing V. It was her autonomous decision while she realized that – if she wanted – she could have continued her actions to reach her initial goal. In order to kill V, additional acts were needed, which means that D withdrew from a murder in the phase of incomplete attempt. Withdrawal at that stage implies that her impunity is not dependent on her effectively preventing a fatal outcome. As a result, she can be punished neither for attempted murder of V nor – even if V finally died in hospital as the result of the stabbing – for completed murder. To be more specific: (a) If V did not die from the wounds inflicted by D, D can be punished only for intentionally causing bodily harm; (b) if V eventually died because of the harm inflicted, D will be found guilty of intentional causing bodily harm resulting in an unintentional death of the victim, which is a separate offense to be perpetrated with so-called mixed mens rea (art. 9 § 3 PCC).

The "active repentance" clause has been present in every Polish Criminal Code (of 1932, 1969, and 1997) and its legitimacy has not been questioned. In practice, courts tend to focus primarily on examining whether the withdrawal from the attempt has met the requirement of voluntariness and – in case of a completed attempt – whether it was the perpetrator who actually prevented the result from occurring.

Vignette 8: Criminal Responsibility of Minors

D is a 13-year-old boy. He abducts and rapes V, a girl of the same age. Should D be punished for a criminal offence?

In the Polish criminal justice system, the age of criminal responsibility changed over time. The first Polish Criminal Code of 1932 provided that only a person who was 13 years of age could be held criminally responsible. However, there was a broad exception that applied to persons between 13 and 17 years of age. It provided that a minor who committed a crime between the age of 13 and 17 was not subject to punishment for an act committed without discernment (i. e., without having achieved mental and moral development to such an extent that he could recognize the meaning of his act and control his conduct). The Criminal Code of 1969 set the age limit at 17 years of age. But the Code provided that a minor who, after reaching the age of 16, committed a crime against life, the crime of rape, robbery, a crime against public security, or intentionally caused a serious bodily injury or a serious health disorder, could be held accountable under the principles set out in the Criminal Code, if this was indicated by the circumstances of the case and the properties and personal conditions of the perpetrator, especially if previously applied educational or corrective measures had turned out to be ineffective. At the same time, if the perpetrator committed an offense between the age of 17 and 18, the court could apply educational or corrective measures intended for minors instead of punishment, if the circumstances of the case and the characteristics and personal conditions of the perpetrator justified it.

The current regulation of the Criminal Code of 1997 is similar to the previous one. It stipulates that anyone who commits a prohibited act after reaching the age of 17 is criminally liable (art. 10 § 1 PCC) but also provides a few exceptions to this principle. Although the principle has not been changed since the enactment of the Code in 1997, the exceptions have evolved.

In relation to a perpetrator who committed an offense between the ages of 17 and 18, the court imposes, instead of punishment, educational, therapeutic, or corrective measures intended for minors, if the circumstances of the case, the degree of the perpetrator's development, and his/her characteristics and personal conditions justify it. This exception has not been modified.

The Code of 1997 makes it possible to hold minors younger than 17 years criminally responsible under certain conditions. Initially, only a minor who, after reaching the age of 15, committed one of the most serious crimes listed in the Code could be punished for a criminal offense, if the circumstances of the case and the level of development of the perpetrator, his characteristics and personal conditions justified it, and in particular if previously applied educational or corrective measures had been ineffective. Currently, this catalogue includes such offenses as the assassination of the President, murder and its aggravated forms, infliction of a grievous bodily harm, taking over control of a waterborne or airborne vessel, rape and its aggravated forms, bringing about a catastrophe in land, water or air traffic, assault on a public officer resulting in a grievous bodily harm, taking a hostage, and robbery.

Under the same personal conditions, even a 14-year-old can be held criminally responsible for aggravated murder and if it must be assumed that the use of educational or corrective measures is not able to ensure his social rehabilitation. This exception came into force on October 1, 2023. The amendment was justified by the Ministry of Justice based on only one opinion commissioned by the Ministry, although police statistics did not indicate the need for such a modification. It has been speculated that the amendment could have been a reaction to the case of a boy who committed murder on the day before his 15th birthday, which would indicate its populist character.

Even in light of the latest amendments, it is clear that a 13-year-old boy who abducted and raped his colleague cannot be held criminally responsible for these offenses. Such a perpetrator is to be dealt with according to the Act on Supporting and Resocialising Minors. This Act's liability regime applies to minors between 13 and 17 years of age; it covers all criminal and fiscal offenses as well as misdemeanours and fiscal misdemeanours. Such cases are decided by the family court, which may impose educational and corrective measures.

Vignette 9: Statute of Limitations

> In 1995, D violently raped V, a 35-year-old woman, using a knife. D managed to escape and was not apprehended until 2023. Traces of his DNA taken from the victim's body leave no doubt that D is the perpetrator. Should D be convicted despite the long delay?

The statute of limitations is a quite complex issue in Polish criminal law. In general, the length of the limitation period depends on (a) the seriousness of an offense and (b) whether it is subject to public or private prosecution.

Since the Criminal Code of 1997 came into force, the time period required to pass for discontinuing proceedings after the commission of an offense has been changed several times. With one exception in 2015, the statutes of limitations were extended. There also exists a separate addition to the limitation period, which extends the general period by ten years whenever criminal proceedings regarding the offense were initiated (or even – starting in October 2023 – whenever the prosecution undertook some procedural activity aimed at determining whether a prohibited act had been committed). A specific regulation moreover suspended the statute of limitations during the COVID-19 pandemic for about one and a half years. This law has, however, been declared unconstitutional by a decision of the Constitutional Tribunal.[18]

According to judgments of the Constitutional Tribunal and the Supreme Court, it is possible to extend the period of limitation retroactively, as long as the statutory time period had not elapsed before the extension was enacted. Only a few authors reject this view, stating that it contradicts the principle of legality (*nullum crimen, nulla poena sine lege praevia*) and the rules of a democratic state of law, specifically the principle of public trust in the state and its laws.[19]

Given that the period of limitation depends, in the first place, on the statutory sentence range of the offense in question, we need to retrace the maximum penalty for aggravated rape in 1995 and then check the statute of limitations by today's standards.

Rape in its basic type has always been an offense subject to the maximum penalty of deprivation of liberty of more than three years. That means that it fell into the scope of application of art. 101 § 1 pt 3 PCC, determining a limitation period of ten years. Given the fact that D managed to escape and was not apprehended, we may assume that no charges were (formally) brought against him. That means that the proceedings should have been discontinued by 2005, because back then an extension of the period under art. 102 PCC required the filing of charges.

However, on 3 August 2005, a new category of offenses was introduced in art. 101 § 1 PCC: offenses subject to the penalty of deprivation of liberty of more than five years (point 2a). That means that if D committed the offense before 3 August 1995 and charges were not filed against him, the proceedings should have been discontinued before this date. On the other hand, if he raped V on 3 August 1995 or after this date, the period of limitation period would extend by five years until 2010, assuming that it is permissible to extend limitation periods retroactively.

The situation will change dramatically if we assume that (1) charges were successfully filed against D and (2) that he committed the offense on or after 3 August 1995. On 3 August 2005, not only was the period of limitation for rape extended, but the additional period for prosecution under art. 102 PCC was likewise extended to

18 12 December 2023 (P 12/22).

19 M. Budyn-Kulik, M. Kulik, *Wybrane aspekty funkcjonowania konstytucyjnej zasady ochrony zaufania na gruncie prawa karnego w perspektywie internalizacji norm prawnych jako warunku jej efektywności*, "Studia Iuridica Lublinensia" 1/2016, pp. 191–192; B. Nita-Światłowska, A. Światłowski, *Przeszkoda procesowa z art. 17 § 1 pkt 6 k.p.k. wobec zmian terminów przedawnienia (kontekst konstytucyjny)*, "Państwo i Prawo" 10/2018, pp. 103–104; M. Nawrocki, *Wpływ zmian terminów przedawnienia na sytuację sprawcy. Glosa do postanowienia Sądu Najwyższego z 26. 10. 2017 r., II KK 192/17*, "Przegląd Sądowy" 2/2019, p. 120.; K. Lipiński, *Modyfikacje terminów przedawnienia karalności przestępstw, przestępstw i wykroczeń skarbowych oraz wykroczeń w związku z epidemią COVID-19*, "Czasopismo Prawa Karnego i Nauk Penalnych" 2/2020, p. 45; M. Kulik, *Zasada odpowiedniego* vacatio legis *jako część zasady przyzwoitej legislacji – uwagi z perspektywy prawa karnego*, „Czasopismo Prawa Karnego i Nauk Penalnych" 1/2021, pp. 68–69; M. Kulik, *Przedawnienie karalności i przedawnienie wykonania kary w polskim prawie karnym*, Warszawa 2014, p. 148; K. Lipiński (in:) *Kodeks karny. Część ogólna. Komentarz*, ed. J. Giezek, Warszawa 2021, pp. 788, 798.

ten years. That means that the period for prosecution would have expired only in 2015.

But there is a further complication in this case: If D committed the offense after 1 July 1995, the limitation period would expire on 1 July 2015, because on this day the additional limitation period (art. 102 PCC) was shortened back to five years (before it was extended back again a few months later).

That means that proceedings against D would have to be discontinued:

a) in 2005 – if charges were not filed against D and he committed the offense before 3 August 1995;
b) in 2010 – if charges were not filed against D and he committed the offense on or after 3 August 1995;
c) in 2010 – if charges were filed against D and he committed the offense before 3 August 1995;
d) on 1 July 2015 – if charges were filed against D and he committed the offense on or after 3 August.

The period of limitation for a rape committed in 1995 thus could be 10, 15 or 20 years, depending on the exact date of the commission of the offense.

If we were to evaluate D's offense under the Criminal Code in its current wording, which entered into force on 1 October 2023, his situation would be quite different. Aggravated rape (including use of a knife) has become a felony subject to a penalty of at least three years of deprivation of liberty. For this group of offenses, there is today a basic 20-year limitation period. Also, since an investigation was initiated, the additional 10-year period would apply, since currently the Code does not require charges to be filed in order to extend the limitation period. That means that by today's standard the proceedings would have to be discontinued only after 30 years since the commission of the rape. The period would be extended even further if the victim was a minor. This regulation, prescribing a more severe penalty for aggravated rape could not, however, be applied retroactively to the offense committed in 1995. At that time, using a knife did not constitute an aggravated form of rape. Retroactivity to the detriment of the perpetrator is prohibited by art. 4 § 1 PCC (*lex severior retro non agit*).

Vignette 10: Life Imprisonment without Parole

The Penal Code of State S provides for imprisonment for life as the maximum penalty for murder, but also authorises the court to order an offender's early release after a minimum of 15 years if the offender is no longer dangerous. Reacting to cases of particularly heinous murders, the legislature of S wishes to introduce a penalty of life imprisonment without any possibility of early release, regardless of the offender's continued dangerousness. Would this amendment be acceptable?

This kind of amendment would not be acceptable in the Polish criminal law system, under the Constitution and European Convention on Human Rights – yet it was enacted among several other populist amendments to the Criminal Code on 7 July 2022 and came into force on 1 October 2023.

The Criminal Code provides as a general rule that an offender may apply for early release after serving half of his sentence (in some cases, e. g., recidivism or acting in organized criminal group, two thirds or three quarters). Until 1 October 2023, an offender sentenced to life imprisonment could apply for conditional release after 25 years. Currently, the minimum time to be served is 30 years. The Code also provides that under specific, exceptional circumstances, the court may extend that "basic" period and impose more severe restrictions (art. 77 § 2 PCC). This provision has been used rarely, in particularly heinous cases. Browsing the database of judgments, we find many more judgments describing when this provision cannot be used than judgments applying it.

Nevertheless, on 1 October 2023, the legislature added two paragraphs to art. 77 PCC, stating:

§ 3 When imposing a sentence of life imprisonment or of imprisonment for a period of not less than 20 years on a perpetrator for an act committed after having been convicted of an offense against life and health, freedom, sexual freedom, public security or an offense of a terrorist nature, the court may order a ban on conditional release;

§ 4 When imposing a sentence of life imprisonment, the court may order a ban on the conditional release if the nature and circumstances of the act and the personal characteristics of the perpetrator indicate that his remaining at large will cause a permanent danger to life, health, liberty or sexual freedom of other persons.

Therefore, formally, there is a legal basis for life imprisonment without the possibility of early release (excluding presidential pardon, which lacks sufficient clarity as to its discretion) for offenses committed on or after 1 October 2023.

During the legislative process, experts and scholars had specifically stated that these provisions violate the Polish Constitution, ECHR, and several soft-law regulations.[20] The draft was nevertheless enacted and came into force – at least formally. This reservation is necessary, because the fact that the provision violates constitutional values (specifically: the principle of a democratic state of law, the dignity of the human being, principles of humanitarianism, and proportionality) as well as international law makes it necessary for the courts to refuse to apply this provision. Article 91.2 of the Polish Constitution states that

> An international agreement ratified with prior consent expressed by statute takes precedence over a statute if the statute cannot be reconciled with the agreement.

In our opinion, art. 77 §§ 3–4 of the amended Criminal Code violates art. 3 ECHR, since in similar cases the European Court of Human Rights stated that some kind of "reducibility (in the sense of the existence of a mechanism affording a not wholly unreal prospect of eventual release) must exist, in law and in practice, at the time of sentencing in order for the requirements of Article 3 to be met in relation

---

20 See for example J. Giezek, D. Gruszecka, K. Lipiński, *Opinia na temat ustawy z dnia 7 lipca 2022 r. o zmianie ustawy – Kodeks karny oraz niektórych innych ustaw (druk senacki nr 762)*, Senat RP – Opinie i Ekspertyzy, Warszawa 2022.

to the nature of the sentence passed".[21] This view has also been expressed in the Polish criminal law literature.[22] Given that art. 77 §§ 3–4 of the amended Criminal Code cannot be reconciled with art. 3 ECHR (which is an international agreement ratified with consent expressed by statute), it cannot be applied in any case under the Polish Constitution, even though they formally are part of statutory law.

Both provisions have not yet been applied in any case. Regardless of constitutional and international inconsistencies, the probability that they will never be applied stems from the fact that their application is optional – the court may but does not have to ban conditional release. In a previous draft, announced by the Minister of Justice – General Prosecutor in 2019, the ban was mandatory. But that draft was amended by the second chamber of Parliament (Senate), and it never entered into force because the Constitutional Tribunal found the procedure in which it was enacted to be unconstitutional.[23]

---

21 ECtHR judgment of 9 July 2013, Case of Vinter and others v. The United Kingdom (Applications nos. 66069/09, 130/10 and 3896/10); see also judgment of 4 September 2015, Case of Trabelsi v. Belgium (Application no. 140/10).

22 B. Nita-Światłowska, *Możliwość orzeczenia kary dożywotniego pozbawienia wolności bez dostępu do warunkowego przedterminowego zwolnienia jako przeszkoda ekstradycyjna wynikająca z Europejskiej Konwencji Praw Człowieka*, "Europejski Przegląd Sądowy" 6/2017; W. Hermeliński, B. Nita-Światłowska, *Kara dożywotniego pozbawienia wolności bez dostępu do warunkowego przedterminowego zwolnienia – refleksje w kontekście gwarancji wynikających z Europejskiej Konwencji Praw Człowieka*, "Palestra" 10/2018.

23 Judgment of 14 July 2020, Kp 1/19.

14. Singapore

By *Wing-Cheong Chan**

General Introduction

Although Singapore is a common law jurisdiction, Singapore's criminal law is statutory in nature. The general principles of criminal liability as well as most of the major offences (such as property offences and acts of violence against the person) are found in the Penal Code 1871 (hereinafter "Singapore Penal Code").

As shown by the title of this law, the Singapore Penal Code was enacted in 1871 when Singapore was a British colony as part of the Straits Settlements at the time. The Singapore Penal Code was an almost exact replica of the Indian Penal Code which was enacted in India about 10 years before. Although Singapore has in this law retained many of the general principles that it shares with other Indian Penal Code jurisdictions (for example, Bangladesh, Pakistan, Malaysia and Sri Lanka), the exact details may have changed over the years through amendments to the Singapore Penal Code or judicial decisions.

As a somewhat unique feature in terms of drafting technique, the Indian Penal Code contains "illustrations" to many of the provisions to show how the law should be interpreted. These illustrations are meant as a guide for the public and for legal personnel.

Owing to the historical origins of the Singapore Penal Code and to Singapore being a former British colony, cases from the Indian Penal Code jurisdictions and other common law jurisdictions such as England are frequently cited in the courts.

Other important Singapore statutes containing criminal offences include the Arms Offences Act 1973, the Misuse of Drugs Act 1973, the Prevention of Corruption Act 1960, and the Road Traffic Act 1961. These laws supplement the Singapore Penal Code.

Vignette 1: Trolley Problem – Killing one Person to Save Many

Five young children are playing on railway tracks. An express train is approaching, and it is too late to stop the train before it hits the children, probably killing them. Operator D recognizes the emergency situation. He electronically flips a switch and thus deflects the train from its regular track to a little-used sidetrack. However, the lone repairman V is busy on the sidetrack, and the deflected train kills V, as D had anticipated. Is D criminally responsible for murder of V?

Even if the *actus reus* and *mens rea* for murder are satisfied, D can rely on the exception found in section 81 of the Singapore Penal Code (also known as the defence of necessity) to avoid criminal liability:

---

* Professor of Law, Yong Pung How School of Law, Singapore Management University.

Nothing is an offence merely by reason of its being done with the knowledge that it is likely to cause harm, if it be done in good faith for the purpose of preventing or avoiding other harm to person or property.

Explanation. – It is a question of fact in such a case whether the harm to be prevented or avoided was of such a nature and so imminent as to justify or excuse the risk of doing the act with the knowledge that it was likely to cause harm.

Illustrations

(a) A, the captain of a steam vessel, suddenly and without any fault or negligence on his part, finds himself in such a position that, before he can stop his vessel, he must inevitably run down a boat B, with 20 or 30 passengers on board, unless he changes the course of his vessel, and that, by changing his course he must incur risk of running down a boat C, with only 2 passengers on board, which he may possibly clear. Here, if A alters his course without any intention to run down the boat C, and in good faith for the purposes of avoiding the danger to the passengers in the boat B, he is not guilty of an offence, though he may run down the boat C, by doing an act which he knew was likely to cause that effect, if it be found as a matter of fact that the danger which he intended to avoid was such as to excuse him in incurring the risk of running down the boat C.

(b) A in a great fire pulls down houses in order to prevent the conflagration from spreading. He does this with the intention, in good faith, of saving human life or property. Here, if it be found that the harm to be prevented was of such a nature and so imminent as to excuse A's act, A is not guilty of the offence.

(c) X, the commander of a naval vessel, is deployed in response to a threat of a terrorist attack against a ferry terminal in Singapore. X receives information that vessel A, with a crew of 6, has been hijacked by terrorists and is approaching the ferry terminal at great speed and is likely to collide into the terminal. There is insufficient time to evacuate the persons at the terminal, which is estimated to be about 100. X orders vessel A to stop her manoeuvre immediately and fires a warning signal. However, vessel A continues her advance towards the terminal. Here, if X gives an order to fire at vessel A to disable it, without any intention to cause harm to the crew members of vessel A, and in good faith for the purpose of avoiding the danger to the persons at the terminal, he is not guilty of an offence. This is so even though he knows that he is likely to cause harm to the crew members of vessel A, if it be found as a matter of fact that the danger which X intends to avoid is such as to excuse him in incurring the risk of firing at vessel A.

This defence is rarely invoked and no case has successfully pleaded it in Singapore to date.

It is clear from the wording of section 81 that its scope extends to murder ("Nothing is an offence [...]"). However, the defence only appears to cover acts done "with the knowledge that it is likely to cause harm" (this is repeated in the Explanation and illustrations (a) and (c)). Academic commentators have suggested that the defence can apply to other mental states as well.[1] Hence, the defence can be used in Vignette 1 even if D had the *mens rea* for murder under any of the limbs to section 300 of the Singapore Penal Code.

---

1 Stanley Yeo, Neil Morgan and Chan Wing Cheong, *Criminal Law in Singapore* (LexisNexis, 2022) para [23.34].

The following must be proved for the defence:

(a) There must be harm to a person or property to be prevented or avoided;

(b) The act done must have been done in good faith for the purpose of preventing the harm;

(c) The harm to be prevented or avoided must be of such nature and so imminent as to justify or excuse the act. This is a question of fact;

(d) The accused was not at fault in creating the situation where the harm sought to be prevented or avoided presented itself.

Requirement (a) is satisfied since the harm to be prevented or avoided is the killing of five young children playing on the tracks.

"Good faith" is defined in section 26B of the Singapore Penal Code as doing something with due care and attention. It is an objective assessment. Requirement (b) is satisfied if we assume that, owing to the emergency situation, D has done what he could in the circumstances to assess the situation and the only viable alternative to prevent or avoid the killing of the young children is to deflect the train to the side-track.

Requirement (c) is also an objective assessment and can be satisfied. The nature of the act (killing of five young children) and its imminence (too late to stop the train) can justify or excuse the act of killing V. The facts in the Vignette are similar to the facts in illustration (a) to section 81.

Requirement (d) is also satisfied in that D was not at fault for creating the danger of colliding into the young children.

In addition, commentators have added two more requirements to section 81 even though they are not expressly found in the provision itself but are implicit in the illustrations:[2] D's response must be both "necessary" and "proportionate". How they operate will depend on the exact circumstances of the case. Whether the conduct is "necessary" concerns the question "whether there was some other viable lawful means of avoiding the peril available to the accused besides committing the crime charged". As for "proportionality", assessment is based on "the social policy considerations, moral values and societal expectations attending the particular circumstances of the case at hand".

Vignette 2: Attribution of Death

D intends to kill his neighbour V. Hidden near V's house, D waits for V and stabs him several times with a knife. V is taken to the hospital, where his wounds are treated. His injuries are not life-threatening and V is kept overnight for observation. During the night, a technical defect in the hospital kitchen leads to the outbreak of a fire, which kills V and other persons. Can D be held criminally responsible for V's death?

---

2 Stanley Yeo, Neil Morgan and Chan Wing Cheong (note 1), paras. [23.21]–[23.31].

The Vignette presents two problems, one concerning the *mens rea* for a fatal offence, the other concerning the *actus reus*. D can only be held criminally responsible for V's death if D has caused V's death. It could be argued that it was the fire that killed V, rather than the knife injuries (which were not life-threatening).

Unfortunately, there are no general provisions in the Singapore Penal Code explaining how causation issues should be resolved. There are only two explanations found in section 299 of the Singapore Penal Code (on the meaning of culpable homicide) that deal with very specific situations:

> *Explanation* 1. A person who causes bodily injury to another who is labouring under a disorder, disease or bodily infirmity, and thereby accelerates the death of that other, shall be deemed to have caused his death.
>
> *Explanation* 2. Where death is caused by bodily injury, the person who causes such bodily injury shall be deemed to have caused the death, although by resorting to proper remedies and skilful treatment the death might have been prevented.

Courts in Singapore have adopted the test for causation found in the common law: there must be both causation in fact and causation in law.[3] The former is the "but for" test – but for a particular event, would the result have happened? Under this test, it can be said that but for D's act of injuring V, V would not have been in the hospital where he was killed by the fire.

Causation in law is about attributing legal responsibility – whether there is a sufficient nexus such that D should be blamed for what happened to V. A common-sense approach is adopted. In cases of intervening acts (such as the hospital fire), the question is whether the intervening act has weakened the nexus between D's act and V's death such that D cannot be said to be a substantial cause of the death (even though D was a factual cause).[4] In one case, the question posed was whether the intervening act had such "causative potency" that D's initial act could not be said to have contributed significantly to the result.[5]

On the facts of Vignette 2, it is likely that D will not be held criminally responsible for V's death on the basis that causation is not proven. D had only caused non-life-threatening injuries and although this was a factual cause of V's death, it was the fire that was the legal cause of V's death.

Vignette 3: Torture to Save a Life

Kidnapper K has abducted an 8-year-old girl G and hidden her in a small cave in the woods. K is trying to extort money from G's parents for her release. The police manage to arrest K. Although being questioned for 24 hours, K steadfastly refuses to disclose where he hid G. Police officer D correctly assumes that G may soon die of thirst if she cannot be found. He therefore severely beats K to make him tell the truth. Fearing even more violence, K eventually leads the police to the cave, where they find G still barely alive. Should D be punished for torturing K?

---

3 See, for example, *Nickson Guay Seng Tiong v PP* [2016] 3 SLR 1079.

4 *Nickson Guay Seng Tiong v PP* [2016] 3 SLR 1079 at [30]–[33].

5 *Ng Keng Yong v PP* [2004] 4 SLR(R) 89 at [67].

Depending on the injuries caused to K, D may be liable for an offence under section 330 or 331 of the Singapore Penal Code:

> 330. Whoever voluntarily causes hurt for the purpose of extorting from the sufferer, or from any person interested in the sufferer, any confession or any information which may lead to the detection of an offence or misconduct, or for the purpose of constraining the sufferer, or any person interested in the sufferer, to restore or to cause the restoration of any property or valuable security, or to satisfy any claim or demand, or to give information which may lead to the restoration of any property or valuable security, shall be punished with imprisonment for a term which may extend to 7 years, and shall also be liable to fine or to caning.
>
> *Illustrations*
>
> (a) A, a police officer, tortures Z in order to induce Z to confess that he committed a crime. A is guilty of an offence under this section.
>
> (b) A, a police officer, tortures B to induce him to point out where certain stolen property is deposited. A is guilty of an offence under this section.
>
> (c) A, a customs officer, tortures Z in order to compel him to confess to a pretended offence against the customs laws. A is guilty of an offence under this section.
>
> 331. Whoever voluntarily causes grievous hurt for the purpose of extorting from the sufferer, or from any person interested in the sufferer, any confession or any information which may lead to the detection of an offence or misconduct, or for the purpose of constraining the sufferer, or any person interested in the sufferer, to restore or to cause the restoration of any property or valuable security, or to satisfy any claim or demand, or to give information which may lead to the restoration of any property or valuable security, shall be punished with imprisonment for a term which may extend to 10 years, and shall also be liable to fine or to caning.

D may try to argue for a defence based on duress, private defence, or necessity. The defence of duress is found in section 94 of the Singapore Penal Code:

> Except murder and offences against the State punishable with death, nothing is an offence which is done by a person who is compelled to do it by threats, which, at the time of doing it, reasonably cause the apprehension that instant death to that person or any other person will otherwise be the consequence:
>
> Provided that the person doing the act did not of his own accord, or from a reasonable apprehension of harm to himself short of instant death, place himself in the situation by which he became subject to such constraint.
>
> *Explanation* 1. A person who, of his own accord, or by reason of a threat of being beaten, joins gang-robbers knowing their character, is not entitled to the benefit of this exception on the ground of his having been compelled by his associates to do anything that is an offence by law.
>
> *Explanation* 2. A person seized by gang-robbers, and forced by threat of instant death to do a thing which is an offence by law – for example, a smith compelled to take his tools and to force the door of a house for the gang-robbers to enter and plunder it – is entitled to the benefit of this exception.

However, it is not likely that this defence will succeed since the threat to G must be one of "instant death". In this case, G's death is not instant ("may soon die of thirst"). Furthermore, D cannot be said to be "compelled by threats" to beat up K.

The right of private defence extends to the protection of other persons as stated in section 97(a) of the Singapore Penal Code:

> Every person has a right, subject to the restrictions contained in sections 98 and 106A, to defend –
>
> (a) his own body, and the body of any other person, against any offence affecting the human body; [...]

It is clear that the right to private defence in this situation has commenced and is still continuing at the time when D caused the injuries to K. D reasonably believes that G may die soon arising from K's act of kidnapping her and refusing to disclose her location, and this belief is still continuing. See section 101 of the Singapore Penal Code:

> (1) The right of private defence of the body starts as soon as the defender reasonably believes that there is danger to the body (either his own or that of any other person) arising from any act which is an offence against the human body or an attempt or a threat to commit the offence, though the offence may not have been committed.
>
> (2) The right of private defence continues as long as the belief of danger mentioned in subsection (1) continues.

However, D's right of private defence is limited by section 98:

> (1) The right of private defence does not extend to the inflicting of more harm than it is reasonably necessary in the circumstances.
>
> (2) There is no right of private defence in cases in which there is reasonable opportunity to have recourse to the protection of a public authority in the circumstances.
>
> *Illustrations*
>
> (a) Z ambushes A in a secluded area and attempts to kill A. A kills Z while fending off Z's attack. A is guilty of no offence because, in the circumstances, A had no reasonable opportunity to have recourse to the protection of a public authority.
>
> (b) Z ambushes A in a secluded area and attempts to kill A. A's right of private defence arises because, at that point of time, A had no reasonable opportunity to have recourse to the protection of a public authority. In the midst of the struggle between A and Z, a police patrol car arrives on the scene. A's right of private defence ceases the moment A had reasonable opportunity to have recourse to the protection of the police.

Hence, the plea of private defence may not be successful if D had inflicted "more harm than is reasonably necessary in the circumstances". This is an objective assessment made by the court.

The defence of necessity (described under Vignette 1) could also be used, but it has been argued by commentators that the defence of necessity should only be used if the situation does not fall within the other defences.[6] However, illustration (c) to section 81 of the Singapore Penal Code suggests otherwise – the scenario there is one of private defence of other persons and yet the defence of necessity is used.

The defence of necessity may succeed in this case since D committed the harm to K in good faith for the purpose of avoiding or preventing G's death. It can also be said

---

[6] See Stanley Yeo, Neil Morgan and Chan Wing Cheong (note 1), para. [23.7].

that the injuries to K are necessary and not disproportionate to the harm to be avoided or prevented (death of G). However, it may be questioned if the "imminence" requirement is satisfied since it may take some time before G dies from thirst.

Vignette 4: Lethal Self-Defence

> R, a well-trained young man armed with a knife, accosts 50-year-old D, who is on her way home from a party in the early morning hours. R threatens her with the knife and takes away her purse filled with 500 € and her wristwatch worth 1,000 €. As R turns to run away, D draws a pistol she is secretly carrying in her jacket, and shoots and kills R in order to retrieve her property. Is D guilty of murder?

Assuming that the *actus reus* and *mens rea* for murder are satisfied, D would nevertheless not be liable for murder but the lower offence of culpable homicide (sections 299 and 300 of the Singapore Penal Code). This is because the "special exception" of exceeding the right of private defence is applicable.

The right of private defence is found in sections 96 to 106A of the Singapore Penal Code. The facts of Vignette 4 concern private defence of D's own property, which falls under section 97(b):

> Every person has a right, subject to the restrictions contained in sections 98 and 106A, to defend – [...]
>
> (b) the property, whether movable or immovable, of himself or of any other person, against any act which is an offence falling under the definition of theft, robbery, mischief or criminal trespass, or which is an attempt to commit theft, robbery, mischief or criminal trespass.

It is clear that D's right to private defence against the robbery had arisen and was continuing at the time, see sections 104(1) and (3) of the Singapore Penal Code:

> (1) The right of private defence of property starts when the defender reasonably believes that there was a danger to property (either his own or that of any other person) arising from any act which is an offence falling under the definition of theft, robbery, mischief or criminal trespass, or which is an attempt to commit such an offence.
>
> [...]
>
> (3) The right of private defence of property against robbery continues as long as the offender causes or attempts to cause to any person death or hurt or wrongful restraint, or as long as the fear of instant death or of instant hurt or of instant personal restraint continues.

However, as stated in section 97, the right of private defence is subject to the two restrictions in section 98 (the text is stated above in Vignette 3).

Although D had no reasonable opportunity to have recourse to the protection of the police in the circumstances because R was about to run away with D's possessions, D inflicted more harm than was reasonably necessary by killing R. D could have prevented the robbery by other means such as threatening to shoot R or by shooting at R but not killing him. What is "reasonable" is objectively assessed.

However, even though the full defence of private defence does not apply, the partial defence under exception 2 to section 300 of the Singapore Penal Code does. Section 300 stipulates 7 situations where culpable homicide is not murder. Exception 2 states:

> Culpable homicide is not murder if the offender, in the exercise of the right of private defence of person or property, exceeds the power given to him by law, and causes the death of the person against whom he is exercising such right of defence, without premeditation and without any intention of doing more harm than is necessary for the purpose of such defence.
>
> *Explanation.* The word "premeditation" means the offender's intention, which was formed prior to the circumstances which gave rise to the act of private defence –
>
> (a) to cause death in section 300(a) or to cause such bodily injury as is mentioned in section 300(b) or (c); or
>
> (b) to do an act knowing that the act is so imminently dangerous in the way mentioned in section 300(d).

As explained above, D was exercising her right of private defence of property, but had exceeded the right given to her and had caused the death of R. Since the killing of R was done without premeditation and without the intention of doing more harm than is necessary to assert her defence, this exception can apply. D will therefore not be guilty of murder but culpable homicide (a lesser offence).

Exception 2 differs from a complete defence in that it only requires D to honestly believe that the harm inflicted was necessary to prevent the robbery. In other words, D must not have the *subjective* intention to inflict more harm than necessary. If she did, the exception will not apply. In comparison, the complete defence requires an *objective* assessment of whether D inflicted more harm than necessary in the circumstances.

Vignette 5: Criminal Responsibility of Subordinates for Systemic Offences

> D is a soldier in the army of a country ruled by a junta of generals who have come to power through a violent coup. When an opposition group demands the return to a democratic system, the government orders the soldiers to shoot and kill any person who resists arrest. Following this order, D kills three young men who take part in a protest demonstration and hit a police officer who tries to arrest them. When D is tried after a change of regime, he says that he did not like to shoot the protesters but that he thought that he had to obey his commanders' orders. D knew that if he had refused to shoot, he might have been demoted, but no physical harm would have occurred to him. Should D be convicted of murder? If so, should his sentence be mitigated because of his situation?

Assuming that the *actus reus* and *mens rea* for murder are satisfied, there are two possibilities. First, D may have a full defence if the defences in sections 76 or 79 of the Singapore Penal Code apply. (The defence of duress found in section 94 of the Singapore Penal Code does not apply since it does not apply to cases of murder and D only thought that he would be demoted if he did not obey – see the text of the provision in Vignette 3).

Section 76 of the Singapore Penal Code states:

Nothing is an offence which is done by a person who is bound by law to do it or justified by law in doing it.

Illustrations

(a) A, a soldier, fires on a mob by the order of his superior officer, in conformity with the commands of the law. A has committed no offence.

(b) A sees Z repeatedly stabbing Y with a knife on a public road. Y dies. A, in the exercise of the power which the law gives to all persons apprehending murderers in the act, forcefully seizes Z, in order to detain Z so that Z can be arrested by the police officers when they arrive. A has committed no offence.

The defence of superior orders concerns situations where a person, usually a public servant, seeks to be exculpated based on the ground that they were obeying the law such as a command of their superior officer.

D is protected via section 76 of the Singapore Penal Code, provided that he is obeying a lawful order. This is shown in illustration (a).

A separate defence is found in section 79(1) of the Singapore Penal Code where the person mistakenly believed that they were bound by law to follow the order:

(1) Unless otherwise provided by written law, nothing is an offence which is done by any person who by reason of a mistake of fact or in ignorance of a fact in good faith believes himself to be bound by law to do it or justified by law in doing it. [...]

Illustrations

(a) A sees Z commit what appears to A to be a murder. A, in the exercise, to the best of his judgment exerted in good faith, of the power which the law gives to all persons of apprehending murderers in the act, seizes Z, in order to bring Z before the proper authorities. A has committed no offence, though it may turn out that Z was acting in self-defence.

(b) A, a police officer, is deployed to perform the duty of screening passengers boarding a flight at the airport. A sees Z, a passenger queuing up to be screened, acting suspiciously. As A approaches Z, Z suddenly shouts aloud that he is carrying a bomb and warns A not to approach further. As A draws his revolver, Z suddenly starts to run away. A, after assessing the circumstances of the case, and to the best of his judgment exerted in good faith, believes that Z has a bomb and will set it off. A shoots Z and Z dies as a result. A has committed no offence, even though it may turn out that Z was not carrying a bomb.

(c) A, a police officer, is deployed to perform patrol duty at an underground train station. A receives information from police headquarters that someone is attempting to plant a bomb in the public transport system. The profile of the suspect is also provided. While patrolling the underground train station, A sees Z, who fits the profile. Z is seen carrying a backpack and behaving suspiciously. A approaches Z and orders him to stop. Z suddenly starts running towards a crowd in the station. A, after assessing the circumstances of the case, and to the best of his judgment exerted in good faith, believes that Z has a bomb and will set it off. A shoots Z and Z dies as a result. A has committed no offence, even though it may turn out that Z was not carrying a bomb.

(d) X, the commander of a naval vessel, is patrolling Singapore territorial waters. X receives information that someone may hijack a vessel in order to commit a terrorist act. X spots vessel A which is proceeding at high speed towards a cruise liner. X orders vessel A to stop her manoeuvre immediately and fires a warning signal. Vessel A instead starts accelerating towards the cruise liner. X, after assessing the circumstances of the case, and to the best of his judgment exerted in good faith, believes that vessel A is going to ram into the cruise liner. X gives an order to fire at vessel A. The persons on board vessel A die as a result. X has committed no offence, even though it may turn out that vessel A was not hijacked nor were there any terrorist on board.

(e) A, an officer of a court, being ordered by that court to arrest Y, and, after due enquiry, believing Z to be Y, arrests Z. A has committed no offence. […]

Section 79 provides D a defence if, by reason of mistake of fact, in good faith believed they were bound by law to obey the order. The defence does not apply if D knew or ought to have known that the order was unlawful.

It should be noted that only mistakes of fact are covered by section 79. Mistakes of law are not a defence (section 79A of the Singapore Penal Code). An example of a mistake of law is where D mistakenly believed that the government had the legal authority to make the order when it did not. Conversely, an example of a mistake of fact is where D mistakenly believes that the factual circumstances are such that the order was warranted.[7]

Alternatively, a partial defence is available under Exception 3 to section 300 of the Singapore Penal Code:

> Culpable homicide is not murder if the offender, being a public servant, or aiding a public servant acting for the advancement of public justice, exceeds the powers given to him by law, and causes death by doing an act which he, in good faith, believes to be lawful and necessary for the due discharge of his duty as such public servant, and without ill will towards the person whose death is caused.

In order to satisfy Exception 3, D must show that:

(a) he is a public servant;

(b) he believed in good faith that killing the three young men was lawful and necessary for the discharge of his duties; and

(c) he did not have any ill will towards the three young men.

The term "public servant" is defined in section 21 of the Penal Code. D would fall within the definition in section 21(1)(a):

> The words "public servant" denote a person falling under any of the following descriptions:
>
> (a) every officer in the Singapore Armed Forces; […]

This provision is an exception to section 79A according to which mistakes of law are not a defence. Exception 3 can succeed even if D made a mistake about the legality of the order, provided all the other elements are satisfied. However, D does not get a full defence. He would be convicted of culpable homicide instead of murder.

Vignette 6: Limits of Consent

V is a 21-year-old ambitious athlete and short-distance runner. He has learned that certain artificial limbs can enhance a runner's speed. He decides that he would

7 This is illustrated by the case *R v SAH Alsagoff* [1946] 2 MC 191.

rather have an artificial limb instead of his right lower leg. He approaches D, a surgeon in private practice, and asks him to amputate his leg below the knee and replace it with an artificial limb. D complies with V's request. Should D be punished for mayhem?

D may have a defence under section 88 of the Singapore Penal Code. (The defence under section 87 of the Singapore Penal Code does not apply since D's act was committed with the intention to cause grievous hurt. The below-knee amputation is a form of grievous hurt, see the definition of grievous hurt in section 320 of the Singapore Penal Code).

Section 88 provides:

Nothing, which is not intended to cause death, is an offence by reason of any harm which it may cause, or be intended by the doer to cause, or be known by the doer to be likely to cause, to any person for whose benefit it is done in good faith, and who has given a consent, whether express or implied, to suffer that harm, or to take the risk of that harm.

Illustrations

A, a surgeon, knowing that a particular operation is likely to cause the death of Z, who suffers under a painful complaint, but not intending to cause Z's death, and intending, in good faith, Z's benefit, performs that operation on Z, with Z's consent. A has committed no offence.

This defence requires the act (that is, the below-knee amputation) to be done for the benefit of V. What constitutes a "benefit" is not defined by the Singapore Penal Code, except that "mere pecuniary benefit" is excluded by section 92. In this situation, it can be argued that V derives more than pecuniary benefit such as mental health by being able to realise his ambition to improve his running speed.

It has been suggested by commentators that whether the act qualifies as a "benefit" should be up to the parties to decide rather than the court.[8] The same commentators have suggested that the requirement of "in good faith" applies to the intention that *V* benefit from the act rather than how carefully D carries out the act.[9]

Section 90 of the Singapore Penal Code explains what does not qualify as consent:

A consent is not such a consent as is intended by any section of this Code –

(a) if the consent is given by a person –
   (i) under fear of injury or wrongful restraint to the person or to some other person; or
   (ii) under a misconception of fact,

   and the person doing the act knows, or has reason to believe, that the consent was given in consequence of such fear or misconception;

(b) if the consent is given by a person who, from unsoundness of mind, mental incapacity, intoxication, or the influence of any drug or other substance, is unable to understand the nature and consequence of that to which he gives his consent; or

(c) unless the contrary appears from the context, if the consent is given by a person who is below 12 years of age.

---

8 Stanley Yeo, Neil Morgan and Chan Wing Cheong (note 1), para. [19.57].

9 Stanley Yeo, Neil Morgan and Chan Wing Cheong (note 1), para. [19.58].

In this scenario, none of the situations in section 90 apply, so D's consent is valid. The consent was freely given by D, with knowledge of the facts that are material to his decision.

Vignette 7: Withdrawal from an Attempt

25-year-old D is deeply upset with her former boyfriend V, who had ended their relationship to be with another woman. To punish V, D plans to stab him with a large knife. D knows that the stab wounds can be fatal and accepts V's death as a possible outcome. When V goes jogging, D attacks him from behind and stabs him in the back three times. V breaks down. D realises that she has injured him but that the injuries will not cause his death. She realises that she could kill him by stabbing him again but decides to leave him alone. Should D be punished for attempted murder?

A withdrawal, even if voluntary due to remorse by D, does not negate liability for an attempted offence.[10] This assumes that the *actus reus* and *mens rea* for the attempt have been satisfied. However, a court can consider the withdrawal as mitigation of the offence in sentencing D.

Note that a possible argument is that if D refrains from committing the murder because of a change of heart, then D did not have the intention to commit it in the first place. Proof of intention is required for liability for attempted murder (section 307 of the Singapore Penal Code).

Vignette 8: Criminal Responsibility of Minors

D is a 13-year-old boy. He abducts and rapes V, a girl of the same age. Should D be punished for a criminal offence?

The minimum age of criminal responsibility in Singapore is 10 years. Only those who are below 10 years old are completely exempted from criminal liability (section 82 of the Singapore Penal Code).

For those who are 10 years old but below 12 years old, it is a defence if they can show that they have "not attained sufficient maturity of understanding to judge of the nature and consequence of his conduct on that occasion".

These provisions in the Singapore Penal Code read as follows:

82. Nothing is an offence which is done by a child below 10 years of age.

83. Nothing is an offence which is done by a child of or above 10 years and below 12, who has not attained sufficient maturity of understanding to judge of the nature and consequence of his conduct on that occasion.

In this case, since D is 13 years old, he can be punished for the offence. However, he will be tried in the Youth Court and there are special orders available for young offenders like him under the Children and Young Persons Act 1993.

There used to be a provision in the Evidence Act that a boy under the age of 13 years is incapable of committing rape, but this was repealed in 1996.

---

10 *PP v Tsao Kok Wah* [2001] 1 SLR(R) 252.

The minimum age of criminal responsibility in Singapore used to be 7 years. This was amended in 2019 and the new age of 10 years came into effect in 2020.

Vignette 9: Statute of Limitations

In 1995, D violently raped V, a 35-year-old woman, using a knife. D managed to escape and was not apprehended until 2023. Traces of his DNA taken from the victim's body leave no doubt that D is the perpetrator. Should D be convicted despite the long delay?

There is no statute of limitations applicable to criminal offences in Singapore. However, with the lapse in time, it will be more difficult for the Prosecution to prove the guilt of the accused beyond a reasonable doubt if the evidence and witnesses are no longer available.

Examples of cases where there had been a long lapse of time between the crime and the conviction include Phey Yew Kok[11] (he was on the run for 36 years) and Haron Ismail[12] (he was on the run for 14 years).

Vignette 10: Life Imprisonment without Parole

The Penal Code of State S provides for imprisonment for life as the maximum penalty for murder, but also authorises the court to order an offender's early release after a minimum of 15 years if the offender is no longer dangerous. Reacting to cases of particularly heinous murders, the legislature of S wishes to introduce a penalty of life imprisonment without any possibility of early release, regardless of the offender's continued dangerousness. Would this amendment be acceptable?

It is likely that the amendment will be accepted in Singapore provided that the law is validly passed by the Legislature. There is no specific provision in the Singapore Constitution against cruel, inhuman or degrading treatment or punishment. In cases brought before the Singapore courts on the mandatory death penalty on the basis of cruel or inhuman punishment, arguments based on legal developments from other parts of the world have been rejected because of the different constitutional history of Singapore.[13]

Singapore is not a signatory to the International Covenant on Civil and Political Rights. But even if it was, Singapore adopts a "dualist" approach where international law obligations do not give rise to individual rights unless adopted by domestic law.

The only ground for challenge is that the law violates the right to equal protection found in Article 12 of the Singapore Constitution:

(1) All persons are equal before the law and entitled to the equal protection of the law.

(2) Except as expressly authorised by this Constitution, there shall be no discrimination against citizens of Singapore on the ground only of religion, race, descent or place of birth in any law or in the appointment to any office or employment under a public au-

---

11 https://www.todayonline.com/singapore/phey-yew-kok-pleads-guilty-corruption.

12 https://www.todayonline.com/singapore/man-62-who-surrendered-after-14-years-fugitive-jailed-getaway-driver-role-office-break-ins-2-decades-ago-1791066.

13 *Yong Vui Kong v PP* [2010] 3 SLR 489.

thority or in the administration of any law relating to the acquisition, holding or disposition of property or the establishing or carrying on of any trade, business, profession, vocation or employment.

(3) This Article does not invalidate or prohibit –
(a) any provision regulating personal law; or
(b) any provision or practice restricting office or employment connected with the affairs of any religion, or of an institution managed by a group professing any religion, to persons professing that religion.

The prevailing approach to assess if a law is in compliance with Article 12 is the "rational classification" test. This only requires that the classification is: (a) based on an intelligible differentia; and (b) that differentia bears a rational relation to the object sought to be achieved by the provision.

It can be argued that the law complies with this test since the distinction as to who is liable to life imprisonment without parole is based on the severity of the offence committed such as heinous murders. The rational relation test will also be satisfied assuming that the object of the law is to impose longer sentences for public protection against those who commit heinous murders (a self-fulfilling and circular argument).

However, there are indications in recent case law that the second step of the test requires a court to consider whether the differential treatment is reasonable.[14] This is a potentially more demanding inquiry depending on the level of generality of the legislative object of the law. For example, if the object of the law is to protect the public from serious offenders, the law may be argued to be under-inclusive if it provides sentences of life imprisonment without parole only for those who commit certain offences as well as over-inclusive since those who commit those offences identified by the law may not pose more danger to the public than other offenders.

Although the Singapore court has recognized that there need not be a "perfect relation" or "complete coincidence" between the differentia and the legislative object of the law for the second test, it has also been said that the relationship "must not be so tenuous as to be incapable of withstanding scrutiny". A high level of scrutiny is demanded where the law has "a significant bearing on an individual's life and liberty".

It is too early to say how the jurisprudence of the court on Article 12 will develop. There are positive signals, but the court has also pointed out that the new approach does not mean "an open-ended mandate to evaluate legislation on the basis of its policy preferences, for that would be outside [the court's] constitutional role".

---

14 See *Syed Suhail bin Syed Zin v Attorney-General* [2021] 1 SLR 809 and *Tan Seng Kee v Attorney-General* [2022] 1 SLR 1347.

15. Turkey

By *Ali Emrah Bozbayındır** and *Rifat Murat Önok***

Vignette 1: Trolley Problem – Killing one Person to Save Many

Five young children are playing on railway tracks. An express train is approaching, and it is too late to stop the train before it hits the children, probably killing them. Operator D recognizes the emergency situation. He electronically flips a switch and thus deflects the train from its regular track to a little-used sidetrack. However, the lone repairman V is busy on the sidetrack, and the deflected train kills V, as D had anticipated. Is D criminally responsible for murder of V?

D could be liable for intentional killing under Article 81 of the Turkish Penal Code. Whether D's tragic choice would exceptionally be justified or excused would spark controversy in Turkish literature, as elsewhere. Yet, in the recent literature, there has been no specific scholarly treatment of the criminal responsibility of the actors in such hypotheticals aside from brief overviews of the community of hazard (*Gefahrengemeinschaft*) cases or the decision of the German Constitutional Court of 15.02.2006 regarding the 2005 Aviation Security Act (*Luftsicherheitsgesetz*).[1] Remarkably, in the older literature, with reference to the case of the Plank of Carneades, it has been argued that the law must refrain from passing judgment and making normative assumptions in such hard cases, and should leave the matter to an area beyond the law.[2]

With respect to the present case, one could possibly debate D's criminal responsibility within the ambit of the so-called emergency rights, that is, self-defence and necessity, which are contained in Article 25 Turkish Penal Code (TPC). One could, however, exclude self-defence without much effort, for this defence requires an imminent attack from an aggressor, which is not the case here. Hence, the possibility of permitting the killing of an innocent non-aggressor, in the present case V, if this will save one or more lives could be discussed within the ambit of the defence of necessity, which Turkish law classifies as an excuse.[3] The definition of necessity contained in Article 25(2) of the TPC reads as follows:

* Professor of Criminal Law at the Faculty of Law, Boğaziçi (Bosphorus) University, Istanbul.

** Associate Professor of Criminal and Criminal Procedure Law at the Faculty of Law, Koç University, Istanbul.

1 Mehmet Emin Artuk et al., *Ceza Hukuku Genel Hükümler* (16th ed., Adalet 2022) 581; Fatih Selami Mahmutoğlu and Serra Karadeniz, *Türk Ceza Kanunu Genel Hükümler Şerhi* (Beta 2017) 539.

2 M. Tahir Taner, *Ceza Hukuku Umumi Hükümler*, (3rd ed., İsmail Akgün Matbaası 1953) 427–428.

3 It is worth noting that there has been a controversy in Turkish literature concerning the legal nature of the defence of necessity. For an overview see R. Murat Önok and Işık Önay, "Hukuk Düzeninin Birliği İlkesi Çerçevesinde Zorunluluk Halinin Hukuki Niteliği" (2019) 77(2) İstanbul Hukuk Mecmuası 847, 895.

> Anyone who has committed an act having been compelled to do so by the necessity of saving himself or others from a grave and absolute danger, which he does not voluntarily cause nor is otherwise avoidable, shall not be held criminally liable, provided the means used to rescue are proportionate to the gravity of the danger and the protected right.

In the present case, there is little doubt that D seeks to fend off a grave and absolute danger to the children. There is also no reason to believe that the danger has been voluntarily caused by D. The defendant may, in a state of necessity, interfere with an innocent person's interests in order to avert imminent danger from himself or from another. As D has provided emergency help to the children, his act would satisfy this condition.

The crucial question, however, is whether the act of killing V would be regarded as proportionate or, more concretely, could be excused. The test of proportionality, along with the requirement of the existence of a qualified danger, allows for a narrow construction of the defence of necessity in Turkish criminal law. According to one view in the literature, if the right to be protected outweighs the right to be violated, the offender may be absolved of criminal liability.[4] According to this view, one could assume that saving five lives by sacrificing one would be excused. It needs to be added that the wording of the provision concerning the defence of necessity does not contain an explicit preclusion of the right to life from the scope of the defence of necessity.[5] One could, therefore, argue that if the life of the defendant or a third person's life is in imminent and grave danger, he may violate an uninvolved, innocent third party's life, for these rights are regarded as equal. If one adopts such an approach, the actor would be excused for killing an innocent third party who acts to save himself. A literal interpretation, therefore, of the wording of the defence of necessity suggests that D's act would be excused since D acts to save five lives; hence, "the means used to rescue are proportionate to the gravity of the danger and the protected right".

To be sure, if a legal system accords a special status to the right to life of an innocent third party within the scope of the defence of necessity, one can arrive at a different conclusion. In Turkish legal literature, there is indeed a long-standing tradition of excluding violations of the right to life from the scope of the defence of necessity. According to this view, a person in a state of necessity cannot be permitted to kill another innocent person, even if his act may save the lives of one or many innocent persons in danger of imminent death. Thus, killing an uninvolved third party, even if this were the only means of persevering one's own life or the lives of others, could not absolve the actor of criminal liability.[6] This view rests upon cultural but also on humanist ideas upholding the sanctity of human life.[7] Thus, the killing of an innocent third party is excluded from the scope of the defence of necessity. The right to life, or the

---

4 Bahri Öztürk and Mustafa Ruhan Erdem, *Uygulamalı Ceza Hukuku ve Güvenlik Tedbirleri Hukuku* (23rd ed., Seçkin 2023) 286.

5 Elif Bekar, *Türk ve Amerikan Ceza Hukukunda Zorunluluk Hali* (Seçkin 2013) 121–122, 177; Timur Demirbaş, *Ceza Hukuku Genel Hükümler* (18th ed., Seçkin 2023) 334.

6 Ibid.

7 Faruk Erem, Ahmet Danışman and Mehmet Emin Artuk, *Ümanist Doktrin Açısından Türk Ceza Hukuku Genel Hükümler* (14th ed., Sevinç Matbaası 1997) 583; İzzet Özgenç, *Türk Ceza Hukuku Genel Hükümler* (19th ed., Seçkin 2023) 487 ff.

preservation of life, is one of the fundamental principles of the Turkish legal system and tradition. It forbids any tendency towards the quantification of human life under any circumstance by furnishing the right to life of an innocent third party with absolute protection. According to this tradition, for instance, throwing a passenger overboard to save the rest of the people on a boat is not permitted.

In such circumstances, however, the state of necessity would be considered a mitigating circumstance within Article 62 of the TPC, which regulates the grounds for discretionary mitigation. It needs to be highlighted that the former Turkish Penal Code contained a more favourable provision for the defendant, which enabled the judge to reduce the sentence considerably if the defendant had violated the condition of proportionality in averting the imminent danger (Article 50 of the former TPC). In the present case, for instance, the defendant's act requires a life sentence, and according to Article 50 of the former TPC, he would have received imprisonment from six years to fifteen years. According to the current Penal Code, he would receive a sentence of 25 years instead of a life sentence if the judge decides to mitigate his sentence.

One could, of course, be inclined towards considering such punishment a rather harsh treatment of D. But suppose the quantification of human life is acknowledged as a principle within the defence of necessity. In that case, it might have a slippery slope effect, which would jeopardise and relativise the sanctity of human life by allowing a defence of necessity if the defendant kills an uninvolved third party. Pandora's box would then be opened. The interpretation given above, by contrast, aligns with the principle of upholding human dignity and the state's responsibility for protecting innocent human lives. One could, as it has been aptly put by criminal law scholars Claus Roxin and Luis Greco, sacrifice, for example, a politician in order to save randomly chosen five innocent persons whom terrorists will shoot.[8] The law must uphold the right to life of innocent third parties by protecting them against unlawful assaults, even if the attack has been a consequence of a state of necessity.

Vignette 2: Attribution of Death

D intends to kill his neighbour V. Hidden near V's house, D waits for V and stabs him several times with a knife. V is taken to the hospital, where his wounds are treated. His injuries are not life-threatening and V is kept overnight for observation. During the night, a technical defect in the hospital kitchen leads to the outbreak of a fire, which kills V and other persons. Can D be held criminally responsible for V's death?

The theory of adequate causation (*uygun illiyet teorisi*) has been the dominant theory in resolving issues relating to causation in the jurisprudence of the Court of Cassation until recently and in civil law. But the theory of the equivalence of conditions and, relatedly, the theory of objective imputation have been gaining ground in Turkish criminal law scholarship. In a nutshell, one could suggest that both the theory of adequate causation and objective imputation have been developed to provide normative corrections to factual causation, that is, to deal with the issues of attribution,

8 Claus Roxin and Luis Greco, *Strafrecht Allgemeiner Teil I* (5th ed., C.H. Beck 2020) 1151.

which could not be resolved through the application of the but-for or *sine qua non* test. In the present case, for instance, D's act is the condition *sine qua non* for V's death, and as D acted with the intention of killing, he would be liable for intentional killing. The theory of adequate causality, however, would provide a normative correction with a further test of foreseeability, according to which the fire in the hospital could not have been adequately foreseen by D, and he would hence solely be responsible for attempted intentional killing.

Recently, a competing theory of German import, the theory of objective imputation, has gained ground in the literature and in the jurisprudence of the Court of Cassation. Indeed, the theory of "objective imputation or attributability" of a result to the perpetrator has recently found large academic interest, with most criminal law textbooks discussing the various criteria potentially applicable in determining the answer. After establishing the existence of a causal link between the perpetrator's act and the result,[9] a further normative assessment must be made with regard to determining whether or not this causal result can be imputed to the perpetrator as his own "work" (or product or creation) rather than being a result created by a third party or external circumstances and coincidence, so as not to extend responsibility beyond sensible and fair limits.[10]

The Court of Cassation has referred to this novel theory in a variety of cases,[11] but has seemingly not relied on it to decide the outcome of the cases,[12] even where the decisive issue seemed to be plainly one of objective attributability.[13]

In a case where the victim had been stabbed by the perpetrator who was acting with homicidal intent, but the victim eventually died due to hepatitis caused by the transfusion of infected blood at the hospital, the Court of Cassation held the perpetrator responsible for completed murder. The Court argued that the perpetrator's action was capable of causing the victim's death and that the victim was killed in connection with that conduct: the resulting death was a natural consequence of the perpetrator's conduct and the causal link between the act of the perpetrator and the result had not been severed since there was no result caused independently of the causal link started

---

9 Mehmet Emin Artuk et al., *Ceza Hukuku Genel Hükümler* (17th ed., Adalet 2023) 373; Öztürk and Erdem (n 4) mn. 390; Demirbaş, *Genel Hükümler* (n 5) 276; Hamide Zafer, *Ceza Hukuku Genel Hükümler (TCK m. 1–75)* (8th ed., Beta 2021) 272.

10 Artuk et al. (n 9) 373; Mahmut Koca and İlhan Üzülmez, *Türk Ceza Hukuku Genel Hükümler* (15th ed., Seçkin 2022) 140; Nur Centel, Hamide Zafer and Özlem Çakmut, *Türk Ceza Hukukuna Giriş* (12th ed., Beta 2023) 283; Demirbaş, *Genel Hükümler* (n 5) 277; Öztürk and Erdem (n 4) mn. 390; Berrin Akbulut, *Ceza Hukuku Genel Hükümler* (10th ed., Adalet 2023) 419.

11 See inter alia Court of Cassation Grand Criminal Chamber judgments of 2013/704, 21.04.2015; 2017/271, 16.05.2017; 2017/269, 14.04.2019; 2017/695, 15.06.2021.

12 In the above-mentioned judgments, the ratio decidendi was not based on objective attributability.

13 For example, in a case where the victim had been injured in a car crash and was later killed due to malpractice or a complication during the subsequent surgery, the Court of Cassation decided that there was no causality between the accident (car crash) and the death (12th Criminal Chamber, judgment of 20/11/2012, K. 2012/24620). It is clear that there is causation in this case, but the problem is the attribution of the result.

by the perpetrator.[14] In our view, in this case, the perpetrator should have been held responsible for *attempted* murder.[15] The problem here is one of a lack of objective attributability of the result to the perpetrator.

Like elsewhere, the applicable criteria for determining the objective imputation of the result to the perpetrator are tentative and yet to be precisely determined. However, in the case at hand, the following criteria[16] – which are not mutually exclusive – could apply:

- There is no attributability where the conduct of the perpetrator did not create a legally relevant (impermissible or reproachable) risk[17] towards the materialization of the result.[18] The risk in question must be reflected in the result that has materialized in the instant case.[19] This criterion would lead to the exclusion of responsibility in the Vignette case: Although D stabbed the victim various times, thus causing an impermissible and non-negligible risk to his life, V's death was not the result of this risk (such as death by bleeding) but the direct consequence of an intervening external factor.
- There is no attributability when the result is the consequence of a risk that falls outside the scope of protection of the criminal norm.[20] In order to determine whether this is the case, the following question must be asked: According to the meaning and purpose of the norm, is the result in the instant case (for example, death due to a crash of the ambulance car on the way to the hospital) the type of result that the prohibition in the norm intends to avoid?[21] According to this criterion, the perpetrator in our case would only be held responsible for attempted murder since the purpose of the prohibition of murder is not to avoid deaths caused exclusively

---

14 Court of Cassation Grand Criminal Chamber 2008,186, 02.06.2009.

15 In the same direction Hakan Hakeri, *Ceza Hukuku Genel Hükümler* (25th ed., Adalet 2021) 177; Özgenç (n 7) 175; Artuk et al. (n 9) 377. Cf. Akbulut (n 10) 299: This author disagrees with the reasoning of the court but argues that the perpetrator is responsible for completed murder because the injury caused by the perpetrator has decreased the bodily resistance and weakened the immunity system of the victim as demonstrated by the short time that it took for the infection to kill him; hence it should be concluded that the injury and the infection jointly caused the death of the victim.

16 The criteria applicable in cases of responsibility aggravated due to the result are not discussed since the perpetrator in our case has acted with intent to kill. If the victim had been wounded with intent to only cause injury, we would have had to discuss the "principle of immediacy". Also, criteria applicable to negligent crimes are not discussed.

17 Öztürk and Erdem (n 4) mn. 393. Hence, "general life risks" or "socially accepted risks", such as buying a person an airplane ticket, do not lead to responsibility in the case of a fatal crash (ibid.; Hakan Hakeri, *Ceza Hukuku Genel Hükümler* (28th ed., Adalet 2023) 187; Akbulut (n 10) 421).

18 Koray Doğan, *Neticesi Sebebiyle Ağırlaşmış Suçlar* (Seçkin 2011) 126; Koca and Üzülmez, *Genel Hükümler* (n 10) 140; Artuk et al. (n 9) 373; Öztürk and Erdem (n 4) mn. 391; Demirbaş, *Genel Hükümler* (n 5) 276.

19 Artuk et al. (n 9) 378; Akbulut (n 10) 421.

20 Koca and Üzülmez, *Genel Hükümler* (n 10) 141; Artuk et al. (n 9) 379; Hakeri, *Ceza Hukuku Genel Hükümler* (n 17) 189; Akbulut (n 10) 430.

21 Akbulut (n 10) 430.

by external factors such as incorrect medical treatment or accidents[22] occurring subsequent to the wounding of the victim.[23] Other writers would argue in the same direction based on considerations such as the actor's lack of domination over the result because of his lack of control over the causal link[24] or his lack of direction or ability to control the result.[25] The rationale here is that there is no attributability with regard to unexpected results, even if causal, which cannot reasonably be calculated or foreseen and which are very unlikely occurrences according to life experience ("atypical causal occurrence").[26]

In conclusion, according to objective attribution criteria applicable to the case, the perpetrator in our case should be held responsible for attempted murder and not completed murder since the unlawful risk created by D has not exactly materialized in the result. In other words, although D intended to kill V, the course of events was not foreseeable, and accordingly, his act did not materialize in the result.

Vignette 3: Torture to Save a Life

Kidnapper K has abducted an 8-year-old girl G and hidden her in a small cave in the woods. K is trying to extort money from G's parents for her release. The police manage to arrest K. Although being questioned for 24 hours, K steadfastly refuses to disclose where he hid G. Police officer D correctly assumes that G may soon die of thirst if she cannot be found. He therefore severely beats K to make him tell the truth. Fearing even more violence, K eventually leads the police to the cave, where they find G still barely alive. Should D be punished for torturing K?

The problem of "preventive" or "life-saving" torture has been debated to some extent in Turkey. In the case at hand, there is an actual and imminent risk of death of the kidnapped victim G, and the person beaten to avoid that harm is the person who is responsible for the attack on G. Therefore, this is a case of self-defence, which is regulated in Article 25 (1) of the Penal Code and is unanimously qualified in both academic writings and judicial practice as a justification, eliminating the unlawfulness of the act.

Article 25 (1) TPC explicitly allows for the exercise of self-defence for the benefit of third persons, as is the case here. The provision applies under the following conditions:

---

22 Hakeri, *Ceza Hukuku Genel Hükümler* (n 17) 190.

23 Indeed, Akbulut argues that there is no attributability where the victim who has been wounded (with intent to kill) is killed because of a totally wrongful medical intervention by the doctor, Akbulut (n 10) 288.

24 Artuk et al. (n 9) 374; Demirbaş, *Genel Hükümler* (n 5) 278.

25 Koca and Üzülmez, *Genel Hükümler* (n 10) 141; Özbek et al., *Türk Ceza Hukuku Genel Hükümler* (14th ed., Seçkin 2023) 262; Demirbaş, *Genel Hükümler* (n 5) 277; Zafer (n 9) 272; Doğan (n 18) 132.

26 Koca and Üzülmez, *Genel Hükümler* (n 10) 141; Özbek et al. (n 25) 262; Zafer (n 9) 273. In these cases, it could also be argued that no legally relevant risk has been created, Akbulut (n 10) 433.

(i) There must be an unlawful attack directed at a right belonging to the perpetrator or a third person,

(ii) The attack must be ongoing or certain to occur or to be repeated,

(iii) There must be a necessity to repel the attack,

(iv) The defensive action must be proportionate to the attack.

Theoretically speaking, in view of the conditions imposed by Article 25 TPC, it could be argued that self-defence may apply in the case of torturing a perpetrator to save the life of a third person. In defence of this approach, it may be argued that although the third paragraph of Article 17 of the Constitution, entitled "Inviolability, material and moral being of the person", protects human dignity in the context of the prohibition against torture and inhuman punishment or treatment, under Turkish Constitutional Law there is no established hierarchy of rights that would grant precedence to human dignity over the right to life. In addition, Article 25 TPC only requires "proportionality" in the defensive action, according to the situation and conditions at the time, which means that, in some cases, it is permissible even to sacrifice a legal interest that could be deemed superior to the one that is sought to be protected.

However, Turkish academic writers dealing with the subject of torture are unanimously against the permissibility of resorting to any type of torture or ill-treatment, even if done with the purpose of saving lives. In fact, accepting any justification (or excuse or ground excluding culpability) for torture is deemed impermissible.[27] Despite the lack of an explicit hierarchy between constitutional rights, the general view is that human dignity, which is the legal value primarily protected through the prohibition of torture, is the highest-ranking right in the legal order, and its sacrifice for the sake of protecting any other legal value would violate the requirement of proportionality.[28] It is further argued with regard to necessity as an excuse for torture that the protective action may not be in violation of the fundamental principles of the legal order[29] – an argument that would also apply to self-defence.

It may be said that Turkey's past negative experience regarding torture and ill-treatment, which has led to many criticisms by international organizations and national and international civil society organizations, has led Turkish academics to avoid opening a debate concerning the justification or excuse of torture.

27 R. Murat Önok, *Uluslararası Boyutuyla İşkence Suçu* (Seçkin 2006) 448 ff.; Timur Demirbaş, *İşkence Suçu* (2nd ed., Seçkin 2016) 103–104; İlhan Üzülmez, *Türk Ceza Hukukunda İşkence Suçu* (Turhan 2003) 154 ff.; Durmuş Tezcan, Mustafa Ruhan Erdem and Rifat Murat Önok, *Teorik ve Pratik Ceza Özel Hukuku* (21st ed., Seçkin 2023) 277–279; Mehmet Emin Artuk et al., *Ceza Hukuku Özel Hükümler* (20th ed., Adalet 2023), 346; Mahmut Koca and İlhan Üzülmez, *Türk Ceza Hukuku Özel Hükümler* (8th ed., Adalet 2022) 345–346; Köksal Bayraktar and R. Barış Erman, "İşkence", in: Köksal Bayraktar et al. (eds.), *Özel Ceza Hukuku, c. II, Kişilere Karşı Suçlar* (On İki Levha 2017) 354; Veli Özer Özbek, Koray Doğan and Pınar Bacaksız, *Türk Ceza Hukuku Özel Hükümler* (16th ed., Seçkin 2021) 285.

28 Tezcan, Erdem and Önok (n 27) 278; Özbek, Doğan and Bacaksız (n 27) 285; Fatih Selami Mahmutoğlu, "İşkence ve Eziyet Suçu", in: Köksal Bayraktar et al. (eds.), *Ord. Prof. Dr. Sulhi Dönmezer Armağanı Cilt II* (TCHD AKDTYK 2008) 1036; Sevi Bakım, *5237 Sayılı Türk Ceza Kanunu'nda İşkence Suçu* (Beta 2008), Demirbaş, *İşkence Suçu* (n 27) 103.

29 Mahmutoğlu (n 28) 136; Hakeri, *Ceza Hukuku Genel Hükümler* (n 15) 391.

In assessing the subject matter, Article 90 *in fine* of the Constitution should also be taken into consideration:

> International agreements duly put into effect have the force of law. (…) In the case of a conflict between international agreements, duly put into effect, concerning fundamental rights and freedoms and the laws due to differences in provisions on the same matter, the provisions of international agreements shall prevail.

Turkey is a party to the 1984 United Nations Convention against Torture and Other Cruel, Inhuman or Degrading Treatment or Punishment, and Art. 2 (2) of the Convention provides that

> No exceptional circumstances whatsoever, whether a state of war or a threat of war, internal political instability or any other public emergency, may be invoked as a justification of torture.

As explained by Zach,[30] the absolute nature of the prohibition means that "all attempts to justify the practice of torture in the 'war against global terrorism' in order to extract information from a suspected terrorist for the purpose of, for example, saving the life of innocent civilians who are in danger of being subjected to an imminent terrorist attack […] clearly violate the absolute prohibition of torture as laid down in Article 2(2) CAT and Article 7 ICCPR".[31]

Further, the European Court of Human Rights has stated many times that the prohibition of resorting to ill-treatment during interrogations and interviews (as well as the prohibition of the use of any evidence obtained by resorting to such conduct) is absolute.[32] Therefore, in line with Article 90 *in fine* of the Constitution and the above, resort to any torture or ill-treatment remains unlawful.[33]

In addition, the official explanation of Article 94 TPC refers explicitly to Article 2 (2) of the UN Convention against Torture and states that this provision stipulates that "torture may not be justified or excused under any circumstance or condition." Finally, we are not aware of any case where the Court of Cassation discussed "preventive torture" (or any other justification or excuse) in relation to torture. However, the above-mentioned Article 2 (2) of the 1984 U.N. Convention against Torture has been cited in a recent case where the Court was discussing the crime of torture.[34]

Summing up, according to Turkish academic writings police officer D should be held responsible for the crime of torture, which is laid down in Article 94 TPC. The "severe beating" under interrogation would be qualified as torture. Therefore, there is no need to discuss whether a distinction may be drawn between torture and

---

30 Gerrit Zach, "Article 2. Obligation to Prevent Torture", in: Manfred Nowak, Moritz Birk, and Giuliana Monina (eds.), *The United Nations Convention Against Torture and its Optional Protocol: A Commentary* (2nd ed., Oxford University Press 2020) 92, mn. 59. Further see Üzülmez (n 27) 155, 157; Demirbaş, *İşkence Suçu* (n 27) 104.

31 Turkey is also a party to the ICCPR.

32 *Tomasi v. France* App no 12850/87 (ECtHR, 27 August 1992) para. 115, *Gäfgen v. Germany* App no 22978/05 (ECtHR [GC], 1 June 2010) para. 87.

33 Bayraktar and Erman (n 27) 355.

34 Court of Cassation Grand Criminal Chamber 2017/753, 25.06.2019.

other ill-treatment falling short of torture with regard to potential justifications and excuses.

The punishment would be 3 to 12 years of imprisonment (5 to 12 years if the victim is a woman), barring aggravating circumstances (which are rather numerous). At most, D may benefit from the general provision of Article 62 TPC on discretionary mitigation of punishment (reduction of the sentence of up to one sixth), but even that reduction could not be based on the motive of the perpetrator since the provision only allows the following factors to be taken into account in deciding whether to apply the reduction: the perpetrator's past, social relations, conduct displaying remorse after the act and during trial, potential effects of the punishment on the future of the perpetrator.

Vignette 4: Lethal Self-Defence

> R, a well-trained young man armed with a knife, accosts 50-year-old D, who is on her way home from a party in the early morning hours. R threatens her with the knife and takes away her purse filled with 500 € and her wristwatch worth 1,000 €. As R turns to run away, D draws a pistol she is secretly carrying in her jacket, and shoots and kills R in order to retrieve her property. Is D guilty of murder?

D would be liable for intentional killing according to Article 81 TPC unless her act exceptionally falls within the Penal Code's ambit of a justification or excuse. First, it is necessary to assess whether D's act satisfied the conditions of self-defence.

Article 25 (1) TPC defines self-defence, which is termed "legitimate defence" (*meşru savunma*), as follows:

> Anyone who has committed an act having been compelled to do so by the necessity of defending his own or another's right against a present unlawful attack, which is taking place, is carried out, or is certain to be repeated, shall not be held criminally liable, provided that the defence was proportionate to the attack according to the circumstances when the defensive action was taken.

First, it needs to be evaluated whether D's act satisfies the temporal element of self-defence. As R has committed an act of robbery against D and ran away, it could be argued that, although the aggressive aspect of his attack against D had ceased, his assault against D's property was still imminent. If D had defended herself while R robbed her, her lethal use of force would have squarely fallen within the scope of the defence. Yet, in the case at hand, only an attack against D's property was still taking place. Therefore, we shall confine our analysis to the use of lethal force in defending one's property.

Historically, the definition of self-defence in the new Penal Code has replaced the rather restrictive definition of this justification, particularly concerning the defence of property.[35] Indeed, the former Penal Code, which was by and large adopted from the Italian Codice Zanardelli, allowed self-defence only if an attack against the person or the chastity of the defendant took place. The defence of property was

35 See Ali Emrah Bozbayındır, „Grundlagen und Grenzen des Notwehrrechts im türkischen Strafrecht" (2015) 127(4) Zeitschrift für die gesamte Strafrechtswissenschaft 1093, 1095 ff.

not considered a right to be protected within the ambit of self-defence. Thus, the defence of property was only authorized in specific provisions of the special part of the Code, such as Article 461, which allowed self-defence in cases of robbery or trespass. But if the attack was only against the defendant's right to property, that situation could not be subsumed under Article 49 of the former Penal Code, the main provision on self-defence. Despite calls in the literature since the early 1940s, the legislature retained the restrictive definition of self-defence.[36] A sea change in this area of law occurred with the adoption of the new Penal Code. The new definition of this defence, as strongly suggested in the official justification of Article 25 TPC, meant a conscious expansion of self-defence to any right, which encompasses the right to property. Since then, the limits of the defence of property have become a bone of contention in Turkish literature. The prevailing approach tends to favour a prohibition of deadly force in defence of property. It has been frequently argued that the requirement of proportionality, and arguably Article 2 ECHR prohibits a recourse to deadly force against property. It should be noted that the operational scope of Article 2 ECHR is disputed in Turkey and elsewhere.

Furthermore, the European Court of Human Rights (ECtHR) has not ruled explicitly on whether state actors or private individuals violate the right-to-life provision of the Convention when they use deadly force in defence of the right to property. The scholarly views in Turkey on this matter, however, interpret the ECHR provision on the right to life as an absolute ban on using deadly force in defence of property.[37] Besides, prevailing literary views contend that the right to property cannot under any circumstances outweigh the right to life; hence, the use of lethal force in order to protect property would never pass the test of proportionality enshrined in Article 25 (1) TPC. The Court of Cassation, however, despite its rather conservative approach towards self-defence in general, has not applied such an exacting test of proportionality as has been firmly suggested in the legal literature, at least in the following case:

> On the night of the incident, the victim C. and his friends, after committing an act of theft at around 05:00 am, came in front of the defendant's market, tried to open the shutters of the market by cutting the lock with iron cutting shears. The defendant I.H. heard that the shutters of the market belonging to him and located on the ground floor of his house were opening; he woke up, went to the balcony of his house, and saw a vehicle in front of the market. He saw that the victim and his friends had parked a car with the doors open, and carried the goods from the market, whose shutters were half open, and loaded them into the vehicle. The defendant wanted to make them escape by shouting, "What are you doing, leave those goods", but the victim and his friends continued their actions while swearing at the defendant. The victim then showed the defendant a knife, which was later found inside the vehicle. The defendant tried to dissuade him from his actions by shouting from the balcony. The victim responded by swearing and saying, "Go in". The defendant went inside, took his licensed gun,

36 Tahir Taner, "Meşru Müdafaanın Genişliği ve Mala Karşı Yapılan Tecavüzlerde Müdafaa", in: *Ebül'ula Mardin'e Armağan* (Kenan Matbaası 1944) 631, 635 ff.

37 Mustafa Ruhan Erdem, "Malvarlığına Yönelik Saldırılara Karşı Meşru Savunma İçin İnsan Öldürme ve Yaşam Hakkı (AİHS m. 2)" [2007] 9 Dokuz Eylül Üniversitesi Hukuk Fakültesi Dergisi 987–998; Seydi Kaymaz, "Malvarlığına Yönelik Saldırılara Karşı Meşru Savunma ve Yaşam Hakkı", in: Ayşe Nuhoğlu (ed.), Feridun Yenisey'e Armağan (Bahçeşehir Üniversitesi Yayınları 2014) 229–269.

went back to the balcony, shouted at the people and shot three warning shots in the air. The victim's friends ran away from the scene at the sound of the gunshot. Victim C. did not run away but got into the vehicle loaded with the materials they had carried from the market and drove it away. When the defendant saw that the vehicle and his goods were being taken away, he shot from the back of the vehicle towards the vehicle. The bullets penetrated the back of the vehicle and hit the victim, who was sitting in the driver's seat, in the back area. The victim died as a result of the bullet wounds.

In this case, the Court of Cassation decided that the defendant's act of firing at the victim, who escaped from the scene with his goods, satisfied the conditions of self-defence. Despite the defendant's efforts to prevent the crime of theft from happening, he could not repel the attack; hence, the victim's injury and death remained within the scope of self-defence; the defendant could not be held responsible for an intentional killing and consequently should not be punished.

This case constitutes an ideal-type example of using lethal force to defend one's property within the confines of self-defence. It is no surprise, however, that this judgment has been criticized in the literature on the grounds that it disregarded the absolute disproportion between the right to life and the right to property.

Accordingly, in the present case, D's act would not be justified, for the act of killing could be regarded as grossly disproportionate owing to the fact that D shot at R without trying to take less intrusive measures to rescue her stolen property. Although the value of the property played a role in Turkish law in defence of property cases until the mid-nineteenth century, the current law does not attach any significance to the value of the stolen goods.

That said, considering the nighttime, the physical strength of the attacker and the violent nature of the attack, D exceeded the limits of self-defence due to an excusable excitement, fear or agitation. In such situations, the Article 27 (2) TPC provides for an excuse, i.e., excessive self-defence. D would hence be excused per Article 27 (2) TPC, which reads:

> If the limits were excessed in the course of legitimate defence as a result of excitement, fear or agitation and can be regarded as excusable, the offender shall not be subject to a penalty.[38]

If the case fails to meet these conditions, D's sentence would be reduced according to Article 29 TPC, which contains the institution of unjustified provocation.[39]

Vignette 5: Criminal Responsibility of Subordinates for Systemic Offences

D is a soldier in the army of a country ruled by a junta of generals who have come to power through a violent coup. When an opposition group demands the return to a democratic system, the government orders the soldiers to shoot and kill any person who resists arrest. Following this order, D kills three young men who take part in a protest demonstration and hit a police officer who tries to arrest them. When D is tried after a change of regime, he says that he did not like to shoot the protesters

38 See further Ali Emrah Bozbayındır, "Meşru Savunmada Sınırın Aşılması" (2012) 7(18) Ceza Hukuku Dergisi 113–135.

39 See Gülşah Bostancı Bozbayındır, *Ceza Hukukunda Haksız Tahrik* (Beta 2013).

> but that he thought that he had to obey his commanders' orders. D knew that if he had refused to shoot, he might have been demoted, but no physical harm would have occurred to him. Should D be convicted of murder? If so, should his sentence be mitigated because of his situation?

Obedience to superior orders is regulated in Article 24 (2)–(4) TPC. Academic views are divided on whether it constitutes a justification or a ground excluding culpability (or an excuse).[40] Article 223 (3)(b) Criminal Procedure Code provides that where a crime has been committed in pursuance of a binding but unlawful order, it shall be decided that there is "no need to inflict punishment due to lack of culpability". In any case, the legal qualification of the provision has no bearing on the answer to our question.

Article 137 (2) of the Constitution provides that "An order the object of which constitutes an offence shall under no circumstances be executed; the person who executes such an order shall not evade responsibility." An "order the object of which constitutes an offence" means that if the order is executed, the act committed pursuant to this order would constitute a crime.[41]

Article 24 (3) TPC confirms the above by repeating the first part of the constitutional provision and further clarifying the second part by stating that "Otherwise, the person implementing and the person giving the order will be [held] responsible". Thus, if an order which entails the commission of a criminal offence is implemented, both the person(s) issuing the order and the person executing it will be held responsible as instigator and direct perpetrator, respectively. Turkish legislation has thus opted for the doctrine of absolute liability.[42]

However, Article 24 (4) TPC then provides that "Where the law prevents the review of the lawfulness of the order, only the person giving the order shall be responsible for its implementation". Although the precise meaning and scope of this provision are subject to different interpretations, academic writers generally agree on the view that Article 24 does not justify or excuse the execution of orders requiring the commission of a criminal offence.[43]

---

40 For extensive information on this matter, Muhammed Demirel, *Amirin Emri – Amirin Emrini Yerine Getirmenin Ceza Sorumluluğuna Etkisi* (On İki Levha, 2014) 51 ff.

41 Selman Dursun, "Türk Ceza Hukuku'nda Emrin İfasının Hukuki Niteliğinin Alman ve İtalyan Ceza Hukuku'yla Karşılaştırmalı Olarak İncelenmesi" (2014) 18(2) Gazi Üniversitesi Hukuk Fakültesi Dergisi 203, 235; Demirel (n 40) 56.

42 Ali Emrah Bozbayındır, *Turkey and the International Criminal Court: A Substantive Criminal Law Analysis in the Context of the Principle of Complementarity* (Nomos 2013) 130. For information on this doctrine, see Demirel (n 40) 228–230; Gökhan Güneysu, *Uluslararası Hukukta Amirin Emrini İfa*, (On İki Levha, 2015) 95 ff.

43 Demirel (n 40) 88 ff.; Serkan Meraklı, "Mazeret Sebeplerinin Türk Ceza Kanunu Bakımından Değerlendirilmesi" [2010] Ceza Hukuku Dergisi 261, 290–291; Olgun Değirmenci, "Türk Ceza Hukukunda Kusurluluğu Kaldıran Neden Olarak Amirin Emrini İfa" (2012) 3(10) Türkiye Adalet Akademisi Dergisi 455, 475–476; Koca and Üzülmez, *Genel Hükümler* (n 10) 346; Demirbaş, *Genel Hükümler* (n 5) 309; Özgenç (n 7) 502; Öztürk and Erdem (n 4) 269; Nur Centel, Hamide Zafer and Özlem Çakmut, *Türk Ceza Hukukuna Giriş* (10th ed., Beta 2021) 309–310. Cf Dursun (n 41) 239–241.

There could be one exception left by virtue of Article 137 (3) of the Constitution: "Exceptions designated by law relating to the execution of military duties and the protection of public order or public security in urgent situations are reserved." The meaning of the word "law" in this context is a statutory law enacted by Parliament. Hence, according to this provision, it would be possible to provide for an exception to Article 24 (3) TPC through an explicit statutory provision.[44]

So, is there any such statutory exception under positive Turkish Law applicable to our case? Interestingly, the answer to this question has been controversial in the literature.

As regards the military hierarchy, Article 41 of the Military Penal Code of 1930, which is a nuanced translation of Article 47 of the German Military Penal Code of 1872, regulates the regime of superior orders in the military under the heading of participation in crime. According to Art. 41 para. 2 Military Penal Code, if an order pertaining to the performance of military service constitutes a crime, the person issuing the order is responsible for this crime. There are two exceptions to this rule (Art. 41 para. 3): a) If the subordinate has exceeded the limits of the order given to him/her; b) If the subordinate knows that the order of the commander concerned an act aiming at the commission of a civil or military crime. This provision has thus opted for the "conditional liability" approach.[45] Accordingly, this provision contains two exceptions to the general *respondat superior* rule in the military hierarchy: the first is a case of *excessus mandanti*, and the second relates solely to the subjective knowledge of the subordinate, according to which the subordinate shall be held criminally liable if he knew that the order was aiming at the commission of a crime.[46] While the wording of comma (b) is a bit ambiguous, it aims at introducing a subjective test: Did the subordinate know that he or she is being asked to commit a crime? If the answer is in the affirmative, he or she cannot evade liability. Hence Article 41 (3) (b) Military Penal Codeprovides for an exception based on a subjective test.[47] However, one could argue in the light of the judgments in the *Dover Castle* and *Llandovery Castle* cases, in which the German Imperial Court applied a subjective test, that the manifest criminality and subjective knowledge tests would in most cases lead to the same conclusions.[48]

The problem is that Article 5 TPC, which entered into force on 1 January 2009, provides that the general provisions of the Penal Code shall apply to "special criminal laws" and "crimes embodying criminal punishment". This provision means that, contrary to the *lex specialis derogat legi generali* rule, the provisions in the "general part" of the Penal Code shall supersede provisions on the same matters in other laws.

---

44 However, some writers argue that this provision only applies to unlawful orders that do not constitute an offence, see Demirel (n 40) 89, 96.

45 Bozbayındır, *Turkey and ICC* (n 42) 131. See Demirel (n 40) 230 ff. and Güneysu (n 42) 100 ff., for variations of this approach.

46 Bozbayındır, *Turkey and ICC* (n 42) 131.

47 Ibid. 131–132.

48 Ibid. 132.

The Penal Code itself is not superior in the normative hierarchy to any other law as there is no concept of "basic law" in Turkish Law. The result is the following:[49] (i) Rules enacted before the entry into force of Article 5 TPC which are incompatible with the general provisions of the TPC shall be automatically superseded by the new rules of the Penal Code; (ii) Despite Article 5 TPC, if the Parliament chooses to enact *after* 1 January 2009 a rule in any statutory law that is incompatible with the general provisions of the TPC, this latter rule will still apply as it is *lex posteriori*.

If we apply the above understanding, it can be argued that Article 41 Military Penal Code has now been superseded by Article 24 TPC.[50] In fact, additional Articles 8–10 Military Penal Code provide for a provisional regime that applies the rules of these provisions and the rules of the Penal Code until a new Military Penal Code is enacted – which has not yet happened. As a result, D should be convicted of murder on account of Article 24 (3) TPC.

On the other hand, even if it were argued that Article 41 Military Penal Code is still in force, the result of our case would not change. Under the subjective test of the Military Penal Code, killing civilian protestors would certainly fall within the exception in Article 41 (3) (b) Military Penal Code, because D would certainly know that the murders he is committing constitute crimes.

Therefore, under Turkish law, D could not escape conviction for intentional homicide.

Further, the mere "threat" of demotion would certainly not qualify as a threat under Art. 28 TPC, which provides for a ground excluding culpability only if there is a "certain" and "grave" threat. This is because the provision requires the harm sought to be avoided should at least be equal to the harm inflicted.[51] In our case, the right to life is sacrificed in order to escape the mere threat of demotion.

Finally, under Turkish Penal Law there is no *specific* provision that would allow the judge to mitigate the punishment due to the defendant having acted under orders. At most, the judge could take this factor into account in determining the "basic punish-

---

49 Koca and Üzülmez, *Genel Hükümler* (n 10) 49–50.

50 Zeynel T. Kangal, *Askeri Ceza Hukuku* (Seçkin 2010) 163; Fahrettin Demirağ, *Türk Ceza Kanununun Genel Hükümleri Işığında Askeri Ceza Kanunu* (Seçkin 2016) 142, 532; Olgun Değirmenci, *Askerî Ceza ve Disiplin Hukuku* (3rd ed., Seçkin 2016) 90; Demirel (n 40) 104 (however, the writer argues (at 105–107) that a revision of the relevant provisions of the MPC is required); Öztürk and Erdem (n 4) mn. 449; Dursun (n 41) 230; Bozbayındır, *Turkey and ICC* (n 42) 133.

51 Hakeri, *Ceza Hukuku Genel Hükümler* (n 15) 398. The Court of Cassation is of the same opinion, see Hale Akdağ, *Ceza Hukukunda Kusurluluğu Kaldıran ve Azaltan Nedenler* (Adalet 2020) 245. For an approach that does not focus solely on a balancing of the competing interests see Özgür Küçüktaşdemir, *Türk Ceza Hukukunda Maddi ve Manevi Cebir* (Seçkin 2012) 100 ff. The author favours an assessment that is based not merely on an objective balancing of the competing legal values at stake but rather on a test of proportionality based on the crime committed and all the circumstances of the case, including the resources subjectively available to the perpetrator in order to protect the threatened right.

ment" (Article 61 TPC),[52] or could rely on Article 62 TPC on discretionary mitigation.

Vignette 6: Limits of Consent

> V is a 21-year-old ambitious athlete and short-distance runner. He has learned that certain artificial limbs can enhance a runner's speed. He decides that he would rather have an artificial limb instead of his right lower leg. He approaches D, a surgeon in private practice, and asks him to amputate his leg below the knee and replace it with an artificial limb. D complies with V's request. Should D be punished for mayhem?

In the present case, D could be liable to punishment for qualified bodily injury, according to Article 87 TPC, which contains, among others, the functional equivalent of the offence of mayhem in Turkish criminal law. D's act of amputating V's right lower leg below the knee satisfies the objective and mental elements of this offence. As D has acted upon V's unequivocal consent, the justifiability of his act under the defence of consent must be assessed. Consent, which constitutes a justification, is defined in the general part of the TPC, which is one of the novelties of the code. Article 26 (2) TPC reads:

> No punishment shall be imposed upon a person acting with the declared consent of a person relating to a right at the complete disposition of that person.

In interpreting the Turkish high courts and literature, the scope of the so-called disposable rights is confined to certain individual rights. While the right to life, for instance, is not regarded within the confines of consent, the right to property, as a rule, constitutes *a prima facie* case of a right at the complete disposition of the consenting party. As regards bodily integrity, grave bodily injuries and seriously disabling injuries are excluded from the scope of consent. Accordingly, consent provides no defence to the causation of injury that can be classified as serious, but it would provide a defence in respect of harm below that level. Indeed, in the interpretation of the Court of Cassation, consent provides a defence solely with regard to minor injuries within the meaning of Article 86 (2) of the TPC, which reads:

> Where the effect of an intentional injury upon a person is minor and can be cured by a simple medical treatment then, upon the complaint of the victim, a penalty of imprisonment for a term of four months to one year, or a judicial fine shall be imposed.

The Court of Cassation, in a case similar to the present one in terms of the irreparable nature of the mutilating injury, has reasoned in the following terms:

> When the incident in question was examined, it was seen that the parties wanted to harm their own bodies arbitrarily, and in the meantime, victim A asked defendant B, who was his friend, to slice off his arm, and the defendant cut the victim's arm with a piece of glass, which is considered a weapon. Although the victim did not complain about the defendant and declared that the incident in question occurred with his consent, the victim's consent will not eliminate the offence in the case under investigation since the person does not have absolute authority to dispose of the rights regarding life and physical integrity. The declaration

---

[52] The factors in question are listed in Art. 61 (1) TPC for the purpose of guiding the determination of the basic sentence between the lower and upper limits of the applicable sanction determined for each crime.

of consent has no significance in bodily injury offences, except for the bodily injury offence requiring a victim complaint.[53]

The judgment of the Court also found support in the literature because the person's bodily integrity cannot be regarded as being at his absolute disposal. Thus, consent to bodily injury should be confined to injuries that a simple medical treatment could cure, due to the overwhelming public interest in protecting the bodily integrity of persons.[54]

One could, therefore, contend that the legal maxim *volenti non fit iniuria* (an injury is not done to one who consents) applies to a limited extent in Turkish criminal law. Although the Court of Cassation's test can be criticized for equating the institution of criminal complaint with that of limits of consent, one could argue that such a test could be suitable for offences of bodily harm since it adopts the gravity of the bodily harm as the determining criterion concerning the validity of consent. This test categorically excludes instances of life-threatening or maiming injuries from the scope of consent irrespective of altruistic or professional motives of the parties involved.[55] Consequently, the holder of the right to bodily integrity is entitled to dispose of it unless it exceeds the boundary of a minor injury and becomes a public issue rather than a private matter between those involved in the act of bodily injury. The power to dispose of bodily integrity is recognized as long as public order and policy concerns do not speak against it. Neither the fact that the act of amputation has been executed by a doctor nor the motives for consenting to the amputation alter this assessment. Although consent is a constitutive element of any medical treatment, it does not follow that any treatment given by a doctor is lawful so long as a patient consents. Furthermore, the patient has no right to demand any treatment, and it is the responsibility of the doctor to offer only treatments that a responsible body of medical opinion would think are suitable. As a rule, a doctor should act for therapeutic purposes. The informed consent of a patient, therefore, shall not render an amputation of a leg, cutting off a finger or putting out of an eye of the patient lawful.[56] Bodily integrity is only to a limited extent regarded as the exclusive interest of the owner, and the primary aim is to protect the injured party from irreversible consequences. Consequently, D's act of amputating V's leg cannot be justified under the defence of consent.

Vignette 7: Withdrawal from an Attempt

25-year-old D is deeply upset with her former boyfriend V, who had ended their relationship to be with another woman. To punish V, D plans to stab him with a large knife. D knows that the stab wounds can be fatal and accepts V's death as a possible outcome. When V goes jogging, D attacks him from behind and stabs him in the back three times. V breaks down. D realises that she has injured him but

53 Court of Cassation 3rd Criminal Chamber, 2011/13581, 16.11.2011; see further Ali Emrah Bozbayındır, "Einwilligung des Betroffenen im türkischen Strafrecht" (2014) 26(2) Journal of Criminal Law, The Korean Criminal Law Association 343–356, 351.

54 Meral Ekici Şahin, *Ceza Hukukunda Rıza* (On İki Levha 2012) 54 ff.; Artuk et al. (n 9) 556.

55 Bozbayındır, *Einwilligung* (n 53) 351 f.

56 Hakan Hakeri, *Tıp Hukuku El Kitabı* (Seçkin 2016) 216.

that the injuries will not cause his death. She realises that she could kill him by stabbing him again but decides to leave him alone. Should D be punished for attempted murder?

According to Article 36 TPC, which is entitled "voluntary withdrawal", a perpetrator shall not be punished for an attempt if he or she voluntarily desists from the executory acts of a crime or prevents with his or her own effort the completion of the crime or the materialization of the result. However, if the completed part constitutes a crime, he or she shall be punished for that crime.

The provision requires an answer to, inter alia, the following questions.

The first one is whether the perpetrator's motive for withdrawal is relevant. According to Turkish academic writings[57] and the Court of Cassation,[58] it is not. In particular, withdrawal requires neither repentance nor remorse,[59] shame,[60] ethical or benign considerations[61] nor any consideration regarding a will to return to lawfulness. In other words, the overwhelming majority view favours a psychological approach which rests upon the distinction between autonomous and non-autonomous motives for withdrawal. According to the dominant academic view, it is important that the perpetrator thought that he or she had the possibility, if he or she wished, to carry on and complete the crime, but decided not to do so (the famous "Frank formula").[62] The Court of Cassation has adopted essentially the same criterion in many cases[63] ("despite having the possibility to continue with the executory acts and realizing the result he wishes [...]"). As long as the actor makes an autonomous decision resulting from free will – and not from constriction by external circumstances –, the withdrawal is considered voluntary.[64]

---

57 Artuk et al. (n 9) 743; Zafer (n 9) 542; Ali Emrah Bozbayındır, "Türk ve Mukayeseli Ceza Hukukunda Gönüllü Vazgeçmede 'Gönüllülük' Şartı" [2018] 1 Galatasaray Üniversitesi Hukuk Fakültesi Dergisi 87, 146.

58 Court of Cassation Grand Criminal Chamber 2014/10–183, 24.03.2015.

59 Doğan Soyaslan, *Teşebbüs Suçu* (Kazancı 1994) 122; Adem Sözüer, *Suça Teşebbüs* (Kazancı 1994) 246; Zafer (n 9) 542; Hakeri, *Ceza Hukuku Genel Hükümler* (n 17) 494.

60 Centel, Zafer and Çakmut (n 10) 479; Hakeri, *Ceza Hukuku Genel Hükümler* (n 17) 495; Koca and Üzülmez, *Genel Hükümler* (n 10), 444; Artuk et al. (n 9) 743; Hale Akdağ, "Gönüllü Vazgeçme" (2013) 3(2) Hacettepe Üniversitesi Hukuk Fakültesi Dergisi 91, 104.

61 Soyaslan (n 59) 122; Akbulut (n 10) 847; Enes Yılmaz, "Suçun Özel Bir Görünüş Şekli Olarak Gönüllü Vazgeçme" (2016) 65(4) Ankara Üniversitesi Hukuk Fakültesi Dergisi 2553, 2580; Bozbayındır, "Gönüllülük" (n 57) 146. In the same direction Court of Cassation 14th Criminal Chamber, 2012/1525, 10.12.2013. Also see Court of Cassation Grand Criminal Chamber, 2014/10–183, 24.03.2015; the perpetrator benefitted from Article 36 for abandoning the crime due to the fact that he did not like the quality of the drug he was being offered for sale.

62 Centel, Zafer and Çakmut (n 10) 478; Özbek et al. (n 25) 490; Erdem (n 4) mn. 647; Demirbaş, *Genel Hükümler* (n 5) 522; Artuk et al. (n 9) 738; Zafer (n 9) 542.

63 See, for example, Court of Cassation Grand Criminal Chamber, 14–600/194, 09.06. 2015.

64 Özbek et al. (n 25) 490; Akbulut (n 10) 847; Soyaslan (n 59) 120–122; Akdağ, "Gönüllü Vazgeçme" (n 60) 103; Koca and Üzülmez, *Genel Hükümler* (n 10) 444; Artuk et al. (n 9) 742; Hakeri, *Ceza Hukuku Genel Hükümler* (n 17) 494.

In the present case, the decision not to carry on is not the result of any external circumstance restricting the perpetrator's autonomy and freedom of action. Therefore, the desistance is voluntary.

A second question is whether mere inaction by the perpetrator suffices for him or her to benefit from Article 36 TPC. According to the "holistic assessment theory", one must first assess whether the executory acts have been completed. By taking into account the legal definition of the offence in question, we must consider the following: If an additional (further) act is required for all the definitional elements of the crime to materialize and if this is possible in the instant case, the execution is not over; if there is no need for any further action for satisfying the elements of the offence, the executory acts have been completed.[65] According to this distinction, in our case the executory acts are not yet over: the injuries are not lethal, and for death to occur, it is necessary – and indeed within the possibility of the perpetrator – to further stab the victim.

According to the holistic theory, if the executory acts are not over the perpetrator must simply stop and remain inactive to benefit from the provision.[66] If the executory acts had been completed, mere inaction would not have sufficed,[67] and an active, conscious and serious personal effort by the perpetrator should have been in place to prevent the crime's completion.[68]

In our case, as we determined that the executory acts are not over, the decision by D to leave the victim alone is sufficient to benefit from Article 36 TPC.

However, at the time of the previous Penal Code, different theories had been put forward to decide whether executory acts had been completed. Under the previous Code, the punishability of the attempt was determined according to whether executory acts were interrupted or whether executory acts had been completed, but the crime could not be completed nonetheless. The new Code does not rely on this distinction, so the matter is no longer the object of much doctrinal debate. Therefore, the theories below, which had been advanced at the time of the previous Code and had different purposes, must be approached with caution.

The majority opinion at that time was based on objective theories. Even today, it may be argued that an objective approach has to be taken to the matter since the TPC is based on an objective understanding of determining whether executory acts have commenced; hence the same criteria should determine whether they have ended.[69]

According to different variations of objective theories, executory acts have been completed if all acts which are necessary and sufficient to realize the typical result

---

65 Akbulut (n 10) 837; Öztürk and Erdem (n 4) mn. 646.

66 Akbulut (n 10) 837.

67 Özbek et al. (n 25) 464; Centel, Zafer and Çakmut (n 10) 476.

68 Akbulut (n 10) 836; Sözüer (n 59) 250; Öztürk and Erdem (n 4) mn. 645; Hakeri, *Ceza Hukuku Genel Hükümler* (n 17) 490.

69 Öztürk and Erdem (n 4) mn. 646; Özgenç (n 7) 577; Artuk et al. (n 9) 731; Sözüer (n 59) 225.

have been committed,[70] or if the acts done so far are objectively suitable to realize the result (and typicity in general).[71] This assessment would be made in light of the knowledge and foresight of an average person of normal life experience.[72] According to this theory, in our case it may be argued that the executory acts were completed, because stabbing someone in the back three times is sufficient and suitable to bring about his or her death. In that case, if we were to further argue that a personal, active and serious effort is needed by the perpetrator to prevent the typical result from occurring, D would not be able to benefit from the provision of Article 36 TPC.

Another popular theory advanced at the time of the previous Code was the "deletion of the traces and effects of the act" theory, which argued that executory acts have not been completed if the perpetrator, at the time when the obstacle arose, had the power to eliminate the traces and effects of the acts committed so far.[73] This theory would also lead to the conclusion that the executory acts were completed in our case: The victim's wounds cannot be undone.

Returning to today's academic views, many authors do not seem to make a distinction based on whether executory acts have been completed. They in any event require an active (and serious) effort by the perpetrator for withdrawal in accordance with Article 36 TPC. The Court of Cassation also went that direction in various cases. In one case, the perpetrator had stabbed an elderly woman (who was a neighbour) various times in a life-threatening way, but had then asked the victim if she was dead and if she would complain against him. Upon learning that she was alive and that she would not complain, he returned to his own flat and told his relatives to check on the victim as "something had happened" to her. The relatives then reached the victim and called an ambulance, which took her to the hospital in time. The Court decided that Article 36 TPC was inapplicable since "there was no serious effort to prevent the result from occurring other than telling his mother that something had happened to the victim". (Interestingly, the Court also argued that the perpetrator's acts were not based on voluntariness.)[74] In fact, in one judgment the Court went so far as to demand that the perpetrator "mobilize all of his or her abilities",[75] thus requiring a very serious personal effort. However, in another case it was deemed sufficient that the perpetrator asked one of his workers to take the victim to the hospital.[76] In any case, an active and personal effort was required in these cases.

In conclusion, according to the majority academic opinion and the case law of the Court of Cassation, D would not benefit from the provision on voluntary withdrawal:

---

70 Sulhi Dönmezer and Sahir Erman, *Nazari ve Tatbiki Ceza Hukuku C I* (12th ed., Beta 1997) mn. 569; Demirbaş, *Genel Hükümler* (n 5) 516.

71 Öztürk and Erdem (n 4) mn. 646.

72 Sözüer (n 59) 223.

73 Sulhi Dönmezer and Sahir Erman, *Nazari ve Tatbiki Ceza Hukuku C I* (11th ed., Beta 1994) mn. 572; Demirbaş, *Genel Hükümler* (n 5) 516; Artuk et al. (n 9) 731. Basically, if the perpetrator had the possibility to "erase" or, so to say, to rewind his or her actions so far as to make its signs disappear, executory acts were considered not to be over.

74 Court of Cassation Grand Criminal Chamber, 2013/1–126, 11.07.2014.

75 Court of Cassation Grand Criminal Chamber, 2011/1–692, 21.02.2012.

76 Court of Cassation 1st Criminal Chamber, 2012/3191, 11.09.2012.

Since her attempt had already been completed a concrete counteraction is required for her to benefit from the institution of voluntary withdrawal; lacking such counteraction on the part of D, she would be punished for attempted murder. In other words, according to the objective approach taken by the legislature concerning attempts and voluntary withdrawal, once an attempt has been completed, simple desistance would not suffice.

Vignette 8: Criminal Responsibility of Minors

D is a 13-year-old boy. He abducts and rapes V, a girl of the same age. Should D be punished for a criminal offence?

Article 31 TPC, entitled "minority of age", divides children into three groups in establishing their responsibility:

- Children who have not completed the age of 12 at the time of the commission of the act bear no criminal liability.[77] However, security measures specific to children *may* be applied.
- Children who have completed the age of 12 but not completed the age of 15 at the time of the commission of the act do not bear criminal liability if they were "unable to perceive the legal meaning and consequences of the act" (capacity to perceive) or if the "capacity to direct their behaviour was not sufficiently developed" (willpower). In this case, security measures specific to children[78] (see Article 56 TPC) *must be* applied. As for the criminal charge, the court will decide that "there is no need to inflict criminal punishment due to lack of culpability" (Article 223 (3)(a) Criminal Procedure Code). If, however, the child has the capacity to perceive and the requisite willpower, he or she will be held criminally responsible, but a mandatory reduction of punishment will apply (12 to 15 years instead of aggravated life sentence, 9 to 11 years instead of a life sentence, reduction by one half and a maximum punishment of 7 years for other crimes).
- Children who have completed the age of 15 but not completed the age of 18 at the time of the commission of the act bear criminal liability, but a mandatory reduction of punishment is applied (18 to 24 years instead of aggravated life sentence, 12 to 15 years instead of life sentence, reduction by one third and a maximum punishment of 12 years for other crimes).

In our case, the perpetrator, being 13 years of age, would fall within the second group. Hence, an expert witness examination would have to take place[79] to determine whether he had the capacity to perceive and the requisite willpower at the time of the commission of the crime. In addition, a "social examination report" is required (Ar-

---

77 Under the previous Penal Code, which was in force from 1926 until 31 May 2005, the requirement was to have completed 11 years of age.

78 These "protective" and "supportive" measures are listed in Article 5 (1) of the Child Protection Act. These measures include counselling, education, care, health, and sheltering.

79 This examination has to be performed by an expert physician, Centel, Zafer and Çakmut (n 10) 411. This could be a forensic science expert, a psychiatrist or another expert physician, Demirbaş, *Genel Hükümler* (n 5) 377.

ticle 35 Child Protection Act). The expert report should refer to issues such as the family environment, social environment, education, physical and mental development of the child.[80] Both examinations (expert witness and social examination) must be conducted.[81] The determination as to the existence of criminal capacity is left to the judge.[82] The judge considers the expert report and the social examination report in conjunction to reach a conclusion.[83]

Academic writers agree that this examination should be done in light of the particular crime.[84] A child may have criminal capacity with regard to a given act but not with regard to a different act. The Court of Cassation is of the same view.[85]

If the result of the examination is positive, D would be held responsible for the crime of "qualified sexual exploitation of minors" (Article 103 (2) TPC), which punishes the insertion of an organ or object into the body of the victim as an aggravated circumstance of the crime. If further aggravating circumstances are absent, the punishment is 16 to 20 years of imprisonment. If further aggravating circumstances exist, the initial punishment could be life imprisonment. On account of Article 31 (2) TPC, D would be punishable by a maximum of 7 years imprisonment.

In addition, D would also be held responsible – and punished cumulatively – for the crime of deprivation of personal liberty regulated in Article 109 TPC, with the further application of the aggravating circumstance laid down in para. 5, namely the commission of the crime with a sexual purpose, and of the aggravating circumstance laid down in para. 3, comma (f), namely the commission of the act against a child. A further aggravating circumstance applies if the act has been committed through violence, threat or deceit (para. 2) – which is likely the case for D since he abducted the victim. Thus, in connection with this deprivation of liberty D would be liable to imprisonment of 6 to 21 years, which would mean, by virtue of Article 31 (2) TPC, that he would be punishable with up to 7 years of imprisonment.

As a final note, there seems to be no academic criticism regarding the *minimum* age requirement in Turkish criminal law. Textbooks dealing with the issue do not seem to object to the determination of the limit at 12 years of age. However, criticism is directed at the fact that punishment has to be imposed on children who had reached the age of 12 and had the capacity to perceive and the requisite willpower at the time of the commission of the act. It is argued that this approach violates the basic principle in Art. 4, comma (i) of the Child Protection Act, which requires that measures consisting of deprivation of liberty and imprisonment should be the last resort.[86] Similarly, it

80 Koca and Üzülmez, *Genel Hükümler* (n 10) 322.

81 Akbulut (n 10) 710. In the same direction, Court of Cassation Grand Criminal Chamber, 2018/154, 18.04.2019.

82 Koca and Üzülmez, *Genel Hükümler* (n 10) 322–323; Akbulut (n 10) 709.

83 Ali Rıza Çınar, *Çocuk Ceza Hukuku* (Yetkin 2020) 58; Demirbaş, *Genel Hükümler* (n 5) 378; Akbulut (n 10) 710.

84 Centel, Zafer and Çakmut (n 10) 411; Artuk et al. (n 9) 634; Hakeri, *Ceza Hukuku Genel Hükümler* (n 17) 366; Koca and Üzülmez, *Genel Hükümler* (n 10) 323; Demirbaş, *Genel Hükümler* (n 5) 378.

85 Court of Cassation Grand Criminal Chamber, 2018/13–154, 18.04.2019.

86 Artuk et al. (n 9) 635; Akbulut (n 10) 706.

is argued that the law should be amended so that the court is empowered to decide on the application of security measures instead of criminal punishment, even where the child has criminal capacity.[87] However, in response to some heinous crimes committed by minors, the government is now contemplating to amend the provisions of Art. 31 but no official proposal has yet been made.

Vignette 9: Statute of Limitations

In 1995, D violently raped V, a 35-year-old woman, using a knife. D managed to escape and was not apprehended until 2023. Traces of his DNA taken from the victim's body leave no doubt that D is the perpetrator. Should D be convicted despite the long delay?

The Turkish legal system recognises the institution of the statute of limitations in two forms: limitation on prosecution and on enforcement.[88] The Turkish statute of limitations is based on a temporal relationship, and the lapse of time bars either prosecution or enforcement of punishment, depending on the particularities of the case at hand. As D was not apprehended until 2023, the time periods for limitations on prosecution, enshrined in Article 66 (1) TPC, are relevant here:

"Unless otherwise provided for by law, criminal proceedings shall be discontinued upon the lapse of:

a) Thirty years for offences requiring a penalty of aggravated life imprisonment;

b) Twenty-five years for offences requiring a penalty of life imprisonment;

c) Twenty years for offences requiring a penalty of imprisonment of not less than twenty years;

d) Fifteen years for offences requiring a penalty of more than five years and less than twenty years;

e) Eight years for offences requiring a penalty of imprisonment of not more than five years or a judicial fine."[89]

In determining the limitation period, the qualified forms of an offence demanding the imposition of a heavier or lighter punishment shall be taken into consideration.[90] As a rule, all offences are subject to the limitation periods listed above. The Penal

---

87 Demirbaş, *Genel Hükümler* (n 5) 380; Nur Centel, in: Celal Ülgen (ed.), *Çocuk ve Genç Adaleti Sistemi Sempozyumu (4–5 Haziran 2005)* (İstanbul Barosu Yayınları 2006) 36.

88 We solve the present case using the current Penal Code. However, as D committed the offence in 1995, the provisions of the former Penal Code should have been applied since that Code's provided for considerably shorter periods of limitation. The relatively long limitation periods in the present Code can be regarded as a reaction to the relatively short limitation periods of the former Code (see Article 102 of the former Penal Code).

89 The time period for the enforcement of penalties is longer since it applies to cases in which the guilt of the offender has already been established. Article 68 (1) TPC provides the following limitation periods on punishment:
a) 40 years for aggravated life imprisonment;
b) 30 years for life imprisonment;
c) 24 years for a term of imprisonment of twenty years or more;
d) 10 years for a term of imprisonment of up to five years and a judicial fine.

90 Article 66 (3) TPC.

Code, however, provides for an exception for the crime of genocide, crimes against humanity, and establishing an organization to commit these offences.[91]

The limitation period shall be determined pursuant to the highest penalty for the qualified version of the offence, which shall be determined on the basis of the evidence recorded in the dossier. In determining the limitation period, the upper limit of the penalty for the crime stated in the law is to be considered.[92]

In the present case, D committed a sexual assault against V, which, according to Article 102 (2) TPC, requires a punishment of not less than twelve years. The upper limit of the penalty to be imposed in cases of aggravated sexual assault is not expressly regulated. Article 49 TPC states that the upper limit should be 20 years for crimes with an indeterminate upper limit. For this reason, the judge should consider 20 years as the upper limit when determining the penalty for the crime of qualified sexual assault (Article 102 f. 2 TPC). For determining the period of limitation, the upper limit of the penalty of the crime stated in the law should be considered (Article 66, para. 4 TPC). In our case, as a rule, the 20-year period should be taken as a basis for determining the period of limitation for the crime of sexual assault (Article 102 f. 2 TPC). Because the knife is considered a weapon and D has used it while committing the offence, his punishment shall be increased by one-half per Article 102 (3) (d) TPC. Thus, the limitation period for D's act is twenty years, as his act can be punished by thirty years of imprisonment. As D committed the offence in 1995, the commencement of the limitation period needs to be determined. The commencement of the limitation period is set out in Art. 66 (6) TPC:

> For completed offences, the limitation period shall begin on the day the offence was committed; for attempted offences, on the day when the last act was committed; for continuous offences, on the day when the continuing act ended; for successive offences, on the date of commission of the last offence, and for crimes committed against children by their direct ascendant or persons who have influence upon them, the limitation period shall begin on the day when the child turns eighteen years of age.

As the period starts running from the day the offence was completed (in the present case, 1995), and there is no indication regarding statutory grounds for tolling or interrupting the running of the limitation period,[93] D's offence was prescribed in 2015. Therefore, he cannot be convicted. Even if the legislature, disturbed by such cases, decides to expand or lift the time limitations on prosecution, this would not impact the present case, for the statute of limitations in Turkish criminal law is subject to the strict legality principle. Article 38 of the Turkish Constitution is explicit on this matter:

> No one shall be punished for any act that does not constitute a criminal offence under the law in force at the time committed; no one shall be given a heavier penalty for an offence other than the penalty applicable when the offence was committed.

---

91 Articles 76 (4), 77 (4) and 78 (3) TPC explicitly provide that the mentioned crimes are imprescriptible.

92 Article 66 (4) TPC.

93 See Article 67 TPC.

The provisions of the above paragraph shall also apply to the statute of limitations on offences and penalties and on the results of conviction.

As a consequence of this provision of the Constitution, the substantive or strict legality principle must also be applied to the statute of limitations, which includes, to be sure, the prohibition of retroactive application of penal norms; the accused will hence be subject to the limitation period in effect at the time of the commission of the criminal act. In light of this provision of the Constitution, the Constitutional Court classifies the statute of limitations as an institution of substantive criminal law, and accordingly, the legislation concerning the statute of limitations has been tested against the criteria of the strict principle of legality.[94] In other words, under the *lex mitior* principle, Article 38 of the Constitution precludes the immediate application of an extension of statutory limitations, for this would be to the detriment of the alleged offender. To be sure, a case that had already been prescribed under the statute of limitations cannot be resuscitated under a new law after the original limitation period has elapsed. Besides, it would also be unwise to hold a person criminally liable after a long passage of time.

Vignette 10: Life Imprisonment without Parole

The Penal Code of State S provides for imprisonment for life as the maximum penalty for murder, but also authorises the court to order an offender's early release after a minimum of 15 years if the offender is no longer dangerous. Reacting to cases of particularly heinous murders, the legislature of S wishes to introduce a penalty of life imprisonment without any possibility of early release, regardless of the offender's continued dangerousness. Would this amendment be acceptable?

Case 1: In Turkey, on New Year's Eve 2017, around 01:15 am, a single gunman entered a famous nightclub on the Bosphorus and shot dead 39 and wounded 71 persons. The mass shooting at an Istanbul nightclub was carried out professionally and claimed by the DAESH terror organisation.

Case 2: In New Zealand, on 15 March 2019, 51 persons were killed after a single gunman opened fire at two Christchurch mosques. Another 89 persons were injured, with one person dying of his injuries seven weeks later.

Both perpetrators of these attacks were sentenced to life imprisonment without parole for each charge of murder by the respective courts of these jurisdictions. In the Turkish legal system, life imprisonment without parole is confined to certain terroristic offences and crimes against the security of the state, like the one described above.[95] Apart from these exceptions, an offender who receives a life sentence would be eligible for early release after serving a minimum term in prison. This minimum term for a life sentence is twenty-four years, and for the so-called aggravated life sentence, thirty years.[96]

---

94 *Sait Özdemir* App no 2015/39 (Turkish Constitutional Court [Anayasa Mahkemesi], 11 October 2018.

95 Code on the Execution for Penalties and Security Measures, Article 107 (16).

96 Code on the Execution for Penalties and Security Measures, Article 107 (2).

Arguably, sentences of life imprisonment without parole are increasingly finding favour in legislatures worldwide. The judge in the Christchurch terror attack case, who sentenced the perpetrator to a whole-life sentence, probably provided one of the best justifications for this form of punishment:

> The question that has arisen for me is how can a free and democratic society adequately respond to a crime of such exceptional seriousness — that takes the lives of innocent men, women and children on such a wholesale scale with such animus, and with such malice and callous indifference? Parliament has provided a sanction for such crimes in the form of a life sentence without parole that can only be imposed in the case of the very worst murders. Its use must be taken to have been intended only when the circumstances clearly warrant its imposition. The unavoidable rhetorical question in sentencing you today is, if not here, then when?
>
> The need to make an order that you serve your sentence without parole does not primarily arise from deterrence nor from the need to protect the community from you, powerful as both considerations are when dealing with an offender capable of such terrible crimes and the necessity of delivering a cogent message that the commission of such an atrocity will be met with the most condign response. However, I am mindful that as the years pass and you become a much older man, the risk you pose could be reassessed. The need for deterrence is also clear, but the deluded motivation of zealots capable of such crimes, with their overvalued beliefs that feed such extreme violence, are less likely to be tempered by the fear of penal consequences no matter how severe.
>
> Your crimes, however, are so wicked that even if you are detained until you die, it will not exhaust the requirements of punishment and denunciation. Those legitimate penological grounds for continued detention will remain. At nearly 30 years of age, you are a relatively young man and the justifications for your continued detention over time may shift as the years pass. Some may change, but I do not consider, however long the length of your incarceration during your lifetime, that it could, even in a modest way, atone for what you have done. Ordinarily, such an approach would be a poor guarantee of just and proportionate punishment, but I consider yours to be one of those exceedingly rare cases that are different."[97]

Justice Mander's remarkable opinion highlights the main arguments favouring a life sentence without parole, that is, some crimes are so heinous that they deserve life-long incarceration for purposes of pure punishment; and some crimes are so wicked that even if the prisoner is detained for the whole of his natural life, it will not exhaust the requirements of retribution and deterrence. It is evident that now, where the death penalty is no longer available, the only suitable punishment in such cases would be incarceration for the rest of the prisoner's natural life. In other words, the emerging approach in sentencing regards life imprisonment not as a finite period short of the prisoner's natural life. One could, therefore, argue that a life sentence without parole is meant to serve retributive demands of the public consciousness and restore public order by communicating such a harsh condemnation to meet the enhanced security needs of the people.

The imposition of an irreducible life sentence has nevertheless been criticised in Turkish literature due to the lack of a prospect of release. The European Court of Hu-

---

97 *The Queen v. Brenton Harrison Tarrant* CRI–2019–009–2468 NZHC 21292 (The High Court of New Zealand, 2020) paras. 182–184.

man Rights, however, made clear that there is no violation of Article 3 ECHR if a prisoner, in fact, spends the whole remainder of his life in prison. If, for instance, an offender continues to be a risk for the whole of his or her life, he or she may not be released because of public security concerns.[98] For the compatibility of such a life sentence with the ECHR, the Strasbourg Court requires that domestic law furnishes a so-called prospect for release. For instance, it has been found that Turkish (and English) whole-life sentences, which have been criticized in the Turkish literature,[99] are incompatible with the European Convention on Human Rights.[100]

A further argument regarding the acceptability of a life sentence without parole would be peculiar to jurisdictions where the abolition of the death penalty is not yet taken for granted or has at least not fully acknowledged by the people. Enhanced life sentences have been designed to meet the need for strict punishment in a given society. It therefore does not come as a surprise that in Turkey the public demands harsh punishment and even, in some instances, the reintroduction of the death penalty after a heinous murder has been committed. Indeed, cases of callous and malevolent murders immensely upset the social order. In the recent past, for instance, a minibus driver abducted a university student he was meant to drive home from university, raped and burnt her while she was still alive; a young man attacked a young girl with a samurai sword for no particular reason and brutally killed her; most recently, a taxi driver took a masked man into the cab because it was cold and was callously killed while the murderer mocked the taxi driver for "trusting him". The whole nation watched the act of murder over the CCTV recording in the car. These acts of murder would be considered to be qualified intentional killings. Because of the elements of premeditation and gruesome killing, the perpetrators in these cases would receive aggravated life sentences with a thirty-year minimum term of imprisonment. Such acts of murder could also be qualified as heinous and exceptionally grave, and an ordinary life sentence would be regarded as unduly lenient. That said, it is open to debate whether judges should in such cases be granted discretionary powers to impose life sentences without parole.

Accordingly, if a legislature in a given polity decides to introduce a penalty of life imprisonment without any possibility of early release, such an amendment would be solely acceptable under strict circumstances and only for certain grave offences as a necessary evil. The heinousness of his offence notwithstanding, a criminal justice system should provide to a person sentenced to life imprisonment without parole the hope for a possibility of release in exceptional circumstances. Such circumstances can render the just punishment initially imposed no longer justifiable in circumstances where, for instance, a prisoner is suffering from a terminal illness or is bedridden or similarly incapacitated.

---

98 Such a sentence, however, could be regarded as a violation of Article 3 of the ECHR if the domestic law does not furnish a prospect for release. *Vinter and Others v. The United Kingdom* App no 66069/09, 130/10 and 3896/10 (ECtHR, 9 July 2013) paras. 108 ff.; see further Öztürk and Erdem (n 4) 557.

99 Özgenç (n 7) 880 f.; Öztürk and Erdem (n 4) 556 ff.; Demirbaş, *Genel Hükümler* (n 5) 749 ff.; Centel, Zafer and Çakmut (n 10) 690.

100 See, for instance, *Vinter and Others v. The United Kingdom* (n 98) paras. 108 ff.; *Kaytan v. Turkey* App no 27422/05, (ECtHR, 15 December 2015) paras. 52 ff.

16. U.S.A.

By *Sara Sun Beale**

Vignette 1: Trolley Problem – Killing one Person to Save Many

Five young children are playing on railway tracks. An express train is approaching, and it is too late to stop the train before it hits the children, probably killing them. Operator D recognizes the emergency situation. He electronically flips a switch and thus deflects the train from its regular track to a little-used sidetrack. However, the lone repairman V is busy on the sidetrack, and the deflected train kills V, as D had anticipated. Is D criminally responsible for murder of V?

The Trolley Problem implicates the justification defense and "choice-of-evils" doctrine. At common law, justification/choice-of-evils was not a defense to intentional homicide.[1] The common law approach reflected the sentiment that the death of an innocent person was at least as harmful as any other potential offense.[2] In other words, no harm could be evil enough to justify the taking of an innocent life.

The drafters of the Model Penal Code (MPC) rejected the common law approach. Model Penal Code § 3.02(1)(a) introduced a general justification defense that did not exclude intentional homicide. It provides that otherwise illegal conduct may be justified (and therefore legal) if the actor believes that the conduct is necessary to avoid a comparably greater harm to himself or another.[3] Acknowledging the supreme value placed on the sanctity of life, the MPC Commentaries argued that "[i]t would be particularly unfortunate to exclude homicidal conduct from the scope of the defense," because "conduct that results in taking life may promote the very value sought to be protected by the law of homicide."[4] If a defendant's intentional homicide resulted in a net saving of innocent lives, for example, then the justification defense should apply.[5]

States have split on whether to follow the restrictive common law or the more expansive MPC approach. New York law incorporates the MPC approach, allowing for the justification defense in a homicide case – though there are slight deviations from MPC § 3.02(1)(a). Other states, such as Kentucky, follow the common law and preclude the justification defense in any charge of intentional homicide.

---

* Charles L.B. Lowndes Professor of Law Emerita, Duke Law School.

1 See John Alan Cohan, *Homicide by Necessity*, 10 Chap. L. Rev. 119, 120 (2006) ("At common law and almost universally in modern law, the necessity defense has been consistently denied in cases where the actor commits intentional homicide in order to avert a greater evil."); *Regina v. Dudley & Stevens*, 14 Q.B.D. 273 (1884) (finding sailors guilty of murder after killing and eating a crew member while lost at sea).

2 See, e.g., *United States v. LaFleur*, 971 F.2d 200, 205 (9th Cir. 1991) ("When the defendant commits murder under duress, the resulting harm – i.e. the death of an innocent person – is at least as great as the threatened harm – i.e. the death of the defendant.").

3 Model Penal Code § 3.02 (Am. L. Inst.).

4 MPC Part I Commentaries, art. 3, at 14 (1985).

5 Ibid. at 15.

a) New York

In New York, the justification defense is codified at Penal Law § 35.05(2), which states in relevant part:

> Conduct which would otherwise constitute an offense is justifiable and not criminal when [...] [s]uch conduct is necessary as an emergency measure to avoid an imminent public or private injury which is about to occur by reason of a situation occasioned or developed through no fault of the actor, and which is of such gravity that, according to ordinary standards of intelligence and morality, the desirability and urgency of avoiding such injury clearly outweigh the desirability of avoiding the injury sought to be prevented by the statute defining the offense in issue.[6]

If the court finds as a matter of law that the defendant has alleged facts sufficient to satisfy these requirements, it must submit the defense to the jury.[7]

The New York law imposes several limits on the defense. First, the harm caused by the person seeking to raise the defense must be necessary to avoid a comparably worse harm.[8] The conduct must be both "warranted by the circumstances" and "reasonably calculated to have an actual effect in preventing the harm." The defense excludes "conduct for which there is a reasonable, legal alternative course of action."[9] The harm caused must also be an "evil" in and of itself,[10] and the defendant must make an affirmative choice to cause such harm in an attempt to avoid the comparably greater harm.[11] Finally, the harm sought to avoid must be imminent, and "a present, immediate threat – i. e., a danger that is actual and at hand, not one that is speculative, abstract or remote."[12]

Applied to the Trolley problem, D would likely be able to assert the New York justification defense against a charge of V's murder.[13] The harm D sought to avoid, the probable death of five children, appears to be imminent and occasioned through no fault of D. The harm to be caused, the death of V, was an affirmative "evil" choice made by D. The remaining two prongs, necessity and comparative desirability, are issues for the jury. Assuming there was no reasonable alternative to protect the children, a jury would likely find that V's death was objectively necessary to protect the children. A more difficult question is whether a jury would find that "ordinary stan-

---

6 N.Y. Penal Law § 35.05(2).

7 See ibid. ("[W]henever evidence relating to the defense of justification under this subdivision is offered by the defendant, the court shall rule as a matter of law whether the claimed facts and circumstances would, if established, constitute a defense."). See *generally* N.Y. Crim. Jury Instr. 2d Penal Law § 35.05(2) (model jury instructions on justification defense).

8 See *People v. Maher*, 79 N.Y.2d 978, 982 (1992) ("It is not for the trial court to hypothesize other reasonable alternatives to the course of action chosen by the defendant.").

9 Ibid.

10 See *Rodriguez*, 16 N.Y.3d at 345 ("To be entitled to such a charge there must be two 'evils'.").

11 See *People v. Jimenez*, 39 N.Y.3d 74, 79 (2022) ("Choice is a necessary prerequisite to this justification defense, hence the common reference to it as the 'choice of evils' defense.").

12 *People v. Craig*, 78 N.Y.2d 616, 624 (1991).

13 This presupposes that, absent the intention to save the children, D would be guilty of murder.

dards of intelligence and morality"[14] deem taking V's life to be objectively more desirable than allowing the death of five children.[15] If the jury does find for D on these two prongs, he would not be criminally liable for V's death.

b) Kentucky

This defense of justification/choice-of-evils would not be available in Kentucky, which explicitly excludes intentional homicide from the defense. In Kentucky, "conduct which would otherwise constitute an offense is justifiable when the defendant believes it to be necessary to avoid an imminent public or private injury greater than the injury which is sought to be prevented by the statute defining the offense charged."[16] But unlike New York law, the Kentucky statute states that "no justification can exist under this section for an intentional homicide."[17] This exclusion of intentional homicide from the defense follows the traditional common law, rather than the more expansive approach taken by MPC § 3.02. Since the Trolley Problem involves the intentional killing of V, in Kentucky D would not be able to invoke the justification defense and D could be convicted of murder.

Vignette 2: Attribution of Death

> D intends to kill his neighbor V. Hidden near V's house, D waits for V and stabs him several times with a knife. V is taken to the hospital, where his wounds are treated. His injuries are not life-threatening and V is kept overnight for observation. During the night, a technical defect in the hospital kitchen leads to the outbreak of a fire, which kills V and other persons. Can D be held criminally responsible for V's death?

V's death as a result of the hospital fire, rather than the stabbing, raises causation issues. In the United States, there are two main approaches to causation: the common law and Model Penal Code (MPC) approaches. Although the analysis differs to some degree, it is unlikely that D could be held criminally responsible for V's death under either approach.

a) The Common Law Approach – California

In homicide cases, the California courts have held that "a cause of the death of [the decedent] is an act or omission that sets in motion a chain of events that produces as a direct, natural and probable consequence of the act or omission the death of [the decedent] and without which the death would not occur."[18]

---

14 N.Y. Penal Law § 35.05(2).

15 The drafters of the MPC would likely find that this net saving of innocent lives is objectively more desirable than the saving of one innocent life.

16 Ky. Rev. Stat. Ann. § 503.030 (West 2023).

17 Ibid.

18 *People v. Cervantes*, 29 P.3d 225, 229 (Cal. 2001) (quoting California Jury Instructions: Criminal § 3.40 (7th ed. 2005)).

Under California's approach, the defendant's conduct must be the proximate cause of the victim's death.[19] Proximate cause turns on the relation between the actor's conduct and the result. Where the defendant's act is directly connected with the victim's death, proximate cause is clearly established.[20] But an intervening cause may preclude liability. The common law approach differentiates between independent and dependent intervening causes, with independent causes absolving the defendant from liability while dependent causes do not. The California courts have held that to be independent, an intervening cause must be an "unforeseeable [...] extraordinary and abnormal occurrence, which rises to the level of an exonerating, superseding cause."[21] California courts ask whether the independent intervening cause itself or the injury it caused were foreseeable to the defendant.[22] If neither the intervening cause nor the actual results were foreseeable, the defendant will be relieved from liability.[23] In contrast, defendants will be held criminally responsible if the intervening cause is dependent, or a "normal and reasonably foreseeable result of defendant's original act."[24] In evaluating foreseeability, it is sufficient that a consequence "might reasonably have been contemplated."[25] Therefore, causation under the common law approach focuses on foreseeability.

Here, the fire that caused V's death is unlikely to be viewed as a reasonably foreseeable result of D's stabbing. The defense will argue that a kitchen fire killing a hospital patient is an unforeseeable, extraordinary, and abnormal occurrence that could not be predicted to result from a stabbing. Though the California courts have recognized that something less than a strong probability may be sufficient for liability,[26] D will likely be successful in claiming that death caused by a fire is not a consequence that might have been reasonably contemplated.

b) The MPC Approach – Pennsylvania

The Model Penal Code defines causation in Section 2.03,[27] and the drafters rejected the common law's focus on proximate cause,[28] opting instead for an approach that

---

19 *People v. Morgan*, 225 Cal. Rptr. 673, 674 (Cal. Ct. App. 1985).

20 See *Cervantes*, 29 P.3d at 229.

21 See ibid. at 232–33.

22 See *People v. Brady*, 29 Cal. Rptr. 3d 286, 295–96 (Cal. Ct. App. 2005) (explaining that proximate cause "revolves around a determination of whether the later cause of independent origin, commonly referred to as an intervening cause, was foreseeable by the defendant or, if not foreseeable, whether it caused injury of a type which was foreseeable").

23 Ibid.

24 *Zemek v. Superior Court*, 257 Cal. Rptr. 3d 729, 745 (Cal. Ct. App. 2020).

25 *Cervantes*, 29 P.3d at 232–33.

26 See ibid. at 233 ("The consequence need not have been a strong probability [...] [t]he precise consequence need not have been foreseen; it is enough that the defendant should have foreseen the possibility of some harm of the kind which might result from his act.").

27 Model Penal Code and Commentaries § 2.03 (Am. L. Inst., Official Draft and Revised Comments 1985).

28 The MPC drafters aimed to do away with "encrusted precedents on proximate causation, by reference to doctrines of dependent supervening and independent supervening causes." Ibid. at § 2.03, cmt. 2 at 258.

premises liability on the actor's mental culpability as to causing a prohibited result. The only strictly causal component of the provision is the but-for-causation analysis in § 2.03(1)(a) MPC, which states that conduct constitutes the cause of a result if "it is an antecedent but for which the result in question would not have occurred."[29] The rest of § 2.03 MPC, however, requires a jury determination of the propriety of allowing the result to influence the defendant's criminality.

Since the vignette includes an attempted homicide, § 2.03(2) MPC[30] governs the causation analysis, and § 2.03(2)(b) MPC governs where the actual result "involves the same kind of injury or harm as that designed or contemplated, but in which the precise injury inflicted was different or occurred in a different way."[31] Section 2.03(2)(b) MPC instructs juries to evaluate causation in such situations based on whether "the actual result involves the same kind of injury or harm as that designed or contemplated and is not too remote or accidental in its occurrence to have a [just] bearing on the actor's liability or on the gravity of his offense."[32] The MPC commentaries make clear that in contrasting the actual result with the designed result, the focus should be on the "specific character and manner of occurrence."[33] The MPC drafters recognized that the variety of situations that raise causation issues "preclude an advance catalogue of premises that can be used mechanically to deduce a solution."[34] Accordingly, the drafters placed the responsibility for making the ultimate causation determination on the jury.

Section 2.03 MPC has had little influence on state criminal codes. Many criminal codes include no causation provision,[35] and only seven states have adopted causation provisions influenced by the MPC,[36] not all of which closely follow the MPC's approach to causation.[37]

---

29 Ibid. at § 2.03(1)(a).

30 This section covers result crimes where "purposely or knowingly causing a particular result is an element of an offense." Ibid. at § 2.03(2).

31 Ibid. at § 2.03, cmt. 3 at 261.

32 Ibid. at § 2.03(2)(b).

33 Ibid. at § 2.03, cmt. 5 at 266.

34 Ibid. at § 2.03, cmt. 3 at 262.

35 Ibid. at § 2.03, cmt. 5 at 265; Paul H. Robinson, *The Model Penal Code's Conceptual Error on the Nature of Proximate Cause, and How to Fix It*, 51 Crim. L. Bull. 1311, 1325 (2015) ("[M]ost states, even those with Model Penal Code-based criminal codes, reject the Code's causation provision. Every modern American recodification – three-quarters of the states – are based in significant part on the Model Code, yet its approach to causation is rejected in forty-three jurisdictions.").

36 See Ariz. Rev. Stat. § 13-203 (LexisNexis 2023); Del. Code Ann. tit. 11, §§ 261–262 (2024); Haw. Code R. §§ 702-214–702-215 (LexisNexis 2023); Ky. Rev. Stat. Ann. § 501.060 (LexisNexis 2023); Mont. Code Ann. § 45-2-201; N.J. Rev. Stat. § 2C:2-3 (2023); 18 Pa. Cons. Stat. § 303 (2023).

37 Hawaii and New Jersey modified MPC subsections 2.03(2)(b) and (3)(b) by adding an inquiry into whether the actual result was dependent on another's volitional conduct to give explicit weight to intervening volitional action as a factor that might relieve an actor from liability. See Haw. Code R. § 702-215 (LexisNexis 2023); N.J. Rev. Stat. § 2C:2-3 (2023). Arizona and Kentucky adopted the language from the MPC draft proposal that asks whether the result "occurs in a manner which the person knows or should know is rendered substantially

Pennsylvania adopted § 2.03 MPC virtually verbatim.[38] Courts in Pennsylvania follow a two-step process to determine causation. First, but-for causation or "cause in fact," must be established by showing the defendant's conduct was "an antecedent but for which the result in question would not have occurred."[39] Second, Pennsylvania courts require a showing of legal cause which necessitates asking "whether the result[s] of defendant's actions were so extraordinarily remote or attenuated that it would be unfair to hold the defendant criminally responsible."[40] Legal cause is established by showing that "the victim's death [was] the natural or foreseeable consequence of the defendant's actions."[41] Pennsylvania courts have recognized that juries must use their common sense and sense of justice to determine "whether the actual result has bearing on the actor's culpability or whether the result was too remote to have such bearing."[42] Normative values should prevent the jury from finding causation "if the fatal result was an unnatural or obscure consequence of the defendant's actions."[43] Thus, as applied by the Pennsylvania courts, the MPC approach to causation also turns on foreseeability. But the MPC invokes foreseeability as a tool to inform the jury's determination of whether it is "just" to hold the defendant accountable, a much narrower use than the common law approach.

Under the MPC approach as applied in Pennsylvania, it is unlikely that D could be held criminally responsible for V's death. The first step of the analysis is satisfied. But for D's stabbing, V would not have been in the hospital when the fire broke out, and V's death would not have occurred. However, the facts likely fail the second step's analysis of legal cause. D has a strong argument that a hospital kitchen fire was "extraordinarily remote or attenuated," making it "unfair to hold [him] criminally responsible."[44] The character and manner of V's death by fire were not similar to the death D intended to result from stabbing. Dying from a hospital fire can hardly be seen as "the natural or foreseeable consequence" of a stabbing.[45] Here, the kitchen fire is a cause wholly unconnected to the defendant, and absent the fire V's stab wounds were not life-threatening. Therefore, it is probable that a jury will view the victim's death from a hospital fire as an "unnatural or obscure consequence" of the defendant's stabbing that should not fairly bear on the defendant's guilt.

---

more probable" by the defendant's conduct instead of the remoteness language adopted by § 2.03(2)(b). See Ky. Rev. Stat. Ann. § 501.060 (LexisNexis 2023); Ariz. Rev. Stat. § 13-203 (LexisNexis 2023).

38 18 Pa. Cons. Stat. § 303 (2023).

39 See ibid. at § 303(a)(1); *Commonwealth v. Rementer*, 598 A.2d 1300, 1305 (Pa. Super. Ct. 1991).

40 *Rementer*, 598 A.2d at 1305.

41 *Commonwealth v. Nunn*, 947 A.2d 756, 760 (Pa. Super. Ct. 2008).

42 *Rementer*, 598 A.2d at 1306, n. 5. Under the MPC approach, "criminal causation has come to involve a case-by-case social determination; i.e., is it just or fair under the facts of the case to expose the defendant to criminal sanctions." Ibid. at 1304.

43 See ibid. at 1306-07.

44 Ibid. at 1305.

45 *Commonwealth v. Nunn*, 947 A.2d 756, 760 (Pa. Super. Ct. 2008).

Vignette 3: Torture to Save a Life

> Kidnapper K has abducted an 8-year-old girl G and hidden her in a small cave in the woods. K is trying to extort money from G's parents for her release. The police manage to arrest K. Although being questioned for 24 hours, K steadfastly refuses to disclose where he hid G. Police officer D correctly assumes that G may soon die of thirst if she cannot be found. He therefore severely beats K to make him tell the truth. Fearing even more violence, K eventually leads the police to the cave, where they find G still barely alive. Should D be punished for torturing K?

The defense of necessity, sometimes referred to as "choice of evils," may justify D's severe beating of K in order to save G's life. Some states follow the common law approach to necessity. Many other states, despite some resistance to doing so, have codified the defense.[46] Where recognized, necessity is a public policy-rooted justification for an individual charged with criminal conduct.[47]

The necessity defense's contours vary across the United States, and whether D would have a defense to criminal charges would depend on the state in which he is prosecuted. The objective reasonableness approach, reflected in New York's statute, limits necessity to objectively reasonable emergency measures that avoid imminent injury. In contrast, other states, including California and Illinois, consider the actor's subjective beliefs as well as objective factors.[48] Finally, Wisconsin offers the most restricted form of the defense, limited to cases involving natural physical forces instead of human actions.

a) Objective Reasonableness – New York

In many U.S. states, the necessity defense's success depends on a series of objective factors, such as whether an emergency existed, how imminent the threatened injury was, and whether the defendant's choice to avoid a harm was reasonable.[49] New York's necessity defense is the most influential statute that takes this approach.[50] It states:

> Conduct which would otherwise constitute an offense is justifiable and not criminal when [...] [s]uch conduct is necessary as an emergency measure to avoid an imminent public or private injury which is about to occur by reason of a situation occasioned or developed through no fault of the actor, and which is of such gravity that, according to ordinary standards of intelligence and morality, the desirability and urgency of avoiding such injury clearly outweigh the desirability of avoiding the injury sought to be prevented by the statute defining the offense in issue.[51]

---

46 Michael H. Hoffheimer, *Codifying Necessity: Legislative Resistance to Enacting Choice-of-Evils Defenses to Criminal Liability*, 82 Tul. L. Rev. 191, 198 (2007) (noting that the need for a necessity defense may be reduced by the availability of prosecutorial discretion in charging and narrow judicial construction of criminal statutes).

47 2 Paul H. Robinson, Criminal Law Defenses § 124 (2023).

48 See *infra* Part I.

49 1 Jens David Ohlin, Wharton's Criminal Law § 15:3 (16th ed. 2023).

50 Hoffheimer, *supra* note 46, at 239.

51 N.Y. Penal Law § 35.05(2) (McKinney 2023).

The New York courts have characterized this as "an entirely objective test," noting it makes no reference "to what the actor intends, or believes to be necessary."[52] A defendant's conduct must have been an emergency response to avoid an imminent injury that was about to occur without any fault of the defendant. The defendant's choice must be objectively reasonable, weighing the harm the defendant averted against the interests protected by the statute in question.[53] The desirability of avoiding one harm must "clearly outweigh" the other harm the defendant caused as measured by "ordinary standards of intelligence and morality." The judge determines whether the defendant has presented sufficient facts to submit the case to the jury,[54] and if submitted the prosecution must disprove the justification beyond a reasonable doubt.[55] The legislative history suggests that the defense is only meant for "rare and highly unusual circumstances."[56]

D might have a successful defense in New York. G, who might die of thirst if not found, faced a present, immediate threat.[57] D's conduct was an emergency response, after alternatives were exhausted, reasonably calculated to reveal G's location.[58] A jury could find that the "ordinary standards of intelligence and morality" warranted D beating K to learn of G's location in time to avoid her death.

b) Mixed Objective and Subjective Approaches – California and Illinois

In other states, the necessity defense requires not only that the actor make a reasonable choice of evils, but also that the actor believe in the necessity of that choice.[59]

aa) California

California recognizes the common law defense of necessity.[60] The defense must be "of an emergency nature, threatening physical harm, and lacking an alternative, legal course of action."[61] A court is required to instruct the jury on the necessity defense where there is evidence sufficient to establish that the defendant violated the law

(1) to prevent a significant evil,

(2) with no adequate alternative,

(3) without creating a greater danger than the one avoided,

(4) with a good faith belief in the necessity,

---

52 *People v. Craig*, 585 N.E.2d 783, 786 (N.Y. 1991).

53 Ibid. at 785–86.

54 § 35.05(2) ("Whenever evidence relating to the defense of justification under this subdivision is offered by the defendant, the court shall rule as a matter of law whether the claimed facts and circumstances would, if established, constitute a defense.").

55 *People v. McManus*, 496 N.E.2d 202, 203 (N.Y. 1986).

56 *Craig*, 585 N.E.2d at 786.

57 See *id.* at 787.

58 See ibid.

59 See MPC Part I Commentaries, art. 3, at 14 (1985).

60 *People v. Garziano*, 281 Cal. Rptr. 307, 308 (Cal. Ct. App., 1991).

61 In re Eichorn, 81 Cal. Rptr. 2d 535, 539 (Cal. Ct. App., 1998).

(5) with such belief being objectively reasonable, and

(6) under circumstances in which he did not substantially contribute to the emergency.[62]

The first triggering condition is not difficult to meet. For instance, the Court of Appeal has held that sleep deprivation could be a "significant evil" in a prosecution for sleeping in a public area.[63] The fourth and fifth prongs of California's test demand that the defendant demonstrate a good faith and objectively reasonable belief in the necessity of an action taken to prevent a "significant" evil. Because these factors turn on good faith and reasonableness, whether necessity exists is generally a question of fact.[64]

D could successfully demand a necessity instruction if the case were prosecuted in California. If it is a significant evil for a person to be deprived of sleep, G's death would certainly be a significant evil. D could claim that after twenty-four hours of questioning, no adequate alternative to obtain G's location existed. K's severe injuries would not create a greater harm or danger than G's death, and D did not substantially contribute to her emergency. D believed in good faith in the necessity of the beating to save G's life. The fact-finder would determine whether this belief was objectively reasonable.

bb) Illinois

Similarly, Illinois codifies a broad necessity defense including both objective and subjective elements. It provides:

> Conduct which would otherwise be an offense is justifiable by reason of necessity if the accused was without blame in occasioning or developing the situation and reasonably believed such conduct was necessary to avoid a public or private injury greater than the injury which might reasonably result from his own conduct.[65]

This defense is not entirely subjective: the defendant must "reasonably" believe in the necessity of the criminal conduct. The statute does require the defendant to have been without blame in creating the situation, but it does not require that the avoided injury be imminent. Once "some evidence" of the defense has been introduced, the prosecution has the burden of disproving the defense beyond a reasonable doubt.[66] Since D was without blame in creating the situation, and he believed that G might die if not found and rescued, it is likely that the court would instruct the jury on the necessity defense, allowing it to determine whether D's belief that his actions were necessary to avoid a greater evil were reasonable.

c) Natural Physical Forces – Wisconsin

Wisconsin's statute provides:

---

62 Ibid. (citation omitted).

63 Ibid.

64 Ibid.

65 720 Ill. Comp. Stat. 5/7–13 (West 2023).

66 *People v. Ferree*, 581 N.E.2d 699, 702 (Ill. App. Ct. 1991).

> Pressure of natural physical forces which causes the actor reasonably to believe that his or her act is the only means of preventing imminent public disaster, or imminent death or great bodily harm to the actor or another and which causes him or her so to act, is a defense to a prosecution for any crime based on that act.[67]

Although the statute recognizes that some circumstances may dictate "[avoiding] a greater evil by bringing about the lesser evil,"[68] Wisconsin limits the defense's applicability to situations caused by natural physical forces such as "storms, fires, and privations."[69] There seem to be two elements within a "natural physical force": first, the court must determine what set the "force" in motion; second, it must ask whether that "force" may be controlled.[70]

Despite the narrow scope of the statutory text, dicta in one case suggested that it might be read broadly enough to reach D's conduct. In a prosecution for heroin possession, the Wisconsin Court of Appeals rejected the defense for a defendant who had chosen to become a heroin addict, but it also stated that its analysis would not preclude future defendants from asserting a medically-related necessity as a defense if they had not been responsible for their condition.[71]

Vignette 4: Lethal Self-Defense

> R, a well-trained young man armed with a knife, accosts 50-year-old D, who is on her way home from a party in the early morning hours. R threatens her with the knife and takes away her purse filled with 500 € and her wristwatch worth 1,000 €. As R turns to run away, D draws a pistol she is secretly carrying in her jacket, and shoots and kills R in order to retrieve her property. Is D guilty of murder?

D's shooting of R implicates U.S. criminal law on self-defense and particularly the use of force to protect one's person or property. Although the use of force in self-defense is a generally recognized defense, the justified use of deadly force is limited to situations of utmost necessity, and U.S. criminal law also makes a distinction between protecting one's life and one's property.[72] Because these facts involve the use of deadly force in protection of one's property, the outcome largely depends on the state law where D is charged.

a) The Model Penal Code

The Model Penal Code (MPC) has served as a blueprint for criminal codes in many states, and as such, presents a natural starting place for analysis. Section 3.06 MPC

67 Wis. Stat. Ann. § 939.47 (West 2023).

68 *State v. Olsen*, 299 N.W.2d 632, 634 (Wis. Ct. App. 1980) (citation omitted).

69 Ibid.

70 *State v. Anthuber*, 549 N.W.2d 477, 480 (Wis. Ct. App. 1996).

71 Ibid.

72 The basic judgment underlying the self-defense justification is that "the preservation of life has such moral and ethical standing in our culture and society, that the deliberate sacrifice of life merely for the protection of property ought not to be sanctioned by law," except in the most serious circumstances. Model Penal Code and Commentaries § 3.06 cmt. 1 at 72 (Am. L. Inst., Official Draft and Revised Comments 1985).

governs the "Use of Force for the Protection of Property."[73] Under § 3.06, "the use of force upon or toward the person of another is justifiable when the actor believes that such force is immediately necessary" to either (a) "prevent or terminate [...] the unlawful carrying away of tangible moving property [...] in his possession," or (b) "to retake tangible movable property, provided that the actor believes that he [...] was unlawfully dispossessed."[74] Therefore, a threshold requirement for the use of force is that the actor believes in the necessity of his conduct. Section 3.06(1)(a) MPC governs situations where an individual is defending an initial aggression against property, while § 3.06(1)(b) MPC applies when one recaptures property after possession has been lost.[75] Since D's purse and wristwatch have just been taken, her use of force may be considered either an effort to "terminate" R's carrying away of her property, or as recaption under § 3.06(1)(a) and (b) MPC. Since R had just turned to run away, D's action might be seen as an effort to "terminate" his carrying away of her property. If this is characterized as "recaption," the force must be "used immediately or on fresh pursuit after such dispossession" and the actor must believe that the person against whom he uses force "has no claim of right to the possession of the property."[76] Both conditions are satisfied here, where D used force immediately after dispossession and R had no claim of right to the stolen items.

However, since D employed deadly force, more stringent limitations on her use of force must also be satisfied under the MPC. The use of deadly force provision was hotly debated by the MPC drafters.[77] The original provision allowed the use of deadly force only to protect one's dwelling, but was expanded after strong opposition to include § 3.06(3)(d)(ii) MPC "to encompass the most serious and potentially violent situations."[78] Section 3.06(3)(d)(ii) MPC permits the use of deadly force where the actor believes that "the person against whom the force is used is attempting to commit or consummate arson, burglary, robbery or other felonious theft" and "has employed or threatened deadly force against or in the presence of the actor."[79] Therefore, under the MPC, D's use of self-defense is probably justified.[80] It is likely D can prove she believed that R was "attempting to commit *or consummate*" a robbery and that he "threatened deadly force" by brandishing a knife.

b) Variations in State Law

Although most U.S. criminal codes now provide a justification defense for the use of deadly force in defense of property, they follow a variety of approaches. Although

---

73 Ibid. § 3.06 at 67.

74 Ibid. § 3.06(1)(a)–(b).

75 Ibid. § 3.06 cmt. 5 at 80.

76 Ibid. § 3.06(1)(b)(i)–(ii).

77 Ibid. § 3.06 cmt. 7 at 91–92.

78 Ibid.

79 Ibid. § 3.06(3)(d)(ii)(A).

80 As a helpful illustrative example, take the MPC drafters' discussion of a scenario that mirrors the Vignette: "one who commits robbery [...] at gunpoint and who is in the course of fleeing [...] may be shot by the victim if in the victim's judgment such force is immediately necessary in order to prevent the consummation of the offense." See ibid. § 3.06 cmt. 7 at 96.

some states adopted the MPC provision virtually verbatim,[81] others have narrowed the MPC's defense. Several states appear to allow the use of deadly force to prevent the commission, but not the consummation of the crime.[82] In these states, D would not succeed in claiming a justification defense since R arguably already committed the robbery, and D's shot was intended to prevent him from consummating the offense as he ran away with her property. Other states limit the justified use of deadly force to the context of one's dwelling.[83] D's use of force clearly falls outside the protection of these defenses.

Following New York's approach,[84] many states now tie the justification for the use of deadly force to an actor's reasonable belief that the other person is committing a forcible crime.[85] New York permits the use of deadly force where an actor "reasonably believes that such other person is committing or attempting to commit a [...] robbery."[86] Therefore, for D to succeed in her self-defense justification in New York, she must prove that she believed deadly force was necessary to prevent the commission of the robbery, and that her belief was reasonable.[87] New York's approach differs from the MPC by including a reasonableness requirement for the use of deadly force.[88] To find that the use of deadly force was justified, the jury must determine whether a reasonable person in the defendant's situation could have had these beliefs.[89] In making this reasonableness determination, the jury should consider all of the "circumstances

81 See, e.g., N.J. Stat. Ann. § 2C:3-6(3); Neb. Rev. Stat. Ann. § 28-1411 (LexisNexis 2024).

82 See, e.g., Del. Code Ann. tit. 11, § 466(c)(2) (2024) (permitting the use of deadly force to protect property if the defendant reasonably believes that the person is "attempting to commit [...] robbery"); Haw. Rev. Stat. Ann. § 703-306(3)(b) (LexisNexis) (the use of deadly force for the protection of property is justifiable only if the person against whom deadly force is used is attempting to commit a [...] robbery"); Ala. Code § 13 A–3–23(a)(3) (LexisNexis 2024) (deadly force is justified where a person reasonably believes another person is "[c]omitting or about to commit a [...] robbery").

83 See, e.g., 18 Pa. Cons. Stat. § 507 (2024) (limiting the justified use of deadly force to situations where there is an unlawful entry into the actor's dwelling); Ky. Rev. Stat. Ann. § 503.080 (LexisNexis 2024) (reserving the use of deadly force justification to situations where the robbery is committed in the dwelling).

84 See Model Penal Code § 3.06 cmt. 7 at 97 n. 49 (listing thirteen codes and proposals that generally follow the pattern in New York's use of deadly force provision).

85 See, e.g., N.Y. Penal Law § 35.15(2)(b) (Consol. 2024) (permitting the use of deadly force where an individual "reasonably believes that such other person is committing or attempting to commit a [...] robbery"); Fla. Stat. Ann. § 776.031(2) (LexisNexis 2024) (permitting the use of deadly force where an individual "reasonably believes that such conduct is necessary to prevent the imminent commission of a forcible felony").

86 N.Y. § 35.15(2)(b).

87 See *People v. Goetz*, 497 N.E.2d 41, 43 (N.Y. 1986).

88 See ibid. at 50 (explaining how drafters in New York were influenced by the MPC, but crucially, inserted the word "reasonably" before "believes"). As the *Goetz* court explained, the MPC takes a two-step approach: 3.06 focuses solely on the defendant's subjective belief. If the defendant meets these criteria, he may still lose the defense if he was reckless or negligent in having the required beliefs; but he would lose the defense only for crimes with a mens rea of recklessness or negligence. See MPC 3.09(2).

89 *Goetz*, 497 N.E.2d at 52.

facing a defendant or his situation."[90] The motive for the use of deadly force may also factor into the reasonableness analysis.[91] Applying this standard, D's use of deadly force might reasonably have been seen to be necessary to prevent the completion of the crime of robbery and thus justified. The totality of the circumstances include the differences between R, a young, fit man with a knife, and D, an unarmed fifty-year-old woman. D's motive for shooting R was solely to try to stop the robbery. A jury could find that a reasonable person in D's situation would believe that the use of deadly force was necessary to terminate the commission of the robbery.

Vignette 5: Criminal Responsibility of Subordinates for Systemic Offenses

> D is a soldier in the army of a country ruled by a junta of generals who have come to power through a violent coup. When an opposition group demands the return to a democratic system, the government orders the soldiers to shoot and kill any person who resists arrest. Following this order, D kills three young men who take part in a protest demonstration and hit a police officer who tries to arrest them. When D is tried after a change of regime, he says that he did not like to shoot the protesters but that he thought that he had to obey his commanders' orders. D knew that if he had refused to shoot, he might have been demoted, but no physical harm would have occurred to him. Should D be convicted of murder? If so, should his sentence be mitigated because of his situation?

In the United States, criminal acts committed by federal soldiers acting within their duties are governed by the Uniform Code of Military Justice (UCMJ).[92] Violations of the UCMJ are adjudicated within the U.S. military through courts-martial[93] and governed by the *Manual for Courts-Martial* (the *Manual*).[94] Military law recognizes a defense of "obedience to orders." The *Manual* provides:

> It is a defense to any offense that the accused was acting pursuant to orders unless the accused knew the orders to be unlawful or a person of ordinary sense and understanding would have known the orders to be unlawful.[95]

---

90 Ibid. at 42.

91 See *In re Jesse C.*, 535 N.Y.S.2d 752 (N.Y. App. Div. 1988) (finding that a reasonable person in the appellant's position would not have thought deadly force was necessary to prevent a robbery from occurring where the appellant shot the victim because he was "angry and mad" instead of to try and stop the robbery).

92 10 U.S.C. Ch. 47.

93 10 U.S.C. § 818(a) ("[G]eneral courts-martial have jurisdiction to try persons subject to this chapter for any offense made punishable by this chapter and may […] adjudge any punishment not forbidden by this chapter[.]"). However, soldiers are not subject to the UCMJ once their service ends; they may be prosecuted in federal court under the U.S. Code for acts committed during their employment. See 18 U.S.C. §§ 3261-67, and Namosha Boykin & Kelechukwu Chidi Onyejekwe, *War Crimes – From the Battlefield to the Courtroom*, American Bar Association (Feb. 4, 2022), https://www.americanbar.org/groups/judicial/publications/appellate_issues/2022/winter/war-crimes-from-the-battlefield-to-the-courtroom/.

94 United States Dep't of Def., Manual for Courts-Martial United States (2024).

95 Ibid. at II–136.

The lawfulness of the order is decided by the military judge.[96] The *Manual*'s "ordinary sense and understanding" test is more stringent than the manifest illegality standard applied in some other jurisdictions.[97]

U.S. courts-martial have convicted defendants for following orders in military conflicts that "a man of ordinary sense and understanding would have known [...] [to be] unlawful,"[98] though the cases may also have met the more stringent manifest illegality test as well. In *United States v. Kinder*, 14 C.M.R. 742 (A.F.B.R. 1954), an airman was ordered by his lieutenant to kill a captured Korean civilian.[99] The airman understood and feared that he would be demoted for failing to obey this order.[100] He killed the civilian and was convicted of premeditated murder and conspiracy to commit murder.[101] The Air Force Board of Review rejected the airman's argument that his obedience to the lieutenant's order should constitute a defense.[102] Acknowledging that good faith compliance may sometimes justify a subordinate's action, the Board of Review held that the order was "so obviously beyond the scope of authority of the superior officer and so palpably illegal on its face as to admit of no doubt of its unlawfulness to a man of ordinary sense and understanding."[103]

In the court martial of Lieutenant William Calley, who was convicted of murdering 22 adults and children in Vietnam, the judge instructed the jury that acts done in compliance with an unlawful order are a defense "unless the superior's order is one which a man of ordinary sense and understanding would, under the circumstances, know to be unlawful, or if the order in question is actually known to the accused to be unlawful."[104] On appeal, the defense argued that the standard of common sense and understanding was too strict, particularly in a battlefield situation. The U.S. Court of Military Appeals ultimately declined to alter the traditional "ordinary sense" standard, because even if Calley were "the most ignorant person in the United States Army in Vietnam [...] he must be presumed to know that he could not kill the people involved here."[105]

Although they are dicta, the opinions of the concurrence and dissent explored alternative formulations of the obedience of orders defense. The majority presented a detailed history of the articulation and application of the "ordinary sense and under-

---

96 Ibid. The judge may instruct the panel not to consider the obedience to orders defense. See *United States v. Griffen*, 39 C.M.R. 586, 588 (1968) ("I tell you as a matter of law that if instructions or orders were [...] given to the accused [...] [they] would have been manifestly an illegal order. You are advised as a matter of law, any such command [...] was an illegal order.").

97 Mark J. Osiel, *Obeying Orders: Atrocity, Military Discipline, and the Law of War*, 86 Calif. L. Rev. 939, 973 (1997).

98 *United States v. Calley*, 48 C.M.R. 19, 27 (C.M.A. 1973).

99 *United States v. Kinder*, 14 C.M.R. 742, 754 (A.F.B.R. 1954).

100 Ibid. at 763.

101 Ibid. at 763.

102 Ibid. at 763.

103 Ibid. at 774.

104 *Calley*, 48 C.M.R. 19, 27 (C.M.A. 1973).

105 Ibid. at 29.

standing" standard.[106] In dissent, Chief Judge Darden characterized that standard as unfair to unsophisticated soldiers or those of somewhat limited intellect.[107] The proper standard, he argued, would require that

> Almost every member of the armed forces would have immediately recognized that the order was unlawful and that the accused should have recognized the order's illegality as a consequence of his age, grade, intelligence, experience, and training.[108]

Judge Darden argued that this test had several important advantages:

> [It] properly balances punishment for the obedience of an obviously illegal order against protection to an accused for following his elementary duty of obeying his superiors. Such a test reinforces the need for obedience as an essential element of military discipline by broadly protecting the soldier who has been effectively trained to look to his superiors for direction. It also promotes fairness by permitting the military jury to consider the particular accused's intelligence, grade, training. Finally, that test imputes such knowledge to an accused not as a result of simple negligence but on the much stronger circumstantial concept that almost anyone in the armed forces would have immediately recognized that the order was palpably illegal and other elements directly related to the issue of whether he should have known an order was illegal.[109]

Concurring in the result,[110] Judge Duncan identified several considerations weighing against abandoning the traditional standard. The first was the deference owed to the *Manual*, which reflects "serious reflection by knowledgeable and concerned personnel" with full regard to the needs of both the armed forces and the accused.[111] More fundamentally, he noted a general problem with any objective standard:

> All tests which measure an accused's conduct by an objective standard – whether it is the test of "palpable illegality to the commonest understanding" or whether the test establishes a set of profile considerations by which to measure the accused's ability to assess the legality of the order – are less than perfect, and they have a certain potential for injustice to the member having the slowest wit and quickest obedience.[112]

Finally, Judge Duncan observed that if any change were to be made, it should be done by Congress and not the court.

If prosecuted in a courts-martial, whether D could successfully claim the obedience of orders defense would turn on whether D knew the orders to be unlawful, or a person of ordinary sense and understanding would have known the orders to be unlawful.

---

106 Ibid. at 28–29.

107 Ibid. at 31.

108 Ibid. at 32.

109 Ibid. at 32.

110 Judge Duncan concurred in the result only because he disagreed with the "presumption" that Calley knew the order to be illegal, which he characterized as a question of fact for the jury. Ibid. at 29.

111 Judge Duncan: "Those who prepared the Manual provision and the President of the United States, the Commander-in-Chief, who approved and made the provision a part of our law, were aware that disobedience to orders is the anathema to an efficient military force." Ibid. at 30 (footnote omitted).

112 Ibid. at 30.

Since a junta of generals has taken over in a violent coup, it is difficult to know what persons of ordinary understanding would understand.

Vignette 6: Limits of Consent

> V is a 21-year-old ambitious athlete and short-distance runner. He has learned that certain artificial limbs can enhance a runner's speed. He decides that he would rather have an artificial limb instead of his right lower leg. He approaches D, a surgeon in private practice, and asks him to amputate his leg below the knee and replace it with an artificial limb. D complies with V's request. Should D be punished for mayhem?

In United States criminal law, consent is rarely a defense against charges involving serious bodily injury. The rationale can be traced back to the common law understanding that the king is the primary victim in violent offenses: by injuring another, you deprive the king of the aid and assistance of one of his subjects.[113] The American Law Institute's Model Penal Code (MPC) incorporated this theory, enumerating three circumstances in which consent to bodily injury acts as a valid defense: (1) when the injury is nonserious, (2) when the injury is a foreseeable result of participation in a legal activity, and (3) when consent otherwise establishes justification, most clearly referring to physical harm sustained as a result of a doctor administering a recognized form of treatment.[114] In the context of such medical treatment, the MPC commentaries point to circumstances in which "social and personal gains obviously warrant the risks inherent in recognized forms of treatment."[115]

State laws on consent now vary widely. One group of states, including Pennsylvania, adopted the language from the MPC almost verbatim. A second group, including North Carolina, have chosen to draft their own statutes implicating the consent defense as it relates to use of force. And a third group of states, including California, still apply the common law approach to consent. Although the analysis varies from state to state, it is unlikely that D would be convicted in Pennsylvania, North Carolina, or California.

a) Pennsylvania

The relevant Pennsylvania statutes, 18 Pa. Cons. Stat. §§ 311(b)(2) and 509(4), closely follow the MPC. Section 311(b)(2) allows a defense of consent to bodily harm when the consent establishes a justification for the conduct under the provisions governing justification.[116] Under § 509(4), use of force is justified if the actor is (1) a "doctor or other therapist," (2) "the force is used for the purpose of administering a recognized form of treatment," and (3) "the treatment is administered with the consent of the patient."[117] While the "recognized form of treatment" standard has not

---

113 Vera Bergelson, *Consent to Harm*, 28 Pace L. Rev. 683, 686–87 (2008).

114 Model Penal Code §§ 2.11(2)(c), 3.08(4) (Am. L. Inst.). Under the Model Penal Code § 211.1, mayhem was incorporated into the general offense of assault. MPC Part II Commentaries at 174 (1985).

115 MPC Part I Commentaries at 395 (1985).

116 18 Pa. Stat. and Cons. Stat. Ann. § 311(b)(2) (West 2023).

117 18 Pa. Stat. and Cons. Stat. Ann. § 509(4) (West 2023).

been interpreted in Pennsylvania courts with respect to § 509(4), cases on analogous issues indicate that the validity of a specific medical treatment is a question for the jury.[118] Although there is no case on point, one scholar concluded that consensual amputations arising from Body Integrity Identity Disorder, a rare disorder causing patients to seek to become amputees, would not be protected under the language of the MPC.[119]

Under Pennsylvania law, D's criminal liability would depend on two factual findings: whether the surgery constitutes bodily harm, and, if so, whether the amputation was a "recognized form of treatment." If the surgery did improve V's quality of life, and left him with no disabilities whatsoever, a jury may find there was no bodily harm. And the availability of surgery as an option for V and D's willingness to perform provide some support for the view that it would be considered an accepted form of treatment. Considering these facts, it is unlikely that D would be subject to criminal liability in Pennsylvania (or other states that adopted the MPC approach).

b) North Carolina

North Carolina has not codified the MPC's language regarding consent to bodily harm. The crime most like mayhem, "Castration or other maiming without malice aforethought," is codified at N.C. Gen. Stat. § 14–29:

> If any person shall, on purpose and unlawfully, but *without malice aforethought*, cut, or slit the nose, bite or cut off the nose, or a lip or an ear, *or disable any limb or member of any other person*, or castrate any other person, or cut off, maim or disfigure any of the privy members of any other person, *with intent to kill, maim, disfigure, disable or render impotent such person*, the person so offending shall be punished as a Class E felon.[120]

While similar offenses provide exceptions for consensual medical treatment, § 14–29 does not.[121]

In 1961, the North Carolina Supreme Court held that consent is not an exception to the crime of maiming, relying heavily on the common law understanding that violent crimes are offenses against the state, not an individual.[122] That case involved a defendant who assisted another in amputating his own finger to collect insurance proceeds, rather than an amputation for some perceived physical benefit.[123] The court found the defendant criminally liable based on the theory that the

118 See, e. g., *Com. v. Salameh*, 421 Pa. Super. 320, 325 (1992) (prescribing of controlled substances); *Butler v. Gross*, No. 1951, 1989 WL 817162 (Pa. Com. Pl. June 1, 1989) (medical malpractice).

119 Bergelson, *supra* note 113, at 688–89.

120 N.C. Gen. Stat. § 14–29 (emphasis added).

121 See, e. g., N.C. Gen. Stat. § 14–28.1(e) (providing a medical exception for a law banning female genital mutilation of a child).

122 *State v. Bass*, 255 N.C. 42, 50 (1961).

123 Ibid. at 43–44.

> Government is deeply concerned, financially and otherwise, for the health of its citizens and that they not become a public charge [...] our commonwealth needs the services of its citizens quite as much as the kings of England needed the services of theirs.[124]

Whether D's actions implicate this statute would depend on whether the surgery "disabled" V's leg, and whether D acted with intent to do so. Since it is unlikely that V would be disabled as a result of the surgery, it is unclear whether the maiming statute would apply to him. If the surgery did indeed increase V's athletic ability, it seems very unlikely that a court would find a disability. Similarly, based on V's intention to increase his athletic ability, and D's willingness to help, it is unlikely that D performed the surgery with any intent to disable V. Considering these factors, D would be unlikely to suffer any criminal liability in North Carolina.

c) California

Like North Carolina, California has not codified the consent defense. California Penal Code § 203 defines the offense of mayhem,[125] which includes three elements: (1) an unlawful act through physical force, (2) that results in an injury which disables or deprives someone of a member of his body, (3) done maliciously.[126] "Maliciously" is further defined by statute as to "import a wish to vex, annoy, or injure another person."[127]

There are some indications that California courts would recognize consent as a defense to mayhem. First, the victim's consent may negate the required malicious intent to "vex, annoy, or injure" the victim. In one case regarding a small injury inflicted by a minor upon his sister, the court noted that her "consent had the effect of eliminating any malice."[128] Similarly, courts have found that a *lack* of valid consent to certain cosmetic procedures is sufficient to establish malice in a charge of mayhem (but without explicitly ruling that affirmative consent would eliminate such malice).[129] Finally, California has imported the common law understanding of disablement: procedures that do "not render the patient impotent or unable to fight for the king" do not constitute mayhem.[130]

It is unlikely that D would be found criminally liable for mayhem in California. As in Pennsylvania and North Carolina, it is unclear whether the limb augmentation would render V "unable to fight for the king" and therefore qualify as deprivation

---

124 Ibid. at 50.

125 Cal. Penal Code § 203 (West) ("Every person who unlawfully and maliciously deprives a human being of a member of his body, or disables, disfigures, or renders it useless, or cuts or disables the tongue, or puts out an eye, or slits the nose, ear, or lip, is guilty of mayhem.").

126 *People v. Ausbie*, 123 Cal. App. 4th 855, 861 (2004).

127 Cal. Penal Code § 7 (West).

128 In re Joshua W., No. F042629, 2003 WL 22940757, at *5 (Cal. Ct. App. Dec. 15, 2003).

129 See, e.g., *People v. Pirnia*, 5 Cal. Rptr. 3d 903, 910 (breast augmentation surgery); *Jessin v. Shasta Cnty.*, 274 Cal. App. 2d 737, 747 (1969) (vasectomies); *People v. Page*, 104 Cal. App. 3d 569, 576 (Cal. Ct. App. 1980) (tattooing); *People v. Winn*, No. B259128, 2016 WL 3356741, at *16 (Cal. Ct. App. June 9, 2016) (tattooing).

130 *Jessin*, 274 Cal. App. 2d at 747 (finding that voluntary vasectomies do not constitute mayhem).

or disablement under the statute. Additionally, a California court would likely view V's valid consent to the operation as eliminating the malice element, therefore acting as a complete defense against mayhem.

Vignette 7: Withdrawal from an Attempt

25-year-old D is deeply upset with her former boyfriend V, who had ended their relationship to be with another woman. To punish V, D plans to stab him with a large knife. D knows that the stab wounds can be fatal and accepts V's death as a possible outcome. When V goes jogging, D attacks him from behind and stabs him in the back three times. V breaks down. D realizes that she has injured him but that the injuries will not cause his death. She realizes that she could kill him by stabbing him again but decides to leave him alone. Should D be punished for attempted murder?

U.S. states would take very different approaches to the question whether D's decision to stop her attack on V after inflicting non-fatal injuries would be a defense to attempted murder. Note, however, that in all states she could be convicted on an assault if the charge of attempted murder failed. Traditionally, U.S. law gave no effect to an individual's withdrawal from the attempt to commit a crime, but the American Law Institute's Model Penal Code (MPC), published in 1962, prompted a reevaluation of this traditional rule in several states. The MPC created a new defense of withdrawal (called "renunciation") from criminal attempt.

U.S. states now take three different approaches to withdrawal from attempt. Some, like California, maintain the traditional approach and would give no effect to D's change of heart. Other states, including New York and Arizona, have adopted a defense of withdrawal (or renunciation), but the criteria of that defense vary. D would likely have a defense in New York, but not in Arizona.

a) The Traditional Common Law – California

California follows the traditional common law rule. Its courts have repeatedly stated that once an "overt act toward the commission of the contemplated offense" has been taken, the fact that the defendant abandoned his or her criminal purpose is not a defense.[131] Thus, D could not escape liability for attempted murder in California.

b) The Model Penal Code Approach – New York

The drafters of the MPC introduced a renunciation defense into American law, and New York adopted a provision modeled on the MPC. Section 5.01(4) MPC states that "renunciation of criminal purpose" will serve as "an affirmative defense [when the perpetrator] abandoned his effort to commit the crime or otherwise prevented its commission, under circumstances manifesting a complete and voluntary renunciation of his criminal purpose." The new defense was intended to serve two functions. It demonstrates that there is no need for punishment or rehabilitation

---

131 *People v. Crary*, 265 Cal. App. 2d 534 (Cal. Ct. App. 1968). See *also People v. Ross*, 205 Cal. App. 3d 1548, 1554 (Cal. Ct. App. 1988) ("[A] person cannot avoid responsibility for acts committed which constitute an attempt to commit a crime [...] by voluntarily abandoning his purpose [...]").

when a defendant voluntarily and completely abandons an attempt, and it encourages would-be criminals to voluntarily abandon their efforts.[132]

New York Penal Law § 40.10(3) mirrors the language of MPC § 5.01(4), recognizing the defense of renunciation.[133] No New York case has held that the defense applies in an attempted murder prosecution when the defendant decided not to kill the victim and terminated a violent attack. But dicta in cases involving attempts to commit other violent crimes suggest that New York courts would recognize the defense in D's case. In prosecutions for attempted kidnapping and attempted rape, the courts rejected the renunciation defense because the defendants had not withdrawn from their attempted crimes of their own volition.[134] Despite the fact that the victims experienced physical harm,[135] in both cases the court stated that the defendants could have successfully relied on the defense of renunciation if they had voluntarily and completely abandoned their criminal purpose due to a "change of heart."[136] Following these precedents, if the jury found that D had voluntarily and completely abandoned her criminal purpose, she would have a full defense to the charge of attempted murder (though not, of course, to her assault on V).

c) A Narrower Renunciation Defense – Arizona

Arizona adopted a statutory renunciation defense, but it is more restricted than the New York provision modeled on the MPC. Arizona law requires not only that defendants completely and voluntarily renounce their criminal intent, but also that they either provide law enforcement with timely warning or otherwise make a reasonable effort to prevent the criminal result.[137] If a defendant fails to take one of these steps, the renunciation defense fails.

---

132 Model Penal Code and Commentaries 359 (Am. L. Inst. 1985).

133 New York Penal Law § 40.10 (3) states: "In any prosecution [...] for an attempt to commit a crime, it is an affirmative defense that, under circumstances manifesting a voluntary and complete renunciation of his criminal purpose, the defendant avoided the commission of the crime attempted by abandoning his criminal effort and, if mere abandonment was insufficient to accomplish such avoidance, by taking further and affirmative steps which prevented the commission thereof."

134 See *People v. Dolan*, 51 A.D.3d 1337, 1340 (N.Y. Sup. Ct. 2008) (rejecting defense in prosecution for attempted kidnapping because defendant fled out of "fear of detection or apprehension"); *People v. Jenks*, 239 A.D.2d 673, 675 (N.Y. Sup. Ct. 1977) (rejecting defense in prosecution for attempted rape because defendant abandoned his criminal efforts due to the "victim's artful persuasion").

135 In both cases, victims experienced physical harm before the attempt was abandoned. *Dolan*, 51 A.D.3d at 1138 (victim was beaten with defendant's fist and firearm); *Jenks*, 239 A.D.2d at 674 (victim was pinned down and touched in her vaginal area). Yet, the courts still stated (in dicta) that the renunciation defense could have been available had their motives for withdrawal been acceptable.

136 *Dolan*, 51 A.D.3d at 1340.

137 Arizona Crim. Code § 13-1005(A) provides: "In a prosecution for attempt [...] it is a defense that the defendant, under circumstances manifesting a voluntary and complete renunciation of his criminal intent, gave timely warning to law enforcement authorities or otherwise made a reasonable effort to prevent the conduct or result which is the object of the attempt [...]".

The Arizona statute also states that

> A warning to law enforcement authorities is not timely within the meaning of this section unless the authorities, reasonably acting upon the warning, would have the opportunity to prevent the conduct or result. An effort is not reasonable within the meaning of this section unless the defendant makes a substantial effort to prevent the conduct or result.

Thus, in Arizona D's renunciation defense would fail, and she would still be liable for attempted murder because she did not give a timely warning to the authorities, seek help for V, or make some other "substantial" effort to prevent V's death. Under New York law, in contrast, affirmative steps to prevent the completion of the crime would have been required only if D's abandonment would have been insufficient to prevent V's death.[138]

Vignette 8: Criminal Responsibility of Minors

> D is a 13-year-old boy. He abducts and rapes V, a girl of the same age. Should D be punished for a criminal offence?

A 13-year-old boy who abducted and raped a 13-year-old girl could face criminal responsibility in any jurisdiction in the United States. As of February 2024, twenty-four states in the U.S.A. have no minimum age of prosecution.[139] The remaining twenty-six states take various approaches, but no minimum age of prosecution is set above age 13.[140] As discussed below, each state has its own statutory regime for the criminal responsibility of minors.

This contribution will focus on the statutory regimes in Alabama, Florida, and Nevada. In Alabama and Florida, D may be prosecuted for rape and kidnapping despite his youth. In Nevada, he would also be subject to prosecution, but would have a defense if he was unaware of the wrongfulness of his conduct.

It is important to note, however, that a related question would also arise: whether D would be prosecuted as an adult or be tried in juvenile court. Although each state has a juvenile court system that handles cases in which juveniles are accused of acts that would be crimes if adults committed them, all states also have transfer laws that allow or require criminal prosecution of some young offenders.

See *also State v. Hanson*, 674 P.2d 850, 853 (Ariz. Ct. App. 1983) (holding defendant was entitled to a jury instruction on renunciation when evidence from the case reasonably supported the conclusion that he abandoned attempted robbery because "the victims were so upset"); *Candelaria v. Lewis*, No. 95-15708, 1996 WL 144218, at *2 (9th Cir. Mar. 29, 1996) (holding defendant would not be able to apply the renunciation defense because, among other reasons, he could not "establish timely warning to law enforcement, and he probably could not establish a reasonable attempt to prevent the crime [of selling cocaine]").

138 New York Penal Law § 40.10 (D).

139 National Juvenile Justice Network, Brief: Charting U.S. Minimum Ages of Jurisdiction, Detention, and Commitment 1 (2024), https://www.njjn.org/uploads/digital-library/UPDATED%20February%202024_Minimum%20Age%20Laws%20for%20Juvenile%20Court%20Jurisdiction%20and%20Confinement.pdf.

140 Ibid.

a) Minimum Ages of Prosecution

As noted, U.S. states split on the question whether to specify a minimum age for criminal liability. Alabama, along with twenty-three other states, sets no minimum age of prosecution and any minor may be punished if the prosecution can establish the elements of a crime. In these states, there is no question that D may be prosecuted and punished for the kidnapping and rape of V.

Other states set various age thresholds for criminal liability, but these thresholds are much younger than 13. For example, the minimum age for some offenses is 7 in Florida[141] and 8 in Nevada.[142] But states with minimum ages of prosecution, such as Florida and Nevada, often vary the age at which a child may be punished depending on the offense charged.

In Florida, children younger than 7 years may be prosecuted for a forcible felony, such as murder, sexual battery, and kidnapping.[143] Thus even if D had been under the age of 7, he could have been prosecuted in Florida because these offenses are categorized as forcible felonies.

In Nevada, there are two significant restrictions on the punishment of young children who are at least 8 years old. Children between the ages of 8 and 10 years are criminally liable only for murder and sexual offenses.[144] Thus even if D had been between the ages of 8 and 10 years, he could have been prosecuted given the nature of the offenses. But Nevada also adds a special limitation on the criminal liability of children between the ages of 8 and 14 years. They are not liable to punishment "in the absence of clear proof that at the time of committing the act charged against them they knew its wrongfulness."[145] Thus, absent "clear proof" that D, at the time of the kidnapping and rape, possessed knowledge of the wrongfulness of the crimes, he may not be convicted in Nevada.

b) Transfer to Adult Criminal Court

State laws on transfer to adult court vary significantly. Most states allow the juvenile court judge to waive jurisdiction over certain cases and transfer them to adult court, and many states exclude certain serious offenses from juvenile court jurisdiction, at least for minors that have reached a certain age.[146]

In Florida, the court would have discretion to transfer D's case to adult court after considering a variety of factors including the "seriousness of the alleged offense to the community and whether the protection of the community is best served by trans-

---

141 Fla. Stat. § 985.031.

142 Nev. Rev. Stat. § 194.010.

143 Fla. Stat. §§ 985.031; 776.08.

144 Nev. Rev. Stat. §§ 194.010; 62F.100.

145 Ibid.

146 See generally Patrick Griffin et al., *Trying Juveniles as Adults: An Analysis of State Transfer Laws and Reporting*, U.S. Dep't of Justice 2 (2011), https://www.ojp.gov/pdffiles1/ojjdp/232434.pdf [perma.cc/MZ23–U9CV] (discussing various state mechanisms for trying juveniles as adults).

ferring the child for adult sanctions," and whether the offense "was committed in an aggressive, violent, premeditated, or willful manner."[147]

In contrast, in Alabama and Nevada, D's case would be adjudicated in juvenile court because he was not 14 at the time of the offense. In Alabama, the prosecutor could have made a motion to transfer the case to adult court if D had been 14 years old at the time of the offense,[148] and if D had been 16 he would not have been subject to the jurisdiction of the juvenile court.[149] Similarly, in Nevada, the prosecutor could have made a motion to transfer D to adult court if he had been 14 years old at the time of the offense.[150] The prosecutor could have moved to transfer the case for a 13-year-old charged with murder or attempted murder.[151]

c) Public Opinion and Legal Change

In the United States, public opinion has driven changes in the age at which criminal charges against minors can be prosecuted in adult court rather than the juvenile court system. A wave of punitive changes swept through the U.S.A. in the early 1990s: Changes enacted in virtually every state during the 1990s made it much easier to prosecute juveniles as adults and increased the sanctions applicable to juveniles. This legislation was part of the "tough on crime" hyperpunitiveness of that period. The juvenile justice legislation paralleled the efforts in the adult criminal justice system to enact "three strikes" and other mandatory minimum punishment statutes, as well as longer sentences in general. Racial imagery and racially based political appeals played an important role in creating the climate that led to the enactment of this legislation. In addition, politicians and the media warned the public that we faced a new breed of youthful superpredators and cold-blooded killers, as well as a demographic threat of a huge increase in juvenile crime.[152]

As one report explained, the changes enacted during this period were intended

> To ease and support the State's decision to punish, hold accountable, and incarcerate for longer periods those juveniles who had, by instant offense or history, passed a threshold of tolerated "juvenile" criminal behavior. [They reflected] the belief that serious and violent juvenile offenders must be held more accountable for their actions. In many instances, accountability is defined as punishment, or a period of incarceration, with less attention paid to the activities to be accomplished during that incarceration.[153]

But U.S. public opinion has shifted, and it is now sharply divided on how the legal system should treat teenagers who commit violent crimes. A 2023 Gallup poll found

---

147 Fla. Stat. § 985.556.

148 Ala. Code § 12-15-203(a). The factors to be considered by the court include the nature of the alleged offense. Id. at 12-15-203(d)(1).

149 Ala. Code § 12-15-204(a)(2) (class A felony).

150 Nev. Rev. Stat. § 62B.390(1).

151 Ibid. at § 62B.390(2).

152 Sara Sun Beale, *You've Come a Long Way, Baby: Two Waves of Juvenile Justice Reforms as Seen from Jena, Louisiana*, 4 Harv. C.R.–C.L. L. Rev. 511, 514 (2009) (footnotes omitted). See also Patricia Torbet et al., State Responses to Serious and Violent Juvenile Crime ix (1996). Washington, DC: Office of Juvenile Justice and Delinquency Prevention.

153 Torbert et al. (note 153) at 59.

that 46 % of respondents favor treating them the same as adults, and 47 % favored giving more lenient treatment in juvenile courts.[154] The poll found that attitudes of Democrats, independents, and younger adults had changed more than those of Republicans and older adults, and college graduates were also more favorable to lenient treatment in the juvenile system. The percentage favoring treatment as adults has decreased significantly in the last two decades.[155]

This shift in public opinion has been reflected in changes in the laws of some states, which no longer automatically charge children under 18 as adults for certain crimes. It is unclear whether these changes reflect a more general reduction in support for punitive criminal justice policies, or a greater understanding of adolescent mental development.[156]

Vignette 9: Statute of Limitations

> In 1995, D violently raped V, a 35-year-old woman, using a knife. D managed to escape and was not apprehended until 2023. Traces of his DNA taken from the victim's body leave no doubt that D is the perpetrator. Should D be convicted despite the long delay?

In many U.S. states, including Maryland, New Jersey, and New York, there are no statutes of limitations applicable to crimes equivalent to first-degree or aggravated rape, and a prosecution against D may be commenced at any time. In other states, such as Oklahoma and Ohio, the general period of limitations has passed, but statutory exceptions for DNA evidence would allow a prosecution to be commenced by 2026 or 2028. On the other hand, in some states the limitations period would have ended for less serious offenses.

a) No Applicable Statute of Limitations

In many U.S. states, there are no statutes of limitations applicable to crimes equivalent to first-degree rape.[157] Accordingly, the state may prosecute D despite the 28-year lapse between the commission of the crime and his apprehension. States vary in whether they exempt all felonies, or only certain violent felonies, from their statutes of limitations. Maryland has no statute of limitations for any felony, including rape.[158] In New Jersey, there is no statute of limitations for sexual assault or aggravated sexual

---

154 Jeffrey M. Jones, Americans Divided on Treatment of Violent Juvenile Offenders, https://news.gallup.com/poll/545021/americans-divided-treatment-violent-juvenile-offenders.aspx (Dec. 4, 2023).

155 Majorities of 65 % in 2000 and 59 % in 2003 felt juveniles aged 14 to 17 who commit crimes should be treated the same as adult criminals. Ibid.

156 See ibid. (noting decreases in other punitive policies, such as the death penalty, as well as factors such as the new understanding of adolescent development).

157 The name of the offense varies from state to state. Maryland and New York describe the offense as first degree rape, but New Jersey calls it aggravated sexual assault. *Compare* Md. Code, Crim. L. § 3-303, N.Y. Penal L. 130.05(1) & N.Y. Penal L. 130.35 *with* N.J. Stat. § 2C:14-2.

158 *State v. Renfro*, 223 Md. App. 779 (Md. 2015) ("Maryland has no statute of limitations on felonies.").

assault.[159] Finally, in New York, there is no statute of limitations for rape in the first degree.[160]

b) Applicable Statutes of Limitations with Exceptions for DNA Evidence

Other states, such as Ohio and Oklahoma, provide limitations periods for violent rape but include exceptions for DNA evidence that would allow a successful prosecution of D if the state acts promptly.

In Ohio, the statute of limitations for rape in the first degree is twenty-five years.[161] Since twenty-eight years have passed since the time of the rape, the statute of limitations would bar D's prosecution unless the state's statutory exception for DNA evidence applies. If a DNA match is made more than twenty-five years after the crime was committed, Ohio allows a prosecution to be commenced within five years of the match determination.[162] Assuming that the DNA match was made just before D was apprehended in 2023, the prosecution would have until 2028 to commence a prosecution in Ohio.

Similarly, in Oklahoma, although the statute of limitations has run, there is an exception for newly discovered DNA evidence. The Oklahoma statute of limitations for rape is twelve years after the discovery of the offense.[163] Assuming that V reported the rape immediately in 1995, the limitations period ended in 2007. Oklahoma provides, however, that a prosecution resting on DNA may be commenced within three years of establishing the identity of the perpetrator through testing.[164] Thus, assuming that the identity of the perpetrator was not established until 2023, D may be convicted in Oklahoma so long as the prosecution is commenced by 2026.

c) Lesser Crimes

If a less serious felony were charged (perhaps because the prosecution is unable to establish the elements of first-degree or aggravated rape), there would still be no limitations period in Maryland, but statutes of limitations would present a greater barrier to conviction in New Jersey and New York.

In New Jersey, when a lesser crime – such as criminal sexual contact – is charged, the statute of limitations is five years from the commission of the offense.[165]

In New York, when a lesser crime – such as second-degree rape – is charged, the statute of limitations is twenty years, but it excludes time when the defendant was continuously out of the state or when the defendant's whereabouts were unknown.[166]

159 N.J. Stat. § 2C:14-2; § 2C:1-6.

160 Penal Law § 130.05(1), 130.35.

161 Ohio Rev. Code Ann. § 2901.13; § 2907.02(2).

162 Ohio Rev. Code Ann. § 2901.13(D)(1)–(2).

163 Okla. Stat. tit. 21, § 1111; Okla. Stat. tit. 22, § 152.

164 Okla. Stat. tit. 22, § 152(C)(2).

165 N.J. Stat. § 2C:14-3. 2; N.J. Stat. § 2C:1-6.

166 Ibid. at 4(a)(i)–(ii).

The statute of limitations may not be extended by more than five years in total.[167] Additionally, New York case law suggests that the statutes of limitations for these offenses may be tolled when DNA evidence provides a new link to the perpetrator to the crime.[168] Thus, if second-degree rape were charged, the prosecution may argue that the statute of limitations should be tolled until the discovery of the defendant's identity was made.

Vignette 10: Life Imprisonment without Parole

The Penal Code of State S provides for imprisonment for life as the maximum penalty for murder, but also authorizes the court to order an offender's early release after a minimum of 15 years if the offender is no longer dangerous. Reacting to cases of particularly heinous murders, the legislature of S wishes to introduce a penalty of life imprisonment without any possibility of early release, regardless of the offender's continued dangerousness. Would this amendment be acceptable?

The U.S. Constitution would not prohibit a federal or state law that imposed a sentence of life without parole (LWOP) on an individual over the age of 18 regardless of that individual's continued dangerousness. But mandatory juvenile LWOP sentences violate the Eighth Amendment of the U.S. Constitution, and some state constitutions impose additional limitations on LWOP sentencing schemes. Finally, LWOP sentences are controversial, and an influential U.S. organization has recommended that states adopt statutory second-look provisions.

a) LWOP and the Federal Constitution

The Eighth Amendment of the U.S. Constitution forbids cruel and unusual punishments,[169] prohibiting excessive sanctions[170] and requiring that punishment fall "within the limits of civilized standards."[171] In response to categorical challenges to the death penalty, the U.S. Supreme Court looks to "the evolving standards of decency that mark the progress of a maturing society"[172] and applies a two-part objective and subjective test.[173] The objective inquiry seeks "guidance in history and from objective evidence of the country's present judgment."[174] This involves surveying other jurisdictions where the same punishment is allowed for similar crimes and jury verdicts.[175] The subjective inquiry is the Court's independent judgment concerning the punish-

---

167 Ibid.

168 See, e.g., *People v. Brown*, 890 N.Y.S.2d 415 (N.Y. 2009) (statute of limitations was tolled until defendant's DNA record was matched to DNA evidence).

169 U.S. Const., amend. VIII ("Excessive bail shall not be required, nor excessive fines imposed, nor cruel and unusual punishments inflicted").

170 *Roper v. Simmons*, 543 U.S. 551, 560 (2005)

171 *Trop v. Dulles*, 356 U.S. 86, 100 (1958) (plurality opinion).

172 *Roper*, 543 U.S. at 561 (citing *Trop*, 356 U.S. at 100–01 (plurality opinion)).

173 See *Coker v. Georgia*, 433 U.S. 584 (1977) (plurality opinion). This case focused on whether a punishment of death for the crime of rape of an adult woman was constitutional. The Supreme Court ultimately held it violated the Eighth Amendment.

174 Ibid. at 593 (plurality opinion).

175 Ibid. at 593–97 (plurality opinion).

ment.[176] It includes consideration of proportionality between the punishment and the offense[177] and the purposes of punishment.[178]

Although this analysis was developed in death penalty cases, the Court has extended it to juvenile LWOP cases. In *Graham v. Florida*,[179] the Court determined that sentencing juveniles to LWOP for non-homicide offenses violated the Eighth Amendment. In *Miller v. Alabama*, [180] the Court held that *mandatory* juvenile LWOP sentences for homicide violated the Eighth Amendment, and that sentencing courts must have discretion to consider a juvenile's diminished culpability and greater prospects for reform.[181] But the U.S. Constitution does not require a court that employs its discretion to sentence a juvenile to LWOP to make an explicit finding of "permanent incorrigibility" or to provide an on-the-record sentencing explanation that will allow an implicit finding of permanent incorrigibility.[182]

Thus the U.S. Constitution would not be violated by a law imposing LWOP on persons who committed murder when they were at least 18, though mandatory LWOP sentences for juveniles would violate the cruel and unusual punishment clause of the Eighth Amendment.

b) LWOP and State Constitutions

aa) Age-Related Restrictions

Many state constitutions prohibit cruel and unusual punishments,[183] and some state constitutions impose additional limitations on LWOP sentences for juveniles as well as a new class categorized as emerging adults. The Massachusetts Supreme Judicial Court held that all juvenile LWOP sentences, including those where the underlying offense is murder, violate the state's constitution because of "the unique characteristics of juvenile offenders."[184] And the Supreme Courts in Washington and Massachusetts have expanded *Miller* to a new class of individuals: emerging adults. The Washington Supreme Court held that its state constitution prohibited mandatory

---

176 Ibid. at 598–600 (plurality opinion) ("[...] the Constitution contemplates that in the end our own judgment will be brought to bear on the question of the acceptability of the death penalty under the Eighth Amendment").

177 Ibid. at 597–600.

178 See, e.g., *id.* at 597–98; *Enmund v. Florida*, 458 U.S. 782, 798–801 (1982); *Atkins v. Virginia*, 536 U.S. 304, 318–21 (2002).

179 560 U.S. at 82 ("if [the state] imposes a sentence of life it must provide him or her with some realistic opportunity to obtain release before the end of that term").

180 *Miller v. Alabama*, 567 U.S. 460, 471–76, 479 (2012) ("We therefore hold that the Eighth Amendment forbids a sentencing scheme that mandates life in prison without possibility of parole for juvenile offenders.").

181 See ibid. at 471–76.

182 *Jones v. Mississippi*, 593 U.S. 98, 104–05 (2021).

183 See William W. Berry III, *Cruel State Punishments*, 98 N.C. L. Rev. 1201, 1205–06 n. 23 (2020) (listing states which have similar cruel and unusual punishment provisions in their state constitutions).

184 *Diatchenko v. District Attorney for the Suffolk Dist.*, 1 N.E.3d 270, 276 (Mass. 2013) (holding that juvenile LWOP in any circumstance is a violation of the state's constitution). Juvenile offenders are defined as those under 18 years old.

LWOP sentences for defendants 18 to 20 years old who were convicted of homicide, because "many youthful defendants older than 18 share the same developing brains and impulsive behavioral attributes as those under 18."[185] As such, the sentencing process must allow consideration of these mitigating factors.[186] In 2024, the Massachusetts Supreme Judicial Court went further and held LWOP unconstitutional for anyone 20 or younger, regardless of the underlying offense.[187]

bb) Offense-Related Restrictions

Two states have granted review to decide whether their state constitutions preclude LWOP sentences for felony murder, which requires no proof of intent to kill when a death occurs during the commission, attempt to commit, or flight from certain felonies. In 2023 the Supreme Court of Colorado granted review on the question of whether an LWOP sentence for felony murder is categorically unconstitutional and/or grossly disproportionate.[188] And in 2024, the Supreme Court of Pennsylvania agreed to hear a case to address whether a mandatory LWOP sentence for felony murder is unconstitutional under the state constitution and/or the Eighth Amendment of the U.S. Constitution.[189]

c) The American Law Institute's Recommendations

In 2023, the American Law Institute (ALI) approved a recommendation that legislatures should seek to enact laws that would allow for the modification of long-term sentences, creating a "'second-look' process for sentence modification available to prisoners who have served exceptionally long terms."[190] The ALI's Principles for Legislation provide:

1. The legislature shall authorize a judicial panel or other judicial decisionmaker to hear and rule upon applications for modification of sentence from prisoners who have served 15 years of any sentence of incarceration.
2. After first eligibility, a prisoner's right to apply for sentence modification shall recur at intervals not to exceed 10 years.[191]

The Principles of Legislation do not have the force of law in any U.S. jurisdiction. But the ALI's prestige will bring attention to the recommendation, which reflects the

---

185 *In re Monschke*, 482 P.3d 276, 280–82, 287 (Wash. 2021) (holding that mandatory life without parole sentences for defendants under 20 violated Article I, § 14 of the Washington Constitution).

186 Ibid. at 287.

187 *Commonwealth v. Mattis*, 224 N.E.3d 410, 428 (Mass. 2024) (extending the protections of *Diatchenko* to those 18 to 20).

188 *Sellers v. People*, No. 22SC738, 2023 WL 3479427 (Colo. 2023) (cert. granted in May 2023).

189 *Commonwealth v. Lee*, No. 180 WAL 2023, 2024 WL 655325 (Pa. 2024) (cert. granted in February 2024).

190 American Law Institute, Principles for Legislation § 11.02 cmt. a at 910.

191 Id., § 11.02(1)–(2).

views of many distinguished members of the ALI. It is too soon to say if any states will adopt such second-look regimes.

III. Synopsis

1. Trolley Problem – Killing one Person to Save Many?

By *Gian Marco Caletti*

Vignette 1

Five young children are playing on railway tracks. An express train is approaching, and it is too late to stop the train before it hits the children, probably killing them. Operator D recognizes the emergency situation. He electronically flips a switch and thus deflects the train from its regular track to a little-used sidetrack. However, the lone repairman V is busy on the sidetrack, and the deflected train kills V, as D had anticipated. Is D criminally responsible for murder of V?

a) Introduction

This Vignette concerns the so-called "trolley problem", which is a well-known issue at the intersection between criminal law[1] and morality.[2]

Although they rarely rely on judicial decisions, the national reports reveal very similar solutions in response to this scenario. Every jurisdiction frames the case within the topic of necessity and, although there are some practical nuances, the commentators' consistent view is that (criminal) law should not blame those who are obliged to face such a tragic choice.

From this perspective, the uniformity of responses to the Vignette seems to reflect a pattern of universal justice. At the same time, the national reports dealing with this dilemma highlight many other interesting indications on a comparative level.

b) Comparing the Trolley Dilemma with Other Traditional Cases of Necessity

Before examining them, however, it is worth taking a closer look at the specific case presented in the Vignette. Although the trolley problem is a classic issue in criminal law, it should not be confused with other traditional cases of necessity or tragic choices and moral dilemmas. Some differences, therefore, should be emphasised.

---

1 See H. Welzel, Zum Notstandsproblem, 63 Zeitschrift für die gesamte Strafrechtswissenschaft (ZStW) 48, 51 (1951); P. Foot, The Problem of Abortion and the Doctrine of the Double Effect, 5 Oxford Review 5 (1967); J.J. Thomson, The Trolley Problem, 94 (6) The Yale Law Journal 1395 (1985).

2 Prof. Michael Sandell's lectures at Harvard University "Justice: What's The Right Thing To Do?" are well known. They are available on youtube, https://www.youtube.com/watch?v=kBdfcR-8hEY.

Duncker & Humblot · Berlin | https://doi.org/10.3790/978-3-428-59449-8.2025.416567

A first point to highlight is that operator D is neither emotionally involved in the situation nor are his rights directly affected in the balancing of interests. He does not kill V to save himself or someone he knows. Circumstances make D a sort of "God" who is entitled to decide who should die and who should not, but without having a direct interest or emotional connection to the people potentially affected by his choice.

This makes the situation different from some typical cases of necessity, such as the shipwreck example[3] or the mountaineer who cuts the rope killing his companion in order to survive. These subjects act to save their own life, while D does not run any risk to his physical safety.

Certain similarities can be established with the situation in which someone has to decide whether to shoot down an airplane hijacked for terrorist purposes before it reaches its target and terrorists accomplish a massacre (the 9/11 case). Nevertheless, there exist several differences, especially the fact that in the present Vignette the repairman V is not in danger before D's act. By contrast, the people on the hijacked plane already are in mortal peril.

There are some similarities with the casuistry of tragic choices in medical health care,[4] such as the case where a surgeon has to decide which of conjoined twins to save by surgery.[5] Upon closer examination, however, in this case there is the substantial difference that both twins are in mortal danger, whereas in the trolley problem V and the children are not simultaneously in danger.[6] V's death occurs only after an active (and causally relevant) conduct of D, who by deviating the train shifts the danger from the five children to the repairman V.

Probably the most similar scenario is that of pandemic triage, in which the medical doctor has to choose which patient should be ventilated in order to survive.[7] But even this scenario presents substantial differences, including the fact that doctors can rely on scientific knowledge for the tragic choice to be made, assessing which patient has the best chance of survival.

In light of these considerations, it can be said that the trolley problem is a truly unique case, in which the choice between human lives takes place in its essence, without personal involvement, without parameters other than numbers. However, this does not mean that it is an entirely unrealistic scenario. At the end of this Synopsis, attention will be drawn to a new application made possible by new technologies.

---

3 See, e.g., the famous case *The Queen v. Dudley and Stephens*, (1884) 14 QBD 273.

4 For an article that concludes that Trolley scenarios are not the ultimate criterion for making ethical decisions in difficult medical cases but that they can serve as an initial intuitive guide, see G. Andrade, "Medical ethics and the trolley Problem" (2019) J Med Ethics Hist Med 12.

5 See, e.g., *Re A (Children) (Conjoined Twins: Surgical Separation)*, [2001] Fam 147.

6 For more considerations on this point, see the Australian national report.

7 For an analysis of the criminal issues of that situation, F.P. Schuster, Coping with Moral Dilemmas in German Criminal Law Theory and Justice: Classical Cases and Modern Variants, Criminal Law Forum, 34(2):1, 2023. In Italy, G.M. Caletti, Il triage in emergenza pandemica, Quaderni Costituzionali, 2020, 3, 616.

c) Establishing Actus Reus and Mens Rea

The first question raised by the trolley problem is whether D commits the offence of murder.

An overview of the surveyed jurisdictions shows that liability for murder requires that D's conduct caused V's death (*actus reus*) and that D acted with intent to kill (*mens rea*). Both of these elements seem to be satisfied in the present case.

It is clear on the facts that D's action – flipping the switch – caused V's death in the relevant manner. *Mens rea*, however, may be more debatable, because D does not directly intend V's death in the sense of acting in order to bring it about.

However, this does not mean that D does not act with intent, since he may have oblique intent to kill V. In common law jurisdictions, oblique intent as defined in *R. v. Woollin* requires D to foresee the result as virtually certain.[8] The test seems satisfied as the Vignette states that D "had anticipated" the death of V.

In civil law countries, on the other hand, the awareness of V's death could amount to indirect intent (the definition of which is very similar to that of oblique intention). D does not want the consequence of his action but knows it is very likely to occur. D goes ahead with his conduct regardless, accepting the unwanted consequence.[9]

In both common law and civil law countries, *mens rea* would exist even if D was not virtually certain of V's death (as in the present case) but foresaw it as probable. In Anglo-American systems, D would be held liable for recklessness, which is based on foreseeing an unreasonable risk. In European systems, on the other hand, the existence of *dolus eventualis* could be recognised. In this form of intent, the actor is not certain that the result will materialise but only knows about the possibility that it may occur. He is culpable because he accepts the risk of the event occurring as a consequence of his *actus reus*[10].

Unanimously, therefore, all national reports seek the answer to the question whether D should be held criminally liable on the ground of defences.

d) Defences: Debate on Necessity between Justification and Excuse

If it is agreed that D commits the offence of murder, the following stage is to consider potential defences. There are three main options here, including self-defence, duress, and necessity, of which the defence of necessity appears as the most promising for D to avoid criminal responsibility.

National reports agree that self-defence cannot negate D's liability. Self-defence would provide a justificatory defence if D used force to protect his interests or those of someone else. A prerequisite, however, is that there is an attack by the person who

---

8 [1998] 4 All ER 103.

9 See, e. g., the Belgian national report.

10 Curiously, the Namibian national report also recognises the existence of dolus eventualis in this case.

subsequently suffers harm, but in the trolley problem there obviously is not any aggressive action taken by V.[11]

In the light of this shared conclusion, any exception to D's liability for murder must be assessed in the framework of necessity. The main question raised by the case then remains whether the necessity defence can be applied to the crime of murder.

The practical solution of each jurisdiction depends on the provisions in national law on justifying and excusing necessity. In legal systems in which necessity has only a justifying effect,[12] D is criminally liable for the murder of V. In contrast, in countries where criminal law also provides for excusing necessity, D's choice is held not blameworthy and so his acquittal is considered the most probable outcome.[13]

According to a widespread opinion, the sacrifice of a life cannot be fully justified by law, not even if it serves to save five other lives as in the present case. Such a sacrifice can at most be excused, if exceptional circumstances such as those characterising the trolley problem exist.

From a comparative point of view, surprisingly, all national reports emphasise the distinction between necessity as a justification and necessity as an excuse.[14] This is not something that can be taken for granted, given the diversity of traditions and the large number of jurisdictions surveyed.

Of course, reports highlight also some regional peculiarities. A Finnish Court, for instance, would most likely solve the case by convicting D of murder but waiving the punishment. In England and Wales, given the justifying nature of necessity, the debate concerns the question whether duress provides a defence to murder.[15]

Germany is another very interesting exception. The German report emphasises that the effect of necessity as an excuse is limited to averting dangers to the actor or to persons close to him. Therefore, D cannot rely on this excuse. At the same time, although the Penal Code does not provide an excuse, some German scholars would grant D an "extra-statutory" excuse if he takes action to save the greater number of lives rather than remaining passive and – in the hypothetical – letting the children be smashed by the train.[16]

Although not made explicit, this seems to be the position with which most commentators agree, based on the argument that, as a matter of fairness, it would be overly harsh to punish D for murder of V although he did what he could to save lives.

---

11 The English national report points out that self-defence can be used exceptionally to justify force on innocent parties, but not in this case.

12 E.g., China, some American States which follow the traditional common law, and Turkey. The only jurisdictions in which justification is likely to be applied are Belgium and those U.S. jurisdictions which follow the MPC.

13 E.g., most Australian jurisdictions, Israel, Poland, Namibia.

14 On this latter category, see J. Horder, *Excusing Crime*, Oxford University Press, 2004.

15 See the national report on England and Wales for details.

16 See German national report for more.

e) Some Possible Origins of a "Kantian" Approach

The approach that emerges from the overview of the reports rejects the utilitarian view that it is permissible to sacrifice one life in order to save a greater number of lives. In this widespread perspective, human life is an inviolable legal interest, the destruction of which cannot be justified and deemed "lawful".

After all, a defence of justification expresses a judgement of moral approval by the legal system, whereas an excuse merely recognises that it is understandable that the defendant acted as he did under exceptional conditions. Some of the reports mention possible origins of this "Kantian" approach, based on the ban on balancing human lives in conflict with others.

A first point is the "sanctity" of human life.[17] This principle seems to have strong roots in the traditional common law, according to which it is invariably forbidden to take the life of an innocent person.[18] Also from the Turkish response, the sanctity of life emerges as a very important value of the legal system.[19]

Some reports from Central Europe also reveal a historical matrix of the ban on balancing human lives like other legal interests. The debate developed around the so-called euthanasia trials in Germany. After the end of the NS period, some doctors who selected disabled people to be killed defended themselves by saying that they did this in order to stay in charge and save the lives of many others. If they had been replaced by other doctors chosen by the regime, even more people would have been selected and killed. Comparable accounts are mentioned in the Dutch and Norwegian reports, since these countries were occupied by German forces.

Finally, the rejection of a utilitarian approach also seems to be driven by possible practical implications. Making the sacrifice of a human life legitimate would lead to a slippery slope in the age of terrorism. In the future, torture in the ticking bomb scenario or the shooting down of a hijacked aircraft could be consistently authorised on the same basis.

f) Final (and Provocative) Considerations

Ultimately, the globally supported idea is that D commits an act that is against the law but which it would be unjust to punish. There is a sense of universal justice that all commentators (including the author of the present Synopsis) share regarding this dramatic example. Regardless of the respective laws and technicalities, no one considers it acceptable to punish D for the tragic choice he makes. This view appears also to reflect social attitudes: the report on Japan mentions a survey showing that 90 percent of Japanese respondents would agree to switch the tracks like D did.[20]

This uniformity of thought gives rise to the suspicion that, hidden behind sophisticated legal arguments, perhaps there is the forbidden calculation – that, in the end,

---

17 See, e.g. D.J. Baker, J. Horder (eds.), *The Sanctity of Life and the Criminal Law. The Legacy of Glanville Williams*, Cambridge University Press, 2013.

18 See the U.S. national report.

19 See the Turkish national report.

20 See the Japanese national report.

the common thought could be that D is right to switch tracks because he saves five children in exchange for one adult.

The circumstance that the potential victims are children also is very important. Children cannot be blamed for putting themselves in danger, while, for example, five drunken adults would be much more subject to blame than the repairman, who is just doing his job.

It would be interesting to understand the legal implications of the opposite scenarios: D switches tracks to save the single man and kills five people, or D doesn't switch the course of the train which is about to kill the five children. Is there a duty to save them? Would it be a case of negligence not to save the five children? Is it certain that D's omission is not criminally relevant?

These seem only provocative speculations, but they may soon have to be answered due to technological evolution. Self-driving cars need clear instructions to deal with scenarios like the trolley dilemma,[21] and criminal law then cannot simply rely on the old adage that "*necessitas non habet legem*" for declaring that it would be unfair to punish the switch man.

---

21 See, e.g., R Jenkins et al. (eds.), *Autonomous Vehicle Ethics: The Trolley Problem and Beyond* (OUP, 2022).

2. Attribution of Death

By *Paolo Beccari*

Vignette 2

D intends to kill his neighbor V. Hidden near V's house, D waits for V and stabs him several times with a knife. V is taken to the hospital, where his wounds are treated. His injuries are not life-threatening, and V is kept overnight for observation. During the night, a technical defect in the hospital kitchen leads to the outbreak of a fire, which kills V and other persons. Can D be held criminally responsible for V's death?

a) Attribution of Death: A First Re-Reading of the Case

The case vignette describes D's intentional stabbing of V and V's death as the final result. Between the act and the result, however, lies the complication of an abnormal course of causation, where an extraordinary event – the outbreak of a fire – intervenes.

We can assume that D intends to kill V at the moment when he stabs him. But V's death does not occur immediately as a result of D's conduct, mainly for two reasons: first, the stab wounds inflicted do not endanger V's life; second, D stops the assault after stabbing V a few times. It is not known why D stopped the assault; he could have done so of his own accord or because something beyond his control intervened (e. g., someone approaching the scene or police sirens sounding in the distance). However, as a logical consequence of the stab wounds, V is taken to the hospital, where his wounds are treated and he is kept overnight for observation. During the night, a new factor intervenes in the causal chain: a technical defect in the hospital kitchen leads to the outbreak of a fire, which causes the death of V and other patients.[1] These events lead to the question whether D, having set the "trigger" for V's hospitalization and eventual death, is guilty of a completed intentional homicide or can only be punished for attempted murder.[2]

b) Two Theories on Causation in Criminal Law and the Notion of "Abnormal Risk"

The decision turns on the fundamental issue of causation in criminal law theory. According to a common concept, every result-related offence requires a conjunction of human conduct and a result through a causal chain.

According to the *Äquivalenztheorie* proposed by the German criminalist von Buri (1873), every antecedent without which the result would not have come into existence should be considered a cause. Under this theory, all necessary conditions are

---

1 The Vignette does not indicate that it was the stab wounds that prevented V from escaping the fire. We can therefore not say that D was responsible for V's death by immobilizing him.

2 This difference is not just an academic question. In most jurisdictions, sentences for completed murder are or can be significantly more severe than those for attempted murder, and there may even be different courts that have jurisdiction for trying the case.

considered to be equivalent. This theory thus does not distinguish between causes and conditions.

One problem with this approach is that one could eliminate one cause after another, and the result would still remain the same; there would thus exist complete uncertainty about the determining cause. Problems also arise when that chain of causation is broken due to the intervention of a "natural event", a non-agential factor that lets the result appear as being caused by a non-human intervention. In such cases, there remains a degree of uncertainty,[3] because even natural events could be read as enhancing human causation. The risk is to endorse a "mechanistic judgement".

To exemplify the concept, let us imagine a relative of the deceased V blaming D for V's death by stating: "He would never have died in the hospital fire if D had not stabbed him!". He could argue that D intended V's death, he stabbed V, and V died; D should therefore be criminally liable for intentionally killing V.[4]

It is true that V would not have died in the hospital fire if D had not injured him, because in that case V's hospitalization would not have occurred. In terms of factual causation, V's death was thus entirely dependent on D's act. Under that approach, a natural event (the fire in the hospital) is placed within a chain of causation set in motion by a human being. By doing so, however, the notion of a "natural result" is distorted. Some legal systems, by following this approach, give "human form" to natural events.[5]

But nothing changes if we replace the outbreak of the fire by some human act. Let us assume, as in the example posed in the German report, that V is in the hospital waiting to be released, when a nurse N in a sudden rage attacks V and kills him. Based on mere factual causation, we could say – diverging from the solution offered in the German report[6] – that V would never have died if D had not caused him to be in the hospital, where he would later meet the "out-of-control nurse".

The key point, then, does not lie in a distinction between human and non-human intervention, but in the ineffectiveness of a mere "but for" (*condicio sine qua non*)

---

3 See report on England and Wales.

4 Cf. the opening of the German report.

5 See Australian report: "certain such natural events will be viewed in the same light as – or, at the least, will be held to be capable of being viewed by a jury in the same light as – the 'free, deliberate, and informed intervention of a second person'", quoting HLA Hart and Tony Honore, *Causation in the Law* (Clarendon Press, 1985, 2nd ed.) 342, discussing *Bush v Commonwealth* (1880) 78 Ky 326. The Australian report also quotes from *The Queen v Hallett*, where the appellant had assaulted the deceased and then left him unconscious on a beach, whereupon the deceased was eventually drowned by the incoming tide. The Court held, without very much hesitation, that "the action of the sea on the deceased" could not be regarded as "breaking the chain of causation".

6 The German report instead concludes that V's death would solely be attributed to N, because her attack "overtook" the causal chain initiated by D. V's death is attributed to N even if D's attack might later have caused V's death. See also the case in the Chilean report of the death of a patient in an ambulance car due to a traffic accident involving the vehicle. Here again, based on factual causation, we could conclude that, had he not been injured, he would not have been in that ambulance car and would not have died in the accident, thus attributing the death to the perpetrator.

test of factual causation, which overextends D's responsibility. All legal systems represented here agree that such a reading of causation in criminal law would be ineffective, unconvincing and unacceptable. See, for example, the criticism of the Japanese report: "The scope of attribution would be too large if attribution required only a causal relationship, because causal chains are endless." Absurdly, in a system of mere factual causation one could hold D's parents responsible for the killing because of giving birth to D, perhaps together with the owner of the kitchen tools shop where D bought the knife. Therefore, most legal systems recognize a so-called prohibition of regress: "If the independent action of third parties is the last relevant cause to lead to a death, one ought not to 'go back' beyond it".[7]

Legal systems thus distinguish between factual and legal causation. Put simply, for legal causation it must be proved that D caused V's death *in a legally relevant way.* Although all legal systems agree that such a re-reading of causation is necessary, the law on causation remains unclear and ambiguous with regard to the criteria to be applied.[8] Legal systems tend to rely on case law for solutions. The main idea, according to the Australian report, is that "a person can be liable for homicide only if his or her conduct substantially [or significantly] contributed to the subsequent death of V, taking into account the actual time at which and the manner in which the death occurred".[9]

Certainly, risk assessment is not simple. In assessing multiple risks and their offensive potential, not all readings of legal causation can be considered satisfactory. For example, in Belgium "all necessary causes remain intact in the causal chain, including faults that only had a limited contribution to the outcome".[10] This theory is one of a "masked factual causation", since D is held responsible for the result whenever his act – if put on the same level as other causes – was a necessary condition of V's death.[11] The Belgian report's assertion that this doctrine is very "victim-friendly"[12] is correct – one can prosecute D for murder in any case in which he provided a necessary causal factor.[13]

Within the framework of legal causation, many legal systems recognize the doctrine of "extraordinary risk", whereby an exception is made to the attribution of an outcome where the risk that materialized was unforeseeable or otherwise totally atyp-

---

7 See Chilean report.

8 See, e. g., Belgian report ("In the absence of a legal definition, the causality issue has been decided by case law") and Singapore Report ("... there are no general provisions in the Singapore Penal Code explaining how causation issues should be resolved"). For Italy, reference is made to G. Fiandaca/E. Musco, *Criminal Law. General Part*, Bologna, 2019, pp. 242–243: "Articles 40 and 41 [of the Penal Code] lend themselves to different readings because they fail to indicate a well-defined and unambiguous model of causation".

9 See Australian report.

10 See Belgian report.

11 Norway's reflection seems relevant on the point: "Where several causes are involved, the assessment varies depending on the causal constellation as the *conditio* requirement cannot be fully maintained in these cases."

12 See Belgian report.

13 Belgian law also does not require any psychological connection (*mens rea*) between the agent and the event, as will be seen in the next section.

ical (*völlig atypisch*).[14] According to that doctrine, it does not matter whether a causal factor is human or natural; what counts is its "exceptionality" compared with a typical causal course.

The three arguments for this solution as expressed in the German report help to explain the idea of an extraordinary risk.

First, "the causal chain between the stabbing and V's death was quite atypical". It is true that the conduct of homicide is not bound to any form and can result from different causal chains, but it is also true that such a causal chain usually does not include a fortuitous fire blaze in a hospital. Yet, "there are several exceptional situations in which the law negates attribution even though causation can be proved. This is the case, for example, when an independent actor (or the victim himself) interfered autonomously and created a new risk which superseded the original risk created by the defendant."[15]

Second, "the prohibition of stabbing persons is not meant to protect anyone from burning to death in a hospital blaze". This argument looks at the purpose of the rule violated by the defendant: a chain of (legal) causation is broken whenever the fact that occurs, even if it is factually attributable to the agent's conduct, does not constitute a concretization of the risk that the rule is meant to prevent. One could say here that the purpose of a statute prohibiting murder refers to violating the interest of individual human life, not other interests, such as public safety or public health; and in the Vignette case, the outbreak of the fire is fortuitous, not brought about by D's willful behavior.

Third, "V's risk of being killed by a fire was not increased significantly by being in a hospital; fires are not more likely in hospitals than in private homes. V's death can thus not be attributed to D's act but to the general 'life risk' (*allgemeines Lebensrisiko*) that a fire can break out and kill persons near the fire". And this – we can say briefly – is "common knowledge", based on rules of common experience.

The notion of risk thus serves as a watershed: if the agent creates by his or her conduct a "legally prohibited risk", effectively increasing the probable occurrence of a harmful event, and if the prevention of that risk is the purpose of the rule violated, then the agent will be punishable for the result.

Outside this kind of "ordinary" risk, anything which constitutes an extraordinary or totally atypical risk will not be attributable to him or her. Under that theory, the notion of a naturally caused result is replaced by the concept of a "legally prohibited risk" (which lumps together the cases of the hospital fire and the "out-of-control nurse"). In this context, an accidental fire in a hospital should be considered an extraordinary risk.

This approach has become the majority view in several legal systems. The Australian report seems to refer to it when stating that, "where an extraordinary event such as the one with which we are concerned intervenes between the conduct of the accused and the death of the deceased, it seems that that event must be regarded

---

14 See German report.

15 Ibid.

as replacing the accused's conduct as the legal cause of the death".[16] Similarly, the report on Chile states that "The leading strand of scholarship holds that the solution is offered by the 'objective attribution/imputation' doctrine. According to this view, a result may not be attributed to a defendant if the naturalistic *conditio sine qua non* is normatively defeated". This doctrine "is based on the notion of 'legally prohibited risk', and a series of specific applications have been developed by doctrine to exclude the attribution of certain results falling outside this kind of risk".[17] The Chinese report explains that "Chinese criminal law has increasingly emphasized the theory of objective attribution (*Lehre von der objektiven Zurechnung*) in discussions on causation issues". Still in the Asian context, the Japanese legal system also defines the theory of objective attribution/imputation of the event as "Japanese-style"[18], confirming its broad acceptance.[19]

This seems to be the dominant doctrine worldwide, having replaced the doctrine of "*condicio sine qua non* under scientific laws" as well as the doctrine of adequate causation, which is based on judgments of probability in daily life.[20]

However, it is interesting to note that there is no shortage of alternative models that contain further aspects. For example, Finnish law "has not been built on the famous German doctrine of 'objective imputation'";[21] still, "An act that is deemed to have occurred more by accident than through negligence is not punishable".[22] This clearly shows that there is no single theory underlying the problem of causation, nor do we currently find a uniform paradigm. Once again, it is therefore important to consider the different sensitivities emerging from the national reports.

c) Subjective Attribution as a Supplement to Objective Attribution (?)

Reports are unanimous in concluding that "it is unlikely that D could be held criminally responsible for V's death".[23] However, even the most widely shared theory,

---

16 See Australian report, which also adds: "At the very least, that should be the case where, as here, the wounds caused by the accused would certainly not have killed the deceased".

17 See Chilean report.

18 See Japanese report.

19 Namibia also seems to have adopted this doctrine by treating the "purpose of the norm" as the basis of liability and introducing the notion of an "abnormal event". The Polish report states "we commonly use objective attribution (*obiektywne przypisanie*, *objektive Zurechnung*) theory" since the early 2000's, and the Turkish report declares that "the theory of objective imputation has gained ground in the Turkish criminal law scholarship and in the jurisprudence of the Court of Cassation". And, finally, the U.S. "Common Law approach" seems to coincide with this German doctrine as it speaks of "an extraordinary and abnormal occurrence, which rises to the level of an exonerating, superseding cause".

20 These two doctrines are mentioned only briefly, but they are still used in some jurisdictions (the former is widely used in Italian jurisprudence, the latter is the one conventionally used in Japan and in Belgian courts).

21 The reporter from Finland declares that "this doctrine has sometimes been discussed in the criminal law literature, but it has not been widely accepted".

22 Section 7 para. 3 Finnish Penal Code (515/2003).

23 See the opening of U.S. report.

i. e., the German doctrine of objective attribution, does not sufficiently explain the final result.

For example, consider the following case, involving an agent D and a victim V as well as an extraordinary event.

> With intent to kill V, D kidnaps him and ties him to the base of a tree in a forest to make him die of hardship. He does so, however, after watching the weather and seeing a thunderstorm approaching. Once V is tied up, D walks away and leaves V without the possibility to move. The thunderstorm arrives, and a very powerful lightning strikes the tree to which V is tied and kills him. Can D be held criminally responsible for V's death?

In this hypothetical, D does not directly kill V, nor is V's life endangered by D's act. The striking of lightning is a risk of everyday life and certainly cannot be controlled by D. At the same time, the lightning could represent an atypical causal result of the killing that D had intended to be brought about by starvation. Yet, the conclusion as to D's criminal responsibility might differ from the Vignette case. The reason may be D's subjective disposition. In the Vignette case, D did not and could not foresee the outbreak of the fire; in the hypothetical posed here, he could have foreseen the fact that V could be killed by lightning. The difference in outcome could thus be explained by a subjective element in the theory of objective imputation.[24]

Various reports in fact mention an element of foreseeability, which pertains to the level of culpability. For example, the Polish report points out that "it is crucial not only to establish a causal link between events (their temporal and local relation) but also to examine whether the result was connected with inadvertence of the defendant".[25]

The Finnish report also explains that "In Finnish (and Swedish) criminal law this situation would be dealt with as a case of excessive reach of culpability, especially criminal intent".[26]

An extraordinary risk then exceeds, on the level of causality, an ordinary scope of risk and the purpose of the rule violated, but also – on the level of culpability – the scope of what the agent could have foreseen.

As the Australian report states, "A death made foreseeable by the accused's conduct has actually resulted from an event that is so unpredictable, and thus 'so independent' of that conduct, as to render the accused's acts 'merely part of the history'".[27] England and Wales also focus on the principle of foreseeability, specifying that "the more foreseeable the intervention was, the more likely that it will *not* break the causal chain".[28] Further indications of foreseeability can be found in other reports.[29]

---

24 See Chinese report.

25 See Polish report.

26 See Finnish report.

27 See Australian report.

28 See report on England and Wales.

29 In Israel, "the case law and part of the literature pose the question whether the course of events that took place, based on a relatively high level of generalization (in contrast to the concrete course of events with all its details), was reasonably foreseen/predicted by D". In Namibia, "In order for an intervening event to qualify as such, it has to be an abnormal one and

It is not an easy task, however, as the Israeli report notes, to know "concretely what is included within reasonable prediction".[30] The idea, as the Italian report puts it, is "not only to prevent any subject from being charged with factors that exceed and deviate from an ordinary causal course, but also any element outside his *mens rea*".[31]

On the other hand, such a subjective approach has been criticized by some Belgian writers as linking completely unforeseeable consequences to indirect causes, thereby undermining legal certainty.[32] This criticism can be overcome by looking at the foreseeability criterion in the context of negligent crimes. Here, the negative limit is drawn at fortuitous events, thus constructing the concepts of foreseeable and fortuitous events as antithetical to each other. If an event is fortuitous, there can be no negligence – which requires foreseeability – since fortuity relates to occurrences outside of what is imaginable and can be the subject of cautionary rules.[33] It is possible, in other words, to discern a complementarity between the two elements, which clarify each other. It can be argued that a typical causal course not only lacks objectively exorbitant occurrences but also is a course of events that a subject can reasonably imagine to occur. Therefore, foreseeability also refers to a "sequence of occurrences" in a "normal" causation course, defined by common experience.

We may therefore bring the two requirements together and regard the non-foreseeability of the result as a complementary aspect of a risk which exceeds the purpose of the criminal rule and an ordinary causal course. This might provide a good meeting point between the approaches in different legal systems. That way, we can also give a proper meaning to the notions of intervening natural and non-agential events (or by a third party, if we still think about the nurse example) as excluding the criminal responsibility of the original actor.[34] Thus, if D – with intent to kill – had stabbed V on the side of a highway, not fatally injuring him but causing him to fall onto the roadway, where V was hit and killed by a car, there would have been neither an extraordinary risk on the causal level nor an unforeseeable risk on the subjective level. Hence D could be held criminally responsible for V's death. In contrast, in the hospital vignette D could perhaps have foreseen a sudden deterioration of V's general condition, but certainly not a fire that developed fortuitously in the kitchen due to a technical defect. Indeed, "Dying from a hospital fire can hardly be seen as 'the natural or foreseeable consequence' of a stabbing".[35] Therefore, in our present case, D cannot be held criminally responsible for V's death and, particularly, for completed murder. As the German report rightly highlights, "One counterargument could be the fact

---

should not be foreseeable by the perpetrator". Californian law likewise decides these cases on the criterion of (un)foreseeability of the result: for the actor's responsibility, it is sufficient that the consequence "might reasonably have been contemplated".

30 See Israel report.

31 See Italian report.

32 See Belgian report.

33 On this point, see, e.g. in Italy G. Fiandaca/E. Musco, *Criminal Law. General Part*, Bologna, 2024, p. 572.

34 See Finnish report: "To put it simply: the danger and the breach of duty that the stabbing meant could not be linked to the outcome due to intervening factors".

35 See the U.S. MPC approach.

that D *intended* to kill V. But even D's intention cannot provide a sufficient link for the necessary 'objective' attribution of V's death to D's act. D cantherefore only be convicted of *attempted* murder of V".[36]

Even in a case such as that of the lightning in the forest (as mentioned above), D might raise the issue of an *aberratio delicti,*[37] pointing out the divergence between what was intended and what was achieved (D wanted death from starvation, V died instead from the lightning strike). As a result, D could not be convicted of intentionally killing V but only of attempted murder.[38]

This is to highlight, once again, the emphasis to be placed on foreseeability when establishing criminal liability in complex causal contexts.

d) Brief Concluding Reflections

In the conjunction of an objective component (risk assessment according to the doctrine of objective attribution) and a subjective one, a universally acceptable meeting point can perhaps be found as the response to the present case (and other similar cases), still respecting the majority causation doctrines being used today in various legal systems.

The link between the two distinct elements – identified at the beginning of this Synopsis – can thus be finally re-defined: quite distinct from a purely factual notion of causation (resolutely excluded by all legal systems involved), this link results from an interaction between the plane of legal causality according to the extraordinary risk formula and the subjective element of foreseeability, which makes the result attributable to the perpetrator on the level of culpability.

---

36 See German report.

37 On the *aberratio* issue, see Chinese report.

38 This is actually stated in a very important ruling of the Italian Supreme Court of Cassation (Cass. pen. Sec. Un., no. 22676 of May 29, 2009) on a drug dealer's liability for a drug addict's death, which echoes the arguments of S. Canestrari, *L'illecito penale preterintenzionale*, Padua, 1989.

3. Torture to Save a Life

By *Mordechai Kremnitzer*

Vignette 3

Kidnapper K has abducted 8-year-old girl G and hidden her in a small cave in the woods. K is trying to extort money from G's parents for her release. The police manage to arrest K. Although being questioned for 24 hours, K steadfastly refuses to disclose where he hid G. Police officer D correctly assumes that G may soon die of thirst if she cannot be found. He therefore severely beats K to make him tell the truth. Fearing even more violence, K eventually leads the police to the cave, where they find G still barely alive. Should D be punished for torturing K?

The analysis will be performed according to the following parameters:

- the final result: punishability or non-punishability;
- the offence: the basis for punishability and for non-punishability – a discussion;
- the distinction between justification and excuse;
- is torture special?
- reference to public opinion;
- reference to implications and history.

The Synopsis concludes with a summary, some preliminary thoughts on the nature of the case, and my view.

a) The Final Result

Punishment states: Australia, Belgium, Chile (with one view supporting a supra-legal excuse), England and Wales (with a differing view of the authors), Finland, Italy, Namibia, Turkey

Non-punishment states: China, Germany, Israel, Japan, Norway, Poland, Singapore, U.S.A.

It has to be underlined that since most states (with the exception of Germany, Israel, and to some extent Poland) did not have to resolve a similar case, the analysis is based on the assessment of academics and often on the difference between majority and minority views.

b) The Offence

There are two basic models:

In most states there is a special offence dealing with extortion of a confession or information by public employees. The exceptions are England with no special offence; Namibia, in which there is no special offence, but the possibility of the direct application of the international norm is mentioned; Germany, in which this type of offence is limited to obtaining evidence for a criminal process and does not extend to interrogations to prevent the commission of a crime. The relevant offences in Germany are an assault perpetrated by a public employee and coercion (*Nötigung*). In Singapore, the offence is not limited to public employees and requires a result. In the Netherlands, the special offence is limited to extortion that causes harm.

In some states (like Israel), coercion to make a confession is a traditional offence, not related directly to international law. In others, it is a specific offence related to torture and inhuman conduct based on international law, in some cases replacing the original old-fashioned offence (Belgium, Chile, Finland). In some states (Norway, Poland, possibly Namibia), the international norm against torture is applied directly.

c) Discussion

It seems that there is a correlation between the centrality of international law in this context and an approach to punishability based on the absolute nature of the international norm against torture. On the other hand, in order to pave a way for acquittal, it is argued either that in the special circumstances of the case the minimal threshold for maltreatment was not crossed or that the prohibition against torture binding states and their agents does not preclude self-defense by citizens, including policemen.

The main basis for punishability (not just prima facie punishability but punishability in effect) is the international norm prohibiting the use of torture and inhuman conduct to achieve information. This is an absolute norm, explicitly excluding exceptions. In most jurisdictions an internal – identical or similar – norm is added, sometimes (as in Australia) with a provision excluding exceptions. In some states, the norm is backed up by the constitution (China, Germany, Norway, according to one view in Chile).

The underlying assumption is that the beating by the police officer in the Vignette was committed in the framework of his public authority (even if he deviated from it); being public and not private, the beating is an act of state violating the international norm. Additional reasons for punishability are exhaustive regulations of police interrogations (China, England, Norway) and a concern about institutional implications of non-punishment (see Wilenmann cited report on Chile). Some legal systems are ready to move from a categorical "no" to torture to an examination of possible defenses, usually self-defense and necessity as justifications, but also prevention of crime (England) and emergency evacuation (Japan). Different arguments have been raised against the application of these defenses: they do not relate to public employees who are to adhere to the principle of legality (specific legal authorization); a lack of reasonableness; a lack of imminence of danger; a lack of necessity, and a lack of proportionality.

Among the states that would not punish D, some regard the act as justified (as self-defense or necessity or both), while others regard the act as unlawful but recognize a personal excuse (necessity, duress of circumstances, excessive self-defense, or a supra-legal necessity excuse). The difference between these two approaches is twofold. It concerns the characterization of the act and the choice between a clear-cut preference and a compromise. The justification approach is based on conceiving the beatings as a private act of protecting another person within the framework of self-defense. In contrast, the excuse approach sees the beatings as a public act, belonging to the role of police; since it is devoid of a specific legal authorization, it is illegal and cannot be justified.

The German report draws our attention to a possible scenario in which it is the parents of the kidnapped child who have gotten hold of the kidnapper. Shouldn't they be allowed to find out where their daughter is hidden, even if that requires the use of force against the kidnapper? At first sight, our heart goes out to the parents. But on second thought, the result becomes less obvious, especially if we put in the place of the parents another person with the same knowledge or suspicion. Is it a good idea, in a state adhering to the rule of law, to privatize the power to investigate and to put it in the hands of private citizens? That would mean to grant citizens the authority to distinguish between a person who withholds information necessary to save a life from immediate danger and a person who is wrongly suspected of having such information. It seems that the power to use physical force to extract the information, to the extent that the law grants such power, should be in the hands of professional experts in interrogation and acquiring information.

The means that will be used by non-professionals may be utterly ineffective, even counter-productive (shutting up someone who could have been convinced to share information if treated differently), and it cannot be expected that less intrusive methods will be used first. This is a clear case in which citizens are required to call upon the authorities. Moreover, the right of a private individual to defend another person should defer to the right and duty of public servants to defend others. Withdrawal of a third person from the conflict (where a police officer can intervene) does not even have the same negative implications as withdrawal, in similar circumstances, of the attacked person herself.

In the end, the unlawful attack is terminated by the kidnapper himself, not by the police officer, similar to a case in which the kidnapper provides the information for money. One can doubt, therefore, whether this is a typical case of self-defense.

It has to be admitted that if our gaze is focused on the two protagonists – the police officer (representing the child and the legal system) and the kidnapper – a lot can be said in favor of the right of the policeman to use force for the sake of saving a life from immediate danger. On the scale of rights, on one side there is the kidnapper's right to bodily integrity and human dignity; on the other side, there is the girl's right to live (a pre-condition for human dignity). The kidnapper's right not to be beaten carries much less weight than the girl's right to life and to human dignity, in fact her right to her humanity, which includes her right to be treated as a goal in herself and not to be turned into a means for extortion. The scale on her side is heavier, even much heavier. The kidnapper, after exposing the child to imminent danger to her life, is under a legal duty to undo his wrongdoing and provide the life-saving information (China). He has full control over his body and dignity. He has the choice to fulfill his duty or to bear the consequences of his refusal. At least subjectively, the duty that he is under and the choice he holds in his hands (mouth) are alleviating the feeling of being humiliated, following from his decision to stay on the criminal, life-endangering track. This might put into doubt the issue of him being "ill-treated" based on crossing a threshold (as mentioned in the Norwegian report): In the opinion of the "man or woman in the street", the kidnapper could not have expected to be treated with kid gloves. The other side of the same coin is the fact that the police officer is not expected to accept the decision of the kidnapper to remain silent. This raises the issue of his culpability. If it is extremely difficult (or even impossible) to expect him to obey the law in these dire circumstances, punishing him violates his human dignity. It follows that he should be excused or at least receive a mitigation of punishment.

Turning to the general phenomenon of using torture or inhuman treatment in interrogations, the leitmotif here is the concern that things will get out of hand and that the danger of a slippery slope will materialize (*Duran* in Chile). What will happen if the beating does not produce a result? Isn't there an inherent motivation to escalate the pressure? At what point does it have to stop? What is the assurance that the suspected person is indeed the one who is involved in the crime and has the information? If torture is efficient in this kind of case, why stop here and not use it in other cases? Regarding the beatings as an act of self-defense is using a big hammer. If it is justified, is there a good enough reason to exclude the confession, or even to impose administrative or disciplinary measures on the police officer?

These concerns put into question the solution of justifying the conduct of the police officer. They create a need for a compromise which avoids an unfair treatment of the police officer but also avoids the negative institutional result of permitting torture in investigations. Rejecting a justification and recognizing an excuse is such a compromise. I will leave open the question whether the compromise is not an illusion. Within state hierarchical institutions, a personal excuse is difficult to swallow, and an excuse is susceptible to becoming a *de facto* justification.

Supporters of a justification offer alternatives to the institutional problem, such as merely taking administrative/disciplinary measures against the officer, including dismissal from office. But is this approach consistent with a justification? And is it really effective?

An argument for a justification is based on a comparison of beatings (in our case) to making use of a weapon by a policeman in compelling circumstances, resulting in grievous bodily harm or even death. How can a beating be forbidden when killing is permitted and justified?

To justify a broader, more intensive protection against torture than against bodily integrity and life it is not necessary to engage in weighing the protected interests. It may be sufficient to point out that the psychological mechanism that deters from maiming or killing is stronger and more effective than the inhibitions against violating human dignity. The strong need to protect dignity stems from its special vulnerability and from the fact that it is more exposed to systematic abuse (a view in Chile). It is the special vulnerability of human dignity in this context (and in historical experience) that is behind the absolute character of the international norm, the need for a deontological border, the need to raise the level of protection to the highest level of the legal order (Turkey).

d) The Distinction between Justification and Excuse

In some states, reference is made to the distinction between justification and excuse (not always in these terms), and in countries such as Poland and Israel, this distinction is the basis of the approach. In Norway, it is presented as a possible approach. If we believe that the acquittal of the policeman is a just result, the distinction between justification and excuse is helpful in explaining this result.

e) The Scope of the Absolute Prohibition Against Torture

In most reports it is assumed that the absolute prohibition covers all forms of inhuman and degrading treatment and not only torture. In two countries (Belgium and Israel) there is an official view (Government or Attorney-General) which limits the absolute character of the norm to torture only.

f) Reference to Public Opinion

Some reports refer to public opinion as supporting an acquittal, especially if there is a trial by jury (Australia, Belgium, Israel).

g) Reference to Implications and History

In some reports, broader implications are discussed: in England, the concern that recognition of necessity may open the door to anarchy and that a relativist approach may undermine the inadmissibility of extorted confessions; in Australia, the concern of breaching the dam is mentioned to introduce alternative ways of treating the situation.

h) A Summary

Factors favoring punishability are

- regarding the action taken by D as an official act performed as a police officer (and not as a private citizen),
- the affinity with international law,
- a recent history of systemic wide-spread official use of torture (Turkish report: "It may be said that Turkey's past negative experience regarding torture and ill-treatment which has led to many criticisms [...] has led Turkish academics to avoid opening a debate concerning the justification or excuse of torture"; Chilean report: the criminal offence of torture was introduced in 2016 "affected by the aftermath of the Chilean dictatorship [...]". Israel is an exception in this regard, explained by the assessment of real risks from terrorism as including ticking bombs), and
- concern regarding the broad implications of non-punishability.

Factors favoring non-punishability are

- the view that self-defense applies also to policemen and that this norm trumps considerations of legality of the executive,
- confidence in the rule of law and a skeptical view of the "slippery slope" scenario,
- reliance on alternative sanctioning of the officer,
- the balancing of interests placing significantly greater weight on the officer's side (who protects both the life and the human dignity of the child),

- justice and fairness toward the officer who acted in an extremely difficult situation in which he could hardly be expected to refrain from taking action, hence no culpability, and
- factual elements: the beatings were applied on the real offender; the force applied on him was limited; no lasting harm was caused; the life of the child was rescued at the last moment.

i) The Nature of the Case

We see here a clash between an international, noble and elevated norm and a strong local public sense – identifying with the police officer, regarding him as a devoted policeman who did the right thing.

From a theoretical point of view, this case raises the issue of the nature and feasibility of absolute norms – how absolute is the absolute? Is it possible to have an absolute norm that provides for just and fair results in all situations, or is it necessary to have some relaxation of the absolute, an escape door? How should we treat conflicts between justice from a broad view of the system as a whole and justice to the individual?

j) My View

Because of the last point, it is not right to generalize, since "justice from a broad view of the system as a whole" depends on the nature of system. The relevant criteria are the depth and strength of the rule of law and the level of terroristic threats. If based on these elements (strong embeddedness of the rule of law and a low level of threats) it can be assumed that the case remains a rather unique exception and will not have broad implications on the system as a whole, the policeman should be excused (preferably through an extra-legal excuse or discretion of the prosecution). Respect to fundamental international norms and the important idea of the absolute protection of human dignity rule out a justification and lead to a relatively weak excuse. If on the other hand, the mentioned criteria lead to an opposite response and it can be assumed that torture would become routinized and systemic, punishability should prevail. The punishment imposed should take into account the special circumstances of the case that reduce significantly D's wrongdoing and his culpability.

4. Lethal Self-Defence

By *Johan Boucht*

Vignette 4

R, a well-trained young man armed with a knife, accosts 50-year-old D, who is on her way home from a party in the early morning hours. R threatens her with the knife and takes away her purse filled with 500 € and her wristwatch worth 1,000 €. As R turns to run away, D draws a pistol she is secretly carrying in her jacket, and shoots and kills R in order to retrieve her property. Is D guilty of murder?

a) Introduction

All jurisdictions surveyed accept self-defence as a justification. The legal structure of self-defence is relatively similar in all of them, distinguishing between the relevant legal interests, temporal limitations, and substantive limitations (necessity and proportionality/reasonableness). While most jurisdictions included in the draft also recognise excessive self-defence as an excuse in some form, some jurisdictions, mainly belonging to the Anglo-American legal tradition, do not. German thinking on criminal law seems to have had considerable influence on the development of the doctrine of self-defence in many jurisdictions, not only in Europe but also in South America and Asia.

In most of the jurisdictions surveyed, self-defence is regulated in the general part of the criminal code, but there are exceptions. For example, in England and Wales self-defence is partly (as regards private defence) developed at common law and partly in the Criminal Law Act 1967, and in Japan the right to self-defence against attacks on property is regulated in a separate act ("Act on Prevention and Disposition of Thefts and Other Related Offenses"), which extends the ordinary rules on self-defence in the Japanese Criminal Code. The synopsis is based on a distinction between self-defence as a justification, making the lawful, and as an excuse, excusing the perpetrator while not affecting the unlawfulness of the act.

b) Self-Defence as a Justification

There are considerable similarities between jurisdictions as regards the interests which can be protected under the rules on self-defence. All jurisdictions accept self-defence for the protection of individual interests, both one's own and those of others, such as physical and sexual integrity as well as property. All jurisdictions therefore accept that D in principle has the right to self-defence to protect both herself and her property against R's unlawful attack on them.

The national reports indicate that a common feature of the rules on self-defence is that a "trigger" in the form of an unlawful attack of some kind is required. For the rules to apply, there has to be, for example, "an illegitimate aggression" (Chile), an "unlawful infringement" (China), an "unlawful attack" (Turkey), or the person must act to "prevent a crime" (England and Wales).

Based on the national reports, it seems that temporal limitations apply in most jurisdictions, although their scope varies. Many jurisdictions distinguish between an on-going attack and an attack which has ended. In several of the national reports (such as Belgium, Chile, Norway, Poland, and Turkey), relevance is thus attached to the fact that R's attack on D's person had ended when R was shot by D and that the attack was merely directed at D's property at this stage. Self-defence by D was therefore no longer warranted by any attack on her person, but only by the attack on her property.

Another aspect of the temporal dimension relates to the distinction between the commission and the completion of the offence, in this case with regard to the theft of D's property. Jurisdictions differ as to whether the theft was completed when R was shot. In some jurisdictions, theft is completed at the time when the possession of the property in question has shifted from the rightful owner to the thief (Finland, Norway and some U.S. states). In these jurisdictions, D can no longer claim self-defence. In Norway, for example, the justification of D's act must therefore be assessed under the rules on "self-enforcement" (section 19 of the Criminal Code), but these rules are considerably stricter as regards the use of force compared to the rules on self-defence. In some other jurisdictions, particularly where German influence has been strong, theft is considered to be on-going until the thief has brought the property into safety, for example to his house (Chile and Germany). This gives self-defence a considerably wider scope of application compared to the former position. In these jurisdictions, R's attack on D's property had not come to an end when D shot R. Self-defence was therefore available even while R was in the process of escaping from the scene of the robbery.

Whether D was entitled to kill R varies amongst jurisdictions that accept that D acted in self-defence. In some jurisdictions, such as Australia, lethal self-defence for the protection of property is ruled out by law. Other jurisdictions accept lethal force for the protection of property in certain situations. Under the U.S. Model Penal Code, lethal force is permitted to protect property provided that the defender believes that such force is necessary. Under these rules, D's act would probably be justified. Similarly, in the state of New York, the use of deadly force is permitted where an actor "reasonably believes that such other person is committing or attempting to commit a robbery", and the defender proves both that he or she believed that deadly force was necessary to prevent the commission of the robbery and that his or her belief was reasonable. In New York, therefore, D's act might be justified as self-defence. Under Chinese law, the victim is entitled to unlimited self-defence, including killing the attacker, in some cases, such as assault, murder, robbery and rape, provided the defence is not "undue". As R's acts amounted to robbery, it is possible that killing R was justified under Chinese law under this rule. Under Japanese law, the right to self-defence is extended to certain property related offences. Provided there is "a present danger to the life, body, or chastity of himself or of someone else", lethal force may be used to prevent a thief from stealing or recovering stolen property, to prevent a person from entering another person's residence where that person carries a deadly weapon or climbs over a gate or barrier, or in order to attempt to remove a person who has entered a residence illegally. As R was in the process of escaping when he was shot by D, these rules would not seem to apply. The use of lethal force can also be justified under Japanese law where there is no imminent danger to one's own or another's life where force is used "out of fear, astonishment, excitement, or dismay". However, the facts as presented in the vignette do not indicate that this was the case here and this exception would therefore not seem applicable.

If lethal self-defence for the protection of property is not permitted directly *ipso iure*, the justification of D's act would in many of the jurisdictions included in this project depend on a normative assessment of all the circumstances of the case. Civil law jurisdictions, and jurisdictions inspired by civil law, tend to distinguish between necessity and proportionality requirements. Necessity means that the least intrusive means for averting the attack must be used. Proportionality involves a separate assessment of whether the necessary defensive act was reasonable in view of the circumstances. Common law jurisdictions and some jurisdictions inspired by common law do not seem to make this distinction; they focus instead on whether the act was reasonable (England and Wales, Singapore), which seems to include both aspects. New York law refers to a necessity requirement, but the considerations involved seem to indicate that necessity also includes a reasonableness/proportionality assessment.

In some jurisdictions, such as Germany, necessity is the main criterion for assessing whether an act in self-defence is justified. Under German law, proportionality is not a relevant criterion unless the legal interest infringed by the attack is of very low value. As the value of D's property which R took possession of was not trivial, this exceptional proportionality assessment would probably not apply, and the German courts might acquit D. Chinese law also focuses on necessity, although the Chinese Supreme Court also requires a certain degree of proportionality between the attack and the self-defensive act (see above about the right to unlimited self-defence). According to the national report, it is likely that D's act would be justified under Chinese law. Under Japanese law, the focus also seems to be more on necessity than proportionality; self-defence is permitted even where there is a disproportion between the interests involved.

Other jurisdictions require that the defence is not only necessary but also proportionate (Australia, Belgium, Chile, England and Wales, Finland, Italy, Norway, Poland, Singapore, and Turkey). Some jurisdictions apply additional normative criteria to clarify the intensity of this assessment. Under both Finnish and Norwegian law, the force must not "clearly exceed what is reasonable". Thus, a considerable margin of appreciation for the benefit of the defender applies *ipso iure.* However, the Norwegian rules on "self-enforcement" (section 19 of the Criminal Code) accept only "reasonable" force and a stricter test than under the rules on self-defence therefore applies.

The circumstances that each jurisdiction considers important in this assessment vary. Several national reports observe that the attack against D's person had ended and was only directed against her property when D fired the pistol; less force may often be used for protecting property than, for example, attacks against an individual's physical integrity. The difference in value between the interests involved ("property v. life") is mentioned in several reports (Belgium, Chile, Italy, Norway, Poland, and Turkey). The value of the property that was stolen is relevant in Germany in assessing whether a proportionality requirement would exceptionally apply, but in most other jurisdictions lethal force may not be used to protect property regardless of its value. The difference in age and fitness between D and R is mentioned by the U.S. report. Two national reports refer to Art. 2 ECHR (the right to life) in support of denying lethal self-defence for the protection of property (England and Wales and Turkey). The risk of danger to D's life in the case of resistance was mentioned in one report (Israel).

In view of the national reports, it seems that most of the jurisdictions which rely on a relative reasonableness assessment would not justify D's act under the rules on self-defence in this case. However, the Turkish report observes that the Turkish Supreme Court has accepted lethal self-defence for the protection of property in some cases; it is therefore not ruled out that D might be acquitted there, although this is unlikely as there were other options available to her. Under Namibian law, D's act might be justified as there was no other way of recovering the stolen property from R.

c) Excessive Self-Defence as an Excuse

Although several jurisdictions would not justify D's action as self-defence, rules on excessive self-defence may nevertheless under certain circumstances excuse the defendant in some of these jurisdictions. Rules on excess may either enable courts to mitigate the sentence or to acquit the defendant altogether. The national reports of some jurisdictions, such as England and Wales, Namibia and the U.S.A., do not make explicit references to excessive self-defence as an excuse.

The content of the rules on excess varies amongst jurisdictions. In some, excess renders the defendant liable for a lesser crime, e. g., manslaughter instead of murder (Australia, Italy, Singapore). In Australia, these rules do not, however, apply to the protection of property; D would therefore not benefit from them in this case. In Singapore, in contrast, a defendant might have a partial defence, and would be convicted of "culpable homicide" (manslaughter), where he "in the exercise of the right of private defence of person or property, exceeds the power given to him by law, and causes the death of the person against whom he is exercising such right of defence, without premeditation and without any intention of doing more harm than is necessary for the purpose of such defence". This seems to apply to D, who would thus be convicted of the lesser offence.

In other jurisdictions, the defendant may either have his or her sentence mitigated or may be acquitted altogether. Most jurisdictions that acknowledge excess as an excuse seem to accept it at least where the defender has used too much force. In some jurisdictions, the rules on excessive self-defence do not apply where the temporal limitations of self-defence have been overstepped (such as Norway); D can therefore not rely on excess as an excuse as she fired the pistol after R had obtained possession of the property. In other jurisdictions (such as Finland), the rules on excess apply both regarding the intensity of the force which has been used and regarding the temporal limits. The fact that D shot R after the attack had ended would therefore not, in principle, exclude her from the scope of excessive self-defence as an excuse. However, the national report indicates that it is unlikely to apply to D in view of the circumstances.

The scope of application of the rules on excessive self-defence as an excuse varies among jurisdictions. Some seem to make application of the excuse contingent on the defendant's subjective state of mind by requiring that she has acted in "temporary mental incapacity" (Belgium), "duress or out of insurmountable fear" (Chile), "mental distress" (Israel), "out of fear, astonishment, excitement, or dismay" (Japan), "fear or agitation" (Poland), or "excitement, fear or agitation" (Turkey). Some jurisdictions also include objective elements in this assessment, such as the "dangerousness and unpredictability of the attack" (Finland).

Many jurisdictions that acknowledge excess as an excuse seem to agree that D cannot be acquitted on this basis. However, there is not unanimity. Under Japanese law, the rules on excess might apply if D was upset (which she might have been). The Turkish report argues that the rules on excess might apply "considering the time, the physical strength of the attacker and the violent nature of the attack" and that D would therefore have "exceeded the limits of self-defence due to an excusable excitement, fear or agitation".

Even if D's actions cannot be fully excused, according to some of the national reports D's sentence could be mitigated. Under Belgian law such a reduction would follow directly from the law (arts. 411 and 414 of the Criminal Code): the sentence must be reduced to a maximum of five years (instead of 30 years) if the homicide has been directly provoked by serious violence against persons. This would seem to apply to D. The Chilean and Turkish reports also argue hold that D's sentence should be reduced. Although the rules on self-defence would not apply to D's case under Norwegian law, excess as a mitigating circumstance also applies to "self-enforcement"; D's sentence might therefore be mitigated in view of the circumstances.

d) Conclusion

The national reports indicate that self-defence is a universally accepted justification. However, in spite of similarities that exist between the participating jurisdictions, the outcome of the case vignette varies. In all jurisdictions, R's violent attack on D gave her some right to defend her interests. All of them seem, in principle, to allow for lethal self-defence in certain situations, albeit not necessarily for the protection of property. In some jurisdictions, D might be acquitted on the ground of self-defence (China, Germany, Namibia and some states of the U.S.). Others would quite clearly not accept the taking of life for the protection of property under the circumstances described in the Vignette (Australia, Belgium, Chile, England and Wales, Finland, Israel, Italy, Norway, Poland, Singapore, and Turkey). In some of the latter jurisdictions, excess as an excuse might nevertheless apply.

How can the national differences then be explained? For example, why do some jurisdictions permit lethal self-defence against attacks on property, whilst others do not? Why do some jurisdictions require the defence to be both necessary and proportionate, while others merely require necessity (possibly with some element of proportionality attached to it)? And why do some jurisdictions apply temporal limits to the use of self-defence that do not apply in other jurisdictions? Explaining national differences is a complex task which is beyond the scope of this synopsis. However, it can be pointed at certain circumstances that may assist in explaining these differences. Where a legal system has been heavily influenced by that of another jurisdiction, it is likely that the position of the "mother rules" will also be transplanted into the other jurisdiction. There may also be cultural-historic reasons for certain national variations. How the self-defence doctrine has developed in a particular jurisdiction may therefore to some degree explain certain features of that system, for example the scope of the doctrine. How the doctrine is justified within a jurisdiction may also carry some explanatory force. Depending on whether self-defence is justified, for example, on grounds of general prevention, on the individual's right to protect his own interests (possibly in combination with a perception that self-defence also serves the protection of public interests), or on the idea that the attacker has forfeited his own rights through the attack might explain certain features of the doctrine in national jurisdictions.

5. Criminal Responsibility of Subordinates for Systemic Offences

By *Ali Emrah Bozbayındır* and *Rifat Murat Önok*

Vignette 5

D is a soldier in the army of a country ruled by a junta of generals who have come to power through a violent coup. When an opposition group demands the return to a democratic system, the government orders the soldiers to shoot and kill any person who resists arrest. Following this order, D kills three young men who take part in a protest demonstration and hit a police officer who tries to arrest them. When D is tried after a change of regime, he says that he did not like to shoot the protesters but that he thought that he had to obey his commanders' orders. D knew that if he had refused to shoot, he might have been demoted, but no physical harm would have occurred to him. Should D be convicted of murder? If so, should his sentence be mitigated because of his situation?

a) Introduction

The national reports on Vignette 5 raise a wide variety of questions regarding the criminal liability of D. In brief, most of the national reports classify D's actions as murder, and they extensively discuss the possible application of the defence of superior orders. The attribution of criminal liability in this Vignette is relatively straightforward, and the fact that D did not like to shoot the protestors does not negate his intention to kill them.[1]

Whereas some national reports imply that the criminal code had been changed to officially permit the fatal shooting of peaceful demonstrators or that such acts would be condoned under the regime, the Vignette is silent on the matter, and it was not, therefore, intended to raise issues connected with *ex post facto* criminalization of acts within the ambit of a post-regime-change law.[2]

On the other hand, some national reports discuss the question whether D's acts could be classified as crimes against humanity instead of ordinary crimes. In many countries, the former qualification would have a bearing on the availability of defences to be invoked.

b) Classification as a Crime against Humanity

Although the Vignette does not provide sufficient information to permit an analysis of whether the acts in question constitute a crime against humanity, several national reports take the context and the possible systematic nature of the offences that have been committed in the junta regime into due regard. The national reports of Belgium, Chile, and Namibia discuss that the accusations against D could be elevated to the level of crimes against humanity, which, according to their definition in customary international law, require that single acts must have been committed within the con-

1 See, for instance, England and Wales, Germany, and Poland.

2 As a result, the applicability of the "Radbruch Formula" and possible exceptions to the prohibition on retroactive application of criminal law are not discussed here. It is of note, however, that the Japanese and Israeli reports approach the matter from this vantage point.

text of a systematic or widespread attack against any civilian population. The Chilean report illustrates this point in the following manner:

> The systematic violation of human rights and the violent rule by the junta highlight the possible applicability of the regulations on crimes against humanity. The circumstances required to elicit these crimes are 1. that the act is committed as part of a widespread or systematic attack against a civilian population, and 2. that such an attack is based on a policy of the state or another organised group as described in the law (art. 1). The facts described in the case fit smoothly within this description. The sentence for homicide as a crime against humanity encompasses the range of common murder and aggravated murder (art. 4).

If, according to the respective national definition, D's acts satisfy the elements of crimes against humanity, his acts would not be treated as ordinary murder. The Belgian report states that if D's acts were classified as murder as a crime against humanity, no justification would be available to him according to article 70 of the Belgian Criminal Code. In Chile, the defence of superior orders is confined to cases where the defendant was acting under duress.

Further, the elevation of the crimes to the status of crimes against humanity would be employed as an argument to justify the retroactive punishment of a person after a regime change under post-regime-change law. Article 7 of the European Convention on Human Rights would provide some guidance in the European context.

Although it does not state it explicitly, the Chinese report takes the context in this Vignette to invoke the concept of perpetration through an organization (*Organisationsherrschaft*). As stated in the report:

> Some scholars invoke the concept of "perpetration through an organization" (Oganisationsherrschaft) to explain this relationship. Proponents of this view argue that, as a mastermind with command authority, the order-giver can establish indirect perpetration by ordering criminal acts through the organizational power structure. This type of domination or control typically applies in cases of state power abuse or systemic offenses, where the front-line perpetrator is a direct perpetrator, and the commander is an indirect perpetrator.

The Chinese solution to the present Vignette considers D a coerced accomplice, a form of duress stipulated in Article 28 of the Chinese Criminal Code. Accordingly, D's punishment should be mitigated, or he should be exempted from criminal liability.

c) Possible Defences

Now we shall turn our attention to possible defences and mitigating factors as discussed in the national reports. The possible defences available in this Vignette would be the defences of superior orders, duress and the prevention of crime (the latter only for England and Wales). D shot the protestors while they were hitting a police officer. The reporters from Chile and England raise the point that the defence of a third party could be considered, depending on the level of aggression exhibited by the protestors.

Although it is not evident from the description in the Vignette that the level of threat would play a determining role in the European context, it is discussed in the Belgian report:

> Article 2 of the ECHR states that a "deprivation of life shall not be regarded as inflicted in contravention of this article when it results from the use of force which is no more than ab-

solutely necessary: (a) in defence of any person from unlawful violence; (b) in order to effect a lawful arrest or to prevent the escape of a person lawfully detained; (c) in action lawfully taken for the purpose of quelling a riot or insurrection". In this case, probably all three grounds could be invoked. It is not clear whether the "hitting" of the officer was life threatening. If so, the shooting might be justified as legitimate defence of others (art. 416 BeCC). If not, and that seems more likely, D's action will be deemed "more than absolutely necessary", especially in light of the ECtHR's strict construction of this criterion (ECtHR McCann and Others v. UK, § 147) and the obligation of states to apply a test of strictly proportionate use of force excluding any margin of appreciation for deprivation of life by state authorities (see also ECtHR Ribcheva and Others v. Bulgaria, § 165).

aa) Superior Orders and Mistake of Law

Recognition of the defence of superior orders and its delimitation is the law's response to the dilemma of a subordinate who finds himself between two conflicting demands, namely an order of his superior that exceeds proper limits and the requirements of domestic or international criminal law. There are two extreme solutions to this dilemma. The first is the doctrine of unconditional obedience and of *respondeat superior*, according to which only the superior who gives the unlawful order is responsible. At the other pole is the doctrine of absolute liability, which gives the subordinate the right to question the lawfulness of any order given to him, and in case the subordinate executes an unlawful order, he is made responsible for his act. Between these two, intermediate views exist. The prevailing moderate approach in many jurisdictions is the conditional liability theory (*obeisance avec reserves*), which, under certain circumstances, considers a subordinate's mistake as to the lawfulness of an order as a defence. The manifest illegality principle is a golden mean between the two extremes. According to this principle, obeying a superior's orders relieves the soldier of criminal responsibility. If, however, an order is manifestly unlawful or, in other words, the illegality of the order is evident on its face, the soldier must refuse to obey it, or he shall be criminally responsible. Most of the reporting countries adhere to one or more forms of the manifest illegality model with regard to the defence of superior orders. For example, Belgian and German law and the Italian case law have adopted the manifest illegality model; the reports of Israel and Finland refer to the manifest illegality of the order to argue that the defence of compliance with superior orders would not excuse D. Some states (Finland, Poland, Turkey, U.S.A.) hold the subordinate responsible if he knew about the illegality of the order. In Poland, the subordinate is responsible if "he intentionally commits a crime while carrying out an order". A wide variety of tests have been developed to ascertain the subordinate's knowledge regarding the legality of an order. Lower thresholds apply in some other countries: in the U.S.A., it is sufficient for the subordinate's criminal liability to show that a person of ordinary sense and understanding would have known the orders to be unlawful, whereas in Finland there is no defence if "the soldier should have understood the unlawfulness of the order and of the act it requires".

Among the jurisdictions included here, Australia and England and Wales do not recognize a superior orders defence, thereby coming close to the doctrine of absolute liability. As suggested in the English national report, such an approach places "junior soldiers in an unenviable position of having to decide between obeying what could be an unlawful order or being court-marshalled for refusing to obey what could be a lawful order". But the English report also states that this argument has little traction on the facts of the present Vignette, because the defendant does not face physical harm, only demotion, and the order, given its disproportionality, could not be regarded as arguably lawful.

In a civil hierarchy, if the subordinate considers an order unlawful, the general rule for public servants is the so-called reflexive obedience.[3] According to this, if a civil servant considers an order from his superior unlawful, the latter must renew the order in writing. If the superior repeats the order in writing, the subordinate who executes the order shall be absolved of any responsibility unless the unlawful but binding order involves a criminal offence.[4]

However, the military codes or manuals of the reporting countries foresee more relaxed norms regarding superior orders. In Germany, for instance, under § 5 of the Military Criminal Code a subordinate who carries out an order to commit a criminal offence is guilty only if he recognizes that the act is unlawful or if that fact is manifest under the circumstances known to him. Applying this test, the German report arrives at the conclusion that it was obvious even to a simple soldier that he was ordered to commit an intentional homicide for which there existed no military necessity or justification. Thus, the Military Code does not provide an excuse for D.

In Finland, the perpetrator is exempt from criminal liability if "the act has occurred under circumstances in which the subordinate could not have reasonably been expected not to carry out the order". But, as the Finnish report explains:

> The order given by the government in the Vignette case is indeed manifestly illegal since it demands a completely disproportionate reaction to demonstrators. It amounts to state terror. The soldier should thus have understood the unlawfulness of the order and of the act ordered. The order is so manifestly unlawful that even the circumstances do not give any reason for an exemption of liability as might be granted according to the second part of the section.

In Italy, an order to shoot at a group of demonstrators during a protest would be clearly unlawful, so that the soldier must not carry it out even if it is a so-called unquestionable order.

Likewise, according to the subjective test contained in the Turkish Military Penal Code, the subordinate could not claim that he did not know that the order was aimed at the commission of a crime because of the clearly unlawful nature of the order that would be obvious to the perpetrator. The same conclusion is reached in the report on Finland.

This also holds true with regard to a stricter subjective test under U.S. military law, which recognizes a defence of obedience to orders in the Manual for Courts-Martial:

> It is a defence to any offence that the accused acted pursuant to orders unless the accused knew the orders to be unlawful or a person of ordinary sense and understanding would have known them to be unlawful.[5]

---

3 See Chile.

4 Chile, Italy, and Turkey are examples.

5 United States Dep't of Def., Manual for Courts-Martial United States (2024) at II–136.

Indeed, the Manual's "ordinary sense and understanding" test is more stringent than the manifest illegality standard applied in some other jurisdictions. In *United States v. Kinder*, for instance, an airman was ordered by his lieutenant to kill a captured Korean civilian; the Air Force Board of Review rejected the airman's argument for a superior order defence by stating that the order in question was "so obviously beyond the scope of authority of the superior officer and so palpably illegal on its face as to admit of no doubt of its unlawfulness to a man of ordinary sense and understanding."[6] Regarding the situation in this Vignette, the report on U.S.A. makes the following observations:

> If prosecuted in a courts-martial, whether D could successfully claim the obedience of orders defense would turn on whether D knew the orders to be unlawful, or a person of ordinary sense and understanding would have known the orders to be unlawful. Since a junta of generals has taken over in a violent coup, it is difficult to know what persons of ordinary understanding would understand.

This assessment makes it explicit that the subjective test regarding the illegality of an order is more context-dependent than the objective tests of manifest illegality outlined above.

The defence of mistake of law is connected with the superior orders defence. Could D escape punishment by arguing that, because of superior orders, he was unaware that he was acting in breach of existing criminal prohibitions?

In a similar vein, the Namibian report suggests that the Government of the Junta is the recognized government. Considering the fact that its orders were only specific to persons who resisted arrest, the Namibian report concludes that the order was not manifestly unlawful in the circumstances prevailing at the time. The Namibian report further states that:

> D's contention is that he was under the belief that he should obey his superiors. Therefore, it can be concluded that he lacked the requisite intent or mens rea to commit murder. The question of whether D ought to have known that the order was unlawful becomes mute by the conclusion that the order was not manifestly unlawful.

On the other hand, the other reports dealing with mistake of law conclude that, under the circumstances of the case, D could not escape punishment. The German report suggests that "even in a state under authoritarian rule, it is evident that persons must not be shot just because they are resisting arrest". The German report refers to the jurisprudence of the Federal Court of Justice in the so-called Wall Guard cases, where the Court denied an unavoidable mistake of law of soldiers who shot and killed fugitives who tried to climb over the fence separating the German Democratic Republic and the Federal Republic of Germany. The Italian report states that D may not invoke the rules on "putative error" because D had to assess for himself the clear unlawfulness of the order and disregard it. The Israeli report argues that even if D was not aware of the illegality of the order, he would not benefit from the defence of obedience to orders since the order was manifestly illegal. Moreover, in Belgium the defence of mistakes regarding the order's illicit character is excluded by statute with regard to crimes against humanity. Likewise, the reference in the Namibian Constitu-

---

6 See the relevant case law in the report on U.S.A.

tion to the binding character of "the general rules of public international law and international agreements binding upon Namibia" means that Art. 33 of the Rome Statute is applicable, and orders to commit genocide or crimes against humanity are deemed to be manifestly unlawful. The report on Namibia nevertheless concludes that, under the circumstances of the case, the order in question was not manifestly unlawful. That is the only report that reaches this conclusion.

bb) Duress

D's fear of being demoted is discussed in the national reports mostly in the context of duress and necessity (or "unsurmountable fear" in Chile). There seems to be consensus here that D's mere concern of being demoted would not satisfy the requirements of duress, necessity or unsurmountable fear.

For instance, the Australian and English reports provide an overview of the common law defence of duress, which is based on a "merciful concession to human frailty". The English report sums up the requirements of this defence as follows:

> Duress applies where the defendant reasonably believes that another has threatened her with death or serious injury (i. e., to herself or to another for whom she is expected to be responsible) unless she commits a specified offence, and D's actions in committing the offence are reasonable in the circumstances.

In D's situation, however, the significant disparity between the threat to D (demotion) and the crimes D committed (three murders) is self-evident.[7] Similarly, D's situation cannot satisfy the elements of excusing necessity; for example, the mere risk of a demotion is not onerous enough to present an excuse under § 35 of the German Criminal Code or the conditions of necessity as set out in Art. 71 of the Belgian Criminal Code. The excuse of duress has been limited to dangers to life, health, and liberty which cannot otherwise be averted. Furthermore, after explaining that D's fear could not be classified under the general defence, the Chilean report highlights the fact that "the degree of fidelity to the law to be expected of a member of the armed forces surpasses greatly the one expected of a common citizen". The Norwegian report arrives at a similar conclusion in its application of the necessity defence in Article 17 of the Norwegian Criminal Code:

> […] it is clear that no physical harm would have come to D had he refused to carry out the orders, only a risk of demotion. As the interest of not being demoted is likely to not be considered a legally protected interest, the first criterion of section 17 would not appear to be satisfied. The rules on necessity would therefore not apply. However, even if they did apply, it is clear that the value of the sacrificed interests, the lives of three protestors, is far greater than the value of those which are saved. D's actions can therefore not in any case be justified.

The Norwegian report also notes that necessity cannot be invoked as a defence because, according to case law, it can never be justified to sacrifice the life of another to save one's own life. Similarly, in Australia duress is not a valid defence when the charge is murder in the first degree as a principal.

[7] For further discussion, see the Australian report.

d) Mitigating Factors in Sentencing

Regarding mitigating factors in sentencing, there are a wide variety of institutions in the jurisdictions included here. The Australian report makes the following observation concerning the possible application of non-exculpatory duress as a mitigating factor in the present case:

> D's factual scenario makes it unlikely that the duress will have significant mitigatory effect. Indeed, it would seem likely that, rather than D's situation affording him mitigation in a sentence, it might, in fact, *increase* the length of any sentence [...]. Because any duress here is very minor, and because D's response to it so disproportionate, it seems likely that the sentencing court would find that D's moral culpability was not reduced on this account. And it would be difficult for a court to conclude that, due to the presence of such duress, D's prospects of rehabilitation were improved or his chances of reoffending reduced.

In England, as there is no applicable defence, this would be a straightforward case of murder. The report on Israel likewise argues that, given the specific circumstances of the case, D should not be able to benefit from any mitigation.

However, in China, "since D can be regarded as a coerced accomplice under Article 28 of the Chinese Criminal Code, his punishment should be mitigated or withheld altogether, depending on the circumstances of the crime."[8]

Under Belgian and Turkish law, mitigating circumstances in Article 81 of the Belgian Criminal Code and Article 62 of the Turkish Criminal Code are an open category, and D could invoke them. In fact, in Belgium, it would even be possible to suspend the sentence.

In Finland, the shooting of civilians would be regarded as wilful killing, but the specific circumstances of the killings would be taken into account as factors mitigating the punishment under Chapter 6 of the Finnish Criminal Code. Likewise, the Chilean report concludes that D should be convicted of murder but that superior orders may have a mitigating effect on his punishment. If the subordinate had tried to suspend or modify the order but was overruled by the superior, the subordinate will not be punished at all. If he just carried out the order without an attempt to avoid it, there is a mandatory mitigation of the sentence.

Under § 5 subsec. 2 of the Germany Military Criminal Law, the Court may reduce the sentence of a soldier who committed a crime he was ordered to commit if his culpability is minor, given the special situation in which he found himself when carrying out the order. Depending on the exact circumstances and the pressure exerted on the soldiers by their superiors, it is quite possible that a court will grant a reduction of sentence to D.

In Singapore, a partial defence would be available, that is, the application of culpable homicide instead of murder. The partial defence is available if the offender, be-

---

8 According to a minority view in China, when a subordinate is aware of the unlawfulness of a command but still carries it out, he can be excused based on the theory of lack of expectation to act in accordance with the norm (*Unzumutbarkeit normgemäßen Verhaltens*), a supra-legal excusatory defense. Due to the unequal power relationship between commanders and subordinates, it is often difficult to expect subordinates to resist unlawful orders, especially in the military, where personnel have the right to dissent but not to refuse orders.

ing a public servant, exceeds the powers given to him by law and causes death by doing an act which he, in good faith, believes to be lawful and necessary for the due discharge of his duty as a public servant and without ill will towards the person whose death he caused. Due to this last condition, this partial defence would probably not be applicable here. If it were to succeed, D would be convicted of culpable homicide instead of murder.

In Poland, there is no separate legal basis for mitigating the sentence. Specifically, there are no grounds for a so-called extraordinary mitigation of the penalty. The Court may, however, take into account the fact that D was a subordinate. Therefore, his guilt was diminished due to the pressure his superior exerted on him. Nevertheless, it would only be possible to include this factor in the process of imposing a penalty within its regular (not mitigated) boundaries.

e) Concluding Remarks

Of the possible approaches toward the defence of superior orders, the doctrine of *respondeat superior*, which provides a complete defence whenever a subordinate obeys the orders of a superior, has not been adopted in any of the jurisdictions under review. The opposite principle of absolute liability seems to be the law in Australia and England, where the defence is ruled out entirely. An exclusion of the defence has also been considered if D's act were regarded as a crime against humanity, because some jurisdictions rule out the defence of superior orders for crimes against humanity.

However, most of the jurisdictions included in this study have adopted rules akin to the manifest illegality test, according to which superior orders provide a defence whenever the order is not manifestly unlawful. Accordingly, the objective test of manifest unlawfulness has been satisfied in the present case, because D was ordered to shoot peaceful protestors. Several jurisdictions have adopted a subjective test according to which the subordinate will be excused if he could not have realized that the order in question was unlawful. Applying this test does not alter the conclusion in the present case. Where the order was to shoot peaceful protestors, it is difficult to argue that such an order was not manifestly illegal, or that the defendant would not have been aware of its illegality.

As there is an overlap between the defence of superior orders and the related defences of duress and mistake of law, reports discuss these defences as well. Most of the reports also exclude these defences. The manifest illegality of the order would indeed preclude any plea that D could not have realized the unlawfulness of the order. And the mere fear of being demoted is not regarded as a threat of violence within the meaning of duress.

As for mitigating circumstances, several reports argue that, on the facts of the case, D should not receive any mitigation of sentence. On the other hand, in some jurisdictions D would be eligible for a mitigation either on the basis of a general provision giving the court discretion to reduce punishment or on the ground that he was carrying out an order. The latter fact could also be taken into account in deciding the penalty within its regular range.

6. Limits of Consent

By *Frank Verbruggen* and *Pieter van Rooij*

Vignette 6

V is a 21-year-old ambitious athlete and short-distance runner. He has learned that certain artificial limbs can enhance a runner's speed. He decides that he would rather have an artificial limb instead of his right lower leg. He approaches D, a surgeon in private practice, and asks him to amputate his leg below the knee and replace it by an artificial limb. D complies with V's request. Should D be punished for mayhem?

The amputation performed by D on V's limb raises questions regarding its legality. Specifically, is such an amputation considered the *actus reus* of an offence? In the affirmative, are there any justificatory grounds that could render the act legal under specific circumstances?

In *all* legal systems there are limits as to what a person can consent to. Not all legal goods are "at the free disposal" of the individual. Across all national responses there appears to be a consensus regarding the disposable nature of property rights – with nuances, such as environmental legislation – and the nearly absolute nature of the right to life (although in some states euthanasia is allowed under strict conditions). The legal good at stake in Vignette 6, physical integrity, occupies a position somewhere between these two extremes in all legal systems.

The question of whether an amputation is the *actus reus* of an offence is answered affirmatively in all national responses. However, some national reports mention a discussion in the national literature about the presence of an *actus reus* in cases of consent (England and Wales, Germany, Japan and California) or of a medical intervention (Australia, Chile, China, Pennsylvania, North Carolina and California), although none of them exclude the possibility that an *actus reus* is present in the case described in the Vignette.

Therefore, the focus of the national reports is on the possibility of justifying what is, in principle, an illegal act. Although all legal systems have some form of grounds of justification that could be applicable, most respondents indicate that D's amputation would not fall within the scope of any of these grounds. Some national responses do not provide a definitive answer, although they tend to lean against a justification. Only two national reports, from Germany and Singapore, conclude that D's behavior would probably be justified under their respective legal frameworks.

In all legal systems, consent can serve as a justification for otherwise illegal conduct. Some of them have a more or less general theory on consent (Italy, Namibia, Norway, Singapore, and Turkey), others allow consent only in specific situations identified by (case) law (Australia, Belgium, Chile, England and Wales, and Germany), although it is clear that all of them put limits on the possibility to consent, and that consent has to meet certain conditions to be valid. Only a minority of the legal systems represented have a specific article on consent (in general or with respect to the offence underlying this Vignette) in their criminal laws (Germany, Italy, Norway, Singapore, Turkey, and Pennsylvania).

Some scholars emphasize the conditions for the validity of consent. The conditions are similar across different legal frameworks. Consent must be given by someone with the legal capacity to do so, and it must be informed, i. e., the individual understands what they are consenting to and is aware of the legal interests at risk and the consequences. Consent must also be given freely, without physical or psychological coercion, and it must be given prior to the act.

All jurisdictions require a certain level of autonomy of the persons deciding about their physical integrity. The vast majority of legal systems distinguish between minor bodily harm and grievous bodily harm, excluding the latter from the right to dispose unless another significant legal interest is at stake. Surgical and medical interventions are universally recognized exceptions, but only if they have a curative or preventive medical purpose. This concept is evolving and subject to cultural differences. Several national reports mention aesthetic surgery as having such a purpose. Additionally, several national reports state that the gravity of the surgical act must be proportionate to the intended benefits. The treatment must also be carried out *lege artis.*

Most legal systems view D's act as neither curative nor preventive, and claim that it lacks proportionality to the intended benefits. Consequently, it is not considered justified behavior, placing D at risk of conviction in many jurisdictions. This presents a peculiar contrast with self-harm, as the latter is generally not criminalized. While the national reports do not specifically focus on this contrast, this observation might add a valuable but complicating perspective for the debate.

In Germany, however, consent can be given as long as the act does not offend common morality. Case law interprets this condition as fulfilled unless the act in question places the consenting party in a concrete danger of death. Since that was not the case, the amputation can be justified by consent according to German law. Similarly, Singapore law allows consent as a justification except in situations where the act is intended to cause death.

The reports from Finland, Norway, and Poland highlight the potential mitigating influence of consent on sentencing.

The current situation might be explained by the historical evolution of criminal law. The classical "enlightened" criminal laws were conceived and codified in the Eighteenth and Nineteenth Centuries. In that period, there was some consensus that property was at the complete disposal of the owner, so it only had to be protected against attacks which the owner did not want. One's life, on the other hand, was not disposable, most likely because Judeo-Christian morality remained dominant. Historically, this tenet had led to the qualification of (attempted) suicide as a felony, a strict attitude towards mercy killings and even abortion. Self-defense and defense of the life of others were the only exceptions. The sanctity of life might have survived as a principle despite the secularization of many states. In common law, it was confirmed in the famous Mignonette case of the House of Lords, which rejected duress or necessity as defenses for murder (*R v Dudley and Stephens* (1884) 14 QBD 273, DC).

The triple evolution of societies, of offences and of the medical possibilities has shattered the self-evident character of these age-old, virtually absolute prohibitions. Whereas historically rape was conceived as an offence against the "family order" and only applied to female victims, it has evolved towards a gender-neutral crime meant to protect sexual self-determination, with the consequence that consent has taken center stage. Abortion has in many jurisdictions evolved from a violation of unborn life to a decision of the woman over her own body, at least within the first stages of pregnancy. The sanctity of life has been called into question in debates on the end of life, euthanasia and assisted suicide, which have led to legalization in some states.

Resistance against these trends is not seldom motivated by religious feelings and sometimes focuses on the vulnerability of the alleged victim, which would affect the validity of consent. As the lack of consent has become the defining feature in sexual offences, some presumably vulnerable groups, especially young people, are deemed incapable of giving valid consent.

For adults, an increasingly liberal and less moralist approach has prevailed in Western countries (but not necessarily in other parts of the world): the interpretation of the fundamental right to privacy and family life has led to a push for decriminalization of homosexual and extramarital relations and the acceptance of some sexual practices between consenting adults that might imply the infliction of some physical pain (sado-masochism). Violent and dangerous sports have been regulated (and condoned) by law, and medical needs as a justification have been interpreted broadly, even to include esthetical interventions. An emphasis on self-determination of the informed patient has begun to replace the former more paternalistic approach of medicine.

All these evolutions have made it more difficult to answer the question why personal choice and self-determination of capable adults is not to be accepted. Two elements in the Vignette seem decisive: on the one hand, the motive of V, success in sports, and on the other, the far-reaching and irreversible effect on his physical integrity. Lesser interventions may be questioned but not criminalized. An Australian hockey player decided to have part of his finger amputated to play at the Olympics, as it had been broken and would take months to heal.[1]

The debate on which medical interventions that improve performance in sports are justified and which are not is eternal and remains controversial, with gender modification surgery as one of the most evident issues. With an expected increasing relevance of sophisticated protheses and implants in the future, the discussion will not end anytime soon. It therefore seems that the consensus on the values is only skin deep: amputation of legs to be more successful in sports is deemed excessive now, but there might be more debate on where exactly the line between acceptable and criminal interventions should be drawn. Body integrity dysphoria as a psychiatric problem has sparked the difficult debate whether it could be justified to perform amputations,[2] for instance when it is feared that without them the patient might commit

---

1 BBC News, 26 July 2024, https://www.bbc.com/news/articles/ckmg7ngkgjeo.

2 Costandi, M., "The science and ethics of voluntary amputation", *The Guardian* 30 May 2012, https://www.theguardian.com/science/neurophilosophy/2012/may/30/1?view=mobile; Dua, A. (February 2010), "Apotemnophilia: ethical considerations of amputating a healthy limb", *Journal of Medical Ethics* 36 (2): 75–8, doi: 10.1136/jme.2009.031070.

suicide or seriously harm himself. Some observers[3] point out the similarity with gender identity disorders, for which many states allow surgery.

It should be pointed out that some harm caused to others is covered by criminal law, regardless of the consent or a request from the victim, whereas self-harm is not. The dominant underlying thought seems to be that people who want to be harmed in a way which most people would consider disproportionate are mentally vulnerable or ill and should be protected against themselves. The same ratio underlies the (new) separate criminalization of inciting persons to commit suicide and other offences regarding "abuse of vulnerability". These tendencies have in common that they deny the person the capacity to decide and render their decisions invalid.

3 Lawrence, A. A. (2006), "Clinical and theoretical parallels between desire for limb amputation and gender identity disorder", *Archives of Sexual Behavior* 35 (3): 263–278, doi:10.1007/s10508-006-9026-6.

7. Withdrawal from an Attempt

By *Alicja Limburska* and *Konrad Lipiński*

Vignette 7

25-year-old D is deeply upset with her former boyfriend V, who had ended their relationship to be with another woman. To punish V, D plans to stab him with a large knife. D knows that the stab wounds can be fatal and accepts V's death as a possible outcome. When V goes jogging, D attacks him from behind and stabs him in the back three times. V breaks down. D realizes that she has injured him but that the injuries will not cause his death. She realizes that she could kill him by stabbing him again but decides to leave him alone. Should D be punished for attempted murder?

The main subject covered by this Vignette is withdrawal from a criminal attempt and its potential role as a defense. Since the responses presented in the national reports vary significantly in the level of detail and the issues discussed, we put together several questions regarding various aspects of the case described in the Vignette in order to systematize the analysis of the source material:

- Does the national regulation recognize withdrawal from a criminal attempt as an independent defense? (1)
- What are the legal consequences of a withdrawal from a criminal attempt? (2)
- What is the justification of the adopted solution? (3)
- What conditions must be met in order to absolve an offender from responsibility for the attempted crime? (4)
- Do the requirements differ depending on whether the attempt is complete or incomplete? (5)
- In case of a successful withdrawal – will the offender be held responsible for crimes completed in the course of the attempt? (6)
- If in a legal system withdrawal from an attempt does not constitute a formal defense, can it affect criminal responsibility in any other way? (7)

(1) Withdrawal from a criminal attempt is recognized as an independent defense in the vast majority of countries represented in the national reports. To be more precise – only 5 out of 16 jurisdictions do not regard withdrawal as a potential ground for exclusion of criminal liability (Australia, England and Wales, Namibia, Singapore, and traditional common law of the U.S.A.). Of the countries that recognize the legal relevance of withdrawal, only the Chilean Criminal Code does not regulate this issue explicitly.

(2) Although national reports define the legal consequences of withdrawal from a criminal attempt differently, it is difficult to say whether these are actual differences or whether the real meaning just has to some extent been lost in translation. Having that issue in mind, we can say that in the majority of the analyzed legal systems a successful withdrawal results in the exclusion of punishability of the act in question ("the

act is not punishable", a perpetrator "shall not be punished for an attempt"). There are, however, some exceptions. First, Israeli law provides that an offender who withdraws from an attempt "shall not bear criminal liability" since "an attempt or preparation is not criminal when the defendant voluntarily withdraws". It is difficult to say which aspect of the offence is reduced (or negated) by a successful withdrawal under Israeli law. Secondly, it seems that in Japan withdrawal negates the perpetrator's guilt, which would suggest that it constitutes a form of an excuse. In any case, the Japanese report is the only one to mention exculpation of the offender as the most far-reaching effect of withdrawal. Interestingly, some legal systems that recognize withdrawal as a defense considered it to be a circumstance that may indicate a lack of intent (e.g., Chile, Japan).

(3) In the legal systems covered by the national reports, recognition of a withdrawal from criminal attempt is usually justified in a similar manner. On the one hand, it is emphasized that there is no need for punishing or rehabilitating an offender who voluntarily changed his or her behavior and refrained from completing the crime. In other words, the aims of punishment have, in a way, already been reached, which justifies the negation of criminal liability. On the other hand, the analyzed institution is very often seen as an encouragement for the perpetrator – "a golden bridge" which offers the offender a safe retreat to lawfulness. Under this perspective, recognizing withdrawal as a defense is in fact an element of criminal policy, weighing the need to punish the perpetrator against the protection of legal interests from further threats. The Japanese report presents two additional, alternative theories: an "illegality reduction theory" assumes that the absence of intent demonstrated by withdrawal reduces the illegality of the act in question, while a "responsibility reduction theory" claims that the condemnation of the offender is diminished due to his voluntary abandonment of his previous intent.

In some cases, even if a withdrawal does not exempt the perpetrator from punishment (or grant him impunity), it may still greatly influence his liability. This statement applies to the criminal laws of Australia, England and Wales, and Singapore. Although the perpetrator in these jurisdictions is held criminally liable, the penalty imposed on him will probably be mitigated.

(4) For obvious reasons, we can consider the prerequisites for withdrawal only where the legal system recognizes such behavior as worthy of mitigating the response of the criminal law. Such conditions appear in 13 countries – regardless of the legal form taken by withdrawal from an attempt. The most important requirement – existing in every examined legal system – is the voluntariness of the decision not to continue with the attempted offence. This condition, sometimes referred to as the spontaneity of a withdrawal (as in Belgium), requires the withdrawal to occur by the own will of the perpetrator. Although some legal systems (e.g., Israel and Poland) seem to demand, on the level of the definition of withdrawal, some kind of "repentance" by the defendant, it seems that in fact even in these jurisdictions acting on his own initiative and without an external influence (i.e., coercion) would be sufficient. Some of the rapporteurs specifically state that the motive for abandoning the intent of completing the offence is not relevant as long as it stems from the free will of the perpetrator. He can be motivated by repentance, remorse, shame or other considerations;

the perpetrator need not have decided to become a law-abiding citizen (Turkey). In other words, the perpetrator only needs to be aware of the possibility of completing the offence and to freely decide not to do so. However, it is worth noting that a court in New York negated the voluntariness of a withdrawal where it was brought about by the "victim's artful persuasion".

(5) Further requirements as to the applicability of the defense depend on whether the attempt the perpetrator withdrew from was completed. In fact, it seems that this distinction – requiring more effort in case of a completed attempt – is present in almost every system recognizing withdrawal as an important factor influencing the attribution of criminal liability or limiting its severity. The rapporteurs were not unanimous on whether the case presented in the Vignette constitutes a completed or an incomplete attempt. Most of them regard it as incomplete (since D would have to undertake further actions to cause V's death). It seems that the uncertainty stems not only from different evaluations of the text of the Vignette but also from differences among the legal definitions of the completion of an attempt. For example, in Turkish criminal law D's attempt would be deemed incomplete under a holistic assessment theory, but not necessarily under objective theories (prevailing at the time when the previous Criminal Code was in force). Also, in some jurisdictions, completion of the attempt is determined subjectively from the perpetrator's point of view (Germany, Norway), whereas others use an objective or semi-objective test, e. g., a "reasonable man" standard or its equivalent.

Regardless of these differences, in every legal system that distinguishes between these two kinds of attempt, requirements differ depending on whether the attempt is completed or incomplete. If the attempt is incomplete, the defendant usually simply needs to refrain from completing the offence by stopping his or her actions. On the other hand, in case of a completed attempt, he or she is required to undertake active measures effectively preventing the result from occurring (e. g., in Chile, China, Finland, Norway, and Italy) or at least to make a sincere (honest, reasonable) effort to prevent the criminal result (Germany, Israel, Japan, and Turkey). Polish criminal law, for example, encompasses both of these possibilities: a completed attempt is not punishable at all if the defendant prevented the result from occurring, and it is possible to extraordinarily mitigate the penalty if he or she tried to prevent the occurrence of the result but failed. It is worth mentioning that the criminal law of Arizona (U.S.A.) stands out from this distinction, since in order to benefit from the renunciation defense under its Criminal Code the defendant is required to provide law enforcement with a timely warning or to otherwise make a reasonable effort to prevent the criminal result.

(6) In all jurisdictions that recognize withdrawal as a defense, a person who voluntarily and completely abandons criminal intent still bears criminal liability for the offence he or she managed to complete on the path to his or her final – later abandoned – purpose. Given the facts presented in the Vignette, this would mean that D would be held liable for inflicting grievous bodily harm on V.

(7) The replies to the vignette reveal that its resolution was somewhat controversial. Some of the rapporteurs had doubts concerning the facts of the case, some about the possible application of law to these facts, and most of them about the legal assess-

ment of the presented case. Some authors expressed doubt whether D really had a change of heart and decided not to kill V, so there might not have been any withdrawal at all. It was also stated (in reports from Australia, England and Wales, and Singapore) that D's behavior may be used as evidence to cast doubt on the prosecution claim that D had the intent to kill V. This might suggest a rather static perspective on intent in common law systems. To mention further controversies: in Chile it is debated whether an attempt is possible with *dolus eventualis*; in China, some scholars claim that in case of repeated harmful acts voluntary abandonment of further actions should be seen as an attempted offence rather than as withdrawal from further acts. Some Israeli scholars in turn claim that there is a requirement of actual repentance of the perpetrator coming from the depth of his or her heart. The reporter from Japan emphasized that D's behavior might be treated as withdrawal in accordance with new theories, whereas traditional theories would require such actions as transporting V to the hospital.

To sum up, a withdrawal from a criminal attempt is widely recognized as a circumstance that affects the scope of the perpetrator's criminal liability. In the majority of jurisdictions, a withdrawal from a criminal attempt results in the negation of punishability of the act in question, which is justified by the lack of a real need to punish a perpetrator who autonomously gives up the initial criminal intent. Recognition of this defense can also be seen as an element of criminal policy of states that decide to grant the defendant "a golden bridge" enabling a safe retreat to lawfulness.

The common basic condition for enjoying the benefits of abandonment is undoubtedly the voluntariness of the decision not to complete the attempted offence. Further requirements as to the applicability of the defense vary depending on whether the attempt was completed or not. While in the case of an incomplete attempt the defendant usually simply needs to withdraw from completion of the offence by stopping his or her actions, in the case of completed attempts further, active measures are required. In any case, even if a withdrawal is successful, the offender will still be held responsible for any crime completed in the course of the attempt. The lack of a formal defense of withdrawal seems to be typical of common law jurisdictions. Even in this case, however, a withdrawal may have an impact on criminal liability by proving lack of intent, or as a factor mitigating the sentence.

8. Criminal Responsibility of Minors

By *Sara Sun Beale*

Vignette 8

D is a 13-year-old boy. He abducts and rapes V, a girl of the same age. Should D be punished for a criminal offense?

As reflected in the chart below, the national responses to Vignette 8 reveal sharp disagreement, and roughly equal numbers favoring three positions: prohibiting punishment because of D's age, permitting punishment, or allowing punishment, depending on additional facts concerning either D's capacity or the harm he caused.

Jurisdiction	Minimum Age	Changes or Special Features	Presumption
Australia	10 NSW but varies among states and territories	Some jurisdictions now 12, others considering 14	Under 14 rebuttable lack of capacity
Belgium	12 Flanders, but varies among 3 communities	12–18 capable of guilt, but juvenile sanctions (Flanders)	
Chile	14		
China	14, but 12 if intentional infliction of bodily harm causing serious disability	14 until 2021, when authorized criminal punishment 12–14 for homicide and most serious assaults	
England and Wales	10	10 prima facie criminal capacity, but in juvenile court	In 1998 abolished rebuttable presumption of lack of capacity (*doli incapax*); in 1993 abolished irrebuttable presumption that boy under 14 was incapable of vaginal or anal intercourse.
Finland	15		
Germany	14		
Israel	12		
Italy	14		
Japan	14		
Namibia	7		7–14, rebuttable presumption of limited capacity
Norway	15	Raised in 1987	

(Continued)

Jurisdiction	Minimum Age	Changes or Special Features	Presumption
Poland	15	17 most crimes;15–17 most serious crimes; 14 aggravated murder	
Singapore	10		10–12 requires proof of sufficient maturity
Turkey	12	12–15 no liability if lacked capacity to perceive or direct behavior	
United States	24 states no minimum age; varies in others, but none below 13	In many states may be transferred to juvenile court	

Seven nations – Chile, Finland, Germany, Italy, Japan, Norway, and Poland – would not permit punishment because of D's age. The minimum age for the imposition of criminal liability in these nations is generally 14 or 15.

In contrast, five nations – Belgium, England and Wales, Israel, Singapore, and the United States – would permit D to be punished. In those countries, the minimum age for criminal responsibility ranges from 10 to 12. However, the national reports for some of these nations state that D would be subject to juvenile sanctions or that his case would be transferred to juvenile court.

Finally, in four nations – Australia, China, Namibia, and Turkey – whether D could be punished would depend on additional facts concerning his maturity and capacity, or the nature of the injury he inflicted. In Australia and Namibia, there would be a rebuttable presumption that D lacked criminal capacity. That presumption was abolished in England and Wales in 1993. In Turkey, there is no liability for defendants aged 12–15 who lacked capacity to perceive or to direct their own behavior. In these countries, the focus would be on D's individual maturity and capacity. In contrast, China focuses on the nature of the offense and harm caused, not D's maturity or capacity. A defendant aged 12–14 can be convicted only of the most serious crimes: homicide or intentional infliction of serious bodily harm causing serious disability. D could thus be liable only if the rape was shown to have been the intentional infliction of serious bodily harm that caused V serious disability.

It should be noted that several of the responses come from nations – Australia, Belgium, and the United States – in which criminal law is delegated to individual states or territories, allowing for different approaches. In Australia, although New South Wales has a minimum age of 10 for liability, in the Australian Capital Territory (ACT) the age has been raised to 12, and there are plans for further increases to 14 in the ACT, Victoria, and Tasmania. In Belgium, it appears from the national report that the minimum age in the three communities is 12, but there are some differences in the approach taken in Flanders, Wallonia, and the Brussels Capital Region. In the

United States, 24 states have no minimum age for criminal liability. Although the remaining 26 states specify a minimum age, none are below 13 for a serious felony.

Several of the national reports describe changes and calls for reform. The United Nations Committee on the Rights of the Child have repeatedly called on Australia and other common law nations to raise the minimum age of responsibility. This recommendation reflects recent research on the capacity of children from developmental psychology and neuroscience. As noted above, one Australian state has recently raised the age of responsibility, and others plan to do so. Belgium has seen a series of changes in the minimum age, most recently a new decree providing that people aged 12–18 are too young to be criminally punished by general sanctions meant for adults. Chile's adoption of the minimum age of 14 reflected the legislators' belief that this was the common age limit in OECD countries, as well as the recommendation of the Interamerican Committee on Human Rights, which has promoted the progressive elevation of the minimum age. Norway increased the minimum from 14 to 15 years in 1987.

Other nations have resisted calls to lower the age of responsibility. England and Wales has been regularly criticized by the United Nations for its comparatively low age of criminal responsibility, but consecutive UK governments have signaled that they will not increase the age.

At least one nation recently lowered the age of criminal responsibility, and there have been calls for similar actions in other nations. In 2021, an amendment to the Chinese Criminal Code lowered the age of criminal responsibility for the most serious crimes. In Germany, highly publicized cases of rape and murder committed by children aged 12 or 13 years renewed the debate about lowering the age, but no action has been taken.

In the United States, public opinion – affected by media coverage and political appeals – swung strongly towards treating juveniles like adults in the 1990s, leading to legal changes in most states, moving many juvenile offenders to the adult criminal court system. But public opinion is now more evenly divided and there is increasing support for more lenient treatment for juvenile offenders.

9. Statutes of Limitation

By *Carla Sepúlveda Penna*

Vignette 9

In 1995, D violently raped V, a 35-year-old woman, using a knife. D managed to escape and was not apprehended until 2023. Traces of his DNA taken from the victim's body leave no doubt that D is the perpetrator. Should D be convicted despite the long delay?

a) Quantitative Summary

In answering the question "Should D be convicted despite the long delay?", five jurisdictions clearly lean towards a yes, or almost certainly yes.[1] Ten jurisdictions decisively answer no.[2] One jurisdiction's stance would depend on the specific charge.[3] Among the jurisdictions where D would probably face conviction, two arrive at this conclusion despite statutes of limitations that would normally bar prosecution after a certain period.[4] In contrast, in all eleven jurisdictions where the offender would not be prosecuted, this result is due to the operation of a limitation period rather than other mechanisms. Additionally, Norway would currently bar prosecution due to the offense being committed in 1995 but has since amended its laws so that a prosecution under similar circumstances today would be possible. This illustrates that beyond the mere existence of time bars, the specific design and their applicability to certain offences vary.

In summary, the responses to the question whether D (regarding the time of the offence) should be punished can be systematised as follows:

Country	Should D be punished?	Applicable time limit
Australia	D should be punished	No time limits generally
Belgium	D should not be punished	Applicable time limit of 10 years
Chile	D should not be punished	Applicable time limit of 5 years
China	Depends on the charge	Applicable time limit of 10 years if simple rape; if aggravated rape, time limit is 20 years; prosecutorial authority may grant leave to prosecute even after that time

1 Australia, England and Wales, Namibia, Singapore, and most of the states in the U.S.A. – which states are considered as a single jurisdiction for the purposes of this count.

2 Belgium, Chile, Finland, Germany, Israel, Italy, Japan, Norway, Poland, and Turkey.

3 China.

4 Namibia and several U.S. states.

(Continued)

Country	Should D be punished?	Applicable time limit
England and Wales	D should be punished	No time limits generally
Finland	D should not be punished	Applicable time limit of 20 years
Germany	D should not be punished	Applicable time limit of 20 years
Israel	D should not be punished	Applicable time limit of 15 years, but DNA evidence allows prosecution for up to 23 years
Italy	D should not be punished	Applicable time limit of 24 years
Japan	D should not be punished	Applicable time limit of 15 years
Namibia	D should be punished	General time limit of 20 years, but crime is subject to death sentence, hence no time limit
Norway	D should not be punished	Applicable time limit of 10 years
Poland	D should not be punished	Applicable time limit of 10 years if offence committed before 03.08.1995; 15 years if committed after 03.08.1995.
Singapore	D should be punished	No time limits generally
Turkey	D should not be punished	Applicable time limit of 20 years
U.S.A. – Maryland, New Jersey, New York	D should be punished	No time limits generally for this offence
U.S.A. – Oklahoma, Ohio	D should be punished	Usual time limit for the offence is 12 or 25 years respectively, but DNA evidence opens a new window for prosecution.

b) Specific Mechanisms: Mandatory vs. Discretionary

In comparative terms, three categories of legal systems emerge among the sampled jurisdictions in dealing with the passage of time concerning "more than minor" offences. The first contains mandatory, categorical rules defining a specified period after which prosecution is barred. The second category includes jurisdictions with similar rules but incorporates exceptions where specified authorities may decide otherwise. The third category features systems where discretion – exercised by various authorities – determines whether a case proceeds to prosecution and punishment.

The first group comprises eleven jurisdictions: Belgium, Chile, Finland, Germany, Israel, Italy, Japan, Namibia, Norway, Poland, Turkey and several U.S. states (New Jersey, New York, Oklahoma, Ohio). All but one feature a sliding scale of time periods, which increase with the greater severity of the offence. The nominal limitation periods for a rape as described in the Vignette ranges from 5 years (Chile at the time of the offence in 1995) to 24 years (Italy). The exception is Namibia, which has only one category of limitation with a period of 20 years for all offences unless punished with death (which has since been abolished).

Norway has a traditional statute of limitation but now excludes rape and other sexual offences (as well as some other crimes), although it did not in 1995. The effects of these changes for the Vignette are clear, as section 3 (1) of the Norwegian Criminal Code is understood to apply, thus excluding the retroactive effect of the change on offences already statute-barred. Other reports also deal with the expected effects of a hypothetical change in their countries' rules on limitation periods,[5] some of which absolutely bar changes applying to offences committed in the past, while others allow a change as long as the period has not yet expired.

The existence of statutes of limitation, as we see, does not necessarily preclude prosecution of the offence. However, it does create a clear, binary solution about the possibility of bringing D to trial and convicting him. For a serious offence such as rape, there is no doubt that the offence ought to be prosecuted if no time bar impedes it, while if the limitation period has run out, no authority can change the legislatively set definition.

This last point is different in China. China has a traditional tiered structure of time periods. The nominal limitation period for rape is 10 years. Yet, for aggravated rape the limitation is extended to 20 years. This enables the use of an exceptional rule, by which approval from the Supreme People's Procuratorate allows the prosecution to proceed even after 20 years. At its discretion, the Procuratorate can base the decision on the specific circumstances of the case and its social impact, maximizing the role of criminal law in punishing crimes, balancing and maintaining fairness and justice, and maintaining social stability.[6] This gives some space to the policy or otherwise discretionary aims of the prosecutorial agency to be considered. The prevailing view, according to the rapporteur, is that the fact that the offence has not been forgotten by society after such a long period is informally required. The Supreme People's Procuratorate is very strict in considering these exceptions. But the mere possibility of the prosecutorial authority to decide about the adequacy of prosecuting an individual case sets the Chinese regulation apart from the traditional structure of statutes of limitation.

The third group of legal systems draws principally on discretion and not on predefined rules to establish whether a case will be prosecuted and punished. Firstly, there is the discretion of the prosecutor. Then, there is the judicial remedy of abuse of pro-

5 Belgium, Chile, Finland, Poland, and Turkey.

6 See Wang Aili (ed.), Explanation of the Criminal Code of the People's Republic of China: Legislative Reasons, and Relevant Provisions, 2021, 261.

cess. Finally, there is the inscrutable space for the jury's decision, which is guided by the judge's instructions.

In these systems – Australia, England and Wales, Singapore, and Maryland – where prosecutions mostly are not bound by the principle of mandatory prosecution for serious offences, there is no categorical time limit. This means that an "old" case will follow the same assessment as any other case, i. e., usually a decision based on the availability of evidence and the public interest in prosecution.

If the prosecutor's decision is to go ahead with the proceedings, a judicial remedy in the form of a stay of proceedings may be requested by the defence. "Stay applications made wholly or partially on the basis of delay are reasonably common (even if, as will be seen, they are very rarely granted)", mentions the report on Australia. The remedy of granting a stay of proceedings due to abuse of process is highly exceptional. In these jurisdictions, delay in itself does not necessarily mean that an abuse of process is likely. The fact of the passage of time needs to be accompanied by other relevant circumstances, such as prejudice and the impossibility to conduct a fair trial. There do not seem to be significant differences between the tests in England and Wales, Australia, and Singapore. The assessment of whether this standard is met is in the hands of the judge. She may reject the application if she considers that the problems mentioned by the defence do not arise, or that even if they are present, they may be reasonably dealt with through instructions to the jury.

Juries occupy the place of a last control.[7] Their decision is guided by the instructions given by the judge, which helps to manage the delay by pointing to possible effects of the passage of time, especially on evidence. The national reporters also highlight that there may be an effect of time on the law, which may prove challenging for juries.

c) Attitudes towards the Effect of the Passage of Time

One salient aspect of comparison lies in the attitude towards "the passage of time" or "delay" itself. While some legal systems consider it to inherently impact on criminal proceedings, others consider that it has no bearing on its own.

Good examples are Australia on the one hand and China and Belgium on the other. For Australia, "the question of delay [...] is not one about the effluxion of time *per se*. Rather, it is concerned with prejudice to an accused *by reason* of that delay". Meanwhile, one view in China suggests "that the statute of limitations marks the temporal limit of a crime's relevance as an unlawful act, suggesting that once this period has expired, the offense no longer constitutes a criminal act". For Belgium, the passage of time restores social peace, thereby questioning the effectiveness and appropriateness of punishment for old offences.

In less philosophical terms, it is also said that there is a "loss of interest of the legal system" (Italy) or that there is a "weakening of the societal impact of crimes over time, leading to the expiration of punitive authority" (Japan). Even if there was a fac-

---

7 The Australian reporter comments that in NSW giving of directions to a jury is "the primary action that may be taken" to protect against the potential unfair consequences of delay.

tual interest or social awareness about a particular crime, these reflections would not be impacted.

The report on Chile expresses a wariness among scholars of the proposition that the state retains its penal power unchanged after a long time, and therefore considers the principle of humanity as a limit to that power. That report also explains that the threat of a prosecution for an extended period of time can have a damaging effect on the individual concerned. This is not the same as an effect of time *per se*, but it might be seen as a normative effect of time on the state's legitimate use of power. However, Chilean law, in contrast to most other systems of statutory limitation, does not consider the passage of time *per se* to be sufficient for barring prosecution. It requires the defendant's "good behaviour" expressed by "no commission of further offences" for the limitation to operate. This expresses a historically older position elsewhere (e. g., Germany) that the passage of time needs to be coupled with some sign of rehabilitation or reform of the offender.

Why does Namibia establish a single time limit of 20 years (although not applicable to the Vignette) after which prosecution is impossible? Assuming there is no magic number but that all numbers are proxies for the relevant legal considerations, what this number does express is a tipping point. The fact that this legislation does not require additional circumstances (such as the ones mentioned in the previous paragraph) demonstrates that either time *per se* is perceived to have an effect or that it is assumed that "enough" happens in 20 years to justify an unconditional limitation.[8]

Beyond the possible effect of the passage of time *per se*, the most commonly mentioned circumstance of "what" happens during that time is the decay of evidence. But the approaches on this point differ. Regimes operating under a jury system seem more reliant on the capacity of the adjudicator to determine whether such an effect has occurred. For instance, an Australian court in Macri held that: "the disadvantages caused by the delay were curable by directions [to the jury] made pursuant to s 165B [Evidence Act 1995]". Going even further, in Jago the court declared that "the vagueness and uncertainty of memory and evidence which is likely to result from delay is more likely to be damaging to the prosecution than to the defence case". In Belgium, by contrast, the emphasis is on avoiding miscarriages of justice, because the disappearance or weakening of evidence "compromises legal certainty and the rights of defence".

d) Legal Change and Trends

Some scholars have recently claimed that there is a crisis of statutes of limitation and that they seem to be receding.[9] One may argue, however, that this institution is quite resilient and is only adapting its contours. On the side of countries relying on

---

[8] It is worth highlighting that since 1995, when the facts in the Vignette took place, Namibia has abolished the death penalty. This means that s 18 (2) of the Criminal Procedure Act containing the exception for offences carrying this sentence and rendering them prosecutable indefinitely has lost applicability. Now all offences fall under the 20-year limitation rule.

[9] For instance, Tinti, Pedro León, "Prescripción, justicia y certeza del derecho." *Revista de la Facultad de Derecho y Ciencias Sociales de la Universidad Católica de Córdoba* 1, 2008, 13–55.

discretion, there also seems to be relative stability. The reporters for England and Wales express the view that "there are no proposals to introduce a general statute of limitations for indictable criminal offences". Based on the findings of this project, it is difficult to say whether there exists a universal tendency towards adopting or limiting statutes of limitation.

With regards to the specific case of sexual offences against adult victims, some countries with statutes of limitation have changed their law in the last few decades,[10] either extending the periods or declaring outright that these offenses are imprescriptible. But many jurisdictions have not followed that trend.[11] The situation is different for sexual offences against minors, where there seems to be a much clearer tendency toward introducing exception clauses.[12] The reasons put forward for these changes, however, do not apply in the same manner to adult victims, as they often rely on the argument of the victims' dependence, their immaturity, and their inability to recognize that they have been victimized. This is most clearly expressed in the report on Turkey, where the exception is not limited to sexual offences but extends to all crimes committed against victims by their direct ascendants or persons who have influence upon them.

There seem to be no major tensions for systems following the discretionary paradigm, which are dealing with the complexities arising from the passage of time mostly through their traditional and general tools. In the case of England and Wales, for instance, even if "staleness" of the offence was a criterion when the Crown Prosecution Service issued its first Codes for Crown Prosecutors,[13] this criterion is now no longer explicitly mentioned as a ground for lack of public interest in prosecution. However, this conclusion cannot be generalised for all areas of the criminal law. The national reporters for England and Wales highlight that in the context of the conflict in Northern Ireland statutory immunity for those who cooperate with investigations was introduced, which has been declared incompatible with the European Convention on Human Rights. For common crimes, legislatures in these jurisdictions make use of their power to establish limitation statutes as they see fit.[14]

Some U.S. states and Israel seem to be isolated in their consideration of DNA evidence, or more generally, biometric identification means, as a sufficient cause to allow for criminal prosecution after limitation periods have expired. No other jurisdiction represented in this survey has adopted such a rule. Besides, in neither case is the prolonging of the period for prosecution unlimited. In Israel the absolute limit is 23 years. Ohio opens a 5-year and Oklahoma a 3-year window to prosecute after the determination of a DNA match.

---

10 For instance, Chile, from 5 to 10 years; Norway, 15 years to imprescriptible; Belgium, moving from 10 to 15 years.

11 Such as China, Finland, Germany, Israel and Japan.

12 These offenses are imprescriptible in Belgium, Chile, and Norway. They have suspended or longer periods of limitation in Finland, Japan, Germany, Poland, and Turkey.

13 Code for Crown Prosecutors of 1985, 1994, 2000, 2004 and 2010.

14 An example is mentioned for Australia by reference to the Australian Securities and Investments Commission Act 2001.

This situation demands reflection on the fact that one frequently advanced justification for statutes of limitation is the alleged decay of evidence. If a piece of evidence is scientifically considered reliable even after 20 or 30 years, should that not lead to a reconsideration of the absolute character of the rule by legislatures? As we have seen in the previous section, some legal systems seem to operate on the belief that the unreliability will probably benefit the defence, while others put more weight on its prejudice against the defence. The fact that other legal systems have not introduced exceptions for DNA or other biometric identification does not mean that they are not considering scientific advances. In Japan, general extensions of the periods of limitation were partly based on advances in investigative technology. This fact, however, did not lead legislatures to change the categorical character of the rule.

e) What about the Values of Justice?

In order to arrive at any conclusion regarding the universality of the justice values at stake in this Vignette, we first need to examine what values have an impact on the solutions offered by the legal systems to the issue of the passage of time for criminal prosecution and conviction.

Many of the arguments offered are (partly) pragmatic and thus not directly related to justice. This includes the arguments regarding evidence, and also the need to provide incentives for the criminal justice organs to move forward with their cases.

The substantive arguments are sometimes regarded as being in tension with each other. This leads the German reporter to conclude that "[i]n the end, it is a policy decision to what extent a temporal limitation of prosecution should be granted; the need to do justice needs to be weighed against a social interest in letting past events rest". In this portrayal, the need to do justice appears one-sided, as if there were no "justice reasons" in favour of limitation and "doing justice" was only about achieving convictions. By contrast, other authors – especially from the civil-law sphere – seem to think that the appropriate use of punishment, and in particular limiting the use of state power, is a matter of justice, or, more specifically, of avoiding injustice or inhumanity.

A doctrinal approach is necessarily oriented towards finding a rationale for the particular features of the legal regime under study. This makes comparison between different systems difficult, as they may not share the underlying priorities in terms of justice. However, even if a more theoretical approach could seem more pertinent, it may be loaded with idiosyncrasy; statutes of limitations (or mechanisms such as abuse of process) are a small particle in a wider procedural and criminal justice setting, which has its own principled priorities. Mechanisms for dealing with possible injustice in prosecuting assume the operation of mandates and powers of criminal justice agents as given. Yet, these vary from jurisdiction to jurisdiction, and other traditional tropes of comparative criminal law also have a bearing here, such as the mandatory versus discretionary prosecution principles, the extent of lay participation, the adversarial or inquisitorial nature of proceedings and trials, and the understanding of the substantive principle of legality.

One conclusion in this regard could be that there seems indeed to be a shared commitment to avoiding injustices arising from prolonged periods of time between the commission of the offence and prosecution, despite the differing mechanisms used to address it. If time limits are introduced, the specific amounts of time permitted to elapse differ (and often depend on the perceived severity of the offence expressed by statutory sentence lengths). This seems to indicate that "doing justice" is more relevant than "not doing injustice" if the offence is more serious, even if most of the time there exists a point where the second value takes over (except for offences declared "imprescriptible").

A final reflection refers to the question whether there are different standards concerning justice regarding sexual offences, and whether impunity is less acceptable in these cases. The consideration that sexual offences cause mental harm to victims that can leave them traumatised for life has allowed for an exceptional extension of limitation to 10 years in Chile, while other crimes with similar sentences are subject to a 5-year limitation period. Moreover, it has been argued that by "the nature itself of these crimes [rape], victims take several years to come to the criminal justice system, and it is reasonable for this to be taken into consideration when defining the limitation period".

The fact that in Finland not only the sentence range but also the legal interest protected by sexual crimes has changed highlights a different aspect of this discussion. Does it make a difference whether a sexual assault is considered a matter of social morality (thus often carrying a lower sentence) or a crime against the self-determination of the individual? Does the community resign itself to the non-prosecution of collective goods sooner than to that of violations of individual interests? Does society forget before the victim does? These questions cannot be answered here but may well be considered in the context of periods of limitation for sexual offences.

10. Life Imprisonment without Parole

By *Andrew Dyer*

Vignette 10

The Penal Code of State S provides for imprisonment for life as the maximum penalty for murder, but also authorizes the court to order an offender's early release after a minimum of 15 years if the offender is no longer dangerous. Reacting to cases of particularly heinous murders, the legislature of S wishes to introduce a penalty of life imprisonment without any possibility of early release, regardless of the offender's continued dangerousness. Would this amendment be acceptable?

a) Introduction

In October 1983, Arthur Hutchinson broke into a family home, where, the Grand Chamber of the European Court of Human Rights ("ECtHR") tells us, "he stabbed to death a man, his wife and their adult son. He then repeatedly raped their 18-year-old daughter, having first dragged her past her father's body."[1] About 33 years later, Alexandre Bissonnette burst into the Great Mosque of Québec armed with a semi-automatic rifle and a pistol.[2] Driven by "hatred, racism, ignorance and Islamophobia",[3] he opened fire on worshippers, killing six people and seriously injuring five others.[4]

In between these dates, on opposite sides of the world, certain children committed crimes of similar enormity to the murder offences just outlined. On 8 September 1988, when they were aged 14 and 16 respectively, Bronson Blessington and Matthew Elliott were in the company of three other young persons at a Sydney railway station. The group formed a plan to abduct and rape a woman. The plan was then promptly put into effect. Members of the group forced a young woman named Janine Balding into her own car at knifepoint. They drove her away and raped her. The car pulled off the road in an outer suburb, whereupon Ms Balding's legs were bound and a scarf was stuffed in her mouth. She was then carried over a fence and to a nearby dam, where she was held underwater and drowned.[5] About five years later, somewhat similar events occurred in the United Kingdom ("UK"). On a day when they were "play[ing] [...] truant from school",[6] Jon Venables and Robert Thompson, both aged ten, abducted a two-year-old boy named Jamie Bulger from a shopping centre. They tortured him, "battered him to death and left him on a railway line to be run over".[7]

---

1 *Hutchinson v The United Kingdom* (European Court of Human Rights, Grand Chamber, Application No 57592/08, 17 January 2017) [10] ("*Hutchinson*").

2 *The Queen v Bissonnette* (2022) SCC 23, [11] ("*Bissonnette*").

3 Ibid. [10].

4 Ibid. [11].

5 *The Queen v Jamieson* (1992) 60 A Crim R 68, 69–70.

6 *V v The United Kingdom* [1999] IX Eur Court HR 111, [7].

7 Ibid.

Cases such as these raise a number of questions. There was widespread public support for the imposition on Hutchinson, Bissonnette, Blessington, Elliott, Venables and Thompson of an irreducible life sentence.[8] But what weight, if any, should be given to public opinion of this sort? Further, in at least some of these cases, the sentencing court was seemingly entitled to regard an irreducible life sentence as proportionate to the seriousness of the relevant offending. But where such a sentence *is* proportionate, is that enough to render it morally permissible? Or is there some reason why, despite its proportionality in particular circumstances, the irreducible life sentence may never properly be imposed?

As is made clear by the national reports in this volume – which are summarised in part 2 of this chapter – different jurisdictions around the world deliver different answers to the questions just posed. In the Asian countries surveyed (China, Japan and Singapore), there is no constitutional obstacle to the enactment of a law that authorises the imposition on an individual of an irreducible life sentence (the same might be true of Chile and Israel[9]) – and it seems that, in at least two of those countries,[10] such sentences are actually being imposed. By contrast, in many of the relevant European countries (namely, Belgium, Finland, Germany, Italy and Norway), such a law could not validly be passed. These countries have all ratified the European Convention on Human Rights[11] (ECHR), article 3 of which prohibits the imposition by a Contracting State of a life sentence that is either de jure or de facto irreducible.[12] That said, even before the European Court of Human Rights (ECtHR) so pronounced, such sentences had been held to be constitutionally impermissible in European states such as Germany and Italy.[13] Poland, Turkey and the UK have also ratified the ECHR. But

8 For example, in the case of Venables and Thompson the deceased child's family had persuaded 278,300 individuals to sign a petition that urged the Secretary of State to allow neither boy ever to be released from prison; and a further 21,281 people had sent to him coupons from the *Sun* newspaper that supported a whole life tariff in Venables' and Thompson's case: ibid. [22].

9 See, respectively, country report Chile and country report Israel. It appears that, at the moment, no Chilean or Israeli legislative provision authorises the imposition of an irreducible life sentence – although, with that said, a life sentence with a non-parole period of 40 years (see country report Chile) would be regarded as irreducible if it were imposed in Europe: *Bancsók and László Magyar v Hungary (No 2)* (European Court of Human Rights, First Section, Application Nos 52374/15 and 53364/15, 28 October 2021) [47].

10 Those two countries are China and Singapore. Regarding China, see country report China and Zhiyuan Guo and Rong Ma, "Life Imprisonment in China", in: Dirk van Zyl Smit et al. (eds.), *Life Imprisonment in Asia* (Palgrave Macmillan, 2023) 83, 87–9. Regarding Singapore, see Benny Tan, "Life Imprisonment in Singapore: Legal and Sociological Perspectives", in: Dirk van Zyl Smit et al. (eds.) (ibid.) 261, 261–2. It seems that de facto life without parole sentences are imposed in Japan; country report Japan and Tepei Ono, "Life Imprisonment in Japan: The Existing Legal System and Alternative Sanctions for the Death Penalty", in: Dirk van Zyl Smit et al. (eds.) (ibid.) 197, 200. Certainly, the death penalty is still being imposed.

11 *Convention for the Protection of Human Rights and Fundamental Freedoms*, opened for signature 4 November 1950, 213 UNTS 221 (entered into force 3 September 1953).

12 *Vinter v United Kingdom* [2013] III Eur Court HR 317, [107]–[110]; *Murray v The Netherlands* (2017) 64 EHRR 3, [99]; *Hutchinson* (European Court of Human Rights, Grand Chamber, Application No 57592/08, 17 January 2017) [42].

13 Country report Germany; country report Italy. See also, e.g., Joshua Kleinfeld, "Two Cultures of Punishment" (2016) 68(5) *Stanford Law Review* 933, 951.

populist governments in the former two countries have resisted the ECtHR's life sentence jurisprudence;[14] and the UK government has exhibited a similar hostility to the relevant Strasbourg Court rulings.[15] Throughout the rest of the English-speaking world, the position is generally the same, or even more punitive. It is true that, in certain southern African states, such as Namibia, the courts have held that irreducible life sentences infringe the human dignity of those upon whom they are imposed and cannot be imposed conformably with constitutional guarantees against "cruel, inhuman or degrading […] punishment".[16] But, in the United States (U.S.A.), life without parole sentences are liberally imposed,[17] including on juveniles[18] – and, while such sentences are not nearly so common in Australia, they are far from unknown. Indeed, the highest court in that country has upheld extraordinary legislative schemes that remove the prospect of parole from a small number of highly unpopular offenders – two of whom were children at the time of their offences.[19]

What is the explanation for the different approaches, across the world, to the permissibility of irreducible life sentences? In part 3, I argue that the reasons various courts have given for holding such sentences to be objectionable might shed some light on this question. In other words, when holding that such sentences cannot validly be imposed, courts have used the language of liberalism and human rights: they have emphasised the human dignity that all of us – even the "vilest of criminals"[20] – possess. Accordingly, it seems unsurprising that such sentences are more likely to be considered unacceptable, and unlawful, in liberal democracies – and, most especially, in jurisdictions where the authorities have seen fit to protect "liberal rights"[21] through the enactment of a human rights charter. That said, certain liberal democracies have adopted a more punitive approach. In many of the Anglophone jurisdictions surveyed, penal populism has prevailed in recent decades, leading governments to "resort […] to measures which in effect negate the democratic membership and entitlements of offenders."[22] During the same time, similar developments appear to

14 Country report Poland; Ergul Celiksoy, "Ongoing Problem of Irreducible Life Sentences in Turkey" (2019) 27 *European Journal of Crime, Criminal Law and Criminal Justice* 320, 334–8.

15 See, e.g., Dirk van Zyl Smit and Catherine Appleton, *Life Imprisonment: A Global Human Rights Analysis* (Harvard University Press, 2019) 46.

16 Country report Namibia. See also *S v Tcoeib* 1999 NR 24 (SC) ('*Tcoeib*'); *S v Gaingob* (SA 7 of 2008) [2018] NASC 4 (6 February 2018) [68] ("*Gaingob*"). The same findings were made by the Constitutional Court of Zimbabwe in *Makoni v Commissioner of Prisons* [2016] ZWCC 8.

17 As noted by, e.g., Kleinfeld (n 13) 955.

18 Country report U.S.A. See also *Jones v Mississippi* 141 S Ct 1307 (2021).

19 Country report Australia. See also *Crump v State of New South Wales* (2012) 247 CLR 1; *Knight v State of Victoria* (2017) 261 CLR 306; *Minogue v State of Victoria* (2019) 268 CLR 1.

20 *Bissonnette* (2022) SCC 23, [2].

21 Mark Tushnet, "New Forms of Judicial Review and the Persistence of Rights- and Democracy-Based Worries" (2003) 38 *Wake Forest Law Review* 813, 814.

22 Nicola Lacey, *The Prisoners' Dilemma: Political Economy and Punishment in Contemporary Democracies* (Cambridge University Press, 2008) 8.

have occurred in Japan.[23] The causes of these populist criminal justice responses are complex, and contested, and this matter cannot be resolved here.[24] What seemingly can be said, however, is that the more harshly individualistic and inegalitarian a society becomes, the more disdainful it will tend to be of the rights of disfavoured minorities such as prisoners – and the more inclined it might be to promote "stigmatising and exclusionary"[25] criminal justice policies. That will perhaps especially be so where that society lacks any recent experience of the kind of tyranny that might make another society think twice about violating the human rights of the unpopular.[26]

b) The Position in the Surveyed Jurisdictions

We can begin our summary of the applicable law by dealing with the three Asian jurisdictions just mentioned. And that can be done briefly. According to the Chinese rapporteur, irreducible life sentences would probably be "unacceptable to the majority of the Chinese criminal law academic community".[27] This opposition, it seems, is based largely on dignitarian concerns. Rather than "respect[ing] individuals", the state that imposes such sentences "treats criminals merely as instruments of negative general deterrence."[28] Furthermore, the Chinese report explains, these scholars hold that "life imprisonment without parole contradicts" the purposes of punishment.[29] It "deprives criminals of the possibility of reintegrating into society";[30] it "forswears altogether the rehabilitative ideal".[31]

So much for the academics. What about the law? The Chinese position seems clear, as does that in Japan and Singapore. In China, "life imprisonment without parole" was introduced in 2015 and operates as an "alternative measure to the death penalty" in certain cases of embezzlement and bribery.[32] Likewise, in Japan, the death penalty remains the maximum penalty for murder – and the Japanese rapporteur assures us that, if ever that penalty were abolished, "the introduction of life imprisonment without the possibility of parole would probably be readily accepted"[33] (perhaps even by scholars?). In Singapore, the position seems essentially the same. In the absence of "a specific provision in the […] Constitution against cruel, inhuman or degrading treat-

---

23 Country report Japan. See too Setsuo Miyazawa, "The Politics of Increasing Punitiveness and the Rising Populism in Japanese Criminal Justice Policy" (2008) 10 *Punishment and Society* 47.

24 Attempts to explain the emergence of penal populism have been made by, e.g., John Pratt, *Penal Populism* (Routledge, 2007) chapter 2 and Julian V Roberts et al., *Penal Populism and Public Opinion: Lessons from Five Countries* (OUP, 2002) chapter 4.

25 Lacey (n 22) 8.

26 For example, as Pratt notes, "the legacy of Nazi Germany" might at least partly explain the moderate penal policies adopted in that country; Pratt (n 24) 161.

27 Country report China.

28 Ibid.

29 Ibid.

30 Ibid.

31 *Graham v Florida* 560 US 48, 74 (2010) (Kennedy J) ("*Graham*").

32 Country report China. See too Guo and Ma (n 10) 87–9.

33 Country report Japan.

ment or punishment", and due to "the different constitutional history of Singapore", the courts have rejected challenges to provisions that mandate the death penalty.[34] In such circumstances, it seems hard to accept that a Singaporean provision that authorised the imposition of irreducible life sentences would be constitutionally suspect.[35]

If we move now from Asia to Europe, we see a more moderate penal approach. "[T]he legal culture in Norway, and indeed in the Nordic countries", the Norwegian rapporteur says, speaks "against very severe punishments."[36] "Traditionally", he continues, "Nordic criminal policy has been characterised as being both humane and rational, with moderate punishment levels, low imprisonment rates and a focus on rehabilitation".[37] It is this focus on rehabilitation that I wish particularly to stress. For, according to the ECtHR in *Vinter v The United Kingdom*, it is not just in the Nordic countries, but elsewhere in Europe too, that "clear support" exists "for the principle that all prisoners, including those serving life sentences, be offered the possibility of rehabilitation and the prospect of release if that rehabilitation is achieved."[38] For example, as is noted in the German country report, the Federal Constitutional Court held in 1977 that, due to art 1(1) of the Basic Law – which provides that "[h]uman dignity" is "inviolable" and must be "respect[ed] and protect[ed]" by "all state authority" – "cruel, inhumane or degrading punishment is prohibited" and the state may not "forcibly deprive" an offender of his or her liberty without giving him or her the "chance of regaining liberty at some point in the future".[39] And, in a series of cases, the Italian Constitutional Court has likewise held that "perpetual punishment" is compatible with art 27 of the Constitution – which provides, relevantly, that "[p]unishments may not be inhuman and shall aim at re-educating the convicted" – only if those subject to such punishment have "the effective possibility of parole".[40]

---

[34] Country report Singapore. The Singaporean rapporteur refers in particular to the Singapore Court of Appeal's decision in *Yong Vui Kong v Public Prosecutor* [2010] 3 SLR 489 ('*Yong Vui Kong*'). One argument made by the appellant in that case was that the mandatory death penalty provisions in the *Misuse of Drugs Act* (Cap 185, 2001 Rev Ed) were invalid due to article 9(1) of the Singapore Constitution, which provides, relevantly, that: "No person shall be deprived of his life [...] save in accordance with law." The impugned provisions, it was said, were not "law", because they provided for the imposition of an inhuman punishment – the mandatory death penalty: at [46]. The court rejected this argument, principally because of the Singapore government's "unambiguous" (at [72]) rejection, in 1969, of a proposal to insert into the Constitution an article that expressly prohibited "torture or inhuman or degrading punishment or other treatment": see [65]. "It is not legitimate for this court", it was said, "to read into Art 9(1) a constitutional right that was decisively rejected by the Government": at [72].

[35] Cf. ibid. As was pointed out in *Yong Vui Kong* [2010] 3 SLR 489 at [6], art 9(1) of the Singapore Constitution "expressly sanctions the death penalty" (as opposed to its mandatory imposition – which, as just noted (see n 34), is nevertheless also constitutionally acceptable). Given that that is so, surely irreducible life sentences may also be imposed?

[36] Country report Norway.

[37] Ibid. This is confirmed by the Finnish rapporteur, who notes that "[i]ntroducing a life sentence without parole would go against the basic principles of Finnish criminal law" and concludes that any proposal to introduce such sentences in Finland "would be rejected": country report Finland.

[38] [2013] III Eur Court HR 317, [114].

[39] BVerfGE 45, 146. See also *Vinter* [2013] III Eur Court HR 317, [69].

[40] Country Report Italy. See also *Vinter* [2013] III Eur Court HR 317, [72].

In light of this European consensus, and because "respect for human dignity" is at the very essence of "the Convention system",[41] the *Vinter* Court held that a life sentence will be compatible with art 3 of the ECHR – which prohibits, relevantly, the imposition of "inhuman or degrading [...] punishment" – only if the prisoner has the "prospect of release and a possibility of review".[42] The review need not be judicial in character.[43] Moreover, the Court did not specify exactly when the review must occur.[44] But it did make it clear what its purpose is. The review's purpose, the Court held, is to "allow [...] the domestic authorities to consider whether any changes in the life prisoner are so significant, and such progress towards rehabilitation has been made in the course of the sentence, as to mean that continued detention can no longer be justified on legitimate penological grounds."[45]

Similar reasoning has been deployed by certain courts outside Europe. For example, in Namibia, the Supreme Court has held that a sentence of life imprisonment will "not be constitutionally sustainable if it effectively amounts to an order throwing the prisoner into a cell for the rest of the prisoner's natural life as if he was [sic] a 'thing' instead of a person without any continuing duty to respect his dignity".[46] And while there might be no constitutional obstacle in Israel or Chile to the enactment of a provision that authorises the imposition of irreducible life sentences, it seems that all life prisoners in these jurisdictions are in fact provided with a realistic possibility of release.[47]

If we return briefly to Europe, however, reference is made to *Vinter* in some of the country reports. For example, the Belgian rapporteurs note that there is some political support for irreducible life sentences in that jurisdiction – and that, but for Belgium's membership of the ECHR, irreducible life sentences would be "possible" there.[48] As

41 *Vinter* [2013] III Eur Court HR 317, [114].

42 Ibid. [110].

43 Ibid. [120]. This aspect of the Court's decision has been criticised. See, e. g., Dirk van Zyl Smit et al., "Whole Life Sentences and the Tide of European Human Rights Jurisprudence: What Is to Be Done?" (2014) 14 *Human Rights Law Review* 59, 71–9.

44 *Vinter* [2013] III Eur Court HR 317, [120]. That said, the Court did "observe that the comparative and international law materials before it" showed "clear support for the institution of a dedicated mechanism guaranteeing a review no later than twenty-five years after the imposition of a life sentence, with further periodic reviews thereafter".

45 Ibid. [119].

46 *Tcoeib* 1999 NR 24 (SC). See too *Gaingob* (SA 7 of 2008) [2018] NASC 4 (6 February 2018) [59]. As the Namibian country report makes clear, the relevant article of the Nambian Constitution is article 8, which provides that: "[t]he dignity of all persons shall be inviolable" (art 8(1)); "[i]n any judicial proceedings [...] respect for human dignity shall be guaranteed" (art 8(2)(a)); and "[n]o persons shall be subject to torture or to cruel, inhuman or degrading treatment or punishment" (art 8(2)(b).

47 Country report Israel and country report Chile. This conclusion is, however, subject to two qualifications. First, if a prisoner is so elderly, at the time of his or her conviction, as to mean that s/he will certainly die before his or her non-parole period expires, there is in fact no realistic possibility of release. Secondly, as stated at n 9, the ECtHR would regard certain Chilean life sentences as irreducible, even though there is seemingly a realistic prospect of release after the prisoner has served many years in prison.

48 Country report Belgium.

it is, however, Belgian law "is in conformity" with *Vinter*, "since 25 years is the maximum" period that a life prisoner will remain in prison before he or she may apply for release.[49] Similarly, the Finnish rapporteur suggests that the ECtHR's case law is one reason why that country's government would be unlikely to propose the introduction of irreducible life sentences.[50]

That said, not all Contracting States to the ECHR have been so compliant. The Polish rapporteurs record that irreducible life sentences breach not just the ECHR but also the Polish Constitution.[51] But, despite this, the purported effect of recent "populist amendments" to the Criminal Code is to empower judges to impose such sentences in certain circumstances.[52] The position is similar in Turkey. In that country, "life imprisonment without parole is confined to certain terror offences and crimes against the security of the state".[53] Nevertheless, irreducible life sentences *can* be ordered in some circumstances, even despite: (i) a number of ECtHR decisions in which that Court has found such sentences to violate art 3 of the ECHR;[54] and (ii) art 17 of the Turkish Constitution, which, like art 3 of the ECHR, prohibits "inhuman or degrading [...] punishment."[55]

A somewhat similar situation exists in England and Wales. In *Vinter*, each of the three – English – applicants had had a whole-life order imposed on them, due to their commission of particularly heinous murders. Were these sentences irreducible or not? The Strasbourg Court held that they *were*. Section 30(1) of the *Crimes (Sentences) Act 1997* (UK) did provide the Secretary of State with the power to release a whole-life order prisoner on licence if he was persuaded that "exceptional circumstances exist[ed] which justif[ied] [...] the prisoner's release on compassionate grounds". And English authority[56] did provide that the Secretary of State was *required* to release the prisoner if his or her continued imprisonment would amount to "inhuman or degrading ... punishment". But there was also the Secretary of State's published policy to consider. According to that policy, the Secretary would exercise his power of compassionate release only if the prisoner was "suffering from a terminal illness" *and* "the risk of re-offending" was "minimal" *and* further conditions could be satisfied.[57] "At the present time", the Strasbourg Court said in *Vinter*, "it

49 Ibid.

50 Country report Finland.

51 Country report Poland.

52 Ibid.

53 Country report Turkey.

54 See, e. g., *Kaytan v Turkey* (European Court of Human Rights, Application No 27422/05, 15 September 2015) [63]–[67]; *Öcalan v Turkey (No 2)* (European Court of Human Rights, Second Section, Application Nos 24069/03, 197/04, 6201/06 and 10464/07, 18 March 2014) [202]–[207]. Note, too, that, in a similar vein to art 91.2 of the Polish Constitution (as to which, see country report Poland), art 90 of the Turkish Constitution provides that: "In the case of a conflict between international agreements, duly put into effect, concerning fundamental rights and freedoms and the domestic laws due to differences in provisions on the same matter, the provisions of international agreements shall prevail over the domestic law."

55 See the discussion in Celiksoy (n 14) 338–44.

56 *The Queen v Bieber* [2009] 1 WLR 223, 238–9 [48]–[49].

57 Prison Service Order 4700, chapter 12.

is unclear whether, in considering [...] an application for release under s 30 by a whole life prisoner, the Secretary of State would apply his existing, restrictive policy [...] or would go beyond the apparently exhaustive terms of that Order" by releasing the prisoner who was being detained incompatibly with art 3 of the ECHR.[58] In such circumstances, the Court could not be satisfied that whole-life orders were reducible life sentences.[59]

The response of the UK government, press and public to *Vinter* was not positive. Indeed, the decision was "met with fierce criticism"[60] from such quarters. In response to this, the Strasbourg Court retreated. The Court did not hold that irreducible life sentences could be imposed compatibly with art 3 ECHR after all. Rather, it held, in *Hutchinson v The United Kingdom,*[61] that it had been wrong to find that UK "whole-life orders" were irreducible life sentences. The matter, it said, had been "clarified"[62] by the England and Wales Court of Appeal ("EWCA") in *The Queen v McLoughlin.*[63] As that Court had found, the *Hutchinson* court indicated,[64] the Secretary of State's policy was "of no consequence".[65] In a case where a "whole-life" prisoner requested compassionate release, the Secretary of State was not entitled to "fetter his discretion by taking into account only the matters" in his policy.[66] Instead, he had to act compatibly with art 3.[67] This, the *Hutchinson* court suggested, would require him to release the whole-life prisoner who had made "exceptional progress towards rehabilitation".[68] And if he were not to do so, the High Court, upon the prisoner's application for judicial review, could do so instead.[69]

As the rapporteurs on England and Wales indicate,[70] despite this dictum it is unclear whether, in the future, any whole-life prisoners will be released on the basis that they have achieved rehabilitation. Far clearer is that the public would react adversely to any such release decision. And that brings me to the final matter that I want to deal with in this part. As indicated in the introduction to this chapter, in certain parts of

---

58 *Vinter* [2013] III Eur Court HR 317, [129].

59 Ibid. [130].

60 Mugambi Jouet, "The Abolition and Retention of Life Without Parole in Europe: A Comparative and Historical Perspective" (2023) 4 *European Convention on Human Rights Law Review* 306, 334.

61 European Court of Human Rights, Grand Chamber, Application No 57592/08, 17 January 2017.

62 *Hutchinson* (European Court of Human Rights, Grand Chamber, Application No 57592/08, 17 January 2017) [39].

63 [2014] 1 WLR 3964 ("*McLoughlin*").

64 *Hutchinson* (European Court of Human Rights, Grand Chamber, Application No 57592/08, 17 January 2017) [39].

65 *McLoughlin* [2014] 1 WLR 3964, 3975 [30].

66 Ibid. 3975 [32].

67 *Hutchinson* (European Court of Human Rights, Grand Chamber, Application No 57592/08, 17 January 2017) [39].

68 Ibid. [55].

69 Ibid. [52].

70 Country report England and Wales.

the English-speaking world there has been much resistance to the idea that irreducible life sentences are off-limits. This is evident in the English press and public's response to *Vinter*. And it is also evidenced by US and Australian law.

Although it prohibits "cruel and unusual punishments",[71] the US Constitution "would not prohibit a federal or state law" from authorising a judge to impose an irreducible life sentence on an adult offender.[72] It is true that such a sentence may not lawfully be imposed on a juvenile offender for a non-homicide offence,[73] or mandatorily for homicide.[74] But when we consider the kinds of child offenders upon whom irreducible life sentences are being imposed, we see how greatly U.S. penal policy differs from that in Europe. In *Jones v Mississippi,* the petitioner, who was 15 at the time, stabbed his grandfather to death after a quarrel between the two that had resulted from the deceased's discovery of Jones's girlfriend in Jones's bedroom.[75] While it seems hard to regard Jones's crime as anything other than a standard case of murder, he is currently serving a sentence of life without parole. And, although the punitiveness on display in the U.S. dwarfs that in other Anglophone jurisdictions,[76] penal populism flourishes in Australia too. One of the cases with which we began was that of Blessington and Elliott. Their crime, the savage rape and murder of Janine Balding, was undoubtedly far more serious than that committed by Jones. But when account is taken of Blessington's and Elliott's youth at the relevant time, and of their extremely troubled upbringings, it is hard to accept that an irreducible life sentence was at all proportionate to the seriousness of their offending.[77] Yet s 154A of the *Crimes (Administration of Sentences) Act 1999* (NSW), among other things, ensures that these two prisoners will not be released from prison until they are "in imminent danger of dying", or are "incapacitated to the extent that [they] [...] no longer [...] [have] the physical ability to do harm to any person", and further conditions are satisfied.[78]

c) What Explains the Different Attitudes to "Life Without Parole"?

At this point, it is necessary to state why exactly irreducible life sentences are considered to be morally objectionable. That is because, once we set out such reasons in clear and precise terms, we can see better why such sentences may not lawfully be imposed in certain jurisdictions – and why certain other jurisdictions take a different

71 U.S. Constitution, 8th Amendment.

72 Country report U.S.A.

73 *Graham* 560 US 48 (2010).

74 *Miller v Alabama* 567 US 460 (2012).

75 141 S Ct 1307, 1312 (2021).

76 van Zyl Smit and Appleton have recorded that, of 64,306 prisoners sentenced to life without parole whom they had been able to identify worldwide, 53,290 were serving their sentences in the U.S.A. And while those commentators had not been able to identify all prisoners sentenced to life without parole, they estimated that, if they had been able to do so, "significantly more than 50 percent" of those prisoners would be in the U.S.A.: van Zyl Smit and Appleton (n 15) 94.

77 As essentially argued by Kirby J in his dissenting judgment in *The Queen v Elliott and Blessington* (2006) 68 NSWLR 1, 39–43 [179]–[207].

78 See country report Australia.

approach. Or, to be more direct, the objections to irreducible life sentences are human rights objections, which find their basis in a liberal suspicion of state power.[79] It is therefore unsurprising that those states in which a liberal culture prevails are far more likely than states with a more punitive, authoritarian culture to hold that irreducible life sentences "must quite simply be excluded from the arsenal of sanctions available to the state".[80]

It is perhaps tempting to argue that irreducible life sentences are contrary to human rights because they punish *disproportionately* those upon whom they are imposed. Indeed, in *Vinter*, the Grand Chamber seemed to flirt with this idea. "[E]ven when a whole life sentence is condign punishment at the time of its imposition", the Court said, "with the passage of time it becomes [...] a poor guarantee of just and proportionate punishment".[81] On reflection, however, and consistently with the views expressed by the Turkish rapporteurs,[82] such reasoning is unpersuasive.

It is true that, in some cases, an irreducible life sentence *will* be disproportionate to the seriousness of the offending that it punishes. Indeed, I have just argued that one of those cases is that of Blessington and Elliott; and the same can be said of another of the cases noted in the introduction to this chapter – that involving Venables and Thompson. Those latter offenders did not have irreducible life sentences imposed on them. But the ECtHR indicated that, if such sentences *had* been imposed, there might well have been a breach of art 3 of the ECHR.[83] The Court was not entirely clear about what the basis for such a violation would have been. But it is submitted that one reason why the Court would have been justified in finding an art 3 breach in such a case is that such sentences would have been "severely disproportionate"[84] to the seriousness of Venables' and Thompson's offending.[85]

When we consider certain cases, however, it is far less clear that an irreducible life sentence would be disproportionate. Consider, for example, the crimes committed by

79 Nearly 40 years ago, Israeli criminologist Leon Sheleff observed that, when it comes to punishment, "[f]ascist regimes of the right and communist ones of the left" can find themselves in "close and strange alignment" with one another. He ascribed this to the shared authoritarianism of these systems of government. Despite the profound ideological differences between fascist and communist regimes, Sheleff said, "they reach similar conclusions about the paramountcy of the state; in the case of right-wing fascism, as a result of the central role that the state plays in the overall ideology, emphasizing tight control over the individual in order to ensure the fairly extensive degree of uniformity essential for the furtherance of the nation's goals; in the case of left-wing communism, as a result of the desire to control the economy in order to achieve the economic goals that are the essence of the ideology": Leon Sheleff, *Ultimate Penalties: Capital Punishment, Life Imprisonment and Physical Torture* (The Ohio State University Press, 1987) 30.

80 *Bissonnette* (2022) SCC 23, [68].

81 *Vinter* [2013] III Eur Court HR 317, [112].

82 Country report Turkey.

83 *V* [1999] IX Eur Court HR 111, [97]. See too *Hussain v The United Kingdom* [1996] 1 Eur Court HR 252, [53].

84 *V* [1999] IX Eur Court HR 111, [93].

85 It is now well established that a grossly disproportionate sentence is an "inhuman or degrading [...] punishment" within the meaning of ECHR art 3. See, e. g., *Vinter* [2013] III Eur Court HR 317, [102].

the two adult offenders with whom we began, Hutchinson and Bissonnette. Or "the slaughter of innocents by Anders Brevik".[86] Or the massacres to which the Turkish rapporteurs refer.[87] As Lippke has suggested, at least some of those who commit crimes like these would seem to "deserve to spend the rest of their lives in prison".[88] In other words, if irreducible life sentences breach the human rights of those upon whom they are imposed, this cannot be because they necessarily punish such offenders disproportionately.

In an important article,[89] the reasoning in which the Supreme Court of Canada has recently approved,[90] Kerr and Berger have pointed out that there are in fact two kinds of punishment that breach constitutional or human rights guarantees against "inhuman or degrading" or "cruel and unusual" punishments. The first, it is true, is a punishment – such as a prison sentence or a fine – that is grossly disproportionate to the seriousness of the offender's crime(s).[91] The problem here lies not with the *type* of punishment – imprisonment and fines are legitimate – but, rather, with the *amount* of punishment that the state inflicts on the individual. In other words, the penalty – say, life imprisonment for "overtime parking"[92] – is clearly excessive when regard is had to the seriousness of the offender's crime and to his or her "specific circumstances".[93] The second type of punishment is different. Penalties such as torture or corporal punishment,[94] for example, are not "inhuman or degrading" or "cruel and unusual" because, and only where, they are (grossly) disproportionate to the seriousness of particular offending. Rather, they fall within a "narrow class of punishments that are cruel and unusual *by nature*".[95] In other words, here, by contrast with grossly disproportionate punishments, the problem is not with the amount of punishment. It is instead with the *type* of punishment that is imposed. The punishment is one that is "intrinsically incompatible with human dignity".[96] Whatever the circumstances, whatever the prisoner has done, it may never be imposed.

In *The Queen v Bissonnette*, the Supreme Court of Canada accepted that the irreducible life sentence is one of those penalties, like torture and corporal punishment –

86 Richard Lippke, "Irreducible Life Sentences and Human Dignity: Some Neglected and Difficult Issues" (2017) 17 *Human Rights Law Review* 383, 396.

87 Country report Turkey.

88 Lippke (n 86) 396.

89 Lisa Kerr and Benjamin Berger, "Methods and Severity: The Two Tracks of Section 12" (2020) 94 *Supreme Court Law Review* 234.

90 *Bissonnette* (2022) SCC 23, [60]. It is not just the Supreme Court of Canada that has accepted that a punishment will be "inhuman or degrading" or "cruel and unusual" in two circumstances – that is, where it is: (i) grossly disproportionate to the seriousness of the offence that it punishes, or (ii) inherently contrary to the human dignity of the punished. See, e.g., *Vinter* [2013] III Eur Court HR 317, [102]–[103]; *O'Neil v Vermont* 144 US 323, 339–40 (1892) (Field J).

91 *Bissonnette* (2022) SCC 23, [61].

92 *Rummel v Estelle* 445 US 263, 274, fn. 11 (1980).

93 *Bissonnette* (2022) SCC 23, [61].

94 Ibid. [66].

95 Ibid. [64] (emphasis added).

96 Ibid.

and the death penalty – that is inherently barbaric.[97] In so holding, the Court deployed reasoning that resembles that of the German Federal Constitutional Court in 1977,[98] the Namibian Supreme Court a couple of decades later in *S v Tcoeib*[99] and the ECtHR in *Vinter*. "Such a sentence", the Court said:[100]

> Is degrading insofar as it negates, in advance and irreversibly, the penological objective of rehabilitation. This objective is intimately linked to human dignity in that it conveys the conviction that every individual is capable of repenting and re-entering society.

And then, later, the Court added that the irreducible life sentence conveys and presupposes that "the offender is beyond redemption and lacks the moral autonomy needed for rehabilitation."[101]

What precisely did the Court mean? It will be recalled that, in *Tcoeib*, it was stated that, where a prisoner has no realistic prospect of parole, he or she is treated as "a 'thing' instead of a person"[102] – and we find a similar focus on objectification in the German Federal Constitutional Court's reasoning. "A criminal offender", it was said, "may not be turned into a mere object in the fight against crime, in violation of his or her constitutionally protected right to be valued and respected as a person in society".[103] Indeed, if a person *were* to be treated as "a mere object of the state", the Court held, this "would be contrary to human dignity."[104] Such human dignity is only respected if the state treats prisoners as "individual[s] with personal autonomy".[105] As the ECtHR made clear in *Vinter*, the state *is* respectful of life prisoners' autonomy if it shows a commitment to their rehabilitation.[106] It is *not* respectful of their autonomy if it treats them as "morally deformed people"[107] who, because they lack the human capacity to reason, cannot be persuaded to reform their ways, and therefore must be "banishe[d]"[108] from social life.

This liberal focus on persuasion, and on preventing the state from treating humans as though they were "things" to be "abandoned",[109] or as hopeless "psychopaths",[110]

---

97 Ibid. [7]–[8].

98 See text accompanying n 39.

99 1999 NR 24 (SC).

100 *Bissonnette* (2022) SCC 23, [8].

101 Ibid. [81].

102 1999 NR 24 (SC); and see text accompanying n 46.

103 BVerfGE 45, 146.

104 Ibid. 145.

105 Ibid.

106 *Vinter* [2013] III Eur Court HR 317, [114]–[119].

107 Kleinfeld (n 13) 941.

108 Ibid. 949.

109 *Tcoeib* 1999 NR 24 (SC).

110 Of course, as Kleinfeld suggests, some offenders *are* psychopaths who presumably cannot be reformed: Kleinfeld (n 13) 1029, 1035. But, as Jeffrie Murphy has pointed out, "[t]here are obvious and grave dangers, calling to mind Nazi Germany, in creating any political or legal authority to decide who is and who is not a person or to count as a person: Jeffrie Murphy, "Moral Death: A Kantian Essay on Psychopathy", in: Jeffrie Murphy, *Retribution,*

seems to go some way towards explaining why the surveyed jurisdictions take the approaches they do to irreducible life sentences. China is not a liberal democracy, and nor is Singapore. Accordingly, it is unsurprising that, in both of these jurisdictions, the state has the power to "write off [...] human being[s] as irredeemable"[111] and impose objectifying punishments on them. Similar remarks can be made about Turkey and Poland at certain points recently. As Pratt and Miao have suggested, because the very purpose of populist governments is to reflect "the public will" as directly as possible, and because such governments are openly contemptuous of expert knowledge, they will normally pursue criminal justice (and other) policies that "override concerns about individual human rights."[112] Accordingly, it is no surprise to see both the Turkish and Polish governments resisting *Vinter*.

More surprising, if it were not so notorious, would be the U.S.A.'s longstanding commitment to "exclusionary justice."[113] As Lacey puts the matter:[114]

> The USA stands [...] as a country with a long democratic tradition, and one which prides itself on its robust constitutional culture and respect for civil rights. Yet its criminal justice system is, in significant respects, of a sort which we would expect to find [...] in one of the countries whose repressive regimes the USA so loudly decries in its foreign policy rhetoric [...]

Why? Commentators have advanced various theories, but it seems clear that it has at least something to do with the American crime wave of the 1970s.[115] And perhaps, too, American individualism and ideas about personal responsibility caused U.S. legislators to react to this crime wave in the harshly punitive manner in which they did.[116] Whatever is the case, the American approach to "life without parole" could not be more different from that taken in many parts of Europe. In turn, the recent history of tyranny and widespread human rights abuses in Europe might be one reason for the culture of penal moderation that exists in many European states. And perhaps it is with an eye to the past that certain southern African countries have done what they can to withstand penal severity. Striking in this regard is Mahomed CJ's statement in *Tcoeib* that the "despair" expressed by the irreducible life sentence seemed to him:[117]

> Inconsistent with the deeply humane values articulated in the preamble and the text of the Namibian Constitution which so eloquently portrays the vision of a caring and compassion-

---

Justice, and Therapy (D Riedel Publishing Company, 1979) 128, 139. And it is not as though the community will be endangered if the state unsuccessfully attempts to rehabilitate a life prisoner. Such a prisoner will remain in prison for life: *Vinter* [2013] III Eur Court HR 317, [108]; and see also Judith Lichtenberg, "Against Life Without Parole" (2018) 11(1) *Washington University Jurisprudence Review* 39, 59.

111 Van Zyl Smit and Appleton (n 15) 300.

112 John Pratt and Michelle Miao, "The End of Penal Populism; The Rise of Populist Politics" (2019) (XLI/2) *Archives of Criminology* 15, 37.

113 Lacey (n 22) 31.

114 Ibid. 30–1.

115 Kleinfeld (n 13) 1021.

116 Ibid. 1025–6.

117 1999 NR 24 (SC) (emphasis added).

ate democracy *determined to liberate itself from the cruelty, the repression, the pain and the shame of its racist and colonial past.*

As was noted above,[118] it is not accurate to view jurisdictions such as Australia and England and Wales in the same light as the U.S.A. But they are not like the Nordic countries or Germany either: when it comes to criminal justice, they are a "hybrid case".[119] This is due largely to the influence of penal populism, which emerged in the last couple of decades of the twentieth century[120] – and which seems easier to describe than explain. Like populism more broadly, penal populism contends that "the public [...] should have a strong influence on penal affairs."[121] It is hostile to the "rights-based claims" of criminal offenders[122] and "seeks opportunities to turn the punishment of offenders into a symbolic spectacle of reassurance and vengeance for an onlooking public".[123] It places emphasis on "victims' voices",[124] venerates "ignorance over intellect",[125] and disdains the "criminal justice expert" and seeks to reduce his or her influence.[126] It has succeeded in the latter enterprise. Crucially, since the 1990s there has been bipartisan political support in many Anglophone jurisdictions for harsh criminal justice responses.[127]

As just noted, the causes of penal populism are not entirely clear. But high levels of inequality and individualism in societies such as Australia and England and Wales might well have something to do with it – as might the long history of political freedom in these countries.[128] Societies in which individuals are seen as the masters of their own destiny, and in which poverty and crime are thus viewed as the fault of the impoverished and criminal, are unlikely to favour penal moderation.[129] And societies that have not seen at close range just where a failure to protect minority rights can lead, might be particularly liable to take a more insouciant approach than they should to the protection of the rights of prisoners.

d) Conclusion

Whether or not "life without parole sentences are *increasingly* becoming favourable to legislatures worldwide",[130] there is certainly a widespread conviction that par-

---

118 See text accompanying n 76.

119 Lacey (n 22) 38.

120 Roberts et al. (n 24) 131.

121 Pratt (n 24) 32.

122 Ibid. 20.

123 Ibid. 30.

124 Ibid. 18.

125 Ibid. 163.

126 Ibid. 19.

127 Ibid. 22. See also Tim Newburn and Trevor Jones, "Symbolic Politics and Penal Populism: The Long Shadow of Willie Horton" (2005) 1(1) *Crime Media Culture* 72.

128 And, in the case of Australia, physical isolation might be a factor.

129 Roberts et al. (n 24) 155.

130 Country report Turkey (emphasis added).

ticular offences are "so grave"[131] as to justify such a penalty. And, as we have seen, many legislatures across the world have acted consistently with such a conviction: irreducible life sentences are being imposed in the U.S.A., Australia, China, Turkey and (seemingly) Singapore – and the Polish and UK governments have expressed some opposition to the idea that such sentences are unlawful and contrary to human rights norms. The death penalty is still imposed in Japan, which seems to make it clear that irreducible life sentences would be accepted there too; and the Chilean legislature has authorised the imposition of sentences that would be regarded as irreducible if passed in Europe.[132] That said, there is far from a worldwide consensus in favour of irreducible life sentences. Such sentences are not imposed in Israel; and, in Namibia and throughout much of Europe, it has been accepted that, however proportionate such sentences might be in particular cases, they violate the human dignity of those upon whom they are imposed and amount to "inhuman or degrading punishment".

I have argued here that, when we examine the reasons that Courts have supplied for holding that irreducible life sentences are incompatible with human rights, we seem to gain some insight into why different jurisdictions have taken different approaches to the permissibility of such sentences. The reasons the Courts have given are liberal reasons. At their heart is an acknowledgement that even those who "commit the most abhorrent and egregious of acts"[133] are "autonomous, responsible"[134] human beings who, consequently, must be reasoned with and not squashed. Unsurprisingly, such an approach has gained far less traction with authoritarian, populist and penal populist governments than it has in jurisdictions where, for whatever reason, a liberal, human rights-respecting culture prevails.

---

131 Matthew Groves, "A Life Without Hope – The Victorian Charter and Parole" (2018) 42(6) *Criminal Law Journal* 353, 371.

132 See n 9.

133 *Vinter* [2013] III Eur Court HR 317 (Concurring Opinion of Judge Power-Forde).

134 Jeffrie Murphy, "Cruel and Unusual Punishments", in: Murphy (n 110) 223, 233.

IV. Concluding Observations

By *Thomas Weigend*

This volume presents the results of an experiment. We wished to test the hypothesis that there exist similar intuitions of justice worldwide, leading to similar solutions in concrete hypothetical cases, regardless of differences in statutory law and in general theories of criminal law. Based on prior comparative studies, we had some reason to think that basic notions of justice do not differ much in different parts of the world.[1] We chose to test this hypothesis by devising ten case Vignettes, seven reflecting theoretical problems of criminal liability and three concerning choices in criminal policy.

Methodological Similarities

On a methodological level, the outcome of our study provides an argument in favor of a "functional" comparison of laws.[2] By and large, the responses from geographically diverse jurisdictions have shown that legal experts from different legal systems can talk to each other with ease. The Synopses, which draw valuable conclusions from parallels between national reports as well as from their differing perspectives, clearly support that point: representatives of geographically and historically vastly different jurisdictions can and in fact tend to discuss the same issues when faced with identical factual situations.[3]

---

1 See *Robinson/Darley*, Intuitions of Justice: Implications for Criminal Law and Justice Policy, 81 Southern California Law Review 1 (2007); *Robinson*, Intuitions of Justice and the Utility of Desert, 2013 (claiming that popular notions of justice are similar in different societies); *Perron*, Rechtsvergleichende Analyse der Untersuchungsergebnisse, in: Eser/Perron (eds.), Strukturvergleich strafrechtlicher Verantwortlichkeit und Sanktionierung in Europa, 2015, 761, 915 et seq. (presenting results of a comparative study of a case of domestic homicide).

2 For overviews of the critique of the functional method by "post-modern" comparative law theorists see *Kischel*, Rechtsvergleichung, 2015, 95 et seq.; *Weigend*, Strafrechtsvergleich, in: Hilgendorf/Kudlich/Valerius (eds.), Handbuch des Strafrechts, vol. 1, 2019, 1055, marginal notes 5–7.

3 This is true although the legal focus is not identical in all responses on the Vignettes. For example, in dealing with Vignette 5 (superior orders as a possible ground of justification or excuse) some respondents emphasize that D possibly committed a crime against humanity, others concentrate on the question of a possible mistake of fact or law, whereas one respondent deals at length with the issue of retroactivity of the law against shooting protesters. But such differing perspectives are to be expected when a brief set of facts is presented without indicating where the legal focus is supposed to be put. Through communication with the rapporteurs, we

Duncker & Humblot · Berlin | https://doi.org/10.3790/978-3-428-59449-8.2025.415909

Similarities and Differences in Outcome

Our initial hypothesis has proved accurate to some extent. Most of the responses from 16 jurisdictions employ similar lines of argument even where the proposed outcomes differ from each other. Different jurisdictions apply similar legal categories and doctrines even if they are named differently. For example, in Vignette 2 (Attribution of Death) almost all participating jurisdictions (with the probable exception of Belgium) require for criminal liability some kind of a close, "normative" relationship between a person's act and the legally relevant result; the existence of a "but for" causal connection is not regarded as sufficient. Likewise, in Vignette 7 (Abandonment of Attempt) all jurisdictions bring similar considerations to bear, even where they lead to differing results.

It is not surprising, however, that the suggested outcomes of the Vignette cases – in spite of the similarity of arguments used – differ from each other in the 16 jurisdictions included in our study. One reason for such differences lies in our choice of problems: We selected "close cases", as to which opposing views tend to be held even within the same jurisdiction.[4] As we show below, differences in outcome do not normally result from jurisdictions' principles of legal theory, for example, on the requirements of justification or on elements of mens rea. Rather, different outcomes are often due to policy choices. Most of these choices are not associated with a jurisdiction's belonging to a particular legal family or even with its general orientation toward strictness vs. leniency, but they depend on each legal system's assessment of the conflicting values and interests at stake in the relevant factual situation. General attitudes play a somewhat greater role in the results of Vignettes 8, 9 and 10, where the limits of criminal liability are set in a more direct way. But even there, we did not detect any consistent clusters of jurisdictions.

Policy Decisions in Vignette Cases

In Vignette 2 (Attribution of Death), we can see in all jurisdictions an effort to limit criminal liability to results that were not only caused in fact by the defendant but also could *ex ante* be expected to follow from his conduct. Normative devices to achieve that result differ, with some jurisdictions preferring the concept of "objective attributability" (*objektive Zurechnung*), others relying on subjective tests ("Could the actor have foreseen this result?"), with both avenues usually leading to the same conclusion. The rationale of limiting attribution is to avoid holding individuals criminally responsible for harm that appears to be the result of "fate" rather than the actor's blameworthy conduct.

In Vignette 3, the absolute prohibition of torture due to policy reasons (to avoid a slippery slope effect toward its frequent use) can be so strong as to override any con-

managed to clear up some factual misunderstandings and thereby harmonize the scope of the legal analysis.

4 *Sara Beale's* report on the United States, covering a great number of different State jurisdictions, shows that very different legal views and solutions co-exist even within one country.

sideration of necessity that may speak in favor of applying torture. That seems to be the case, e. g., in Belgium, Turkey, and according to one view in China. Other jurisdictions put greater weight on the individual rights of the persons potentially affected by the person to be tortured (e. g., Australia, Israel) and would therefore permit the use of force to extract information in certain situations. In Israel, this decision seems to be influenced by the country's experience with terrorism.

Vignette 4 (Limits of Self-Defense) involves several policy issues related to the situation of self-defense. One question concerns the temporal extension of the right to defend oneself, which can be differentiated between defending one's life and health and defending one's property. The other issue is proportionality: may an attacker justifiably be killed if only the attacked person's property is at stake? In that regard, the legal systems under study here propose different answers: In Germany, for example, a person may, if necessary, kill a thief to protect his property. But in a greater number of jurisdictions (e. g., Australia, Belgium, Chile), deadly self-defense in that situation is explicitly prohibited, and other jurisdictions probably arrive at the same result by using the requirement of proportionality (e. g., China, Israel, Italy, Turkey). As *Johan Boucht* correctly points out in the Synopsis on this Vignette, the extent of a possible justification or excuse in situations of an illegal attack probably is influenced by the rationale of allowing self-defense: systems which regard self-defense as an instrument for (also) defending a public interest may be more inclined to grant liberal defense rights than systems that base the right to self-defense only on the individual interests of the attacked person or on the idea that an attacker has forfeited some of his rights.

The responses to Vignette 5 (Superior Orders) reflect a broad spectrum of policy attitudes to the relationship between commanders and subordinates in a military context. There are the extreme solutions of a justification or excuse provided for the soldier even if the order was clearly illegal (Chile, Japan) and granting no excuse whatsoever (Australia, England, Israel[5], Poland, Turkey, Norway in peacetime); and there is the intermediate solution of excusing the subordinate unless the order was manifestly illegal or its illegality was known to the subordinate (Finland, Germany, Italy, Namibia[6], U.S.A.). As with many other Vignettes, the lists of jurisdictions that have adopted any one of these three options do not follow any perceivable pattern with regard to legal tradition or the political system in place.

Vignette 6 (Amputation by Consent) presents the issue of the limits of consent in criminal law. Here, only a minority of jurisdictions would acquit the doctor who amputated the athlete's leg, based on the justificatory effect of the patient's consent (Germany, Japan, Singapore, some U.S. States). Many other jurisdictions have chosen to limit the effect of consent to injuries that are not serious (Australia, Norway, Poland) and/or not permanent (Finland, Italy, Namibia, Turkey). Separate grounds of justification are provided for operations that are medically indicated (e. g., Belgium, Chile, China, Germany), but this would not apply to the Vignette case. The

5 *Mordechai Kremnitzer* explains that Israeli law will provide "no support of dictatorship by law, hence no leniency for the soldier".

6 Interestingly, *Pilisano Masake* and *Inonge Mainga* state that the superior's order in Vignette 5 would not be regarded as manifestly illegal in Namibia.

somewhat paternalistic stance of most jurisdictions, which contrasts with their liberal attitude toward self-harming activities, has been linked to the ancient notion that one's body does not entirely belong to oneself but to God (Israel) or to the sovereign (U.S.A.). But the persistence of paternalism in many jurisdictions even in the 21st century is astonishing. There may exist fundamentally differing attitudes toward the balancing between individual autonomy and societal interests.

In Vignette 7 (Abandoning Attempt), different attitudes toward taking into account a person's abandonment of an attempted offense become apparent. Some jurisdictions (e.g., Belgium, Chile, Finland, Germany, Israel, Italy, Norway, Poland) grant full impunity (except for other offenses already completed) if the defendant voluntarily gave up the attempt, either by stopping to act or (if the relevant result would come about without further action) by actively preventing the result from occurring. In other jurisdictions (e.g., Australia, England, Namibia, Singapore, some States of the U.S.), the offender will be punished even if he desisted, but his sentence will be reduced. Some jurisdictions (Belgium, China) distinguish between incomplete attempts (not punishable if abandoned) and completed attempts (punishable even if the defendant has actively prevented the result). Here, the line-up of the more restrictive jurisdictions coincides with a common-law heritage. But the main source of the differing outcomes seems to lie in the rationales for punishing attempts: If the attempt offender is regarded as punishable mainly because of his bad intention, the fact that he changed his mind can only partially reduce the blameworthiness of his prior illegal intention. If, on the other hand, the main interest of the system lies in avoiding the occurrence of harm, it makes sense to build a "golden bridge" for the defendant to make him prevent the harm.

Vignette 1 (The Trolley Problem) may be an exception from the dominant role of policy decisions for the resolution of Vignette cases. Here, the general attitude toward the value of an individual life appears to be the crucial factor: Some legal systems follow a utilitarian course allowing for a mathematical comparison of lives saved vs. lives sacrificed and therefore would justify D's act (e.g., Belgium, Japan, U.S. Model Penal Code). The majority of jurisdictions represented in this study, however, would not justify the killing of an innocent person (e.g., Chile, England, Germany, Namibia, Norway, Poland, Turkey) and would at most grant D an excuse.

Vignettes 8, 9 and 10 require policy decisions on the extension of the criminal law over young persons and over time, and on the maximum penalty to be imposed.

Regarding the minimum age of criminal responsibility (Vignette 8), there exists an astonishingly broad scope of legal standards, reaching from having no age limit at all (24 States of the U.S.) to a minimum age of 15 years (Finland, Norway). Many legal systems have opted for intermediate solutions, such as an individual assessment of a teenager's understanding of normative concepts (Belgium, Germany, Namibia, Turkey) or a referral to family or juvenile court, which is expected to tailor the official reaction to the individual needs of the offender (Australia, Chile, Germany, Italy, Japan, Poland, Singapore, U.S.). Interestingly, there is no common trend to be observed with regard to changing age limits: some jurisdictions have recently lowered the minimum age of criminal responsibility (Belgium, China for most serious crimes), whereas others have raised it (Australia, Norway). It seems that historical traditions and recent experience with the effect of non-criminal responses to juvenile offenses have a significant impact on such policy decisions.

Vignette 9 (Statutes of Limitation) likewise presents a broad spectrum of solutions. Here, we can see a kind of watershed between common-law and civil-law jurisdictions: Legal systems historically based on the common law typically have no prescription of criminal prosecution for serious offenses, but prosecutors tend to have discretion and judges may dismiss "stale" cases, especially where it would be unfair to the defendant to hold a trial after many years (e. g., Australia, England, Singapore, some U.S. States). By contrast, "Continental" legal systems invariably have statutes barring prosecution after a given number of years have passed since the commission of the offense, with the length of the period often depending on the seriousness of the crime (e. g., Belgium, Chile, China, Germany, Italy, Norway, Poland, Turkey; same applies to Namibia and some States of the U.S.). Prescription of prosecution is based on different considerations, most frequently on the argument that the impact even of serious crime on society tends to decrease over time. In recent years, some legal systems have extended the period for the prosecution of sexual offenses (Germany, Japan, Norway), perhaps because the long-lasting impact of these offenses on victims has gained greater recognition.[7] It has aptly been observed, however, in the Synopsis written by *Carla Sepúlveda*, that certain features of the criminal process, such as the principles of mandatory vs. discretionary prosecution and the adversarial vs. inquisitorial style of proceeding, also have an impact on the necessity and importance of statutes of limitation.

The responses to Vignette 10 show that some legal systems provide for sentences of life imprisonment without a possibility of early release (Australia, China, England, Israel), sometimes based on a perceived need of retribution for very serious crime (Australia, Israel), sometimes as a response to the continuing dangerousness of offenders (Italy), sometimes as an alternative to the death penalty (China, Japan). But in many jurisdictions, life sentences without the possibility of release have come under heavy criticism for being disproportional (Chile) or even for violating the prisoner's human dignity (Germany, Israel, a minority view in China). A compromise solution seems to be security detention of chronically dangerous offenders (Belgium, Germany), which leaves open the possibility of release when the dangerousness has subsided.

Factors Explaining Policy Differences

A brief analysis of the responses to the ten Vignettes has led us to the conclusion that there are no universally equal intuitions of justice that would lead to the same or very similar outcomes for each Vignette. But there are globally similar features of *arguing* about criminal responsibility.

All legal systems are facing the conflict, typical of criminal law, between the need to establish clear and precise conduct rules and offense definitions and, on the other hand, leaving some leeway for courts to take exceptional situations into account, thus

[7] See *Carla Sepúlveda* in her Synopsis on Vignette 9.

enabling judges to arrive at solutions that do justice to the individual defendant.[8] This inherent conflict in the creation and application of criminal law has been resolved differently in the legal systems under review here. But there seems to exist a worldwide tendency toward creating legal mechanisms that permit an individualization of justice. In some jurisdictions, the concepts of individual responsibility (culpability) serve that purpose by allowing courts to maintain the validity of the general rule (by negating a justification) while at the same time acquitting the individual defendant, absolving him from personal responsibility for his act or for the harm he caused (see, e.g., Israel, Norway and Poland, Vignette 3). In cases of self-defense, several jurisdictions provide for an excuse if the attacked person went beyond what was necessary due to an understandable overreaction to a sudden assault (Chile, Germany, Japan, Poland and Turkey, Vignette 4). Other jurisdictions do not grant a full excuse in this situation but reduce the charge from murder to manslaughter (Australia, Finland and Singapore, Vignette 4). If guilt cannot be negated, the law will permit the court to impose a very lenient sentence in order to acknowledge a conflict which made it difficult for the defendant to comply with the legal obligations (see Finland, Vignette 1; Belgium and Norway, Vignette 3; Poland and Turkey, Vignette 4, Norway and Poland, Vignette 6; Australia and Japan, Vignette 7). Looking at the various solutions proposed for the perennial conflict between clear general rules and individualized justice, we cannot detect any pattern that would make it possible to identify systematic preferences for one or the other of these goals.

Although we did not find any set of factors that would permit us to identify among the 16 jurisdictions groups that would consistently follow the same principles or policies, there are some features that seem to have a discernible influence on criminal policy decisions.

One such factor is the existence of constitutional principles relating to criminal law. Obvious examples are the principles of legality (*nullum crimen sine lege*) and of proportionality between the offense and the sanction. Respect for human dignity is a further overarching principle, which however can work in favor of offenders (e.g., exclusion of certain penalties) as well as potential victims of state-sponsored violence (e.g., norms prohibiting the use of torture, as in Vignette 3; see Germany, Namibia).

Another layer of protection of individual rights can be provided by international conventions, most importantly the European Convention on Human Rights. In some jurisdictions, obligations under international law supersede national legislation, which can have an impact on the prohibition of torture (Vignette 3, see Belgium, Norway, Turkey). A defendant's right to have his case decided within a reasonable time (Art. 6 sec. 1 ECHR) has an impact on the issue of prescription (Vignette 9, Belgium). And the U.N. Convention on the Rights of Children has in some jurisdictions (Australia, Belgium, England) been cited in the context of setting a minimum age of criminal responsibility (Vignette 8).

One fault line between legal systems that has often been mentioned in comparative legal literature is the division between common law and civil law jurisdictions. In our

---

[8] For a thoughtful analysis of this problem, see *Mordechai Kremnitzer*, Synopsis on Vignette 3.

sample, there are four jurisdictions with a strong "common law" heritage (Australia, England, Singapore, U.S.A.), eight systems more or less bearing the features of "civil law" (Belgium, Chile, Finland, Germany, Italy, Norway, Poland, Turkey), and four jurisdictions with strong traditions of their own and varying influences of the English and the Continental traditions (China, Israel, Japan, Namibia). When we look at the Vignettes used in this study, the proposed solutions to the problem cases do not follow the common law/civil law divide. Take, for example, Vignette 6 concerning the limits of consent to a non-medically indicated amputation of a leg: The most "liberal" outcome (justification of the doctor performing the surgery) has been proposed by the respondents from Germany, Japan and Singapore, whereas the surgeon's conviction for causing grievous bodily harm (albeit with a lenient sentence) would be the expected outcome in common law countries, such as Australia and several U.S. States, as well as in many "civil law" jurisdictions, e.g., Finland, Italy, Norway, Poland and Turkey.

There do exist, however, a few typical characteristics of dealing with problem cases in legal systems of English-speaking countries. One such characteristic is the "subjectivisation" of grounds of justification, as exemplified in Vignettes 3 and 4. Under English law, the defense of duress of circumstances (Vignette 3) does not require proof of the objective existence of a risk to an important legal interest but only of the defendant's reasonable belief that there is a risk of that kind. Similarly, in deciding on the reasonableness of an aggressive response to an attack, English courts will acquit the defendant if he genuinely believed that circumstances existed which would make his act reasonable, even if it was not in fact reasonable (Vignette 4).[9] In many American jurisdictions, the defense of self-defense also requires no more than the actor's *belief* that the use of force is immediately necessary to avert an attack.[10] By contrast, "Continental" legal systems typically regard an act as justified only if it was objectively necessary to reject an illegal attack or an imminent danger to a legal interest. Any error on the part of the defender making him believe that he was in fact in a situation of legitimate self-defense will only be considered as negating or (if the mistake was negligent) reducing his blameworthiness (see, e.g., Germany, Norway, Vignette 4).

Another characteristic of common law systems is a tendency to use open-ended terms whose interpretation in any given case is left to the court (which often means: to a jury of lay persons). Singapore law on the defense of necessity (Vignette 1) explicitly states that "it is a question of fact in such a case whether the harm to be prevented or avoided was of such a nature and so imminent as to justify or excuse the risk of doing the act [...]"; and in England and Wales a finding of intention to kill is left to the jury without being bound by specific criteria, so as to leave some "moral elbow room" to the jurors (England, Vignette 1). Similarly, the question of whether an event

---

9 See Section 76 of the Criminal Justice and Immigration Act 2008, as quoted in the national report on England and Wales.

10 See § 3.06 Model Penal Code as quoted in the U.S. report on Vignette 4. The laws of Singapore as well as of New York and some other States of the U.S.A. require a "reasonable" belief, thus introducing an objective prerequisite for justification. Similarly, in Australia the defense of self-defense is available only if it is "reasonably possible" that the defendant believed that his conduct was necessary to avert an attack (see report on Australia, Vignette 4).

can be attributed to the person who provided a "but for" cause for the event is left to the jury in Australia, England, Singapore and the U.S.A. (Vignette 2). Typical fluid expressions used in legislation of common law jurisdictions are "reasonable" and "fair" as conditions of non-punishability of the defendant's conduct, with the decision on whether the defendant acted "reasonably" being left to the finder of fact without further guidance (see, e.g., England, Vignette 3 (issue of "duress" left to the jury); Australia, England, U.S.A., Vignette 4). In Australia, the question of whether it would be "unfair" to proceed against the defendant many years after the commission of a crime is left to the judge (Vignette 9).

These examples show that common law jurisdictions tend to place great faith in the sense of justice and fairness of the "common people" who sit as a jury. This tendency can work in favor of the defendant but can also be detrimental to him, especially where his conduct (or his personality and social background, as they appear at the trial) conflicts with the moral views of the majority. An emphasis on moral attitudes is also reflected in some value judgments of common law jurisdictions, for example, a stricter attitude toward persons who commit an attempt of a crime but later withdraw from it, thus preventing the occurrence of harm (Australia, England, Vignette 7). The judicial principle of *stare decisis* also makes for greater conservatism and a lower speed in adapting to social change (see England, Vignette 1, with regard to extending the defense of necessity to acts of killing).

In civil law systems, by contrast, we tend to see a greater emphasis on providing for just and fair dispositions by well-formulated criminal statutes which ideally leave very little room for judicial discretion. Legislatures seek to foresee, to the extent possible, factual situations that may arise and to devise formulations that can be applied to these situations. The strict application of the principle of legality (*nullum crimen sine lege*) relies on the ability of the democratically elected legislature to formulate precise and easily understandable criminal laws which at the same time cover exactly the conduct that is to be incriminated. This emphasis on precisely written laws not only aims at protecting citizens from arbitrary repression by organs of the state but also reflects a particular model of distributing state power between the legislative and the judicial branches.

Beyond the common law/civil law divide, historic connections between jurisdictions can play a role in explaining similarities between them. Among the common law systems, England has historically played a leading role. But the United States has developed its own laws and legal standards (differing from State to State) in the 250 years of independence from England, and the same is true for Australia. On the "Continental" half of the board, Germany has long had an influential role, which extended even to such far-away countries as Chile, China and Japan. In the responses to the Vignettes from these countries, we can now and again find references to German legal theories.[11] But it seems that these instances of adopting arguments and legal constructs from German legal theorists are diminishing over time,[12] in

11 See, e.g., Vignettes 1 (China), 2 (China, Poland, Turkey – "objective attribution"), 6 (Chile), 7 (Japan).

12 See *Weigend*, Internationale Strafrechtswissenschaft nach deutschem Modell?, Goltdammers Archiv für Strafrecht 2020, 27, 32 et seq.

line with the loss of influence of "grand dogmatic theories" in the legal debate in Germany itself.[13] It has correctly been pointed out that the social conditions and ethical standards of each country, especially its own concept of criminal justice, slowly but inevitably push historical ties to (formerly) "leading" foreign legal systems into the background (see Japan, Vignette 2; China, Vignette 4).

In some instances, a country's historical experience appears to play a significant role in shaping its attitude toward individual criminal law problems. This is shown in the responses to Vignette 3 (Torture to save a life). Here, the respondents from Japan and the U.S.A. do not even mention the issue of torture; and whereas Turkey clearly rejects any tolerance of a policeman's violence, Israel – probably in light of its experience with terroristic threats – seems to accept torture under specific circumstances.

Policy Decisions on Sanctioning

Vignettes 8, 9 and 10 have been designed to reveal differences among legal systems with regard to the extension of criminal law. From the responses, we can say that some jurisdictions (e. g., Australia, U.S.A.) have more punitive solutions on maximum and minimum punishments, age of responsibility, and the possibility of criminal prosecution even many years after the commission of the offense, whereas the two Nordic countries in our sample tend to be more hesitant to apply criminal sanctions in "borderline" situations. It is difficult to decide, however, whether such differences mainly result from historical traditions (e.g., of having no minimum age of criminal responsibility and no statutes of limitation in the United States) or from conscious policy choices. We can only surmise that an emphasis on retribution and deterrence as the main purposes of punishment leads to greater punitiveness, whereas a greater concern for rehabilitation of the offender has the opposite effect. Given the checkered picture of responses from our 16 jurisdictions, we would in any event hesitate to suggest the existence of ties between particular "legal cultures" and the punitiveness of criminal policy.

Conclusion

Our experiment has demonstrated both the beauty and the limits of comparison in criminal law. Despite (or rather: because of) the wealth of ideas and information provided by the national respondents and the authors of the Synopses, we are faced with a welter of legal materials which can hardly be systematized; much less do they lend themselves to suggesting simple, one-dimensional factors responsible for the features of any national criminal law. Different notions of justice in criminal matters have turned out not to depend on any jurisdiction's "system" of criminal law nor on the

---

13 In Germany, the former "schools" of criminal law which tended to dominate the scholarly debates (associated with names like Karl Binding, Franz von Liszt, Hans Welzel, Günter Jakobs, and Claus Roxin) have recently given way to a more pluralistic, mosaic-like landscape of criminal law scholarship.

overall orientation of its criminal policy. Arguments in all systems tend to have a similar structure; but the mix of determinative factors (historical, ethical, political) is different in each jurisdiction reviewed.

On the other hand, our overview shows that each legal system seeks to arrive at "just" conclusions, weighing the conflicting needs of safeguarding important individual and societal interests, protecting victims of crime, taking account of (sometimes conflicting) values and aims of punishment, and providing outcomes that can be accepted as fair both by the defendant and the community at large. In problem cases as represented in our Vignettes, these outcomes often differ from each other; but they invariably tend to reflect a genuine effort of the legal system to reach fair results.

Comparison demonstrates that justice in criminal cases can look different and can be achieved in different ways. There is thus no reason for any single legal system to claim superiority and to try to convert others. If any jurisdiction has managed to resolve a problem in a particularly persuasive way, we can expect that the work of comparatists will spread the word and will encourage other systems to emulate that foreign idea (if it can be made to fit into the domestic system). But such success stories of individual ideas cannot be expected to be frequent. The main lesson from our endeavor thus is that many different avenues can lead to justice.

Perhaps more importantly, the results of our experiment suggest that justice in criminal matters is not an absolute but a contingent concept. What is regarded as "just" in difficult criminal cases or borderline policy issues depends on a multitude of factors, for example, a jurisdiction's historical experience, cultural background, social conditions, and general value system (for example, the relative emphasis on individual freedom vs. social coherence). Justice may thus be served in different legal systems by diametrically opposed outcomes. Our comparative study teaches us equanimity, humility and tolerance when facing different ideas of justice from a global perspective.

V. List of Contributors

Sara Sun Beale is Charles L.B. Lowndes Professor of Law Emerita at Duke Law School, Duke University, Durham, NC.

Paolo Beccari is a PhD candidate in Criminal Law at the Department of Legal Studies, University of Bologna.

Johan Boucht is Professor of Criminal Law at BI Norwegian Business School in Oslo.

Ali Emrah Bozbayındır is Professor of Criminal Law at the Faculty of Law, Boğaziçi (Bosphorus) University, Istanbul.

Gian Marco Caletti is Senior Researcher in Criminal Law at the Department of Legal Studies, University of Bologna

Steven Cammiss is Associate Professor in Law at the University of Birmingham.

Wing-Cheong Chan is Professor of Law at the Yong Pung How School of Law, Singapore Management University.

John J Child is Professor of Criminal Law at the University of Birmingham.

Sam J Cole is Assistant Professor in Criminal Justice at the University of Birmingham.

Thomas Crofts is Associate Dean and Professor at the Department of Law and Behavioural Sciences, City University of Hong Kong.

Andrew Dyer is Associate Professor at Melbourne Law School, University of Melbourne.

Elisa Hoven is Professor of German and Foreign Criminal Law, Criminal Procedure Law, Economic and Media Criminal Law at the University of Leipzig.

Mordechai Kremnitzer is Professor Emeritus of Law at The Hebrew University of Jerusalem and Senior Fellow at the Israel Democracy Institute.

Alicja Limburska is Assistant Professor at the Department of Substantive Criminal Law, Faculty of Law, Administration and Economics, University of Wrocław, and attorney-at-law, Bar Council in Wrocław, Poland.

Konrad Lipiński is Assistant Professor, Department of Substantive Criminal Law, Faculty of Law, Administration and Economics, University of Wrocław, and attorney-at-law, Bar Council in Wrocław, Poland.

Arlie Loughnan is Professor of Criminal Law and Criminal Law Theory at Sydney Law School, University of Sydney.

Inonge Mainga is practicing attorney at Inonge Mainga Attorneys, Namibia.

Pilisano Masake, is Associate Dean of the School of Human Sciences and Education, Department of Social Sciences, at Namibia University of Science and Technology.

Kimmo Nuotio is Professor of Criminal Law at the University of Helsinki.

Rifat Murat Önok is Associate Professor of Criminal and Criminal Procedure Law at the Graduate School of Social Sciences and Humanities, Koç University, Istanbul.

Duncker & Humblot · Berlin | https://doi.org/10.3790/978-3-428-59449-8.2025.415910

Carla Sepúlveda Peña is Assistant Professor of Law at Universidad Adolfo Ibáñez, Chile.

Michael Peng is Solicitor at the Commonwealth Director of Public Prosecutions in Sydney and Sessional Lecturer in Criminal Law at the University of New South Wales.

Pieter van Rooij is a PhD candidate and Research and Teaching Assistant at the Institute of Criminal Law at KU Leuven.

Zhiwei Tang is Postdoctoral Researcher in Criminal Law at the KoGuan School of Law, Shanghai Jiao Tong University.

Tomoko Utsumi is Professor at the Graduate School of International Social Sciences, Yokohama National University.

Frank Verbruggen is Professor at the Faculty of Law and Criminology and Head of the Institute of Criminal Law at KU Leuven.

Thomas Weigend is Professor Emeritus of Criminal Law at the University of Cologne.